PRAISE FOR *THE BIBLE AND HOMOSEXUAL PRACTICE*

"This is a brilliant, original, and highly important work, displaying meticulous biblical scholarship, and indispensable even for those who disagree with the author."—**James Barr**, Distinguished Professor of Hebrew Bible, Emeritus, Vanderbilt University

"Gagnon has offered a learned, judicious, and comprehensive examination of the biblical testimony. . . . His book is fair and compassionate, and should become a major resource for those taking the scriptural witness seriously."—**Brevard S. Childs**, Sterling Professor of Divinity (Hebrew Bible), Emeritus, Yale Divinity School

"Gagnon makes his point clear in defending the non-acceptance of homosexual relationships on biblical grounds. In its learnedness, his book will without doubt be in the vanguard of its position and cannot be ignored in future debate even by proponents of discordant views."—**Martti Nissinen**, Professor of Hebrew Bible, University of Helsinki (author of *Homoeroticism in the Biblical World*)

"This work contains the most sophisticated and convincing examination of the biblical data to date and puts the data in the context of ancient culture. The implications for the present are drawn in a prudent and well-argued manner. The book thus makes an essential contribution to defusing the emotionalism that surrounds the discussion. Even someone who advocates a different position will be able to appreciate this advantage of the book."—**Jürgen Becker**, Professor of New Testament, Christian-Albrechts University

"Gagnon's work provides, in my judgment, the most thorough and satisfying analysis and evaluation of the biblical texts yet produced. It is abreast of the latest literature, scrupulous in its exegesis, and sensitive to hermeneutical questions. It is a study that no serious scholar will want to ignore."—**David F. Wright**, Senior Lecturer, Ecclesiastical History, The University of Edinburgh

"I know of no comparable study of the texts and interpretive debates that surround homosexual behavior. . . . Gagnon's approach to the issue grasps the complexity of the debate, and does so with much compassion. Although the work is not polemical in tone, it also becomes clear that some widely quoted authorities and contemporary advocates of sexual liberation in this area have misread the historical and textual data and misused contemporary scientific, classical argument and pastoral evidence."—**Max L. Stackhouse**, Stephen Colwell Professor of Christian Ethics, Princeton Theological Seminary

"This is an impressive study that moves the discussion forward in an important and hotly contested area of Christian ethics. It articulates and defends the traditional view, but is delightfully free of tired traditional arguments. Nothing is taken for granted. . . . The book is at one and the same time hard-hitting, carefully nuanced, irenic, practical, and fair. It is a necessary read for any who are seriously concerned with Christian sexual ethics."—**John Nolland**, Professor of New Testament, Trinity College

THE BIBLE AND HOMOSEXUAL PRACTICE

TEXTS AND HERMENEUTICS

ROBERT A. J. GAGNON

Abingdon Press
Nashville

THE BIBLE AND HOMOSEXUAL PRACTICE
TEXTS AND HERMENEUTICS

Library of Congress Cataloging-in-Publication Data

Gagnon, Robert A. J., 1958-
   The Bible and homosexual practice : texts and hermeneutics / Robert A.J. Gagnon.
     p. cm.
   Includes bibliographical references and index.
   ISBN 0-687-08413-X (alk. paper)
   1. Homosexuality—Biblical teaching. I. Title.

BS680.H67 G34 2001
241'.66—dc21

                                                                        00-049341

01 02 03 04 05 06 07 08 09 10—10 9 8 7 6 5 4 3 2

MANUFACTURED IN THE UNITED STATES OF AMERICA

For my wife, Carol

CONTENTS

Acknowledgments

Writing a book on a controversial subject requires considerable encouragement along the way. The following scholars were kind enough to read the manuscript and write gracious publicity notices about its importance for the homosexuality debate: James Barr, C. K. Barrett, John Barton, Richard Bauckham, Jürgen Becker, Brevard S. Childs, C. E. B. Cranfield, J. Andrew Dearman, James D. G. Dunn, I. Howard Marshall, Ulrich Mauser, Scot McKnight, Bruce M. Metzger, Douglas J. Moo, Jerome Murphy O'Conner, Terry C. Muck, James B. Nelson, Martii Nissinen, John Nolland, Marion L. Soards, Max L. Stackhouse, Frank Thielman, Duane F. Watson, Stephen Westerholm, and David F. Wright.

Special thanks are extended to colleagues at Pittsburgh Theological Seminary who provided support, counsel, and prayer during the writing of this book. I am blessed to be at an institution that honors the right of each faculty member to state and publish sincerely held convictions. The experience of writing this book has deepened, rather than diminished, my conviction that one cannot expect to be the beneficiary of academic freedom unless one extends the same grace to others.

Finally, I would like to thank the following people: Joseph R. Cockrell, M.D., who during different stages of the manuscript's production selflessly read it with a psychiatrist's and neurologist's eye and made many helpful suggestions for improvement; the members of my Thursday-night house church group who prayed me through the process of writing this book; and my wife, Carol, and daughters, Caris and Eliana, whose lives are inextricably bound with my own and who shared in the sacrifices associated with this book.

To God and the Lord Jesus Christ be the glory.

Abbreviations

General

acc.	accusative (case)
aor.	aorist (tense)
B.C.E.	Before the Common Era
ca.	circa
C.E.	Common Era
cf.	confer, compare
ch(s).	chapter(s)
circ.	circumstantial (participle)
d.	died
Dtn	Deuteronomic law code (Deuteronomy 12–26)
Dtr	Deuteronomistic (history, writer); Deuteronomist
esp.	especially
H	Holiness Code (Leviticus 17–26)
impf.	imperfect (tense)
indic.	indicative (mood)
J	Jahwist or Yahwist source (of the Pentateuch)
lit.	literally
LXX	Septuagint
midd.	middle (voice)

MS(S).	manuscript(s)
MT	Masoretic Text
NT	New Testament
OT	Old Testament
P	Priestly Source (of the Pentateuch)
par.	parallel (denotes the existence of parallel verses in one or more other canonical Gospels)
Q	Sayings Source common to Matthew and Luke
Q/Luke	a Lukan saying with a parallel in Matthew but not Mark; hence Q
R	Rabbi or Rab
sc.	*scilicet*, obviously, namely, no doubt
s.v.	*sub verbo*, under the word
viz.	*videlicet*, namely
v(v).	verse(s)

Names of Bible Translations

ASV	American Standard Version
CEV	Contemporary English Version
JB	Jerusalem Bible
KJV	King James Version
MOFFATT	*The Bible: A New Translation*, James Moffatt
NAB	New American Bible
NASB	New American Standard Bible
NEB	New English Bible
NIV	New International Version
NJB	New Jerusalem Bible
NJPS	*Tanakh: The Holy Scriptures*, Jewish Publication Society Translation
NLT	New Living Translation
NRSV	New Revised Standard Version
PHILLIPS	*The New Testament in Modern English*, J. B. Phillips
REB	Revised English Bible
RSV	Revised Standard Version

Names of Biblical Books (with the Apocrypha)

Gen	Amos	Eccl	1–4 Macc	Gal
Exod	Obad	Lam	Pr Azar	Eph
Lev	Jonah	Esth	Pr Man	Phil
Num	Mic	Dan	Sir	Col
Deut	Nah	Ezra	Sus	1–2 Thess
Josh	Hab	Neh	Tob	1–2 Tim
Judg	Zeph	1–2 Chr	Wis	Titus
Ruth	Hag	1–4 Kgdms	Matt	Phlm
1–2 Sam	Zech	Add Esth	Mark	Heb
1–2 Kgs	Mal	Bar	Luke	Jas
Isa	Ps (Pss)	Bel	John	1–2 Pet
Jer	Job	1–2 Esdr	Acts	1–3 John
Ezek	Prov	4 Ezra	Rom	Jude
Hos	Ruth	Jdt	1–2 Cor	Rev
Joel	Cant	Ep Jer		

Secondary Sources: Journals, Major Reference Works, and Series

AB	Anchor Bible
ABQ	*American Baptist Quarterly*
AGJU	Arbeiten zur Geschichte des antiken Judentums und des Urchristentums
ANET	*Ancient Near Eastern Texts Relating to the Old Testament.* Edited by J. B. Pritchard. 3d ed. Princeton, 1969
AOAT	Alter Orient und Altes Testament
BAGD	Bauer, W., W. F. Arndt, F. W. Gingrich, and F. W. Danker. *Greek-English Lexicon of the New Testament and Other Early Christian Literature.* 2d ed. Chicago, 1979
BDB	Brown, F., S. R. Driver, and C. A. Briggs, *Hebrew and English Lexicon of the Old Testament.* Oxford, 1907
BDF	Blass, F., A. Debrunner, and R. W. Funk. *A Greek Grammar of the New Testament and Other Early Christian Literature.* Chicago, 1961
BECNT	Baker Exegetical Commentary on the New Testament

Bib	*Biblica*
BibInt	*Biblical Interpretation*
BIS	Biblical Interpretation Series
BJRL	*Bulletin of the John Rylands University Library of Manchester*
BK	*Bibel und Kirche*
BN	*Biblische Notizen*
BNTC	Black's New Testament Commentaries
BRev	*Bible Review*
BSac	*Bibliotheca sacra*
BTB	*Biblical Theology Bulletin*
BTZ	*Berliner Theologische Zeitschrift*
BZAW	Beihefte zur ZAW
CBET	Contributions to Biblical Exegesis and Theology
CBQ	*Catholic Biblical Quarterly*
CHALOT	Holladay, W. L., *A Concise Hebrew and Aramaic Lexicon of the Old Testament.* Grand Rapids, 1971
ChrCen	*Christian Century*
CRINT	Compendia rerum iudaicarum ad Novum Testamentum
CSR	*Christian Scholar's Review*
DJG	*Dictionary of Jesus and the Gospels.* Edited by J. B. Green and S. McKnight. Downers Grove, 1992
DPL	*Dictionary of Paul and His Letters.* Edited by G. F. Hawthorne and R. P. Martin. Downers Grove, 1993
EBib	*Etudes bibliques*
EDNT	*Exegetical Dictionary of the New Testament.* Edited by H. Balz, G. Schneider. ET. Grand Rapids, 1990–1993
EKKNT	Evangelisch-katholischer Kommentar zum Neuen Testament
EncJud	*Encyclopaedia Judaica.* 16 vols. Jerusalem, 1972
EvQ	*Evangelical Quarterly*
ExAud	*Ex auditu*
ExpTim	*Expository Times*
FRLANT	Forschungen zur Religion und Literatur des Alten und Neuen Testaments
FRR	*Family Research Report*
HALOT	Koehler, L., W. Baumgartner, and J. J. Stamm, *The*

	Hebrew and Aramaic Lexicon of the Old Testament. Translated and edited under the supervision of M. E. J. Richardson. 4 vols. Leiden, 1994–1999
HBT	*Horizons in Biblical Theology*
HNT	Handbuch zum Neuen Testament
HTKNT	Herders theologischer Kommentar zum Neuen Testament
HTR	*Harvard Theological Review*
IBC	Interpretation: A Bible Commentary for Teaching and Preaching
ICC	International Critical Commentary
IDBSup	*Interpreter's Dictionary of the Bible: Supplementary Volume.* Edited by K. Crim. Nashville, 1976
ITC	International Theological Commentary
ITQ	*Irish Theological Quarterly*
JAAR	*Journal of the American Academy of Religion*
JBL	*Journal of Biblical Literature*
JE	*The Jewish Encyclopedia.* Edited by I. Singer. 12 vols. New York, 1925
JETS	*Journal of the Evangelical Theological Society*
JHistSex	*Journal of the History of Sexuality*
JHomosex	*Journal of Homosexuality*
JPSTC	The Jewish Publication Society Torah Commentary
JPT	*Journal of Psychology and Theology*
JRE	*Journal of Religious Ethics*
JSNT	*Journal for the Study of the New Testament*
JSOT	*Journal for the Study of the Old Testament*
JSOTSup	*Journal for the Study of the Old Testament: Supplement Series*
KD	*Kerygma und Dogma*
KEK	Kritisch-exegetischer Kommentar über das Neue Testament (Meyer-Kommentar)
KNT	Kommentar zum Neuen Testament
LÄ	*Lexikon der Ägyptologie.* Edited by W. Helck, E. Otto, and W. Westendorf. Wiesbaden, 1972
LCC	Library of Christian Classics. Philadelphia, 1953–
LCL	Loeb Classical Library

LSJ	Liddell, H. G., R. Scott, H. S. Jones, *A Greek-English Lexicon.* 9th ed. with revised supplement. Oxford, 1996
MNTC	Moffatt New Testament Commentary
NAC	New American Commentary
NCB	New Century Bible
NIB	*The New Interpreter's Bible*
NICNT	New International Commentary on the New Testament
NICOT	New International Commentary on the Old Testament
NIDNTT	*New International Dictionary of New Testament Theology.* Edited by C. Brown. 4 vols. Grand Rapids, 1975–1985
NovT	*Novum Testamentum*
NTD	Das Neue Testament Deutsch
NTS	*New Testament Studies*
OBT	Overtures to Biblical Theology
OTL	Old Testament Library
OTP	*Old Testament Pseudepigrapha.* Edited by J. H. Charlesworth. 2 vols. New York, 1983
QR	*Quarterly Review*
RAC	*Reallexikon für Antike und Christentum.* Edited by T. Kluser el al. Stuttgart, 1950–
RlA	*Reallexikon der Vorgeschicte.* Edited by M. Ebert. Berlin. 1924–1932
RNT	Regensburger Neues Testament
SBL	Society of Biblical Literature
SBLDS	Society of Biblical Literature Dissertation Series
SIHC	Studies in the Intercultural History of Christianity
SJT	*Scottish Journal of Theology*
SNTSMS	Society for New Testament Studies Monograph Series
SP	Sacra pagina
Str-B	Strack, H. L., and P. Billerbeck. *Kommentar zum Neuen Testament aus Talmud und Midrasch.* 6 vols. Munich, 1922–1961
SVTP	Studia in Veteris Testamenti pseudepigraphica
TBei	*Theologische Beiträge*
TDNT	*Theological Dictionary of the New Testament.* Edited by G. Kittel and G. Friedrich. Translated by G. W. Bromiley. 10 vols. Grand Rapids, 1964–1976

TDOT	*Theological Dictionary of the Old Testament.* Edited by G. J. Botterweck and H. Ringgren. Translated by J. T. Willis, G. W. Bromiley, and D. E. Green. 8 vols. Grand Rapids, 1974–
Them	*Themelios*
THKNT	Theologischer Handkommentar zum Neuen Testament
TJT	*Toronto Journal of Theology*
TLNT	*Theological Lexicon of the New Testament.* C. Spicq. Translated and edited by J. D. Ernest. 3 vols. Peabody, Mass., 1994
TPINTC	TPI New Testament Commentaries
TynBul	*Tyndale Bulletin*
USQR	*Union Seminary Quarterly Review*
VC	*Vigiliae christianae*
VT	*Vetus Testamentum*
VTSup	Vetus Testamentum Supplements
WBC	Word Biblical Commentary
WTJ	*Westminster Theological Journal*
WUNT	Wissenschaftliche Untersuchungen zum Neuen Testament
WW	*Word and World*
ZEE	*Zeitschrift für evangelische Ethik*
ZG	Max Zerwick and Mary Grosvenor, *A Grammatical Analysis of the Greek New Testament.* Rev. ed. Rome, 1981
ZNW	*Zeitschrift für die neutestamentliche Wissenschaft und die Kunde der älteren Kirche*
ZTK	*Zeitschrift für Theologie und Kirche*

Primary Sources: Ancient Texts

Apocrypha and Septuagint

2 Esd	2 Esdras
1–4 Macc	1–4 Maccabees
Sir	Sirach / The Wisdom of Yeshua ben Sira / Ecclesiasticus
Sus	Susanna
Tob	Tobit
Wis	Wisdom of Solomon

Old Testament Pseudepigrapha

2 Bar.	*2 Baruch (Syriac Apocalypse)*
2 En.	*2 Enoch (Slavonic Apocalypse)*
4 Ezra	*4 Ezra*
Gk. Apoc. Ezra	*Greek Apocalypse of Ezra*
Jos. Asen.	*Joseph and Aseneth*
Jub.	*Jubilees*
L.A.B.	*Liber antiquitatum biblicarum* (= Pseudo-Philo)
L.A.E.	*Life of Adam and Eve*
Let. Aris.	*Letter of Aristeas*
Ps.-Phoc.	Pseudo-Phocylides
Sib. Or.	*Sibylline Oracles*
T. 12 Patr.	*Testaments of the Twelve Patriarchs*
T. Ash.	*Testament of Asher*
T. Benj.	*Testament of Benjamin*
T. Dan	*Testament of Dan*
T. Gad	*Testament of Gad*
T. Iss.	*Testament of Issachar*
T. Jos.	*Testament of Joseph*
T. Jud.	*Testament of Judah*
T. Levi	*Testament of Levi*
T. Naph.	*Testament of Naphtali*
T. Reu.	*Testament of Reuben*
T. Sim.	*Testament of Simeon*
T. Zeb.	*Testament of Zebulun*
T. 3 Patr.	*Testaments of the Three Patriarchs*
T. Ab.	*Testament of Abraham*
T. Isaac	*Testament of Isaac*

Dead Sea Scrolls and Related Texts

1QS	*Serek Hayaḥad* or *Rule of the Community*
CD	Cairo Genizah copy of the *Damascus Document*
11QT[a]	Temple Scroll[a]

Philo

Abr.	*On the Life of Abraham (= De Abrahamo)*
Alleg. Interp.	*Allegorical Interpretation (= Legum allegoriae)*
Animals	*On Animals* (or *Whether Animals Have Reason*) *(= De animalibus)*
Cher.	*On the Cherubim (= De cherubim)*
Contempl. Life	*On the Contemplative Life (= De vita contemplativa)*
Decal.	*On the Decalogue (= De decalogo)*
Dreams	*On Dreams (= De somniis)*
Good Person	*That Every Good Person Is Free (= Quod omnis probus liber sit)*
Hypoth.	*Hypothetica*
Migr.	*On the Migration of Abraham (= De migratione Abrahami)*
Names	*On the Change of Names (= De mutatione nominum)*
QE	*Questions and Answers on Exodus (= Quaestiones et solutiones in Exodum)*
QG	*Questions and Answers on Genesis (= Quaestiones et solutiones in Genesin)*
Spec. Laws	*On the Special Laws (= De specialibus legibus)*

Josephus

Ag. Ap.	*Against Apion*
Ant.	*Jewish Antiquities*
J.W.	*Jewish War*

Mishnah, Talmud, and Related Literature

To distinguish the same-named tractates in the Mishnah, Babylonian Talmud, Jerusalem Talmud, and Tosefta, the following abbreviations are used before the title of the tractate: *m.*, *b.*, *y.*, or *t.*

ᶜAbod. Zar.	*ᶜAbodah Zarah*
Ber.	*Berakot*

ʿEd.	Eduyyot
Giṭ.	Giṭṭin
Hal.	Ḥallah
Ker.	Kerithot
Ketub.	Ketubbot
Ned.	Nedarim
Nid.	Niddah
Pesaḥ.	Pesaḥim
Qidd.	Quiddušin
Sanh.	Sanhedrin
Šabb.	Šabbat
Yebam.	Yebamot

Targumic Texts

Tg. Ps.-J.	Targum Pseudo-Jonathan

Other Rabbinic Works

Gen. Rab.	Genesis Rabbah
Lev. Rab.	Leviticus Rabbah
Mek. R. Shim.	Mekilta of Rabbi Simeon
Pesiq. Rab.	Pesiqta Rabbati
Pirqe R. El.	Pirqe Rabbi Eliezer
S. ʿOlam Rab.	Seder ʿOlam Rabbah

Apostolic Fathers

Barn.	Barnabas
Did.	Didache
Ign. Eph.	Ignatius, To the Ephesians

New Testament Apocrypha and Pseudepigrapha

Acts John	Acts of John
Apos. Con.	Apostolic Constitutions and Canons
Eg. Gos.	Egerton Gospel
Gos. Naz.	Gospel of the Nazarenes

Gos. Thom.   Gospel of Thomas
Pap. Oxy. 1224 Oxyrhynchus Papyrus 1224
Ps.-Clem.   Pseudo-Clementines

Classical and Ancient Christian Writings

Achilles Tatius, *Leuc. Clit.* (= *Leucippe et Clitophon* or *The Adventures of Leucippe and Cleitophon*)
Aristides, *Apol.* (= *Apology*)
Aristotle, *Eth. nic.* (= *Ethica nichomachea* or *Nicomachean Ethics*)
Artemidorus, *Onir.* (= *Onirocritica* or *The Interpretation of Dreams*)
Athenaeus, *Deipn.* (= *Deipnosophistae*)
Cat. Cod. Astrol. Graec. (= *Catalogus Codicum Astrologorum Graecorum*)
Cicero, *Dom.* (= *De domo suo*); *Leg.* (= *De legibus*); *Phil.* (= *Orationes philippicae*)
Clement of Alexandria, *Paed.* (= *Paedagogus*)
Dio Chrysostom, *Disc.* (= *Discourses*)
Epictetus, *Diatr.* (= *Diatribai [Dissertationes]*)
Eusebius, *Praep. ev.* (= *Praeparatio evangelica* or *Preparation for the Gospel*); *Dem. ev.* (= *Demonstratio evangelica* or *Demonstration of the Gospel*)
Hippolytus, *Haer.* (= *Refutatio omnium haeresium* or *Refutation of All Heresies*)
John Chrysostom, *Hom. Rom.* (= *Homilies in the Epistle to the Romans*)
Justin, *1 Apol.* (= *First Apology*)
Juvenal, *Sat.* (= *Satirae*)
Maximus of Tyre, *Or.* (= *Orations*)
Nilus, *Ep.* (= *Epistulae*)
Origen, *Comm. Matt.* (= *Commentary on the Gospel of Matthew*); *Fr. 1 Cor.* (= *Fragments from Commentaries on the First Epistle to the Corinthians*); *Fr. Exod.* (= *Fragments from Commentaries on Exodus*)
Ovid, *Metam.* (= *Metamorphoses*)
Philostratus, *Ep.* (= *Epistulae*)

Plato, *Phaedr.* (= *Phaedrus*); *Prot.* (= *Protagoras*); *Symp.* (= *Symposium*);

Plutarch, *Mor.* (= *Moralia*): *Dial. Love* (= *Moralia: Dialogue on Love* = *Amatorius* = *Erōtikos*); *Beasts* (= *Moralia: Whether Beasts Are Rational* = *Bruta animalia ratione uti*); *Lyc.* (= *Lycurgus*)

Pollux, *Onom.* (= *Onomasticon*)

Pseudo-Aristotle, *Probl.* (= *Problemata*)

(Pseudo-) Cyril of Alexandria, *Homil. Div* (= *Homiliae diversae*)

Pseudo-Lucian, *Affairs* (= *Affairs of the Heart* or *Amores*) (153-54)

Rhet. Her. (= *Rhetorica ad Herennium*)

Rufinus, *Sent. Sext.* (= *The Sentences of Sextus trans. by Rufinus*)

Sacra Parall. (= *Sacra Parallela*)

Seneca, *Ep.* (= *Epistulae morales* or *Moral Epistles*)

Stobaeus, *Anth.* (= *Anthologium*)

Theodoret, *Hist. eccl.* (= *Historia ecclesiastica* or *Ecclesiastical History*)

Theophilus, *Autol.* (= *Ad Autolycum* or *To Autolychus*)

INTRODUCTION

The Personal Risks Inherent in Writing Such a Book

"You ought to have your head examined." "What were you thinking?" Such expressions are used in American culture to express incredulity at the actions of another who puts him or herself needlessly at risk. Surely such expressions are never more apropos than when a seminary professor writes a book about the Bible passages that deal with homosexuality and the interpretation of these texts, and especially when one does so from the perspective taken in this book.

The reasons for calling into question the good sense of such a person are readily apparent. The debate now raging on the subject of homosexuality in the church and the wider culture is nothing short of fierce. To jump into the fray with both feet is to invite attack, often vicious attack. One can hardly be surprised by this volatile state of affairs. Simply put, sex matters. The powerful mating instinct built into the human species, with its enormous potential for both pleasure and pain, consumes an extraordinary amount of our time and energy as we attempt to figure out how to satisfy it and domesticate it, with whom and when, so as to maximize pleasure and minimize pain to ourselves and others. The mating instinct can be harnessed to build families, contribute to a stable and nurturing society generally, and promote happiness; but it can also destroy these social goods. Consequently, much is at stake on nearly any issue involving sexual ethics.

In the cultural, political, religious, and academic arenas of our lives, issues related to homosexuality and homosexual persons are pervasive and hotly contested. Protests and counterprotests over the portrayal of homosexuals in the media seem constant. Public and private policy debates rage about such issues as antidiscrimination laws regarding housing and employment; hate-crime legislation; statutes that redefine marriage and/or grant domestic partner status to homosexual couples; educational and training programs that promote tolerance and diversity; the public support for the arts; qualifications for military service; and allocations for AIDS research. The church—local congregations and denominational bodies—divides because of fierce disagreements about the status of homosexual Christians, their relationships, and their qualifications for ministry. One side appeals to the explicit statements in Scripture regarding same-sex intercourse, the structures of God's creation, principles of sexual holiness, two millennia of church tradition, the influence of environment on the development of homosexuality, the dearth of long-term and monogamous homosexual relationships, and the negative health effects of homosexual behavior. The other side points to genetic causation, the fruit of caring homosexual relationships, the antiquated worldview and obsolescence of other parts of Scripture, and such Christian virtues as tolerance and inclusion. In the academy today, speaking one's mind is especially perilous for those who question the morality of same-sex intercourse. Opposing intolerance of the sexual practices of others functions as a badge of intellectual open-mindedness and membership among the avant-garde of cultured society—part of a cherished self-perception of being on the "cutting edge." There is an undeniable, built-in bias among many of the intellectual elite against advocates of traditional sexual values. Attitudes toward homosexuality cohere with this wider bias. It is into this context that I put forward my own best argument, well aware of the risks.

In the politics of personal destruction, the first risk is to be labeled *homophobic*, a label which conveys the impression of a psychiatric disorder. This label is employed as part of an overall strategy of intimidation to forestall genuine debate and belittle vocal dissenters. Moral disapproval of sinful behavior, of behaviors that are destructive to individuals and/or society, or contrary to God's will, is different from fear and must be distinguished if the conversation is to proceed.

A second risk is that of being labeled *intolerant*, perhaps applied as a global descriptor of personhood and not just with respect to a negative stance toward same-sex intercourse. It is important to be clear about the definition of tolerance and its place among Christian virtues. While tolerance may be a virtue in many instances, love holds a superior place in a Christian worldview (1 Cor 13:13). Love and tolerance overlap but are not identical concepts. The Bible describes a God who loves the entire world but does not tolerate sin. In fact, in the few instances when words that could be translated as tolerance or intolerance occur in the biblical text, they generally appear in contexts that *condemn* tolerance of wickedness and immorality in the midst of God's people. Rev 2:20 is a case in point: "But I have this against you: you tolerate (*apheis*) that woman Jezebel, who calls herself a prophet and is teaching and beguiling my servants to practice fornication (*porneusai*) and to eat food sacrificed to idols" (NRSV).[1] Of course, the scant positive use of *tolerance* and *tolerate* in English translations does not mean that the concept of tolerance receives little play in the Bible.

---

1. The translation "you tolerate" is given by nearly all major English committee translations of this verse. RSV uses the word *tolerate* only once elsewhere, outside the Apocrypha, in Esth 3:8 (Haman's slander to the king that the Jews "do not keep the king's laws, so that it is not for the king's profit to tolerate them" [similarly, REB, NAB, NIV; NASB: "to let them remain"], *lĕhannîhām, hipᶜîl* of *nwḥ* = "set down; leave, let, allow, leave alone"); cf. 2 Esd 15:8 ("neither will I tolerate their wicked practices"); 3 Macc 1:22 (bolder Jews would not "tolerate" the king's wicked plans). To these instances NRSV adds: Ps 101:5 ("A haughty look and an arrogant heart I will not tolerate" [most: "endure"], from *yākal* = "be able; endure"); Mic 6:11 ("Can I tolerate wicked scales . . . ?" [RSV, NIV, NAB: "Shall I acquit"; REB, NJB: "Can I connive at"], from *zākâ* = "be pure, blameless, justified, regarded as righteous" [qal] or, if vocalized as a piel, "justify [the use of]"); Rev 2:2 ("I know that you cannot tolerate evildoers" [similarly, NAB, NIV; RSV: "bear"; NASB: "endure"; REB: "abide"; NJB: "stand"], *bastazō* = "bear, endure, carry" [BAGD]; cf. Sus 1:57 ("would not tolerate your wickedness"). In addition to Esth 3:8; Rev 2:2, 20, NAB translates "tolerate" in Gen 34:7 (Shechem's rape of Dinah was an act which "could not be tolerated," lit., "should not be done," *nipᶜal* of *ᶜāsâ*); 2 Tim 4:3 ("For the time will come when people will not tolerate (*anexontai*) sound doctrine" [RSV, NASB: "endure"; NRSV, NIV: "put up with"; REB: "stand"; NJB: "accept"], *anechō* = "endure, bear with, put up with" [BAGD]).

Jesus' injunction against judging (Luke 6:37) and his chastisement of hypocrites who were eager to take the speck out of another's "eye" but blind to the log in their own (Luke 6:41-42)[2] are two texts that come quickly to mind. Nor is the Bible itself immune from the criticism of intolerance at specific points. Nevertheless, the biblical data should give a person pause before trumpeting tolerance as *the* central Christian or biblical virtue. Toleration of immoral sexual practices was a vice, not a virtue. So, rather than elevate tolerance to the highest position, one might do better to lift up one of the Christian virtues that Paul cites as fruits of the Spirit in Gal 5:22-23: "love, joy, peace, patience, kindness, goodness, faith/faithfulness, gentleness, and self-control." Unlike the word *tolerance*, none of these virtues implies any reduction of moral resolve against sinful behavior. *If* same-sex intercourse is indeed sin, then an appeal to tolerance is largely misplaced.

Third, critics of homosexual behavior risk being labeled *exclusive* and *resistant to diversity*. As with the use of the words *tolerant* and *intolerant*, such labels obscure the real conflict; namely, whether one determines that the behavior in question is sinful/harmful or not. No one on either side of the homosexuality debate wants to be inclusive of harmful behavior or widen diversity to include sin.

A fourth risk taken by biblical scholars or theologians who write anything critical of homosexual behavior is that of being labeled *uncritical*. However, critical scholarship by no means leads in a straight line to the conclusion that the biblical texts condemning same-sex intercourse ought to be dismissed, though some seem to presume this as a matter of course. Most people in the church mean by *critical* that one cannot read everything the Bible says at face value. In other words, the text must be read through a hermeneutical lens, the ancient context and contemporary currents must be considered, and some measure of openness must be given to the possibility that a given author or authors of a biblical text may be reflecting personal or cultural biases. With this approach I am in basic agreement. However, on this issue, as on any other, if a clear, unequivocal, and pervasive stance in the Bible can be

---

2. Note, though, the concluding statement for the latter, which presupposes an appropriate mode for admonishing others against evil: "*First* take the log out of your own eye, *and then* you will see clearly to take the speck out of your brother's eye."

shown to exist—across the Testaments and accepted for nearly two millennia of the church's existence—then the burden of proof lies with those in the church who take a radically different approach to the issue. In any case, uncritical scholarship in the use of the Bible is not restricted to any one side of the theological spectrum.

Fifth, others may accuse scholars who publicly question the morality of homosexual behavior of *holding on to* outmoded moral standards or *primitive understandings of sexuality*. But such labels beg the question of how one knows what is outmoded. Is something outmoded simply because it has a long pedigree? To the contrary, the antiquity and durability of a given prohibition against immoral conduct often indicates its workability, effectiveness, and elasticity as a cultural model rather than its contemporary irrelevance.

Sixth, some may contend that writing a book such as this risks *endowing the homosexuality debate with unmerited importance*. Of course we all lament the amount of time, energy, and resources that has been expended on the issue. Apparently, however, people on the whole feel that the one thing worse than having church and society devote such great efforts to the issue is giving up and allowing the other side to control all policy, public and private, secular and religious. The amount of attention devoted to the homosexuality debate is related not just to the importance of the issue (in the Bible and empirically) but to the absence of a clear consensus from which to formulate policy decisions, and the fact that a fundamental shift in attitudes hangs in the balance.

Finally, some will charge that a book such as this *promotes violence against homosexuals*, even though readers of this book receive not the slightest encouragement to be anything less than loving in personal dealings with homosexuals. While antihomosexual violence deserves to be vigorously denounced, it does nobody any good to ignore the dangerous way in which isolated and relatively rare incidents of violence against homosexuals have been exploited to stifle freedom of speech and coerce societal endorsement of homosexual practice. Four points are pertinent here. First, if proponents of same-sex intercourse really have a paramount interest in curtailing acts of violence against homosexuals, the best thing for them to do is to hold up models of civil discourse among people who oppose same-sex intercourse. Second, a lesson can be learned from the tradition of Jesus' reaction to the woman caught in adultery in John 7:53–8:11, ironically a favorite proof text for Christians who advocate the acceptance of homosexual behavior. In the story, Jesus does not back down in his opposition to adultery despite the fact that adulterous women in Israel faced the prospect of mob violence; he calls adultery a sin and commands the woman to change her ways (8:11). His solution is not to tolerate adultery but to make a distinction between the community's assessment of the act as immoral and the application of the death penalty. Third, there is no end to the kinds of moral discourse that can be squelched when the distinction between polite but critical rhetoric on the one hand and violent extremists on the other is ignored.[3] By that same logic, for example, the United States in the nineteenth century should have endorsed the practice of polygamy in order to avoid violence against polygamists. Fourth, statistically more significant than hate crimes against homosexuals are the harmful effects of various forms of homosexual behavior on homosexuals themselves: serious health risks (such as AIDS) associated with anal intercourse and rampant promiscuity; "pick-up murders," in which a gay man kills an anonymous sex partner; and high rates of domestic violence and sadomasochism among homosexual couples. Societal tolerance of homosexual practice results in a higher incidence of experimentation with bisexual and homosexual practice among youth, with all its attendant negative side effects. None of this even touches the negative effects that homosexual behavior can have on a person's relationship with God. One may then ask, which is the more humane rhetoric? Rhetoric that out of a sense of compassion fosters same-sex intercourse, or rhetoric that out of a sense of compassion rejects same-sex intercourse while promoting kindness to homosexuals and management of homoerotic impulses?

---

3. Unfortunate acts of violence have occurred in conjunction with many otherwise noble movements: the civil rights movement for African Americans; the resistance on American college campuses to the Vietnam War; the struggle against apartheid in South Africa; environmental groups (case in point: the "Unabomber"); and the cause of Palestinians, to name a few. If the logic of gay rights activists were applied to these causes, then all of these movements should have been or should be quashed. Indeed, avid supporters of homosexual practice would have to stifle themselves since some critics of their cause have become the target of death threats, drive-by shooting into their homes, arson, and other forms of harassment.

Motivation for "Coming Out of the Closet"

Acknowledging Personal Regrets

In recent years, as an occasional speaker in church forums I have been involved on a small scale in the debate over ordaining "self-affirming, practicing" homosexuals. Often at such forums there are moving presentations both by those who have "come out of the closet" to proclaim that their homosexuality is part of God's good creation, and by those who have gone one step further by coming out of the homosexual lifestyle. The homosexuality debate is generally not pleasant for those who speak out publicly against homosexual behavior—at least it has never been for me. Not only does it leave one vulnerable to the host of stereotypes treated above and position one squarely against the cultural norms prevailing in most of the media, academy, and secular establishment, but it also forces one to uphold standards of righteousness when keenly aware of one's own imperfections and need for grace. It also compels one to emphasize the negative and define boundaries rather than to discuss more uplifting core elements of the faith.

Perhaps worst of all is the knowledge that a rigorous critique of same-sex intercourse can have the unintended effect of bringing personal pain to homosexuals, some of whom are already prone to self-loathing. This is why it needs to be emphatically stated that to feel homosexual impulses does not make one a bad person. I deplore attempts to demean the humanity of homosexuals. Whatever one thinks about the immorality of homosexual behavior, or about the obnoxiousness of elements within the homosexual lobby, homosexual impulses share with all other sinful impulses the feature of being an attack on the "I" or inner self experiencing the impulses (Rom 7:14-25). The person beset with homosexual temptation should evoke our concern, sympathy, help, and understanding, not our scorn or enmity. Even more, such a person should kindle a feeling of solidarity in the hearts of all Christians, since we all struggle to properly manage our erotic passions. A homosexual impulse, while sinful, cannot take shape as accountable sin in a person's life unless one acquiesces to it. Thus a reasoned denunciation of homosexual behavior and all other attempts at nurturing and justifying homosexual passions is *not,* and should not be construed as, a denunciation of those victimized by homosexual urges, since the aim is to rescue the true self created in God's image for a full life.

Still, a distinction in one's head and a distinction in one's heart are two different things. For homosexuals a denunciation of homosexuality may *feel* like an indictment of homosexuals. Regrettably, some of this pain may be unavoidable in the hope of doing away with the greater pain of living outside of God's redemptive plan. There can be no healthy transformation so long as homosexuals live in a world of unreality, including the unreality of false notions about Scripture's view of homosexuality. When a homosexual holds out hope that something in the teachings of Jesus or in the Bible generally speaks positively about same-sex erotic unions, naturally there is going to be disappointment and sadness upon the discovery that nothing of the sort exists. One is reminded here of Paul's sober retrospect on his "tearful letter" to the Corinthian believers:

> For though I grieved you in the letter, I do not continue to have regrets—though I used to have regrets, for I see that letter (though only for a short time) grieved you. Now I rejoice, not because you were grieved but because you were grieved into repenting. For you were grieved in a godly manner (lit., in accordance with God), in order that you would in no way be caused loss or damage by us. For a godly grief (lit., a grief in accordance with God) produces a repentance which leads to a salvation free of all regret; but the grief of the world produces death. (2 Cor 7:8-10)

For Paul, causing the Corinthian community sorrow was not the objective. Indeed, Paul regretted that they had to feel any sorrow at all, though from Paul's perspective it was unavoidable. The objective was rather to wake up the Corinthians to the seriousness of the matter at hand so that the end result might be something greater than emotional tranquillity: the salvation of those involved.

Three Generic Reasons for Speaking Out

For me, there are three generic reasons for speaking out against same-sex intercourse which override the personal risks. The first two have to do with the two commandments of the law singled out by Jesus as the greatest—two principles on which every ethical decision should be based. The third has to do with the urgency of the time.

First, regarding the vertical dimension to human existence, devotion to God ought to take precedence over every other consideration: "You shall love Yahweh your God with all your heart, and with all your soul, and with all your might" (Deut 6:5; cited in Mark 12:30, 33 par.). The whole of what we do and who we are should proceed from a desire to please the sovereign God who created humankind and is working to redeem it. Jesus' vision of God's kingdom or reign involves a transcendent reality above and yet to come, a reality that God's people are called on to seek and to pray for beyond all else. Of course such assumptions about God's reign do not settle once and for all which side of the issue one should come down on as regards homosexuality. However, I am persuaded that to love God with one's whole being and to pray for the coming of God's rule entails submitting one's pursuit of sexual pleasure to the revealed will of God. To suppose that God does not have much interest in regulating the human sex drive, one of the most powerful and potentially destructive human impulses, is both counter-intuitive and in direct conflict with Scripture. From a Judeo-Christian standpoint, it is a truncated vision of reality to accept various forms of sexuality merely because the participants involved give their consent to a given sex act. The first consideration must always be what God wants. God calls us to live holy lives subject to the divine will and not according to our own desires. In my view, the Bible, though not the only witness to God's will and not immune to hermeneutical scrutiny, is the single most important element for discerning that will. As I will argue, the Bible speaks unequivocally and forcefully to the issue of homosexuality.

Second, regarding the horizontal dimension of human existence, it matters how humans act in relation to one another. Here the definitive injunction is to "love your neighbor as yourself" (Lev 19:18; cited in Mark 12:31, 33 par.; Matt 5:43; 19:19; Rom 13:9; Gal 5:14; Jas 2:8). Jesus in the parable of the good Samaritan (Luke 10:29-37) expanded the meaning of *neighbor* (*rēʾăkā* = a companion from one's kinship group, a fellow Israelite) to embrace anyone whom one would want to act like a neighbor to oneself in one's own hour of greatest need, including enemies, aliens, and outcasts.[4] Jesus interpreted *love* to mean doing to other people whatever you would want them to do to you (the Golden Rule, Luke 6:31 par.). Such love demands an aggressive search for the lost and their reintegration into the sphere of God's redemptive work.

In contemporary society the command to love is often misconstrued as tolerance and acceptance. The concept is richer than that. True love "does not rejoice over unrighteousness but rejoices with the truth" (1 Cor 13:6). The immediate context of the love commandment in Lev 19:18 underscores the moral dimension of love:

> You shall not hate your brother in your heart. *You shall firmly reprove your fellow-countryman* and so not incur guilt because of him. You shall not take revenge and you shall not hold a grudge against any of your people and you shall love your neighbor as yourself. I am Yahweh. (Lev 19:17-18)

Love and reproof are not mutually exclusive concepts. If one fails to reprove another who is engaged in self-destructive or community-destructive behavior, or any conduct deemed unacceptable by God, one can hardly claim to have acted in love either to the perpetrator or to others affected by the perpetrator's actions. Without a moral compass love is mere mush. Without taking into account God's will for holy living, love turns into affirmation of self-degrading and other-degrading conduct. This means that true love of one's neighbor does not embrace every form of consensual behavior. What constitutes an expression of love to one's neighbor depends significantly on how one assesses the benefit or harm of the neighbor's behavior. If indeed homosexual behavior is sin and an obstacle to the fullness of life available in Christ, then the church has an obligation both to protect the church from the debilitating effect of sanctioned immorality and to protect the homosexual for whom more is at stake than the satisfaction of sensual impulses. If a person is about to touch a live wire or encour-

---

4. For a helpful, up-to-date discussion of Jesus' interpretation of Lev 19:18 in relation to early Judaism, see Gerd Theissen and Annette Merz, *The Historical Jesus: A Comprehensive Guide* (Minneapolis: Fortress, 1998), 381-94.

age others to do so, it is not a kindness to affirm that person's behavior or to remain silent. In my opinion, despite the best of intentions by many heterosexual champions of same-sex erotic unions, affirming homosexual behavior is not the loving thing to do, either for the church and society as a whole or for homosexuals. Love for one's neighbor requires one to speak out against such behavior, sometimes firmly. Godly love is responsible love.

The third justification for speaking out is the urgency of the time we live in. The window of opportunity for speaking out against homosexual behavior is closing. Nothing less than intellectual integrity, free speech, and a potentially irreversible change in the morality of mainline denominations are at stake in this vital area of sexual ethics. Many homosexuals are not out to foist acceptance of their behavior on the public but are simply people with hurting souls who need our sympathy and understanding help. Many heterosexuals who see nothing inherently wrong with homosexual behavior are tolerant of those who disagree. Yet a growing number of zealous crusaders for gay "rights" are working hard to stifle vocal disagreement with the homosexual agenda by fostering a public characterization of those who refuse to go along as reactionary, dangerous characters (on a par with racists or misogynists), even exerting institutional pressure to fire, not hire or license, or retard the promotion of vocal dissenters.

Personal Reasons for Speaking Out

The three reasons given above for speaking out against homosexual behavior can be generic to anyone who views such behavior as harmful or contrary to God's will. In addition to these reasons, my own particular interest in the subject derives from personal relationships with homosexuals in the church, some of whom have struggled with their homosexual urges (successfully or not), others of whom have not struggled. Of these interactions three stand out.

While I was an undergraduate at Dartmouth College in the late-1970s, a Christian student who had been attending the student fellowship group of which I was a member "came out of the closet." He no longer made a secret of his homosexual orientation and now affirmed his intent to engage in sexual relations with other males. No direct action was ever taken by the student fellowship group, but their stance on homosexuality was fairly evident, and the student of his own accord soon tapered off, and later ended, his participation. I had a conversation with him shortly after he had "come out." I simply tried to listen to him, to extend love. He saw no need to struggle with his homosexual impulses any longer because, at least in part, he was receiving affirmation from the official Dartmouth community to celebrate his homosexuality. Why not choose the path of least resistance, particularly when one is receiving praise for doing so? We graduated and went our separate ways. The fact that he had attended the same Christian group, as well as the perceptible impact that the homosexual lobby on campus had on him, made the interaction memorable.

Later, as a graduate student at Harvard Divinity School, I became involved in a church that had a ministry to people struggling with homosexual impulses. There I became friends with a man who had stopped pursuing sexual relations with other men and had married a Christian woman. As a child, he had experienced his father to be a cold and distant personality. He had difficulty feeling like "one of the boys" and shied away from typically male forms of socialization. Now, with the help of counseling, he had found contentment in a committed heterosexual relationship. In times of high stress, his same-sex desires would reemerge, yet he remained faithful to his wife, much like any heterosexual person who, in marriage, is committed to keeping his/her vows but remains susceptible to temptation through unsolicited sexual desires. To me he is an example of sober hope for those struggling with their homosexuality.

Recently I had the opportunity to get to know a mild-mannered and thoughtful homosexual man. Michael (not his real name) enjoys attending a church that happens to take an unequivocal stance against same-sex unions. By his own account he attends this particular church because, despite members' views on homosexuality, he feels the warmth of believing fellowship and worship there, as well as a strong acknowledgment of Christ's lordship. He is not secretive about his homosexuality to members of the church, or about his active role in an AIDS ministry. Michael grew up in the church, had a strained relationship with his father, who died when Michael was eleven, and is now HIV-positive but asymptomatic. Michael does not appear to be emotionally torn by the conflict between the pronouncements of Scripture and his homosexual behavior. He does think that there is a chance that God will judge him severely for his conduct. It is not altogether clear who is witnessing to whom, but his presence creates an interesting environment in which the church demonstrates kindness without giving up its historic stance against same-sex intercourse.

While the above three cases provide an interesting spectrum, I make no pretense that these three homosexual men constitute a representative sample of all homosexuals. My point in mentioning them is simply to indicate one of the factors that generated my interest in the subject of homosexuality. For me, they put a human face on the debate about homosexuality and serve as a reminder to me both of the intractable character of sexual desire and of the possibility for change.

The Argument of This Book

The objective of this book is to demonstrate two main points. First, there is clear, strong, and credible evidence that the Bible unequivocally defines same-sex intercourse as sin. Second, there exist no valid hermeneutical arguments, derived from either general principles of biblical interpretation or contemporary scientific knowledge and experience, for overriding the Bible's authority on this matter. In sum, the Bible presents the anatomical, sexual, and procreative complementarity of male and female as clear and convincing proof of God's will for sexual unions. Even those who do not accept the revelatory authority of Scripture should be able to perceive the divine will through the visible testimony of the structure of creation. Thus same-sex intercourse constitutes an inexcusable rebellion against the intentional design of the created order. It degrades the participants when they disregard nature's obvious clues, and results in destructive consequences for them as well as for society as a whole. These consequences include matters of health (catastrophic rates of disease and shortened life expectancy) and morals (unstable and destabilizing patterns of sexual behavior where short-term and non-monogamous relationships constitute the rule rather than the exception).

The focus of this book on *same-sex intercourse* or *homosexual practice*, as opposed to homosexual *orientation*, is a reflection of the Bible's own relative disinterest toward motives or the origination of same-sex impulses. What matters is not what urges individuals feel but what they do with these urges, both in their fantasy life and in their concrete actions. Even so, it will be argued that scientific research to date does not support the assertion of many proponents of homosexual behavior that homosexual orientation is primarily due to genetic causation. Rather, the most that can be claimed is that homosexuality arises from a complex interplay of genes, intra-uterine and post-uterine biological development, environment, and choice. Genes, if they have any effect at all on a predisposition to homosexuality, are likely to play an indirect and partial role, not a dominant one.

While book-length treatments of homosexuality by biblical scholars or church historians supportive of homosexuality have appeared in a steady stream since 1980 (particularly those by Boswell, Scroggs, Edwards, Countryman, Brooten, and Nissinen), those by biblical scholars who question the legitimacy of homosexual behavior are fewer and more recent. Examples of the latter are books by three New Testament scholars, Ronald Springett (1988), Marion Soards (1995), and Thomas Schmidt (1995); and a book by an Old Testament scholar and pastor, Donald Wold (1998). Mention should also be made of the significant articles or chapters by Richard Hays (on the hermeneutical appropriation of Scripture) and David Wright (especially on the meaning of 1 Cor 6:9), as well as a recent book by theologian and ethicist Stanley Grenz.[5] Wold's book focuses on the ancient Near Eastern

---

5. John Boswell, *Christianity, Social Tolerance, and Homosexuality: Gay People in Western Europe from the Beginning of the Christian Era to the Fourteenth Century* (Chicago: University of Chicago Press, 1980), esp. pp. 61-117; Robin Scroggs, *The New Testament and Homosexuality: Contextual Background for Contemporary Debate* (Philadelphia: Fortress, 1983); George R. Edwards, *Gay/Lesbian Liberation: A Biblical Perspective* (New York: Pilgrim, 1984); L. William Countryman, *Dirt, Greed, and Sex: Sexual Ethics in the New Testament and Their Implications for Today* (Philadelphia: Fortress, 1988) esp. pp. 104-29; Bernadette J. Brooten, *Love Between Women: Early Christian Responses to Female Homoeroticism* (Chicago: University of Chicago Press, 1996); Martti Nissinen, *Homoeroticism in the Biblical World* (Minneapolis: Fortress, 1998); Ronald M. Springett, *Homosexuality in History and the Scriptures: Some Historical and Biblical Perspectives on Homosexuality* (Washington, D.C.: Biblical Research Institute, 1988); Marion L. Soards, *Scripture and Homosexuality: Biblical Authority and the Church Today* (Louisville: Westminster, 1995); Thomas E. Schmidt,

background and the Old Testament but gives relatively little attention to the New Testament data. The book by Soards provides helpful information and insights, particularly on the relationship of biblical authority to the Reformed tradition. However, the treatment of the biblical texts is deliberately brief and written in a popular style, leaving room for a more rigorous and detailed assessment of the Bible and its hermeneutical relevance. To some extent this need is met in the books by Springett and especially Schmidt. Yet I believe there is still a need for carrying the discussion of biblical texts further, including such areas as the implicit motive clause for the Levitical prohibitions; the meaning of *para physin* ("beyond or contrary to nature") in early Jewish literature and its relation to Paul's understanding of the phrase; Jesus' position on sexual ethics and compassion; and a more thoroughgoing

Straight and Narrow? Compassion and Clarity in the Homosexuality Debate (Downers Grove: InterVarsity, 1995); Donald J. Wold, *Out of Order: Homosexuality in the Bible and the Ancient Near East* (Grand Rapids: Baker, 1998); Stanley J. Grenz, *Welcoming But Not Affirming: An Evangelical Response to Homosexuality* (Louisville: Westminster John Knox, 1998). The articles or chapters by Richard B. Hays are: "Relations Natural and Unnatural: A Response to John Boswell's Exegesis of Romans 1," *JRE* 14 (1986) 184-215; "Awaiting the Redemption of Our Bodies: The Witness of Scripture Concerning Homosexuality," *Homosexuality in the Church* (see below), 3-17; *The Moral Vision of the New Testament: A Contemporary Introduction to New Testament Ethics* (San Francisco: Harper, 1996), ch. 16 (pp. 379-406). The works by David Wright are: "Homosexuals or Prostitutes? The Meaning of *Arsenokoitai* (1 Cor. 6:9, 1 Tim. 1:10)," *VC* 38 (1984): 125-53; "Homosexuality: The Relevance of the Bible," *EvQ* 61 (1989): 291-300; "Early Christian Attitudes to Homosexuality," *Studia Patristica* 18 (1989): 329-34; *The Christian Faith and Homosexuality* (rev. ed.; Edinburgh: Rutherford House, 1994; a twenty-nine-page pamphlet). Significant collections of essays on both sides of the debate include: Jeffrey S. Siker, ed., *Homosexuality in the Church: Both Sides of the Debate* (Louisville: Westminster/John Knox, 1994; contributors are from various theological disciplines); Robert L. Brawley, ed., *Biblical Ethics and Homosexuality: Listening to Scripture* (Louisville: Westminster John Knox, 1996; contributors are all biblical scholars, mostly Presbyterian seminary professors); Choon-Leong Seow, ed., *Homosexuality and Christian Community* (Louisville: Westminster John Knox, 1996; a collection of essays by professors at Princeton Theological Seminary); and David L Balch, ed., *Homosexuality, Science, and the "Plain Sense" of Scripture* (Grand Rapids: Eerdmans, 2000; half of which consists of essays by biblical scholars). In each collection, contributions from scholars opposed to same-sex intercourse are in a distinct minority: four or five out of thirteen in Siker; two out of nine in Brawley; three or four out of thirteen in Seow; and four out of eleven in Balch. The collection edited by Balch became available to me too late to be thoroughly integrated into my book. See my review article, *HBT* 22 (2000): 174-243.

response to recent criticisms of the Bible's view of homosexuality as misogynistic and outdated. A major aim of this book is to lift up in a more rigorous and scholarly way than has been done till now the argument of the complementarity of male and female in material creation as a key argument in early Judeo-Christian opposition to same-sex intercourse.

The four chapters that follow this introduction examine the biblical witness that speaks directly to the issue of same-sex intercourse. Chapter 1 treats: the ancient Near Eastern background; the creation stories in Genesis 1–3; the story of Ham's sin in Gen 9:20-27; the narrative of Sodom and Gomorrah in Gen 19:4-11, and various other ancient interpretations of the sin of Sodom; the narrative of the rape of the Levite's concubine in Judg 19:22-25; the question of homosexual cult prostitution in Israel; various issues relating to the laws in Lev 18:22 and 20:13; and the narrative of the relationship of David and Jonathan in 1 Samuel 18–23 and 2 Samuel 1. Chapter 2 focuses on the meaning of the *para physin* ("contrary to nature") argument in early Judaism, particularly in Philo and Josephus, against its Hellenistic background. Chapter 3 begins the discussion of the early Christian witness against same-sex intercourse, with an exploration of Jesus' stance. Chapter 4 treats extensively the Pauline literature, specifically Rom 1:24-27 (arguably the single most important biblical text) and the vice lists in 1 Cor 6:9 and 1 Tim 1:10.

In chapter 5, I turn my attention from "what the texts meant" in their original context to "what the texts mean" in a contemporary setting. Having established that the biblical texts that speak directly to the issue of same-sex intercourse express unambiguous opposition to it and do so in large part on the credible grounds of the anatomical, procreative, and interpersonal complementarity of male and female, it becomes crucial to ask whether this opposition should continue to have normative status in communities of faith more than nineteen hundred years later. In this chapter I identify and critique seven main arguments that have been employed to circumvent the enduring validity of the biblical witness.

My hope in writing this book is threefold. First, I hope to contribute to a better understanding of the biblical witness regarding same-sex intercourse. Second, I hope to help remove some "dead ends" in the homosexuality debate. My third hope is of ultimately promoting the greater health of the church and of the homosexuals to whom the church is called to minister. Of course, many readers will remain supportive of homosexual relationships even after reading this book. But it is hoped that there will be fewer attempts to minimize the biblical witness through appeals to such erroneous arguments as the exploitative nature of homosexuality in antiquity; the Bible's alleged concern to preserve male dominance in sexual expression; the absence of any conception of an innate homosexual orientation in antiquity; or the paucity of biblical references that speak directly to the issue. Assessments of the credibility of the Bible's stance should be focused on three points: (1) above all, the revelatory authority of the Bible on an issue of moral practice that the Bible strongly and consistently condemns as grounds for exclusion from the redeemed community of God; (2) the witness of nature (to which the Bible itself points), that is, the complementarity of male and female sex organs as the most unambiguous clue people have of God's intent for gender pairing, apart from the direct revelation of the Bible; and (3) arguments from the realm of experience, reason, and science.

1. The Witness of the Old Testament

Anyone wanting to know about the Old Testament's witness to homosexual practice will expect an exegete to focus primarily on two sets of texts: first, the narrative of the destruction of Sodom and Gomorrah in Gen 19:4-11 (within the epic written by the Yahwist, J); and, second, the legal proscriptions found in the section of Leviticus known as the Holiness Code (H), 18:22 and 20:13. Indeed, attention to these texts is justly deserved. Yet a proper treatment of same-sex intercourse in the Old Testament requires expanding discussion to other key areas. First, it is necessary to set the stage by examining the ancient Near Eastern background. In what ways did Hebrew attitudes toward homosexual practice reflect or differ from the larger cultural horizons? To what extent can gaps in our understanding of the ancient Israelite worldview be filled in by other ancient Near Eastern data? Second, the creation stories in Genesis 1–3 are important for grappling with a broader vision for male and female sexuality, at least on the part of the framers of P (the Priestly Writing) and J. Even though the creation accounts are directed toward other purposes, they provide guidance for the interpretation of homosexual intercourse. Third, two other narratives have an important bearing on the question of the Bible's attitudes toward same-sex intercourse: the story of the curse of Ham in Gen 9:20-27 (J); and the account of the rape of the Levite's concubine in Judg 19:22-25 (within the Deuteronomistic History, Joshua through 2 Kings), which closely approximates Gen 19:4-11. Fourth, the question of homosexual cult prostitution during the period of the divided monarchy is pertinent for assessing attitudes toward homosexual practice held by the architects of Deuteronomic law (Dtn) and the author of the Deuteronomistic History (Dtr). Finally, the question of whether the relationship between David and Jonathan had any homoerotic aspects requires discussion.

I. The Ancient Near Eastern Background

Recent summaries and analyses by David Greenberg, Martti Nissinen, Donald Wold, and Saul Olyan provide a helpful starting point for describing ancient Near Eastern perspectives on homosexuality.[1] Our overview will be ordered according to the amount of information available for a given region or ethnic group: Mesopotamia, Egypt, the Hittite kingdom in the Anatolian peninsula, and Canaanite territory.

Mesopotamia

Most of our data regarding homosexual behavior in the ancient Near East comes from Mesopotamia. Here there are four primary sources of information: laws, magical texts (omens, incantations), myth and ritual practice, and epic stories.[2]

---

1. David F. Greenberg, *The Construction of Homosexuality* (Chicago: University of Chicago Press, 1988), 96-99, 124-35; Nissinen, *Homoeroticism*, 19-36, 144-52 (notes); Wold, *Out of Order*, 43-61; Olyan, " 'And with a Male You Shall Not Lie the Lying Down of a Woman': On the Meaning and Significance of Leviticus 18:22 and 20:13," *JHSex* 5 (1994): 192-95; Springett, *Homosexuality*, 33-48. Also: J. Bottéro and H. Petschow, "Homosexualität," *RlA* 4 (1975), 4:459-68; W. Westendorf, "Homosexualität," *LÄ* 2 (1977), 2:1272-74; Karl Hoheisel, "Homosexualität," *RAC* 16 (1994): 294-97; Gordon Wenham, "The Old Testament Attitude to Homosexuality," *ExpTim* 102 (1990-91): 359-61; Marvin H. Pope, "Homosexuality," *IDBSup* (1976): 415-16; Derrick Sherwin Bailey, *Homosexuality and the Western Christian Tradition* (New York: Longmans, Green & Co., 1955), 30-37; H. A. Hoffner, Jr., "Incest, Sodomy, and Bestiality in the Ancient Near East," *Orient and Occident* (ed. H. Hoffner; AOAT 22; Neukirchen: Butzon & Bercker, 1973), 81-90.

2. Greenberg cites other evidence: "Anal intercourse was part of the sexual repertoire: it is depicted in figurative art from Uruk, Assur, Babylon, and Susa as early as the

(1) Middle Assyrian Laws

Same-sex intercourse goes unmentioned in Mesopotamian law codes until the Middle Assyrian Laws of the late second millennium B.C.E. Laws 19 and 20 (tablet A) address the matter:

> If a man [or: a seignior; i.e., an aristocrat] furtively spreads rumors about his comrade [or: neighbor], saying: "Everyone has sex with him" [or: "People have lain repeatedly with him"], or in a quarrel in public says to him: "Everyone has sex with you [or: People have lain repeatedly with you], I can prove the charges," but he is unable to prove the charges and does not prove the charges, they shall strike him 50 blows with rods; he shall perform the king's service one full month; they shall cut off (his hair?) [better: they shall castrate him] and he shall pay one talent of lead.

> If a man [or: a seignior] has sex [or: lay] with his comrade [or: neighbor] and they prove the charges against him and find him guilty, they shall have sex [or: lie] with him and they shall turn him into a eunuch.[3]

The word for "comrade" or "neighbor," *tappā'u,* denotes "a man of equal social status, or a man who was otherwise socially involved with the perpetrator, like a neighbor or a business partner."[4] The verb for "have sex with," "lie with," *niāku,* means "have sex as the dominant (i.e., penetrating) partner."[5] It is unclear whether the verb implies rape. It seems unlikely for A §19, but probable for A §20.[6] Presumably,

---

beginning of the third millennium B.C. There is no evidence that fellatio or cunnilingus was practiced, either heterosexually or homosexually. . . . Zimri-lin, king of Mari, and Hammurabi, king of Babylon, both had male lovers; Zimri-lin's queen refers to them matter-of-factly in a letter" (*Construction,* 126).

3. Translation by Martha Roth, *Law Collections from Mesopotamia and Asia Minor* (Atlanta: Scholars Press, 1995); cited in Nissinen. Material in brackets is from the translation of T. Meek in *ANET,* 181.

4. Nissinen, *Homoeroticism,* 26. It is not entirely clear whether the term *tappā'u* puts the primary emphasis on equal social status or spatial proximity (for example, a member of one's clan or village).

5. Cf. A §18, which has a similar form to A §19 but replaces the charge with "Everyone has sex with your wife."

6. So Olyan and Greenberg. Nissinen is unclear whether rape or a nonviolent sexual subjection by a dominant partner is at issue in A §20. Wold questions whether force

if the "comrade" in A §20 wanted to be penetrated, he would have no grievance to bring to the courts, and the man doing the penetrating would not be criminally liable.

In the case of both laws it was apparently regarded as degrading and shameful for a man to be penetrated as if he were a woman, regardless of whether the passive partner was a voluntary participant. To be routinely penetrated by other men was to be treated as a "man-woman" and hence made inferior in honor and status to those doing the penetrating. The principle of *lex talionis* explains the punishment: just as the penetrator deprives the penetrated man of his manhood, so too the penetrator will be denied his manhood by being castrated. It is thus assumed in both laws that no self-respecting man would want to be penetrated by another man. In light of this, Nissinen's comment may be misleading: "It cannot be said that Middle Assyrian Laws would take into consideration a case in which two men were involved as equals in a voluntary homoerotic relationship and for mutual satisfaction." It is not just that "neither homosexual acts nor heterosexual acts were considered as being done by two equals."[7] There was something wrong or strange about *any* man who wanted to be penetrated as if he were a woman. Nevertheless, although such a man was an object of scorn or pity, he was not prosecuted.

Because The Middle Assyrian Laws were oriented toward protecting the rights of men in their dealings with other men of roughly the same social circles, all that can be inferred from the absence of a law protecting a man from being "mounted" by a social superior and/or one not living in spatial proximity is that the former had no recourse in the courts. In the nature of things, a social inferior (for example, a foreigner or resident alien, a prisoner of war, a slave) might have been expected to put up with the same-sex passions of a superior. The active partner, though, apparently did not incur shame, even when his behavior had to be criminalized to protect others. Indeed, his actions were taken as a sign of his superior social standing and power over the one

is implied in A §20. The consensus is that A §19 refers to a false charge of voluntary prostitution. But is an exchange of money necessarily inferred? Is the receptive partner thought of as someone with an erotic desire for penetration? Or is he too weak to protect his own manly honor? Or is he all of the above?

7. *Homoeroticism*, 26.

penetrated. This was certainly true of homosexual rape,[8] but probably it would also have been true when the passive partner was a willing participant. In short, the laws were interested in applying criminal sanctions only to two specific cases of (male) same-sex intercourse: a man who slandered another man with the charge of being *repeatedly* penetrated by other men; and a man who *coercively* penetrated another man of similar social status and/or belonging to the same clan. The penalty for such acts was severe (castration), though less than the maximum penalty of death prescribed for some cases of adultery (see A §§12-13).

(2) *Magical Texts*

In the Babylonian omen text, *Šumma ālu* (pre-seventh century B.C.E.), five of thirty-eight omens involve homosexual intercourse.[9] Two of them are positive omens: "If a man copulates with his equal from the rear, he becomes the leader among his peers and brothers"; and "If a man copulates with a male cult prostitute (*assinnu*), a hard destiny (or: care, trouble) will leave him." The first confirms that the man who penetrated a male in his social circle lowered the latter's status in relation to himself.[10] The second indicates a form of homosexual intercourse that received societal acceptance or at least tolerance: sex with a male cult prostitute. A third omen, involving sex with a courtier (*gerseqqû*), appears to be moderately negative ("terrors will possess him for a whole year and leave him").[11] Two other omens foretell a "hard destiny": a man in prison who desires to mate with men "like a male cult prostitute" and a man who copulates with his house-

---

8. For examples, see ibid., 26-27.
9. For translations, see Nissinen, *Homoeroticism*, 27; A. Kirk Grayson and Donald B. Redford, *Papyrus and Tablet* (Englewood Cliffs: Prentice-Hall, 1973), 149 (quoted in Greenberg, *Construction*, 126-27).
10. This is not necessarily a contradiction of Middle Assyrian Law A §20. Omens neither prescribe nor proscribe behavior.
11. Several things in this third example are unclear: the precise meaning of *gerseqqû* (a member of the court? the chief family assistant? a eunuch?), and the reason why the omen is negative, or even whether the omen is negative at all (Greenberg, citing the translation of Grayson and Redford, reads: "For one whole year the worry which plagued him will vanish" [127]).

47

born slave. The prison omen reflects societal disgust for a man who takes on the role of male cult prostitute without in fact being one (that is, one who practices without a valid license to do so). The situation of sex with one's slave is less clear. Was having sex with one's slave an ill omen because "a sexual connection would erode a master's authority over his slaves," or because "a slave born at home is comparable to a family member," or because the slave's social status was too low?[12]

Another text, an Almanac of Incantations, speaks favorably of "love of a man for a woman," "love of a woman for a man," and "love of a man for a man." The last mentioned category suggests that same-sex intercourse between two men in Mesopotamia could be construed as something other than a power trip by a dominant partner.[13]

(3) Myth and Ritual Practice: Male Cult Prostitutes

As an omen text cited above indicates, there was a certain acceptability in Mesopotamian society for sex with an *assinnu, kurgarrû,* or *kuluʾu* (words sometimes translated as "male cult prostitutes").[14] They were closely connected with the goddess Inanna (her Sumerian name) or Ishtar (her Assyrian name), who was identified with Venus (masculine as the morning star and feminine as the evening star)—hence, a goddess possessing androgynous features and traits. In the mythic story, Inanna's (or Ishtar's) Descent to the Underworld, cult prostitutes helped free the goddess from the underworld.[15] In keeping with their role in the myth, their liminal state between two sexes, and their status as devotees of the goddess, they were thought to possess magical power that could deliver people from sickness or other troubles, or bring people success against enemies. They dressed like women, wore

---

12. For the first view, Greenberg, *Construction*, 127; for the second, Nissinen, *Homoeroticism*, 28; for the third, Wold, *Out of Order*, 48.
13. Nissinen's confident assertion that the incantation "can scarcely be interpreted as referring to mutual love between two equal and consenting male citizens" is overstated (*Homoeroticism*, 35). Such an interpretation appears to contradict his own reading of the Gilgamesh Epic.
14. Nissinen provides a helpful discussion of them (*Homoeroticism*, 28-34). See also Greenberg, *Construction*, 94-106, esp. 95-97; Springett, *Homosexuality*, 41-45.
15. See *ANET* 52-57, 106-9; Stephanie Dalley, *Myths from Mesopotamia* (Oxford: Oxford University Press, 1989), 154-62.

makeup, carried with them a spindle (a feminine symbol), and engaged in ecstatic dance and ritual self-torture (probably including self-castration, like the *galli* of Hellenistic and Roman times); some may have been born hermaphrodites. The goddess, it was believed, had transformed each into a "man-woman" or even a "dog-woman" (with "dog" denoting a disgusting transformation of masculinity and possibly also intercourse in a doglike position). There is good evidence that they offered their services for a fee as the receptive partner in anal intercourse.[16] Ideally, a man who had intercourse with an *assinnu* did so as a means of accessing the power of the goddess herself. Although the role of the *assinnu*, *kurgarrû*, or *kuluᵓu* was institutionalized, they were often treated with great disdain. In addition to the epithet "dog," they were said to have been created from the dirt under the god Enki's nails, a mere "broken jar." One text speaks of them as those "whose masculinity Ishtar changed into femininity to strike horror into people—the bearers of daggers, razors, pruning-knives and flint blades who frequently do abominable acts to please the heart of Ishtar." Another text refers to their detestable lot in life: "Bread from the city's ploughs [a euphemism for penises] shall be your food, the city drains shall be your only drinking place, the drunkard and the thirsty shall slap your cheek."[17]

---

16. In addition to the omen text cited above and the "plough" text cited below, Nissinen refers to the following texts: "When the *kalû* wiped his anus, (he said): 'I must not excite that which belongs to my lady Inanna' "; "When a ['man-woman'] entered the brothel, he raised his hands and said: 'My hire goes to the promoter. You are wealth, I am half' "; "Men take into their houses *kurgarrûs* who deliver them children"; and another *Šumma ālu* omen, which predicts that a man will experience a need to have sex with another man "like an *assinnu*." "Male cult prostitutes" is thus a fair designation for one of their functions in Mesopotamian society. Greenberg regards such a conclusion as "inescapable" (*Construction*, 97-98). Nissinen thinks it "possible," though he regards "homoeroticism" as only a "side-issue" (*Homoeroticism*, 33-35). Wold states with regard to these cult functionaries that "it is not possible to deduce . . . a pattern of homosexual practice in the religious sphere at this time" (*Out of Order*, 49). Elsewhere, though, he speaks of same-sex intercourse with male cult prostitutes as a reality of ancient Mesopotamian society (ibid., 48, 51).

17. The first text is the Epic of Erra 4.52-56 (eighth century B.C.E. or earlier; Dalley, *Myths from Mesopotamia*, 305), the second Ishtar's Descent to the Underworld 101. See the following seventh-century B.C.E. curse on a monument praising the victory of the Assyrian king Esarhaddon over the king of Egypt: "If somebody

(4) The Gilgamesh Epic

Some interpret The Gilgamesh Epic as depicting a homosexual relationship between Gilgamesh, the oversexed superhuman king of Uruk, and Enkidu, the uncivilized wild man created by the gods as a suitable partner for Uruk.[18] Enkidu is described as a man with a hairy body and "tresses like a woman."[19] A harlot with whom Enkidu falls in love describes Gilgamesh to him as a man whose "whole body is charged with seductive charm." Gilgamesh relates to his mother a dream in which "a sky-bolt (*kiṣru*) of Anu kept falling upon me. . . . I loved it as a wife, doted on it. . . . You treated it as equal to me" (a possible word play with *kezru*, a "male with curled [i.e., dressed] hair," and *kezertu*, a female devotee of Ishtar, a cult prostitute). In a second dream Enkidu is likened to an "axe" (*ḥaṣṣinnu*, a possible word play on *assinnu*). Gilgamesh's mother interprets his love for Enkidu "as a wife" to mean that the latter will be a friend who never forsakes Gilgamesh; that is, she does not interpret the erotic connotations of the dream to mean an erotic relationship in reality. When Gilgamesh and Enkidu finally meet, Gilgamesh defeats Enkidu in a fight. Then they "kissed each other, and formed a friendship." The story of their relationship never explicitly mentions sexual intercourse between the two. When Enkidu eventually dies, Gilgamesh laments his death with the words: "My friend has covered his face like a bride. . . . Enkidu, my friend whom I love so much." The degree to which one describes the relationship as homosexual depends on how much one wants to read between the lines. Nissinen characterizes their relationship as

---

moves this monument, removes my name from it and writes his own name instead . . . , let Ishtar transform his masculinity into femininity and put him tied in front of the feet of his enemy." All three texts are cited in Nissinen.

18. The story begins with a complaint by the nobles of Uruk to the gods regarding Gilgamesh's sexual abuse of young men and women alike: "The nobles of Uruk are worried in their chambers: 'Gilgamesh leaves not the son to his father; day and night is unbridled his arrogance. . . . Gilgamesh leaves not the maid to her mother, the warrior's daughter, the noble's spouse!'" (translation by E. A. Speiser in *ANET* 73-74).

19. The translations are primarily by Dalley, *Myths from Mesopotamia*, cited in Nissinen.

an accentuated masculine asceticism. . . . Eroticism is important first
and foremost as the impetus to the transformation which leads first
from savage sexual behavior to mutual love, and finally away from
physical sex. . . . Especially noteworthy is the equal relationship
between the men, with no clear social or sexual role division. . . . This
exemplifies less a homoerotic than a homosocial type of bonding,
which is often strong in societies in which men's and women's worlds
are segregated.[20]

Greenberg, who argues in favor of a homosexual relationship, has a different take on the question of equality. "Though Enkidu was certainly
not effeminate, he is analogized to a female prostitute by virtue of the
subordinate sexual role he played after being defeated by
Gilgamesh."[21] Both Greenberg and Nissinen compare the relationship
to that of David and Jonathan, and Achilles and Patrocles in the *Iliad*.
The analogy of David and Jonathan, however, might rather speak for
an intimate but entirely nonsexual relationship. Wold contends that
"Nothing in the language of the epic is suggestive of a homosexual relationship."[22] Certainty is not possible. If the story expresses approval of
a man offering himself for penetration (mutual, consenting, or otherwise), it is in tension with the Middle Assyrian Laws. Perhaps one
should speak of a deep platonic admiration or even attraction between
Gilgamesh and Enkidu.

Egypt

Since no legal codes have been discovered in ancient Egypt, it is even
more difficult to assess Egyptian attitudes to same-sex intercourse than
it was for Mesopotamia. The evidence, such as it is, is conflicting.[23]
(1) Although the Egyptian pantheon of gods (like the Mesopotamian
pantheon) included hermaphroditic deities, there is no evidence of
homosexual cult prostitution. However, a positive, metaphorical use of

---

20. *Homoeroticism*, 24.
21. *Construction*, 113.
22. *Out of Order*, 49.
23. Greenberg provides a good summary (*Construction*, 127-35). See also Wold, *Out of Order*, 56-59; Nissinen, *Homoeroticism*, 19, 144 nn. 1-3.

homosexual imagery in relation to the gods can be found in coffin texts; for example: "I will swallow for myself the phallus of Re" and "his (viz., the earth god Geb's) phallus is between the buttocks of his son and heir."[24] Another coffin text, though, uses the metaphor of same-sex penetration to express fearlessness regarding a god's ability to do him harm: "[The god] Atum has no power over me, for I copulate between his buttocks."[25]

(2) There is an account of Pharaoh Pepi II (ca. 2400 B.C.E.) making regular secret nocturnal visits to an unmarried general, Sisene, apparently for homosexual intercourse. It is unclear whether such a relationship would have been viewed at the time as a scandal because of the homosexual connotation.[26] A tomb for two manicurists and hairdressers of Pharaoh Niuserre (ca. 2600 B.C.E.) pictures the two men holding hands, embracing, and touching noses. Pharaoh Ikhnaton (ca. 1370 B.C.E.) is depicted in intimate scenes (nudity, chin-stroking) with his son-in-law and probable co-regent Smenkhare. The former is drawn with a feminine physique and the latter is given titles of endearment normally reserved for Ikhnaton's concubines and queen.[27]

(3) In one version of the myth of Horus and Seth (ca. 1160 B.C.E.), the gods are deliberating about which of the brothers should rule Egypt. When Seth reveals that he had "played the male role" with Horus, successfully ejaculating his semen "between Horus' buttocks" while the latter was asleep, the gods "screamed aloud, and belched and spat on Horus' face." However, Horus is able to turn the tables on Seth by mixing some of the sperm in Seth's food.[28] Temple inscriptions at Edfu from the Ptolemaic period (third–second centuries B.C.E.) convey a similar theme: Horus eats lettuce (whose juice is identified with semen)

---

24. Raymond O. Faulkner, *The Ancient Egyptian Coffin Texts* (Warminster: Aris and Phillips, 1973), 2.162, 264.

25. Coffin Texts VI, 258 f-g (Westendorf, "Homosexualität," 1272).

26. Greenberg argues that "it does not necessarily follow that Egyptians of the time viewed homosexuality negatively" (*Construction*, 129). Wold argues differently: "Since the reign of Pepi II was long and corrupt, it possibly reflects a part of that decay" (*Out of Order*, 56).

27. Greenberg, *Construction*, 130.

28. Ibid., 131; Grayson and Redford, *Papyrus and Tablet*, 76.

so that he can ejaculate into Seth's anus.[29] Both accounts are *primarily* about aggression, not homosexual desires.[30] Yet they do indicate that shame is associated with being a receptive male partner.

(4) The Book of the Dead (fifteenth century B.C.E.) contains two confessions in which the deceased proclaims in his defense, "I have not defiled myself. . . . I have not been perverted; I have not had sexual relations with a male lover (or: boy)" (ch. 125).[31] The Edfu inscriptions mentioned above also contain a prohibition against coupling with a *nkk* or *ḥmw*, terms associated with either an effeminate coward or a receptive male partner. The active role is thus condemned in both pieces of evidence.[32] In a late Heracleopolitan inscription, a man declares, "I did not wish to love a youth. As for a respectable son who does it, his (own) father shall abandon him in court."[33] Here both adult-insertive and youth-receptive homosexual acts are viewed as reprehensible, perhaps even subject to criminal prosecution.

Overall, the evidence for approval of some forms of same-sex intercourse is not as strong in Egypt as in Mesopotamia. Egyptian toleration of same-sex intercourse appears to have been greater early in its history rather than later. In a few dynasties at least, a small number of Pharaohs and court officials engaged in homosexual practice. As in Mesopotamia, there was a tendency to stigmatize the receptive male partner (though not a universal tendency) and to regard aggressive penetration of another man as proof of superiority. There is also evidence of attitudes that deplore the actions of the insertive partner, though the severity of societal censure is not clear.

---

29. Greenberg, *Construction*, 132; J. Gwynn Griffiths, *The Conflict of Horus and Seth* (Chicago: Argonaut, 1969), 45-46.
30. However, homosexual desire on the part of Seth cannot be ruled out. Springett cites a papyrus fragment found in Kahun: "The Majesty of Seth said to the Majesty of Horus, How beautiful are your buttocks!" (*Homosexuality*, 35-36; quoted from Griffiths, *Conflict*, 42). See H. Te Velde, *Seth: God of Confusion* (Leiden: Brill, 1977), 55, 59.
31. *ANET* 34-35. Greenberg contends that such confessions do not imply that an insertive partner had committed a grave offense (*Construction*, 134).
32. Greenberg argues for a restriction of such attitudes to "priests and moralists." A much earlier text, The Instructions of Vizier Ptahhotep (mid–third millennium B.C.E.) warns only against forcing a "vulva-boy" to have sex against his will (*Construction*, 134).
33. Wold, *Out of Order*, 59.

The Hittite Empire (Anatolia)

Hittite law (second millennium B.C.E.) forbids sexual relations between father and son, apparently on the grounds that it is incestuous, not homosexual.[34] No other mention of same-sex intercourse is made in Hittite literature, even though their law code mentions related sexual impurities such as incest, bestiality, adultery, and rape. Whether the silence indicates societal approval of same-sex intercourse or the rarity of the practice in Hittite culture cannot be determined.

Ugarit/Western Semites/Canaan

Ugaritic literature and art discovered to date gives no hard evidence of homosexual practice, though it does of bestiality and incest.[35] Both the Levitical Holiness Code (Lev 18:1-5, 24-30; 20:22-26) and the Deuteronomistic History (1 Kgs 14:24)[36] speak of homosexual intercourse as one among many "abominations" for which God drove out the Canaanites and other nations before Israel. If the story of Ham ("the father of Canaan") "seeing his father's nakedness" refers to an act of same-sex intercourse, then the Yahwist too would have regarded this practice as typical of the Canaanite population. The attestation of three independent sources, along with the persistence of male temple prostitutes in Israel during the era of the divided monarchy, speaks against an entirely imaginative reconstruction of the past by any one biblical author.[37]

Summary

In the ancient Near East one cannot speak either of uniform approval or uniform disapproval. Viewpoints varied among different

---

34. "If a man violates his own mother, it is a capital crime. If a man violates his daughter, it is a capital crime. If a man violates his son, it is a capital crime" (Law 189; *ANET* 196).
35. However, Delbert Hillers has referred to the Canaanite goddess Anath as one who, like Ishtar, "takes away men's bows, that is, who changes men into women" ("The Bow of Aqhat," *Orient and Occident*, 74).
36. The Deuteronomistic Historian appears to make a connection between Rehoboam's Ammonite mother (1 Kgs 14:21) and the introduction of "high places, pillars, and Asherim . . . and male temple prostitutes" (14:23-24).
37. Contra, e.g., Bailey, *Homosexuality and the Western Christian Tradition*, 37.

population groups (ethnic, socioeconomic, religious) and during different periods of history. Unfortunately, laws regulating homosexual practice can be found in only one legal code, The Middle Assyrian Laws. Since no legal codes from Egypt have survived, nothing can be concluded from the absence of specific regulations there. The silence emanating from Hittite legal material and from Ugaritic literature and art is difficult to interpret, though independent testimony from J, D/Dtr, and H emphatically attributes homosexual practice to the non-Israelite ethnic groups in Canaan.

The two Middle Assyrian Laws that pertain to same-sex intercourse characterize "lying with" a man as an inherently degrading act for the male who is anally penetrated. To be known as a man with whom many other men have slept could severely damage one's standing in the community—so much so that a man who falsely accused another man of such was liable to castration. Homosexual rape was also grounds for castration. The implication of the penalty is that the man who played the female role in male-male intercourse lost his manhood. A man who attempted to deprive another man of his manhood, without the latter's consent, would himself be deprived of manhood through castration. In Lev 18:22; 20:13, the characterization of homosexual intercourse as "lying with a man as though lying with a woman" conveys a similar thought. However, there are also significant differences.

The Middle Assyrian Laws did not criminalize *any* consensual homosexual practice. Possibly they even permitted homosexual rape of a man of lower social status or of a man who did not belong to one's clan or village. Both Assyrian magical texts, on the one hand, and Egyptian myth, magic, and coffin texts, on the other, were able to put a positive spin on the "conquest" achieved by men who forced other males to be penetrated anally. (However, some Egyptian inscriptions, along with two confessions in The Book of the Dead, stigmatize the behavior not only of consenting passive partner but also of the dominant homosexual partner—though it is not clear how badly.) In one or two Mesopotamian texts and in two Egyptian tomb scenes homosexual love appears to be extolled. Homosexual cult prostitution was apparently an accepted part of Mesopotamian society. The masculinity of certain men had been transformed into femininity by the goddess Ishtar. Although such men were held in extremely low esteem, their behavior was understood to be forced on them by the goddess. Intercourse with such a "dog/man-woman" could bring good fortune on oneself. So the negative attitude toward homosexual practice in the ancient Near East, even in The Middle Assyrian Laws, was hardly uniform and total.

The Levitical laws, however, criminalized not only the behavior of all homosexual rapists but also the behavior of both partners in a consensual act of same-sex intercourse. Both have committed an abominable act. They also applied the same sanctions to Israelite and resident alien alike and made no concessions for homosexual intercourse with a person of unequal social status. According to The Middle Assyrian Laws, the maximum penalty for homosexual libel and homosexual rape was castration (in addition to blows with a rod, fines, and a limited period of forced labor). In the Levitical laws, the penalty for homosexual intercourse was death for both the passive partner (presumably, consenting) and the active partner (whether acting with the consent of the passive partner or not). The level at which the Levitical laws stigmatize and criminalize all homosexual intercourse, while not discontinuous with some trends elsewhere, goes far beyond anything else currently known in the ancient Near East.[38]

II. Genesis 1–3: Creation Stories

The creation stories of Genesis 1–3 do not speak directly to the issue of homosexual practice. However, they do supply us with a general understanding of human sexuality, set within the broader context of God's grand purposes at creation. As such, important implications for acceptable sexual practice arise out of them. The scholarly consensus holds that Genesis 1–3 is the product of two different authors or

---

38. For similar verdicts, see Wold, *Out of Order*, 59; Olyan, " 'And with a Male . . .'," 194-95. Nissinen, while contending that "other ancient Near Eastern sources display sexual ethics, taboos, and gender roles basically similar to those in the Hebrew Bible," also acknowledges: "Unlike the sources from classical antiquity, the Holiness Code does not even make any difference with regard to the social status of the partners; the prohibition concerns all male couplings even if the social stratification is otherwise widely recognized in its proscriptions" (*Homoeroticism*, 42, 44).

schools: Gen 1:1–2:4*a* can be traced to the Priestly writer (P); Gen 2:4*b*–3:24 to the Yahwist (J).

When looking at P's view of human sexuality, one has to first step back and assess the overall purpose behind the writing of Genesis 1, then ask how the author's view of human sexuality fits into those purposes. The description of God's act of creating the heavens and the earth in Genesis 1 has as its ultimate purpose the justification of a holy day of rest on the seventh day. This is evident not only from the uniqueness of the seven-day schema among creation stories of the ancient Near East, but also from the fact that eight acts of creation require a doubling up of creative acts on days three (dry land and vegetation) and six (land creatures and humans), and from the conclusion in 2:1-3, which stresses the precedent for the command to sabbath rest in God's own rest.

The creation of human beings corresponds closely to the attention given to sabbath rest. This is so because only human beings, made in God's image and given the task of ruling the creation on God's behalf (cf. Ps 8:5-8), are capable of doing the following two things: (1) responding to God's command to rest after every six days from the work of subduing (not exploiting) the earth; and (2) consciously worshiping the Creator on the seventh.[39] The pinnacle of God's creative work is thus human beings as creatures capable of receiving and carrying out commands from God in relation to the rest of creation. Filling or populating the earth with humans is a precondition for ruling it, and procreation is a precondition for filling the earth. The complementarity of male and female is thereby secured in the divinely sanctioned work of governing creation.

> [26]And God said, "Let us make *ʾādām* (man, an earthling, humankind) in our image (*běṣalmēnû*), in accordance with our likeness (*kidmûtēnû*), and let them have dominion over the fish . . . birds . . . cattle . . . wild animals . . . and over every creeping thing. . . ."

---

39. See Claus Westermann, *Genesis 1–11: A Commentary* (Minneapolis: Augsburg, 1984 [German orig., 1974]), 157-58; Donald E. Gowan, *From Eden to Babel: A Commentary on the Book of Genesis 1–11* (Grand Rapids: Eerdmans, 1988), 28-29; idem, "Genesis and Ecology: Does 'Subdue' Mean 'Plunder'?" *ChrCent* 87 (1970): 1188-91.

²⁷And God created the *ʾādām* in his image,
in the image of God he created it (or: him),
male and female he created them.⁴⁰

²⁸And God blessed them and God said to them, "Be fruitful and multi-
ply and fill the earth and subdue it and have dominion over the fish . . .
the birds . . . and every living thing. . . ." (Gen 1:26-28)

Is the sexual complementarity of men and women, then, contingent
on procreation? The argument might be made that since the present
problem of the earth is not underpopulation but overpopulation, the
mandate for heterosexual coupling need no longer be the norm.⁴¹
Doubtlessly, the Priestly writer would have responded: Should humans
then mate with animals to avoid procreation? Or has God changed the
complementarity of male and female anatomy? God's intent for human
sexuality is imbedded in the material creation of gendered beings, irrespective of the globe's population. "Male and female he created them"
probably intimates that the fullness of God's "image" comes together
in the union of male and female in marriage (not, one could infer, from
same-sex unions).⁴² Marriage is not confined only to procreation, a
point certainly made by the Yahwist in his treatment of the creation of
the female human. Perhaps, too, even in the event of overpopulation,
the Priestly writer would have insisted on the necessity of fulfilling the
mandate to "be fruitful and multiply." First, for humans in general, a
procreative purpose for marriage avoids a detachment of sexuality
from stable family structures (though P might have allowed for fewer
children per couple). Second, for God's people in particular, procreation is vital because God's people play a special role in discerning
God's will for the created order and for communicating that will to the
next generation.

---

40. Cf. 5:1: "On the day when God created *ʾādām*, in the likeness (*bidmût*) of God he
made him (or: it), male and female he created them; and he blessed them and
called their name *ʾādām* on the day when they were created."
41. See, *inter alios*, Richard E. Whitaker, "Creation and Human Sexuality,"
Homosexuality and Christian Community, 11-12.
42. *Contra* Phyllis A. Bird in two articles republished in *Missing Persons and Mistaken
Identities: Women and Gender in Ancient Israel* (OBT; Minneapolis: Fortress, 1997):

In the Yahwist's version of creation, Gen 2:4b–3:24, the human is made even more of a focus of God's attention than in Genesis 1. The ʾādām is formed before plants and animals (2:5) "from the ground (ʾādāmâ)" and receives life from God's breath (2:7). God delayed the creation of plants until the creation of ʾādām to till the ground and

---

"'Male and Female He Created Them': Genesis 1:27b in the Context of the Priestly Account of Creation," 123-54 (*HTR* 74 [1981]); and "Genesis 1–3 as a Source for a Contemporary Theology of Sexuality," 155-73 (*ExAud* 3 [1987]). See now also: Bird, "The Bible in Christian Ethical Deliberation Concerning Homosexuality: Old Testament Contributions," *Homosexuality, Science, and the "Plain Sense" of Scripture*, 166-68. Bird believes that the sexual differentiation described in 1:27 has an extremely limited function. P, who among the Pentateuchal authors took the most care in maintaining God's transcendence and in avoiding anthropomorphic descriptions, would have been repulsed by the notion that God possessed any form of sexuality (pp. 142, 151, 160). Rather than relate sexual differentiation to the divine image, P views sexual differentiation as a feature that makes humans unlike God and like other creatures (pp. 142-43, 158, 168). Indeed, whereas sexual differentiation of other creatures can be assumed, it must be explicitly stated in the case of humans because being made in God's image implies the absence of such differentiation (pp. 142, 160). Thus, the "parallel statements of v. 27 must be understood as sequential, not synonymous" (p. 158). "It relates only to the blessing of fertility, making explicit its necessary presupposition. It is not concerned with sexual roles, the status or relationship of the sexes to one another, or marriage" (p. 149; cf. p. 162). "P's statement concerning human sexuality . . . focuses solely on its biological nature" (p. 170).

Bird pushes her argument too far. It is obvious that, *contra* Bird, the clauses in v. 27 are not sequential but parallel; the sequence is between (not within) verses: from v. 26 ("Let us make . . .") to v. 27 ("God created . . .") and then to v. 28 ("God blessed them and said . . ."). Bird's reading virtually requires reading 1:27c (and 5:1c) as standing in an adversative relationship to the preceding two clauses: ". . . in the image of God he created it/him, [but] male and female he created them." Yet this is manifestly not what the absence of an adversative conjunction implies. While other creatures also share in sexual differentiation, human sexual differentiation is distinctive in that it is connected with, or follows from, the special status of being made in God's image. P's emphasis on divine transcendence would not have been compromised if he had regarded complementary differences between male and female humans as bringing out different facets of the divine image (for example, God as ruler and God as nurturer). That the creation of "male and female" would have held for P no implications regarding "the status or relationship of the sexes to one another, or marriage" is hard to accept, given the following verse with its command to procreate. To suppose that P viewed marriage as solely "biological," as if for P marriage was just a mechanical and impersonal relationship void of mutual affection, is to posit for P a view of sexuality out of step with the rest of the Hebrew Bible. The exuberance of the command to "be fruitful and multiply" hardly intimates that husband and wife should "hold their noses" while having sexual

keep the "garden in Eden" in shape (2:5, 8-9, 15). Animals were formed for the express purpose of providing companionship and support for the *ʾādām*, that he might have "a helper as his counterpart" (*ʿēzer kĕnegdô*),[43] for "it is not good for the *ʾādām* to be alone." Yet they were found to be unsuited for that role (2:18-20). The solution that God arrived at was not the independent creation of another *ʾādām*, a replica of the first, but rather to "build" a complementary being from a portion of *ʾādām*'s own self, a "rib" (2:21-22).[44] That the unique complementarity of male and female is being stressed in the narrative is evident from *ʾādām*'s response when this new being was presented to him (now clearly a "him"): "This at last is bone from my bones and flesh from my flesh; to this one shall be given the name 'woman' (*ʾiššâ*) for from man (*ʾiš*) this one was taken" (2:23). Only a being made

---

intercourse, doing their best to restrain sexual passion for one another. As such, "male and female he created them" has important implications for human sexuality, both in conjunction with and apart from procreation.

43. As J. Andrew Dearman notes: "The term 'helper' (*ʿēzer*) does not imply inferior status but one who supplies what is lacking. The Lord is the 'help/helper' of Israel (see Ps 121:1-2)" ("Marriage in the Old Testament," *Biblical Ethics and Homosexuality*, 65 n. 4); similarly, Gowan, *From Eden to Babel*, 46; Carol Meyers, *Discovering Eve: Ancient Israelite Women in Context* (New York: Oxford University Press, 1988), 85; Terence E. Fretheim, "Genesis," *NIB* 1:352. "The comment that her husband 'shall rule over her' [3:16] . . . probably reflects the cultural primacy of the man in subsistence efforts (farming, gathering, and herding). . . . The intensive process of birth and nurture kept the mother closer to the domicile as manager of the household, although her duties were not limited to child rearing. . . . These circumstances of labor and 'hierarchical' gender roles result from the disobedience of the man and the woman; they are not 'creation mandates' but prospective explanations of physical existence outside the garden" (Dearman, "Marriage," 56; similarly, Bird, "Male and Female," 152-53; "Genesis 1-3," 165-66). It is interesting that while J views the subordination of women to men as a product of the fall (implying the woman's equal status pre-fall), he unmistakably views the divine authorization for (and only for) heterosexual marriage as a pre-fall phenomenon. Those who argue that the case for validating homosexual behavior is comparable to the case for validating women's equal status overlook this point.

44. The precise meaning of *ṣēlāʿ* is not clear since nowhere else is it used of part of a human body; normally, it denotes the side of an object. A third-century C.E. rabbi, Samuel bar Nahman, thought of Adam as an androgynous being that was sliced in half, down the side: "When God created Adam, he created him facing both ways; then he sawed him in two and made two backs, one for each figure" (*Gen. Rab.* 8:1; cited by George Foote Moore, *Judaism* [Cambridge: Harvard University Press, 1927–30], 1.453, 3.137).

from ʾādām can and ought to become someone with whom ʾādām longs to reunite in sexual intercourse and marriage, a reunion that not only provides companionship but restores ʾādām to his original wholeness. The woman is not just "like himself" but "from himself" and thereby a complementary fit to himself. She is a complementary sexual "other."[45]

This is the very point made by the narrator in the next verse: "Therefore a man (ʾîš) shall leave his father and his mother[46] and become attached[47] to his woman/wife (ʾiššâ) and the two will become one flesh" (2:24). The sexual union of man and woman in marriage, of two complementary beings, in effect makes possible a single, composite human being. So great is the complementarity of male and female, so seriously is the notion of "attachment" and "joining" taken, that the marital bond between man and woman takes precedence even over the bond with the parents that physically produced them. A descriptive statement about the creation of woman thus provides etiological justification for prescriptive norms regarding marriage.[48] It is important that in the Yahwist's version of the creation of man and woman, attention is focused not on the goal of procreation (childbearing receives mention only in 3:16)[49] but rather on the relational (including physical/sexual) complementarity of male and female, that is, on the companionship and support provided by heterosexual marriage.[50]

It will not do to argue that nothing is said here about the legitimacy of homosexual relationships.[51] Even though an evaluation of same-sex

---

45. *Contra* Whitaker, "Creation and Human Sexuality," 9.

46. "The woman in his day might have no choice but to leave her home, because her father arranged a marriage for her; so it is the man, who had more freedom, of whom J speaks" (Gowan, *From Eden to Babel*, 49).

47. Or: join, stick, cling, cleave, be united (*dābaq*).

48. Bird argues that, as etiologies, Gen 1:26-28 and Gen 2:22-24 explain "why things are the way they are," not why they should be this way ("The Bible in Christian Ethical Deliberation," 167). The dichotomy is artificial. Often—and surely this is the case here—etiologies do both, providing additional sanction for why things should continue to remain as they are.

49. Gen 3:16 makes a woman's "pain in childbearing," not childbearing itself, the punishment for eating from the tree of the knowledge of good and evil.

50. See Westermann, *Genesis 1–11*, 234.

51. Even though they are not happy about this conclusion, Danna Nolan Fewell and David M. Gunn accept it: "Just as relations with parents and children are

intercourse is not the point of the text, legitimation for homosexuality requires an entirely different kind of creation story.[52] Only a being made from man can be a suitable and complementary counterpart for him. The language of the narrative is, of course, mythic. The Yahwist "presumes that his hearers know that he did not shape the imagery himself, but is passing on very ancient traditions formed long ago."[53] Yet the story remains authoritative for conveying that the obvious complementarity (and concordant sexual attraction) of male and female witnesses to God's intent for human sexuality. Male and female are "perfect fits" from the standpoint of divine design and blessing. Male and male, or female and female, are not.[54]

Hence, already at the start of the canon, in the description of human origins in Genesis 1–3, a justification for male-female union is provided: the physical, interpersonal, and procreative sexual complementarity of male and female. As we shall see, this motif will reappear as a continuous thread in the Old Testament, early Jewish, and New Testament critiques of same-sex intercourse as "contrary to nature."

---

diminished, so, too, are excluded relations between people of the same sex. The 'helper corresponding to [like-opposite]' the human/man is a sexual 'opposite.' According to this claim, human sexuality is clearly monogamous exogamous heterosexuality: one partner, outside the family, of the opposite sex. Partnership, according to this agenda, demands sexual and familial difference" (*Gender, Power, and Promise: The Subject of the Bible's First Story* [Nashville: Abingdon, 1993], 29).

52. Cf. the creation myth concocted by Aristophanes in Plato's *Symposium*, discussed in ch. 5.I. George R. Edwards somehow arrives at the conclusion that because Adam may have been an androgynous being before the creation of woman "the foundations of creationist homophobia" are dissolved ("A Critique of Creationist Homophobia," *Homosexuality and Religion* [ed. R. Hasbany; New York: Haworth, 1989], 112). I cannot make out the logic of his argument.

53. Westermann, *Genesis 1–11*, 230.

54. Whitaker attempts to split the hermeneutical application of Genesis 1 and Genesis 2: "Genesis 1 emphasizes God's sovereign power; Genesis 2 highlights human freedom"; Genesis 1 expresses an outdated "procreational model," while Genesis 2, with its model of "sexuality as companionship, as the sharing of tasks [and] as the enjoying together of the fruits of our labors and of each other, fits easily into contemporary society" ("Creation and Human Sexuality," 11-12). Cf. also Bird, who similarly emphasizes the differences between J's "psychosocial" portrait of sexuality and P's merely "biological" portrait ("Male and Female," 152-53; "Genesis 1–3," 170-71). To drive such a wedge Whitaker has to ignore completely the motif of the exclusive complementarity of male and female genders and the Yahwist's own exclusive sanctioning of male-female sexual union in 2:23-24. The notion of

III. Genesis 9:20-27: Ham's Act and Noah's Curse

In Gen 9:20-27, the Yahwist tells the story of how it came to be that the Canaanites were subjugated to the Israelites.

[20]Noah, a man of the soil, was the first to plant a vineyard. [21]When he drank some of the wine, he became drunk and was uncovered[55] in the middle of[56] his tent [22]and Ham, the father of Canaan, saw the nakedness[57] of his father (*wayyar*ʾ . . . *ʾēt ʿerwat ʾābîw*) and told (it) to his two brothers outside. [23]And Shem and Japheth took the (Noah's?) outer garment[58] and put (it) on the shoulders of the two of them and walked backwards. And they covered the nakedness of their father, with their faces turned the other way,[59] and they did not see the nakedness of their father. [24]When Noah woke up from his wine (that is, drunkenness), he came to know[60] what his youngest son had done (*ʿāśâ*) to him. (9:20-24)

Noah then cursed Canaan, the son of Ham, declaring that Canaan would become the slave of "his brothers," Shem (= Israel) and Japheth (= the Philistines?). God would give the land of Canaan to Israel but would also "make space for Japheth" by permitting Japheth to "live in the tents of Shem" (9:25-27).

"attachment" or "joining" in 2:24 may not be limited to the act of sexual intercourse but it certainly includes it (as the following verse's comment about an unashamed nakedness suggests). The Yahwist recognizes that (a) the "parts fit" male to female only and (b) a holistic, personal complementarity is achieved only in opposite-sex unions. A man can never be a complementary sexual "other" for another man. P and J (and the traditions they draw on) may emphasize different aspects of male-female complementarity but they are in complete agreement over the exclusive claim to complementarity possessed by heterosexual unions.

55. *wayyitgal*, *hitpaʿel* of *gālâ*. Some translate as a reflexive, "uncovered/exposed himself" (*HALOT*, NASB, NJPS; the translations in the commentaries of Wenham, Hamilton, Mathews); BDB as a passive, "was uncovered"; most as a mediating stative, "lay uncovered/naked." The difference between the reflexive and passive senses is that between Noah taking off his own clothes and someone else entering the tent to undress Noah.

56. Or: inside (*bĕtôk*).

57. Specifically, genitals.

58. Or: mantle, wrapper; bed covering (*śimlâ*). "They used 'a cloak' to cover Noah, that is, the outer daytime garment also used as a blanket at night (Exod 22:26)" (Gordon J. Wenham, *Genesis 1–15* [WBC; Waco: Word Books, 1987], 200).

59. Lit., "and their faces backwards" (*ûpĕnêhem ʾăhōrannît*).

60. That is, learned, found out (*wayyēdaʿ*).

What was Ham's horrible crime? A simple interpretation of the text indicates that the Canaanites were cursed because the father of their eponymous ancestor Canaan saw his father Noah lying in his tent naked and provoked Noah's ire. That a literal "seeing" was involved, nothing more, is suggested by the attribution of Shem's and Japheth's "not seeing" to keeping their faces turned away from Noah. Moreover, Noah's "uncovered" state is rectified by putting Noah's cloak over him.[61]

However, as Wold notes, there are problems with this interpretation.

> Was there a custom that children did not even look into the tent of their parents? How could Ham have known that his father was naked when he opened the tent flap? Perhaps, in his innocence, he meant only to speak with his father. Or, more altruistically, perhaps he knew that his father had taken too much wine and needed assistance of some sort. Perhaps Ham saw his naked father and entertained lewd thoughts (i.e., lusted after him), but did nothing about it. If so, this incident would be one of the earliest examples where an individual is made liable to a curse or penalty for merely intending to do something. . . . Scholars who accept the literal view maintain that Ham only saw his nude father, but they must defend a custom about which we know nothing. They must also presume an immoral intention based on the severity of the curse imposed by Noah. A further problem with this view is that it does not explain why the curse was pronounced on Ham's son Canaan and not on Ham himself.[62]

These problems are resolved satisfactorily when one understands this story as an instance of incestuous, homosexual rape. Wold and

---

61. Cf. Umberto Cassuto, *A Commentary on the Book of Genesis* (Jerusalem: Magnes, 1984), 2.148-51; Wenham, *Genesis 1–15*, 200; Victor P. Hamilton, *The Book of Genesis: Chapters 1–17* (NICOT; Grand Rapids: Eerdmans, 1990), 323; Kenneth A. Mathews, *Genesis 1–11:26* (NAC; Nashville: Broadman & Holman, 1996), 418-20; Gowan, *From Eden to Babel*, 108-9; and Fretheim, "Genesis," 404. According to Westermann, it was "a question of the obligations of the son to take care of his father who has become heavy with wine, as in the Aqht myth (cf. *ANET*, p. 150, ll.32-33). . . . Ham's outrage consists in not covering his father" (*Genesis 1–11*, 484-85, 488). For the disgrace of being uncovered, he cites Exod 20:26; 2 Sam 6:16; 10:4-5; Lam 4:21; and Hab 2:15. Yet, contra Westermann, Gen 9:22-23 is clear that "Ham's outrage" is not so much failing to cover his father as "*seeing* his father's nakedness." Moreover, Noah expresses consternation over what Ham "had done to him," not what he failed to do for him.
62. Wold, *Out of Order*, 66-67.

Nissinen, among others, have made a convincing case for this inter-pretation.[63]

First, the story appears to place Ham inside the tent, suggesting an action beyond peeking into the tent. Gen 9:22 clearly states that, after seeing his father's nakedness, Ham "told (it) to his two brothers *out-side*." The Septuagint is even more explicit, adding (or translating from a different Hebrew version) that Ham "went out and told . . ." (*exelthōn*). What was he doing inside the tent? Possibly the tent was understood to be off-limits to the sons, explaining why Shem and Japheth were "outside" and unaware. The fact that v. 23 refers to Shem and Japheth taking "*the* outer garment" suggests that the garment was Noah's.[64] How did Noah's garment happen to be outside the tent? The most like-ly answer is: Ham brought it out when he went back outside. Why would Ham have brought out Noah's garment? A possible answer: Ham brought the garment out as proof of what he "had done" to his father. It was the evidence he needed to establish bragging rights.

Second, when Noah woke up, "he learned what his youngest son had *done* to him"—not the expression one would expect to describe an unintended glance or even voyeurism.[65] If *wayyitgal* is translated "and

---

63. Ibid., 69-76; Nissinen, *Homoeroticism*, 52-53. Springett considers such an inter-pretation possible (*Homosexuality*, 77-78). Cf. Hermann Gunkel, *Genesis* (Macon: Mercer University Press, 1997; trans. of 3d Germ. ed., 1910), 80; Gerhard von Rad, *Genesis: A Commentary* (rev. ed.; OTL; Philadelphia: Westminster, 1972; orig. Germ. ed., 1949), 137; J. E. Bruns, "Old Testament History and the Development of a Sexual Ethic," *The New Morality* (ed. W. Dunphy; New York: Herder and Herder, 1967), 75-76; Anthony Phillips, "Uncovering the Father's Skirt," *VT* 30 (1980): 41; Nahum M. Sarna, *Genesis* (JPSTC; Philadelphia: Jewish Publication Society, 1989), 66; Christoph Levin, *Der Jahwist* (FRLANT 157; Göttingen: Vandenhoeck & Ruprecht, 1993), 119; Schmidt, *Straight and Narrow?*, 88, 193 n. 6; Seth Daniel Kunin, *The Logic of Incest: A Structuralist Analysis of Hebrew Mythology* (JSOTSup 185; Sheffield: Sheffield Academic Press, 1995), 174-75; Athalya Brenner, *The Intercourse of Knowledge: On Gendering Desire and 'Sexuality' in the Hebrew Bible* (BIS 26; Leiden: Brill, 1997), 107-109; O. Palmer Robertson, "Current Critical Questions Concerning the 'Curse of Ham' (Gen 9:20-27)," *JETS* 41 (1998): 177-88, esp. p. 180. Marc Vervenne alludes vaguely to the text's condemnation of the "erotic aberrations of the *Umwelt*" ("What Shall We Do with the Drunken Sailor? A Critical Re-examination of Genesis 9.20-27," *JSOT* 68 [1995]: 33-55).

64. Gunkel, *Genesis*, 80.

65. As Robertson remarks, "It seems very unlikely that Noah would have had any remembrance of a mere look from his son while he was in a state of drunkenness"

THE BIBLE AND HOMOSEXUAL PRACTICE

he was uncovered" rather than "and he uncovered himself," it "leaves the door open" for asking: who uncovered Noah? The continuation in 9:22 (which need not be separated from 9:21 with a period) intimates that Ham committed the unspeakable act.

Third, and most important, the language of "uncovering" and "seeing the nakedness of" connects up with similar phrases denoting sexual intercourse.[66] Leviticus uses the phrase "uncover the nakedness of" to denote incest (18:6-18; 20:11, 17-21; also in 18:19, of sexual intercourse with a woman during her menstrual cycle). The same phrase is used elsewhere in the Bible of prostitution and adultery, and of rape and/or public exposure for adultery.[67] In Lev 20:17, the expression "sees his/her nakedness" is used to describe sibling incest; in other instances, the phrase "seeing the nakedness of" may imply an opportunity for rape.[68]

Fourth, the claim that the text is concerned with Ham's homosexual rape of his father is bolstered by the depiction of homosexual rape in a Mesopotamian omen text and the Egyptian myth of Horus and Seth (both cited above); in other words, as attempts at emasculating, disgracing, and demonstrating one's power over a rival. By raping his father and alerting his brothers to the act, Ham hoped to usurp the

---

("Curse of Ham," 179). Wold takes up the question of whether the narrator could have the "evil eye" (i.e., visual witchcraft) in mind and concludes: "In my opinion, the idea is not far-fetched, but it is purely speculative. . . . no extant [ancient Near Eastern] text describes the punishment of a person for merely looking at someone who is naked" (*Out of Order,* 68).

66. The famous divorce text in Deut 24:1 probably also means by "a nakedness of some sort," an objectionable act of sexual intercourse. For the phrase "uncover the nakedness of," *HALOT* translates: "sleep with."

67. Ezek 22:10 ("in [Jerusalem] they uncover their fathers' nakedness") may refer to incest with one's mother or stepmother (cf. Lev 18:7-8; 20:11; also, Deut 22:30; 27:20, "uncovering his father's skirt," of incest with a stepmother); contra Anthony Phillips, who interprets "the nakedness of your father" in Lev 8:7a and "uncovering his father's skirt" in Deut 22:30 and Ezek 22:10 as a reference to sex with one's father ("Uncovering the Father's Skirt," 38-43). Regarding metaphors for prostitution and adultery, see Ezek 16:36; 23:18; and for rape and/or public exposure in an adultery trial, Isa 47:3; Ezek 16:37; 23:10; 23:29.

68. For the "uncovering nakedness"/"seeing nakedness" parallel, see Isa 47:3; Ezek 16:37 (cited above). For "seeing nakedness" as an opportunity for rape, see Lam 1:8-10; Hab 2:15; Nah 3:5.

authority of his father and elder brothers, establishing his right to succeed his father as patriarch.

Fifth, the brothers' actions in "covering their father's nakedness" and taking great pains not to look at their father is compatible with an interpretation of "seeing another's nakedness" as sexual intercourse. The brothers' actions play on the broader meaning of the phrase. Not only did the brothers not "see their father's nakedness" in the sense of having intercourse with him, but also they did not even dare to "see their father's nakedness" in a literal sense. Where Ham's act was exceedingly evil, their gesture was exceedingly pious and noble.

Sixth, understanding Ham's action as incestuous, homosexual rape of one's father explains the severity of the curse on Canaan. According to Lev 18:24-30; 20:22-26, the reason God decided to "vomit out" the Canaanites from the land was their participation in such "abominable practices" (coercive or voluntary) as incest (mentioned most often in Leviticus 18, 20) and same-sex intercourse (singled out for special mention as an "abominable practice"). The etiological thrust of Gen 9:20-27 lies at the forefront: The Canaanites deserve to be dispossessed of the land and made slaves because they are, and always have been, avid practitioners of immoral activity. In the new post-diluvian world, it was their ancestor that committed the most heinous act imaginable—not just rape, but incest; not just incestuous rape, but homosexual intercourse; not just incestuous, homosexual rape, but rape of one's own father, to whom supreme honor and obedience is owed. It is, in effect, in the Canaanites' blood to be unremittingly evil. Canaanite proclivity to homosexual rape is hinted at by J in Gen 10:19 when he mentions the fact that the territory of the Canaanites extended as far south as Sodom and Gomorrah. The etiological character of the story about Ham also explains why the curse fell on Canaan rather than Ham. The story was being transmitted at a time when Canaan alone—not Egypt, Cush, and Put, Ham's other "sons"—had been dispossessed by Israel. History had shown that the curse on Ham was really a curse only on Canaan. And the punishment eminently fit the crime (*lex talionis*). Just as Ham committed a heinous act with his "seed" (sperm), so too the curse fell on his "seed" (son, descendants).[69]

---

69. This explanation also renders superfluous the old hypothesis (adopted by

Thus it is likely that the narrator charged Ham with committing a heinous act of incestuous, homosexual rape of his father. This interpretation of Gen 9:20-27 is not unique in the history of interpretation. Three Greek translations of 9:22 (those of Aquila, Symmachus, and Theodotian) substitute *tēn aschēmosynēn* ("shamefulness") for *tēn gymnōsin* ("nakedness")—the same Greek term employed by the LXX in the phrase "uncover the nakedness of" throughout Lev 18:6-19 and 20:11, 17-21 (referring to incest). It is also applied by Paul to homosexual intercourse in Rom 1:27. "Perhaps Aquila, Symmachus, and Theodotian intended to imply that Ham committed a homosexual act with his father, but this implication is not necessary, as they might have chosen *aschēmosynē* to render *ʿerwat* and to mean nothing more than nakedness."[70] The Babylonian Talmud (*Sanhedrin* 70a) records a debate between Rab and Samuel (early third century C.E.) about the meaning of "had done to him" in Gen 9:24: "Rab and Samuel [differ], one maintaining that he castrated him, while the other says that he had homosexual relations with him."[71]

The relevance of the story for discussing contemporary homosexual-

---

Wellhausen, Gunkel, von Rad, and others) that 9:22 originally read just "Canaan" rather than "Ham, father of Canaan."

70. Albert I. Baumgarten, "Myth and Midrash: Genesis 9:20-29," *Christianity, Judaism, and Other Greco-Roman Cults* (ed. J. Neusner; Leiden: Brill, 1975), 3.66. Cf. Wold, *Out of Order,* 69-70; James L. Kugel, *Traditions of the Bible* (Cambridge: Harvard University Press, 1998), 222. The targums on Gen 9:22 (*Onqelos, Neophyti, Pseudo-Jonathan*; cf. the Peshitta) indicate that Ham "told his two brothers in the street" (i.e., he was indiscrete in relating what he saw). Another tradition states that "while he was asleep, his shame was uncovered. Ham laughed at his father's shame and did not cover it, but laughed about it and mocked" (*Cave of Treasures* [E] 21:3).

71. "He who maintains that he was castrated [reasons thus:] since [Noah] cursed [Ham's] fourth son, [Ham] must have injured [Noah] with respect to [having] a fourth son. But he who says that [Ham] had homosexual relations with [Noah] draws an analogy between 'and he saw' written twice," both in Gen 9:22 and Gen 34:2 (where Shechem "saw" Dinah and lay with her by force; *b. Sanh.* 70a). The tradition of castration appears also in: Theophilus of Antioch (late–second century C.E.), *Autol.* 3.28; and *Tg. Ps.-J.* 9:24. Baumgarten argues that the "later versions of the castration are not based on some pre-existing tradition, but were creations of the second century A.D." to explain why the curse fell on Ham's fourth son and not on Ham himself ("Myth and Midrash," 69, 71). "Homosexuality remains an attractive possibility" (ibid., 64 n. 56).

ity is complicated by other factors. Gen 9:20-27 is not just about same-sex intercourse but also about other grave offenses: rape, incest, and dishonoring one's father. Perhaps Ham is condemned for the latter three offenses, not the same-sex component of the act? Yet for the Yahwist, whose view of Canaanite sexual immorality appears to have been similar to that espoused in Levitical law, Deuteronomic law, and the Deuteronomistic History, it can hardly be doubted that the element of same-sex intercourse was an important compounding factor leading to the curse.

This is confirmed by the way in which Levitical law frames the discussion of incest and same-sex intercourse. None of the prohibitions of specific forms of incest in Lev 18:6-18; 20:11-21 mentions acts of incest between two males. There are no explicit prohibitions of intercourse between a father and a son (or son-in-law, or stepson), or grandfather and grandson, or a man and his brother (or stepbrother, or brother-in-law), or an uncle and a nephew.[72] Clearly, this is not because incestuous same-sex intercourse was permitted (see the placement of the prohibition against same-sex intercourse in 20:13 in the midst of a series of incest prohibitions). Rather, its occurrence was probably considered so rare and heinous that no explicit prohibition was required

---

72. Obviously, when the Levitical laws against incest forbid, for example, sexual intercourse with one's mother or sister-in-law or aunt, they are referring to incest committed by men against women; that is, "you" refers to Israelite males (see 18:23: "You shall not have sex with any animal . . . , nor shall any woman . . ."). The prohibition against sexual intercourse with "your father, which is the nakedness of your mother; she is your mother" refers to intercourse with one's mother, not one's father (18:7; cf. 18:8; and *Jub* 33:1-17: when Jacob discovered that his son Reuben had lain with his concubine Bilhah, he "was very angry with Reuben because . . . he had uncovered his father's robe"). The Levitical laws against incest are directed at men, not women, apparently because the potential for uncontrollable domestic abuse lay not with women but with men (who were in positions of domestic authority, whose physical strength lent itself to abuse, and whose proclivity to sexual immorality was considered greater). Incidentally, Frederick W. Bassett appeals to the wording of Lev 18:8 as a basis for arguing that Ham had sex not with Noah but with Noah's wife (Ham's mother), making Canaan a child of incest ("Noah's Nakedness and the Curse of Canaan," *VT* 17 [1971]: 232-37). The key problem with this theory is that Gen 9:20-27 is quite explicit that Noah's own nakedness is at issue. See the critique by G. Rice, "The Curse That Never Was," *JRT* 29 (1972): 5-27, esp. 11-13.

other than the general prohibitions in Lev 18:22; 20:13. Homosexual intercourse was understood to cut across all categories of sexual immorality, constituting its own distinct sin.

Furthermore, in Gen 19:30-38 the Yahwist recounts another story of offspring taking sexual advantage of their father's state of drunkenness. The Yahwist finds the circumstances distasteful and undoubtedly employs the story to slander the origins of the Moabites and Ammonites. However, the degree of revulsion expressed by the Yahwist for this case of heterosexual incest is nothing like the degree of revulsion registered toward Ham's act of homosexual incest (certainly one can sympathize with the motives of the daughters of Lot: the desire for progeny; compare the Tamar-Judah episode in Gen 38). Thus incestuous homosexual practice counted as two heinous acts, not one: incest and homosexual practice.

Nissinen points out that the story "does not speak of Ham's homosexual orientation but his hunger for power."[73] Whether the Yahwist thought that Ham's aggressive act was carried out entirely apart from any depraved, same-sex lust cannot be known with any certainty. Nissinen, though, is certainly correct that Ham's behavior was significantly motivated by a lust for power. Does that mean that the story does not speak to consensual and loving homosexual acts? The question of homosexual orientation was surely irrelevant to the denunciation of same-sex intercourse, just as any debate about an orientation toward incest (or bestiality) would have been irrelevant. It was the act that mattered.

As with Lev 18:22; 20:13, the author probably regarded every act of male same-sex intercourse as detestable since the penetrated male, at the moment of penetration, inherently functions as a female—whether the act of same-sex intercourse is coercive or consensual. We have also seen a similar disdain in ancient Near Eastern texts both for men who rape other males and for males who willingly offer their bodies to other men (male cult prostitutes partly exempted).

Gen 9:20-27 takes an even more stringent approach. Whereas in the ancient Near East generally there were some mixed signals about homo-

---

73. *Homoeroticism*, 53.

sexual behavior, especially as regards the status of the one doing the penetrating, the narrator in Gen 9:20-27 is unequivocal in his condemnation of Ham. If Ham's intent was to use anal penetration of his father as a means of establishing the dominance of his lineage over that of his brothers, his plan backfired, for he brought upon his descendants a horrific curse.

IV. Genesis 19:4-11: The Story of Sodom and Gomorrah

Traditionally, Gen 19:4-11 has been regarded as the classic Bible story about homosexuality. However, to the extent that the story does not deal directly with consensual homosexual relationships, it is not an "ideal" text to guide contemporary Christian sexual ethics. Nevertheless, many go too far when they argue that the story has little or nothing to do with homosexual practice; that, instead, the story is only about inhospitality or rape.[74] As with the story of Ham's incestuous, homosexual rape of Noah, the inherently degrading quality of same-sex intercourse plays a key role in the narrator's intent to elicit feelings of revulsion on the part of the reader/hearer.

In Genesis 18, Abraham is visited by three "men," who (according to the narrator) are Yahweh and two angels. After Abraham's and Sarah's show of hospitality to the visitors (18:1-8) and an assurance from one of the visitors that Sarah would give birth to a son (18:9-15), Yahweh informed Abraham that the two angels were being sent to Sodom to see if the "outcry" against the people of Sodom and Gomorrah concerning their "grave sin" was true (18:20-21; cf. 19:13). In the meantime, Abraham secured from Yahweh an agreement not to destroy Sodom (the residence of his nephew Lot) if ten righteous people could be found (18:22-33). When the two angels arrive, only Lot acts hospitably by taking the visitors into his home and exhibiting further kindnesses (bows, washes their feet, makes them a feast; 19:1-3).

---

74. Even Richard Hays, who affirms the biblical witness against homosexual activity, has stated: "The notorious story of Sodom and Gomorrah—often cited in connection with homosexuality—is actually irrelevant to the topic" ("Awaiting the Redemption of Our Bodies," 5). Bird qualifies this: "I believe [Hays] is right in insisting that this text does not address the cases under consideration today, but I do not think it can be dismissed as testimony to the OT's attitude toward homosexual activity" ("The Bible in Christian Ethical Deliberation," 147).

[4]Before they could lie down,[75] the men of the city, the men of Sodom—from young to old, all the people, from one end (of the city to the other)[76]—surrounded the house. [5]They called to Lot and said to him, "Where are the men who came to you tonight? Bring them out to us so that we may know (= have intercourse with) them. [6]Lot went out to the doorway to (meet) them and shut the door behind him. [7]He said to them, "No,[77] my brothers, do not act wickedly. [8]Here are two daughters of mine who have not known (= had intercourse with) a man. Let me bring them out to you; and do to them according to that which is good in your eyes;[78] only do not do a thing to these men for they have come under the shelter[79] of my roof." [9]But they said, "Step away over there!"[80] And they said, "This guy[81] came to live as an immigrant[82] and he has the nerve to act like a judge![83] Now we will act more wickedly toward you than toward them."[84] And they kept putting intense pressure on[85] the man[86] Lot and stepped forward to break down the door. [10]But the men

---

75. Or: go to bed/sleep (*yiškābû*). Possibly the writer is setting the stage for the abomination of men lying with men (compare the same verb in Lev 18:22; 20:13).

76. *miqqāṣeh*: lit., "from the end/edge/border/extremity/outskirts," an abbreviation for *minhaqqāṣeh ʾel haqqāṣeh* (Exod 26:28; 36:33); thus, "from one end (of the city) to the other" (*HALOT*, Westermann; for similar terms elsewhere *HALOT* translates: "without exception," or "every single one of them"). Cf. BDB: "A condensed term for what is included within the extremities = the whole," here "in its entirety." The emphasis in this verse is on the wickedness of every inhabitant of Sodom (at least every male), justifying the city's complete destruction (18:22-33).

77. Or: I beg you; please (*ʾal nāʾ*).

78. Most render idiomatically: "as you please" or "what(ever) you like/want/wish."

79. *ṣel*: "shadow, shade (as protection)"; "shelter" (most), "protection" (NIV, NJB).

80. *geš* (*qal* imptv. *nāgaš*) *hālĕʾâ*: lit., "step forward or approach thither."

81. Lit., "the one" (*hāʾeḥād*), but as contemptuous address.

82. *lāgûr*: "to dwell as alien and dependant" (*HALOT*); "to stay as foreigner and sojourner" (*CHALOT*); "to sojourn, dwell (as a newcomer, *gēr*, without original rights)" (BDB). Lot is reminded, however much he has tried to integrate into Sodomite society, that he remains an outsider without legal rights and protection (Sarna).

83. *wayyišpōṭ šāpôṭ*: "act like a judge" (*HALOT*); "act as a lawgiver/judge/governor" (BDB). The intensifying sense of the infinitive absolute following a finite verb probably carries the sense of outrage and indignation that I have tried to convey with the phrase "has the nerve to."

84. "More wickedly" probably means to kill Lot, not just commit homosexual rape against him.

85. *wayyipṣĕrû . . . mĕʾōd: pāṣar* = "urge, coerce" (*HALOT*); "push, press upon" (BDB).

86. NJPS: "the person of" (*hāʾîš*); so too the translation of E. A. Speiser, *Genesis* (AB; Garden City: Doubleday, 1964), 136.

reached out their hands and brought Lot into the house with them and shut the door. [11]They struck the men who were at the doorway of the house with blinding light,[87] from small to great, so that they grew tired (of trying)[88] to find the doorway. (Gen 19:4-11)

The angels then confirmed to Lot that Yahweh had sent them to destroy the city (19:12-14). In the morning, Lot, his wife, and his two daughters were coaxed by the angels out of the city (19:15-23). Sodom and Gomorrah and all the cities of the Plain (except Zoar) were then destroyed and Lot's wife, looking back, was turned into a pillar of salt (19:24-26). Later, while living in a cave in the hills, Lot's two daughters get him drunk and "lay with" him on two consecutive nights "so that we may preserve offspring through our father." From these acts of incest Moab and Ben-ammi were born (19:30-38).

Derrick Bailey, followed by John Boswell and John McNeill, argues that "know" in Gen 19:5 meant "get acquainted with," not "have sexual intercourse with."[89] It is true that the Hebrew verb $yāda^c$ ("to know") is used in a sexual sense only fifteen other times out of nine hundred forty-three uses in the Hebrew Bible (though six of these are found in Yahwistic material in Genesis alone).[90] Even so, the immediate context (Lot's offer to give the men of Sodom his "two daughters who have not 'known' a man," 19:8) and the close parallels in the related

---

87. *sanwērîm* (elsewhere only in 2 Kgs 6:18): "dazzling light" (*CHALOT*), "blinding light" (Speiser, NJPSV, NAB, NJB), "blinding flash" (Hamilton); less likely, "sudden blindness" (BDB), "blindness" (NRSV, REB, NIV, NASB, Westermann). Speiser and Sarna argue strongly for the first sense over the second. The angels "thereby abandon their human disguise" (Speiser).

88. *wayyilʾû* (*qal* impf. *lāʾâ*): "grow weary; (+ inf.) become tired of, give up" (KBS); "be weary, impatient" (BDB). Cf. "they wearied themselves trying to find" (NASB; similarly, Westermann, RSV); "they became exhausted trying to find" (Hamilton). Speiser and Sarna, however, argue for the following sense: "they could not (or: were unable to) find/reach" (most); "they were helpless to find" (NJPS).

89. Bailey, *Homosexuality*, 3-4; Boswell, *Homosexuality*, 93-94; John J. McNeill, *The Church and the Homosexual* (Kansas City: Sheed, Andrews and McMeel, 1976), 54-55.

90. J: Gen 4:1, 17, 25; 19:8; 24:16; 38:26. The other uses in the Hebrew Bible are Num 31:17, 18, 35; Judg 11:39; 19:22, 25; 21:11; 1 Sam 1:19; 1 Kgs 1:4. Cf. in the OT Apocrypha: Jdt 12:16; Sus 11, 39; in the NT: Matt 1:25; Luke 1:34. Bailey speaks of ten other uses, not fourteen; he naturally discounts the parallel in Judg 19:22, and also omits Num 31:17, 18; Judg 21:11.

story of the Levite's concubine in Judg 19:22, 25 (which clearly use "know" in the sense of "have sexual intercourse with") leave little room for doubting the sexual connotation. In looking at the meaning of words, to paraphrase a slogan from the real estate industry, three things are most important: context, context, context. Few scholars today, even among supporters of homoerotic behavior, adopt Bailey's argument.[91]

Certainly the reason given by Lot for not handing over the men ("for they have come under the shelter of my roof") suggests his intention to act as a proper host in accordance with the high value placed on hospitality by ancient convention.[92] Both the safety of his guests and his own honor are at stake. Beyond that, it is difficult to say from the story's perspective how much of Lot's desire to give up his own daughters instead of offering himself is due to plain self-interest,[93] how much is due to a devaluation of women in ancient culture,[94] and how much is

---

91. Cf. the refutation of Bailey and Boswell by Wold, Grenz, Springett, Nissinen, Edwards, Greenberg, Scroggs; James B. De Young, "The Contributions of the Septuagint to Biblical Sanctions Against Homosexuality," *JETS* 34 (1991): 158-65; Guenther Haas, "Exegetical Issues in the Use of the Bible to Justify the Acceptance of Homosexual Practice," *CSR* 26 (1997): 387-88; and Lynne C. Boughton, "Biblical Texts and Homosexuality: A Response to John Boswell," *ITQ* 58 (1992): 142-43.

92. In addition to Gen 19:1-3, the issue of hospitality is also highlighted in Abraham's display of hospitality to the angelic visitors in Gen 18:1-16; in the "outcry against Sodom and Gomorrah" which appears to be coming from outside of these cities, probably from travelers seeking temporary lodging (hence the disguise of the angels as travelers; 18:20-21; 19:13); and Lot's plea that the visitors not be harmed, "for they have come under the shelter/protection of my roof" (19:8).

93. Cf. Gen 12:13 and 20:2, 11, where Abraham twice passes Sarah off as his sister to avoid being killed. In these two stories, though, Abraham is in far greater danger than Sarah; in the Sodom episode, Lot is in no greater or lesser danger than his two daughters. J. Gerald Janzen tentatively suggests that by offering his daughters, Lot sought "to shock the men of the city to their senses" (*Abraham and All the Families of the Earth: A Commentary on the Book of Genesis 12–50* [ITC; Grand Rapids: Eerdmans, 1993], 64).

94. The story of Lot's daughters copulating with their drunken father (19:30-38) may indicate the daughters' revenge for their father's earlier offer to the men of Sodom. This in turn suggests a less than positive opinion of Lot's actions on the part of the Yahwist. "Really, there is no need to make excuses for [Lot], as far as the biblical perspective is concerned. In all the stories about him, the soundness of Lot's judgment is never the point at issue; the opposite, in fact, is more than once indicated" (Bruce Vawter, *On Genesis: A New Reading* [Garden City: Doubleday, 1977], 236).

due to the revulsion felt for same-sex eroticism. Ultimately, however, since the story is used as a type scene to characterize the depth of human depravity in Sodom and Gomorrah and thus to legitimate God's decision to wipe these two cities off the face of the map, it is likely that the sin of Sodom is not merely inhospitality or even attempted rape of a guest but rather attempted homosexual rape of male guests.

As with Gen 9:20-27, the perversion of same-sex male intercourse appears to be an integral part of this story, along with other factors. Just as one form of illicit copulation (between angels and women) contributed to the earlier cataclysm of the great flood in Genesis 6 (an important element in the general "wickedness of humankind," 6:5), so too another form of unnatural sexual relations (between men) served as a key contributing factor in the cataclysmic destruction of Sodom and Gomorrah.[95] The story in Gen 19:1-14 is just one event, but a vital one in epitomizing the towns' widespread wickedness (cf. 18:20: "how very grave their sin!").

Middle Assyrian Law A §20 proscribes homosexual rape precisely because of the homosexual element. This is clear enough from the implicit application of the *lex talionis* in the punishment (castration) and by the preceding law (MAL A §19) regarding the great social disgrace of being known as a person with whom other men have had intercourse. To "lie with a man as though lying with a woman" (Lev 18:22; 20:13) was to treat a man as though his masculine identity counted for nothing, as though he were not a man but a woman. To penetrate another man was to treat him like an *assinnu*, like someone whose "masculinity had been transformed into femininity." Thus three elements (attempted penetration of males, attempted rape, inhospitality), and perhaps a fourth (unwitting, attempted sex with angels),[96]

---

95. Wenham, "Homosexuality," 361; followed by J. Glen Taylor, "The Bible and Homosexuality," *Them* 21 (1995): 5. The links between the stories of the Flood and of the destruction of Sodom and Gomorrah are multiple. The two stories are often coupled in early Jewish and Christian literature. Later rabbinic interpretation included same-sex intercourse among the sins of the generation of the Flood (*b. Sanh.* 108a; *Gen. Rab.* 26.5; 27.3; *Lev. Rab.* 23.9). Cf. Wold, *Out of Order,* 70; Samuel H. Dresner, "Homosexuality and the Order of Creation," *Judaism* 40 (1991): 309-21.

96. Notwithstanding Jude 7, the fact that the intended victims are identified by the

combine to make this a particularly egregious example of human depravity that justifies God's act of total destruction. It may well be that inhospitality and social injustice constitute the overarching rubric for the story, as subsequent interpretations of the event indicate. Yet what makes this instance of inhospitality so dastardly, what makes the name "Sodom" a byword for inhumanity to visiting outsiders in later Jewish and Christian circles, is the specific form in which the inhospitality manifests itself: *homosexual* rape.

The demand of the men of Sodom to have sex with Lot's visitors, along with their subsequent threat to "act more wickedly toward you [Lot] than toward them [the two visitors]" (19:9), climaxes and establishes beyond doubt the utterly evil character of the city's inhabitants that had been alleged on other grounds earlier in the narrative (13:13; 18:20-33). The inhospitality here was not a minor breech of etiquette such as neglecting to set out the best dinner plates and utensils. It was not just a case of failing to take a traveler into one's home, to wash his feet, to offer food, shelter, and protection.[97]

Leland White, Daniel Boyarin, and Martti Nissinen, among others, posit that the intent of the Sodomites was to challenge Lot's honor as a resident alien by dishonoring Lot's guests.[98] This being the case, one

---

narrator as angels would not justify the magnitude of divine judgment since there is no indication given in the story line that the men of Sodom are aware of the visitors' true identity. Possibly, though, there is condemnation for failure to recognize angels in their midst or to take the appropriate precautions in case the visitors proved to be angels (cf. Heb 13:2; *T. Asher* 7:1, cited below).

97. For a discussion of hospitality in the Old Testament, see Weston W. Fields, *Sodom and Gomorrah: History and Motif in Biblical Narrative* (JSOTSup 231; Sheffield: Sheffield Academic Press, 1997), 54-67. Fields considers "the primary motif of the Sodom, Gibeah, and Jericho traditions" to be "the treatment of the 'stranger in your gates'" (p. 188). "The misbehavior against a [*gēr*, "sojourner, resident alien"] is compounded by the sexual nature of the abuse or intended abuse, and . . . such sexual improprieties eventuate in communal punishment" (p. 187). According to J. A. Loader: "Their sin is a three-in-one-matter. They violate the sacred law of *hospitality* and in so doing give themselves over to *depravity of a homosexual nature*. . . . At the same time it must be said that the sin here is not just a private homosexual act, but homosexual *mob rape*" (*A Tale of Two Cities: Sodom and Gomorrah in the Old Testament, early Jewish and early Christian Traditions* [CBET 1; Kampen: Kok, 1990], 37).

98. Cf. 19:9. The men of Sodom interpret Lot's offer of his daughters as an insult to their status as citizens of Sodom. As a lowly resident alien, Lot has no right to dic-

cannot say that their desire was to have homosexual sex "unless we want to believe that all the men of Sodom are homosexual."[99] The truth is that no one can say precisely how the Yahwist construed the motives of the men of Sodom (beyond generic evil), though a reasonable conjecture might be a combination of homoerotic or bisexual lust on the part of at least some of the crowd and an aggressive intent to dominate and humiliate strangers to Sodom by forcing on them an abominable and shameful practice. A strict either/or interpretation, *either* homosexual/bisexual lust *or* an aggressive disgrace of visitors, goes beyond the wording of the text and imposes a distinction that did not always hold true in the ancient world. As we have seen, homosexual desire was not unknown in the ancient Near East, not to mention ancient Greece. Heterosexual rape is an act of aggression, but it is usually not void of all sexual desire. There was no need for the Yahwist to stress the intentions of the inhabitants that lay beyond their demand to have sex with Lot's male visitors. Whether each and every man in the mob aimed solely at pure violence and domination, or whether some hoped to take advantage of the strangers for a sexual thrill as well, matters little to the

---

tate to the men of Sodom those with whom they are allowed to have sex. Victor H. Matthews points out that Lot had already committed a violation of hospitality customs when, despite his own status as a resident alien, he took the initiative to bring the visitors to his house. Only a citizen had the right to represent the city at the city gate ("Hospitality and Hostility in Genesis 19 and Judges 19," *BTB* 22 [1992]: 3-11).

99. Leland J. White, "Does the Bible Speak About Gays or Same-Sex Orientation? A Test Case in Biblical Ethics: Part I," *BTB* 25 (1995): 20; similarly, Daniel Boyarin, "Are There Any Jews in 'The History of Sexuality'?" *JHSex* 5 (1995): 348-53; Edwards, *Gay/Lesbian Liberation*, 26-27, 46; Matthews, "Hospitality," 5; H. Darrell Lance, "The Bible and Homosexuality," *ABQ* 8 (1989): 144; Simon B. Parker, "The Hebrew Bible and Homosexuality," *QR* 11 (1991): 6-8; Nissinen, *Homoeroticism*, 48-49. Nissinen refers to the myth about Horus and Seth, Assyrian legal and omen texts, and the use of the phallus as a mode of ritual dominance in ancient Greece. Athens' defeat of Persia in 460 B.C.E. is depicted as a Greek man holding his erect penis as he approaches a bent-down Persian (Figure 3 in Nissinen's book). Statues of the Phrygian god Priapus, portrayed with a large penis, were often placed in strategic locations of homes and gardens to warn intruders of the fate that awaited them (ibid., 48). Cf. Kenneth Dover: "human societies at many times and in many regions have subjected strangers, newcomers and trespassers to homosexual anal violation as a way of reminding them of their subordinate status" (*Greek Homosexuality* [2d ed.; Cambridge: Harvard University Press, 1989], 105).

story line—and certainly would have mattered little to the visitors. The stress is entirely on the mob's horrible plans for mistreating the seemingly helpless visitors—not just *that* they wanted to mistreat them but *the way in which* they chose to mistreat them. As with the author(s) of the Levitical prohibitions, the Yahwist is less concerned with motives than with the act of penetrating a male as if he were a female, an act that by its very nature is demeaning regardless of how well it is done.[100]

To suggest that the story does not speak to the issue of homosexual behavior between consenting adults, even in an indirect way, is misleading. Undoubtedly for the Yahwist, the difference between consenting homosexual intercourse and coerced homosexual intercourse was that in the former both participants willingly degraded themselves while in the latter one of the parties was forced into self-degradation. The burden of proof is entirely on those who would assert otherwise, particularly given the Yahwistic material in Genesis 2–3 that gives etiological sanction only for marriage and sex between male and female, the story of Ham's homosexual rape of his father, the exclusively heterosexual relationships portrayed throughout the Yahwistic source, and the general consonance between the Yahwist and the legal material of the Pentateuch in assessing abhorrent sexual practices. While the story of Sodom, because of the added factors of inhospitality and rape, is not an ideal passage for studying the Bible's views on same-sex intercourse, it nevertheless remains a relevant text.[101]

---

100. Cf. Schmidt, *Straight and Narrow?*, 89; Wright, "Homosexuality: The Relevance of the Bible," 292; Westermann, *Genesis*, 1.301; Speiser, *Genesis*, 142; Victor P. Hamilton, *The Book of Genesis: Chapters 18–50* (NICOT; Grand Rapids: Eerdmans, 1995), 34-35; Gunkel, *Genesis*, 207; von Rad, *Genesis*, 217. The view held by Gunkel and von Rad that the angels were depicted as handsome youths is drawn more from Josephus and Philo than from Genesis 18–19.

101. According to Nissinen, it is "misleading to speak of the 'author's antagonism towards homosexuality' or claim that 'he condemns homosexuality.'" His concluding comment that, other than in the context of aggression, "the Yahwist's attitude towards same-sex interaction remains unknown" is unconvincing. It is not borne out by his own examination of the ancient Near Eastern background. Moreover, it seems to be contradicted by his admissions that gang rape of a man "inevitably has a homoerotic aspect" and that "the homoerotic means of [disgracing Lot's guests] . . . , of course, is condemned as part of the bad behavior of the Sodomite scoundrels" (*Homoeroticism*, 48-49). A similar criticism can be made against Bird who says, on the one hand, "the ancient Israelites had no experience or conception of male homoerotic relations as consensual or expressive of a com-

Other Early Interpretations of the Sin of Sodom

Sometimes the argument is made that, since later biblical texts mention things other than homosexuality as the sin of Sodom and
Gomorrah, Gen 19:4-11 must not have anything negative to say about
homosexual conduct.[102] Four groups of Bible texts stand out.[103]

(1) Isaiah likens the devastation of the country around Zion to that
of Sodom and Gomorrah, refers to the leaders of Judah as "you rulers
of Sodom," labels their offerings and incense an "abomination," and
then proceeds to accuse them of having blood on their hands because
they have not given justice to the oppressed, the orphan, and the
widow (Isa 1:7-17). These themes resemble the Yahwist's motif of
Sodom's hostility toward the vulnerable among them, visitors (the
angels), and resident aliens (Lot).

(2) Ezekiel states that "the sin" of Sodom consisted of the fact that
"she and her daughters (i.e., the towns in Sodom's territorial orbit)
had pride (or: arrogance), an oversatiation from food, complacency (or:

---

mitted relationship"; and, on the other hand, "It is not clear whether [the Israelite
authors] viewed homoerotic activity among the inhabitants of these wicked cities
as consensual and habitual or only as perverse sport with visitors. They do appear
to suggest, however, that no Israelite male would consent to engage in homoerotic relations" ("The Bible in Christian Ethical Deliberation," 148).

102. Cf., *inter alios*, Edwards, *Gay/Lesbian Liberation*, 44-54.
103. Usually the cities of Sodom and Gomorrah are mentioned as examples of extreme
evil, of God's resolve to wipe out evil, and/or of utter devastation at God's hands
for evil committed, without any further elaboration of the nature of that evil:
Deut 29:23; 32:32; Isa 3:9; 13:19; Jer 23:14; 49:18; 50:40; Lam 4:6; Amos 4:11;
Zeph 2:9; Hosea 11:8; Matt 11:23-24; Luke 17:28-29; Rom 9:29; Rev 11:8. Jer
23:14 picks up on the theme of sexual immorality in the Sodom story: "But in the
prophets of Jerusalem I have seen a more shocking thing: they commit adultery
and walk in lies; they strengthen the hands of evildoers, so that no one turns from
wickedness; all of them have become like Sodom to me, and its inhabitants like
Gomorrah" (NRSV). Cf. *Jub.* 13:17 ("the men of Sodom were great sinners");
22:22; 36:10; Wis 10:6-8 (in their wickedness "they passed wisdom by"); *4 Ezra*
2:8-9; 3 Macc 2:5 ("acted arrogantly . . . notorious for their vices"); *Gk. Apoc. Ezra*
2:19; 7:12; *T. Naph.* 4:1; *T. Abr.* 6:13 (B); *m. Sanh.* 10:3. For a thorough discussion of traditions about Sodom and Gomorrah in the OT, early Jewish, and early
Christian literature, see Loader, *A Tale of Two Cities*, 75-138; also, Fields, *Sodom
and Gomorrah*, 155-84. Loader refers to the general "lack of interest in Sodom"
in Qumran texts and contrasts that disinterest with the great interest shown by the
Samaritan *Memar Marqah* (third to fourth century C.E.; *Tale*, 124-26).

unconcern) brought on by peace and quiet; and she (Sodom) did not take hold of the hand of the poor and the needy (i.e., did not help them). And they grew haughty and *committed an abomination* (*wataᶜ ăśênâ tôᶜēbâ*)[104] before me and I removed them when I saw it" (16:49-50).[105]

The context is a comparison of the "abominations" of Jerusalem/Judah with those of her "sisters" Samaria and Sodom. In ch. 16, Jerusalem's "abominations" are idolatrous actions (image making, child sacrifices, foreign alliances). The effect of such actions on the covenant with Yahweh is communicated (as often in the prophets) through the metaphor or allegory of the unfaithful wife (here adultery, paying others for sex, lustful abandon to other lovers). Thus, on the level of allegory, Jerusalem's "abominations" are sexual sins; on the level of reality, Jerusalem's "abominations" are idolatrous practices.

At first glance, Ezekiel's description of Sodom's sin appears to focus exclusively, or at least primarily, on the sin of social injustice. A robust economy at Sodom (cf. Gen 13:10) led to complacency and pride which, in turn, led to a callous indifference toward the plight of "the poor and needy." It is commonplace among proponents of same-sex intercourse to assert that Ezekiel did not interpret the sin of Sodom in terms of sexual immorality, at least not in its own right.[106]

Yet can such an assertion be justified? The passage does not explicitly state that the "abomination" consisted of a failure to attend to the poor and needy. Since the Hebrew word for "abomination" (*tôᶜēbâ*) is the same word used in the Levitical prohibitions for homosexual intercourse, it is conceivable that Ezekiel is alluding to the same.[107] The overtone of sexual immorality in the surrounding allegory lends sup-

---

104. "Abomination" is often rendered by translators in the plural. However, a collective singular is questionable, particularly given Ezekiel's liberal use of the plural throughout the chapter (16:2, 22, 36, 43, 47, 51, 58).

105. The final phrase can be rendered as "when I saw (it)" or "as you have seen," depending on whether the verb is read as a first-person singular (MT) or as a second-person singular (some Hebrew and Greek manuscripts and the Vulgate).

106. E.g., Bailey, Boswell, Boyarin, Nissinen, Lance.

107. Moshe Greenberg intimates that the abomination was homosexual anal intercourse (*Ezekiel 1–20* [AB; Garden City: Doubleday, 1983], 289). According to Leslie Allen, "Sodom's shocking or abominable conduct in v. 50 may well be a reflection of homosexuality. . . . But the specification of Sodom's sins highlights

port for such an interpretation. However, this identification could be questioned. The plural "abominations" (*tôʿēbôt*) is applied elsewhere in Ezekiel to a wide array of vices, including sins of social injustice, so it is possible that "abomination" here does refer to failure to help the poor and needy. One must decide whether the progression in 16:49-50 consists of three steps or four. Is the progression: (1) abundance; (2) flagrant disregard of God's will; (3) callous indifference toward the poor (= abomination)? Or should the "abomination" be viewed as a fourth stage: (4) abominable same-sex intercourse? Alternatively, "abomination" may have in view the rape of helpless visitors sheltered by a resident alien, made doubly offensive by the inherent degradation of same-sex intercourse, as a particularly vivid instance of crimes against "the poor and the needy."[108]

---

the city's arrogance or pride in materialistic comfort and excess, coupled with a lack of concern for the poor" (*Ezekiel 1–19* [WBC; Dallas: Word, 1994], 244).

108. Was Ezekiel unaware of the tradition enshrined in Genesis 19? Did he have access to an independent tradition about Sodom? Greenberg suggests that Ezekiel merely extrapolated from the reference in Gen 13:10, 12-13 about the abundant fertility of the plain of the Jordan and embellished it further by analogy to the social injustice pervading Jerusalem in his own day (similarly, Allen; Walther Zimmerli (*Ezekiel* [Hermeneia; 2 vols; Philadelphia: Fortress, 1979], 1.350). Westermann, however, concludes that "the prophets rely on a tradition that is independent of Gen. 19" (*Genesis*, 1.298-99; similarly, Speiser, *Genesis*, 142). Loader provides the most sophisticated analysis of the tradition history. Already in the pre-monarchic period, "the basic motifs of what we call the Sodom tradition" may have existed: the association of Abraham and Lot with Sodom, Sodom as a paradise of sorts, "a non-Israelite story of several gods who visited the area and a non-Israelite story of the origin of Moab and Ammon," and the image of Sodom as "a wicked city which was destroyed and thus became a barren wasteland." "The Sodom Cycle [in Genesis 18–19] itself was composed in the seventh century B.C.E. and thus could not influence the preaching of the earlier prophets. . . . *There is evidence of literary dependence of Ezekiel 16:50 on the Genesis story* [18:20]. During the various stages of the exilic period the . . . story of Genesis 18–19 was known. . . . The [pre-exilic] prophetic perspective lived on (Lm 4) and in the later phases . . . was used to ridicule foreign kings and to criticise favouritism in the administering of justice. All of this does not mean that the tradition used by the pre-exilic prophets is *older* than the tradition used by the author of Genesis 18–19" because both drew on the same pre-monarchic "Sodom tradition" (*A Tale of Two Cities*, 72-74; my emphasis). "Ezekiel's social motif is essentially the same as that of the Sodom Cycle. For . . . the sexual violence of the Sodomites is also a form of social violence or oppression" (ibid., 65; my emphasis).

Ezek 18:10-13 provides an intriguing double use of *tô⁀ēbâ* that may solve the dilemma:

¹⁰But if he has born to him a son who is a ruffian (or: a violent person; a burglar), a shedder of blood, and he does any of these things— ¹¹although he (viz., his father) has not done any of these things: he eats on the mountains, or defiles his neighbor's wife, ¹²oppresses the poor and needy, commits robbery, does not return a pledge, or lifts up his eyes to the idols, *commits an abomination* (*⁀āśâ tô⁀ēbâ*), ¹³lends at interest and takes an extra charge, shall he (viz., the son) then live? [or: he shall certainly not live]. *He committed all these abominations* (*ʾēt kōl hattô⁀ēbôt hāʾēlleh ⁀āśâ*);[109] he shall certainly be put to death. His blood shall be on himself.

It is apparent that "he commits an abomination" does not directly refer back to the clause "he oppresses the poor and needy" because the clause "or he lifts up his eyes to the idols" intervenes between the two expressions. This in turn suggests that the clause "he committed an abomination" in 16:50 does not refer back to the preceding "she did not take hold of the hand of the poor and the needy." Moreover, there is little reason to believe that "he commits an abomination" in 18:12 alludes to the immediately preceding clause (idolatry) or the following clause (interest-bearing loans) since it appears as just one element among many in an ongoing list.[110] There are no indications in the Hebrew that a break in thought has occurred either just before or just after the clause, as if the clause represented a sort of parenthetical declaration about all the sins being mentioned.[111] The concluding summary, "He committed *all* these abominations," plays that role. The clause "he commits an abomination" must then refer to a distinct act of its own, perhaps so heinous in the author's view that it could be described only by way of metonymy.

The explanation for the singular and plural uses of *tô⁀ēbâ* in 18:12-13 probably lies with the similar phenomenon in Leviticus 18, part of the Holiness Code (Leviticus 17–26). A summary following a list of for-

---

109. As with 16:50, most translators render the singular as a plural.
110. Contra REB ("and joins in abominable rites") and Allen, *Ezekiel 1–19*, 264, 276 ("he engages in a shocking practice, in that he lends at interest . . .").
111. Contra Zimmerli, *Ezekiel*, 1.383. MT's placement of a *sillûq* at the end of the clause should be ignored.

bidden sexual relations in Lev 18:6-23 characterizes all of the preceding acts as "abominations" (tôʿēbôt, 18:24-30, with the plural appearing in 18:26, 27, 29, 30). However, in all of the Holiness Code only homosexual intercourse is singled out for special mention within the list as "an abomination" (18:22 and 20:13). The point is probably the same for Ezek 18:10-13; all of the preceding acts are "abominations," but there is one specific act that deserves the label above all others: homosexual intercourse. The phrase in Lev 20:13 is nearly an exact match with Ezek 18:12: "they committed an abomination" (ʿāśû tôʿēbâ). The lists of evil actions in Ezek 18:5-9, 10-13, 14-18, each of which overlaps the others significantly, bear very strong connections to the Holiness Code, so a tie to Lev 18:22; 20:13 ("an abomination") and 18:26-30 ("abominations") is likely.[112] The two other singular uses of tôʿēbâ in Ezekiel (22:11; 33:26), like all the occurrences of tôʿēbâ in Leviticus (singular and plural),[113] refer to sexual sins as well.[114] Therefore, the evidence indicates that the singular tôʿēbâ in Ezek 16:50 refers to the (attempted)

---

112. "In many of these short legal rulings [in 18:5-18] there are clear echoes of laws of the Book of the Covenant, of Deuteronomy, and especially of the Holiness Code. Over against this the verbal contacts with the classical Decalogue are surprisingly small" (Zimmerli, Ezekiel, 1.380). The prohibition against adultery in Ezek 18:6, 11, 15 matches Lev 20:10. "Lev 25:17 (H; further Lev 19:33; 25:14) is particularly close to Ezekiel's formulation" of oppression (ynh) in 18:7, 12. Robbery (gzl) in Ezek 18:7, 12, 16 "is not mentioned either in the laws of the Book of the Covenant or those of Deuteronomy, but is found in H in Lev 19:13." Showing pity to the needy in Ezek 18:7, 16 is alluded to in Lev 19:9-10. In 18:8, 13, 17 the prohibition against taking interest "stands particularly close to H in the wording of its formulation" (Lev 25:35-37). "The formulations of the Holiness Code in Lev 19:15, 35 are also very close in language" to the pair of pronouncements concerned with conduct in courts of law in Ezek 18:8. "The same is true of the concluding statement [in Ezek 18:9, 17] which demands obedience to Yahweh's laws and statutes, which has quite close counterparts in Lev 25:18; 26:3" (ibid., 380-81). If "he commits an abomination" does not refer to homosexual intercourse, it may refer to "approaching a woman during her menstrual period" (cf. Lev 18:19; 20:18), which is mentioned in Ezek 18:6 (cf. 22:10) but not picked up in the next two lists in 18:10-13, 14-18.

113. The four plural occurrences of tôʿēbâ in Lev 18:26-30 and the two singular occurrences in Lev 18:22 and 20:13 account for all the usages of the word in Leviticus. This indicates the close association of tôʿēbâ with sexual sin in the Holiness Code. Ezekiel appears to have broadened the usage beyond sexual sin when employing the plural tôʿēbôt but still limited the use of the singular tôʿēbâ to sexual sin.

114. Ezek 22:10-11 reads: "In you they uncover their fathers' nakedness; in you they violate women in their menstrual periods. One commits [an] abomination with

83

commission of atrocious sexual immorality at Sodom, probably the homosexual intercourse proscribed in Lev 18:22; 20:13.

In that case, an important literary nexus would be created between the Holiness Code (or the circles out of which the Holiness Code grew) and the Yahwist's epic (or an independent tradition similar to Gen 19:1-11), by way of the sixth-century exilic prophet-priest Ezekiel. For we are contending that Ezekiel interpreted the actions of the men of Sodom in Gen 19:1-11 in the light of Lev 18:22; 20:13 (or prototypes of these texts). In both contexts, the commission of immoral sexual acts led, or is said to lead, to "removal": Sodom's destruction and Canaan's

---

his neighbor's wife; another lewdly defiles his daughter-in-law; another in you defiles his sister, his father's daughter" (NRSV). Here the *tôʿēbâ* is clearly adultery; the sins discussed immediately prior and following are likewise sexual sins (various forms of incest, sex with a menstruating woman). The singular "abomination" refers to a specific type of act; it is not a collective singular. The chapter is introduced with God's command to Ezekiel to declare to Jerusalem "all its abominations." Again, the singular *tôʿēbâ* is reserved for sexual sin, even though all the acts discussed in ch. 22 are collectively referred to as abominations. As with ch. 18, allusions to the Holiness Code abound; 22:10-11 is closely tied to Leviticus 18 and 20.

According to 33:25-26, 29, "You eat flesh with the blood, and lift up eyes to your idols, and shed blood; shall you then possess the land? You depend on your swords, you commit *[an] abomination*, and each of you defiles his neighbor's wife; shall you then possess the land? . . . Then they shall know that I am Yahweh, when I have made the land a desolation and a waste because of all their abominations that they have committed" (NRSV modified). Once more, the singular *tôʿēbâ* occurs in a wider context of vices, all of which are collectively labeled "abominations." Given the explicit description of adultery as an "abomination" in 22:11, it is tempting to treat "you commit [an] abomination" and the immediately following clause "each of you defiles his neighbor's wife" as an instance of hendiadys ("you commit an abomination by each of you defiling . . ."). However, the clause "commits an abomination" in 18:12 is distinct from the clause "defiles his neighbor's wife" in 18:11. The close association with adultery in 33:26, though, suggests one of the sexual sins mentioned in Leviticus 18 as the referent for "abomination" (probably same-sex intercourse; alternatively, incest or sex with a menstruating woman). Cf. Greenberg, *Ezekiel 21–37* (AB; New York: Doubleday, 1997), 685: "Although in Ezekiel this epithet ["commit abominations"] usually attaches to idolatry . . . , in 22:11 it denotes sexual immorality (as in the Holiness Code, e.g., Lev 18:26-30). Since the terms of our clause are obviously related to those of 22:11, it is plausible to take them in a sexual sense (*Rashi specifies sodomy*, to which the epithet is applied in Lev 18:22; 20:13)" (my emphasis). As with 16:50 and 18:12, many translate the singular as a collective plural.

dispossession. We have already observed a similar link between the story of Ham's act of incest and homosexual intercourse in Gen 9:20-27 and the laws in Leviticus 18. In both texts the Canaanites are said to have been disinherited from the land of Canaan because of their abominable commission of such forbidden sexual sins as incest and homosexual intercourse. A connection between Lev 18:22; 20:13 and Gen 19:1-11 in Ezekiel's thinking would also mean that Ezekiel defined one of two concrete manifestations of sin at Sodom as sexual immorality (the other being social injustice).

Even this analysis, though, does not get at the deeper sin of Sodom from Ezekiel's perspective. Ezekiel thought that the inhabitants of the city became "prideful" and "haughty" as a result of the city's prosperity, and in their prosperity they *both* neglected the poor *and* committed a particularly abominable act of sexual immorality. The two evils are linked by a flagrant disregard of God's own priorities, putting the human self at the center of the cosmos. In Ezekiel's view, the overarching rubric for the sin of Sodom is not inhospitality or homosexual behavior but human arrogance in relation to God. The focus is theocentric.[115]

A similar theocentric focus appears in the earliest known interpretation of Ezek 16:49-50. Yeshua ben Sira (a teacher of wisdom living in Jerusalem, ca. 200–180 B.C.E.) wrote that God "did not spare those living in the place where Lot sojourned, whom he regarded as abominable[116] on account of their pride (or: arrogance)" (Sir 16:8). "Pride" was a central negative concept for ben Sira (as for wisdom literature generally), treated as the antithesis of the humility necessary for attaining wisdom. In Sir 10:12-18, ben Sira states that

---

115. In the opinion of Fields, "The sexual perversion of Sodom is alluded to by the references to gross sexuality both preceding and following the pericope concerning Sodom in Ezekiel 16, but it is secondary for Ezekiel's sense of the tradition. . . . He saw, therefore, that the main point of the story was a polemic against mistreatment of the [gēr] as exemplified by the Sodomites' mistreatment of Lot" (*Sodom and Gomorrah,* [171-]179, 184). Is it not more accurate to say that, in *Ezekiel's* view, the main point of the Sodom story is human arrogance in relation to God and God's will, a human moral autonomy or self-determination which works itself out in neglecting to aid "the poor and needy" and in the commission of immoral sexual acts against those without legal protection (the resident alien and travelers)?

116. Or: loathed, abhorred, detested (*ebdelyxato,* related to the noun *bdelygma,* "abomination").

the beginning of pride is when a human withdraws from the Lord, and his heart withdraws from his Maker. For the beginning of pride is sin, and the one who clings to it will pour forth abomination. Because of it the Lord brings on them unheard-of calamities, and utterly destroys them. . . . The Lord lays waste the lands of the nations and destroys them to the foundations of the earth. He removes some of them and destroys them, and erases the memory of them from the earth. Pride has not been created for human beings, nor violent (or: furious, stubborn) anger for those born of women.

The description reads like an indirect commentary on the cataclysmic destruction of Sodom. Pride, by definition, is the rejection of the Creator and the divinely sanctioned order of creation. Genesis 1–3, Lev 18:22; 20:13, and, as we shall see below, Rom 1:26-27 all suggest that same-sex intercourse was rejected on the grounds that it constituted a violation of the anatomical and procreative sexual complementarity of male and female in creation—by definition an instance of pride, a supplanting of God's design in creation for sexuality in favor of one's own design.

However, the context of Sir 10:12-18 points in the first instance to the social injustice (*adikia*) of the rich and powerful against the lowly (10:8, 14-15, 18), getting angry with one's neighbor "for every injury," and "violent anger." Since 10:12-18 does not directly mention Sodom, we can expect the application to be tailored to the specific needs of the author's subject matter rather than to the story of Sodom itself. In close proximity are warnings about sexual sin (sex with a prostitute, adultery, fornication, 9:1-9). Elsewhere ben Sira can speak of sexual sin too as the product of arrogance and an absence of the fear of the Lord. "The one who sins against his marriage-bed says to himself, 'Who can see me? . . . The Most High will not remember sins.'. . . So it is with a woman who leaves her husband . . . her disgrace will never be blotted out. Those who survive her will recognize that nothing is better than the fear of the Lord . . ." (23:18, 22, 26-27).[117] Consequently, it is possible that in 16:8 ben Sira interpreted the sin of Sodom as both violent

---

117. The context also speaks of incest and fornication (23:16-17) and an adulterous woman (23:22-26). Other texts in Sirach treating sexual immorality include 7:22-26; 19:2; 41:21-22.

injustice toward strangers and immoral sexual conduct toward the same; or as hostile behavior toward "sojourners," climaxing in an act of homosexual rape.[118] The theme of hostility toward visitors is confirmed by Wis 19:13-14, though given an odd twist. The Egyptians in the time of Moses "suffered justly for their own evil acts, for they practiced a more grievous hatred of strangers. For others (the citizens of Sodom?) did not receive/welcome visitors whom they did not know, but these (viz., the Egyptians) enslaved guests and benefactors."[119]

(3) In the New Testament, an early strand of Jesus tradition (Q) hands down words of Jesus that compare the greater culpability of those who treat Jesus' messengers inhospitably with the lesser guilt incurred by the people of Sodom. "Whenever you enter a town and they do not receive you, as you go out of that town shake off the dust from your feet. I tell you, it shall be more tolerable on the day (of judgment) for Sodom than for that town" (Luke 10:10-12 par. Matt 10:14-15).[120]

(4) Jude 7 characterizes Sodom and Gomorrah as cities "that committed sexual immorality [*ekporneusasai*] and went after other flesh." The reference to sexual immorality is ambiguous (though it probably refers to homosexual acts), while the clause "went after other flesh" probably refers to their attempt to copulate with Lot's angelic visitors. In other words, the two actions (committing sexual immorality and pursuing angels) are to be treated as related, but distinct, actions. Less likely, the two actions are to be regarded as a unitary concept (a hendiadys): they "practiced sexual immorality by going after other flesh." Since Gen 19:1-11 nowhere intimates that the men of Sodom were aware that the visitors were angels, or that the men desired to have sex

---

118. James B. De Young is more confident that "abomination" refers directly to homosexual behavior in Sirach ("A Critique of Prohomosexual Interpretations of the Old Testament Apocrypha and Pseudepigrapha," *BSac* 147 [1990]: 439-42).

119. By any account this is a strange reading of the Sodom episode (if indeed the author is alluding to Sodom). For he compares Sodom's treatment of strangers favorably with Egypt's treatment of the Hebrews. Can the author be referring to attempted homosexual rape as merely an "unwelcoming act" and preferable to Pharaoh's treatment of the Hebrews?

120. This is essentially the reconstruction of the Q saying by the International Q Project headed by James Robinson. "Q" is the alleged written source behind the sayings material common to Matthew and Luke but not found in Mark.

with angels, this interpretation appears strained. A better understanding is that in their lust for sexual intercourse with other men, the men of Sodom inadvertently put themselves in the sacrilegious position of pursuing sexual intercourse with angels. "In like manner" the false believers, against whom Jude wages combat, had through their lust for immoral sexual behavior come into conflict with the angelic guardians of this world order. The sexual freedom of the former required the rebuttal and slander of the latter. Second Peter 2:6-10, partly dependent on Jude 7, speaks of the "licentious conduct of the lawless" Sodomites and God's judgment on them as a lesson to "those who indulge the defiling passion of the flesh." Thus both Jude 7 and 2 Pet 2:6-10, like some texts in the Pseudepigrapha,[121] connect the sin of Sodom with passions for sexual immorality, not failure to provide social justice or inhospitality.

---

121. Occasionally early post-biblical Jewish texts refer to the sexual immorality of Sodom and Gomorrah without being more specific. In *Jub.* 16:5-6, the Sodomites are described as "cruel and great sinners and they were polluting themselves and they were fornicating in their flesh and they were causing pollution upon the earth"; 20:5-6 attributes their destruction to "their fornication and impurity and the corruption among themselves with fornication." Two texts from the *Testaments of the Twelve Patriarchs* also have vague references to sexual immorality: *T. Levi* 14:6 "predicts" of the Israelites that "your mixing [= sexual intercourse] will become like Sodom"; according to *T. Benj.* 9:1, "you will commit sexual immorality, the sexual immorality of the Sodomites, and will perish . . . and shall resume illicit acts with women." That the "sexual immorality" in question has to do, at least partly, with same-sex intercourse is intimated by the wording of *T. Naph.* 3:4. After referring to gentiles changing "the order" of nature by devoting themselves to idols, "Naphtali" leaves the following charge to his descendants: "But you, my children, shall not be like that, (instead) knowing (or: discerning, recognizing) in the firmament, in the earth and in the sea and in all the pieces of workmanship the Lord who made all these things, in order that you may not become like Sodom, *which exchanged the order of its nature*" (*hētis enēllaxan taxin physeōs autēs*). The parallel reference to idolatry in 3:3 and the parallels with both Rom 1:18-27 (a two-step "exchange" of "nature" in committing idolatry and same-sex intercourse) and the descriptions in Philo of inhabitants of Sodom (and practitioners of same-sex intercourse in general) as acting "contrary to nature" confirm that the author has in mind same-sex intercourse as a violation of the sexual complementarity of male and female manifest in human anatomy and procreative function (cf. Loader's observation: "In this context the changing of its order by Sodom can only refer to the homosexual aspirations of the Sodomites mentioned in Genesis 19:5" [*A Tale of Two Cities*, 82]). The author probably also

The above overview demonstrates two main strands of interpretation regarding Sodom's sin(s): one that focused on sins of social injustice or inhospitality; another that stressed sexual immorality. Some authors weave the two themes together. In the case of those who mention only the first strand, social injustice or inhospitality, it would be a mistake to conclude from their silence about any homosexual sin at Sodom that they did not regard homosexual intercourse as exceedingly sinful. Some pre-exilic and exilic prophets may have had access only to a tradition about the evil at Sodom that contained no mention

---

included a reference to attempted intercourse with angels, given the reference in 3:5 to the angelic "Watchers" who "likewise exchanged the order of their nature" by copulating with human females and given too the exhortation in *T. Asher* 7:1 not to become "like Sodom which did not recognize the Lord's angels and perished forever" (cf. Jude 7). It is difficult to say whether homoerotic intercourse or intercourse with angels is most in the foreground (Bailey thinks the latter, although he acknowledges the presence of both elements; *Homosexuality*, 14-18). *Second Enoch* 10:4; 34:1-2 (long recension, manuscript P only) definitely refers to the sin of Sodom as male-male intercourse but the dating is difficult.

Rabbinic texts also mention the sexual dimension of Sodom's sin, but primarily as a means of underscoring the inversion of the social order. In *Gen. Rab.* 49-51, there is some mention of an agreement on the part of the men of Sodom to subject to homosexual rape all strangers and to take their money (cf. *t. Soṭ* 3:11-12). Also, the destruction of the city before sunrise is compared to an abortion carried out at night by an adulterous woman. Otherwise, a discussion of the sexual aspect is omitted. According to *b. Sanh.* 109a-b, Rabbi Jehudah (†299 C.E.) attributed four types of evil to Sodom: (1) their being "wicked with their bodies" (i.e., sexual immorality); (2) money or mistreatment of the poor; (3) blasphemy; and (4) bloodshed. A similar list appears in *Targum Pseudo-Jonathan, Targum Onqelos* ("Now the men of Sodom were wicked with their wealth, and they were sinful with their bodies before the Lord, exceedingly") and *Targum Neofiti* ("And the people of Sodom were wicked toward one another and sinful with sexual sins and bloodshed and idolatry before the Lord, exceedingly") on Gen 13:13. The focus of *b. Sanh.* 109a-b is on the Sodomites' arrogance arising out of their prosperity, their greed for money, their perverse legal system, and especially their callous and cruel treatment of strangers and the poor. One tradition refers to a charitable act on the part of one of Lot's daughters on behalf of a poor man in the city, for which she was burned (*Pirqe R. El.* 25). Loader concludes: "In Rabbinic circles the wickedness of the Sodomites was proverbial. . . . Rabbi Jehudah's idea of 'bodily' sin, the sexual aspect, is well attested. . . . It is, however, mostly subsumed under his idea of the Sodomite 'sin with money' and 'with bloodshed', i.e., the socio-economic aspect of the wickedness of Sodom is predominant in the Rabbinic texts. . . . The social aspect is developed by the logic: wealth-parsimony-social oppression" (*A Tale of Two Cities*, 116; cf. *Lev. Rab.* 23.9, which may allude to homosexual desire). See also Kugel, *Traditions of the Bible*, 331-34.

of attempted homosexual rape. Even the Yahwist's version of the Sodom cycle in Genesis 18–19 views the story in 19:1-11 as a definitive proof of a larger truth; namely, that the "great outcry" that had come to God regarding the "very grave sin" of Sodom and Gomorrah was accurate (18:20-21). The abuse of outsiders who sought lodging in Sodom and Gomorrah undoubtedly took other forms in addition to homosexual rape. Some other interpretations imply that the Sodomites perpetrated evils on its own citizenry, not just outsiders. Writers would be free to select elements of the Sodom tradition that most spoke to their contemporary situation.

Even if, contrary to what we have argued, the texts in Ezekiel and Jude were construed as making no reference to homosexual intercourse, one still would have little basis for inferring that these authors were somehow neutral about homosexual practice. Ezekiel was a Zadokite priest. His message within the prophetic corpus of the canon shows the deepest concern for the kinds of purity law enshrined in Leviticus 17–26. Both he and the author of Jude are among the more "orthodox" and conservative of the writers of the Bible. It is unimaginable that either of them would have adopted a more liberal stance on the question of homosexuality. Any putative silence on their part about homosexual intercourse would have to be attributed to the *ad hoc* nature of their writings. In a desire to make tradition or Scripture relevant to their audience, they highlighted elements in the Sodom story that spoke to the issues of their own day. If same-sex intercourse were not an issue among their readers, there would have been little need to address it explicitly.

The stance of Jesus on homosexual behavior will be dealt with in ch. 3. Suffice it for now to say that inhospitality and homosexual practice were probably not mutually exclusive categories for Jesus.[122] In the Jesus saying cited above, Sodom is singled out as the most atrocious example of inhospitality mentioned in the scriptures of Israel (a reasonable interpretation given the cataclysmic judgment of God on the city). What made it so atrocious? Many factors, to be sure, but the height of the town's evil was epitomized by the attempt to rape visiting

---

122. Schmidt, *Straight and Narrow?*, 87.

strangers and a resident alien, and, worse still, sexual intercourse with males: emasculating Lot's guests by treating them not in accordance with their nature as males but as females to be penetrated in anal sex. What gives the Jesus saying an unusual twist is its assertion that, as bad as the inhospitality of Sodom was (and it *was* bad), those towns that refuse to listen to Jesus' messengers proclaiming salvation before the Day of the Lord will be charged with even greater inhospitality.

Jesus' likely awareness of the homoerotic dimension to the sins of Sodom is confirmed not only by the presence of Gen 19:4-11 in his scriptures but also by the fact that the two most prominent Jewish writers of the first century C.E., Philo and Josephus, interpreted Gen 19:4-11 to refer explicitly to homosexual acts.[123] Both Philo (a Jew from Alexandria, Egypt) and Josephus (who lived in Israel for the first thirty years of his life, thereafter Rome) also cited other sins of the people, such as arrogance, inhospitality to strangers, gluttony, drunkenness, and adultery, all sins due to the extreme wealth and excess prosperity of these cities.[124] For Philo and Josephus homosexual conduct was merely the most outrageous example of a much wider range of sinful excess. This validates the observation that some of the other applications of the Sodom story (arrogance, inhospitality, social injustice) were not necessarily made to the exclusion of a critique of homosexual intercourse.

V. Judges 19:22-25: The Rape of the Levite's Concubine

This story parallels closely the story of Sodom and Gomorrah.[125] Here a certain Levite from the hill country of Ephraim had just

---

123. Cf. Philo, *Abr.* 133-41; *QG* 4.37; Josephus, *Ant.* 1.194-95, 200-201 (discussed in the next chapter). Josephus also speaks about Sodom's evil in *J. W.* 4.483-85; 5:566.
124. Cf. Loader, *A Tale of Two Cities,* 86-104.
125. Parallels between the two texts have been noted at least since the time of Pseudo-Philo (*L.A.B.* 45:2; first century B.C.E.). It is difficult to discern the precise relationship between the two texts. Literary dependence is likely given the significant verbatim agreement between Gen 19:4-8 and Judg 19:22-24. Most scholars date J prior to the Deuteronomistic History; so it is not surprising that most think that the motif of attempted homosexual rape of the Levite came into being through assimilation to the story of Sodom (cf. Wellhausen, Gunkel; J. Alberto Soggin,

negotiated in Bethlehem with his father-in-law for his concubine's return.[126] En route to Ephraim they and a male servant stopped off at Gibeah (in Benjamin). They waited for a time in the public square "but no one took them in to spend the night." Finally, an old man (also originally from the hill country of Ephraim, not a Benjamite) took them in.

[22]While they were enjoying themselves, the men of the city, worthless men,[127] surrounded the house, pounding on the door. They said to the

---

Judges [OTL; Philadelphia: Westminster, 1981], 282, 288; Bailey, Edwards; Nissinen too leans in this direction). However, Susan Niditch has argued that "Issues of style, plot, theology, integrality, and correspondence between medium and message point to a relative chronology for the Sodomite theme as employed in Genesis 19 and Judges 19–20, and the Judges account appears to be the prior version" ("The 'Sodomite' Theme in Judges 19–20: Family, Community, and Social Disintegration," *CBQ* 44 [1982]: 375-78; similarly, von Rad and Westermann). Niditch's arguments have been criticized by Stuart Lasine, who points (1) to features in the Judges story that heighten the gravity of the offense (cf. Gen 19:8, "Let me bring them out to you; and do to them that which is good in your eyes; only to these men do not do a thing," with Judg 19:24, "Let me bring them out; *and violate them* and do to them that which is good in your eyes; but to this man you must not do this *disgraceful* thing") and (2) to blind motifs (the offer of the old man's daughter is never developed in the Judges narrative and may be a vestige of the offer of Lot's two daughters; contra Lasine, though, the offer of the old man's daughter may prepare the reader for the problem in Judges 21 regarding the offer of daughters to the surviving Benjamite males). Cf. Lasine, "Guest and Host in Judges 19: Lot's Hospitality in an Inverted World," *JSOT* 29 (1984): 37-59, esp. 38-41; followed by Marc Brettler, "The Book of Judges: Literature as Politics," *JBL* 108 (1989): 411. According to Lasine, Judges 19 invites the reader to contrast the behavior of Lot as host with that of the old man (the latter offering his own guest's concubine and explicitly instructing the mob to "violate" both his own virgin daughter and the Levite's concubine instead) and the action taken by Lot's angelic guests and the Levite (the latter thrusting his own concubine outside). If the account in Judg 19:22-25 is dependent on the account in Gen 19:4-11, it would represent the earliest known interpretation of the latter.

126. Susan Ackerman identifies the concubine as a "secondary wife" to the Levite rather than as "a woman who is part of a man's harem but is not one of his actual wives" (the narrative describes the Levite as the woman's "husband" [v. 3] and her father as the Levite's "father-in-law" [vv. 4, 7, 9]). The former exercised more "autonomy and authority" than the latter (*Warrior, Dancer, Seductress, Queen: Women in Judges and Biblical Israel* [New York: Doubleday, 1998], 236).

127. Lit., "men of the sons of worthlessness / uselessness / wickedness" (ʾanšê bĕnê bĕliyyaʿal; KBS, BDB); "worthless, good-for-nothing, base fellows" (BDB), "villains" (*HALOT*), "a perverse lot" (NRSV), "scoundrels" (NJB), "hell-raisers" (Boling), "toughs" (Soggin).

old man, the master of the house, "Bring out the man who has come to your house so that we may know (= have intercourse with) him." [23]The man, the master of the house, went out to them and said to them, "No, my brothers, do not act wickedly. Since this man has come to my house, do not do this disgrace (*nĕbālâ*).[128] [24]Here are my virgin daughter and his concubine. Let me bring them out; and violate[129] them and do to them that which is good in your eyes; but to this man you must not do this disgraceful thing (*dĕbar hannĕbālâ*)." [25]But the men were unwilling to listen to him; so the man seized his concubine and thrust her outside to them. They knew (= had intercourse with) her and they abused[130] her all night until the morning. When dawn began to break, they let her go.

The woman dragged herself to the door and collapsed. In the morning "her master/husband" (*'ădônêhâ*) got up and found her lying at the door. When she did not answer his command to "get up," he put her on his donkey and, on returning home, cut her up into twelve pieces. The parts were distributed through emissaries to the various tribes, as a summons to holy war against the tribe of Benjamin (the battle and aftermath are described in chs. 20–21).

Similar questions to those raised by the story of Sodom appear here. Was the owner of the house willing to sacrifice his daughter and the Levite's concubine to the mob, rather than let them have the Levite, because of the inferior social status of the women? Or was it because

---

128. *nĕbālâ*: "senselessness, foolishness, disgrace, disgraceful folly (esp. of sins of unchastity)" (BDB); "stupidity, folly, insulting behavior; willful sin, sacrilege" (*HALOT*); "senseless disgrace" (Boling); "disgraceful thing" (NIV); "vile thing" (NRSV, Soggin); "outrage" (REB); "crime" (NAB); "infamy" (NJB); "impiety" (Soggin).

129. *'annû*: "1. oppress; humiliate (a woman by an enforced marriage; Deut 21:14; 22:24, 29)"; "2. do violence to; a. rape (a woman; Gen 34:2; 2 Sam 13:12, 14, 22, 32; Judg 19:24; 20:5; Lam 5:11)"; "abuse" (Ezek 22:10-11); c. "overpower" (*HALOT*); "humble, mishandle, afflict" (BDB); "ravish" (NRSV, NAB, Boling, Soggin), "abuse" (REB), "ill-treat" (NJB); NIV's "use" is too weak.

130. *wayyit'allĕlû* (*hitpa'el* of *'ll*): "deal with someone wantonly, play a dirty trick on"; (*poel* = "deal severely with, treat violently, injure"; *HALOT*); "dealt wantonly/ruthlessly with" (BDB); "abused" (*HALOT*, BDB, REB, NAB, NIV), "wantonly raped" (NRSV), "ill-treated" (NJB), "vilely mistreated" (Boling), "violated" (Soggin).

male rape of a female was considered less heinous than homosexual intercourse? Given the poor treatment of the concubine throughout the story, it can hardly be doubted that her life was viewed by the old man (and by the Levite) as worth less than her husband's. Even though she too was a guest (unlike the old man's daughter), she was a guest of significantly lesser stature than her husband. When the old man twice implored the men of the city not to do this "senseless, disgraceful thing" or "appalling act" (nĕbālâ, 19:23-24), a good part of what he had in mind was the inhospitable humiliation and subduing of a traveler through forced sex. Thus he could say with reference to the women: "violate (humiliate, overpower, subdue) them," that is, rather than violate the Levite (19:24). The Levite could later refer to what happened to his concubine, along with the attempt on his own life, as a nĕbālâ (20:6; cf. 20:10). Indeed, in recounting the events at Gibeah, the Levite says nothing about an attempted homosexual rape; only the words "they intended to kill me" (20:5). Quite apart from a homosexual assault, the heterosexual rape and murder of the traveler's concubine was alleged to be the greatest atrocity committed by Israelites since the days of the exodus from Egypt (19:30).[131]

The theme of inhospitality is clearly marked at the beginning of the narrative by the comment that "no one took them in to spend the night" when they sat down in the city square. As with the Sodom story, the only one who extended an offer of lodging was a man who was not native to the city.[132] So one could argue that the Gibeah incident is not so much about homosexual practice as about inhospitality manifested in a vicious rape and murder. Nissinen, following Boyarin, can state:

> The main cause for offense in the story of Gibeah is the heterosexual assault on the Levite's wife. Perhaps not surprisingly, no later interpreter of the story, ancient or modern, has condemned heterosexual

---

131. The pronouncement was made by either the Levite (so the LXX: the Levite instructed his emissaries to say, "Has such a thing ever happened . . . ?") or by those who saw the concubine's dismembered body (so the Hebrew Masoretic Text).
132. For the theme of inhospitality, see Matthews, "Genesis 19 and Judges 19," 6-10.

behavior because of this text, although it is structurally equivalent to the story of Sodom, which has been used to condemn homosexuality.[133]

In other words, people do not draw the conclusion that all heterosexual intercourse is bad from a story about heterosexual rape; why should they draw the conclusion that all homosexual intercourse is bad from a story about attempted homosexual rape?

The logic sounds convincing until one stops to reflect on the historical and literary contexts for the narrative in Judges 19–21. The Deuteronomistic History, as we shall argue below, takes a clear stance against homosexual intercourse as an abominable violation of God's standards for human sexual expression. It is itself dependent on the Deuteronomic law code for its moral valuation of various acts, a work which also takes a demeaning view of homosexual intercourse (referring to homosexual cult prostitutes as "dogs"). As noted in connection with the narrative about Sodom and Gomorrah, similar views were held by the authors of pentateuchal material and in the ancient Near East generally. In these contexts, how is it possible to reasonably argue that homosexual intercourse *per se* did not add to the dimension of horror for the old man, for the Levite, and for the narrator of the story? Repugnance for male penetration of males must have been a significant factor in twice designating the demand for sexual intercourse with the Levite as a *nĕbālâ* much greater than that involving intercourse with the old man's daughter and the Levite's concubine. It was an act that underscored the perversion of the Israelite men of Gibeah.[134] A similar conclusion was reached by Susan Niditch:

---

133. Nissinen, *Homoeroticism,* 51; cf. Boyarin, "Are There Any Jews in 'The History of Sexuality,'" 351.
134. Indeed, if (as some argue) the motif of homosexual rape is secondary, from the standpoint of tradition history, there can be no other credible reason for its addition than to intensify the abhorrent character of the Benjamites. In retelling the story, Josephus expunges any reference to the demand by the men of Gibeah to have sexual intercourse with the Levite (*Ant.* 5.136-49). Given Josephus's contrasting approach to the Sodom story (where he emphasized the homosexual dimension), the probable reason for the omission was to absolve Israelites of any suspicion of homoerotic tendencies (Scroggs, *Homosexuality,* 90; Edwards, *Gay/Lesbian Liberation,* 41).

In Judges 19, the unwelcome attack has the additional negative feature
of homosexuality. . . . The threat of homosexual rape is thus a doubly
potent symbol of acultural, non-civilized behavior from the Israelite
point of view. . . . homosexual rape is not merely an attack against an
individual. It threatens proper family-concepts and . . . the greater community of Israelites. . . . the Benjamites' rape of a female is hypotheti-
cally less of an abomination than the homosexual attack. [135]

Niditch explains the subsequent terse statement of the Levite to the
tribal assembly at Mispah ("they intended to kill me," Judg 20:5) as
due to "uncomfortableness in the tradition about reemphasizing the
homosexual aspect of the attack."[136] One can read between the lines:
Homosexual rape is inferred from the next statement, that "they
raped (^{c}innû) my concubine until she died." Another possible explanation for the failure to mention homosexual rape in Judg 20:5 is
that the narrator wanted to underscore the disreputable character of
the Levite himself. The Levite sought to exaggerate the danger to his
own person in order to rationalize his own complicity in the atrocity.

---

135. "The 'Sodomite' Theme in Judges 19–20," 368-69. Ken Stone is right to stress
that, from the narrator's perspective, the truly heinous element of the crowd's
demand to have sex with the Levite is the treatment of a man as if he were a
woman, that is, as someone who is penetrated in sexual intercourse. However, he
overplays the misogynist dimension of the narrator's horror of male-male intercourse by focusing almost exclusively on "gender hierarchy"; that is, on placing
the Levite in the shameful position of a socially inferior sexual object (a woman)
rather than sexual subject ("Gender and Homosexuality in Judges 19: Subject-
Honor, Object-Shame?" *JSOT* 67 [1995]: 87-107; idem, *Sex, Honor, and Power
in the Deuteronomistic History* [JSOTSup 234; Sheffield: Sheffield Academic
Press, 1996], 69-84). All men, at one time or other in their lives, exist in subordinate relationships to other classes of men. The mere fact of being put in a position of social submission to others does not constitute an inherent form of
demasculinization. Moreover, while the author of the book of Judges accepts
male headship over women as the norm, the author shows little embarrassment
at the commanding role played by Deborah as a judge over Israel (chs. 4–5). It
is also surely a questionable assumption that our own culture should take
absolutely no account of fundamental physiological and psychological differences between male and female, as if "being a man" and "being a woman"
amount to the same thing. Both cultural exaggeration and cultural minimization
of divinely created sexual differences between men and women are problematic.
136. "The 'Sodomite' Theme in Judges 19-20," 371.

Consistent with this is the fact that he "forgets" to mention his role in thrusting his concubine outside.[137]

The fact that the men of the city proceeded to rape the concubine raises doubts that the original demand to have sex with the Levite stemmed in part from exclusive homosexual passions, for some or all of the perpetrators.[138] Rape is obviously an act that has to do with aggression, dominance, control, and humiliation of another. However, heterosexual rape often occurs in conjunction with sexual desire. Homosexual rape would appear to require some degree of sexual stimulation, if for no other reason than that sexual stimulation is usually required for erection, and erection for penetration. A strict either/or approach to the question of motivation (intent to do harm vs. sexual passion) is unwarranted for this story. In any case, the text itself is silent on the question of internal sexual motivation. As in the case of the Yahwist's rendition of the story of Sodom, the narrator here is concerned with describing evil actions, not with psychologizing the motives of the perpetrators of this vile act. Rather than argue that the narrators of the twin stories of Sodom and Gibeah would have changed their perspective on homosexual intercourse had they only had a modern understanding of sexual orientation, it is more plausible to say that it probably would not have made any difference to them.

Excursus: The Image of Women in Judges 19–21

Beyond the issue of same-sex intercourse, the story raises a number of concerns about the treatment of women.

(1) The concubine or secondary wife of the Levite is nameless and silent throughout the story, a symbol of her devaluation as a person.

---

137. Certainly the Levite in failing to protect his own concubine would have suffered dishonor. A third explanation for why homosexual rape is not explicitly mentioned in Judg 20:5 is the secondary and late insertion of the theme in 19:22-25.

138. Cf. Boyarin, "Are There Any Jews in 'The History of Sexuality,'" 352 ("the acceptance of a 'heterosexual' substitute shows that the people of Gibeah are not being anathematized as 'homosexuals'"). For the sake of accuracy, it is worth mentioning that the men of the city turned down the old man's offer to send out his daughter and the Levite's concubine as substitutes for the Levite (19:25). Stone makes the point that when the men of Gibeah abuse the Levite's concubine they intend to abuse the Levite through her ("Judges 19," 100-101).

(2) At the beginning of the story the narrator states that the Levite's "concubine became angry with him (Greek/Old Latin; Heb.: prostituted herself against him), and she went away from him to her father's house at Bethlehem" (19:2). When the Levite went to Bethlehem to "speak tenderly to" his concubine in the hopes of bringing her back to the hill country of Ephraim, her fate appears to be largely in the hands of her father and her husband (19:1-9). Only the two men are explicitly mentioned as being present at the feasts. The text indicates that the woman's acquiescence is important (otherwise in her anger she might run away again and there would be no point to the Levite "speaking tenderly to" her), but the formal decision about her return ultimately rested with the two key men in her life.

(3) The decision about where to spend the night, Jebus or Gibeah, is debated by the Levite and his male servant. The concubine appears not to have any input (19:10-13).

(4) The old man at Gibeah took it upon himself to offer not only his daughter but also the Levite's concubine to the men of the city for sexual intercourse (19:24). The Levite "seized his concubine and put her out" the door in order to save himself from the mob (19:25). At no time was the concubine ever consulted.

(5) The concubine's "master/husband" does not open the doors of the house again until morning, when it is time for him to leave. His intent in opening the door is not to rush out to his battered concubine but rather "he went out to go on his way" (19:27). As Lasine notes, "He acts as though he were in a hurry to get on the road to beat the morning traffic."[139] His response to his concubine lying at the door is curt: "Get up, we are going" (19:27-28). When his concubine does not answer, it occasions no remark from the Levite. The text notes only that "he put her on the donkey and the man set out for his home" (19:28).

(6) Upon arriving home, he dismembered her (the MT, unlike the LXX, does not even make clear that the concubine is dead), sending her twelve pieces to the twelve tribes in a call for holy war against the Benjamites (19:29). In chopping her up, he puts the punishment of the Benjamites above a decent burial for his concubine.[140] In his accompanying message he (according to the MT) does express outrage at the events of the previous day (19:30). Later at Mispah he refers to the attempt on his own life and the rape and killing of "my" concubine as a "vile outrage" (NRSV) or "monstrous crime" (NAB;

---

139. "Guest and Host," 45.
140. See Lasine, who stresses the "perversity" of the Levite's action vis-à-vis Saul's dismemberment of the oxen in 1 Samuel 11 (ibid., 41-43).

20:5-6).[141] The narrator does not comment on whether the Levite's outrage was due solely to the destruction of his "property" and offense to his honor, or whether there was an element of compassion toward his deceased concubine. The behavior of the Levite throughout the story, though, suggests the former.

(7) As an addendum, at the end of the tribal war against the Benjamites, surviving Benjamite soldiers are advised by the tribes to abduct two hundred young female dancers at the yearly festival at Shiloh and to make them their wives so that the tribe of Benjamin would not be "blotted out" (21:15-24). This they do, without the consent of the young women. Forcible abduction appears to be the only way to get around the tribes' previous pledge not to give any of their daughters in marriage to the Benjamites (21:1), even if it is by means of a mere technicality (Ackerman refers to it as "sheer casuistry").[142]

As a narrative with a descriptive rather than a prescriptive quality, the actions of the old man, of the Levite, and of the tribal muster in "sacrificing" women (like the action of Lot in offering his daughters to the men of Sodom) are not necessarily presented with the narrator's approval. Judges 19–21 begins with the notice "In those days, when there was no king in Israel . . ." (19:1) and ends with the notice "In those days there was no king in Israel; all the people did what was right in their own eyes" (21:25). With these notices "the editor signals that the whole Judges 19–21 complex depicts a world gone grossly awry" (so Ackerman).[143] As Nissinen puts it, "The narrator depicts the dishonored Levite not as an innocent victim but as a coward. . . . The Levite's manly honor is challenged not only by the men of Gibeah but also by the narrator, who uses this horrifying incident as an example of the anarchy that

---

141. Heb. *zimmâ ûněbālâ*; *zimmâ* means "an infamy, shameful or lewd behavior, wickedness, immorality, depravity."

142. For a discussion of the terrors of the text for women, cf. Phyllis Trible, *Texts of Terror: Literary-Feminist Readings of Biblical Narratives* (Philadelphia: Fortress, 1984), 65-91; Ackerman, *Warrior, Dancer, Seductress, Queen*, 235-40, 250-57, 275-76; Lasine, "Guest and Host," 37-59; Cheryl J. Exum, *Fragmented Women: Feminist (Sub)versions of Biblical Narratives* (Valley Forge: TPI, 1993), 170-201; idem, "Feminist Criticism: Whose Interests Are Being Served?" *Judges and Method* (ed. G. Yee; Minneapolis: Fotress, 1995), 83-86; Gale A. Yee, "Ideological Criticism: Judges 17–21 and the Dismembered Body," *Judges and Method*, 161-67. According to Yee, Judges 17–21 was composed by the Deuteronomist to support Josiah's destruction of cult centers outside Jerusalem. The country Levites are shown to be both "corrupt opportunists intent on financial gain" (Judges 17–18) and "heartless individuals who foment civil war to avenge attempts to dishonor them" (Judges 19–20; p. 167).

143. *Warrior, Dancer, Seductress, Queen*, 257.

allegedly prevailed in Israel before the monarchy was established."[144] Niditch argues that the harsh actions of the Levite exceed any misogynist tendencies that might be found in the Old Testament generally. "In contrast [to Abraham's treatment of Sarah in Genesis 12], Judges 19 has the Levite prepared to sacrifice his concubine to a violent mob to save himself. . . . His crass command, 'Get up; let's go,' might be assessed as a reflection of a world-view in which women are regarded as no more than chattel. Yet though the OT law subordinates women to men, the woman is understood as a human being under the man's protection."[145]

This is not to say that women in ancient Israel were normally "liberated" by contemporary standards. There are prescriptive laws in the Torah that clearly indicate significantly inferior status and fewer legal rights for women, at times even treating them as nearly non-persons from a modern perspective (the virtual property of their fathers or husbands). Deut 22:28-29, for example, prescribes the following penalty to a man who rapes an unattached virgin: he is to pay a bridal price to her father, marry the young woman, and to give up his right of divorce. Some consideration is given to the woman. In such a culture her prospects for marrying anyone else would be remote; permanent marriage even to such a brute might be better than the extreme hardship of never marrying. But the father's rights are paramount. Similarly, if a young woman who is promised in marriage is raped, the rapist is to be killed because "he violated his neighbor's wife" (Deut 22:23-27).[146] Despite such inequalities, the narrator of Judges 19–21 does portray the gang rape and murder of the concubine as an utterly heinous crime and appears to treat the Levite's callous and cowardly behavior toward his concubine as deplorable.

VI. Homosexual Cult Prostitution in Israel

There is good evidence of homosexual cult prostitution in Israel during the period of the divided monarchy.[147] A number of texts speak of the existence of *qĕdēšîm* (sg. *qādēš*, twice used as a collective), literally,

---

144. *Homoeroticism*, 51; similarly, Lasine, "Guest and Host," 50.
145. "The 'Sodomite' Theme in Judges 19-20," 370-71.
146. See Carolyn Pressler, *The View of Women Found in the Deuteronomic Family Laws* (BZAW 216; Berlin: de Gruyter, 1993).
147. Cf. esp. the discussions by Greenberg, *Construction*, 94-100, 140; Nissinen, *Homoeroticism*, 39-41. Greenberg is confident of its existence, while Nissinen considers it "possible." Also: B. A. Brooks, "Fertility Cult Functionaries in the Old Testament," *JBL* 60 (1941): 232-43.

"holy/sanctified men," "consecrated men," "men dedicated to the deity" (Deut 23:17-18; 1 Kgs 14:24; 15:12; 22:46; 2 Kgs 23:7; Job 36:14). The term is usually rendered in standard English translations to denote men at cult sites who engaged in homosexual prostitution: "male temple (or cult, shrine, sacred) prostitutes."[148]

> There shall not be a *qĕdēšâ* (the female counterpart of the male *qādēš*) from among the daughters of Israel and there shall not be a *qādēš* from among the sons of Israel. You shall not bring the earnings[149] of a female prostitute/harlot (*zônâ*) or the wages[150] of a "dog" (*keleb*) into the house of Yahweh your God for (viz., in payment or fulfillment of) any vow, because both of them are an abomination (*tôʿēbâ*) to Yahweh your God. (Deut 23:17-18 [MT: 18-19])

> Rehoboam, son of Solomon, reigned in Judah. . . . and the name of his mother was Naamah the Ammonite. Judah did evil in the sight of Yahweh. . . . They even built for themselves high places (*bāmôt*), and pillars (*maṣṣēbôt*), and Asherah poles (*ʾăšērîm*) on every high hill and under every green tree. And even *qādēš* were in the land. They (viz., the people of Judah) conformed their behavior to all the abominations (*tôʿēbôt*) of the nations which Yahweh dispossessed[151] before[152] the descendants of Israel. (1 Kgs 14:21-24)

> Asa (grandson of Rehoboam) got rid of the *qĕdēšîm* from the land and removed all the idols which his ancestors had made; and he also removed his mother Maacah from the position of queen mother because she had made a disgraceful image for Asherah. And Asa cut down this disgraceful image of hers and burned it in the wadi Kidron; but the high places were not removed. (1 Kgs 15:12-14)

> The rest of the *qādēš* who had been left in the days of Asa his father, he (Jehoshaphat) removed completely[153] from the land. (1 Kgs 22:46 [MT: 47])

---

148. So NRSV, REB, NAB, NIV, NJB, NLT, CEV, NASB. *HALOT* has "consecrated, cult prostitute."
149. Or: fee, pay, wages, hire (*ʾetnan*); *HALOT*: gift, reward.
150. Or: pay, price, earnings, money (*mĕḥîr*).
151. Or: drove out.
152. Or: from the presence of, away from, for, because of.
153. Or: burned, exterminated; expelled, banished (*biʿēr*).

He (Josiah) tore down the houses (or: quarters, apartments) of the *qĕdēšîm* which were in the house of Yahweh, where the women did weaving for Asherah.[154] (2 Kgs 23:7)

The godless in heart put on[155] anger. They do not cry for help when he chains them. Their life-breath dies/expires in their youth, and their life at the same time as[156] the *qĕdēšîm*.[157] (Job 36:13-14)

The following arguments speak in favor of identifying the *qĕdēšîm* with men "whose masculinity had been transformed into femininity" by a goddess (Asherah? Astarte?)[158] and one of whose cultic functions was to offer their bodies to other men for same-sex intercourse. Deut 23:17-18 appears to make a strong connection, if not outright identification, between the *qādēš* and his female counterpart the *qĕdēšâ* on the one hand and a "dog" and a prostitute (*zônâ*) on the other hand.[159]

---

154. Or: wove garments/ veils/ hangings (*ʾōrĕgôt*) for Asherah; "wove coverings for the Asherah pole" (NLT); "wove sacred robes for the idol of Asherah" (CEV).

155. Or: lay up, cherish, harbor (*yāśîmû*).

156. BDB: in the form of, as; others: among (*bĕ*). The synonymous parallelism with the preceding line suggests that "in (the time of) their youth (*bannōʿar*) parallels "in (the time of) the *qĕdēšîm*" (*baqqĕdēšîm*); that is, those who harbor anger in their hearts live a miserable existence and die young, just like the *qĕdēšîm* are known to do.

157. REB ("short-lived as male prostitutes") is to be preferred to NJB ("live among the prostitutes in the temple").

158. The texts in 1–2 Kings suggest a connection with Asherah (Athirat). 2 Kgs 23:7 speaks of "the houses of the *qĕdēšîm* which were in the house of Yahweh, where the women did weaving for Asherah." The *assinnu, kurgarrû,* and *kuluʾu* were well known for carrying a spindle for weaving, a symbol of women's work. Asherah was the wife of El; hence the link with Yahweh, who shared many of the traits of El (cf. the Kuntillet ʿAjrûd inscriptions: "I have blessed you by Yahweh of Samaria and his Asherah"). She was also the chief goddess of Tyre and Sidon (with whom close ties existed in Israel from Solomon on, roughly at the time when the *qĕdēšîm* are mentioned in the Deuteronomistic History). As a fertility goddess and the "Mother of the Gods," she bears some resemblance to the later figure of Cybele, the Great Mother, with whom the *galli* were associated. One of her epithets is *qdš* ("holy place, holiness"). Some see a close relation, possibly identification at times, between Asherah and Astarte (Baal's consort). The latter was the Canaanite equivalent to Ishtar (and later model for Atargatis, with whom the *galli* were also associated). Cf. the entries "Asherah," "Ashtoreth," and "Atargatis" in *The Anchor Bible Dictionary.*

159. Possibly, Deut 23:17 refers to sacred prostitution and Deut 23:18 refers to non-

The two other occurrences of *qĕdēšâ* in the Bible (Gen 38:21-22; Hos 4:14) also link it with the term *zônâ*, "prostitute, harlot."[160] The slur "dog" was applied to the *assinnu*, the "men-women" devoted to Ishtar who feminized their appearance, probably underwent castration, and for a fee allowed themselves to be penetrated anally by other males. The Syrian *galli* who performed a similar role in their devotion to the goddesses Atargatis or Cybele during the Hellenistic and Roman periods were called "holy" (*hieroi*).[161] The remark in 1 Kgs 14:24 that the people of Judah "conformed their behavior to all the abominations (*tôʿēbôt*) of the nations which Yahweh dispossessed" sounds remarkably like the summary in Lev 18:24-30, which followed a listing of sexual offenses that singled out in particular same-sex male intercourse as an "abomination."

Job 36:14 indicates that the *qĕdēšîm* were thought to live a miserable existence that led to an early death.[162] This is consistent with the despised, degrading and debilitating lifestyle that characterized the sexual transformation and anal-receptive prostitution associated with the *assinnu*. If the *qĕdēšîm* were simply cultic functionaries who had no connection to profligate sexual acts, it is difficult to see why the author would have used them as the epitome of those who lead short lives. Surely the point of comparison with the *qĕdēšîm* is not anger per se but rather the deleterious effects of harbored anger and atrocious sexual immorality, two forms of self-destructive behavior, on the quality and length of life.

---

religious prostitution. Nissinen alludes to "the Akkadian *qadištu*, which is a class of female devotees with a disputed sexual function, and the Ugaritic *qdš*, which also belongs to cult personnel, albeit without a clearly defined role or connection to sexual acts" (*Homoeroticism*, 40).

160. "When Judah saw her (Tamar), he mistook her for a harlot/prostitute (*zônâ*). . . . [Later] he (the Adullamite sent by Judah to recover his pledge) asked the men of the place, 'Where is the *qĕdēšâ* . . . ?' But they answered, 'There was no *qĕdēšâ* here.' So he went back to Judah and told him, '. . . the men of the place said there was no *qĕdēšâ* there' " (Gen 38:15, 21-22); "I shall not punish your daughters when they become prostitutes / play the whore (*tiznênâ*) . . . , for the men themselves go aside with the whores/prostitutes (*hazzōnôt*) and sacrifice with the *qĕdēšôt*" (Hos 4:14).

161. Nissinen, *Homoeroticism*, 40-41.

162. Schmidt, *Straight and Narrow?*, 93.

Some have argued that the *qĕdēšîm* may have serviced barren women rather than men.[163] Such a supposition, though, presupposes a custom that cannot be documented for the ancient Near East, whereas the same-sex role of the *assinnu, kurgarrû,* and *kuluʾu* (who, owing to castration, were certainly unsuitable partners for heterosexual intercourse and impregnation) does provide good evidence for homosexual cult prostitution. Moreover, the theory of male-to-female cult prostitution is difficult to harmonize with the attention given by Israelite society to guarding the sexual purity of their women.[164] The harsh descriptions of the *qĕdēšîm* in 1–2 Kings (1 Kgs 14:24: *"even qādēš were in the land"*) and Job 36:14, along with the epithet of "dog" in Deut 23:18, suggests a degree of revulsion more suited to *same-sex* male cult prostitution.

Many centuries later, John of Patmos could write:

> Outside (the new Jerusalem) are *the "dogs"* and the sorcerers and the fornicators *(pornoi)* and the murderers and the idolaters and everyone who loves and practices lying. (Rev 22:15)

"Dog" (Gk. *kyōn*; pl. *kynes*) was a pervasive epithet in antiquity.[165] It has been suggested that the Jesus saying in Matt 7:6 ("Do not give that which is holy to the dogs") used "dogs" as a general term for contemptible people; less likely a term for gentiles.[166] However, it is pos-

---

163. E.g., Bailey, *Homosexuality,* 52-53; Boswell, *Homosexuality,* 99; Scroggs, *Homosexuality,* 71.

164. At different periods of Israelite history, men sometimes had concubines or harems; women never did. It is unlikely that there would have been much of a market in Israel for men to take their barren wives to a local high place to be impregnated by male cult prostitutes, particularly given that paternity would then be held by the male cult prostitute (or Asherah, a *female* goddess?), not the husband, creating all sorts of problems related to legitimacy, inheritance rights, and the like.

165. Cf. David E. Aune, *Revelation* (3 vols.; WBC; Nashville: Nelson, 1998), 3.1223. In the OT, it could be used as a general insult (1 Sam 17:43; 24:14; 2 Kgs 8:13; Isa 56:10-11). The Cynics co-opted the slanderous term. Jews could use it generally of gentiles (Mark 7:27-28 par.; *Ps.-Clem* 2.19.1-3; cf. Str-B 1:724-26). Christians could apply it to the unbaptized (*Did.* 9:5), or to Christian heretics and degenerates (Phil 3:2; 2 Pet 2:22; Ign., *Eph.* 7:1).

166. Dale C. Allison and W. D. Davies, *The Gospel According to St. Matthew* (3 vols.; ICC; Edinburgh: T. & T. Clark, 1988, 1991, 1997), 1.675; Ulrich Luz, *Matthew 1–7* (CC; Minneapolis: Augsburg Fortress, 1989), 419. Mark 7:27-28 par. uses the diminuative *kynarion* (pl. *kynaria*) of gentiles.

sible that the saying alludes to Deut 23:18 since "what is holy" (*to hagion*) could be a play on words with *qādēš* (*qōdēš* = "a holy thing, a votive offering"). The advice not to give what is holy to the dogs could be a logical reversal of the command not to allow "dogs" to give money received from abominable practices to the holy place (the temple) as a votive offering (cf. the emphasis on holiness in Lev 19:2; 20:7, 26 as a contrast to abominable sexual acts).

In any case, "dogs" can hardly mean gentiles in the context of Revelation where the author envisioned "a great multitude . . . from every nation . . . standing before the throne . . . robed in white" (7:9). Though a general reference is possible, it is more likely that in a vice list focusing on sexual immorality and cultic practices the text hearkens back to Deut 23:18. This is confirmed by the parallel vice list in Rev 21:8:

> But as for cowards and the faithless (or: unbelievers) and *the abominable* and murderers and fornicators and sorcerers and idolaters and all the liars, their share shall be in the lake that burns with fire and sulfur, which is the second death.

The reference to "the abominable" (*ebdelygmenois*) matches up with "dogs" in 22:15. The perfect passive participle of *bdelyssomai* appears also in Lev 18:30 (LXX), which refers to the "abominable practices" of the Canaanites (including incest and same-sex intercourse). The related noun, *bdelygma* ("abomination"), is the word chosen by the LXX to translate Hebrew *tôʿēbâ* in Lev 18:22 and 20:13.[167] The existence of male (same-sex) cult prostitutes was well known to Jews of the period, as Philo's comments testify (see the next chapter). Thus the most likely explanation is that the term "dogs" in Rev 22:15 *primarily* has in view emasculated male cult prostitutes, without excluding a wider reference to any who engage in homosexual practice.[168]

---

167. Cf. *2 Enoch* 34:2: "And all the world will be reduced to confusion by . . . [abominable] fornications, [that is, friend with friend in the anus, and every other kind of wicked uncleanness which it is disgusting to report]." The dating of 2 Enoch is in great dispute and the parts in brackets are read in only one of the three or four most significant manuscripts of the shorter recension.

168. Aune thinks the connection to homosexual behavior is possible. Schmidt thinks it is a "suggestive but not compelling" explanation (*Straight and Narrow?*, 98). Bruce Metzger regards it as probable (private communication).

Some contend that the *qĕdēšîm* were a piece of Deuteronomistic fiction.[169] Such a conclusion appears unlikely in view of the date of the writings in question. Second Kings 23:7 reports that King Josiah "tore down the houses of the *qĕdēšîm* which were in the house of Yahweh, where the women did weaving for Asherah." This is an extremely specific point, and it has to do with activity transpiring in the temple precincts itself, not in some remote area of the hill country. The Josianic reform, including this action of tearing down the houses of the *qĕdēšîm*, was part of a series of steps that Josiah took immediately after the discovery of "the book of the law/covenant" in the temple in 622 B.C.E. (2 Kgs 22:8–23:3), a book that most scholars identify as Deuteronomy 12–26 (the section of Deuteronomy containing the law code). That means Josiah's action against the *qĕdēšîm* in the temple precincts was likely taken as a direct result of the laws in Deut 23:17-18 regarding the *qĕdēšîm* or "dogs."

Some (Frank Moore Cross, Richard Elliott Friedman, and others)

---

169. Phyllis Bird, for example, regards them as an imaginative construct, without any historical basis in reality ("The End of the Male Cult Prostitute," *Congress Volume Cambridge 1995* [VTSup 66; ed. J. A. Emerton; Leiden: Brill, 1997], 37-80). Cf. E. J. Fisher, "Cultic Prostitution in the Ancient Near East? A Reassessment," *BTB* 5 (1976): 225-36; Robert A. Oden, *The Bible Without Theology* (San Francisco: Harper & Row, 1987), 131-53 (Oden, though, does not discuss the evidence for the sexual role of the *assinnu, kurgarrû,* and *kuluʾu*); Joan Goodnick Westenholz, "Tamar, *qĕdēšâ, qadištu,* and Sacred Prostitution in Mesopotamia," *HTR* 82 (1989): 245-65; Tikva Frymer-Kensky, *In the Wake of the Goddesses* (New York: Free Press, 1992), 199-202. For other literature that questions the existence of male same-sex cult prostitutes in Israel, cf. Nissinen; Greenberg; Olyan, " ' And with a Male . . .'," 181-2 n. 6; Karel van der Toorn, "Prostitution (Cultic)," *ABD* 5 (1992): 510-13; Elaine A. Goodfriend, "Prostitution (OT)," ibid., 507-9. In her most recent treatment ("The Bible in Christian Ethical Deliberation"), Bird—under the heavy influence of Nissinen's work—appears to have moderated her earlier stance that the existence of homosexual cult prostitutes in Israel is without historical grounding. With regard to the Mesopotamian *assinnus* et al., she makes such comments as: "their role in homoerotic encounters is disputed and evidence for their sexual activity is almost exclusively inferential. . . . It is difficult to estimate the incidence of male prostitution. . . . If the *assinnus* and/or related classes supported themselves as male prostitutes, they had a cultic role to fall back on . . ." (ibid., 159-60). Bird remains skeptical about the historical veracity of homosexual cult prostitutes in Israel: "The interpretation of *qādēš/qĕdēšîm* in DH [the Deuteronomistic History] as a class of male homosexual prostitutes misinterprets religious polemic as social history" and exhibits "no firsthand knowledge of the institution they condemn" (ibid., 173). At the same time, in commenting on Deut 23:17-18, she appears open to

argue for two editions of the Deuteronomistic History, the first written before Josiah's death in 609 B.C.E. and the second written soon after the Babylonian destruction of Jerusalem in 587 B.C.E. (i.e., less than twenty-five years later), perhaps by the same author. That would mean that 2 Kings 23 was written very close in time to the event it describes and by someone with superb access to court archives—possibly someone who was an eyewitness to the Josianic reform and who played an integral role in that reform.[170] All of this speaks well of the accuracy of the information in 2 Kgs 23:7.

The Deuteronomistic Historian reports that *qĕdēšîm* appeared in Judah during the reign of Rehoboam. Why not speak of their presence in Canaan during the periods of the conquest and tribal confederacy? Why not also mention their presence in Israel (the northern kingdom) if he were making up their existence? He subsequently mentions that Rehoboam's grandson Asa "got rid of the *qĕdēšîm* from the land" (1 Kgs 15:12). Yet, later, he notes that the "rest of the *qādēš* who had been left in the days of Asa his father, he (Jehoshaphat) removed completely from the land" (1 Kgs 22:46). Why even bother to mention that Jehoshaphat finished the job, when he makes no inference in 15:12 that Asa had failed to make a clean sweep of the *qĕdēšîm*? It does not sound like the kind of detail that an historian would make up. The Deuteronomistic Historian otherwise makes no explicit mention of

---

assuming their existence: "If [Deut 23:17-18] provides evidence for an accepted (or at least tolerated) form of homosexual practice, then it is instructive that it is in the form of prostitution, a commercial form of sex. . . . If *the prohibition of homoerotic relations [in Deut 23:17-18]* is primarily concerned with the violation of male honor, . . . then the male prostitute, like his female counterpart, provides a safe, though despised, object as one who stands outside the normal system of sexual honor" (ibid., 171; my emphasis). In this and her earlier article she accepts the view that the Deuteronomistic Historian, at least, emphasized "the repugnant associations [of the *qĕdēšîm*] with male homosexual activity" ("The End of the Male Cult Prostitute," 75).

170. Frank Moore Cross, *Canaanite Myth and Hebrew Epic* (Cambridge: Harvard University Press, 1973), 274-89. Friedman makes the interesting suggestion that Jeremiah, in collaboration with his scribe Baruch, wrote both editions of the Deuteronomistic History (Jeremiah's ministry began in 627 B.C.E., Jer 1:2). Friedman, and others (e.g., Baruch Halpern), think that Deuteronomy 12–26 was an old work that came from Levitical priests at Shiloh (*Who Wrote the Bible?* [New York: Harper & Row, 1987], 96-149).

the existence of *qĕdēšîm* in Judah in the two centuries between the reign of Jehoshaphat (ca. 873–849 B.C.E.) and the reign of Josiah (ca. 640–609 B.C.E.); hardly what one would expect of a historian obsessed with reading an imaginary construct back into the period of the divided monarchy. Then, too, one has to explain the reference to *qĕdēšîm* in Job 36:14, which does not lie within the Deuteronomistic orbit. Given the existence of the *assinnu, kurgarrû,* and *kuluʾu* in Mesopotamia, there seems to be little reason to doubt the accuracy of the reports of *qĕdēšîm* in both Deuteronomic law and the Deuteronomistic History.

Yet *even if* the *qĕdēšîm* were a literary fiction, the texts would still be relevant to the discussion of same-sex intercourse in the Bible. For they demonstrate the attitude toward same-sex intercourse adopted by both the authors/transmitters of Deuteronomic law and the Deuteronomistic Historian. It can hardly be denied that these two groups (and the author of Job 36:14) regarded the *qĕdēšîm* as homosexual cult prostitutes.[171] Cult association is established by the name "holy/consecrated ones" and by the connection to Asherah. The element of prostitution is clear from Deut 23:17-18 (fees for services rendered) and the connection to *qĕdēšôt,* who elsewhere are identified as harlots. The same-sex dimension is suggested by the label "dogs," by history-of-religions parallels, and by the unlikelihood of male heterosexual prostitution. One can quibble how big a role same-sex intercourse played in the life of *qĕdēšîm,* or for that matter *assinnus* (as Nissinen does). Regardless, it can scarcely be doubted that these biblical authors put the dimension of *same-sex* prostitution at the forefront of their own reasons for being utterly disgusted with the existence of *qĕdēšîm* in Israel.

One might then counter, "Okay, these biblical authors were opposed to male, same-sex cult prostitution. But that only tells us what the author believed about consensual homosexual practice conducted in the context of idolatrous cults and prostitution, not the kind of loving expressions of homosexuality we witness today." Such a rationale would overlook the ancient Near Eastern context. The Mesopotamian evidence explored at the beginning of this chapter makes clear that the *most* acceptable form of same-sex intercourse—not the least acceptable—

---

171. Cf. De Young, "The Contributions of the Septuagint," 165-77.

was precisely same-sex intercourse conducted in a religious context. Otherwise, for a man to want to be penetrated by another man was *generally* regarded as disgraceful.

The *assinnu*, *kurgarrû*, and *kulu³u* could be tolerated because their femininity was the goddess's doing, not their own. When the biblical authors rejected homosexual cult prostitutes—and surely not just because they were connected to Asherah, as the epithet "dogs" indicates—they were in effect rejecting the whole phenomenon of homosexual practice. They were repudiating a form of homosexual intercourse that was the most palatable in their cultural context. If they rejected that particular form of homosexual practice, how much more all other forms? Certainly the prohibition against cross-dressing in Deut 22:5 puts this beyond doubt (any obscuring of male-female sexual differences is "an abomination [*tô῾ēbâ*] to Yahweh your God, everyone who does these things"), as does the absolute form of the prohibition in Lev 18:22 and 20:13.[172]

In his discussion of *assinnu*, Nissinen argues:

> [I]t is misleading to affiliate *assinnu* with our concept of homosexuality. After all, there is no way of knowing whether they were sexually oriented toward men—or, if emasculated, toward anybody. We can speculate, of course, that men who looked for this role already had a homosexual orientation or a transvestite need and were better able to express it in that role or that they felt themselves otherwise incapable of fulfilling the requirements of the male role in a patriarchal society. Their gender identity certainly changed along with the change of gender role and after the eventual castration. Moreover, there may have been persons among them who were transsexual or born intersexed. All this is beyond modern knowledge.[173]

Yet all such considerations were also irrelevant to the biblical authors because it was the act that counted most, not the reasons for doing it (unless, of course, a man was the unwilling victim of same-sex rape).

---

172. Grenz appears reluctant to affirm the existence of *homosexual* cult prostitution in Israel, apparently because of his concern that some scholars have used this view to justify a limitation on Lev 18:22 and 20:13 (*Welcoming But Not Affirming*, 41-42). His concern is praiseworthy but ultimately misguided.
173. *Homoeroticism*, 34.

Probably there were some *assinnus,* and some *qĕdēšîm,* who were not homosexually oriented at the time they entered their roles; probably, too, there were some who were. The same could be said for those who had sex with male cult prostitutes: some may have engaged in the act for purely religious or pragmatic reasons (for example, as a means of obtaining the goddess's help on some matter), others may have participated in whole or in part because of a homosexual inclination. The bottom line for biblical authors: it did not matter why people willingly engaged in same-sex intercourse, just as it was unnecessary to parse the motivations of those who participated willingly in incest, bestiality, adultery, fornication, or heterosexual prostitution.[174]

The existence of homosexual cult prostitutes in Judah was a recurring problem. At least this was so in the roughly fifty years from the start of the reign of Rehoboam to the start of the reign of his great-grandson Jehoshaphat (922–843 B.C.E.) and in the period leading up to the Josianic Reform two centuries later (622 B.C.E.).[175] Their presence makes it possible that some Judeans did participate in homosexual practices, particularly in conjunction with a resurgence of the Asherah cult. Precisely how many may have participated cannot be determined. However, the phenomenon had enough official endorsement in the late–seventh century that *qĕdēšîm* (along with other devotees of Asherah) could be housed even in the temple precincts. The Deuteronomistic Historian regarded tolerance of their behavior as completely incompatible with Yahwistic faith and practice; they were an "abomination" to the Lord (Deut 23:18; 1 Kgs 14:24). This viewpoint is consistent with the viewpoint held by the Yahwist and the authors/transmitters of the Levitical Holiness Code.[176]

---

174. Accordingly, when I speak of "homosexual practices" or "homosexual cult prostitutes" I am not assuming homosexual orientation.

175. Possibly the *qĕdēšîm* were reintroduced in the reign of Josiah's grandfather, Manasseh, who set up a carved image of Asherah in the temple (2 Kgs 21:7). It is surprising, though, that the Deuteronomistic Historian does not specifically mention them when he lists the abominable practices associated with Manasseh's reign, for which Judah was allegedly punished by God with the Babylonian exile. Is this omission due to the author's faithfulness to his archival records, mentioning the *qĕdēšîm* only when archival materials for a given reign make specific mention of them? Again, this testifies to the Deuteronomistic Historian's restraint in plugging in the theme of the *qĕdēšîm* into his source material.

176. The question remains of why the Deuteronomic Code does not contain a law like

VII. Leviticus 18:22; 20:13: Laws

"With a male you shall not lie as though lying with a woman; it is an abomination." (Lev 18:22)

wĕʾet zākār lōʾ tiškab miškĕbê ʾiššâ tôʿēbâ hîʾ.

"And a man who will lie[177] with a male as though lying[178] with a woman, they have committed an abomination, the two of them; they shall certainly be put to death; their blood be upon them." (20:13)

wĕʾîš ʾăšēr yiškab ʾet zākār miškĕbê ʾiššâ tôʿēbâ ʿāśû šĕnêhem môt yûmātû dĕmêhem bām.

Unlike stories, commands have a definite prescriptive or proscriptive (not just descriptive) function. Both of these commands occur in the context of a larger block of laws (Leviticus 17–26) that many scholars refer to as the Holiness Code (H), a law code which urged all Israelites (not just the priests) to keep the land (not just the sanctuary) unpolluted through holy obedience to the commands.[179]

---

the one found in Lev 18:22; 20:13. It comes closest with Deut 23:17-18. Based on the observations we have already made, it seems unlikely that those who formulated the Deuteronomic Code had any more positive outlook on homosexual intercourse than did those who formulated the Holiness Code, though it is an open question what penalty would have been thought appropriate. Possibly Deuteronomic law crystallized in a period when the only type of homosexual intercourse practiced in Israel was in the context of cult prostitution and even then only rarely.

177. The verb *sākab*, when used of heterosexual intercourse, usually has the man (the active partner) as the subject. There are two exceptions to this general rule. In Gen 19:32-35 the daughters of Lot "lay with" their drunken father "so that we may preserve offspring through our father." In 2 Sam 13:11, Amnon "took hold of (his sister Tamar) and said to her, 'Come, lie with me, my sister.' "

178. The Hebrew word for "male" is *zākār* (Gk. *arsēn*), while the Hebrew word for "lying" is *miškāb* (also "place of lying, bed"; Greek *koitē*). At a later date rabbis and Christians (the latter perhaps through Hellenistic Jews) coined from these words a new word for men who functioned as the active partner in same-sex intercourse: Hebrew *miškab zākûr* (lit., "lying with a male") and Greek *arsenokoitēs* (lit., "a man who lies with a male," "a man who goes to bed with a male"; 1 Cor 6:9; 1 Tim 1:10). Cf. Scroggs, *Homosexuality*, 83, 108.

179. The date and integrity of H, as well as its relationship to P (P in Leviticus = chs. 1–16), is far from settled in scholarly circles. The consensus position, if such a

111

Six features of these two commandments are important for establishing their hermeneutical relevance.

---

position can be said to exist still, is that Leviticus in its final form (and thus P as a whole) is an exilic or early post-exilic work (sixth century) and that H was absorbed by P. Some parts of H may be pre-exilic (e.g., chs. 18–19) while other parts are exilic or even early post-exilic. Ezekiel appears to know much of the legislation in H; some think also that the final compiler of H knew Ezekiel. There is debate over whether H should even be treated as an originally independent law code. For helpful summaries, cf. Henry T. C. Sun, "Holiness Code," *ABD* 3:254-56; Baruch A. Levine, "Leviticus, Book of," *ABD* 4:319-20; idem, *Leviticus* (JPSTC; Philadelphia: Jewish Publication Society, 1989), xxv-xxx; Erhard S. Gerstenberger, *Leviticus: A Commentary* (OTL; Louisville: Westminster, 1996), 4-10; Martin Noth, *Leviticus: A Commentary* (rev. ed.; OTL; Philadelphia: Westminster, 1977), 10-15, 127-28. Jacob Milgrom has argued that both P and H are pre-exilic works and that H was P's redactor. According to Milgrom, P was composed not later than 750 B.C.E.. H was a response by priestly circles in Jerusalem to eighth-century prophetic critiques of the cult, a response that attempted to integrate morality with cult through the rubric of holiness. H then is to be associated with the reforms of Hezekiah. The close links between Ezekiel and H (cf. especially the lists of sins in Ezekiel 18 and 22 with Leviticus 18–20) indicate a pre-exilic date. Cf. Milgrom, *Leviticus 1-16* (AB; New York: Doubleday, 1991), 1-35; also, Israel Knohl, *The Sanctuary of Silence: The Priestly Torah and the Holiness School* (Minneapolis: Fortress, 1995). J. Joosten has recently argued from the "ideational framework" of Lev 17–26 (viz., the focus on the land, the attention to the obligations of the resident alien, and the stress on Yahweh's holy presence in his earthly sanctuary) that "the Holiness Code can best be understood against the background of a rural milieu in Judah of the pre-exilic period" (*People and Land in the Holiness Code: An Exegetical Study of the Ideational Framework of the Law in Leviticus 17–26* [VTSup 67; Leiden: Brill, 1996], 9-16, 203-7). Friedman contends that P was composed by an Aaronite priest in Jerusalem during the reign of Hezekiah as an alternative to the newly combined JE epic and to promote centralization of the cult in Jerusalem around the authority of the Aaronite priesthood. The author brought together a variety of collections of laws, including the Holiness Code which "might originally have been a separate Aaronid document" (*Who Wrote the Bible?* 207-16).

Regardless of the date of H as a document, whether pre-exilic, exilic, or early post-exilic, most agree that H contains legal material that is considerably older than the date of the final compilation. If, as we have argued above, Ezekiel makes reference to homosexual intercourse in partial dependence on H or the circles from which H stems, then 18:22 and 20:13 must represent pre-exilic sentiment (and one could also throw into the mix the data discussed above from the Yahwist, the Deuteronomic law code, and the Deuteronomistic Historian). It is misleading, then, for some scholars to treat Lev 18:22 and 20:13 (or worse, opposition to homosexual practice itself) as if they were late creations of the post-exilic period (e.g., Nissinen, *Homoeroticism*, 37-38, 43; Greenberg, *Construction*, 191-95).

(1) Lev 18:22 occurs in a larger context of forbidden sexual relations that primarily outlaws incest (18:6-18) and also prohibits adultery (18:20), child sacrifice (18:21), and bestiality (18:23). These prohibitions continue to have universal validity in contemporary society. Only the prohibition against having sexual intercourse with a woman "in her menstrual uncleanness" (18:19) does not.

(2) The degree of revulsion associated with the homosexual act is suggested by the specific attachment of the word *tôʿēbâ*, "abomination," "an abhorrent thing," or "something detestable, loathsome, utterly repugnant, disgusting,"[180] intimating a particularly revolting and conspicuous violation of boundaries established by God against the defiling behavior characteristic of other peoples. In the concluding summary in 18:24-30 all the practices mentioned in the chapter are described as "abominations" (18:26-27, 29-30); yet in the preceding list of specific commands in 18:6-23 the word is mentioned only in conjunction with same-sex male intercourse. Once again in Leviticus 20, where penalties are prescribed for many of the forbidden acts of Leviticus 18–19, the word is applied specifically only to sexual intercourse between males (20:13). In short, in the entire Holiness Code—indeed, in the entire priestly corpus of the Tetrateuch—the only forbidden act to which the designation "abomination" is specifically attached is homosexual intercourse.

(3) The penalty is extreme: death (20:13).[181] This penalty exceeds that

---

180. *HALOT*: abomination, abhorrence ("Greuel, Abscheu").

181. Probably by stoning, as with those who sacrifice their children to Molech (Lev 20:2), blasphemers (Lev 24:13-23), sabbath violaters (Num 15:32-36), and rebellious sons (Deut 21:18-21) (cf. *m. Sanh.* 7–8 for a list of those who are to be stoned; 7:4 refers to stoning men who have sex with males). Lev 18:22 does not have a penalty attached specifically to its proscription, owing to the apodictic form of the prohibitions in ch. 18, but rather is attached to the "collective penalty" at the end of the chapter (Levine, *Leviticus*, 135). This collective penalty is twofold. First, there is a penalty on the nation as a whole: If the people of Israel commit these practices as the Canaanites did before them, "the land will vomit you out" (i.e., exile of the nation; 18:24-28). Second, there is a penalty on the individual perpetrators of these offenses: "Everyone who commits any of these abominations, the persons who do so will be cut off from the midst of their people" (18:29). The penalty imposed in 18:29 is the *kareth* penalty (from *kārat*, "to cut off"). Precisely what this "cutting off" entails is a matter of scholarly debate. Some argue that the meaning is excommunication and/or the death penalty, imposed by

required by the Middle Assyrian Laws (castration). Homosexual conduct was not merely prohibited but also regarded as a supreme offense, a penalty consistent with its description as an "abomination."[182] In ch. 18 homosexual intercourse is listed along with other forbidden sexual acts for which a person should be "cut off from their people" (18:29). Failure on the community's part to take action against offenders would lead to expulsion of the whole community from the land of Canaan, just as the previous inhabitants had been expelled for such practices (18:24-30).

---

the community. Others (e.g., Wold, Milgrom) contend that the *kareth* penalty was a penalty imposed by God alone, not the community, and could take many different forms: premature death, a blotting out of the offender's name by terminating the family line (cf. Lev 20:20-21: "they shall be childless"), and/or not permitting the offender to rejoin his ancestors in the afterlife (this last punishment closely approximates the denied inheritance in the kingdom of God of which Paul speaks in 1 Cor 6:9-10). How the *kareth* penalty for 18:22 is to be related to 20:13 is not entirely clear and depends in part on how one views the historical relationship of ch. 20 to ch. 18 (cf. below). In ch. 20 one of the offenses listed in ch. 18 receives both the *kareth* penalty and a communal sentence of death (those who sacrifice their children to Molech; vv. 2-5); others receive only the sentence of death (20:9-16) or only the *kareth* penalty (20:6, 17-19) or only the punishment of childlessness (20:20-21). According to Wold, whose dissertation was on the *kareth* penalty, "Leviticus 20 adds the death penalty whereas chapter 18 has only *kareth*. If one supposes that these penalties are mutually exclusive, some distance may be placed between the two chapters, assigning the latter perhaps to a period when the social nucleus in ancient Israel shifted from the family to the community and then to the state. One could imagine under these circumstances that chapter 20 was written as a separate document. However, I think that the penalties are not mutually exclusive and assign the composition of Leviticus 20 to a period congruent with or shortly after that of Leviticus 18" (*Out of Order*, 99; see also pp. 97-98, 137-48). On the *kareth* penalty generally, cf. Milgrom, *Leviticus*, 457-60.

182. In the list of penalties given for violations of the commandments in Leviticus 20, the only other acts that are specifically connected with the death penalty are: child sacrifice (20:2), cursing one's parents (20:9), adultery (20:10), some forms of incest (20:11-12), marriage to a wife and her mother (20:14), and bestiality (20:15-16). While the penalty may strike us as severe, all of the acts remain reprehensible in our contemporary context. David L. Bartlett argues that, because the death penalty is prescribed for same-sex intercourse, contemporary opposition to same-sex intercourse must be called into question ("A Biblical Perspective on Homosexuality," *Foundations* 20 [1977]: 136). This is a strange argument. Are the laws against adultery and incest irrelevant guides for sexual ethics because the death penalty is no longer prescribed? Paul did not demand that the Corinthian believers put to death the man engaged in incest but he did urge them to expel

(4) Unlike the proscription of homosexual rape in the Middle Assyrian Laws, the laws in Lev 18:22 and 20:13 are unqualified and absolute. They neither penalize only oppressive forms of homosexuality nor excuse either party to the act.[183] The general term "male" (*zākār*) is

---

the man from the community (1 Corinthians 5). According to the story of Jesus' treatment of the woman caught in adultery, Jesus swept aside the death penalty without ignoring Scripture's negative valuation of the act ("sin no more"; John 8:1-11). Grenz explains the difference between the two covenants as follows: "In contrast to ancient Israel, the New Testament community is not localized within a particular physical land given them through divine promise. Consequently . . . eradication of those who commit abhorrent offenses occurs through excommunication (which is connected with spiritual death) rather than through the death penalty itself" (*Welcoming But Not Affirming*, 47). While I would not want to argue a complete disinterest in the land among early Christians, there is definitely a shift in NT texts toward "spiritualizing" and "eschatologizing" the believer's sphere of interest (e.g., Matthew 5–6; John 4:21-26; 2 Cor 10:2-6; Gal 4:25-26; Eph 6:12; Hebrews 11–12).

183. Olyan believes that 18:22 reflects an earlier formulation than 20:13, in which only the dominant, insertive partner (not the receptive partner) was punished (" 'And with a Male . . . '," 186-88). He is not alone in regarding Leviticus 20 as stemming from a later time than Leviticus 18 (cf. Gerstenberger, *Leviticus*, 288-89). Yet his position about only the insertive partner being punished in 18:22 is a case of reading too much out of too little. First, even if 20:13 were a later formulation, it would represent the earliest commentary on the meaning of 18:22; namely, that both partners in homosexual intercourse were liable to the death penalty. Presumably, 20:13 would have been formulated by the same priestly circles as those that formulated 18:22. Is this not the best evidence we have of how the formulators of 18:22 would have understood their own proscription? Second, *all* of the proscriptions in Leviticus 18 (minus 18:21 which does not deal with intercourse) address only the dominant, active partner (usually the male). The only proscription directed specifically to both males and females is the law concerning bestiality in 18:23, an exception easily explained on the assumption that women were regarded as the initiators in any intercourse with animals. By Olyan's reasoning, the authors of the laws against incest would have held only the men accountable for incest, even in cases where the woman was a willing participant or even prime instigator (in contradistinction to penalties prescribed for both participants in 20:11-21). We would also have to assume that the formulators of the prohibition against having sex with "your neighbor's wife" in 18:20 never intended to penalize the wife in an adulterous affair. Yet all the evidence we have from ancient Israelite law indicates that women involved in adulterous affairs were punished with death, if they were willing participants in the act (Num 5:11-30; Deut 22:13-27; Lev 20:10; Ezek 16:38-41; 23:45-48). The reason why Lev 18:22 focuses on the active male partner is because the passive male partner, the one penetrated, takes the place of the female and the female is not directly addressed in the prohibitions of ch. 18. By analogy with the laws against incest and adultery,

used, not "your neighbor" (*rē'ăkā*, one of equal status or from the same region or clan)[184] or "boy, youth" (*na'ar*). The question of whether the homosexual relationship is pederastic or not does not enter the picture. The prohibition applies not only to the Israelite but also to the non-Israelite who lives among God's people (18:26).[185] There are no limitations to cultic prostitution.

(5) Contrary to the contemporary trend of Jewish and Christian communities to accommodate to the prevailing cultural approbation of homosexuality, the entire context of the Holiness Code stresses the distinctive holiness of the people of God. God's people are to imitate the holiness and purity of their God and not the abominable and

---

we should assume that both consenting partners in the "abominable act" were liable to punishment. Taylor adds also two other considerations that speak to the mutual consent of the participants: the prohibitions use simply the verb "lie" rather than another expression that would imply rape (such as "seize and lie"); and the accountability clause in Lev 20:13, "their blood be upon them" ("The Bible and Homosexuality," 5).

184. Olyan, " 'And with a Male . . .'," 196.
185. Jacob Milgrom's contention that the prohibition against homosexual acts is applicable only to Jews and to those non-Jews that live in Israel (18:26) is true only in the most pedantic sense ("Does the Bible Prohibit Homosexuality?" *BRev* 9:6 [Dec. 1993]: 11 and "How Not to Read the Bible," *BRev* 10:2 [Apr. 1994]: 14, 48). Strictly speaking, the concluding exhortation in 18:24-30 only speaks to the question of the effect that sin has on the land of Israel by those who live in Israel. However, if one carried Milgrom's interpretation to its logical conclusion, diaspora Jews and gentiles alike would be exempt from the commands regarding incest, bestiality, and child sacrifice, not to mention (if one were to draw on the prohibitions in chs. 19–20 as well) sorcery, cursing one's mother and father, adultery, idolatry, stealing, cheating, lying, false witness, slander, oppression of the poor, etc. The text is speaking to the situation of residents of Israel; it is not, however, granting license to all who live outside the land (cf. Ezekiel's affinities with the Holiness Code in his commands to exiled Jews). That it addresses one situation does not make it irrelevant to others, particularly in a case involving gender confusion, a matter that cuts across ethnic lines. There is much that the Bible does not chastise the nations for, yet few would conclude from this that all such conduct meets with God's approval. In any case, in the Second Temple period and beyond, Jews and Christians certainly regarded Lev 18:22; 20:13 as binding outside the boundaries of Palestine. Milgrom himself notes that some rabbis included homosexuality under the Noahide Laws binding on non-Jews (*b. Sanh.* 58a; Maimonides, *Kings* 9:5). According to Luke, one of the four binding requirements in the "Apostolic Decree" placed on gentile believers outside Palestine was to abstain from *porneia* (Acts 15:20, 29; 21:25), a word that undoubtedly included same-sex intercourse (see ch. 5.V).

defiling practices of other peoples (18:1-5, 24-30; 19:2). "You shall be holy to me; for I Yahweh am holy, and I have separated you from the other peoples to be mine" (20:26). The commands of God, and not the consensus of the surrounding culture, must shape the behavior of God's people. The relation of church/synagogue to culture is, at least in part, supposed to be reforming rather than conforming.

(6) As we shall see, it is a prohibition carried over into the New Testament. The position adopted by Paul in the New Testament is not an aberration but is consistent with the heritage present in his Scriptures. The two covenants are in agreement.

The Meaning of tôʿēbâ

According to John Boswell,

> The Hebrew word "toevah" . . . does not usually signify something intrinsically evil, like rape or theft (discussed elsewhere in Leviticus), but something which is ritually unclean for Jews, like eating pork or engaging in intercourse during menstruation, both of which are prohibited in these same chapters. It is used throughout the Old Testament to designate those Jewish sins which involve ethnic contamination or idolatry. . . . the Levitical enactments against homosexual behavior characterize it unequivocally as ceremonially unclean rather than inherently evil.[186]

The distinction is odd in view of the way in which the word is used in Lev 18:22, 26-30; 20:13. The word tôʿēbâ is restricted in Leviticus to

---

186. Boswell, *Homosexuality*, 100-102. For a rebuttal of his attempt to perpetuate the distinction especially in the LXX, see Wold, *Out of Order*, 110-12. A position similar to Boswell's is taken by Bird: "The term tôʿēbâ is concentrated in . . . cultic contexts, where it serves to characterize practices as . . . 'taboo'. . . . It is not an ethical term, but a term of boundary marking. . . . it describes a feeling of abhorrence or revulsion that requires or admits no rational explanation. . . . It points to a nonrational and preethical judgment" ("The Bible in Christian Ethical Deliberation," 151-52, 157). As we shall see, the Levitical proscriptions of homosexual intercourse, like most other proscriptions to which tôʿēbâ is attached in Ezekiel and elsewhere, do indeed carry with them at least an implied rational explanation for the proscribed behavior. Indeed, Bird herself implicitly admits of such an explanation for the Levitical proscriptions when she posits as their raison d'être an aversion to putting a male in the subordinate status of a female (ibid., 157).

forms of sexual immorality that can be characterized in three ways: (1) a sexual act regarded by Yahweh as utterly detestable and abhorrent; (2) a sexual act which rendered the individual participants liable to the death penalty or being "cut off" from God's people; (3) a sexual act which, if left unpunished by the nation, put the entire nation at risk of God's consuming wrath, God's departure from the midst of the people, and expulsion of the people from the land of Canaan (18:22, 26-30; 20:13). Homosexual intercourse is singled out among other abominable sexual acts in Leviticus 18 and 20 as a form of sexual misconduct particularly worthy of the designation *tôʿēbâ*. It is difficult to see how one can speak of this or other acts in Leviticus 18 and 20 as "ceremonially unclean rather than inherently evil" for the author or even for ourselves. Whatever one does with the proscription of sex with a menstruating woman, there is no basis for asserting that "'toevah'... does not *usually* signify something intrinsically evil." As Greenberg states:

> Leviticus does recognize forms of ritual uncleanness that are not morally condemned, e.g., childbirth, seminal emission, heterosexual intercourse, and menstruation. Purification from these pollutions is accomplished quite simply through bathing and sacrifice. The word *toevah* is not used to refer to these conditions, nor are they punished. . . . Idolatry was not simply unclean; it was a grave offense. . . . That intercourse with a menstruating woman is also classified as an abomination along with homosexuality is an indication not, as Boswell suggests, that the latter offense was considered trivial, but rather that the former was considered extremely grave.[187]

Outside of Leviticus, *tôʿēbâ* appears most frequently in Ezekiel (forty-three times), the exilic priest-prophet who demonstrates close ties with the legislation found in the Holiness Code. Ezekiel expands the application of the word *tôʿēbâ* to a wide array of offenses. In the rest of the Old Testament, the word occurs sixty-eight times: twenty-two times in Proverbs, seventeen times in Deuteronomy, eight times in Jeremiah, and twenty-one times scattered elsewhere in the Old Testament.[188] The "abominations" most frequently involve the worship

---

187. Greenberg, *Construction*, 195-96; cf. Wold, *Out of Order*, 107-14.
188. Gen 43:32; 46:34; Exod 8:26; 1 Kgs 14:24; 2 Kgs 16:13; 21:2, 11; 23:13; Isa 1:13; 41:24; 44:19; Mal 2:11; Ps 88:8; Ezra 9:1, 11, 14; 2 Chron 28:3; 33:2; 34:33; 36:8, 14.

of other gods (Deut 7:25-26 and very often), including sacrificing one's children to pagan gods (Deut 12:31 and often) and practicing sorcery, divination, and necromancy (Deut 18:9-12; 2 Kgs 21:2, 6). The word is also used often of sexual sins: adultery (Ezek 18:6, 11, 15; 22:11; Jer 7:9); incest (Ezek 22:10-11); intercourse with a woman during her menstrual period (Ezek 18:6; 22:10); cross-dressing (Deut 22:5); remarrying one's divorced spouse after remarriage to another (Deut 24:4, probably an act of fraud for acquiring dowry money); and bringing a prostitute's fee to the temple as payment of a vow (Deut 23:18). As noted in our discussion of biblical interpretations of the Sodom story, tô‘ēbâ probably refers to homosexual intercourse in Ezek 16:50; 18:12; 33:26.

In addition to the above, the following also constitute "abominations" in various texts: murder (Jer 7:9; Ezek 22:6; Prov 6:17); swearing falsely (Jer 7:9; Ezek 22:9, 12; Prov 6:19); habitual lying (Prov 6:16; 12:22; 26:25-28); oppressing or not aiding the poor, aliens, widows, and orphans (Ezek 16:47-52; 18:7, 12, 16; 22:7, 29); a "false balance" used to cheat the poor (Prov 11:1; 20:10, 23); robbery, extortion, and charging interest to Israelites (Ezek 18:7-8, 10-13, 16-17; 22:12, 29; cf. Jer 7:9); treating father and mother with contempt (Ezek 22:7); wicked people (Prov 3:32 and often in Proverbs); the arrogant (Prov 6:16; 16:5); one who creates family strife (Prov 6:19); "one who justifies the wicked and one who condemns the righteous" (Prov 17:15); the hypocritical incense, sacrifice, or prayer of the wicked (Isa 1:13; Prov 21:27; 28:9); cheating God by sacrificing an ox or sheep that has a defect (Deut 17:1); profaning the sabbath (22:8, 26); marriage to someone who worships a different god (Mal 2:11); and putting foreigners in official positions in the temple (i.e., people without devotion to Yahweh, Ezek 44:6-8). In Deut 14:3 animals that are not to be eaten because of their uncleanness are referred to as "abhorrent things," but eating them is not said to be an "abomination." Moreover, the last-mentioned reference (cf. Ezek 22:8, 26), along with the prohibition against intercourse with a menstruating woman, are not representative of the kinds of behavior delimited by the word. Thus Boswell's contention that tô‘ēbâ "is used throughout the Old Testament to designate those Jewish sins which involve ethnic contamination or idolatry" is misleading.

Saul Olyan criticizes the translation "abomination" not for what it intimates but for what it does not. "The conventional translation 'abomination' suggests only what is abhorrent; it does not get across the sense of the violation of a socially constructed boundary, the reversal or undermining of what is conventional, but viewed as established by the deity."[189] To be sure, the issue of "boundaries" is important for the meaning of the term. Leviticus 18–20 (cf. Deut 12:29-32) requires the Israelites to abstain from the very practices of the Canaanites that led to the defiling of the land of Canaan and the land's "vomiting" them out. However, terms such as "socially constructed" and "conventional" should not leave one with the false impression that *tôʿēbâ* is applied only or even primarily to antiquated notions of ritual purity. The word is generally applied to forms of behavior whose abhorrent quality is readily transparent to contemporary believers. Worshiping other gods, child sacrifice, incest, bestiality, adultery, theft, oppressing the poor, false testimony in court against another person, and deceit are not oddities of a superstitious, pre-Enlightenment people whose sole function was to keep the people of God separate from the surrounding culture. It is contextually clear that what is generally meant by *tôʿēbâ* is something that "*Yahweh* hates" (Deut 12:31; Prov 6:16). The passage of time produces changing conceptions of what is detestable to God (as well as changing civil penalties) but, in this case, what is striking is the high degree of continuity between the values of Israelite culture and post-Enlightenment culture.

The Question of the Contemporary Authority of Levitical Law

These considerations, both the six salient features of the Levitical prohibitions against homosexual intercourse and the application of the word *tôʿēbâ* to "intrinsically evil" acts, should give anyone pause before rejecting the relevance of these commandments for our contemporary setting. However, the case is not completely airtight. Paul taught that the law of Moses, the contingent expression of God's will given on Mount Sinai, had been abrogated in Christ. Continuity in much of the divine will remains because the same God who gave the Sinaitic code is also the God of Jesus Christ. Yet because of the Christian conviction

---

189. S. Olyan, " 'And with a Male . . .'," 180 n. 3.

of a change in dispensations, the witness of these two laws from Leviticus has to be tested against the New Testament witness.

The Holiness Code is very much concerned with matters of purity and many of the requirements no longer have force today; for example, the forbidding of sex with a woman during her menstrual cycle (18:19; 20:18), the prohibition against breeding two different kinds of animals, sowing with two different kinds of seed, or wearing clothes made of two different materials (19:19), or the command not to round off the hair on one's temples or mar the edges of one's beard (19:27). Some of these commands may have arisen out of traditional taboos regarding the sacral quality of blood and semen, a concern not to mimic fertility practices of the Canaanites, a desire for consistency in maintaining clear social boundaries and the divinely ordained categories of creation, and/or the intent to symbolize Israel's "set apart" status (that is, its separate and pure devotion to God).

Obviously, one cannot simply say: it is in the book of Leviticus so obey it. On the other hand, it would be a mistake to regard the statutes in the Holiness Code as consisting of largely irrelevant purity regulations. Indeed, most of Leviticus 18–20 can be thought of as an expanded commentary on the ten commandments, with prohibitions against idolatry and witchcraft, stealing and lying, adultery and incest; and commands to honor one's parents, keep the sabbath, and to "love one's neighbor as oneself" (Lev 19:18). Ritual and moral, eternal and contingent, are combined in the profile of holiness developed in Leviticus 17–26. Christians do not have the option of simply dismissing an injunction because it belongs to the Holiness Code. The same God who gave the laws of the Mosaic dispensation continues to regulate conduct through the Spirit in believers. A substantial case must be made for affirming conduct that was regarded with such revulsion.

Paul himself, the very apostle who proclaimed salvation in Christ "apart from the law," clearly believed that there was considerable continuity in the divine will across the two covenants in matters of sexual ethics. That Paul consciously formulated his opposition to same-sex intercourse in the light of Levitical prohibitions is evident from the following. Paul's stance against incest in 1 Corinthians 5 echoes the incest laws in Lev 18:6-18 (cf. the description "father's wife" in 1 Cor 5:1 with Lev 18:7-8 LXX). His reference to same-sex intercourse, along with other vices, as "worthy of death" in Rom 1:32 may have had in view the penalty of death prescribed for homosexual intercourse in Lev 20:13. His use of the word *aschēmosynē* ("indecency, indecent exposure") in Rom 1:27 coincides with its usage twenty-four times in Lev 18:6-19; 20:11, 17-21 (LXX) to describe various illicit sexual acts. The word *akatharsia* ("uncleanness, impurity") in Rom 1:24 appears also in Lev 18:19; 20:21, 25 (LXX).[190] Finally, the very term that Paul employed for men who take other males to bed, *arsenokoitēs* (1 Cor 6:9), is a compound formed from the words in Lev 18:22; 20:13 (LXX) for "male" and "lying."

Does the Influence of Leviticus on Paul Undermine His Moral Credibility?

Bernadette Brooten is a strong advocate for the view that Rom 1:26-32 "directly recalls" Lev 18:22 and 20:13. However, rather than treat this as an argument that supports the contemporary relevance of the Levitical prohibitions, Brooten believes that Paul's connections to the Holiness Code constitute a good reason for *disregarding* Paul's stance on same-sex intercourse. Such connections, she argues, demonstrate that Paul's position was based on antiquated views of impurity, defilement, and shame that cannot be considered normative for our own time. With regard to the forbidden sexual relations in Leviticus 20, Brooten contends that neither age nor consent factored into penalties. A minor and a person raped would suffer the same penalty as the adult perpetrator because purity, not moral agency, was the issue. "Likewise for Paul, consent and coercion do not play a role in his condemnation

---

190. Cf. 1 Thess 4:3-7, where Paul urges the Thessalonians to "abstain from sexual immorality" (*porneia*), to choose a wife on the basis of "holiness" (i.e., her holy character) and not on the basis of lustful passion "like the gentiles/nations who do not know God," to refrain from coveting sexual intercourse with another man's wife, "for God did not call us to uncleanness (*akatharsia*) but in holiness." This text makes a number of points of contact with Leviticus 18 and 20: the emphasis on holiness in sexual conduct, the importance of distinguishing oneself from the sexual immorality that typified the gentile world, and the characterization of sexual immorality as "uncleanness" (see also Rom 6:19 and 1 Cor 7:14 for the holiness/uncleanness contrast; and "uncleanness" as a sexual vice in Gal 5:19; 2 Cor 12:21).

of homoeroticism." The concern of both the Levitical code and Paul was solely for "the holiness and purity" of the community, not the rights of the individual victim.[191]

Brooten's argument is flawed. First, although it is true that the laws in Leviticus 20 do not explicitly make exceptions for those who cannot give consent, neither do they explicitly condemn such. Brooten's case is simply a dubious argument from silence. She suggests that Lev 20:14, a law against taking a "wife and her mother" and carrying the penalty of burning all three participants, would have taken effect if a father raped his minor daughter, thus resulting in the burning not only of the perpetrator but also of the victim and the "nonperpetrating" mother.[192] However, her hypothetical scenario would appear to be discounted by the wording: a man deliberately "takes (viz., in marriage or by common consent, not rapes) a wife (ʾiššâ; a woman, not a girl) and her mother." The language also indicates that the ʾiššâ was not the man's own natural child. Elsewhere in Leviticus 20 the refrain "their blood [be] upon them" (vv. 11-13, 16, 27; v. 9 has "his . . . him") suggests a measure of consent on the part of all the human parties involved, each of whom are justly held accountable for their own executions (cf. 2 Sam 1:16: "Your blood be on your head; for your own mouth has testified against you . . .").[193] The priestly distinction between

---

191. See Brooten, *Love Between Women*, 294 (see pp. 281-94). Similar positions are taken by: Bird, "The Bible in Christian Ethical Deliberation," 151-57 (who, even though admitting that Lev 20:13 is "without clear cultic associations," contends that the "lack of interest in essential ethical criteria [such as questions of age, initiative, or consent] is strikingly clear in the assessment of penalties. In all of the cases in ch. 20, both of the sexual partners are subjected to the same punishment, including the animal," thereby limiting the usefulness of Lev 20:13 for contemporary sexual ethics); and Schoedel, "Same-Sex Eros," 52, 68-71.

192. Brooten, *Love Between Women*, 291.

193. Admittedly, the formula is also used in the case of bestiality to justify the execution of both human and animal (20:15-16); but the justification for holding an animal responsible may have been different from the justification given for holding a human responsible (an animal can be held accountable apart from intent because animals are more expendable than humans); or the animal may have been viewed as a willing participant (cf. Exod 21:28-32: an ox that gores a person is to be stoned). Levine speaks of an "attribution of moral norms to the animal kingdom," citing Gen 6:7; 9:5; Jonah 3:7-8; *m. Sanh.* 7:4 (*Leviticus*, 138). Certainly

sins that are "inadvertent" or "unintentional" and sins that are committed "high-handedly" or "deliberately" is well known and attests to
levels of culpability based on deliberate moral intent.[194] Deut 22:23-27
penalized an engaged virgin for having intercourse with another man
only if she did not cry for help; a cry for help indicated rape and the
victim of a rape was not penalized.[195] Hence, Brooten has little on
which to base her claim that Lev 20:13 would have condemned to
death a "boy raped by an adult male."[196]

Second, if there is little basis for arguing that Lev 20:13 condemned
to death victims of homosexual rape, there is even less reason for arguing that Paul held such a position. The whole point of the argument in
Rom 1:18-32, and one that provides the basis for drawing a parallel
with the Jew in 2:1–3:20, is that the gentiles who are subjected to God's
wrath in the present and in the future Day of the Lord are "without
excuse" precisely because of a conscious and deliberate suppression of
the truth (1:18-20). They are liable to judgment not because they don't
know "that those who do such things are worthy of death" but because
they do know (1:32). Furthermore, the discussion of same-sex intercourse in 1:26-27 makes clear that Paul was applying his condemnation
only in cases where mutual choice and gratification on the part of both
partners was involved ("inflamed with their yearning for one another,
males with males committing indecency"). This picture of judgment
based on willing consent is also confirmed by Philo's discussion in *Spec.*

---

the rationale for sentencing a person who curses a parent was the deliberate
undertaking of the action: "for every man who curses his father or his mother shall
surely be put to death; his father or mother he cursed; his blood [is] on him"
(20:9).

194. E.g., Lev 4:2, 13-14, 22-23, 27-28; 5:2-5, 15, 17-18; 6:4; 22:14; Num 15:22-31;
35:15; Deut 4:42; 19:4; Josh 20:3, 9.

195. Brooten argues that the preceding law against lying with another man's "wife"
(Deut 22:22) lacks such a distinction between consent and coercion so that Deut
22:23-27 must apply the distinction only in the specific case of a betrothed virgin
(ibid., 291 n. 93). Yet it is difficult to discern why an engaged virgin who cried out
would be excused but not a married woman (particularly since the former, though
engaged, is already designated "his neighbor's wife" in 22:24). Surely the distinction in Deut 22:23-27 supplied a principle operative in 22:22 and in other cases
as well.

196. Ibid., 292. Cf. *Sipra Qedoshim Pereq* 10.11 on Lev 20:13 (369[a]) which exempts
underage boys from punishment.

Laws 3.37-38. There is no evidence anywhere in Paul's letters that those victimized by the sins of others (sexual or otherwise) were held morally accountable. Indeed, all the parenesis in Paul presupposes active and willing moral agents.

Brooten presumes that, because Paul did not specifically mention factors of consent or coercion in his discussion of the case of incest in 1 Corinthians 5, these issues were irrelevant to his decision to have the man expelled from the community. She writes:

> Note that Paul's judgment does not reflect moral categories that we might employ today, such as coercion or consent. . . . For example, the father's wife could have initiated intercourse with her stepson while he was still a minor, and the present relationship could, therefore, continue what we would call an earlier victimization of the man while he was still a boy.[197]

This is special pleading. The fact that Paul did not explicitly mention issues of consent or coercion in 5:1-8 in no way implies that abuse of a minor would have been irrelevant for Paul. Paul and the Corinthians knew the circumstances; if they were aware that both parties were consenting adults there would have been no need for Paul to bring up such issues. Contemporary readers are picking up the conversation in midstream. Absolutely nothing can be inferred regarding Paul's inattention to issues of coercion and consent. If anything, the language, "someone *has* his father's wife" (5:1), indicates that the male involved was not only a consenting adult but also the active partner in the relationship.

Third, even *if* Leviticus 20 mandated death for perpetrator and victim alike (a point which I do not concede), that still would not lead to the conclusion that the list of forbidden sexual practices enumerated there has little moral force for contemporary society. It might mean that *additional* considerations, other than those which we might identify as "moral," accounted for the particular severity of the penalty or its application to all parties regardless of consent. Yet it does not necessitate the view that the entire foundation on which the prohibition was built was essentially amoral. Indeed, it may merely buttress the moral

---

197. Ibid., 291.

focus on the inherently degrading character of the act itself for its participants and its destabilizing effects on the community, making any talk about the positive moral intent of the participants irrelevant. Contemporary moral standards still exclude nearly all of the prohibited acts of Leviticus 18 and 20, which is itself testimony to their fundamentally moral grounding.

According to Stephen F. Bigger:

> Pollution restrictions were not directly concerned with moral questions and most have no bearing on morality, but *in some cases (such as in sexual matters) morality was in practice encouraged by fear of pollution.* Mary Douglas commented: "The fact that pollution beliefs provide a kind of impersonal punishment for wrongdoing affords a means of supporting the accepted system of morality."[198]

People's fears of the consequences of a particular form of behavior, including fears of social disintegration and fears of angering the deity by flouting the order visible in creation, lead to the construction of purity systems as safeguards against unintentional or intentional transgressions. Purity regulations associated with sexual activity often serve the social function of protecting females "from sexual advances in the domestic sphere," reducing "the possibility of domestic tension" and "jealousy," and maintaining a stable line of descent. For example, in the case of the prohibition of a man being married to a woman and her mother at the same time (18:17; 20:14, cited above), the

> prime concern of the legislator was not the impurity of incestuous relationships but the inter-relationship between the two women involved. Such a marriage would cause bitter tension within the domestic sphere since, of two women who should have enjoyed equal status, one was in fact dependent upon the other. Both women would find their conflicting dual roles impossible to reconcile.[199]

---

198. "The Family Laws of Leviticus 18 in their Setting," *JBL* 98 (1979): 195. The quote of Douglas is from *Purity and Danger* (London: Routledge & Kegan Paul, 1966), 133. "When the sense of outrage is adequately equipped with practical sanctions in the social order, pollution is not likely to arise. Where, humanly speaking, the outrage is likely to go unpunished, pollution beliefs tend to be called in to supplement the lack of other sanctions" (ibid., 132).
199. "Family Laws," 193-96, 201.

Purity and morality are not necessarily antithetical concepts in Leviticus; in Paul they never are.

Particularly in the area of sexuality, where the potential for abuse is greatest because of the addictive character of sexual pleasure and the self-justification that invariably follows, laws may appear to be more inflexible and harsh than need be the case for every individual violation. In contemporary societies the visceral negative reactions experienced by most citizens, which accompany the legal condemnations of certain forms of forbidden sexual conduct, serve the same role as the purity rules of old. Theoretically, the case could—and has—been made that some sexual relationships between adults and minors may be healthy (for example, between a twenty-one-year-old man and a mature fourteen-year-old girl). One could also argue that even sexual relationships between siblings have positive potential when they involve consenting adults who have taken steps to ensure that intercourse will not lead to conception. However, most contemporary Western legal systems do not make exceptions for these cases because of the justified fear that exceptions would lead to a weakening of society's resistance across the board against pedophilia and incest. Most instances of pedophilia and incest pose a threat to the health and stability of families and society. Consequently, the interests of the many must be given priority over the interests of the few. A rigid and visceral societal stance against *all* manifestations of pedophilia and incest is required to banish even the thought of it from the vast majority of people. Such a point was made in Plato's *Laws* at one point in the conversation between the Athenian stranger and Megillus of Sparta:

> Ath.: Even at present...most men, however lawless they are, are effectively and strictly precluded from sexual commerce with [some] beautiful persons,—and that not against their will, but with their own most willing consent.
> Meg.: On what occasions do you mean?
> Ath.: Whenever any man has a brother or sister who is beautiful. So too in the case of a son or daughter, the same unwritten law is most effective in guarding men from sleeping with them, either openly or secretly, or wishing to have any connexion with them,—nay, most men never so much as feel any desire for such connexion.

Meg.: That is true.

Ath.: Is it not, then, by a brief sentence that all such pleasures are quenched?

Meg.: What sentence do you mean?

Ath.: The sentence that these acts are by no means holy, but hated of God and most shamefully shameful. And does not the reason lie in this, that nobody speaks of them otherwise, but every one of us, from the day of his birth, hears this opinion expressed always and everywhere, not only in comic speech, but often also in serious tragedy. . . . (838A-C; [R. G. Bury, LCL])

In a similar way, the conjunction of purity and prohibition in the priestly laws of the Torah, particularly those having to do with sexual intercourse, often had the effect of strengthening (not detracting from) moral considerations. To state that the Holiness Code and other law codes of the Bible are concerned with issues of purity and pollution, sanctification and shame, is not to establish their irrelevance for contemporary moral discourse. In many cases it signals a staunchly moral stance.[200]

Why the Prohibition of Male Same-Sex Intercourse?

Apart from comparing the law against same-sex intercourse with other laws in the Holiness Code that are no longer regarded as binding, there have been more sophisticated attempts at undermining the Levitical prohibitions against homosexual behavior by spelling out an implicit motive clause that ceases to hold true in a modern context. We describe below four different ways of explaining the rationale behind the prohibitions in 18:22; 20:13.[201]

---

200. Wold emphasizes the correlation between the degree of impurity associated with a given transgression on the one hand and the intentionality and moral severity of the transgression on the other (*Out of Order*, 121-36).

201. Gerstenberger attributes the proscriptions, without justification, to a fear of demons (*Leviticus*, 254, 297). The two laws in The Middle Assyrian Laws having to do with homosexual intercourse have nothing to do with a fear of demons. Undoubtedly the authors of the Holiness Code feared the wrath of God; but the question still remains: why did they think that God viewed homosexual intercourse as utterly detestable?

(1) The Connection with Idolatry?

Some have argued that the reason for the prohibition against males having intercourse with males is because of the connection of such behavior with idolatry.[202] They point to two indications in the context of Lev 18:22; 20:13. First, the prohibition against homosexual intercourse in 18:22 immediately follows the prohibition against sacrificing one's child to Molech (18:21). Second, the warnings against following the practices of the Canaanites at the beginning and end of ch. 18 (vv. 1-5, 24-30; also 20:22-26) suggest that 18:22 has in view homosexual cult prostitutes (the *qĕdēšîm*) and their clients. Intercourse between males was not inherently bad but bad because of its typical associations. Lacking such a cultural context for homosexual practice in our own times, we are free to disregard these prohibitions.

Few today give this argument much credence and for good reason. The repetition of the prohibition against homosexual intercourse in 20:13 does not follow immediately upon the references to child sacrifice in 20:2-5, but rather is sandwiched in between prohibitions of adultery and incest (20:10-12) and prohibitions of incest and bestiality (20:14-16). The link with child sacrifice in Lev 18:21 probably involves

---

202. Cf. Jürgen Becker, "Zum Problem der Homosexualität in der Bibel," *ZEE* 31 (1987): 39-41, 55 (though he adds: "To be sure, the Old Testament and Judaism also show how for the sake of the high ethical esteem of marriage all other sexual activities are forbidden"); Letha Scanzoni and Virginia Ramey Mollenkott, *Is the Homosexual My Neighbor? Another Christian View* (San Francisco: Harper & Row, 1978), 59-61 (who also allude to ceremonial uncleanness); Norman H. Snaith, *Leviticus and Numbers* (NCB; London: Nelson, 1967), 126; S. R. Driver, *Deuteronomy* (ICC; Edinburgh: T. & T. Clark, 1896), 264. Edwards not only argues that Lev 18:22 and 20:13 have in view these male cult prostitutes but also, astoundingly, infers that the absence from the prophetic books of any critique against such figures confirms their openness toward same-sex intercourse (*Gay/Lesbian Liberation*, 54-68). Boswell does not think the *qĕdēšîm* engaged in sex with males but he does view *tô'ēbâ* as implying ceremonial uncleanness owing to "idolatrous sexuality" (*Homosexuality*, 99-101). Bailey also denies any homosexual connotation to the *qĕdēšîm* and puts a different spin on the link to idolatry. "Such acts are regarded as 'abomination' not ... because they were practised by Egyptian or Canaanite idolaters (for of this there is no proof), but because, as a reversal of what is sexually natural, they exemplify the spirit of idolatry which is itself the fundamental subversion of true order" (*Homosexuality*, 59-60).

nothing more than threats to the sanctity of the Israelite family.[203] Or, as Wold puts it:

> The Molech cultus . . . consisted of a sexual element and is therefore categorized as $tô^cēbâ$; it is the sexual aspect of the cultus that places it in the list of crimes in Leviticus 18, not its idolatrous element. Giving one's seed to Molech may have involved cultic prostitution of some kind, dedicating a child to the idol, or even child sacrifice. . . . The idolatry of Molech worship is incidental to the sexual nature of this crime in this context. . . . The sex crimes of Leviticus 18, with the possible exception of Molech worship, were not cultic in nature.[204]

There is also an inconsistency in the application of 18:21 on the part of those who use it to limit 18:22 to cultic contexts. Those who contend that the broadly worded proscription against same-sex intercourse should be confined to cultic prostitution do not contend that the narrowly worded proscription of child sacrifice to Molech[205] had no implications for other forms of child sacrifice. It is not likely that 18:21 was formulated as narrowly as it was in order to leave the door open for child sacrifice to other pagan gods besides Molech, or even to Yahweh. Clearly the authors and framers had in mind all kinds of child sacrifice— indeed, infanticide of any sort. By what rationale, then, is a narrow proscription to be taken broadly but a broad proscription only narrowly?

I do not doubt that the circles out of which Lev 18:22 was produced had in view homosexual cult prostitution, at least partly. Homosexual cult prostitution appears to have been the primary form in which homosexual intercourse was practiced in Israel. However, male cult

---

203. Olyan suggests that it is a late insertion into the series of laws in 18:19-23 (" 'And with a Male . . .'," 198).
204. *Out of Order*, 119.
205. On the problem of the name "Molech," see the commentaries. "Archaeological evidence from Punic and Phoenician sacrificial inscriptions has shown that a simple sacrificial term stands behind the expression *lammōlek*: 'present as a thanksgiving or votice offering.' Children's bones at sacrificial sites attest the custom of sacrificing infants. Very early, however, the expression was already misunderstood as a reference to a particular god 'Molech' . . . whose name evokes the notion of 'king' in its consonants and 'disgrace' in its vowels" (Gerstenberger, *Leviticus*, 253, 292).

prostitution was not the only context in which homosexual intercourse manifested itself in the ancient Near East generally. It was merely the most acceptable context for homosexual intercourse to be practiced in Mesopotamia, certainly for those who played the role of the receptive partner. In our own cultural context we think that the banning of male cult prostitution does not take into account consensual, non-cultic, loving homosexual relationships. In the cultural context of the ancient Near East the reasoning has to be reversed: to ban homosexual cult prostitutes was to ban all homosexual intercourse. In any case, the authors of Lev 18:22 could have formulated the law more precisely by making specific reference to the qĕdēšîm (as in Deut 23:17-18), if it had been their intent to limit the law's application. That they did not do so suggests that they had a broader application in mind. Moreover, the Levitical rejection of same-sex intercourse depends on Canaanite practices for its validity about as much as the rejection of incest, adultery, and bestiality.[206]

Just as an uncompromising devotion to the one god, Yahweh, stood out in the Holiness Code (and the Hebrew Bible generally) against the background of the polytheism of the ancient Near East, so too an uncompromising stance against male-male sexual intercourse distinguished this legal corpus from those of surrounding cultures. What is unclear is why the distinctiveness of Israel's attitude to same-sex intercourse should translate hermeneutically into contemporary irrelevance. In fact, it ought to do the opposite. There were many other Canaanite practices that the Israelites did not reject. That homosexual behavior among the native peoples of Canaan was rejected was undoubtedly due to the fact that it came into conflict with *pre-existing*, traditional Israelite cultural values. For Israelites to maintain such

---

206. Cf. Gerald T. Sheppard, "The Use of Scripture Within the Christian Ethical Debate Concerning Same-Sex Oriented Persons," USQR 40 (1985): 22: "I do not think that the texts in Leviticus can be read from a historical perspective as applicable only to cult prostitution because they stand in the context of other laws regulating general immoral conduct such as incestuous relationships, adultery, and bestiality. I find Edwards's historical speculation concerning the restriction of the abomination formula to cultic violations weak and uncompelling" (this is from an OT scholar who affirms same-sex unions). See also Wright, "Homosexuality: The Relevance of the Bible," 293.

adamant opposition in the face of a spectrum of only qualified opposition and even toleration in the ancient Near East required a conscious and deliberate effort on their part. "That Canaanites practised homosexuality no doubt enhanced Israel's aversion to it . . . , but it is not the fundamental motive for it."[207]

(2) A Procreative Dead End

Some scholars believe that the injunction against same-sex male intercourse was due exclusively or primarily to the fact that such intercourse "wastes seed" and could not lead to procreation.[208] The implication is that the modern-day population explosion and the widespread acceptance of contraceptives in Jewish and Protestant circles would seem to render an objection to homosexuality irrelevant in our own context. Five considerations speak in favor of procreation as at least *a* factor in prohibiting same-sex male intercourse. First, such an interpretation coheres with a possible implicit motive clause for each of the forbidden practices in Leviticus 18 (incest, intercourse with a menstruating woman, adultery, child sacrifice, homosexual intercourse, bestiality): they all pose "a threat to the integrity of the Israelite lineage" (Eilberg-Schwartz) or constitute "affronts to procreation" (Biale). Second, the issue of procreation ties in with the command to "be fruitful and multiply" which, according to the creation story in Genesis 1 (P), is one of two great commands that God gave to the human species (Gen 1:28; the other is to "subdue" and "have dominion over"

---

207. Wenham, "Homosexuality," 362.
208. Milgrom, "Does the Bible Prohibit Homosexuality?" 11 (the loss of semen or spilling of seed "symbolizes the loss of life") and "How Not to Read the Bible," 48 ("The basis for the ban [on homosexuality] . . . is the need for procreation, which opposes, in biblical times, the wasting of seed"); Sarah J. Melcher, "The Holiness Code and Human Sexuality," *Biblical Ethics and Homosexuality*, 98-99 (who argues that the issue of procreation keys into a concern for "patrilineal inheritance of the land": "if their system of land tenure fails . . . , the 'sons of Israel' will find themselves to be landless"); Howard Eilberg-Schwartz, *The Savage in Judaism* (Bloomington: Indiana University Press, 1990), 183; David Biale, *Eros and the Jews* (New York: Basic Books, 1992), 29; Thomas B. Dozeman, "Creation and Procreation in the Biblical Teaching on Homosexuality," *USQR* 49 (1995): 175-76, 179, 189 n. 24; Fewell and Gunn, *Gender, Power, and Promise*, 106-8 (who cite also the negation of the passive partner's maleness).

the earth). Third, given the designation of male sperm as "seed" and some history-of-religions parallels, it may be that ancient Israelites conceived of the man's sperm as containing the whole of life, with the woman's body being nothing more than a "field" or "soil" that supplies the nutrients (blood and milk) to stimulate the seed's growth (cf. Philo, *Spec. Laws* 3.39). Male sperm is life itself, so the wasting of it in intercourse with other males is regarded as a serious offense.[209] Fourth, in the first century C.E. both Philo and Josephus viewed the wasting of seed in non-procreative sex as one of the problems with homosexual intercourse (Philo also expresses concern for the feminization of the passive partner). Fifth, the fact that women do not emit "seed" and therefore cannot waste it may help to explain why same-sex female intercourse goes unmentioned in the Holiness Code.

Nevertheless, it is unlikely that the non-procreative aspect of same-sex male intercourse constitutes the sole or even primary reason why such behavior is banned in the Holiness Code. First, the various behaviors prohibited in Leviticus 18 can be linked under a common rubric only when that rubric is stretched beyond "failure to procreate." Incest (including that between in-laws) and adultery were prohibited even though (and partly because) such sex acts could result in procreation. Sex between a woman and an animal is arguably prohibited because it does not result in procreation, yet it does not result in a loss of *human* "seed." Child sacrifice destroys what is procreated but it is not a failure to procreate. Once the heading for Leviticus 18 broadens beyond "failure to procreate" to "a threat to the integrity of the Israelite lineage" or "affronts to procreation," the implicit motive clause for the interdictions against male-male intercourse need no longer be restricted to "wasting seed" in the strict sense of failing to procreate. Second, if failure to procreate were the central concern, it is puzzling that a number of other sexual acts that do not lead to pro-

---

209. White, "Does the Bible Speak About Gays or Same-Sex Orientation?" 17-18. White apparently perceives this pre-modern, androcentric understanding of conception as a reason for the focus of the Levitical same-sex prohibitions on the male only, and thus a reason for disregarding these prohibitions. However, the opposite conclusion could be drawn: Since we now know that conception and life is equally due to the woman (indeed, more so), a faithful contemporary appropriation of these prohibitions would entail their expansion to forbid lesbian sex.

creation were left out, such as heterosexual sex during a woman's pregnancy. The death penalty (or, indeed, any penalty) was not prescribed
for masturbation even though it resulted in loss of semen (the issue in
Gen 38:8-10 is not masturbation itself but rather failure to fulfill kinship obligations in levirate marriage). Third, it seems unlikely that the
highly emotive reference to intercourse between males as an "abomination" can be limited to a failure to procreate. Is it reasonable to say
that from the standpoint of the framers and transmitters of these prohibitions the fundamental problem with bestiality was that it did not
produce offspring? Surely there was a different level of revulsion
expressed for bestiality and homosexual intercourse than there would
have been in the case of heterosexual sex with a "barren" woman (as
Philo makes clear in *Spec. Laws* 3.33-50).

(3) Contact of Semen with Excrement?

The same kinds of critique against "failure to procreate" as the
implicit motivating clause for the prohibition of homosexual intercourse can also be made against another theory. According to Saul
Olyan, "male-male anal intercourse may have been proscribed in order
to prevent the mixing of two otherwise defiling substances [—excrement and semen—from mingling in the body of the receptive partner],
and thereby prevent the defilement of the land of Israel."[210]
While this, like the procreation argument, may be a secondary factor in the rejection of homosexual intercourse, it would appear to be
subordinated to the larger category of mixing non-complementary
genders. Lev 18:22 and 20:13 make no mention of dung (contrast the

---

210. Olyan, " ' And with a Male . . . '," 203. Steven Bigger thinks that the laws in 18:19-
    23 come under the rubric of "misuse of semen": mixing semen and menstrual blood
    (18:19); commingling the semen of two different men in the same woman (18:20);
    emitting human semen into an animal or animal semen into a woman (18:23) ("The
    Family Laws," 202-3). "Misuse of semen" is a broad generalization that does not
    require Olyan's conclusion that the problem is mixing semen with excrement.
    Bigger himself suggests that the reason why homosexual intercourse involved "the
    misuse of semen" was that it was "seen by the Hebrews as an unnatural variant of
    heterosexuality," just as the "confusion" caused by bestiality "may have referred to
    the mixing of different types of semen in the receptive animal or woman, or the
    confusion of species and social roles" (p. 203). Yet the category of "misuse of
    semen" is still not broad enough to encompass the case of child sacrifice in 18:21.

explicit mention of menstruation in 18:19 and blood flow in 20:18), but they do speak explicitly of gender discomplementarity ("as though lying with a woman"). Of the five other prohibited acts in Leviticus 18 (incest, intercourse with a menstruating woman, adultery, child sacrifice, bestiality), only one probably bases the prohibition on a mixing of two antithetical bodily secretions. In the case of the law regarding bestiality, which is in closer proximity to the law regarding homosexual intercourse than is the law concerning intercourse with a menstruating woman and which bears a stronger resemblance, the paramount violation is the merger of two different kinds of creatures that should never be merged. The transfer of semen from human to beast or beast to human, like the preceding act of penetration, is significant insofar as it conveys that merger. Similarly, to make the commingling of semen with excrement the main concern behind the interdiction in 18:22 and 20:13 is to miss the fundamental concern to which the penetration into the "dirty" anal orifice and the semen transfer point: an abhorrent violation of the gender boundaries for sexual intercourse. Furthermore, if the central concern in 18:22 and 20:13 was the mixing of semen and excrement, then why was there no corresponding prohibition against *heterosexual* anal intercourse? One might compare the similarly worded proscription against cross-dressing in Deuteronomic law (Deut 22:5; cf. 23:1 [MT 23:2] on the exclusion of eunuchs from "the assembly of Yahweh"). This command has nothing to do with semen and everything to do with maintaining gender distinctions.[211]

(4) Gender Discomplementarity as a Violation of the Created Order

Thus there are good grounds for asserting that the primary problem with male-male intercourse is the more general concern that it "mixes" two things that were never intended to be mixed.[212] The issue of procreation would be a specific concern within this larger category. The refrain in 18:22 and 20:13, "as though lying with a woman," is the best

---

211. Boyarin stresses the relevance of this law ("Are There Any Jews . . .," 342-44).
212. Mary Douglas has pointed out that "holiness requires that different classes of things shall not be confused. . . . Holiness means keeping distinct the categories of creation. . . . Incest and adultery (Leviticus 18:6-20) are against holiness, in the simple sense of right order" (*Purity and Danger*, 53).

indication we have of what the primary concern was; namely, behaving toward another man as if he were a woman by making him the object of male sexual desires. That is an "abomination," an abhorrent violation of divinely sanctioned boundaries—in this case, gender boundaries established at creation. The issue of mixing appears elsewhere in the Holiness Code. Both bestiality and sex with one's daughter-in-law were referred to as a *tebel* ("an appalling *mixture* or confusion," 18:23; 20:12)[213] and on grounds other than that semen was lost. Maintaining pure categories extended even to forbidding the breeding of "two kinds" of animals, sowing one's field with "two kinds" of seed, and putting on a garment made of "two kinds" of material (Lev 19:19; cf. Deut 22:9-11). While the last set of prohibitions strike us as quaint,[214] the interdiction of bestiality and incest does not. The priestly version of the creation story in Genesis 1 emphasizes that each of the creatures in the sea, in the sky, and on the earth were created "according to its kind" (also vegetation; Gen 1:11-12, 21, 24-25).

All the laws in Lev 18:6-23; 20:2-21 legislate against forms of sexual behavior that disrupt the created order set into motion by the God of Israel. Each of the laws has as its intent the channeling of male sexual impulses into a particular pattern of behavior, a pattern conducive to the healthy functioning of a people set apart to serve God's holy purposes.[215] Within that general intent, though, the reasons for banning specific forms of sexual behavior vary.[216]

---

213. The word appears only in these two verses in the OT. It is related to the verb *bālal*, "to mix, confuse"; hence, "mixture, confusion, shamefulness, disgracefulness" (*HALOT*); "confusion, violation of nature or the divine order" (BDB); "perversion" (NRSV, NIV, NLT, NASB, Levine), "violation of nature" (REB, NJB; cf. NLT), "abhorrent deed/thing" (NAB).

214. Note too the difference in penalties: sowing one's vineyard with a second kind of seed merely leads to forfeiting the whole yield; the sower is not killed (Deut 22:9).

215. According to Dearman, the rejection of homosexual acts and bestiality "is probably based on the same presuppositions proposed in our analysis of the creation accounts. Homosexuality and bestiality do not conform to the description of existence 'according to their kind,' and the sexual unions they represent are incapable of 'reproducing.' This is only consistent with humankind as male and female. . . . All the forbidden sexual relations in Lev 18:6-23 threaten the proper function of the family" ("Marriage in the Old Testament," 58-59). Cf. Grenz, *Welcoming But Not Affirming*, 46.

216. Calum M. Carmichael has proposed an interesting explanation for the selection and order of the commandments in Leviticus 18–20: interpretation of the narra-

The laws against incest (18:6-18) may have had as many as four aims: (1) protecting females (both blood relations and in-laws), including girls, in the intimate context of an extended family from the predatory sexual habits of male family members; (2) reducing sexual temptations within the family and preventing infidelity, which breeds alienation and distrust in one's spouse and could result in the dissolution of a family; (3) reducing intergenerational conflict, disorder, and dishonor that would arise through sexual rivalry within the family; and (4) ensuring healthy offspring by limiting inbreeding.

The law against intercourse with a menstruating woman (18:19; cf.

---

tive traditions about Israel's first ancestors, primarily in Genesis (*Law, Legend, and Incest in the Bible: Leviticus 18–20* [Ithaca: Cornell University Press, 1997], 60-61, 182-85). For example, in Lev 18:19-23, the "lawgiver" moved from Genesis 18, where Sarah expects renewed fertility and thus the resumption of menstruation (Lev 18:19: prohibition of intercourse with one's menstruating wife); to Gen 21:22-34, where Sarah comes close to committing adultery with Abimelech (18:20: prohibition of adultery); to Genesis 22, where God requires Abraham to offer up Isaac as a burnt sacrifice (18:21: prohibition of child sacrifice); then the theme of fire taking the lawgiver back to Genesis 19, where Sodom is consumed by fire for homosexual rape of guests (18:22: the prohibition of homosexual intercourse); and the theme of sexual abuse of a visitor calling to mind the rape of Dinah by Shechem (Genesis 34), whose father's name Ham means "ass" and whose actions weakened Jacob's "house, the house of the Ox" (Genesis 49) (18:23: prohibition of bestiality). With regard to Lev 20:12-14, the lawgiver moved from intercourse between Reuben's brother Judah and his daughter-in-law Tamar (Genesis 38; the prohibition against sex with one's daughter-in-law in Lev 20:12); to Tamar's image as a cult prostitute and the associated concept of homosexual cult prostitution (the prohibition against homosexual intercourse in Lev 20:13); to the thought that Tamar had a sexual relationship with a father and his sons (the prohibition of the equivalent male offense, intercourse with a wife and her mother, Lev 20:14). It is difficult to know what to make of Carmichael's proposal. Some of the connections (especially the one to bestiality) seem to be quite a stretch; but, then again, most of the midrashic associations made by ancient writers are indeed enormous exegetical stretches. Whether the redactor(s) of the laws in Leviticus 18–20 would have had access to the stories in Genesis is debatable. Yet if Carmichael is correct, it would be further evidence for the connections between H's prohibitions of homosexual behavior on the one hand, and both the Yahwist's story of Sodom's destruction and the Deuteronomistic Historian's description of homosexual cult prostitutes on the other hand. It would mean that the legislators of the Holiness Code understood both the sin of Sodom and the chief abominable activity of the homosexual cult prostitutes to be homosexual intercourse (not rape of a guest and not cultic prostitution).

15:19-24) may have had in view taboos against mixing a medium and symbol of life (semen ejaculated during intercourse) and a medium and symbol of death (menstrual blood flowing out). Life-creating fluids must be separated from life-destructive fluids (a separation of kinds). A woman's flow of death-bearing menstrual blood may have been taken by ancient Israelites as a natural sign from God that access by life-creating semen was undesirable (an argument from nature). The menstrual period was the time that God had given women to cleanse their bodies from impurity as a prelude to renewing a cycle of fertility (a sabbath of sorts from sex). It was not the time for men to intrude with procreative designs. Deliberate intercourse during a menstrual period not only had the effect of "wasting seed" but also of putting one's own desires at cross-purposes with God's timing. Men were required to exercise self-restraint and wait for divinely created processes to run their course. Not to be overlooked as well are other possible factors: the sheer repulsive effect that the appearance of menstrual blood has had on most men in all cultures, eliciting a visceral response against men not similarly repelled; and concerns for the woman's privacy and pain.[217]

The goals of the other laws in 18:20-24 do not require as much explanation. The law against adultery (18:20) is obviously designed to protect the integrity and stability of the marriage bond from interference by males outside the extended family. The law against sacrificing newborn children (18:21) is a safeguard against destroying the fruit of a married couple's procreative efforts. As noted above, the law against bestiality (18:23) thwarts a revolting sexual mixing of two different kinds of species, one created "in God's image" and one not so created.

The particularly "abhorrent" character of homosexual intercourse cannot be explained solely or primarily by its lack of procreative potential. Rather, it is to be traced to its character as a flagrant transgression of the most fundamental element of human sexuality: sex or gender. Homosexual intercourse requires a radical "gender bending" of human sexuality by the very creatures whom God placed in charge of the good, ordered creation. Such an act constitutes a conscious denial of

---

217. See the discussion in Milgrom, *Leviticus 1–16*, 940-41, 948-53, 1001-4; Wold, *Out of Order*, 132.

the complementarity of male and female found not least in the fitted-ness (anatomical, physiological, and procreative) of the male penis and the female vaginal receptacle by attempting anal intercourse (or other forms of sexual intercourse) with another man. Anal sex not only con-fuses gender, it confuses the function of the anus as a cavity for expelling excrement, not receiving sperm.[218] Gender complementarity between male and female is expressed not only in basic sexual anato-my but also in a more holistic sense, as suggested by the Yahwist's depiction of woman's creation out of man's "rib."

Unlike in ancient Greek culture,[219] where the appropriateness of homosexual intercourse was evaluated on the basis of status (the male penetrated must be of lower status), the critique against homosexual intercourse in ancient Israelite culture appears to have been based in the first instance on the absence of gender complementarity between males. Status degradation was at best a secondary consideration.[220] The absence of any loopholes in Lev 18:22 and 20:13 for homosexual inter-course with lower-status members of society undermines Nissinen's

---

218. The kind of mixing that takes place in homosexual intercourse is of a different character from the other forms of mixing cited above. Instead of being a mixing of two dissimilar things, it is a mixing of two similar but noncomplementary things. The prohibition in Lev 18:22 and 20:13 was not a mindless application of the rule that forbade mixture of different kinds, a principle that (rigorously applied) might have led to the assumption that *same*-sex intercourse was more appropriate than heterosexual intercourse (as some Greeks thought). Rather, it was a reflective assessment of the interlocking nature of male-female sexuality lacking in male-male relationships.

219. Ancient Near Eastern culture in general lies somewhere between the position of ancient Israel and ancient Greece on the question of status. The penetrated male was usually regarded as "feminized" by the act of homosexual intercourse. At the same time, The Middle Assyrian Laws do not criminalize consensual homosexual intercourse, and some ancient Near Eastern texts suggest acceptance or at least tolerance of some forms of homosexual intercourse (such as sex with social infe-riors, foreigners, or homosexual cult prostitutes).

220. According to Boyarin, in the biblical culture "penetration of a male constituted a consignment of him to the class of females, but, rather than a degradation of status [as in Greco-Roman culture], this constituted a sort of a mixing of kinds, a generally taboo occurrence in Hebrew culture. . . . God-given categories must be kept separate. . . . Thus when one man 'uses' another man as a female, he causes a transgression of the borders between male and female . . . the issue does not seem to have been status so much as an insistence on the absolute inviolability of gender dimorphism" ("Are There Any Jews in 'The History of Sexuality,'" 341-43,

emphasis on the disgracing of "manly honor." Even though Nissinen acknowledges that "the Holiness Code does not even make any difference with regard to the social status of the partners," he argues that the Holiness Code treats homosexual intercourse between men in 18:22 and 20:13 as abhorrent primarily because it reduces one of the men involved to the *degrading status* of a woman. "Sexual contact between two men was prohibited because the passive party assumed the role of a woman." The issue, Nissinen implies, is not gender but "gender roles"; and by "gender roles" he means the presumption of male superiority and dominance over women in antiquity.[221] The inference Nissinen would like us to draw is clear. In contemporary Western society, where women are regarded as the social equals of men, the Levitical prohibitions of homosexual intercourse not only make little sense, they are based on a premise offensive to modern sensibilities.

By way of response to Nissinen, we can admit that in ancient Israel, as in the ancient Near Eastern generally, there were misogynistic atti-

---

348). See also Thomas M. Thurston, "Leviticus 18:22 and the Prohibition of Homosexual Acts," *Homophobia and the Judaeo-Christian Tradition* (ed. M. L. Stemmeler and J. M. Clark; Dallas: Monument, 1990: the anally receptive male does not conform to the class "male"); and, for the rabbinic position, Michael L. Satlow, "'They Abused Him Like a Woman': Homoeroticism, Gender Blurring, and the Rabbis in Late Antiquity," *JHSex* 5 (1994): 1-25: unlike the Romans who understood sexual penetration politically, "Palestinian rabbinic discourse on homoeroticism is characterized by two traits: concern over gender boundaries, and the divinely ordained limits on sexuality" [p. 23]). Where I would differ strenuously from Boyarin (and Michel Foucault) is over his conclusion that we now know better than to link sexual identity with gender (p. 353). Gender and sexuality ought to be coupled. That the Levitical prohibitions are silent on the question of sexual orientation (e.g., not distinguishing between bisexuals and homosexuals or addressing the question of genetic predispositions) does not make the proscriptions in Lev 18:22; 20:13 irrelevant. Rather, it makes the issue of the special category of the "homosexual" irrelevant for the rejection of such practices (contra also Nissinen, *Homoeroticism*, 44). Since the Levitical prohibitions are based on the Creator's design for the creation, not on human desires for alternative expressions of sexuality, participation in homosexual intercourse by men with an "exclusive homosexual orientation" would have made no difference to the legislators. Would awareness of an "exclusive orientation to bestiality" have made sex with animals any more tolerable for the legislators of the Holiness Code?

221. *Homoeroticism*, 42-44, esp. p. 44; similarly, Brenner, *The Intercourse of Knowledge*, 139-43; Fewell and Gunn, *Gender, Power, and Promise*, 107-8; and Bird, "The Bible in Christian Ethical Deliberation," 149, 157.

tudes toward women. A man putting himself in the sexual role of a woman in ancient Israel would have diminished his social station considerably. However, it was not just the abandonment of traditional male-female hierarchichal roles that made homosexual intercourse such an abhorrent act. If surrendering dominant male social status were the real issue behind the proscriptions of Lev 18:22; 20:13, we would expect the legislators of the Holiness Code to have made subversion of male hierarchy punishable by death, not just the "symptom" of homosexual intercourse. We would expect the authoritative role of "judge" Deborah in Judges 4 to have been "judged" an abomination in ancient song and the subsequent narrative tradition. We would expect the Yahwist to have traced the husband's "rule" over his wife to conditions in the garden of Eden rather than regard it as part of the curse on Eve for listening to the serpent (Gen 3:16). We would wonder why the Priestly writer likewise failed to ground male superiority and dominance over women in his creation account; why he speaks only of the collective rule of humans over the rest of creation, their differentiation into male and female, and their duty to procreate (Gen 1:26-31).[222] The implication of all these texts is that there was something antecedent and more essential than male hierarchy in the created order: human sexuality as expressed in male and female pairing.

Further, why should the Holiness Code have been so absolute in its prohibition of homosexual intercourse if status were the primary issue? Why not permit, as The Middle Assyrian Laws seem to have done, high-status men to coerce sex with low-status men, or permit all consensual homosexual acts? Or why not permit homosexual intercourse in instances where the two male partners were social equals and alternated active and passive roles? Why even regard the male object of another man's affections as standing in for a female, rather than adopt a model closer to the practice of Greek pederasty? The answer to these

---

222. Whether H was aware of P's creation account or not depends on the relative dating one assigns the two documents. If H used P, he probably accepted P's (and J's) version of creation, since he supplied no alternate account. If P incorporated H into his work, then P presumably interpreted H's proscriptions of homosexual intercourse in the light of his own account of creation. Even if H did not know P, his understanding of creation could hardly have been much different with respect to the exclusive sexual pairing of male and female.

questions is apparent. The unqualified character of the prohibitions in Lev 18:22 and 20:13 intimates a more fundamental problem with homosexual intercourse than mere status: a distortion of gender itself, as created and ordered by God. At issue was not so much status differentiation as sexual differentiation. Males were created by God, anatomically and otherwise, for pairing with an "other," not a "like," of the same species. The thinking of the legislators of the Holiness Code was apparently not "Men should not take on the role of women in sexual intercourse because women are inferior beings" but rather "Men should not take on the role of women in sexual intercourse because God created distinct sexes, designed them for sexual pairing, and did so for a reason." While status inversion and gender inversion are related concepts, they are not identical. The latter, not the former, is the main concern behind the Levitical laws.

As we shall see, Paul's own reasoning, grounded in divinely given clues in nature, is similar even though the terminology employed is Hellenistic. Hence, the most likely reason why homosexual intercourse was viewed as wrong in Lev 18:22 and 20:13 was that it mixed two partners in sexual intercourse that God the Creator never intended to be joined: two males. For one man to "lie with" another man in the manner that men normally "lie with" a woman was to defile the latter's masculine stamp, impressed by God and evident in both the visible sexual complementarity of male and female and in the sacred lore of creation. The very integrity and health of the family unit was also undermined. Inability to procreate and misuse of semen were important secondary factors in the critique.

The Absence of an Explicit Critique of Same-Sex Female Intercourse

One ambiguity remains: Are Lev 18:22 and 20:13 only prohibiting (anal) intercourse between men? Both Olyan and Boyarin think that is the case. Olyan compares the phrase "the lying down of a woman" in Lev 18:22 and 20:13 with the phrase "the lying down of a male" in Num 31:17-18, 35; Judg 21:11-12, where a female virgin is defined as someone who does not "know a man with respect to the lying down of a male" and a non-virgin is defined as someone who knows a man in that respect. Since the difference between being a virgin and a non-virgin is penetration of the vagina, it would appear that the comparable phrase for male-male intercourse would imply penetration of a male anal orifice as if it were a female vaginal orifice.[223] Boyarin cites texts from the Babylonian Talmud that indicate that the only type of male-male intercourse regarded as worthy of stoning was anal penetration (*b. Nid.* 13b);[224] that women who "rubbed" other women were not disqualified from marrying priests (*b. Yebam.* 76a and *Šabb.* 65a-b);[225] and that a woman was not guilty of adultery (and thus subject to stoning) if she had intercrural intercourse with another man but she was guilty if she had vaginal or anal intercourse.[226] There is therefore a good case for asserting that Lev 18:22; 20:13 had in mind intercourse between males that involved anal penetration.

However, if this were true, it would still be erroneous to conclude (as both Olyan and Boyarin do) that other forms of homoerotic contact would be permitted. Such a conclusion is akin to arguing that, because any particular corpus of law in the Old Testament explicitly proscribes only penetrative intercourse in the case of incest, adultery, fornication, rape, and bestiality, we can assume that fondling one's stepmother, or a neighbor's wife, or a virgin, or an animal would be acceptable behavior in ancient Israel (cf. the Hebrew idiom "uncover her nakedness" for sexual intercourse).[227] One can of course go quite far in sexual stim-

---

223. Olyan, " 'And with a Male . . .'," 184-86; followed by Nissinen, *Homoeroticism*, 44.
224. Intercrural ("between the thighs") male intercourse was merely a sin comparable to masturbation.
225. Harlots, defiled women, and divorced women were so disqualified. Women who engaged in rubbing against each other's genitals were guilty of "mere lasciviousness/obscenity." For a more negative assessment of lesbian intercourse, see *Sipra Aḥaré* 8.7, which lists among the practices of the Egyptians and Canaanites that must not be copied (Lev 18:3) men marrying men and women marrying women.
226. Boyarin, "Are There Any Jews . . . ?" 336-40, 345-47; cf. also Satlow, "Homoeroticism," 1-25; Brooten, *Love Between Women*, 66-70. It is dangerous to extrapolate from the thought world of the rabbis to the thought world of the framers of the Holiness Code—and not only because of the significant passage of time. The absence of an explicit prohibition in the Torah against nonpenetrative homosexual sex and against lesbianism was almost certainly a major factor in the reticence of the rabbis, a reticence reinforced by the characteristic rabbinic reluctance to apply capital punishment.
227. According to Deut 22:13-21, if at some point during marriage a wife was charged

ulation without technically engaging in intercourse. As the Talmudic examples cited above indicate, such fondling may constitute a lesser transgression of the law that is not subject to the death penalty but would still be considered a transgression.

The primacy of penetration for defining sexual intercourse may *partly* explain why the Holiness Code leaves out lesbian relationships.[228] In such acts there is no penetration by a male organ and no transfer of semen—two acts that effect in a real sense a climactic merger of beings and definitively and unambiguously cross boundaries. A similar rationale helps to explain why the prohibition of bestiality (Lev 18:23; 20:15-16), unlike that of same-sex intercourse, is applied to both men and women: apparently it was thought that women could be penetrated by male animals. There probably were

---

by her husband with not having been a virgin at the time of their wedding, the parents of the woman were given an opportunity to supply proof of their daughter's pre-marital virginity: a cloth used to cover the wedding-night bed with the bloodstains incurred from her first experience of vaginal intercourse. If such a cloth could not be produced, then the woman was considered not to have been a virgin on her wedding day. As a consequence she would be stoned. For legal reasons, then, vaginal penetration became the defining act of sexual intercourse. However, common sense dictates that if a husband *caught* his wife engaging in various consensual sexual acts with another man (holding hands, mouth-to-mouth erotic kissing, exposed breasts, oral stimulation of the penis [fellatio] or vagina [cunnilingus], etc.), her actions would not have been taken as a minor offense. If a man was caught passionately kissing a cow on the mouth or masturbating on a cow, but no penetration occurred, probably this too would have been considered a major offense. If a man approached his stepmother and they engaged in an array of sexual acts short of vaginal penetration, it is likely that this would have qualified as incest. In all of these examples, whether the penalties imposed would have been less severe than a death sentence is beyond knowing. Can anyone seriously argue, though, that the offenses would have been treated as minor, let alone condoned as acceptable behavior? If not, on what basis can one argue that various homosexual acts shy of anal penetration would have been tolerated? Surely in ancient Israel any homosexual acts involving the anus or the penis in any way (for example, fellatio or intercrural sex) would have been treated as a serious offense, not just penile penetration of the anus. Attempts to restrict in a rigid way the application of Lev 18:22 and 20:13 to male anal intercourse must be viewed as an ultra-legalism of sorts. The law codes of ancient Israel made no pretense to covering explicitly every conceivable violation of the covenant with Yahweh. Most commandments were suggestive of a wider field of unacceptable behavior.

228. Cf. Wold, *Out of Order*, 116.

other factors accounting for why lesbian intercourse goes unmentioned. It may have been thought of as a transgression of the covenant but one meriting a punishment less severe than death.[229] Possibly lesbianism was unknown to the Israelites and/or Canaanites (it goes unmentioned in other legal materials from the ancient Near East) so there was no need to legislate it out of existence.[230] We hear of male homosexual cult prostitutes in ancient Israel but not female homosexual cult prostitutes. In a society dominated by men and with a high view of chastity it might have been impossible for a sustained lesbian relationship to develop. It could be taken for granted that Israelite women would go on to marry men, regardless of what experimentation took place with other women before marriage. Female-to-female eroticism would thus constitute no danger to Israelite family structures or determination of paternity. In the end, one cannot know what the precise reason for its exclusion from Lev 18:22; 20:13 was.[231] What we do know is that both Paul in Rom 1:26 and *The Sentences of Pseudo-Phocylides* 192 (a Jewish text from roughly the same time period as Paul), not to mention the Church Fathers, expanded the prohibitions in Leviticus to forbid lesbian intercourse explicitly.

---

229. Cf. Greenberg, *Construction*, 190 n. 35: The fact that lesbianism is not mentioned "may mean that lesbianism was not considered wrong, but more likely it meant that it was handled by fathers and husbands, rather than by public authorities."

230. Cf. Gerstenberger, *Leviticus*, 297 ("Was love between women considered harmless or even advantageous? This . . . does not seem persuasive. . . . Men were the ones creating these prescriptions. . . . Perhaps they simply knew nothing or too little about the lesbian activities of their own mothers, wives, daughters, and female slaves."). Nissinen thinks that women's homoeroticism goes unmentioned because a "woman could not lose her manly honor, and it was inconceivable to think of a woman in an active role in a sexual act. Neither did female same-sex activity challenge male domination. Therefore, women's homoeroticism did not pose as big a problem as that of men" (*Homoeroticism*, 43; see also Bird, "The Bible in Christian Ethical Deliberation," 152). Similarly, Fewell and Gunn argue that "the most fearful prospect for patriarchy is the possibility that males might not be 'men,'" not that females might "usurp men's dominant functions" (*Gender, Power, and Promise*, 107). The problem with this view is that it does not explain why in the Greek and Roman world female homosexuality was often considered more appalling than male homosexuality—precisely because of the challenge it posed to male supremacy.

231. "[I]n the current state of research we cannot definitively explain the lack of a prohibition of female-female sexual contact in ancient Israelite law. In the end, the most plausible explanation may simply be that the lawmakers generally showed greater interest in males and their behavior" (Brooten, *Love Between Women*, 62; similarly, Brenner, *Intercourse of Knowledge*, 143-44).

Incidentally, it is helpful to remember that had the first chapter of Romans not been preserved for posterity, one might have falsely concluded on the basis of 1 Cor 6:9 that Paul opposed only same-sex *male* intercourse. So the argument from silence with regard to Levitical prohibitions is dubious at best. We also know that Jesus and the early church expanded the definition of sexual intercourse to include the interior lust of one's heart toward another. For such communities of faith, the prohibitions in Lev 18:22; 20:13 could not be restricted to male *anal* intercourse.

VIII. David and Jonathan

Only after treating explicit OT references to same-sex intercourse is it possible to put into proper perspective the stories about David and Jonathan in 1 Samuel 18–23 and David's eulogy for Jonathan in 2 Samuel 1. It is sometimes alleged that David and Jonathan had a homosexual relationship which the narrator suppressed.[232] A review of the story and of the expressions used to describe their relationship will make clear the problems with this allegation.[233]

David's first encounter with Jonathan occurred shortly after David slew Goliath. David was brought before King Saul.

---

232. One author has regarded the relationship of Jonathan and David as so important for the homosexual cause in the church that he entitled his book accordingly: Tom Horner, *Jonathan Loved David: Homosexuality in Biblical Times* (Philadelphia: Westminster, 1978), esp. pp. 26-39. A more recent attempt to argue for a homosexual dimension is: S. Schroer and T. Staubli, "Saul, David, und Jonathan—eine Dreiecksgeschichte?" *BK* 51 (1996): 15-22. Schroer and Staubli focus on alleged parallel terminology in the David and Jonathan cycle and the Song of Solomon. Cf. Greenberg, *Construction*, 114: "homophilic innuendos permeate the story." Both Greenberg and Nissinen refer to the relationships between Gilgamesh and Enkidu and between Achilles and Patrocles as parallels. Whether either of these relationships involved sexual intercourse is a matter of debate. Nissinen argues that Gilgamesh's encounter with Enkidu marks a taming of the wild sexuality of each. No such motif appears in the stories about Jonathan and David.

233. The definitive refutation of a homophile reading of the text has been given by Markus Zehnder, "Exegetische Beobachtungen zu den David-Jonathan-Geschichten," *Bib* 79 (1998): 153-79. Zehnder responds to the claims made by Schroer and Staubli. He rightly points out that the occasional connections with language in the Song of Solomon are due to the fact that "close, non-erotic relationships of friendship stand in terms of content in close proximity to intimate romantic relationships" (p. 177).

¹When (David) had finished speaking to Saul, the soul of Jonathan was bound (*niqšĕrâ*) to the soul of David, and Jonathan loved (*wayyeʾĕhābēû*) him as his own soul. ²Saul took him that day and would not let him return to his father's house. ³Then Jonathan made a covenant with David, because he loved him as his own soul. ⁴Jonathan stripped himself of the robe that he was wearing, and gave it to David, and his armor, and even his sword and his bow and his belt. ⁵David went out and was successful wherever Saul sent him. . . . ¹⁵When Saul saw that he had great success, he stood in awe of him. ¹⁶But all Israel and Judah loved David; for it was he who marched out and came in leading them. (1 Sam 18:1-5, 15-16 NRSV)

Here Jonathan's love of David is portrayed as part of a much larger love affair of the people of Israel with David, a love affair based on David's zeal for Yahweh and his military prowess in the context of a life-and-death struggle with the Philistines (18:5). Rather than responding in jealousy as his father Saul soon would, Jonathan offered his complete loyalty to David. In making a covenant with David he adopted David into the royal "house" or family (an extension of Saul's action in not letting David return to his father's house).

David and Jonathan had in effect become "kin," with all the mutual privileges and obligations that such a relationship entails. The two now relate as brothers, not as a romantic couple (cf. 2 Sam 1:26: "my brother Jonathan"). Mention of the fact that Jonathan's "soul" (i.e., "life," *nepeš*) "was bound to" David's soul no more expresses erotic love than do the words of Judah to Joseph in Gen 44:30-31: If Judah returns to his father Jacob without Benjamin, Jacob will die because "his (Jacob's) soul is bound up with (*qĕšûrâ*) his (Benjamin's) soul." The verb *qāšar* usually refers to a binding together of people for political purposes.[234] In effect, Jonathan is assuring David that he has hitched his fortunes to those of David, politically and emotionally. Whatever happens to David happens also to Jonathan. If David hurts, Jonathan hurts. If David rejoices, Jonathan rejoices. Consequently, if David becomes king, Jonathan has every reason to rejoice.

The relationship between Jonathan and David cannot be divorced from the context of the royal court: Jonathan is the king's son and

---

234. About 21 of its 44 occurrences convey the sense of "conspiring."

rightful heir to the throne; but David is God's apparent choice to lead Israel. The two have formed a deeply personal, but nonetheless political, alliance. Two points underscore this. First, the language of love is typical of covenant-treaties between an overlord and vassals or between two political rulers of roughly equal power. For example, future vassals of the Assyrian king Ashurbanipal were instructed, "You must love [him] as yourselves."[235] King Hiram of Tyre is described as a "lover" or "friend" of David's (1 Kgs 5:1).[236] Likewise, all Israel and Judah "loved" David because he successfully led them in battle. Saul was correct to construe this adulation as a sign of crumbling loyalties to his own reign. In an attempt to deceive David, Saul sent word to David that "all [the king's] servants love you" (18:22).

Second, Jonathan's act of handing over his robe, armor, and "even" his sword, bow, and belt was not only an extraordinary token of heartfelt commitment to love David "as his own soul" and to protect him at any personal cost; it was also an act of political investiture. "The passing of arms from the lesser to the greater... seems to have had political implications in the Ancient Near East."[237] Ironically, Saul attempted to clothe David with his armor for David's battle with Goliath (1 Sam 17:38-39). After David defeated Goliath, he took Goliath's own sword and killed him, then put Goliath's armor in his tent (1 Sam 17:51, 54). Second Kings 11:10 reports that the priest Jehoiada brought out David's spears and shields when the time came to usurp Queen Athaliah's rule with the coronation of her grandson Joash. Jonathan's robe (měʿîl) too is probably to be regarded as a royal accoutrement. Giving it to David symbolizes the transfer of the office of heir apparent.

---

235. Cited by P. Kyle McCarter, *1 Samuel* (AB; Garden City: Doubleday, 1980), 342. Schroer and Staubli point to Cant 1:7; 3:1-4 ("you whom my soul loves") as an erotic parallel but there "soul" is the subject, not the object (cf. the similar phrase in Ps 11:5 in a nonsexual context). The phrase "love as one's own soul" is closer to the non-erotic command in Lev 19:18 to "love your neighbor as yourself" (Zehnder). The vast majority of the occurrences of the noun "love" (ʾahābâ) and the verb "to love" (ʾāhab) in the Old Testament have nothing to do with erotic love.

236. MT 5:15. Cf. 2 Sam 19:6 (MT v. 7). The word for "friend" is ʾōhēb, a cognate of ʾāhab, "to love."

237. J. A. Thompson, "The Significance of the Verb *Love* in the David-Jonathan Narratives in 1 Samuel," *VT* 24 (1974): 334-38; Springett, *Homosexuality*, 72-73.

Only three chapters earlier, the accidental tearing of Samuel's robe (*mĕ^cîl*) by Saul is followed by Samuel's declaration that God "has torn the kingdom of Israel from you . . . and given it to a neighbor of yours who is better than you" (1 Sam 15:27-28). "Jonathan is shown here to transfer his privilege of succession willingly to David out of his admiration and affection for him and . . . loyalty."[238]

Later, when Saul spoke with Jonathan and all his servants about killing David, Jonathan secretly relayed to David his father's plot because he "delighted very much" or "took great pleasure" (*ḥāpēṣ mĕʾōd*) in David (19:1). The verb *ḥāpēṣ* carries no sexual connotation in context, as the previous occurrence in 18:22 indicates ("See, the king is delighted with you, and all his servants love you; now then, become the king's son-in-law" [NRSV]). It denotes simply that David found favor in Jonathan's eyes, including political favor.[239]

After Saul's attempts on David's life, David flees. When he visits Jonathan he asks what wrong he has done to deserve such treatment. Jonathan assures David that his father does nothing without consulting him. David is less confident: "Your father knows well that I have found favor in your eyes; and he thinks, 'Do not let Jonathan know this, or he will be grieved'" (1 Sam 20:3). David then devises a plan by which he may discover Saul's intentions and urges Jonathan not to betray him: "Do *ḥesed* (i.e., show loyalty, faithfulness, kindness) to your servant, for you have brought your servant into a covenant of Yahweh[240] with you" (20:8). The use of the self-deprecating expression "your servant" underscores

---

238. McCarter, *1 Samuel*, 305; similarly, Bruce C. Birch, "The First and Second Books of Samuel," *NIB* 2:1120, 1133.

239. The word on occasion carries sexual overtones (Gen 34:19; Deut 21:14; Esth 2:14; Cant 2:7; 3:5; 8:4; each time with reference to a man's wife or betrothed), but usually it does not (e.g., Num 14:8; 2 Sam 20:11; 22:20; 1 Kgs 10:9; 2 Chr 9:8; Esth 6:6-11; Ps 18:19; 22:8; 41:11; Isa 62:4; Mal 2:17; 3:1). The dimension of political allegiance and loyalty is evident in 2 Sam 20:11: "Whoever delights in Joab, and whoever is for David, [let him follow] after Joab." From time to time mention is made of God "delighting in" David or Solomon (2 Sam 15:26; 22:20 [= Ps 18:20]; 1 Kgs 10:9; 2 Chr 9:8). "It is thereby implied that Jonathan's 'delight' in David corresponds to the will of God" (Zehnder, "David-Jonathan-Geschichten," 161).

240. H.-J. Zobel understands "a covenant of Yahweh" in the sense of "an all-inclusive covenant" ("*ḥesed*," *TDOT* 5:53); cf. NRSV: "a sacred covenant." For the meaning of the word *ḥesed*, cf. Katherine Doob Sakenfeld, *Faithfulness in Action: Loyalty in Biblical Perspective* (OBT; Philadelphia: Fortress, 1985), esp. pp. 8-15.

the political dimension of the proceedings. Jonathan in turn reassures David that he will disclose any knowledge he may have of his father's plans to harm David (20:12-13). He renews his covenant with David, with the additional stipulation that David never extirpate Jonathan's lineage:

> [14]"If I am still alive, do with me the *ḥesed* of Yahweh; but if I die, [15]never cut off your *ḥesed* from my house, even if Yahweh were to cut off every one of the enemies of David from the face to the earth." [16]Thus Jonathan made a covenant with the house of David, saying, "May Yahweh seek out the enemies of David." [17]Jonathan made David swear again by his love for him; for he loved him as he loved his own soul." (1 Sam 20:14-17 NRSV modified)

Jonathan recognizes that the Lord is on the side of David. He knows that his father's attempt to destroy David will bring God's wrath. Just as he is willing to risk his very life for David, he asks David to spare his lineage from the divine retribution that is surely coming upon all David's enemies.

When David did not show up at the king's table, Saul flew into a rage and said to Jonathan:

> [30]"You son of a perverse, rebellious woman (*naʿăwat hammardût*)![241] Do I not know that you have chosen the son of Jesse to your own shame (*lĕboštĕkā*) and to the shame (*lĕbōšet*) of your mother's nakedness (*ʿerwat*)? [31]For as long as the son of Jesse lives upon the earth, neither you nor your kingdom shall be established. Now send and bring him to me, for he shall surely die." [32]Then Jonathan answered . . . , "Why should he be put to death? What has he done?" [33]But Saul threw his spear at him to strike him. . . . [34]Jonathan rose from the table in fierce anger and ate no food . . . , for he was grieved for David, and because his father had disgraced him (*hiklimô*). (1 Sam 20:30-34 NRSV)

Saul shames Jonathan by declaring him to be, in Saul's eyes, the equivalent of a bastard offspring of an adulterous wife. Although Jonathan's

---

241. Literally, "son of a perverse (perverted, wayward, wrongdoing) woman of rebellion." *HALOT*: "You bastard of a wayward woman."

mother is slandered, the insult is clearly aimed at Jonathan. The reference to his mother as an adulteress conveys Saul's sense of betrayal. He accuses Jonathan of aligning himself with David, his family's own enemy, and thereby ruining his own chances to become king. From Saul's perspective, such a course of action would not only be shameful for Jonathan but would also bring shame on his mother to have borne such an offspring as this (hence "to the shame of your mother's nakedness").[242] Saul may have viewed Jonathan's avoidance of the mantle of leadership as an unmanly shirking of responsibility, but it is Jonathan's acquiescence to David's political ascendancy, not Jonathan's adoption of the female role in a homosexual relationship with David, that Saul is referring to.[243]

When Jonathan communicated to David his father's reaction, David

> bowed three times, and they kissed each other, and wept with each other; David wept the more. Then Jonathan said to David, "Go in peace, since both of us have sworn in the name of Yahweh, saying, 'Yahweh shall be between me and you, and between my descendants and your descendants, forever.'" (1 Sam 20:41-42 NRSV modified)

David's threefold bowing to Jonathan speaks to the political overtones of the farewell. David and Jonathan are in extreme distress because Saul's actions have made it clear that he has set his house against the house of David. David and Jonathan know that they might never see one another alive again. Understandably, their departure from each other is emotional, just as it would be between father and son or between two brothers. There is nothing inherently homosexual about

---

242. "Jonathan, says Saul, has disgraced his mother's genitals, whence he came forth" (McCarter, *1 Samuel*, 343).

243. Cf. Joab's rebuke of David, who mourned for the death of his rebellious son Absalom instead of celebrating his troops' victory: "Today you have covered with shame the faces of all your officers who have saved your life today, . . . and the lives of your wives and your concubines, for love of those who hate you and hatred of those who love you (ʾōhăbêkā, lit., your lovers). You have made it clear today that commanders and officers are nothing to you; for I perceive that if Absalom were alive and all of us were dead today, then you would be pleased" (2 Sam 19:5-6). In the same way, Saul viewed Jonathan's loving loyalty to David as a betrayal of his own family: love for one who would bring about the demise of Saul's house amounts to hatred of those who bore him. Note, too, in 2 Sam 19:5-6 "love" has political rather than erotic overtones.

two men kissing each other in ancient Near Eastern society.[244] These were not erotic kisses but kisses of sorrow that conveyed the deep emotional pain of a committed friendship and alliance cleft by circumstances beyond their control.

Subsequently, Jonathan visited David while the latter was on the run. There Jonathan explicitly stated his conviction that David "shall be king over Israel, and I shall be second to you" and, for a third time, made a covenant with David (1 Sam 23:16-18). The political side of the relationship is unambiguous.

When David later learns of the deaths of Saul and Jonathan, he bemoans Jonathan's fate in endearing terms:

> I am in distress because of you, my brother Jonathan; you were very dear to me ($n\bar{a}^c amt\bar{a}$ $l\hat{i}$ $m\check{e}^{\jmath}\bar{o}d$);[245] your love to me was more wonderful to me than the love of women. (2 Sam 1:26)

Jonathan's repeated display of (non-sexual) kindness to David at a time when Jonathan was in a position of power, selflessly risking his own life

---

244. Of 27 occurrences of the Hebrew verb "to kiss" ($n\check{s}q$, qal and pi^cel), 24 contain no erotic component. Of the three that do, two are from the Song of Solomon (1:2; 8:1; cf. Prov 7:13). Of the 24 that do not, 15 refer to kisses between relatives, usually between fathers and sons or between brothers. Four refer to two unrelated males kissing, again with no sexual connotation: 1 Sam 10:1 (Samuel-Saul); 2 Sam 15:5 (Absalom-people); 19:40 (David-Barsillai); 20:9 (Joab-Amasa). Cf. Zehnder, "Die David-Jonathan-Geschichten," 163. For weeping in association with kissing, cf. Gen 45:15 (Joseph joyously kissing and weeping upon his brothers after revealing his true identity); 50:1 (Joseph weeping over and kissing his just deceased father Jacob). For bowing down and kissing, cf. Exod 18:7 (Moses-Jethro).

245. HALOT gives the meaning "be friendly with" for the verb $n\bar{a}^c am$ in 2 Sam 1:26. One could translate "you were an intimate friend of mine" or even "you were very lovely to me," "a delight to me," "a source of pleasure to me." Although two (and only two) of the 26 occurrences of the root n^cm are used in a sexual sense (Cant 1:16 [adjective]; 7:7 [verb]), n^cm no more has a sexual connotation in 2 Sam 1:26 than it does three verses earlier. There David extols *both* Saul and Jonathan as "beloved and lovely" ($hanne^{\jmath}\check{e}h\bar{a}b\hat{i}m$ $w\check{e}hanne^c$ $\hat{i}mim$)—surely David was not referring to Saul's erotic attractiveness to other males. Elsewhere the verb is used of the pleasantness, loveliness, beauty, attractiveness, or delight of the land of Israel (Gen 49:15; cf. Ezek 32:19); knowledge (Prov 2:10); the psalmist's words to God (Ps 141:26); and those who stand for what is right (Ps 141:6). Cf. T. Kronholm, "$n\bar{a}^c am$," TDOT 9:469-70, who says the word is being used in 2 Sam 1:26 of intimate friendship, not erotic love.

and certainly his own kingdom, surpassed anything David had ever known from a committed erotic relationship with a woman. No more and no less than this is the point of David's eulogy of his dear friend. David subsequently lived up to his covenant agreement with Jonathan by restoring the fortunes of Jonathan's crippled son Mephibosheth (2 Samuel 9).

None of these texts, taken singly or as a collective whole, provide persuasive support for a homosexual relationship between Jonathan and David. On no occasion does the narrator ever refer to sexual intercourse between David and Jonathan. The verbs *šākab* ("to lie") and *yādac* ("to know") are never employed.[246] David's heterosexual vigor was hardly in question, as the texts that speak of his many wives, concubines, and children attest (1 Sam 18:17-29; 25:39-43; 2 Sam 3:2-5, 13-16; 5:13-16; 11). Indeed, after David's first encounter with Jonathan in ch. 18, the attention of the narrator shifts to Saul's attempts to thwart marriage between one of his daughters and David. It is clear enough from the Bathsheba episode that David could be erotically stimulated by the sight of a pretty woman bathing (2 Sam 11:2-5). Jonathan too was married and had children (1 Sam 20:42; 2 Samuel 9). Of course, heterosexual desires do not necessarily preclude homosexual desires. Yet the narrator's willingness to speak of David's heterosexual sex life puts in stark relief his complete silence about any sexual activity between David and Jonathan or any sexual activity with men after Jonathan's death.

One could argue that the narrators have worked hard, but not entirely successfully, to suppress the details of a homosexual relationship. However, such a theory flies in the face of an important fact. At neither of the two most important stages of the tradition history of the narrative, whether during the composition of the Succession Narrative[247] or at the time of its editing and incorporation into the Deuteronomistic History, is there any indication that the narrators were in the slightest bit concerned about a possible homosexual misunderstanding. Indeed, far from censoring, the narrators did their best to play up the relationship between Jonathan and David. The more covenants and the greater the emotional bond between these two, the

---

246. Zehnder, "Die David-Jonathan-Geschichten," 167, 176.
247. Essentially 1 Sam 16:14–2 Sam 5:10 minus editorial insertions.

merrier. Why were the narrators unconcerned about a hint of homosexual scandal? The answer is obvious: nothing in the stories raised any
suspicion that David and Jonathan were homosexually involved with
one another. Only in our own day, removed as we are from ancient
Near Eastern conventions,[248] are these kinds of specious connections
made by people desperate to find the slightest shred of support for
homosexual practice in the Bible.[249]

Viewing the relationship of Jonathan and David in purely personal
terms grossly distorts the purposes of the narrators. The personal
dimension is significant, but primarily insofar as it conveys a political
point: David is not a rogue usurper of the kingdom of Saul and
Jonathan. The transition of royal power to David came with Jonathan's
own blessing and even initiative. David was not an enemy of the house
of Saul but in some respects its staunchest supporter. Some compan-
ions destroy each other "but there is a lover/friend ($^{\jmath}\bar{o}h\bar{e}b$) who sticks[250]
closer than a brother" (Prov 18:24). David and Jonathan had the latter
type of relationship and it was one which was completely asexual.[251]

---

248. "Men's homosociability apparently was not part of the sexual taboo in the biblical
world any more than it is in today's Christian and Islamic cultures around the
Mediterranean" (Nissinen, *Homoeroticism*, 56).

249. An even more desperate attempt is the claim that Ruth and Naomi were involved
in a lesbian relationship. Cf. the critique in Springett, *Homosexuality*, 78-80.

250. The verb here, *dābēq*, is the same verb used in Gen 2:24 to refer to a man "cleaving" to his wife in a one-flesh relationship; yet there is obviously nothing sexual about
the reference in Prov 18:24. This again points up the flaw of construing the David-
Jonathan relationship as sexual on the grounds that some of the terminology used
to describe that relationship is *occasionally* used of sexual relationships elsewhere.

251. Nissinen admits that "[m]odern readers probably see homoeroticism in the story
of David and Jonathan more easily than did the ancients." Yet he then clouds the
issue and waffles by asserting that *the text "leaves the possible homoerotic associations to the reader's imagination. . . .* In this sense it can be compared to the love
of Achilles and Patroclus (in Homer's *Iliad*) or the love of Gilgameš and Enkidu
. . . [where] *erotic expressions of love are left in the background and only to be
imagined,* and there is no distinction between active and passive sexual roles.
Perhaps these homosocial relationships, based on love and equality, are more
comparable with modern homosexual people's experience of themselves than
those texts that explicitly speak of homosexual acts that are aggressive, violent
expressions of domination and subjection" (*Homoeroticism*, 56; emphasis added;
cf. p. 158 n. 98: contra Greenberg, "there is . . . no indication" that the
Deuteronomistic editors deleted a homosexual relationship from the story).

This sounds like double-speak. Is attributing a homoerotic dimension to the

IX. Conclusion

Old Testament texts that speak to the issue of same-sex intercourse are sufficiently widespread to claim the existence of a pervasive viewpoint within the Old Testament canon.

The Yahwist's (J's) stance toward intercourse between males is evident in three stories: the creation of woman, Ham's homosexual rape of his father, Noah, and the attempted rape of Lot's angelic visitors by the men of Sodom. In the creation story, intercourse between a man and a woman is justified on the grounds that woman was formed from man. Marriage in general and sexual intercourse in particular is thus evaluated as an attachment of two complementary beings into "one flesh," a reunion with one's sexual "other." No such justification is, or can be, provided for same-sex unions. The stories about Ham and Sodom deal not only with homosexual intercourse but also with other factors: incestuous rape of one's father in the case of Ham, rape of vulnerable visitors and resident aliens in the case of Sodom. In both stories, however, homosexual intercourse is made a key component in characterizing an event as a "type scene" of unprecedented evil, vindicating God's subjugation of the descendants of Ham (the Canaanites) and the complete destruction of Sodom. In line with The Middle Assyrian Laws, if the Yahwist regarded homosexual rape as an act that brought great shame on the man raped, he can hardly have approved of those who willingly allowed themselves to be "lain with as a woman."

Both the Deuteronomic law code and the Deuteronomistic Historian

---

story eisegesis or not? Nissinen cannot have it both ways. Simply because the text does not explicitly deny that David and Jonathan are having sex is no license to imagine that they are. Nissinen's reasoning is the equivalent of saying that when the Gospels depict Jesus as saying "Let the little children come to me" they are leaving possible pedophilic connotations to the reader's imagination. It also defies logic to draw a comparison, as Nissinen does, between the relationship of David and Jonathan, which Nissinen admits probably did not involve any sexual intercourse, with modern *homosexual* relationships, which are homosexual precisely because they involve same-sex intercourse. Nobody questions the value of intimate friendships between members of the same sex. It is only when sexual intercourse is introduced into a same-sex relationship that important moral issues are raised. If the relationship of David and Jonathan did not entail an erotic component, then there is nothing in that relationship to validate what homosexuals are asking the church to validate: same-sex intercourse.

deal primarily with the phenomenon of homosexual cult prostitution. We argued on the basis of ancient Near Eastern parallels that this was the most acceptable manifestation of receptive homosexual behavior in Israel's cultural environment. If even this form of homosexual intercourse could not be integrated into the Yahwistic faith, then none could be. The epithet "dog," as ancient Near Eastern parallels show, conveys an expression of particular disgust for the receptive partner in male homosexual intercourse. The prohibition against cross-dressing in Deut 22:5 gets at the same concern for maintaining lines of distinction in maleness and femaleness. The story of the attempted homosexual rape of the visiting Levite, along with the subsequent rape and death of the Levite's concubine (Judg 19:22-26), epitomizes and climaxes the sad state of affairs in the pre-monarchical period: everyone did what was right in his/her own eyes. Its close parallels with the story of Sodom underscore the Deuteronomistic Historian's basic agreement with the Yahwist's position toward homosexual intercourse.

The position of the Priestly writer (P) and the author(s) of the Holiness Code (H) toward same-sex intercourse is clear. The importance given to procreation and to ordering creation according to various "kinds" precludes any openness on P's part toward same-sex intercourse, regardless of whether P knew H. The straightforward declaration that God created male and female for sexual union and blessed that union, and no other, with the capacity to be fruitful and multiply leaves same-sex unions without place in the structures imbedded by God in creation. The framers of the Holiness Code, like the Yahwist, understood Canaanite participation in incest and same-sex intercourse to be two key reasons why God vomited the Canaanites out of the land. They explicitly declared all sexual intercourse between males to be abominable or utterly detestable to God and worthy of the sentence of death. In taking such a severe and comprehensive stance towards male homosexual behavior, Lev 18:22 and 20:13 represent a level of revulsion toward same-sex intercourse without parallel in the ancient Near East. The framers were neither blindly imitating the cultural trends of their own day, nor responding in idiosyncratic fashion to the trauma of exile and restoration. They were not reacting negatively to same-sex intercourse primarily because of its connections to idolatry or because of its impurity owing to the contact of semen with excrement. Not even its procreative incapacity accounts for the degree of abhorrence generated by homosexual intercourse. Rather, H was responding to the conviction that same-sex intercourse was fundamentally incompatible with the creation of men and women as complementary sexual beings. For a man to have sexual intercourse with another male as though the latter were not a male but a female violates God's design for the created order. It puts another male, at least insofar as the act of sexual intercourse is concerned, in the category of female rather than male. It is nothing short of a rebellion against the way in which God made humans to function as sexual beings. We argued, too, that a focus on anal intercourse between males did not imply acceptance of other forms of homosexual behavior, including female homosexual behavior. While recognizing the obsolescence of some of the laws of the Holiness Code in relation to the moral behavior of Christians, we pointed to three factors as evidence for the enduring validity of Lev 18:22 and 20:13: (1) the grounding of these proscriptions in transcultural creation structures; (2) the fact that the closest analogies appear in the proscriptions to incest, adultery, and bestiality—forms of sexual behavior that continue to be rejected by contemporary communities of faith; and (3) Paul's conscious appropriation and endorsement of the Levitical standards against homosexual intercourse for Christian churches not under the Mosaic law.

Among the prophets, it is likely that Ezekiel characterized homosexual intercourse as an "abomination" and connected it with the story of Sodom. Even though the rest of the prophetic corpus is silent about the matter of same-sex intercourse, the role of prophets as spokespersons of God who enforced and creatively applied the old covenant law of the league makes it highly unlikely that any would have condoned same-sex intercourse.

The clear and unequivocal position of the Hebrew Scriptures against homosexual intercourse provides an important backdrop to a discussion of the New Testament's witness. However, because the views of late Second Temple Judaism were also shaped by trends within the broader cultural milieu of the Greco-Roman world, a discussion of the New Testament witness must be preceded by a discussion of further developments in early Judaism.

2. Same-Sex Intercourse as "Contrary to Nature" in Early Judaism

The relevant texts about same-sex intercourse from the New Testament remain ahead of us, but before we turn to them a survey of extra-biblical Jewish teachings will help to place the early Christian teachings in context. In this chapter I look briefly at works that date roughly from 200 B.C.E. to 200 C.E.[1] Given the fact that actual instances

---

1. Hellenistic Jewish authors are of course indebted to the views of Greco-Roman philosophers and moralists who likewise opposed homosexual intercourse. I note parallel arguments throughout the discussion. However, one cannot assume precise agreement in all particulars, since (1) the views of Jewish writers were also shaped by their Scriptures and (2) they did not follow every argument used by Greco-Roman writers. For Greco-Roman views on homosexuality, see Nissinen, *Homoeroticism*, 57-102, 158-74; Greenberg, *Construction*, 106-23, 141-60, 196-210, 228-41; Dover, *Greek Homosexuality*; Scroggs, *The New Testament and Homosexuality*, 17-65; David Halperin, John Winkler, and F. Zeitlin, eds., *Before Sexuality: The Construction of Erotic Experience in the Ancient Greek World* (Princeton: Princeton University Press, 1990); David M. Halperin, *One Hundred Years of Homosexuality: And Other Essays on Greek Love* (New York: Routledge, 1990); Wayne R. Dynes and Stephen Donaldson, eds., *Homosexuality in the Ancient World* (New York: Garland, 1992); Boswell, *Homosexuality*, 61-87; John J. Winkler, *The Constraints of Desire: The Anthropology of Sex and Gender in Ancient Greece* (New York: Routledge, 1990); Amy Richlin, *The Garden of Priapus: Sexuality and Aggression in Roman Humor* (rev. ed.; New York: Oxford University Press, 1992); eadem, "Not Before Homosexuality: The Materiality of the *Cinaedus* and the Roman Law Against Love Between Men," *JHSex* 3 (1993): 523-73; Rabun Taylor, "Two Pathic Subcultures in Ancient Rome," *JHSex* 7 (1997): 319-71; David Cohen,

of homosexual behavior among Jews of this period are not attested,[2] the number of texts that speak directly to the issue of homosexual intercourse are sufficiently numerous and unanimous to ensure an accurate assessment of what Jews thought. These texts provide a bridge between Old Testament Scripture and the Jewish matrix of early Christianity. They help us in determining what Jesus and the authors of New Testament texts who are silent about the issue of homosexuality probably believed. Moreover, they supply us with some sense of the rationale behind early Jewish and Christian positions on the issue, particularly the meaning of "contrary to nature" for Paul in Rom 1:26. As we shall see, the evidence suggests that early Judaism was unanimous in its rejection of homosexual conduct. We are unaware of any dissenting voices.

The relevant texts are primarily from Philo and Josephus. Philo was a Jewish philosopher from Alexandria, Egypt, who lived ca. 10 B.C.E.–45 C.E. Josephus was a Jewish priest, general, and historian who lived ca. 37–100 C.E. He lived in Jerusalem for about the first thirty years of his life and then took up residence in Rome under the patronage of the emperor. Philo addresses homosexual sex in *On the Life of Abraham* 135-37; *Special Laws* 1.325, 2.50, 3.37-42; and *On the Contemplative Life* 59-62. Josephus does so in *Jewish Antiquities* 1.200-201 and *Against Apion* 2.199, 273-75. I discuss these texts in detail below.

"Laws, Society and Homosexuality in Classical Athens," *Past and Present* 117 (1987): 3-21; idem, *Law, Sexuality, and Society: The Enforcement of Morals in Classical Athens* (Cambridge: Cambridge University Press, 1991); Michel Foucault, *The History of Sexuality* (3 vols.; New York: Random House, 1978–86); Saara Lilja, *Homosexuality in Republican and Augustan Rome* (Helsinki: Societas Scientiarum Fennica, 1983); Carola Reinsberg, *Ehe, Hetärentum und Knabenliebe im antiken Griechenland* (Munich: C. H. Beck, 1989); Harold Patzer, *Die griechische Knabenliebe* (Wiesbaden: F. Steiner, 1982); Gundel Koch-Harnack, *Knabenliebe und Tiergeschenke: Ihre Bedeutung im päderastischen Erziehungssystem Athens* (Berlin: Gebr. Mann, 1983); Paul Cartledge, "The Politics of Spartan Pederasty," *Proceedings of the Cambridge Philological Society* 207 (1981): 17-36; Springett, *Homosexuality*, 83-113; and Furnish, *Moral Teaching of Paul*, 58-66. The fullest discussion of lesbianism in antiquity is in Brooten, *Love Between Women*; for bisexuality, see Eva Cantarella, *Bisexuality in the Ancient World* (New Haven: Yale University Press, 1992); and Mark D. Smith, "Ancient Bisexuality and the Interpretation of Romans 1:26-27," *JAAR* 64 (1996): 223-56.
2. A specific case is reported for ca. 300 C.E., when Rabbi Yehudah ben Pazzi caught two men having sex in an attic (*y. Sanh.* 6.4, 23c).

Other references also exist, however, and corroborate the stance of Philo and Josephus. In the *Letter of Aristeas* 152 (ca. 200–100 B.C.E., Alexandria?), the author tells us that Jews are morally superior to the gentiles in that the latter "not only draw near to (or: procure) males but also defile their mothers and even their daughters. We [Jews] are quite separated from these practices." In *Sibylline Oracles* 3 (ca. 163–45 B.C.E., Alexandria), we read that when the Romans come to dominate the world, "immediately compulsion to impiety will come upon these men. Male will have intercourse with male and they will set up boys in houses of ill-fame . . . and it will throw everything into confusion" (184-87); the Jews "are mindful of holy wedlock, and do not engage in impious intercourse with male children, as do . . . many nations . . . , transgressing the holy law of immortal God" (596–600); and "avoid adultery and indiscriminate (or: confused) intercourse with males" (764).[3]

The Sentences of Pseudo-Phocylides 190-92, 212-14 (ca. 50 B.C.E.–100 C.E., Alexandria?) urges that "the limits of sexual intercourse set by nature" not be transgressed by "intercourse between males," "nor should females imitate . . . the sexual role of men." *The Testaments of the Twelve Patriarchs* (of uncertain date and location: ca. 150 B.C.E.–200 C.E. in Syria?) speaks disparagingly of "corrupters of boys" (*paidophthoroi*; *T. Levi* 17:11) and of Sodom, which "exchanged the order of its nature" (*T. Naph.* 3:4). In *Sibylline Oracles* 5 (ca. 70–132 C.E., Egypt) the writer declares, "With [Rome] are found adulteries and illicit (or: unlawful) intercourse with males" (166), and predicts a future time when there will be no "illicit (or: unlawful) love of boys" (430; cf. 387, which condemns Rome for "pederasty"). *Mishnah Sanhedrin* 7:4 (ca. 200 C.E.) states: "These are they that are to be stoned: he that has sexual intercourse with his mother, his father's wife, his daughter-in-law, a male, or a beast. . . ."[4] Wisdom of Solomon 14:26 (ca. 30 B.C.E.–50 C.E., Alexandria) might also be added: idolatry is the source of every evil, including "change of birth/origin" (see p. 298 n. 10).

---

3. The translation of texts from the *Sibylline Oracles* is by J. J. Collins in *OTP*.

4. Cf. *Tg. Ps.-J.* 20:13 on Lev for the punishment of stoning. In another text, Rabbi Judah is said to have cautioned, "Two unmarried men may not sleep in the same cloak," though the majority ("the sages") permitted this (*m. Qid.* 4:14). Commenting on this text, *t. Qid.* 5:10 states simply, "Israel is not suspected"; that is, the men of Israel, unlike the gentiles, are not as a rule prone to such a temptation.

In addition, depending on how they are dated, two texts from *2 (Slavonic) Enoch* may be included. *Second Enoch* 10:4 reads, "This place [of torment], Enoch, has been prepared for those who do not glorify God, who practice on earth the sin which is against nature, which is child corruption in the anus in the manner of Sodom, of witchcraft. . . ."; 34:1-2 reads, "God convicts the persons who are idol worshipers and sodomite fornicators, and for this reason he brings down the flood upon them. . . . all the world will be reduced to . . . abominable fornications, that is, friend with friend in the anus, and every other kind of wicked uncleanness which it is disgusting to report."[5]

The texts I cite above address homosexuality explicitly. However, many other texts supply strong inferential evidence for Jewish opposition to homosexual intercourse, including those that broadly forbid *porneia* ("sexual immorality" as defined by Mosaic law). Another case in point: The Qumran community did not expressly forbid same-sex intercourse, but it did proscribe punishments for any member who even accidentally exposed his genitals to another (male) member (1QS 7:12-14). This, plus its strict adherence to the Mosaic law, makes its opposition to homosexual intercourse clear. Indeed, given the severe stance against homosexual intercourse in the Levitical laws, it is inconceivable that any non-apostate Jew in antiquity would argue for the legitimacy of male-male sexual intercourse. Even Paul, who argued vigorously that the Sinaitic code had been abrogated for those who believed in Jesus as Christ, remained staunchly opposed to same-sex intercourse.

Most of the Jewish authors proscribing male homosexual behavior speak of a "male/man" having sex with another "male/man," thus reflecting the terms used in Lev 18:22; 20:13. However, it is also evident that in most (if not all) of these instances the author primarily had in mind the standard model for homosexual relationships in Greco-Roman culture; namely, pederasty.[6] Nevertheless, this does not mean

---

5. F. I. Andersen dates *2 Enoch* to the end of the first century C.E. but acknowledges "a long and complex process of collecting and editing" and, in any case, the references to sodomy in these passages are found only in one manuscript (P) of the long recension, possibly a late gloss (*OTP*, 1.94-7, 119 n. l, 158 n. 34a).
6. Scroggs also makes this point, though he is incorrect to imply that Jewish authors saw no wider reference to the Levitical law than pederasty. By pederasty we mean

that other forms of homosexual intercourse were unknown to Jews or that a more positive stance might have been adopted for homosexual intercourse between comparable-age partners. They recognized that the laws in Lev 18:22; 20:13 applied to all male-male intercourse, regardless of the relative age, status, or active/passive role of the participants.[7] So, while the Jewish critique is aimed primarily at pederasty, the arguments used cover a wider sweep of same-sex intercourse.

Jews, like Greek and Roman critics of same-sex intercourse, rejected homosexual conduct on the ground that it was "contrary to (or: against) nature" (*para physin*).[8] Apart from the obvious and central fact that the law forbade same-sex intercourse, there were four reasons why only intercourse between male and female was considered to be "in accordance with nature" or "natural" (*kata physin*). The first two are of primary importance: (1) Homosexual intercourse cannot lead to procreation; and (2) homosexual intercourse represents an affront to God's sexual stamp on males and females by uniting two non-complementary sexual beings (with emphasis on the inherent degradation of males penetrated as if females). The next two reasons are of secondary importance: (3) Homoerotic desire constitutes an excess of passion; and (4) homosexual intercourse is not practiced even by animals.

---

erotic love between a mature man and a boy in the developmental stage between puberty and the sprouting of body hair. But caution is required: "boy" (*pais*) could be used of any junior partner in a homosexual relationship, even one who was full-grown.

7. As we shall see below, the Jewish critique of same-sex intercourse never singles out age disparity as the chief evil of pederasty.
8. Scroggs identifies nine arguments against pederasty in the Greco-Roman world: (1) "laws existed which protected youths against sexual assault and which placed restrictions on freeborn prostitutes"; (2) "platonic love is a cover-up" for same-sex erotic passions; (3) "pederasty is effeminate," leading in particular to a "feminizing" of the young passive partner; (4) "pederasty lacks mutuality," since it does not bring pleasure to the youthful passive partner; (5) "pederastic relationships are impermanent"; (6) pederasty breeds "greediness in youths," who learn to expect gifts in exchange for sexual favors and thus skirt prostitution; (7) pederasty breeds jealousy in the active partner; (8) "pederasty is contrary to nature (*para physin*)," in that it does not lead to procreation, is not even practiced by animals, and causes the effeminate passive partner to find fault with nature for making him a man; (9) "women provide superior possibilities than boys" for giving sexual pleasure and providing companionship (*The New Testament and Homosexuality*, 49-62). Argument 8 (contrary to nature) is more prominent in Greco-Roman sources than Scroggs's short

I. Procreation

Procreation is God's clue, given in nature, that the male penis and female vagina/womb are complementary organs. No other sexual activity results in new life. Therefore the only acceptable form of sexual intercourse is between a man and a woman. Yet the argument of Jewish writers did not stop there. Any union formed in the knowledge that no procreation could result (male-male, female-female, human-beast, or even male with infertile female) constitutes sexual passion for its own sake, little more than unbridled lust void of societal responsibility. No longer contributing to populating the earth, such passion demonstrates disregard for the preservation of the human race. Moreover, passion of this sort, exercised beyond nature's and society's control, could only have destructive effects. Concern for the sanctity of male "seed" was also at issue. Philo, and others, reasoned that since sexual stimulation of the male results in ejaculated semen, and since too this seed must have been given by God for a purpose, sexual stimulation must have as its divine purpose the release of seeds for procreation. Moreover, since only fertile women could provide "the deep-soiled and fruitful fields" capable of sustaining the growth of the seed, all unions that did not have procreation in view were forbidden.

Rejection of same-sex intercourse on the grounds that it resulted in an infertile union was commonplace among Greeks and Romans. The classic texts are from Plato's *Laws*, particularly the statement in 636C: "When male unites with female for procreation, the pleasure experienced is held to be in accordance with nature (*kata physin*), but contrary to nature (*para physin*) when male mates with male or female

---

treatment intimates; indeed, some of the other arguments he cites can be included under this heading (3-5, 9). *All* of the arguments adduced by Jewish writers of the period can be brought under the rubric that same-sex intercourse is "contrary to nature." According to Nissinen, "Sex between men (and between women) was regarded as 'against nature' for two reasons: (1) It did not lead to procreation. . . . What is at stake here, however, is not only the anatomical necessity, but also (2) the breakdown of the role structure that had been considered 'natural.' For men this meant that the passive partner's masculine role was changed into a feminine role— the submissive role of the male passive party that was considered 'unnatural.' For women what was involved was just the opposite—they went beyond the passive role that was considered 'natural' for them" (*Homoeroticism*, 88).

with female." Here the issue is curbing self-indulgent passions that do not lead to the stability and growth of the state but rather destabilize the family unit by turning men's affections away from their wives and from the procreation and nurture of children.[9] The first-century Stoic philosopher Musonius Rufus wrote:

> Men who are not wantons or immoral are bound to consider sexual intercourse justified only when it occurs in marriage and is indulged in for the purpose of begetting children, since that is lawful, but unjust and unlawful when it is mere pleasure-seeking, even in marriage. But of all sexual relations those involving adultery are most unlawful, and no more tolerable are those involving males with males, because the daring and flagrant act is contrary to nature (*para physin*; XII).[10]

---

9. According to Plato's "Athenian," laws should be implemented which govern "using in accordance with nature (*kata physin*) the intercourse leading to the procreation of children, on the one hand abstaining from the male and not deliberately killing the race of humans, nor 'sowing into rocks and stone,' where it can never take root and grow, and on the other hand abstaining from every female field in which you would not desire what you have sown to grow. This law . . . has countless good qualities. For, first, it is laid down in accordance with nature (*kata physin*), and it keeps men from erotic rage and insanity and all kinds of adulteries and all excesses in drink and food, and it makes men to be truly fond of their own wives" (838E-839A). One of two laws should be enacted: "Either that no one should venture to touch anyone . . . except his own wedded wife, and should not sow unacceptable and illegitimate seed in concubines, nor unfruitful seeds in males contrary to nature (*para physin*); or we could ban intercourse with males entirely, and if a man had intercourse with any woman except (his wife, he would) . . . be disqualified from any civic commendation" (841D-E). The translations in LCL (trans. R. G. Bury) and Dover's *Greek Homosexuality* were consulted.

10. Modified translation of C. Lutz (*Musonius Rufus* [New Haven: Yale University Press, 1947]). The fact that male-male intercourse is singled out (with adultery) as particularly revolting suggests a broader reason for its rejection than its sterile quality, probably having to do with the relegation of the male passive partner to the role of a woman. This comes out clearly in a later work, the Pseudo-Lucianic *Amores* or *Affairs of the Heart* (ca. 300 C.E.), in which Lycinus recounts a debate by two men concerning the merits of love for women and love for boys. Charicles, a Corinthian, defends the superiority of male love for women: "Since there was no way possible for anything to be born from one, she (Aphodite) cleverly devised a twofold nature (*diplēn physin*) in each (*sc.* species). For, after she had graciously bestowed to males their own means of sowing seed (*katabolē spermatōn*; i.e., capacity for ejaculating sperm), had made plain that the woman was a [vessel], a holder of seed (*gonē*), and had mixed in both genders a common longing (*koinos pothos*; i.e., a desire for the opposite sex), she yoked together the one (*sc.* gender) with the other, having

Of course the argument from procreation is not limited to Greco-Roman sources. We have seen in ch. 1 that procreation is also a factor in the affirmation of heterosexual unions in Gen 1:27-28 and the rejection of homosexual intercourse in Lev 18:22; 20:13.

Among post-biblical Jewish authors, Josephus and Philo also witness to this view. As Josephus succinctly put it: "What are our marriage laws? The law recognizes only sexual intercourse (or: mixing, union) that is in accordance with nature (*kata physin*), the (intercourse a man has) with a woman, and that only for the procreation of children" (*Ag. Ap.* 2.199). Later in the same work he writes of "sexual intercourse with males which is contrary to nature (*para physin*) and without restraint" and accused the Greeks who attributed "to the gods sexual

---

written down (*katagrapsasa*; or: prescribed) a divinely sanctioned rule of necessity, that each of the two (*sc.* genders) remain in their own nature (*idia physis*), and that neither should the female be masculinized (*arrenousthai*) contrary to nature (*para physin*) nor too should the male be softened (*malakizesthai*; or: made effeminate) in an improper (or: unseemly, indecent) manner (*aprepōs*). . . . In the beginning . . . life was in obedience to the authority of the laws that nature (*hē physis*) framed. . . . But little by little, descending from that magnificent height into the pits of pleasure (*hēdonē*), time was cutting strange and peculiar paths to enjoyment. Then wantonness (*tryphē*; or: softness, daintiness, luxury, indulgence), daring all, transgressed the laws of nature herself (*tēn physin autēn parenomēsen*). . . . And who then first looked with the eyes at the male as (*sc.* though) at a female . . . ? One nature (*physis*) came together in one bed. But seeing themselves in one another they were ashamed neither of what they were doing nor of what they were having done to them but, as they say, sowing on barren rocks, they exchanged (*antikatēllaxanto*) great disgrace for a little pleasure (or: they bought a little pleasure at the cost of great disgrace [so M. Macleod, LCL]). Indeed, the daring of some men cut its way forward into tyrannical force so much that it went as far as to commit sacrilege against nature (*tēn physin hierosulēsai*; or: to rob nature's temple) with a knife (viz., by self-castration). By emptying the male quality (*to arren*) out of the males they found the limits of pleasure expanding (*parelkonta*; or: being prolonged). But the wretched and unlucky, (*sc.* castrating themselves) in order that they may be boys more (*epi pleon*; or: for longer), do not even remain men any longer, an ambiguous riddle of twofold nature (*amphibolon ainigma diplēs physeōs*), neither kept for what they have been born nor having that to which they passed over" (19-21; my translation). There are many similarities with the presentation of Rom 1:18-32: passions for the same sex as a devolution from the anatomical and procreative fittedness of male and female present in nature ever since creation; love for the same sex as an instance of being mastered by one's passion (not content with the desire for the opposite sex implanted in them); the obscuring of gender differentiation through same-sex intercourse (leading even to attempts to feminize the passive partner in bodily appearance); and the characterization of same-sex passion as shameless and disgraceful.

intercourse between males" of "inventing an excuse for their pleasures, which were disgusting and contrary to nature" (*para physin*; ibid., 2.273-75).[11] Philo defended God's actions in wiping out Sodom and Gomorrah as an act of compassion for the whole world. If the Greeks and barbarians had imitated the homoerotic practices of the inhabitants of Sodom,

> the cities would have been made desolate, one after another, as though emptied by a disease of plague proportions. Yet God, because he had taken pity as savior and lover of humankind, increased in the highest degree possible the unions of men and women (which were) in accordance with nature (*kata physin*), (unions) having come into being for the sake of the procreation of children. But because he bitterly hated those (unions) which were strange and unlawful, he extinguished them . . . [Philo goes on to mention the destruction of Sodom as a monument to God's hatred of homosexual intercourse]. (*Abr.* 136-37)

In commenting on Lev 20:13, Philo cites the following as one of the reasons why the law was justified in condemning the active and older "lover" in pederastic same-sex intercourse:

> He pursues a pleasure that is contrary to nature (*para physin*) and does his part to make the cities desolate and empty of inhabitants by destroying (*diaphtheirōn;* or: wasting) the procreative sperm. . . . And, finally, because in the manner of a bad farmer he allows the deep-soiled and fruitful fields (of women) to lie barren by forming designs that aim at their sterility, and from which practices (viz., intercourse with other males) absolutely no growth can be expected, he works hard both day and night to achieve these ends. (*Spec. Laws* 3.39)

Similarly, in *Contempl.* 62, Philo blames the active lover for sterility, childlessness, and the desolation of cities.[12] Given his emphasis on

---

11. The translations of Josephus and Philo are my own.
12. "For they practice as an art the depopulation of cities and scarcity of the best kind of people and barrenness and sterility, who imitate those unskilled in farming, sowing instead of the deep soil of the plain the somewhat salty fields or stony and hardtrodden places, which (acts) are naturally incapable of growing anything and destroy (*phtheirei;* or: waste) the deposited seeds" (alluding perhaps to Plato, *Laws* 838E).

procreation, one may wonder if Philo considered all individual acts of sexual intercourse between husband and wife to be illicit when the wife was found to be sterile after years of marriage, including those that took place in the years after menopause. However, for him, the issue was whether the possibility of procreation was one reason for entering into a marital union in the first place.[13]

In contemporary Western culture, the development of effective birth control methods and problems with overpopulation make many question whether the norm that sexual intercourse should always and only be undertaken for the purposes of procreation is not outmoded. Nevertheless, at least one element presupposed in this ancient critique

---

13. Thus, in the matter of marriage to an infertile woman: "One must reproach also those who plough 'a hard and stony land.' And who could these be but those who bond (sexually) with sterile women? For in the hunt for mere uncontrolled pleasure, like the most lustful of men, they willfully and intentionally destroy (*diaphtheirousin;* or: waste) their procreative sperm. For what other reason can they have in giving themselves in marital pledge to such women? Certainly not in the hope of children, a hope which they know must necessarily become unfulfilled (*atelē*); but rather (they do this) because of an exceedingly insane desire and an incurable absence of self-control. So then all the men who marry young women in ignorance at the time of their capacity for having easy births or of the opposite, when they ascertain at a much later date from their inability to have children that they are sterile, do not send them away, are deserving of our pardon, for they give way to intimacy (*synētheia*), a most irresistible (*biastikōtatos;* or: forcible, constraining) thing, and are unable to dissolve the charms of old love stamped on their souls as with a seal by lifelong companionship. But all who woo to be their bride, women who, being infertile, have already been proven to be so by other husbands, copulating simply in the manner of pigs or goats, should be engraved as antagonists of God on monuments listing the impious. For while with the Lover of animals and of humans the aim is, through every kind of care, to effect preservation and continuance for all created things, they who practice as an art (*technazontes*) to extinguish the seed at the same time as the sowing (*katabolē*) are confessedly enemies of nature" (*Spec. Laws* 3.34-36). It is wrong to marry a woman that one has good reason to believe is infertile but acceptable to keep (and, presumably, to continue to have sex with) a woman whose infertility is discovered or comes to pass years later. On the other hand, Philo gives as the reason for the law's prohibition of intercourse with a menstruating woman (Lev 18:19) that the husband must "stand in awe of the law of nature," remembering "not to emit without purpose (*ateleis*) procreative sperm for the sake of a pleasure that is untimely and in poor taste. . . . But if the menstrual period should stop, he may now boldly sow the procreative sperm, no longer fearing the destruction (*phthora;* or: wasting) of what is to be sown" (*Spec. Laws* 3.32-33; see the comments by David Winston, *Philo of Alexandria* [CWS; Ramsey, N.J.: Paulist Press, 1981], 368-69 n. 425).

of same-sex intercourse remains credible. The fact that the semen ejaculated by the penis "takes root" (we would say, "effects the fertilization of an egg") and nurtures life only when penetration of a woman's vagina occurs is clear and convincing proof of God's exclusive design in nature for heterosexual intercourse. God/nature obviously intended the female vagina to be the complementary sex organ for the male penis. In addition, for the sake of society, there is some sense to tying the desire for sexual intercourse with the development of responsible and stable family structures. This is not a critique sufficient in itself since it would involve a similar critique of single-parent homes or a woman who marries after menopause, but it is a contributing factor to the overall assessment of the undesirability of same-sex unions.

II. Gender Discomplementarity

The second main reason why same-sex intercourse was rejected as "contrary to nature" extends from reproductive capability to the anatomical fittedness of the male penis and the female vagina. Since the obvious receptacle given by nature for the male penis was the female vagina, penetration of a male amounted to treating the male as if he were a female and thereby "emasculating" him—a blatant case of anatomical gender transgression.

In effect, the willingly penetrated male takes up a complaint with nature for failing to supply him with a vagina. In Hellenistic and Roman Imperial culture, "the passive partner" in a homoerotic relationship,[14] either on his own initiative or by way of encouragement or coercion from "the active partner,"[15] took the process of feminization a step further by braiding and adorning his hair or growing it long, putting on makeup and perfume, adopting feminine mannerisms, wearing women's clothes, plucking facial and body hair, or (in extreme cases) undergoing castration. Overlaying this critique of a rebellion against one's God/nature-given gender was the standard hierarchical conception of male-female status in antiquity: females were inferior and subordinate to men. By putting themselves in the position of being "mounted"

---

14. *Ho paschōn*, "the one who is 'done' or acted upon, the 'doee.' "
15. *Ho drōn*, "the one who does, the doer."

by other men, the passive partners were regarded as willingly taking on not only a gender role contradictory to their anatomy but also the inferior nature and status of the woman. The position of the active "man on top" conveys his superior status, while the position of the passive partner conveys his inferiority, a status akin to that of a woman.[16]

The classic text among Greco-Roman authors comes from Plato's *Phaedrus* 250E, quoted in the late–first century in Plutarch's *Dialogue on Love* 751D-E:

> If union contrary to nature (*para physin*) with males does not destroy or curtail a lover's tenderness, it stands to reason that the love between men and women, being natural will be conducive to friendship developing in due course from favor.... But the union with males, either unwillingly with force and plunder, or willingly with weakness (or softness: *malakia*) and effeminacy (*thēlutēs*), surrendering themselves, as Plato says, "to be mounted in the custom of four-footed animals and to be sowed with seed contrary to nature (*para physin*)"—this is an entirely ill-favored favor, shameful and contrary to Aphrodite.[17]

Once more, as in the case of the argument from procreation, the argument from "anatomical gender transgression" traces not only back to Greco-Roman culture but also back to the Jewish scriptures. The Levitical prohibitions rejected the blurring of the male gender associated with a man lying with another male "as though lying with a woman" (18:22; 20:13). The primary factor that accounted for the

---

16. Dover, *Greek Homosexuality*, 91-109. Cf. Nissinen, *Homoeroticism*, 68, 73, 79, 83.
17. Translation by Scroggs. The text in Phaedrus describes the actions of the active partner in active verbs; Dover thinks it refers to heterosexual sex (*Greek Homosexuality*, 163), though it is clearly used of homosexual intercourse in Plutarch. For other Greco-Roman texts on this theme, see Pseudo-Lucian, *Affairs*, 19-21 (cited above); Cicero, *Dom.* 139 (it is inappropriate for a male to act "as a woman among men"); idem, *Phil.* 2.44-45 (slandering Mark Antony's boyhood role as a male prostitute and a live-in "beloved" of a male lover); Juvenal 2; 6.40-138; Athenaeus, *Deipnosophists* 13.565B-C, 605D; Dio Chrysostom, *Disc.* 7.133, 135-36, 151-52; 77/78.36 (homoerotic men try to make women of boys, creating "a far worse and more unfortunate breed . . ., weaker than the female and more effeminate"); Seneca, *Ep.* 47, "On Master and Slave," 7. Cf. Nissinen, *Homoeroticism*, 80-87; and Scroggs, *The New Testament and Homosexuality*, 53-55.

description of such an act as an "abomination" was not the status degradation of the male but the mixing of kinds; that is, using another male sexually as if he were a female.

Several Jewish authors and texts speak of the disgusting aspect of same-sex intercourse, alluding in general to the blatant transgression of male-female anatomical complementarity and in particular to the feminization of the male gender that occurs in the case of the passive partner. In commenting on the insatiable passions of the Sodomites, Josephus speaks of same-sex intercourse as an act that would "dishonor (Lot's) guests" (*Ant.* 1.200-201). In *Against Apion* he notes that the law forbids any sexual intercourse that does not lead to procreation, even among heterosexual unions, but particularly "abhors the union of males with males" (2.199). Sexual intercourse between males was characterized by "pleasures which were disgusting and contrary to nature (*para physin*)" (2.275). For Josephus, male-male intercourse had an abhorrent quality that extended beyond the concern of infertile unions because it blurred the gender distinctions sanctified by God. The first-century (B.C.E.) author of *Sib. Or.* 3.596-600 labeled pederasty as "impious intercourse with male children." The author of *Testament of Levi* called pederasts "corrupters of boys" (17.11). Finally, the first-century (C.E.) author of the *Sentences of Pseudo-Phocylides* gives the following injunctions:

> Don't transgress the limits of sexual intercourse set by nature with (or: for) unlawful love. Not even to animals themselves is intercourse between males pleasing. Nor should females imitate in any way the sexual role of men. . . . Having long hair is not appropriate for males, but for voluptuous women. Guard the youthful beauty of a well-formed boy; for many rage for sexual intercourse with a male. (190-92, 212-14)[18]

Philo, though, is our primary source for understanding first-century Jewish attitudes toward anatomical and social "gender bending" in

---

18. A literal translation of 190-92 is: "Don't transgress the marriage-beds of nature with (or: for) unlawful Cypris ["Cypris" is another name for the goddess of love and passion, Aphrodite; cf. Ps.-Phoc. 3: "nor rouse male Cypris"; and *Sib. Or.* 5.430: "unlawful Cypris of boys"]. Not even animals themselves do male marriage-beds please. Nor should females in any way imitate the couch (or: marriage-bed) of men." Cf. the commentary in P. W. van der Horst, *The Sentences of Pseudo-Phocylides* (SVTP; Leiden: Brill, 1978), 237-40, 249-51 (also 110-11 on verse 3).

homoerotic intercourse. He described the homoerotic actions of the men of Sodom as a "throw[ing] off from their necks the law of nature":

For not only in being madly desirous of women (*thēlymanountes*) were they destroying marriages of others (*allotrious;* or: marriages of foreign-ers) but also, although they were men, (they began) mounting (*epibain-ontes*) males, the doers (*hoi drōntes,* the active partners) not standing in awe of (*aidoumenoi*) the nature (*physis*) held in common with those who had it done to them (*hoi paschontes,* the passive partners). . . . Then, little by little, by accustoming those who had been born men to put up with feminine things, they equipped them (*kateskeuasan autois;* or: furnished them, prepared them, set them up) with a female disease (*thēleia nosos;* or: a disease of effeminacy)—an evil that is hard to fight against—not only feminizing their bodies with softness (*malakotēs;* or: effeminacy, weakness) and disintegration (lit., breaking into pieces, *thrypsis;* or: softness, weakness, daintiness, especially by debauchery or luxury) but also bringing their work to completion by making their very souls more degenerate. (*Abr.* 135-36)

The "law of nature" here is the principle that nature teaches us that only sexual intercourse with a female in faithful marital union is legiti-mate; thus, adultery too is contrary to nature (cf. Plato, *Laws,* 841D-E). However, sexual intercourse between men is an even greater viola-tion of natural law than adultery because it violates the very category of gender or sex "nature."[19] The "mounting" of another man emascu-lates that man, first because it treats his male gender as if it were, like the female gender, anatomically suited for sexual penetration; and sec-ond because it puts the male in the inferior status of the female, the passive "doee" rather than the active doer. Penetration is the first stage of feminization. The second stage occurs when the active partner encourages the passive partner to take on female appearance and life-

---

19. Cf. Philo, *Spec. Laws* 2.50: The wicked misuse their sex organs "for abominable lusts and forms of intercourse forbidden by all laws. He *not only* attacks in his fury the marriage-beds of others, *but even* plays the pederast and forces the male type of nature to debase and convert itself into the feminine form, just to indulge a polluted and accursed passion." Also, Philo, *Hypoth.* 7.1: "If you are guilty of pederasty or adultery or rape of a young person, even of a female, *for I need not mention the case of a male,* similarly if you prostitute yourself or allow or purpose or intend any action which your age makes indecent, the penalty is death."

style ("softness"). Philo emphasizes the culpability of the active partner for "not respecting (standing in awe of, fearing, showing regard for, *aidoumenoi*)" the male gender of the passive partner.

Philo comments on the negative effect on both passive and active partners as he discusses Plato's *Symposium* in *Contemplative Life* 59-61:

> Nearly the whole of Plato's *Symposium* is about love (*erōs*), not simply about men mad after (*epimanentōn;* viz., madly in love with) women or of women (mad) after men—for these desires pay tribute to the laws of nature—but about men (mad) after males, differing from them only in age. . . . For the greatest part of it (viz., the *Symposium*) intersperses throughout (the theme of) the common and vulgar love, (a love that) on the one hand takes away (*aphairoumenos;* or: robs, deprives of) manliness (*andreia*), the most useful virtue of life in time of war and in time of peace, and on the other hand works (*enapergazomenos;* or: produces) a female disease (*thēleia nosos;* or: a disease of effeminacy) in their souls and renders androgynous (*androgynous kataskeuazōn;* or: equips/prepares to be men-women, male-female hybrids) those who should have been trained in all the pursuits that make for strength. And having inflicted indignities/outrages (*lymēnamos*) on their boyhood and having guided them into (*agagōn eis;* or: reduced them to) the rank and condition of a beloved girl (*erōmenē*), it also does damage to the lovers (*erastai,* the active partners) as regards the most essential matters: body and soul and property. For the mind of the pederast (*paiderastēs,* the lover of boys) is necessarily oriented toward the darling boy (*ta paidika*), since it is quick-sighted (*oxydorkounta;* or: attentive) toward this one alone but blinded toward all other interests, both private and public; and the body necessarily wastes away (*syntēkesthai;* or: melts away, dissolves) through desire (*epithymia;* or: lust), and especially if a failure (viz., in securing the boy's affections) should ensue; and his property is necessarily diminished from two sides, both from neglect of it and from expenses incurred in pursuing his beloved. Now another greater evil, a pandemic one, grows up alongside (viz., the ones already mentioned) as well. For they practice as an art (*technazontai*) the depopulation of cities. . . .

The active partner is again the primary object of Philo's scorn. Sexual intercourse between two males is unnatural because it turns the passive partner into a "male-female hybrid" and destroys his manly courage, while it corrupts the active partner by consuming all his energies with a passion unbounded by familial and societal obligations. A third problem with homosexual attraction is that it threatens to depopulate urban areas. In his remarks, Philo rejects implicitly the arguments put forward by Phaedrus, Pausanias, and Aristophanes in the *Symposium* for the purity of enduring homosexual love (see ch. 5.I).[20] Philo was not ignorant of pro-homosexuality arguments; he simply refused to accept the validity of such arguments, given the prohibitions in the Torah, the obvious anatomical and procreative complementarity of male and female, and the host of negative individual and corporate side effects of same-sex intercourse. To be sure, as in *Abr.* 135-36, there are misogynist elements in Philo's argument: references to the "disease" of femaleness, treating courage as a distinctly male virtue, and regarding women as mere recipients of erotic love. Yet when we rightly reject these anti-female elements, we do not, thereby, diffuse the whole of Philo's negative assessment of homosexual relationships.

> There has barged into the cities like a raucous religious procession another evil, greater by far than the one just mentioned (viz., men who desire to marry women known to be sterile), pederasty (*to paiderastein*, boy-loving), which formerly was a matter of great reproach (*oneidos;* or: disgrace) even to be mentioned, but now is a matter of boasting not only for the doers (*hoi drōntes,* the active partners) but also for those who have it done to them (*hoi paschontes,* the passive partners) who, accustoming themselves to be infected with a female disease (*nosos thēleia;* or: a disease of effeminacy), drain away both their souls and their bodies (*diarreousi*), leaving no ember (*empyreuma,* live coal covered with ashes) of the male gender (*tēs arrenos geneas;* or: of the male birthright, stock) to smolder (*hypotyphesthai*), thus conspicuously braiding and adorning in various ways the hairs of their heads, and scrubbing and

---

20. Immediately after the text cited above, Philo, appealing to the wisdom of the Torah, rejects the anthropogonic myth spun by Aristophanes in *Symp.* 189D-190 to justify same-sex unions: "I maintain silence about the mythical fictions, particularly the double-bodied people. . . . For all these (fictions) are seductive, capable of enticing the ears by means of the newness of the idea; which (fictions) those on familiar terms with Moses, having learned from the earliest age to love the truth, look down upon with an abundance of contempt, continuing undeceived" (63).

painting (*hypographomenoi;* or: writing over, tracing) their faces with white pigment and orchils (*phykē,* prepared from seaweed and used as rouge by women) and similar things, and anointing themselves richly with fragrant perfumes . . . and with devotion practicing as an art (*technazontes*) to transform the male nature (*physin*) into female they do not blush; concerning whom it is fitting (*axion*) that those who obey the law as their authority desire them to be killed (*phonan*), which (law) commands that the man-woman (*androgynos*) counterfeiting the coin of nature (*to physeōs nomisma parakoptonta*) be put to death unavenged, not being allowed to live a day—indeed, not even an hour, being a disgrace (*oneidos*) to himself and his household and his country and to the whole human race. And let the pederast (*ho paiderastēs*) recognize that he remains under the same penalty, since he pursues a pleasure that is contrary to nature (*para physin*) and does his part to make the cities desolate and empty of inhabitants by destroying (*diaphtheirōn;* or: wasting) the procreative sperm. And, moreover, he deems it worthwhile to become a guide and teacher of the greatest of evils, unmanliness (*anandria*) and effeminacy (*malakia;* or: softness), by prolonging the bloom of the young and feminizing (*ekthēlynōn*) the flower of their prime, which (time of life) was intended for gymnastics training and being made fit as regards bodily strength and might. And, finally, . . . in the manner of a bad farmer he allows the deep-soiled and fruitful fields to lie barren. . . .

And the cause, I think, is the prizes offered among many of the countries for want of self-control and for effeminacy (*malakia*). One can see then these veritable men-women (*androgynoi*) always walking in a pompous manner through a full marketplace, even going in front of processions at the festivals, and having obtained by lot as unholy ones holy duties, and beginning the religious ceremonies of mysteries and their initiation rites, and participating in the secret rites of Demeter. Those of them who were trying to stretch still further their youthful beauty reached after (*ōrechthēsan;* or: yearned for, desired) a more complete change into women and in the process cut off their procreative organs. Wearing purple robes . . . , they march in front . . . [Philo, after noting the deterrent effect on such behavior that would obtain if society instituted the penalty of capital punishment prescribed by Moses, goes on to talk about an "even worse" offense: bestiality]. (*Spec. Laws* 3.37-42)[21]

---

21. See *Spec. Laws* 1.325: The law "puts away beforehand all the unworthy from the holy assembly, starting with the men-women (*androgynoi*) who are infected with the female disease (*hē thēleia nosos*), who by counterfeiting the coin of nature (*to*

Philo conceives of the passive partner as a willing participant in the erasure of his own masculine gender, an accomplice to transforming his "male nature to the female" through the deliberate application of feminine hairstyle, makeup, and perfumes and, in extreme cases, castration. In Philo's view, both he and the active partner, who likewise works to counteract the effects of male puberty on the younger, passive partner, are justifiably deserving of the death sentence pronounced by the law.

As with the argument from procreation, the argument based on gender bending contains elements foreign to most contemporary ways of thinking about gender and homosexuality. The denigration of women as inferior to men, the constricted definition of certain virtues as "manly," and the interpretation of the supine or prone female posture in sexual intercourse as a sign of weakness and status inferiority are offensive in the modern context. The well-defined roles of active partners and passive partners, the age disparity (an older man with a teenage boy or young man), and, in particular, the active attempt often made to feminize the appearance of the passive partner do not characterize all contemporary expressions of homosexuality. Despite the differences between then and now in terms of both conceptualization and practices, one fact remains indisputable: in the very act of male-male intercourse one partner (or both, if active-passive roles alternate) is taking the place of a woman. As far as the fittedness of the sex organs is concerned, only a woman is anatomically complementary to a man. For a man to take on that role is an obvious distortion of the gender distinctions endowed in nature by God.

Two other arguments have secondary significance in Hellenistic Jewish critiques of same-sex intercourse as "contrary to nature."

III. Excess Passion

In their descriptions of the sins of the men of Sodom, both Philo and Josephus describe a man's desire for sexual intercourse with other males

---

physeos nomisma parakoptontes) force their way into the passions and outward forms of licentious (*akolastos;* or: intemperate) women. For it (the law) drives away eunuchs and those who have the generative organs cut off (see Deut 23:1), who both husband (*tamieuontas;* or: manage, control, regulate) the flower of their prime, in order that it might not wither quickly, and restamp the male appearance into a female form." See also: Josephus, *J. W.* 4.560-63.

as an insatiable overflow of lust beyond heterosexual intercourse. In *Abr.* 135, after noting that the chief source of all the sins of the Sodomites was the extreme wealth of the inhabitants owing to high annual crop yields, Philo states:

> Unable to bear the satiety, they bolt like animals and shake off the yoke of the law of nature *(ton tēs physeōs nomon)* from their necks, chasing after very strong drink and food delicacies and unlawful forms of copulation *(ocheia,* a word normally used to describe covering or impregnating by male animals, not humans). For not only in being madly desirous of women were they destroying marriages of others but also, although they were men, (they began) mounting males. . . . In the process of trying to beget children they were given convincing proof of their error *(ēlenchonto)* inasmuch as they were sowing procreative sperm without purpose *(atelēs).* Yet this proof was of no help, since they were conquered by a more forcible desire *(epithymia;* or: lust).[22]

Similarly, in *Ant.* 1.200-201 Josephus states:

> The Sodomites, on seeing these young men of remarkably fair appearance whom Lot had taken under his roof, were bent only on violence and outrage to their youthful beauty. Lot adjured them to restrain their passions and not to proceed to dishonor his guests, but to respect their having lodged with him, offering in their stead, if his neighbors were so licentious, his own daughters to gratify their lust. But not even this would content them.

In our own day, homoeroticism is no longer regarded as merely an excess of passion by people who have become bored with the normal parameters for heterosexual intercourse. This is not to say, though, that there is no connection between the two worlds of thought, ancient and

---

22. So also *Spec. Laws* 3.43. Philo explains bestiality as stemming in part from excessive catering to the appetites of the belly: "They received their first training in food delicacies and drunkenness and other pleasures of the stomach and of the areas below the stomach, but then, after they had been satiated, they broke out into insolence (or: wantonness; *exubrisan*)—for satiety naturally gives birth to insolence *(hybris;* or: wantonness)—with the result that from the consequences of *(hypo)* a damaged understanding they no longer begin to rave and to be mad after people, whether males or females, but even after unreasoning animals."

modern. A rampant promiscuity along with a host of other addictive behaviors that often accompany it remains characteristic of many segments of homosexual male culture. This suggests male homosexual relationships are plagued both by the absence of a female partner to curb the excesses of male sexuality (prone as it is to visual stimulation and extremes in pluriform sexual behavior) and by an insatiable yearning for the completion of gender identification, which translate into inadequate self-control. What the ancient writers understood to be excess passion in general we may recognize as a constant grasping for fulfillment in things that ought to be shunned.

The ancient view of homoeroticism as excess passion and its implications for our interpretation of New Testament perspectives on homosexuality will be dealt with at greater length in section III of ch. 5. Suffice it to say here that Philo and Josephus employed the excess-passion argument as a way of denigrating a form of behavior that *on other grounds* had been shown to be "contrary to nature," not the other way around. In other words, rather than coming to the conclusion that same-sex intercourse was wrong because it arose out of excess passion, they assumed that the wrongness of same-sex intercourse proved an excess of passion. For them, homoeroticism was a passion unbounded by the healthy norms to which nature and law pointed. Accordingly, for Philo adultery and bestiality were not in the first instance wrong because they were manifestations of excess passion but wrong because both destroyed the enduring union between male and female human beings established by God in nature and law. For this reason, the argument from excess passion cannot be considered an argument of the first order regarding why same-sex intercourse was viewed in antiquity as "contrary to nature." One cannot suppose that Philo and Josephus would have adopted a different view of homoeroticism had they conceived of it as an exclusively same-sex orientation with some connection to genetic predispositions. Philo knew Plato's *Symposium* and the arguments given there for the innateness and naturalness of same-sex love but rejected such arguments out of hand. The Levitical prohibitions and the sexual complementarity of male and female taught him that, however innate homosexual urges might be, they ran counter to God's design for sexuality in nature.

IV. Animal Heterosexuality

Another minor argument for the unnaturalness of same-sex intercourse was an appeal to the norm of heterosexuality in the animal kingdom. The argument appears in the works of some Greco-Roman philosophers and moralists. The classic text is in Plato's *Laws*, where the Athenian speaker contends that a strong case can be made for "following nature" and outlawing

> joining with males and boys in sexual intercourse as though with females, adducing as evidence the nature of animals and pointing out that (among them) male does not touch male for sexual purposes, because that is not natural. . . . Our citizens must not be worse than birds and many other animals which . . . when they reach (the) age (for breeding) pair off male with female according to instinct and female with male and for the remaining time they . . . (remain) firm to their first agreements of love. (836C, 840D-E)

Likewise, in Plutarch's *Whether Beasts Are Rational* (ca. 100 C.E.), Gryllus, who had been turned into a pig by a spell from Circe, now refused Odysseus's offer to be turned back into a man: "Until now the desires of animals have involved intercourse neither of male with male nor of female with female. . . . even men themselves acknowledge that beasts have a better claim to temperance and the non-violation of nature in their pleasures" (990D-F).[23] In early Jewish texts, the primary reference to this argument is found in Pseudo-Phocylides: "Don't

---

23. The translations in LCL and by Dover were consulted for the quote from *Laws*; LCL and Scroggs for the quote from Plutarch. Cf. Pseudo-Lucian, *Affairs* 22: "If each man were established on the rules which Providence ordained for us, we would be satisfied with intercourse with women and life would be free (*ekathareuen*; lit., would be clean) from every reproach. Doubtless among animals, who are able to debase nothing (viz., of the coin of nature stamped on them) by an evil disposition, the order (*nomothesia*; or: legislation, law code) of nature is kept undefiled. Lions are not mad after (*epimainontai*) lions, but Aphrodite at the appointed time calls forth their yearning for the female. A bull, leader of the herd, mounts (*epithornytai*; or: covers, copulates with) cows, and a ram fills the whole flock with his sperm. What else? Do not, among wild swine, boars chase after sows? And male wolves mingle with female wolves in sexual intercourse? And, speaking generally, neither the male birds whirring in the air nor all the male

transgress the limits of sexual intercourse set by nature with (or: for) unlawful love. Not even to animals themselves is intercourse between males pleasing" (190-91).[24] Modern zoology recognizes this as an over-simplification, yet as a general observation or as an observation applied to many species it retains persuasive force. In other words, we human beings should emulate not the worst of animal behavior but the best.[25]

V. Conclusion

Jewish authors writing within a century or two of Jesus' birth employed two main arguments to justify their labeling of same-sex intercourse as "contrary to nature" and opposite-sex intercourse as "in accordance with nature." First, they drew evidence from the unique capacity for procreation of heterosexual intercourse. Second, they

---

creatures who have their wet portion under the water assigned to them by lot, nay, not even any living male creature on land, yearn for intercourse with a male, but the decrees of Providence remain unmoved (*akinēta*; or: unchanged, inviolate). But you who are vainly praised for your understanding, a wild beast as truly worthless, you humans, by what new disease were you provoked to transgress law and engage in wantonness (*hybris*; or: lewdness, outrage, insolence) against one another? What blind insensibility have you poured down upon your soul that you had missed the mark in both directions, fleeing what you should pursue and pursuing what you should flee from? And if all, one by one, chose to emulate things such as this, there will not be even one (*sc.* left)" (22; my translation). In Ovid, *Metam.* 9.731-34, a woman who experiences sexual passion for another woman laments that she desires what not even animals desire. There were, however, writers in antiquity who recognized the presence of homosexual activity among some animals (including Aristotle and Pliny the Elder). See Brooten, *Love Between Women*, 273-74.

24. In *On Animals* 49, Philo mentions in passing that animals are given to less sexual vice than humans, including refraining from same-sex intercourse.

25. Cf. Schmidt, *Straight and Narrow?*, 134-35 and the literature he cites on p. 211 for contemporary studies on homosexuality among animals. "Numerous studies of the animal kingdom reveal indiscriminate mounting behavior, usually to express roles of dominance and submission, but animals do not engage in long-term homosexual bonding as humans do. Some monkeys and apes mount or fondle each other to the point of sexual arousal, but even this behavior involves numerous qualifications: most important, the behavior does not continue when the individual matures and has a heterosexual option. The consensus of research is that 'no evidence has as yet emerged to suggest that any nonhuman primate studied to date would rate a 6 [exclusively homosexual] on the Kinsey scale of heterosexuality/homosexuality' " (citing L. A. Rosenblum).

understood the anatomical complementarity or fittedness of the male and female sex organs and the gender-transgressing feminization of the receptive homosexual partner as evidence of homoeroticism's misdirection. Criticisms of homoeroticism, third, as an excess of passion and, fourth, as a form of behavior that even animals have the sense to reject were ancillary to the primary arguments.

Each of the two main arguments contains elements that contemporary assessments of sexuality would find unacceptable. The argument from procreation extends to a claim that all sexual unions entered into must have as their goal the production of offspring. The argument from penetration characterizes the receptive female role as a sign of status inferiority unbecoming to males. Nevertheless, the core of both arguments remain persuasive in a contemporary context, containing as they do a recognition of the fundamental biological complementarity of men and women, a divine and natural stamp of maleness and femaleness that is blurred by same-sex intercourse. Apart from Scripture, the clearest indications as to God's design for human sexuality come from the anatomical fit and functional capacity of male and female sex organs. On the one hand, there is an obvious and "natural" fittedness of the male penis and the female vagina. This fittedness is confirmed not only by the dimensions of the two organs but also by the tissue environment of the vagina (its relative sturdiness against rupture and its cleanliness when compared to the rectal environment), the capacity of both penis and vagina for mutual sexual stimulation (penial glands and the clitoris), and their capacity for procreation. Neither the male anal cavity (the orifice for expelling excrement) nor the mouth (the orifice for taking in food) are likely candidates for what God intended as a receptacle for the male penis.

Passion for persons of the same gender, on the other hand, is not compelling evidence for the legitimacy of same-sex intercourse. Homosexual passion is not supported by any anatomical and procreative complementarity. Further, it is universally acknowledged that not every innate urge should receive societal (let alone divine) approbation.[26] The modern-day attempt to divorce sexual identity from physi-

---

26. One can point to both innate sexual urges (e.g., for multiple partners, children, animals, and siblings) and innate nonsexual urges (e.g., an explosive temper, greed, anxiety).

cal biology [27] is not a sign of the mature socio-scientific wisdom of our age but rather of sophistic folly.

As we prepare to turn to the New Testament texts on homosexuality, it is, finally, important to note not only what these early Jewish texts include in their arguments but also what is missing. The exploitative aspects of same-sex intercourse were not cited by Jewish writers as a fundamental reason for it being "contrary to nature," except insofar as all same-sex intercourse was regarded as inherently exploitative. That same-sex intercourse customarily involved a mature man as the active partner and teenage boys as passive recipients is stated or clearly implied in most of the texts but is not central to the rejection of same-sex intercourse. The focus is generally on the transgender aspect of the intercourse rather than on the age disparity.[28]

Philo did treat at length the deliberate and exploitative feminization of the passive partner by the active partner. Yet he evaluated this as a *further* step in the process of feminization which had already begun when the passive partner made himself "available" for the penis and sexual desire of the active partner. Moreover, in line with the Levitical prohibitions, Philo and Josephus regarded both partners as worthy of death, not just the active partner, because both were willing participants in this gender-bending activity.

The notion that first century Jews, such as Jesus and Paul, would have given general approval to a homosexual lifestyle if they had only been shown adequate examples of mutually caring and non-exploitative same-sex relationships is fantastic. More or different information about same-sex intercourse would not have changed the verdict for any first-century Jew because the anatomical, sexual, and procreative complementarity of male and female unions, in contrast with those between female and female or male and male, would have remained indisputable.

Despite the Hellenistic coloring of the phrase "contrary to nature" and the borrowing of philosophical and moral arguments from Greeks, the understanding of Josephus, Philo, and other Jewish writers of the period is consistent with the twin themes of Scripture that we identi-

---

27. E.g., Halperin, *One Hundred Years of Homosexuality*, 25.
28. The texts in *Sib. Or.* 3 and 5 may be an exception to this rule.

fied earlier. The consistent return to the arguments of the anatomical and procreative complementarity of male and female will be especially important for assessing what Paul meant when he asserted that same-sex intercourse was "contrary to nature," and for our interpretation of his words. In the meantime, however, we turn to Jesus and the task of assessing his views on homosexuality.

3. THE WITNESS OF JESUS

When Christians find a specific teaching of one or more New Testament authors to be unappealing, Jesus is often held up as a counterweight. For example, if many New Testament writers emphasized hierarchical structures in their theology, church polity, and domestic arrangements, Jesus did away with hierarchies. If New Testament writers were disinclined to invert the social order, Jesus proclaimed an ethic that fully included women, sinners, the physically challenged, and gentiles. If New Testament writers surrendered to the bourgeois material interests of their own day, Jesus put a premium on social justice to the poor. If New Testament writers were intolerant of non-traditional forms of sexual expression, Jesus elevated tolerance to the level of a core value, particularly in the area of sexual ethics. After close study of the texts themselves, such contrasts between Jesus and those who followed after him appear simplistic and in need of qualification, but they nonetheless remain fixed stereotypes in the minds of many.

Given such constructs, it is understandable that many proponents of same-sex relationships put a positive spin on the silence of Jesus as regards homosexual behavior. Although there are one or two places where reference to same-sex intercourse is remotely possible,[1] the

---

1. Based on a parallel with a text from the Babylonian Talmud (b. Nid. 13b, see below), it is not impossible that Jesus' reference in Mark 9:42 to "causing one of these little

collective body of Jesus tradition includes no statement to the effect that same-sex intercourse is good or bad. Some combine this silence on the subject with Jesus' embrace of sinners and emphasis on love and conclude that Jesus would not have criticized responsible and loving expressions of homosexual and lesbian conduct. At the very least, they allege, we cannot say with any reasonable degree of certitude that Jesus opposed such relationships in principle.

---

ones to sin" originally referred to pederasty. Cf. Will Deming, "Mark 9.42–10.12, Matthew 5.27-32 and *b. Nid.* 13b: A First-Century Discussion of Male Sexuality," *NTS* 36 (1990): 130-41. "The offense against the 'little ones' . . . appears to be either pederasty or some other form of [heterosexual] child molestation, equivalent to the rabbinic 'playing with children' " (ibid., 134). Schmidt appears to accept the connection between Mark 9:42 and pederasty (*Straight or Narrow?* 93-94). There are, however, several problems with this reading. First, Deming himself admits that "little ones" does not refer to actual children in its Markan context: "Mark seems to understand the 'little ones' in 9.42 as Jesus' disciples, thus ruling out the idea that this verse now refers to pederasty" (p. 138). Second, Mark's interpretation of the "little ones" as disciples is buttressed by similar uses of the phrase elsewhere in Jewish apocalypticism. Zech 13:7 (part of which is quoted in Mark 14:27) mentions the "little ones" against whom God will turn his hand, probably referring in context to the one third of the Israelites who will be severely purified, but not destroyed, at the time of God's judgment (cf. Carol and Eric Meyers, *Zechariah 9–14* [AB; New York: Doubleday, 1993]: 389). CD 19:9-11 interprets Zech 13:7 to refer to "the poor of the flock" who "will escape at the time of visitation." Similarly, *2 Bar.* 48:19-20: "Look at the small ones who submit to you, and save those who come to you. . . . For these are the people whom you have elected." Third, even *b. Nid.* 13b ties in "those who play with children" only tangentially into the discussion of committing adultery "with the hand." Ultimately it interprets the phrase "those who play with children" to refer to "those who marry young girls who have not yet reached the age of child-bearing" rather than pederasts. All in all, the suggestion that Mark 9:42 originally referred to pederasty is possible but not probable.

Another instance that has been cited is Matt 5:22: "But I say to you that everyone who is angry with his brother will be liable to judgment; and whoever says to his brother, *raka*, will be liable to the sanhedrin (council); and whoever says, 'Fool' (*mōre*), will be liable to go into the Gehenna (hell) of fire." A few have argued that *raka* is from the Hebrew *rak* (here with a vocative ending *-a*), meaning "tender, soft, weak, sensitive." According to Greenberg, "the phrase refers to passive effeminate male homosexuals. The case for this reading is strengthened when it is recalled that in Akkadian the syllable *raq* is used as a prefix to denote a woman's name or occupation. It appears in compounded form in the words for a woman, a particular kind of nun, and the female genitals. The Akkadian symbol derives from the Sumerogram for a woman. It has also been suggested that the Greek word *moros* . . . refers to a male homosexual aggressor. This reading makes the threatened punishment far more plausible" (*Construction*, 211; citing: Friedrich Schulthess, "Zur Sprache der

Contrary to the above view, the silence of Jesus on the subject, combined with other factors, makes Jesus' opposition to same-sex intercourse historically probable. Indeed, the word "silence" can only be used in a very constricted sense. Jesus made no *direct* or *explicit* comments on same-sex intercourse, just as he made no direct comments about many other important subjects. In a larger sense, though, Jesus was not silent about same-sex intercourse inasmuch as the inferential data speaks loud and clear about Jesus' perspective. Four points confirm this claim. First, understood in the context of first-century Judaism, it is very unlikely that Jesus would have adopted a fundamentally different stance toward same-sex intercourse, particularly given Jesus' general approach to the Mosaic law. Second, Jesus' appeal to Gen 1:27 and 2:24 in his discussion of divorce (Mark 10:1-12) confirms his embrace of an exclusively heterosexual model of monogamy. Third, Jesus' positions on other matters having to do with sexual ethics were generally more—not less—rigorous than those of his surrounding culture. Fourth, the ways in which Jesus integrated demands for mercy and righteous conduct in his teaching and ministry do not lend

---

Evangelien. Anhang. A. *racha* (*raka*), *mōre*," ZNW 21 [1922]: 241-43; Warren Johansson, "Whosoever Shall Say to His Brother, *Racha*," *Cabirion and Gay Books Bulletin* 10 [1984]: 2-4. Additional support for this interpretation is the use of *malakoi* ("soft ones") in 1 Cor 6:9 and elsewhere in Greek literature to refer to the effeminate, passive homosexual partner. Greenberg toys with the possibility that "Jesus' denunciation of those who speak abusively to others about their homosexual practices, unaccompanied by any condemnation of the practices themselves, implies a defense of those who engage in them" (*Construction*, 211). Actually, it would imply the opposite. A parallel would be Middle Assyrian law A§19, which prescribes the penalty of castration for anyone who spreads unsubstantiated rumors that a certain "comrade" is a frequent object of sexual intercourse with other men. In effect, Jesus would be saying, "To refer in anger to another man as an effeminate homosexual, when you know he is not, is so egregious that it will incur discipline (expulsion?) from the community. There is more than one way to 'murder' a person's character." However, whether *raka* should be given this sense is doubtful. Commentators usually equate it with Aramaic *rêqā'*, which means something like "empty head, blockhead, idiot" (Hebrew *rêq*, "empty"; Syriac *raqa*, used often to call servants), a relatively harmless insult. Cf. the commentaries by Allison and Davies; Luz; Donald A. Hagner, *Matthew* (2 vols; WBC; Dallas: Word, 1993, 1995), 1:116; Joachim Jeremias, "*raka*," *TDNT* 6:973-76, who cites similar interpretations from the Church Fathers; and Str-B 1.278-79, who give multiple examples in rabbinic literature. Jeremias's comment on Schulthess's interpretation is to the point: "this sense is not attested" (p. 974 n. 5).

support for the view that Jesus might have taken a positive or neutral approach to same-sex intercourse. We will now flesh out these four points in greater detail.[2]

I. The Context of Ancient Judaism and Jesus' View of Torah

The univocal stance against homosexual conduct, both in ancient Israel and the Judaism of Jesus' day, makes it highly unlikely that Jesus' silence on the issue ought to be construed as acceptance of such conduct. Jesus was not shy about expressing his disapproval of the conventions of his day. Silence on the subject could only have been understood by his disciples as acceptance of the basic position embraced by all Jews. If Jesus had wanted to communicate affirmation of same-sex unions he would have had to state such a view clearly since first-century Judaism, so far as we know, had no dissenting voices on the matter. Without a clear statement none of his disciples would have made such a logical leap.

Moreover, nothing in the authentic Jesus tradition suggests that Jesus abrogated the Torah during his earthly ministry. According to Matt 5:17-18 (cf. Luke 16:16-17), Jesus states, "Do not think that I have come to abolish the law or the prophets; I have come not to abolish but to fulfill. . . . not one tiny iota or one tiny letter stroke (*keraia*) shall pass away from the law until all things come to pass."[3] At several

2. In his discussion of "Jesus and Homosexuality" (*Homoeroticism*, 118-22), Nissinen unfortunately does not bother to explore the question of whether Jesus was opposed to same-sex intercourse. He should have; it has enormous implications for the overall thesis of his book. He primarily addresses whether or not Jesus was a homosexual, given his singleness and given the "homosociability" of Jesus' relationship with the beloved disciple in John. He draws the obvious conclusion that there is no evidence that Jesus ever engaged in homoerotic behavior with other males. He also discusses the saying of Jesus about those who make themselves eunuchs for the sake of the kingdom of heaven (Matt 19:10-12). He speculates that some of Jesus' followers who renounced marriage may have been homosexuals who were incapable of finding sexual satisfaction in heterosexual marriages. I am not sure what Nissinen's point is here. Nissinen himself acknowledges that inherent in the concept of "eunuchs for the kingdom of heaven" is the requirement of giving up all sexual activity. One can only conclude that the saying gives absolutely no support for same-sex intercourse.
3. Both the interpretation of this passage and its authenticity are hotly debated (many, perhaps most, attribute it to a reactionary Jewish-Christian source). My point in

points, Jesus did prioritize the law's core values and even amended the law by closing loopholes and expanding its demands. This much is clear from the six antitheses that follow in Matt 5:21-48.[4] It is possible that

citing it, though, is similar to Matthew's: however we describe Jesus' distinctive teaching in relation to the Mosaic law, at the end of the day we cannot say that Jesus abrogated the law or any part of it (though he did prioritize some parts of the law over others). The version of the saying in Luke 16:16-17 leads to a similar conclusion: "The law and the prophets were (respected) until John; from that time forward the kingdom of God is being proclaimed and everyone tries to force entry into it (*eis autēn biazetai;* viz., by twisting scripture to justify why they do not heed my proclamation of the kingdom). But it is easier for heaven and earth to pass away than for one tiny letter stroke (*keraia*) of the law to fall" (i.e., the law itself will serve as your judge). (Matt 11:12-13 appears to have split off a portion of the Q saying to form a separate saying about John the Baptist.) Most (e.g., the International Q Project) understand Luke 16:16 to best represent the original Q saying and to mean that the law is of limited temporal duration (i.e., it lasts only until John). But this is precisely what it cannot mean in its immediate Lukan context. Luke 16:17 is quite emphatic: no portion of the law, not even a tiny letter stroke will be rescinded. The sayings before and after 16:16-17 refer to attempts on the part of people to get around the law's core values in order to satisfy their own ungodly desires, whether for wealth or sex. The Pharisees allegedly were trying to get around the law's advocacy of giving away one's wealth to the poor (16:14-15). As the story about the rich man and Lazarus in 16:19-31 makes clear, the rich man and his brothers are without excuse when they fail to give alms, for the instruction to do so is clear in "Moses and the prophets" (16:31). Similarly, men divorce their wives and marry divorced women (16:18), taking advantage of the loophole in Deut 24:1-4 to satisfy their adulterous intent, which conflicts with God's will in making the two "one flesh" and God's expressed hatred for divorce in Mal 2:14-16. Jesus characterizes both cases of willful distortion of Scripture as "forced entry" into the kingdom. Their contrived efforts, however, will come to nought in the end because Scripture itself will condemn their self-serving sophistry on the day of the Lord. Consequently, far from limiting the relevance of the law, Luke 16:16-17 establishes its enduring value as an entry requirement for the kingdom of God.

4. The antithetical formulation "You have heard that it was said . . . , but I say to you . . . ," is due to Matthean redaction in antitheses 3 (divorce), 5 (eye-for-an-eye), and 6 (hate your enemy), but probably pre-Matthean for antitheses 1 (killing/anger), 2 (lust), and 4 (oaths). In all cases the basic content of the teaching contained in the antitheses is drawn from pre-Matthean tradition. Cf. Dale C. Allison, *Jesus of Nazareth: Millenarian Prophet* (Minneapolis: Fortress, 1999), 185-86 (following Bultmann); Luz, *Matthew*, 274-79; Jürgen Becker, *Jesus of Nazareth* (New York: de Gruyter, 1998), 288-89. According to Theissen and Merz, "[T]he meaning of the antithetical form is: 'You have heard that once (on Sinai) it was said (by God) to our forefathers: You shall not kill. But I say to you (going beyond that but not in contradiction to it). . . .' The Torah is not interpreted, not criticized, not done away with, but transcended" (*The Historical Jesus*, 364).

Jesus did not demand the death penalty for certain sexual sins such as adultery and prostitution, although he clearly maintained his opposition to such behavior (cf. below). But at no time did Jesus overturn a specific prohibition of the law, let alone a prohibition of non-cultic, sexual behavior serious enough to warrant the death penalty, which is precisely what he would have had to do with regard to the prohibition of homosexual conduct in Lev 18:22; 20:13.[5] The ban on divorce is not an exception here because the Mosaic law neither prohibited permanent marriages nor commanded divorce; it only allowed divorce. Nor does eating with sinners or touching a leper violate a specific prohibition of the law. The fact that Jesus healed on the sabbath was not a frontal assault on the command to observe the sabbath but rather an interpretation consistent with the humane purpose for which the sabbath law was given.[6] The issue of food laws is more thorny. In Mark 7:15 (cf. *Gosp. Thom.* 14:5), Jesus declares, "there is nothing which goes into a person from the outside which can defile him, but the

---

5. On Jesus' view of the law as one lying well within the bounds of Torah-observant Judaism, cf. esp. the works of E. P. Sanders: *The Historical Figure of Jesus* (London: Penguin, 1993), 205-26; *Jesus and Judaism* (Philadelphia: Fortress, 1985), 245-69; *Jewish Law from Jesus to the Mishnah* (Philadelphia: TPI, 1990); "The Life of Jesus," *Christianity and Rabbinic Judaism* (ed. H. Shanks; Washington, D.C.: Biblical Archaeological Society, 1992), 70-73. For other general treatments: Theissen and Merz, *The Historical Jesus*, 354-72; Joachim Gnilka, *Jesus of Nazareth: Message and History* (Peabody: Hendrickson, 1997), 208-22; William R. G. Loader, *Jesus' Attitude Towards the Law* (WUNT 2/97; Tübingen: Mohr Siebeck, 1997). Although Sanders contends that "Jesus did not think that the written law was wrong and should be repealed, nor did he say to his followers that they should disobey aspects of it," there were "two points where Jesus asserted his own authority in ways that were objectionable or potentially objectionable" (*The Historical Figure of Jesus*, 225). The first is Jesus' commandment to "let the (spiritually) dead bury the (physically) dead" (Q/Luke 9:59-60), which Sanders regards as in sharp tension with the decalogue commandment to honor one's parents. Nevertheless, it was "a one-time-only incident." The second point is more serious: his free association with "sinners and tax collectors." This will be treated at the end of this chapter. Becker is more open to viewing Jesus as one who is willing to violate the cultic requirements of the Torah in view of the overriding realization of God's kingdom; at the same time Becker stresses Jesus' intensification of social ethics, including sexual ethics (*Jesus of Nazareth*, 271-308).

6. A desire to avoid such a misunderstanding may account for Matthew's omission of the saying in Mark 2:27: "The sabbath came into being for the sake of human beings, not human beings for the sake of the sabbath."

things which come out of a person are the things which defile a person." Jesus then privately explains to the disciples "in a house" (a typical Markan redactional motif) what the saying means (7:17-18). Mark adds the parenthetical assertion: "making/declaring all foods clean" (7:19*b*). Mark apparently understood this saying of Jesus to be abolishing all dietary laws. Yet, if the saying goes back to Jesus, it is not likely that Jesus himself would have drawn such a conclusion. Certainly the subsequent disputes in early Christianity over dietary matters are difficult to explain on the assumption that Jesus clearly abolished food laws (cf. Galatians 2, Romans 14). It is probably not accidental that the Matthean parallel strikes the phrase (Matt 15:17); Matthew apparently thought that Mark had overreached himself. Jesus probably intended the saying as a hyperbolic contrast: what counts most is not what goes into a person but what comes out.[7] There is no evidence elsewhere that Jesus abrogated food laws, though it is likely that he diminished their importance relative to "the weightier matters of the law" (Matt 23:23). Since Jesus upheld the law, his silence on the issue of homosexuality indicates his acceptance of the teachings of Hebrew Scripture, which as we have seen is unanimous in its rejection of same-sex intercourse.

Although Jesus does not explicitly refer to same-sex intercourse in extant Jesus tradition, implicit references exist. In Mark 7:21-23, Jesus interprets his saying about what defiles a person as follows: "for it is from ... the human heart that evil intentions come: sexual immoralities (*porneiai*) ... adulteries ... licentiousness. ... All these evil things come from within and defile a person." No first-century Jew could have spoken of *porneiai* (plural) without having in mind the list of forbidden sexual offenses in Leviticus 18 and 20 (incest, adultery, same-sex intercourse, bestiality).[8] The statement underscores that sexual behavior

---

7. Cf. Allison and Davies, *Matthew*, 2.527-31; Sanders, *Jewish Law* (Philadelphia: TPI, 1990), 28; Theissen and Merz, *The Historical Jesus*, 365-67; Loader, *Jesus' Attitude Towards the Law*, 518. Regardless of Mark's view on food laws, he did believe that "sexual immoralities" of the kind outlined in scripture were actions that genuinely defiled a person (7:21-23).

8. In this particular saying, the sin of adultery is listed separately so the plural likely has incest most in view, along with same-sex intercourse and bestiality, probably also fornication and prostitution.

does matter. If Jesus made this remark, he undoubtedly would have understood homosexual behavior to be included among the list of offenses.[9] Admittedly, the arguments against the authenticity of the saying are strong. It is only singly attested in independent sources and it occurs in the context of a private, explanatory discourse (spots often identified with Markan or pre-Markan redaction).[10] But even if Jesus did not utter this precise saying, it is likely that at least at this point Mark correctly interpreted the import of Jesus' saying about "what defiles a person" (7:15) given Jesus' concern for sexual behavior (see below).

The second instance of an implicit reference to same-sex intercourse occurs in Jesus' response to the rich man who inquired about the requirements for eternal life (Mark 10:17-22; cf. *Gos. Naz.* 16). According to Mark, Jesus began by reciting portions of the decalogue, including the prohibition of adultery (Mark 10:19). Given that Philo regarded the seventh commandment against adultery (LXX: sixth) as a rubric embracing the "special laws" against incest, pederasty, bestiality, prostitution, and other matters pertaining to sexual intercourse (*Spec. Laws* 3.1-82), it is probable that implicit in Jesus' embrace of the seventh commandment against adultery was a rejection of all same-sex intercourse. In favor of tracing the incident back to the historical Jesus is the christologically offensive response of Jesus, "Why do you call me good?" (10:18), as well as several characteristic elements of Jesus' ministry and message: the rigorous demand of Jesus' call to discipleship, here to "sell what you own and give to the poor" (10:21); hostility toward wealth; and intensifying the demands of the law to close

---

9. P. D. M. Turner, "Biblical Texts Relevant to Homosexual Orientation and Practice," *CSR* 26 (1997): 441.

10. Such private settings, however, can also be occasions when Mark inserts alternate traditions (e.g., Mark 10:10-12), though 7:21-23 is clearly commentary on the saying in 7:15 (either by Jesus or the early church). Some also add that the use of a vice list demonstrates the Hellenistic origins of the saying; yet vice lists appear in Palestinian Jewish literature as well. Cf. Rudolf Bultmann, *History of the Synoptic Tradition* (rev. ed.; New York: Harper & Row, 1963), 17-18; Allison and Davies, *Matthew*, 2.518-19; Robert A. Guelich, *Mark 1–8:26* (WBC; Waco: Word Books, 1989), 373. Not surprisingly, the Jesus Seminar colors the sayings black: "The Fellows were virtually unanimous in rejecting 7:20-23 as coming from Jesus" (*The Five Gospels* [ed. R. W. Funk, et al.; New York: Macmillan, 1993], 70). Robert H. Gundry believes that the vice list "represents Jesus' teaching" (*Mark: A Commentary on His Apology for the Cross* (Grand Rapids: Eerdmans, 1993), 366.

loopholes.[11] In the case of the rich man, it was not enough that he kept the commandments, though keeping these was an essential prerequisite to "inheriting eternal life" and "having treasure in heaven" (10:17, 21). Even if the story were a later concoction of the post-Easter church, it would still be historically likely that Jesus accepted the commandments of the decalogue as normative and illustrative of a broader sweep of the Torah's legislative authority. Again, while Jesus does not address issues of same-sex intercourse explicitly, his silence can be taken as acceptance of the Levitical standards and, further, what implicit evidence remains bolsters this conclusion. Strong implicit evidence can also be found in the discussion of divorce in Mark 10:1-12.

II. Jesus on Genesis and Male-Female Complementarity

In the discussion of divorce in Mark 10:1-12, Jesus is portrayed by Mark as appealing to both Gen 1:27 ("God made them male and female") and Gen 2:24 ("for this reason a man shall leave his father and mother and will be joined to his wife and the two will become one flesh"). Jesus then adds the comment: "So they are no longer two but one flesh; thus what God joined together, let no one separate" (10:6-9). This suggests that, at least in Mark's view, Jesus accepted the model for marriage and sexual union presented in Genesis 1–2.

Jesus, then, understood that marriage was ordained by God "from the beginning of creation" (10:6) as the union of a man and a woman, not of a man and another man, or a female and another female. He shows no awareness, much less acceptance, of any other pattern—even though no Jew in antiquity could have been oblivious to homosexual

---

11. "Mark's editorial work has gone into the introduction (v. 17a), and for the rest it is accurately constructed and conceived as a unity: the sayings of Jesus are significant only as answers to the questions" (Bultmann, *History of the Synoptic Tradition*, 22). Gundry (*Mark*, 559-69) and Allison and Davies (*Matthew*, 3.40) also defend its authenticity. The Jesus Seminar colors the sayings in 10:17-22 gray, indicating a likelihood that Jesus did not utter these words. Their argument with regard to citing the decalogue is weak: "citing the commandments is scarcely a distinctive statement" (*Five Gospels*, 91). This is precisely the point where, historically, Jesus would probably not have been distinctive in his outlook. The distinctive element in this pericope is that Jesus goes even further in his demand.

relationships among many Gentiles. There was no need for him to comment on whether homosexual unions should be permitted and, if so, whether his stance on divorce and remarriage should apply to them too. The creation texts authorized only one type of sexual union. It would have been a foregone conclusion for him that homoerotic relationships and human-animal unions, both proscribed in Leviticus, were unacceptable. The whole point of Jesus' stance in Mark 10:1-12 is not to broaden the Torah's openness to alternative forms of sexuality but rather to narrow or constrain the Torah's sexual ethic to disallow any sexual union other than a monogamous, lifelong marriage to a person of the opposite sex.

In Gen 2:18-24, "Adam," the human creation from the "ground" (<i>ʾădāmâ</i>), is literally dismembered. His side is split open in order to provide for him the companionship of a complementary being. Marriage between a man and a woman reunites these representatives of the two genders into "one flesh," and is not simply a union of two individuals. The missing part of man is found in woman and vice versa. Sexual intercourse or marriage between members of the same sex does not restore the disunion because it does not reconnect complementary beings. An alternate pattern of sexuality requires an alternate creation myth.

In short, there simply was no place in the Genesis account to accommodate an etiology for same-sex unions, non-exploitative or otherwise. It would be preposterous to suggest that Jesus might have been comfortable with qualifying the worldview of Genesis 1–3 or with entertaining an alternate anthropogony. Jesus' unreserved embrace of this creation account and his bold appeal to it as a means to ending a concession in the Law establishes his commitment to one—and only one—model for sexual reunion.

Can the dialogue in 10:2-9, or something close to it, be traced back to the historical Jesus? Against authenticity only one strong argument comes to mind: single attestation. Yet even the Jesus Seminar acknowledges that a number of singly attested dominical sayings go back to the historical Jesus. Possibly, too, one might argue that the dialogue fits well in the context of post-Easter discussion about the meaning of the independent dominical saying on divorce in

10:11-12.[12] Is there a good reason, though, why the discussion could not have been initiated during Jesus' ministry? To be sure, the question of the Pharisees appears abrupt: "Is it lawful for a man to divorce his wife?" However, such abruptness is not atypical of chreia or pronouncement stories. In any case, the appeals to Genesis 1–2 can be considered apart from the setting in a controversy with Pharisees.[13] Given the authenticity of some sort of saying on Jesus' part forbidding divorce and/or remarriage (see below), it would be strange indeed if Jesus never provided justification for this radical prohibition. It makes good historical sense that when Jesus prohibited divorce/remarriage altogether, it raised the obvious question among either his opponents or his disciples: what about Moses (specifically the allowance for divorce in Deut 24:1-4)? Indeed, it would be amazing if the question had not been raised. It also makes good historical sense that Jesus would have appealed to one scripture text as a way of trumping another scripture text, rather than simply revoking Moses altogether.[14] In 10:5-6

12. The way Mark sets up the two independent traditions (10:2-9, 11-12) suggests the opposite mind-set. Mark presents the saying in vv. 11-12 as a further rationale for Jesus' teaching in vv. 5-9. 10:5-9 asserts *that* divorce is wrong, based upon Genesis 1–2. Mark 10:11-12 gives the reason why: divorce leads to adultery. So, for Mark, it is not just a case of 10:2-9 explaining the saying in 10:11-12 (which it does do by giving scriptural grounds) but also of 10:11-12 explaining the controversy dialogue in 10:2-9. This indicates that 10:2-9 constitutes at the very least an independent *pre*-Markan tradition.

13. Dale Allison speculates that the context not only for the divorce saying in Mark 10:11-12 but also for the sayings about lusting in one's heart (Matt 5:27-28) and getting rid of body parts that cause one to stumble (Mark 9:43-48) has to do with the particular temptations faced by Jesus' disciples. Some disciples may have been away from their spouses for long stretches at a time, in close association with members of the opposite sex and especially subject to sexual temptation. Out of concern for both the reputation of his ministry and the eschatological fate of his followers, Jesus made such pronouncements "to put a damper on sexually unlawful thoughts." As regards the divorce logion, Allison sees his proposal as complementing Mark's setting rather than contradicting it ("Men and Women: Some Interpretive Possibilities (Matt 5:27-28; Mark 9:43-48; Matt 10:11-12)," *Feminist Companion to the Jesus Tradition* [eds. A.-J. Levine and V. Phillips; Sheffield: JSOT, forthcoming]).

14. Cf. CD 4:20-21: "They [= non-Essene Jews] will be caught twice in fornication: by taking two wives during their lifetime, whereas the principle of creation is 'male and female he created them' (Gen 1:27)."

Jesus explains that he is not abolishing the Mosaic law. Moses himself was simply making a concession to human "hardness of heart." But how did he know that? An appeal to the way things were before the fall provides plausible grounds for overriding Moses' concession. The teaching on divorce in Matt 5:31-32, like the antitheses in general, takes a similar approach to closing the loopholes in the Mosaic law, even though an explicit appeal to God's perfect will operative pre-fall (*Urzeit*) and in the coming kingdom of God (*Endzeit*) is not made. Even if the dialogue in Mark 10:5-9 were a church creation, it would likely be an accurate reflection of the kind of reasoning Jesus employed to justify his radical utterance about divorce. Certainly, too, regardless of the historicity of 10:5-9, Jesus accepted the authority of Genesis 1–2 and its sanction of one particular model of marriage: heterosexual monogamous unions.[15]

III. Deconstructing the Myth of a Sexually Tolerant Jesus

The discussion of divorce makes a nice segue into a broader look at Jesus' attitude toward sex. One of the main reasons why proponents of

---

15. Bultmann thought that "the debate [in Mark 10:2-9] certainly derives from the Church; it is set out in an unified way, though use is made of material from the polemics of the Church. The awkwardness of the construction shows its artificiality" (*History of the Synoptic Tradition*, 27). He also acknowledged, however, that it is "probable that the way in which Mk. 10:2-9 sets one quotation of scripture against the other actually goes back to Jesus. For, so far as I know, this was unheard of among the Rabbis. They often enough constructed an aporia out of two apparently contradictory texts of scripture, but only in order to pass on to its solution" (ibid., 49-50). According to Allison and Davies, "we find it hard to imagine that Jesus, given his environment, in which divorce was widely taken to be permitted by the Torah, ever delivered his controversial judgement as a blunt declaration, devoid of argument or any reference to the problem of Deut. 24:1-4. . . . the appeal to Genesis and so to the beginning of things coheres with his eschatological outlook" (*Matthew*, 3.8). In Sanders' view, "I think it highly likely that Jesus also appealed to the order of creation in order to criticize divorce. . . . An ideal world or society will be like paradise before the sin of Adam: the two become one flesh" (*The Historical Figure of Jesus*, 200; similarly, *Jesus and Judaism*, 257: "It is likely on intrinsic grounds that Jesus gave a religious reason for his limitation"). Also favoring authenticity is David R. Catchpole, "The Synoptic Divorce Material as a Traditio-Historical Problem," *BJRL* 57 (1974): 92-127. The Jesus Seminar colors the Jesus sayings in Mark 10:2-9 gray (cf. below).

same-sex intercourse often think that they can enlist Jesus in their cause is that they labor under a popular misconception; namely, that Jesus was far more tolerant on sexual matters than his Jewish contemporaries. The reverse conclusion is likely to be closer to the truth. On matters relating to sexual ethics Jesus often adopted stricter, not more lenient, demands than most other Jews of his time. In other words, his expectations regarding sexual purity, in some respects at least, exceeded the expectations both of the Torah and of traditions prevailing in Jesus' day.

The clearest and most important example of Jesus' intensification of the Torah's sexual ethics occurs in the case of the divorce logion. Scholars universally recognize that Mark's treatment of the divorce issue in 10:2-12 contains a saying in 10:11-12 that has parallels in Q (the double tradition in Matthew and Luke) and in Paul. The material in boldface type represents what can be isolated as the three independent strands of tradition (four, if one counts Mark 10:2-9).

Q/Matthew 5:31-32

It has been said: whoever divorces his wife should give to her a certificate of divorce. But I say to you that **everyone who divorces his wife**, except for a matter of sexual immorality, causes her to be led into **adultery, and** whoever **marries a divorced woman commits adultery.**

Q/Luke 16:18

Everyone who divorces his wife and marries another commits **adultery, and** the one who **marries a woman divorced** from her husband **commits adultery**.

Mark 10:11-12

And he says to them, **Whoever divorces his wife and marries another commits adultery against her. And if she, after divorcing her husband, marries another, she commits adultery.**

Matthew 19:9

But I say to you that **whoever divorces his wife,** not for sexual immorality, **and marries another** commits **adultery.**

197

1 Corinthians 7:10-11

Now to those who have married I give this command, not I but the Lord, that
a wife not be separated from her husband,—
but if in fact she is separated, she should remain unmarried or else be reconciled to her husband
—and a husband not divorce his wife.

The precise content of the saying varies slightly in the different traditions.

(1) In 1 Cor 7:10-11, Paul appeals to Jesus tradition for his instruction on divorce; but he is not necessarily quoting it. He understood Jesus to be forbidding divorce for both husband and wife.[16] Parenthetically, Paul qualifies this tradition, stating that a wife may be separated from her husband if she does not get remarried. In other words, the real issue is remarriage, not divorce. Since this interpretation is reflected in the version of the saying in Q and Mark, it is possible that this qualification is a Pauline paraphrase of Jesus tradition as well. Regardless, Paul does moderate Jesus' position by allowing a believer to divorce an unbelieving spouse if the spouse wishes to have the marriage dissolved (7:12-16).

(2) There is some ambiguity about the original Q version. Both versions agree that a man who marries a divorced woman commits adul-

---

16. Some have argued that Paul has refashioned the tradition to conform to Greco-Roman practice where wives have the right to divorce their husbands. However, Paul's use of a passive verb ("be separated") for the woman is consistent with actual Jewish practice. Although in theory Jewish women did not have the right of divorce, in practice there were indirect mechanisms in place to get around such prohibitions (cf. *m. Ket.* 7:10; 13:10). Not even the version in Mark 10:12, which speaks explicitly of a woman divorcing her husband, is necessarily an attempt at updating the original saying of Jesus to a Hellenistic context. "For Palestine and the East, too, a legal tradition diverging from the majority tradition has been demonstrated according to which women could also take the initiative in divorce; this may be attested in the Elephantine papyri, in the divorces of Herodian wives, and possibly in the letters of divorce from the Wadi Murabba'at (e.g. P. Mur 19), in PsPhilo, *Antt.* 42, 1 and in traces in the Talmud" (Theissen and Merz, *The Historical Jesus*, 362 n. 34; citing Monika Fander, *Die Stellung der Frau im Markusevangelium* [Altenberge: Telos, 1989], 200-57).

tery—a dictum which, if obeyed, would force the divorced woman to remain single the rest of her life. Yet the versions divide on whether a man who divorces his wife (a) himself commits adultery when he remarries (Luke) or (b) causes his wife to commit adultery when she remarries (Matthew). The latter is more likely to be original.[17] However, Matthew also accepted the version in Mark; namely, that a man who divorces his wife and remarries commits adultery (19:9). In any case, the basic sense is that a divorced person who remarries commits adultery. As in 1 Cor 7:10-11, divorce is prohibited but primarily because it leads to remarriage which in turn constitutes adultery. Matthew adds an exception clause based on his interpretation of the motive clause for divorce in Deut 24:1: "except for sexual immorality."[18] Matthew, like Paul, liberalizes this saying of Jesus, apparently

---

17. "Given Luke's fondness for [*heteros*, 'another']. . . , this could be Lukan redaction under the influence of Mk 10.11-12. . . . This possibility is buttressed by the fact that, in chapter 19, the Matthean formulation follows Mk 10.11 and does not conform to 5.32" (Allison and Davies, *Matthew*, 1.528). The International Q Project, however, tentatively accepts Luke's version. According to Robert H. Gundry, Matthew changed the reading to stress "the responsibility of the husband to have compassion on his wife. . . . Matthew has deduced that if a man makes himself an adulterer by marrying a divorced woman . . . , the divorced woman herself also commits adultery by remarrying—and her first husband ought to prevent it by not freeing her" (*Matthew: A Commentary on His Handbook for a Mixed Church Under Persecution* (rev. ed.; Grand Rapids: Eerdmans, 1994], 90). John Nolland accepts the Matthean version as genuine but thinks the sense of the phrase *poiei autēn moicheuthēnai* is "causes her to be 'committed adultery against,' " "causes her to be the victim of adultery." In other words he thinks Matthew's wording is original but means essentially the same thing as Luke's "and marries another commits adultery" ("The Gospel Prohibition of Divorce: Tradition History and Meaning," *JSNT* 58 [1995]: 27-30 [the paraphrases are mine]). While I would not rule out such an interpretation, it faces the problem that in extant literature we have no examples of the passive *moicheuō* being used of a woman having adultery committed against her. Moreover, unlike the version of the Q saying in Luke, Matthew's version makes no explicit mention of the divorced man remarrying.

18. There has been debate whether Matthew means by *porneia* "sexual immorality" in general (adultery, incest, bestiality, same-sex intercourse) or a specific case of such (adultery or incest). A restriction to incest alone is not likely, particularly given the example of Joseph's near "divorce" of Mary in Matt 1:19. A general reference is probable, with adultery being the "high frequency" concern in marital breakups. Cf. the commentaries by Allison and Davies, Hagner, Luz, and Gundry; also, Robert H. Stein, "Divorce," *DJG*, 195; Hays, *Moral Vision*, 354-55; Dale Allison, "Divorce, Celibacy, and Joseph (Matt 1.18-25 and 19.1-12)," *JSNT* 49 (1993): 3-10.

concluding that a strict reading of the saying was too hard to follow and in conflict with scripture (i.e., Jesus must have intended an exemption for men victimized by adulterous wives).[19]

(3) In Mark 10:11, as in Luke 16:18, a man who divorces his wife commits adultery when he remarries. Mark's additional statement in 10:12 about a wife not divorcing her husband reflects a legal situation (viz., women initiating divorce) that Matthew's community apparently did not recognize; hence Matthew strikes the clause. Once more Matthew editorializes with an exception clause for sexual immorality. Matthew also adds an addendum to the story that reflects his awareness of the severity of Jesus' teaching, for the disciples conclude that, if divorce is prohibited, then "it is better not to marry" at all (19:10).[20] The saying in Mark 10:11-12 is set within a controversy dialogue between Jesus and the Pharisees in which Jesus prohibits divorce (10:2-9).

Despite some differences in detail there is basic agreement that Jesus forbade divorce and did so on the grounds that (1) divorce invariably led to remarriage and (2) remarriage while one's first spouse was still alive constituted adultery. In terms of the tradition's authenticity, multiple attestation from early independent sources could hardly be stronger.

In addition to the criterion of multiple attestation, the divorce logion also passes the test of the criterion of distinctiveness or dissimilarity. Jesus' teaching on divorce was virtually unique, not only in relation to the Greco-Roman world but also in relation to his own Palestinian Jewish culture. Deut 24:1-4 presumes that divorce is allowable for a man if his wife "does not find favor in his eyes because he found in her *a nakedness of a thing*" (*ʿerwat dābār*, a sexual indecency of some sort). Despite Mal 2:13-16 ("I hate divorce, says Yahweh"), in first-century Judaism there was general agreement that the husband had a right to divorce. Disagreement between the two great Pharisaic parties (the

---

19. Again, in Matt 1:19, Joseph is regarded as "righteous" not for refusing to consider divorce but rather for trying to end the engagement quietly so as to avoid public disgrace for Mary.

20. Jesus' ensuing remark "not everyone can accept this teaching" refers to the disciples' conclusion that it is better to remain single. Not so, says Jesus. While a single state is preferred ("let anyone accept this who can"), not everyone has received the gift to remain single (19:11-12; a similar point is made by Paul in 1 Corinthians 7).

House of Shammai and the House of Hillel) occurred only over the precise meaning of the phrase "nakedness of a thing" in Deut 24:1. According to a tradition preserved in the Mishnah:

> The School of Shammai say: A man may not divorce his wife unless he has found sexual immorality in her, for it is written, "Because he has found in her indecency in anything" (Deut 24:1). And the School of Hillel say: [He may divorce her] even if she spoiled a dish for him, for it is written, "Because he has found in her indecency in anything" (Deut 24:1). Rabbi Akiba says: Even if he found another fairer than she, for it is written, "and if she does not find favor in his eyes." (Deut 24:1; m. Git. 9:10, H. Danby [slightly modified])

Matthew's exception clause "except on the grounds of sexual immorality" thus reflects an agreement with the Shammaiite interpretation of Deut 24:1.[21] For the Hillelites, a husband had a right to divorce his wife for any reason whatsoever. So far as we know, the only Jews who *may* have strictly prohibited all divorce (and even this is doubtful) were the Essenes.[22]

Since Jesus' alleged opposition to all divorce leading to remarriage was distinctive to his Jewish environment, it is not likely to have been made up. This is especially so because we have evidence from both Paul and Matthew that some early Christian communities found the

---

21. Gundry argues, though, that Matthew is stricter in this respect: "he has not forsaken Jesus' prohibition of a second marriage for the husband, not even though the wife is guilty of unchastity" (*Matthew*, 90-91; this is also the majority opinion in the patristic period). Did Matthew forbid remarriage even for men who divorced adulterous wives? The decision is difficult. Despite the position of the exception clause in Matt 19:9 (between "whoever divorces his wife" and "and marries another"), the most natural reading of this verse is that only men who divorce their wives on grounds other than sexual immorality are guilty of adultery when they remarry (cf. Stein, "Divorce," 193). In favor of Gundry's reading, though, is that Matt 5:32a counts as adultery the remarriage of a woman who was divorced on grounds other than adultery (cf. below). If Matt 19:9 means that a man who divorces his wife on the grounds of adultery can remarry without himself committing adultery, then Matthew had two different rules, one for men and one for women (cf. Becker, *Jesus of Nazareth*, 292). I am not sure what the solution is.

22. According to 11QT[a] 57:17-19 and CD 4:20–5:14 a man is to be the husband of only one wife. 11QT[a] 57:17-19 refers to the king only and may be prohibiting polygamy, not divorce; CD 4:20–5:14 is ambiguous but might be prohibiting divorce.

teaching too severe and so made exceptions for a spouse's sexual infidelity (Matthew) or for a spouse's unbelieving status (Paul). Thus in addition to the criterion of distinctiveness the logion also passes muster on the criterion of embarrassment. The exception-clauses prove the rule, so to speak. Finally, the divorce logion satisfies the criterion of coherence. Jesus' opposition to divorce is consistent with other authentic teachings of Jesus regarding anger and the necessity of forgiveness, the intensified definition of adultery (even lust in one's heart), letting one's "yes" be "yes" (fidelity to marriage vows), not returning evil for evil, and loving even one's enemy—a veritable recapitulation of the antitheses in Matt 5:21-48. So well does the divorce logion satisfy the criteria of authenticity that it is no exaggeration to say that if any Jesus saying preserved in antiquity is authentic it is this one.[23]

Such a conclusion regarding the historical Jesus' opposition to divorce/remarriage is extremely important for gaining a holistic portrait of the historical Jesus. This one position taken by Jesus shatters the stereotype of a figure who was completely accepting and tolerant of the behavior of others, especially the sexual behavior of others.[24]

---

23. Sanders refers to the divorce logion as "the best-attested tradition in the gospels. . . . We can hardly think that the early Christians invented the prohibition: they found it very difficult and had to modify it. . . . We may be certain that the prohibition of divorce on the grounds that remarriage is adultery goes back to Jesus" (*The Historical Figure of Jesus*, 198-200). This is the majority opinion in scholarship today. However, the Jesus Seminar has taken the extraordinary step of giving the divorce logion at best only a gray color. "The Fellows of the Jesus Seminar were almost evenly divided on the question of authenticity." The main reason for rejecting the saying as authentic appears to be: (1) the variations in the transmission of the saying; and (2) that "the roles of Jesus and the Pharisees [in Mark 10:2-12] seem reversed: here the Pharisees view the Mosaic law as permitting divorce, whereas Jesus cites the scripture in support of a more stringent view" (*Five Gospels*, 89; cf. p. 360). The first argument actually supports the authenticity of the saying because it demonstrates clearly the independence of the various sources. Moreover, there is enough common agreement among the various traditions to give us a good idea of what Jesus said. The second argument is simply an instance of personal prejudice based on a cardboard, one-dimensional stereotype of Jesus consistent with a contemporary bias toward sexual freedom. To his credit, John Dominic Crossan, a prominent member of the Seminar, acknowledges the authenticity of the divorce logion (*The Historical Jesus: The Life of a Mediterranean Jewish Peasant* [San Francisco: HarperCollins, 1991], 301-2).

24. Jesus' stance on divorce is also critical for assessing claims Jesus made about himself. Although Jesus did not in this instance (or any other) abrogate the law, he

Rather than adopt a more liberal stance toward divorce, Jesus closed this loophole in the Law.[25] It shows how seriously he took the prohibition against adultery in the decalogue. Not only did he not condone adultery, he also expanded the definition of adultery to embrace the remarriage of divorced men and women. Not only did he uphold the sanctity of the marriage vow, he regarded that vow as absolutely indissoluble[26] and, incidentally, forbade polygamy in the process.[27]

Some scholars have attempted to explain away the contemporary offense of Jesus' teaching on divorce by stressing that it was liberating to first-century Jewish women. In ancient Jewish culture, men had the right of divorce, not women, so eliminating divorce and remarriage

---

clearly took upon himself the extraordinary authority to amend the Torah to render its own core principles more internally consistent.

25. One might make the point that since the contemporary church now adopts a more lenient position on divorce than it once did, the same could be done for homosexuality. See pp. 442-43 for rebuttal.

26. Some scholars prefer to view Jesus' saying about divorce as less a binding community regulation or legal (halakic) ruling and more a piece of moral exhortation (parenesis), an ideal, or intentional hyperbole, with Matthew mistakenly converting it into the former (e.g., Allison and Davies, *Matthew*, 1.532; Hagner, *Matthew*, 1.125-26, 2.550-51; Stein, "Divorce," 197-98). Granted, Jesus was not operating in the context of an institutionalized religious movement with formal sanctions. If this is all one means by the distinction between community rule and moral exhortation, then the position is unobjectionable. However, if one means that Jesus was expressing a view without any disciplinary "teeth," or a view that was little more than an ideal to strive for, then I think this is a misreading. It is likely that Jesus' view on divorce and remarriage would have carried binding authority for his disciples. Divorce and remarriage are not actions that one undertakes accidentally or in the heat of the moment. They require extended deliberation and calculation. Luz is more on target. He rightly notes that Paul, Mark, and Matthew all understood the saying as a command from the Lord whose observance was required by members of the church. "In view of this unanimous finding in early Christianity it seems problematic to charge [Matthew] with making a law of an ethical demand of Jesus. Of course, Jesus has not founded a community with a legal form. But his demand is, so to speak, a 'potential' law for eschatological Israel at the dawn of the kingdom of God. The contrast between law and parenesis does not fit the matter" (*Matthew 1-7*, 303-4). "Jesus possibly formulates a new 'halakah' only at two points": "the prohibition against remarriage"; and "the prohibition against swearing" (Theissen and Merz, *The Historical Jesus*, 362).

27. The divorce sayings express concern about a person having sex with another person while a former sexual partner was still alive. Given that concern, Jesus could hardly have approved of sex with multiple married partners in a polygamous relationship.

withdrew from men the autocratic and arbitrary authority to rid themselves of wives that displeased them. The plight of women, not sexual
purity, was Jesus' main concern.[28] While there is an element of truth in
this position (cf. Mark 10:11: "commits adultery against *her*"), it can
hardly suffice as the main impetus for Jesus' radical new step. In none
of the versions of the saying is there any explicit indication that Jesus
acted out of unilateral concern for women. At the forefront of all the
versions is the issue of adultery, a severe violation of sexual norms. If
his concern had only been for the equal dignity of women, Jesus could
have expanded the right of divorce and declared divorce to be an equal
prerogative of women. Instead, he judged divorce itself to be immoral.
Moreover, he forbade remarriage not only for the husbands who initiated divorce but also for their wives who were victimized by it.[29]

---

28. Crossan, for example, argues that the "opposition here is not just to divorce. . . .
The attack is actually against 'androcentric honour . . .' " (*The Historical Jesus*, 301-
2; following John S. Kloppenborg, "Alms, Debt, and Divorce," *TJT* 6 [1990]: 195-
96); similarly, Theissen and Merz, *The Historical Jesus*, 371; Elizabeth Schüssler
Fiorenza, *In Memory of Her* (New York: Crossroad, 1989), 143.

29. The prohibition against marrying a divorced woman appears only in the Q saying
but it is implied in the Markan and Pauline versions, inasmuch as all the sayings
presuppose that the dissolved marriage is still in force. In God's eyes the divorced
woman and the divorced man are still married to their previous spouses. Hence sex
with a divorced woman, whether in the context of remarriage or not, is the same
as sex with a married woman; it is adultery. The first clause in Matt 5:32 ("everyone who divorces his wife . . . causes her to be led into adultery") gets at the same
point from the side of the woman. If a man commits adultery when he marries a
divorced woman, it follows that the divorced woman in such a relationship also
commits adultery. The wording in Matthew speaks precisely to the question of a
woman who is divorced on grounds other than sexual immorality (as Matthew's
exception clause makes clear); the expression "causes her to be led into adultery"
suggests that the woman had not previously committed adultery. It matters not
why the woman was divorced; a woman divorced for burnt toast would still be committing adultery if she remarried. To spare her this fate, Jesus (according to Matt
5:32a) forbade the husband from divorcing his wife for any reason (except,
Matthew inserts, in cases where the wife has committed an act of sexual immorality; he cannot make her into an adulteress because she has already made herself an
adulteress). In other words, in all the sayings Jesus' fundamental concern starts
with the definition of adultery itself: sex with another person while one's spouse
(former or current) is still alive. The issue of victimization is a concern, as 5:32a
suggests. But it is not the paramount concern. The woman victimized by a husband's frivolous divorce does not escape the charge of adultery when she remarries. In our contemporary context our first concern is the rights of the victim. Jesus'

Some will view Jesus' stringent ethic as unloving. The essence of love in Jesus' understanding, though, was not maximizing free self-expression for others. For Jesus, love involved orienting others away from self-interest and in the direction of the interests of the kingdom of God, inculcating in others a desire to love their comrades with the same love that they extend to themselves. Fidelity to the covenant of marriage and to a relationship still binding in God's eyes, in short, love for one's spouse, takes precedence over sexual self-actualization. Love is a two-edged sword: God grants it and demands it of those who receive divine love.

Jesus' saying on divorce shows how seriously he construed the restriction of sex to one person of the opposite sex within the bond of matrimony. Another saying of Jesus points in the same direction:

> You have heard that it was said, "You shall not commit adultery." But I say to you that everyone who looks at a woman with a view to desiring (or: lusting after) her (*pros to epithymēsai*) has already committed adultery with her in his heart. (Matt 5:27-28)[30]

Not only is it a matter of great urgency to confine sexual intercourse to one's wife, but it is also a matter of great urgency to constrain one's sexual thoughts as well. It is not enough to refrain from fornication and adultery. One must also refrain from actively imagining one's sexual involvement with another woman.

The case for tracing Matt 5:27-28 back to the historical Jesus is not

---

first concern was sexual purity. Correctly, Luz, *Matthew 1–7*, 301-2; Becker, *Jesus of Nazareth*, 293-94. Also, Amy-Jill Levine: "Since Jewish women had marriage contracts which would have made divorce economically prohibitive for most husbands, so strict a teaching was not needed to protect them from being cast aside. . . . it is unlikely that eliminating the possibility of divorce would be beneficial to women trapped in loveless or violent marriages. These injunctions might best be seen as having a theological rather than a social motivation, attempting to reestablish the relationship between woman and man as it existed . . . before the Fall" ("Matthew," *The Women's Bible Commentary* [Louisville: Westminster/John Knox, 1992], 255).

30. Although the phrase "commit adultery" is used, it would be perverse to limit the application of the saying only to the marriage setting. Fornication was not a lesser sin in Jesus' time; virginity was very highly prized. The phrase "commit adultery" does intimate, however, that Jesus was not condemning sexual desire for one's own wife.

as strong as the divorce saying. It is attested only here (though cited also in Justin Martyr, *1 Apol.*, 15.1-4).[31] However, 5:27-28 is consistent with Jesus' broad interpretation of adultery in the divorce saying, as well as with his stress on interior attitude and his penchant for making difficult demands. As Dale Allison has pointed out, the teaching on lust, along with the teaching on murder/anger in the first antithesis (5:21-26) bears structural similarities with the saying about what defiles a person (Mark 7:15; *Gos. Thom.* 14:5) and the saying about attending to the inside of the cup (*Gos. Thom.* 89; Luke 11:39-41 par. Matt 23:25-26). All these sayings start with an accepted teaching or practice which Jesus then relativizes by an appeal to the interior condition. Since the sayings on defilement from within and washing the inside of the cup are often considered authentic Jesus sayings (given a pink rating by the Jesus Seminar, for example), there are good reasons for tracing the saying about an adulterous heart back to the historical Jesus.[32]

---

31. Allison and Davies (*Matthew* 1.522; also Allison, *Jesus of Nazareth*, 176 n. 28) cite the following Jewish and pagan parallels: "I have not had intercourse with any woman other than my wife, nor was I promiscuous by lustful look" (*T. Iss.* 7:2); "Do not look at a woman with a lustful eye" (*T. Isaac* 4:53); "Know that you are an adulterer even if you merely think of committing adultery" (Rufinus, *Sent. Sext.*, 233); one should not commit adultery "either with the eye or with the heart" (*Mek. R. Shim.* 111); "Even he who visualizes himself in the act of adultery is called an adulterer" (*Lev. Rab.* 23:12; *Pesiq. Rab.* 24:2); "Today, when I saw a beautiful woman, I did not say to myself, Oh, that I could possess her. . . nor did I go on to fancy her in my arms" (Epictetus, *Diatr.* 2:18). Luz cites also *T. Benj.* 8:2 ("For the person with a mind that is pure with love does not look on a woman for the purpose of having sexual relations"); *b. Hal.* 1 ("Whoever looks at a woman with [lustful] intention is counted as one who sleeps with her"). For additional rabbinic parallels, cf. Str-B 1.299-301. It is interesting that the comparison/contrast in Matt 5:27-28 is made not with the tenth commandment ("you shall not covet/desire [LXX: *epithumēseis*] your neighbor's wife") but with the seventh commandment ("you shall not commit adultery"). As with the conjunction of two texts from Genesis 1–2 in Mark 10:6-9, Jesus may be combining two commandments "to make perfectly clear the sort of conduct consonant with the Creator's intention" (Allison and Davies, *Matthew*, 1.523), in agreement with developing trends in Judaism (Luz, *Matthew*, 291).
32. *Jesus of Nazareth*, 186-87. Luz believes that "Content deliberations speak in favor of attributing [the saying] to Jesus" (*Matthew 1–7*, 291); similarly, Becker, *Jesus of Nazareth*, 289-91. On the basis of typical Matthean diction, Gundry contends that "the evidence for composition by Matthew is overwhelming" (*Matthew*, 87). Yet, with the exception of *pros* plus an articular infinitive, the words are too common-

It is questionable whether Jesus thought "committing adultery in one's heart" was as serious an offense as "committing adultery in one's body" (the implied parallel). Certainly the community of disciples could do little to regulate the private thought life of individuals in their ranks. "Heart adultery," unlike "body adultery," is less public in its manifestation and therefore more difficult to police. Nevertheless, as the saying which immediately follows the adultery-in-one's-heart text suggests, adulterous thoughts stimulated by sight and touch could, in Jesus' view, get a person's "whole body" thrown into Gehenna (hell).

> If your *right eye* threatens to be your downfall (lit., causes you to stumble, trips you up; *skandalizei*), take it out and throw it away from you, for it is advantageous for you that one of your members be lost/destroyed and that your whole body not be thrown into Gehenna. And if your *right hand* threatens to be your downfall, cut it off and throw it away from you, for it is advantageous for you that one of your members be lost/destroyed and not your whole body go off into Gehenna. (Matt. 5:29-30)

There is a parallel set of sayings in Mark 9:43-48 regarding the hand, foot, and eye, which Matthew reproduces in a more concise form in Matt 18:8-9:

> And if your *hand* threatens to be your downfall, cut it off; it is better for you to enter into life maimed than with two hands to go off into Gehenna, into the unquenchable fire. And if your *foot* threatens to be your downfall, cut it off; it is better for you to enter into life lame than with two feet to be thrown into Gehenna. And if your *eye* threatens to be your downfall, throw it out; it is better for you to enter into the kingdom

---

place in the Greek language to draw any conclusions about Matthean creation. The Jesus Seminar colors Matt 5:27-28 black, indicating that Jesus definitely did not say it, on the grounds that the "injunction against lust occurs commonly in Israelite tradition" (*Five Gospels*, 142). Some continuity with Jewish tradition should be expected—Jesus was, after all, a Jew. It is difficult to say, given the parallels cited above, how radical Jesus was in relation to his own cultural context. The texts cited above, however, cannot be claimed as representing the views of the "common person." Luz sees the distinctiveness of Jesus' message in the context of Jesus' ministry, where male and female followers were brought together in a close working relationship. It is easier not to lust when one is not fraternizing with women on a regular basis (*Matthew 1–7*, 296-97).

of God one-eyed than with two eyes to be thrown into Gehenna, where their worm does not die and the fire is not quenched. (Mark 9:43-48)

The doublet in Matt 5:29-30 may represent an independent (non-Markan) piece of tradition, though certainty is not possible.[33] The association of the expendable eye and hand in 5:29-30 with sexual sin in 5:27-28, along with the close proximity to the divorce text in Mark 10:2-12, suggests that Mark 9:43-48 may originally have had to do with sex as well. The sexual connotation resonates with a similar tradition found in *b. Nid.* 13b.[34] If a sexual connotation was intended, the eye probably refers to a lustful glance, the hand to masturbation, and the foot either is a euphemism for the penis or refers to how one might race toward tempting situations.[35] Three features of the saying point to its authenticity: the theme of giving up all for the sake of the coming kingdom, the offensive nature of self-mutilation for some Jewish circles (cf. Deut 14:1; 1 Kgs 18:28; Zech 13:6), and the use of hyperbole for shock value (which caused concern among Christians who took the saying literally).[36]

---

33. Luz thinks 5:29-30 is derived from Q. Hagner refers to it as a variant tradition. Allison and Davies, and Gundry regard Mark as the source.

34. *B. Nid.* 13b comments on *m. Nid.* 2:1: "The hand that oftentimes makes examination [of the private parts] is, among women, praiseworthy [because it is necessary to determine menstrual cleanness]; but among men—let it be cut off." The commentary includes: an interpretation of Isa 1:15 as a reference to "those that commit masturbation with their hands"; an interpretation of the seventh commandment as prohibiting adultery with the "hand" or the "foot"; and a statement from R. Tarfon that the hand that touches the male member is to "be cut off upon his belly," which is preferable to going "down into the pit of destruction."

35. So Deming, "Mark 9.42–10.12," 130-41; Allison, *Jesus of Nazareth*, 179-82.

36. Cf. Allison, *Jesus of Nazareth*, 187-88; Werner Zager, *Gottesherrschaft und Endgericht in der Verkündigung Jesu* (BZNW 82; Berlin: de Gruyter, 1996), 210-23; Becker, *Jesus of Nazareth*, 59. Luz refers also to the Semitic language background and the double tradition in Matthew and Mark (*Matthew 1–7*, 292). Bultmann accepted the originality of Matt 5:29-30 (*History of the Synoptic Tradition*, 86). Gundry argues that literal self-mutilation is intended; the saying does not contain hyperbole (*Mark*, 514, 525). The Jesus Seminar colors the sayings in both Mark and Matthew gray, largely on the erroneous assumption that Jesus did not proclaim an apocalyptic message. "The context of these warnings is probably the final judgment and the threat of Gehenna (Hell). If so, these sayings do not go back to Jesus." The "radical contrast" appealed to some Fellows of the Seminar. "The majority held that, although the sayings may have originated with

The impression one gets from Matt 5:27-32 is that Jesus took sexual sin very seriously—in some respects more seriously than the prevailing culture in first-century Palestine.[37] He regarded all sexual activity (thoughts and deeds) outside of lifelong marriage to one person of the opposite sex as capable of jeopardizing one's entrance into the kingdom of God. In relation to our own cultural context, Jesus' views on sex represent on the whole a staunchly conservative position. Those who find in the Gospels a Jesus who is a prophet of tolerance, who forgives and accepts all (except, perhaps, the intolerant), regardless of behavioral change, have distorted the historical reality. However, since even such a distorted view contains an element of truth, it is necessary to detour for a moment to discuss those whom Jesus approached in his ministry and what he required of them.

Jesus they have been remodeled to suit the circumstances of the primitive Christian community" (*Five Gospels*, 142, 86).

37. To the sayings discussed above one could add two additional ones: Jesus' pronouncement that in their resurrected state people "neither marry, nor are given in marriage but are like angels in heaven" (Mark 12:25); and Jesus' expression of admiration for those "eunuchs who have made themselves eunuchs for the sake of the kingdom of heaven" (Matt 19:12). Both texts portray a Jesus who is concerned to circumscribe carefully the role of sex in human life. The former indicates that Jesus did not think people would have sex in their resurrected state; sex is only for this age. The latter shows that Jesus extolled the virtues of giving up sex entirely for the pragmatic consideration of devoting oneself to the mission of proclaiming the coming kingdom of God. To be sure, these texts are not in direct contradiction to the positive message about human sexuality in Genesis that Jesus cites in his discussion of divorce in Mark 10:2-9. The joining of man and woman in a permanent bond of marriage is proclaimed by Jesus as God's own doing (10:9). Yet that arrangement will become obsolete when humans are resurrected to angelic form. Even in this age, and all the more as the kingdom of God approaches, God has endowed some with the capacity to forgo marriage and sex altogether (Matt 19:10-11; cf. 1 Corinthians 7). For a careful discussion of these texts, their authenticity as sayings of the historical Jesus, and their contribution to our understanding of Jesus as "millenarian ascetic," cf. Allison, *Jesus of Nazareth*, 172-216, esp. 175-78, 182-85; also p. 53. The categorization of Jesus and Jesus' message to others as "ascetic" has to be used with caution: it has both "yes" and "no" elements. Allison himself acknowledges that Jesus was a "worldly ascetic" or "relatively tame" ascetic like Paul (ibid., 214-15). Certainly Jesus' own unmarried status and his itinerant day-to-day lifestyle would have set him off from his own culture as someone with ascetic tendencies. The same can be said for Jesus' critique of wealth and of storing up earthly treasures, as well as the call to a discipleship of suffering. Allison is right in

IV. Love and Righteousness in the Ministry of Jesus

What makes Jesus' emphasis on a higher ethical standard so remarkable is that it was combined with a vigorous outreach to the "lost sheep of the house of Israel" (Matt 10:6; 15:24). As the parable of the lost sheep intimates, Jesus was willing to take the chance of leaving 99% of the "sheep" unprotected from attack by "wolves" to go after the 1% who were lost (Q/Luke 15:3-7; *Gos. Thom.* 107). Jesus had compassion on the crowds drawn to him "because they were like sheep without a shepherd" (Mark 6:34 par.). He demonstrated concern for Israelites whom he felt to be without adequate religious leadership: those untrained in the law, "sinners and tax collectors," the poor, the persecuted, women, children, the physically challenged, the sick, and those possessed with "unclean spirits" (demoniacs). These were people that Jesus believed had fallen through the cracks, both in terms of receiving instruction regarding upright living and having the opportunity to experience the power of God that delivers. "Those who are well have no need of a physician, but those who are sick; I have come to call not the righteous but sinners" (Mark 2:17; cf. *Pap. Oxy.* 1224). In view of the coming kingdom of God with its attendant judgment on the wicked, Jesus launched an all-out effort to seek and find these "lost

---

not taking the slander of Jesus as a "glutton" in Q/Luke 7:31-35 at face value (contra Funk, Crossan, and others). It is the language of character assassination, and it is not likely to reflect reality. The Qumran sectarians characterized the temple priests and the Pharisees as immoral degenerates. We do not take that language very seriously and we should not take the slander by Jesus' opponents too seriously either. At the same time, this text, as well as the discussion about fasting in Mark 2:18-20, shows that Jesus' ascetic tendencies, such as they were, were not on the same order as those of John the Baptist or even the Pharisees. In some ways, Jesus was more of an ascetic than the Pharisees, in other ways less so. In relation to the freewheeling lifestyle of contemporary Western society, Jesus would certainly be classed as an ascetic (obviously not "the proverbial party animal" that Robert Funk proclaims him to be, as Allison notes). In any case, the sayings in Mark 12:25 and Matt 19:12 confirm that Jesus was not a man who was "sexually liberated" in the modern sense. He was not someone that advocated that people "find themselves" through sexual experimentation with various types of people and unions. Jesus clearly approved of only two forms of sexual experimentation: (1) sexual thoughts and actions directed solely toward one's permanent opposite-sex spouse; or (2) complete abstinence from sexual intercourse and erotic fantasies. Anything else he regarded as abhorrent to the will of God.

sheep," and, like a physician, to heal these "sick ones," thereby reinte-grating them into the community of the redeemed. He also extended to them the proleptic blessings of the coming kingdom through his ministry of healing and exorcism.

The terminology of *the sick* and *lost* employed by Jesus to describe his targeted audience does not encourage the view that Jesus refrained from passing judgment on their moral character. In Mark 2:17 *the sick* does not refer in the first instance to the physically sick who are in need of physical healing but to sinners in need of salvation, including tax collectors (2:15-16). *Healing* implies transformation; transforma-tion implies repentance. Without reform of one's prior sinful conduct there can be no recovery. Jesus came not to affirm the sin of the sinner but rather to restore sinners to wholeness by leading them out of sin.

Similarly, the designation *the lost* implies a deficiency in moral char-acter, a straying from the path of righteousness. *Finding* the lost means returning them to the redeemed community characterized by a holy mode of behavior. Luke 15 contains a series of three parables con-nected by the theme of lostness: the lost sheep (vv. 3-7), the lost coin (vv. 8-10), and the lost (prodigal) son (vv. 11-32). Luke clearly identi-fies the lost as sinners (15:1-2, 7, 10, 13, 21, 30). The lost son is even identified with a dead person or corpse (15:24, 32). In the first two parables, the point is that when a sheep, even one out of a hundred, or a lost coin, even one of little value, is lost a person expends an enor-mous amount of effort to find and restore it. Just so, a father, even over a grossly irresponsible and insensitive son, experiences great joy when the lost son is recovered. In this same manner, God rejoices when the wayward of Israel repent of their sins and renew their covenant rela-tionship.

The addendum to the story of the lost son, the response of the older brother, infers that it is not only the irresponsible and immoral who are lost (15:25-32). Those who react with resentment to the joyous reinte-gration of formerly wayward family members are also lost. A similar point is made in the parables about the vineyard laborers (Matt 20:1-16) and the Pharisee and the tax collector (Luke 18:9-14). These three parables are sometimes interpreted to mean that the very act of impos-ing moral standards on others is wrong. Yet none of the characters in question are criticized for expecting right conduct from others. The older brother's outrage over the squandering of the family fortune by his younger brother is not labeled unjust; the vineyard laborers who worked all day are not maligned for expecting that some work will be required for those who receive pay; the Pharisee is not faulted for regarding as deplorable the behavior of thieves, adulterers, and tax collectors who exploited the poor (Luke 15:11). Rather, these characters are criticized for their distorted self-understanding. The elder brother has to be reminded by his father that "you are always with me and everything that is mine is yours" (Luke 15:31). He was incapable of giving his younger brother a joyous reception because he felt that there was a direct connection between paternal love/favor and years of faithful service. He had forgotten, too, how much he had received and was still receiving from his father. The vineyard laborers who worked all day mistakenly assumed that the landowner had to give each laborer what he or she justly deserved and not a penny more; moreover, that the landowner could not dispense with his own property as he pleased (Matt 20:13-15). The Pharisee had forgotten that, despite all his righteous acts, he was still wholly dependent on God's ongoing mercy. Because he trusted in his own righteousness, he lacked the requisite humility for responding to sinners with compassion rather than contempt (Luke 18:9, 11, 13-14). All had lost the sense of gratitude and humility that flows from an awareness of standing under perpetual grace. They could only begrudge a generous response to others less deserving than themselves. Their sin was not that of expecting repentance from others but rather that of setting up barriers to thwart that repentance.

What was distinctive about Jesus' ministry was not that he refused to make judgments about the conduct of others, or even that he lowered his moral standards. On the contrary, in many areas he elevated those standards. What was distinctive was his incredibly generous spirit even toward those who had lived in gross disobedience to God for years. He expended enormous effort and exhibited great compassion in the search for the lost. Jesus did not wait for the lost to come to him. He went looking for them. He invited them to participate in God's gracious kingdom, extended to them his powers of healing, and entered their homes for table fellowship. He did not approach sinners with contempt or condescension. When sinners responded favorably to his message, they were not treated as second-class members of God's people but welcomed without reservation to the banquet. Jesus joyously welcomed the penitent as if their life had always been characterized by faithful service. There was no probationary period or recrimination for past wrongs and no suspicions about the genuineness of their repentance. Instead, he threw a party for them which celebrated their return. Their mere humble "yes" to Jesus was enough to put their past behind them. In effect, Jesus was declaring a national amnesty from past offenses for all those who followed him. To many observers Jesus had made matters all too easy for the reprobate.

All of this should serve as a wake-up call to those in the church on both sides of the theological aisle. For liberals who think that an aggressive outreach to those on the margins of society entails acceptance without transformation and a diminishment of the church's moral standards, Jesus' ministry provides incontrovertible proof that the church can practice radical love without sacrificing "one iota or one letter stroke" from God's demands for righteous conduct. For conservatives who think that upholding holiness means complete separation from and contempt for the wicked of the world, Jesus' ministry demonstrates that righteousness can be wed with love. When either love or righteousness is sacrificed, the church proclaims a truncated gospel.

As regards the church's response to practicing homosexuals, there must be a willingness to fraternize with them in a spirit of humility and to offer God's forgiveness merely on the basis of a penitent spirit. Such a posture toward practicing homosexuals has nothing to do with changing the church's assessment of homosexual practice as a perversion of the created order. Indeed, it demands such an assessment as a necessary precondition to finding and healing the homosexual. Jesus did not confuse love with toleration of all behaviors and neither should the church. A comparison of two types of stories brings this point home: stories about sexually wayward women and stories about tax collectors.

The truly scandalous component of Jesus' ministry was not his association with the poor, the physically disabled, or even women generally but rather his close contact with "sinners and tax collectors" (Mark 2:15-17; Q/Luke 7:33-34). *Sinners* referred to Jews who were "fundamentally outside the covenant" because they "systematically or flagrantly" transgressed God's law, from the standpoint of the one using the term. It was not a term for the common people.[38] Among the sinners with whom Jesus may have been associated were women known as prostitutes and adulteresses.[39] According to Matt 21:31-32 (with a distant parallel in Luke 7:29-30), Jesus told the chief priests and elders that "the tax collectors and prostitutes (*pornai*) are going into the kingdom of God ahead of you. For John came to you in the way of righteousness and you did not believe him, but the tax collectors and the prostitutes believed him." Here Jesus connects believing prostitutes with John the Baptist, not himself, though by extension one may infer that prostitutes were also attracted to Jesus' message. Luke tells the story of a woman "who was a sinner in the city"[40] who entered the house of a Pharisee where Jesus was dining, bathed Jesus' feet with her tears, dried his feet with her hair, repeatedly kissed his feet, and anointed them with ointment from an alabaster jar she was carrying (7:36-50). The text does not say that Jesus had ever dined with her but does portray Jesus as allowing her to touch his feet in spite of the protests of his host (7:39). Another story, a late scribal insertion into the text of the Gospel of John, tells how the scribes and Pharisees came to Jesus while he was sitting in the temple, bringing with them a woman who had just been caught in the act of adultery (7:53–8:11).[41] In John 4 Jesus at the well of Jacob at Sychar (Shechem?) dialogues with a Samaritan woman who had five husbands and was now living with a man out of wedlock. The scandalous nature of the contact is suggested by the narrator's comment: "his disciples . . . were astonished that he was speaking with a woman" (4:27; her Samaritan ethnicity contributes to the scandal). Although the arguments in favor of the his-

---

38. Sanders, *The Historical Figure of Jesus*, 227; also, idem, *Jesus and Judaism*, 174-211.

39. Luke 18:11 suggests other types of sinners. The Pharisee thanks God that he is not like other people such as "robbers (*harpages*), unrighteous (or dishonest, economically unjust) people (*adikoi*), adulterers (*moichoi*), or even like this tax collector."

40. Precisely what her misdeed was, the text does not say; but it is likely to have been of a sexual nature (fornication, adultery, or prostitution are the obvious candidates).

41. The insertion is made mostly by manuscripts of the Western tradition (notably D, some Old Latin manuscripts). The oldest witnesses and those of the best text family (Alexandrian) do not contain the passage. A few manuscripts insert the material at other points in John's Gospel (after 7:36, 7:44, or 21:25) or after Luke 21:38. Style and vocabulary also speak against Johannine derivation.

torical authenticity of each of these stories are not strong, the fact that Jesus was known to have women followers and to associate freely with sinners provides adequate grounds for believing that some of the sinners affected positively by Jesus' ministry were women charged with sexual sin.[42]

It is largely the influence of these three stories that accounts for the widespread conclusion that Jesus did not think sexual misconduct was a big deal. Do these stories support the weight of such a conclusion?

In the case of the sinful woman who anoints Jesus' feet, it is evident from Jesus' parable about the creditor and two debtors that divine forgiveness of the woman's debts/sins is not an end in itself. Instead, it initiates a new life characterized by intense loyalty and devotion to the one who has forgiven much (7:41-43, 47). The parable of the unforgiving servant in Matt 18:23-35 makes the same point from a different angle. God expects forgiveness to transform the life of the person forgiven. If it does not, the forgiveness is retracted. The woman demonstrates clearly by her actions that she has put herself entirely at the service of Jesus, ready to do whatever he commands. It is inconceivable that this woman, abounding in love for God and intensely grateful for forgiveness, will now continue in whatever activity earned her the notoriety of being a sinner. Luke, who more than any other New Testament author stresses repentance, certainly could not be illustrating that repentance and transformation are non-essential features of the Christian life.

As for the story of the woman caught in adultery, Jesus removes adultery from the list of capital offenses: "Let anyone among you who is without sin be the first to throw a stone at her" (8:7). When Jesus assures the woman, "Neither do I condemn (katakrinō) you" (8:11), he

---

42. Cf. Sanders, *The Historical Figure of Jesus*, 229; Theissen and Merz, *The Historical Jesus*, 371. Kathleen E. Corley makes the helpful observation that, given the slander of Jesus as a drunkard and a glutton, and the sexual revelry associated with pagan banquets, "the image created by such an accusation would . . . include prostitutes of various sorts; courtesans, flute girls and the like. . . . Moreover, tax collectors, as a stereotype of despicable people, were rhetorically connected in Greco-Roman literature with those who trafficked in prostitution, particularly the 'brothel-keepers' " ("Prostitute," *DJG*, 643; cf. idem, *Private Women, Public Meals* [Peabody: Hendrickson, 1993]).

is not saying that neither he nor anyone else has a right to think negatively of the woman's actions. Unfortunately, all too often in our own time this is precisely how the story is heard. We reason: "A woman who commits adultery may have had good reasons for doing so; who are we to judge since we cannot know the circumstances or walk in her shoes? Even if the woman did not have good reasons, we are all sinners and all sin is basically equal." "Casting the first stone" then takes on a whole new meaning. It no longer means a literal stone but rather any critical stance toward a person who commits adultery and remains unrepentant. Such interpretations hopelessly distort the sense of the story. *Condemn* here means to "execute the sentence of stoning," and stoning refers to real stones, capital punishment, not a moral judgment about adultery.[43] The problem with capital punishment is that it is terminal: it does not provide the offender with a second chance to demonstrate repentance. Anyone who has sinned ought to know the importance of being given a second chance; hence, only the one who is without sin has a right to cast a stone. Jesus' rescue of the woman from a fate stipulated by the Mosaic law itself (Deut 22:23-24; cf. Lev 20:10) constitutes an extraordinary gesture of mercy, obviously designed to stimulate gratitude and obedience in the woman. His parting words to her, "from now on sin no more" (8:11), demonstrate two crucial points: (1) Jesus and the Pharisees agree fully on the evaluation of adultery as sin; and (2) Jesus expects this act of incredible mercy, this making alive again of a woman who for all intents and purposes was as good as dead (as with the prodigal son), to deter the woman from ever committing adultery again.

Finally, in the case of the Samaritan woman at the well, it is evident that the dialogue is conceived by the Fourth Evangelist as Jesus' attempt to "evangelize" the woman. The first course of action is not to reform her moral life but to bring her to the realization that Jesus is somebody greater than Jacob who built this particular well, that he is in fact the Messiah, "the Savior of the world" (4:25-26, 42).[44] The trans-

---

43. Cf. Wright, *The Christian Faith and Homosexuality*, 17.
44. The point of comparison (in John's retelling) should not be between Jesus and Jacob, but Jesus and the well, inasmuch as Jesus after his death will become the sole dispenser of the spring of "living water" (= the Spirit; 4:10-15, 23-24; cf. 7:38-39).

formation of the woman is evident from 4:39: "Many Samaritans from that city believed in him because of the woman's testimony." The "convertee" had become the converter. Elsewhere in the Fourth Gospel it is abundantly clear that true faith in, and love for, Jesus leads to a transformed life. "If you love me, you will keep my commandments" (14:15; cf. 14:21). Without such a transformation it is impossible to continue to "abide" in Jesus (15:10).

In sum, the stories about Jesus' encounters with women who were considered sexual *sinners* do not support the conclusion that Jesus was soft on sexual *sin*. He did allow these women to come into close contact with him. He did not fear the stigma attached to associating with such people. He advocated mercy as a means of stimulating repentance and devotion to God rather than support the death penalty. He understood that those who were forgiven the most would stand a good chance of loving the Forgiver the most. Such people made excellent candidates for receiving Jesus' message about the coming kingdom and for obeying his teaching. Jesus forgave sexual sins, like all other sins, in the expectation of transformed behavior. They were to go and sin no more.

Further, Jesus' treatment of sexual sinners was not any different from his treatment of other types of sinners. This becomes clear in the case of a second group of texts: those having to do with tax collectors. The story about the wealthy tax collector named Zacchaeus is the most revealing text as regards how Jesus interacted with tax collectors (Luke 19:1-10). Where the women cited above were marginalized by their sexual misconduct, Zacchaeus was marginalized perhaps because of his collaboration with an oppressive foreign power, but certainly because of the well-founded suspicion that he himself was profiting through extortion. He is a much less sympathetic character than the aforementioned women. Although it is common today to view Jesus as primarily concerned with helping the poor, the offensiveness of Jesus' fraternization with tax collectors is often missed.[45] Few today who would

---

45. Perhaps we have heard a minister compare the tax collectors of the first century with the Internal Revenue Service and its abuses. The comparison is woefully inadequate. The IRS is a branch of the very government we elect; a part of our system of taxation with representation. In addition, the average IRS official is not extorting money from taxpayers and pocketing the excess.

argue that sexual purity was a low-priority issue for Jesus based on Jesus' free association with sexual sinners, would also argue that Jesus was soft on issues of economic exploitation based on his free association with economic sinners.

The parable about the Pharisee and the tax collector ("publican") also loses its offensive and scandalous quality whenever the connection between tax collectors and economic exploitation of the poor is lost (Luke 18:9-14). At the end of the parable the tax collector goes home "justified" in God's eyes, while the Pharisee does not. A typical reaction might be: "Good! The Pharisee is a pompous and judgmental religious prude. It is about time that he gets his comeuppance." Such a reaction, however, would overlook the fact that, as bad as the Pharisee might seem in the modern cultural context (not his own), at least he was not exploiting the poor for his own personal economic gain. When Jesus extols the virtue of the tax collector's humility ("all who humble themselves will be exalted," 18:14), he is obviously not condoning or excusing the severity of the tax collector's offensive behavior. Presumably, the tax collector does not resume his old practice of defrauding the poor after beating his chest in the temple and pleading with God to "be merciful to me, a sinner" (18:13). His penitent spirit is a sign of true repentance. Conversely, the problem with the Pharisee is not his righteous conduct, but rather his self-righteous attitude. Jesus is lifting up the one of the two who has the best chance of leaving the temple with a heart open to God's demands for human compassion.

It is not surprising that when Jesus invited himself to Zacchaeus's home, "all who saw it began to grumble . . . , 'He has gone to be the guest of one who is a sinner' " (19:7). What is crucial for our purposes is that Jesus' fraternization with Zacchaeus clearly does not convey Jesus' acceptance of Zacchaeus's behavior. Jesus exclaimed that "Today salvation has come to this house" only after Zacchaeus had announced his intention to give half of his possessions to the poor and to pay back four times as much of whatever he had defrauded others (19:8-9; cf. 3:12-13).

The concluding words to the story about Zacchaeus, "the Son of Man came to seek out and to save the lost" (19:10), apply equally well to the stories about women sinners. We can apply these same words to our ministries to homosexual persons. In the true spirit of Jesus, to seek and to save practicing homosexuals does not mean confirming their homosexual fantasies or conduct. It means actively seeking out and sharing a meal with them, taking the message of the kingdom to them, and demonstrating through our own interest in them that God values them. It also means remembering our differences from Jesus, knowing that we too are sinners, numbered among those whom Jesus has sought out, recipients of his forgiveness. This is the difficult work of reconciliation, which avoids the two easy paths of toleration and isolation.

The passages discussed above seem, at the very least, to imply that Jesus expects those whom he forgives to repent, leaving behind forever their sinful behavior. E. P. Sanders, however, contests this reading. He argues that the scandal of Jesus' association with the sinners/wicked of Israel cannot be accounted for if the latter followed the normal channels for expressing repentance. His argument requires an extended response. He writes:

> It is not that Jesus disliked repentance and thought that people should never feel remorse and pray for forgiveness. He favoured all this. . . . But . . . Jesus is not to be defined as a preacher of repentance. . . . he was not a repentance-minded reformer. . . . Jesus was a friend of tax collectors and sinners—not of former tax collectors and sinners. . . . Jesus, I think, was a good deal more radical than John. . . . Did he hope that they would change their ways? Probably he did. But "change now or be destroyed" was not his message, it was John's. Jesus' was, "God loves you."[46]

According to Sanders, Luke is primarily responsible for the picture of Jesus as a preacher of repentance. Repentance was at best only a minor theme in Jesus' message (Q/Luke 10:10-15 and 11:29-32; Matt 21:31-32; Luke 13:2-5).

What are we to make of Sanders's contention?[47] Was repentance essential for "sinners and tax collectors" in order to be a follower of

---

46. *The Historical Figure of Jesus*, 232-36. See also idem, *Jesus and Judaism*, 206-10. With many scholars, Sanders attributes the summaries in Mark 1:15; 6:12, which refer to repentance as a hallmark of Jesus' message, to Markan redaction.

47. For critiques, cf. Dale Allison, "Jesus and the Covenant: A Response to E. P. Sanders," *JSNT* 29 (1987): 57-78 (reprinted in *The Historical Jesus* [eds. C. A. Evans and S. E. Porter; Sheffield: Academic Press, 1996], 61-82); Bruce Chilton, "Jesus and the Repentance of E. P. Sanders," *TynBul* 39 (1988): 1-18.

Jesus and/or inherit the coming kingdom of God? The conclusion appears inescapable that Jesus did think so. Part of the problem with Sanders's theory is that a discussion of the place of repentance in Jesus' message cannot be limited to the actual occurrence of the word. In many different ways besides the explicit sayings given above, Jesus' teachings make clear that repentance, transformation, and obedience to the will of God are essential for salvation; without them, judgment and destruction ensue.[48]

Most would agree with Sanders that Jesus prioritized some elements of the law above others and, in cases of internal conflict within the law, the core values took precedence. Nevertheless, this is not the same thing as asserting that obedience to the law was of secondary importance. For example, when Jesus stated that whoever did not "hate" his parents could not be his disciple (Q/Luke 14:26; Gos. Thom. 55), he was not saying that the fifth commandment to honor one's parents had been overturned. Indeed, taken at face value, such an interpretation

---

48. For example, only those who do the will of God belong to Jesus' family and will enter the kingdom (Mark 3:34-35; Gos. Thom. 99). The door to eternal life is narrow and few will find it; many who knock on the door at the end will be turned away with the words "I do not know you" (Q/Luke 13:23-27). The weeds will be separated from the wheat and thrown into the fire (Matt 13:24-30, 36-43; Gos. Thom. 57:1-4); the bad fish in the net will be thrown out (Matt 13:47-50; Gos. Thom. 8); salt that loses its taste will be thrown out (Q/Luke 14:34-35; Mark 9:48-50); the goats will be separated from the sheep (Matt 25:31-46). The person that does not do what Jesus says is like a person who builds a house on sand; such a person faces destruction (Q/Luke 6:49). Those who want to follow Jesus must take up their cross and deny themselves; otherwise, they will lose their lives (Mark 8:34-37; Q/Luke 17:33; John 12:25; Gos. Thom. 55:2). Those who do not do anything with the investment God gave them will have even the little they do have taken away (Q/Luke 19:11-27; cf. Mark 4:25; Gos. Thom. 41). The coming of the Son of Man will precipitate cataclysmic destruction of the wicked as in the days of Noah and Lot (Q/Luke 17:26-27; Luke 17:28-29). Those who are not awake or ready when the Son of Man returns will be destroyed (Q/Luke 12:39-40, 42-48; Matt 25:1-13; Gos. Thom. 21:5; cf. Gos. Thom. 79; Luke 11:27-28). The coming Son of Man will be ashamed of, and deny, anyone ashamed of Jesus "in this adulterous and sinful generation" (Mark 8:38; Q/Luke 12:8-9). For discussions of the theme of judgment in Jesus' teaching, cf. Marius Reiser, Jesus and Judgment (Minneapolis: Fortress, 1997); Becker, Jesus of Nazareth, 53-80; Allison, Jesus of Nazareth, 46 n. 142, 102-22; Theissen and Merz, The Historical Jesus, 264-69 ("All in all, there is no reason to deny that Jesus preached judgment. The tradition of this is too broad"), 377 ("Jesus' eschatological ethic [is] an ethic of repentance").

would violate Jesus' own elevation of the command to love one's neighbor (Lev 18:19), not to mention love of enemy. Jesus was simply recognizing that love of God is the first and greatest commandment, trumping all other duties, even filial duties (though compare the caution in Mark 7:9-13 against using religious devotion as an excuse for violating the fifth commandment). Two or more rulings of the Mosaic law could come into conflict in any given situation and require one to arbitrate in favor of the central values of the law.

Jesus was willing to relax some elements of the law in favor of intensifying others and did so in ways that troubled some of his contemporaries. Some requirements, particularly those commonly described as ritual or cultic in nature (sabbath law, sacrifice, purity requirements), took a back seat to the two central commandments to love God and neighbor (Mark 12:28-31). However, the former were far from being abolished. Jesus also displayed extraordinary generosity and compassion to sinners in order to win them over to the kingdom. At the same time he intensified the law's demand in a number of areas, for example: (1) sexual ethics (though relaxing the death penalty); (2) love of neighbor, stranger, and enemy; (3) forgiving others of debts/sins, not remaining angry at or slandering one's brother or sister; (4) independence from material possessions, giving to the poor; (5) telling the truth, not swearing by oath; (6) humble service of others, surrendering desires for status and honor; and (7) not being ashamed of Jesus, willingness to be persecuted for his sake. In most of these areas, we have sayings of Jesus indicating that failure to comply leads to exclusion from the kingdom of God. Given these intensified demands and the eschatological penalty attached to violators, it is difficult to agree that Jesus "was not a repentance-minded reformer." The specific vocabulary of repentance *may* not have been as prominent in Jesus' teaching as it was in that of John the Baptist; and John *may* not have cozied up to the wicked as much as Jesus did.[49] Nevertheless, to characterize Jesus' message as "God loves you," in contrast to John's proclamation

---

49. In the view of Theissen and Merz, "whereas John the Baptist lived in expectation of an imminent end . . . , in which repentance could only be shown only [*sic*] by the symbolic action of baptism, for Jesus God grants time for an ethical proof [of repentance]" (*The Historical Jesus*, 377).

of "change or be destroyed" is a tremendous oversimplification. There are plenty of sayings in the Jesus tradition, many of them multiply attested, which make quite clear that the latter view, "change or be destroyed," was a staple of Jesus' teaching.

So while it is true that the most important thing for inclusion in the kingdom was "accepting Jesus and following him," it is not possible to drive a wedge between Jesus' message and the Mosaic law. It is not likely that Jesus only "hoped" his followers "would change their ways." To some extent Sanders's point that Jesus did not require repentance "as normally understood" is valid. The charge that Jesus was "a friend of tax collectors and sinners" implies that Jesus did not go about securing the repentance of sinners in ways that others found socially acceptable. Possibly his methods did not conform to Pharisaic oral law. Yet Sanders goes further in suggesting that Jesus did not require tax collectors to "do what the law stipulates in order to become righteous." How does he know that? Sanders acknowledges that Zacchaeus exceeds the demands of the law in his willingness to pay back four times as much to those he defrauded (Luke 19:8; no mention of sacrifice is made) but he regards the whole account as imaginative. He admits that Jesus told the healed leper to show himself "to the priest and offer for your cleansing what Moses commanded" (Mark 1:44) and that he commanded that anyone angry with a brother or sister should first be reconciled "and then come and offer your gift" (Matt 5:24). Yet he treats these texts as anomalies. The only narrative about Jesus' association with tax collectors, besides the Zacchaeus story, is Mark's account of the call of Levi the tax collector and of Jesus eating at Levi's home with other tax collectors (Mark 2:14-17). Sanders points out that nowhere in this text does it say that Jesus required the tax collectors to repay those defrauded, add a 20% fine, sacrifice a ram, and give up shady practices.

Strictly speaking, Sanders is correct, but we can hardly expect the story to tell us every detail. Jesus' parting line that those who are sick need a physician (2:17) implies that moral transformation was Jesus' objective.[50] I do not know whether in every single encounter with a tax

---

50. Allison's observation is apt. "How often do the Gospel narratives really give opportunity for the notice that Jesus demanded restitution be made by 'sinners'? I count only two: the pericope of the tax collector in Mk 2.13-17 par. and the account of Zacchaeus. Of these, one does refer to restitution and the other simply passes over

collector Jesus required them to go through the entire course of repentance prescribed in the law. I suspect that he did but I cannot prove it; neither can Sanders disprove it. Sanders's position is supported by the fact that Jesus, consistent with trends in his own time, seems not to have advocated the death penalty for adultery (this is likely even if the story of the woman caught in adultery is fictional). Yet how might Jesus have reacted if prostitutes continued to prostitute themselves or tax collectors continued to grow wealthy by fleecing the poor *after* they had begun following him?

As regards prostitutes who continued to ply their trade: We know that Jesus thought that if a person remarried while the first spouse was alive such a person committed adultery. The inference here is that sex with more than one person currently alive is an egregious sin. Is it conceivable that Jesus denied married couples their lawful right to divorce and remarry while at the same time permitting prostitutes who followed him to continue to have unlawful sex with many strangers, and for money? What would be the reasoning here? Jesus is very concerned about adultery, even expanding its definition and declares that one's eschatological fate hinges on sexual purity. Is it likely, then, that he would allow active prostitutes among the ranks of his followers? Jesus' opinion about divorce and remarriage is as historically verifiable as anything we know about Jesus. Sanders, however, is only guessing when he states that "Jesus did not want the wicked to remain wicked in the interim, but he did not devise a programme that would enable tax collectors *and prostitutes* to make a living in less dubious ways."[51] This guess is not easily harmonized with Jesus' known positions on sexual ethics.

As regards tax collectors who continued to exploit the poor, we know that Jesus believed that amassing wealth could be an impediment to entering the kingdom of God—indeed, making it almost impossible for

it in order to address more pressing topics. Thus the alleged absence of evidence on the issue at hand may be due to the nature of our sources, not the nature of Jesus' ministry" ("Jesus and the Covenant," 70).

51. *The Historical Figure of Jesus*, 234 (my emphasis). Whether Jesus would have insisted that tax collectors who followed him give up their occupation is not clear. Unlike prostitution, tax collection (at least collecting customs duties) was not an inherently evil practice and Jesus did instruct his followers to pay taxes to the emperor (Mark 12:13-17; *Gos. Thom.* 100; *Eg. Gos.* 3).

the rich to be saved. We know too that Jesus sometimes advocated that his followers sell all they had and give to the poor in order to inherit the coming kingdom. Finally, we know from the beatitudes and other Jesus traditions that Jesus sided squarely with those who were materially oppressed. Yet Sanders would have us believe that, although Jesus certainly did not approve of tax collectors profiting from the misery of the poor, he could live with their ongoing exploitation of them. How can Jesus have railed against outsiders for failing to be generous with their resources and yet not have reined in his own followers who did much worse? It defies common sense. Furthermore, the Lord's Prayer and the parable of the unforgiving servant clearly demonstrate that "debt" forgiveness of others is essential to remaining under God's forgiveness, while Jesus' insistence on dispensing with oaths emphasizes the necessity of telling the truth in all occasions. How could a tax collector who followed Jesus extort money through threats, lies, and underhanded dealings without violating with impunity these basic elements of Jesus' teaching? Jesus' whole proclamation of the coming kingdom of God presupposes radical obedience to the will of God the King.

The key argument that Sanders employs for justifying his conclusion that Jesus did not insist on repentance is that other Jews would not have opposed Jesus if Jesus had made repentance mandatory among his followers. Can the offense caused by Jesus' association with the poor be explained in any other way? It can. It is possible that Jesus did not in all cases first approach those who needed to repent with a call to repentance. He ate with them. He also stressed the coming kingdom of God, God's special invitation to the wicked and outcasts of society, and the fact that in many ways the sinners might be in a better position to receive God's rule than the self-righteous and arrogant. It *may* also be the case that in *some* circumstances he took a few shortcuts by not insisting that a sacrifice be offered or a fine paid. This is no more than a possibility, certainly not a probability. Moreover, he spent most of his time dealing with the wicked, not hanging out with the religious authorities of the day. The whole program would have looked subversive to those outside his circle. Would not such an aggressive outreach to the wicked, along with the implied criticism of the self-righteous, be enough to generate the criticism of Jesus?

Slander is not usually renowned for its accuracy. We should expect the criticism of Jesus' association with the wicked to be exaggerated. The reasoning might have gone something like this: "Jesus is arrogating to himself a level of authority to forgive sins that we find offensive. He is spending an inordinate amount of time with shady characters. Why is it that such people are flocking to him and not to us? He *must* be cutting corners. He *must* be affirming their wicked ways." We find a similar slander in the case of Paul: Paul allegedly advocated that people should "do evil things in order that good things might come" (Rom 3:9). Yet we know that Paul did not adopt such a position. Why could Jesus' opponents not have drawn similarly false conclusions about Jesus' neglect of repentance for the wicked?

Sanders's position on Jesus and repentance is a curiosity in relation to his view on Jesus and eschatology. Sanders has always insisted that Jesus maintained an apocalyptic worldview. An integral part of his argument for an apocalyptic Jesus is the fact that both John the Baptist and the early church clearly proclaimed a coming kingdom.

> What moves the expectation of a [coming, apocalyptic] new order from being a mere possibility to a higher status, a meaning that we may confidently attribute to Jesus, is that this is what John the Baptist thought and this is what Jesus' followers thought after his death. Jesus must fit his context: his followers could not have misunderstood him entirely.[52]

The question is, why does Sanders not adopt the same approach to the issue of repentance? Both John the Baptist and the early church clearly proclaimed a gospel of repentance. Moreover, as with apocalyptic sayings, there are sayings of Jesus throughout the various strata of tradition that link failure to reform with eschatological destruction. Indeed, the two themes, apocalypticism and "change your ways or die," are closely connected. In early Jewish and Christian literature, we never find the former without the latter.

In conclusion, there is no good evidence that Jesus would have permitted followers to commit adultery, get divorced and remarried, prostitute themselves, have sex with animals, or have sex with members of the same sex, just as there is no good evidence that Jesus would have allowed tax collectors who claimed to be his disciples to continue to

---

52. "The Life of Jesus," 62.

exploit others for their own material gain. The evidence we do have strongly suggests that Jesus believed that people who did not repent of sexual immorality or economic exploitation would not have a place in the coming kingdom of God. Probably he would have asked followers who persisted in such conduct to repent; if they did not repent, he likely would have made clear to them that they were no part of his movement.

Before closing the discussion of love and righteousness in Jesus' ethics, it is necessary to say something about the parable of the Good Samaritan (Luke 10:28-35) since appeal to this parable is often made by those attempting to legitimate same-sex intercourse in the church. Advocates of homosexual practice contend that the homosexual in the church is the new "Samaritan" in our midst, whom we must recognize as our "neighbor."[53] There is no question that such an argument has a certain appeal. However, the parable, certainly in its present Lukan context (10:25-29, 36-37), does not condone a homosexual lifestyle any more than it does other forms of sexually immoral conduct such as adultery, incest, and bestiality. Rather, it forces the hearer to reconceptualize an "enemy" into a "neighbor."

In its present context the parable expands on the meaning of "neighbor" put forward by the lawyer who asks "Who is my neighbor?" (10:29). The latter seeks to restrict the meaning of the word so that he might claim fulfillment of Lev 19:18 in spite of his hostility to certain groups of people such as the Samaritans. Jesus broadens the lawyer's perspective by reorienting his angle of vision. Instead of asking the question "Who is my neighbor?" from a vantage point of security, the lawyer is taught to ask the question from the vantage point of one lying half-dead by the side of the road. Then the answer will be "A neighbor is one who could potentially offer aid to you during your hour of greatest need." That is the person whom one ought to love as oneself. One is to identify not with the "good Samaritan" but with the person lying half-dead. The command to "Go and do likewise" (10:37b) is not a com-

<hr />

53. Cf., *inter alios*, Herman C. Waetjen, "Same-Sex Sexual Relations in Antiquity and Sexuality and Sexual Identity in Contemporary American Society," *Biblical Ethics and Homosexuality*, 114; Scanzoni and Mollenkott, *Is the Homosexual My Neighbor?*, ch. 1 ("Who Is My Neighbor?") and ch. 3 ("The Homosexual as Samaritan"); Edwards, *Gay/Lesbian Liberation*, 128-9.

mand to become a neighbor to another instead of asking "Who is my neighbor?" It is a command to show the same kind of mercy to a hated Samaritan that could be shown to oneself by a neighborly Samaritan in one's time of crisis (cf. 10:37*a* where the Samaritan is identified as "the one who showed him mercy"). In short, the parable is a brilliant visualization of the Golden Rule. The lawyer should do to the Samaritan as he would have the Samaritan do to him.[54]

Jesus was not telling the lawyer to affirm the Samaritan's belief system. The Samaritan sect rejected the Davidic covenant, denied that Jerusalem was the holy mountain, and dismissed the canonical authority of the Prophets. To the Samaritan worldview as represented by the woman in John 4:22, the Johannine Jesus responds, "You worship what you do not know; we worship what we know, for salvation is from the Jews." Nor was Jesus stating that whatever lifestyle the Samaritan adopted was to be treated as acceptable. He was asserting that the lawyer should respond to the Samaritan in love, not hate, acting with as much vigor in the Samaritan's best interest as he would be inclined to act in his own self-interest. In the contemporary case of the homosexual that means doing what is best for the homosexual, not necessarily what the homosexual lobby thinks is best. In other words, Christians should treat the homosexual as a friend to be converted over to the path of life, not as an enemy to be consigned to the path of death.

V. Conclusion

Jesus did not overturn any prohibitions against immoral sexual behavior in Leviticus or anywhere else in the Mosaic law. He did not regard sexual ethics as having diminished importance in relation to other demands of the kingdom. It is highly unlikely that he would have held some sort of secret acceptance of homosexuality in the face of uniform opposition within the Judaism of his day. Clearly, he did not adopt more liberal positions on other matters of sexual ethics such as divorce and adultery. Instead, he was more demanding than the Torah, not less. He would have understood the tension between his affirmation of

---

54. Cf. my article, "A Second Look at Two Lukan Parables: Reflections on the Unjust Steward and the Good Samaritan," *HBT* 20 (1998): 1-11.

the model of male-female union in Genesis 1–2 and the alternative model presented by same-sex unions. Consequently, the idea that Jesus was, or might have been, personally neutral or even affirming of homosexual conduct is revisionist history at its worst.

The portrayal of a Jesus as a first-century Palestinian Jew who was open to homosexual practice is simply ahistorical. All the evidence leads in the opposite direction. Why, then, did Jesus not make an explicit statement against homosexual conduct? The obvious answer is that Jesus did not encounter any openly homosexual people in his ministry and therefore had no need to call anyone to repentance for homosexual conduct. He also did not address other sexual issues such as incest and bestiality, but that hardly indicates a neutral or positive stance on such matters. What is clear from the evidence that the texts do offer is that the historical Jesus is no defender of homosexual behavior. To the contrary, Jesus, both in what he says and what he fails to say, remains squarely on the side of those who reject homosexual practice. At the same time, the model of Jesus' behavior toward sexually immoral people can be compared with the model of Jesus' behavior toward those who routinely exploit others for economic gain. The church can and should recapture Jesus' zeal for all the "lost" and "sick" of society, including those engaged in homosexual practice. Concretely, this means visiting their homes, eating with them, speaking and acting out of love rather than hate, communicating the good news about God's rule, throwing a party when they repent and return home, and then reintegrating them fully into communities of faith.

4. THE WITNESS OF PAUL AND DEUTERO-PAUL

As we have seen, the Old Testament is unanimous in its rejection of homosexual practice. So, too, are the Jewish authors in the centuries just before and after Jesus' birth. These are important witnesses for Christians to consider in determining the church's current moral stance, but they are not by themselves determinative. Jesus did not speak directly to the issue. However, he confirms the authority of the Old Testament witness against same-sex intercourse both in his silence and in related teachings. Christian teaching has a firm foundation but awaits additional articulation. It is left, then, to Paul to provide clear instruction for the churches of his day, and ours, on same-sex intercourse. It is to Paul that we now turn and, in particular, the key texts of Rom 1:24-27 and the vice lists in 1 Cor 6:9 and 1 Tim 1:10.

I. Romans 1:24-27

With good reason, Rom 1:24-27 is commonly seen as the central text for the issue of homosexual conduct on which Christians must base their moral doctrine. This is true for several reasons. It is the most substantial and explicit discussion of the issue in the Bible. It is located in the New Testament. It makes an explicit statement not only about same-sex intercourse among men but also about lesbianism. And it occurs within a substantial corpus of material from a single writer, which allows the interpreter to properly contextualize the writer's stance on homosexuality. Rom 1:24-27 is also the most difficult text for proponents of homosexual behavior to overturn. My own translation, along with translation notes, follows immediately. In the remainder of the section, I interpret these verses in relation to Paul's larger corpus and in response to the interpretative strategies of those who seek to defend homosexual practice despite Paul's clear rejection of this behavior.

Translation and Translation Notes[1]

[24]Therefore (i.e., because of human preference for idols over the living God), in the context of these desires of their hearts, God gave them over

---

1. In addition to the standard lexicons (LSJ, BAGD, MM, Zerwick-Grosvenor, *EDNT, NIDNTT, TDNT,* and *TLNT*), standard NT translations were consulted (RSV, NRSV, NAB, NJB, NEB, REB, NIV, NASB, ASV, KJV, NLT, CEV, and MOFFATT) and numerous commentaries: Martin Luther, *Lectures on Romans* (trans. W. Pauck; LCC; Philadelphia: Westminster, 1961 [German original, 1516]); John Calvin, *The Epistles of Paul the Apostle to the Romans and to the Thessalonians* (trans. R. MacKenzie; Grand Rapids: Eerdmans, 1960 [1st Latin ed., 1540]); Charles Hodge, *Commentary on the Epistle to the Romans* (rev. ed.; New York: Garner, 1882 [1835, 1864²]); Heinrich A. W. Meyer, *Critical and Exegetical Handbook to the Epistle to the Romans* (New York: Funk & Wagnalls, 1884 [German original, 1872]); Frederic Godet, *Commentary on St. Paul's Epistle to the Romans* (vol. 1; Edinburgh: T. & T. Clark, 1883); William Sanday and Arthur C. Headlam, *A Critical and Exegetical Commentary on the Epistle to the Romans* (ICC; 4th ed.; Edinburgh: T. & T. Clark, 1900); Theodor Zahn, *Der Brief des Paulus an die Römer* (KNT; Leipzig: A. Deichert, 1910); Karl Barth, *The Epistle to the Romans* (6th ed.; London: Oxford University Press, 1933 [German original, 1918]); Hans Lietzmann, *An die Römer* (HNT; Tübingen: Mohr [Siebeck], 1928); C. H. Dodd, *The Epistle of Paul to the Romans* (MNTC; New York: Harper, 1932); Adolf Schlatter, *Romans: The Righteousness of God* (Peabody, Mass.: Hendrickson, 1995 [German original, 1935]); Anders Nygren, *Commentary on Romans* (Philadelphia: Fortress, 1949); P. M.-J. Lagrange, *Saint Paul Épitre aux Romains* (Ebib; Paris: J. Gabalda, 1950); Otto Michel, *Der Brief an die Römer* (KEK; 5th ed.; Göttingen: Vandenhoeck & Ruprecht, 1955, 1978⁵); Otto Kuss, *Der Römerbrief* (vol. 1; RNT; Regensburg: Friedrich Pustet, 1957); Franz J. Leenhardt, *The Epistle to the Romans* (Cleveland: World Publishing, 1961 [French original, 1957]); C. K. Barrett, *The Epistle to the Romans* (rev. ed.; BNTC; Peabody: Hendrickson, 1957, 1991²); John Murray, *The Epistle to the Romans* (NICNT; Grand Rapids: Eerdmans, 1959); Karl Barth, *A Shorter Commentary on Romans* (Richmond: John Knox, 1959); Hans W. Schmidt, *Der Brief des Paulus an die Römer* (THKNT; Berlin: Evangelische Verlagsanstalt, 1962); Matthew Black, *Romans* (2d ed.; NCB; Grand Rapids: Eerdmans, 1973,

to an uncleanness consisting of their bodies being dishonored among themselves [25]— the very ones who exchanged the truth about God for the lie and worshiped and served the creature rather than the creator, who is blessed forever, amen.[2] [26]Because of this God gave them over to dishonorable passions, for even their females exchanged the natural use (of the male as regards sexual intercourse) for that which is contrary to nature (i.e., sexual intercourse with other females); [27]and likewise also the males, having left behind the natural use of the female (as regards sexual intercourse), were inflamed with their yearning for one another, males with males committing indecency and in return receiving in themselves the payback which was necessitated by their straying (from the truth about God).

Romans 1:24

Therefore (i.e., because of human preference for idols over the living God). Gk. *dio* ("therefore, for this reason, on which/this account, so"). The para-

---

1989[2]); Ernst Käsemann, *An die Römer* (3d ed.; Tübingen: Mohr [Siebeck], 1974; ET Grand Rapids: Eerdmans, 1980); C. E. B. Cranfield, *A Critical and Exegetical Commentary on the Epistle to the Romans* (vol. 1; ICC; Edinburgh: T. & T. Clark, 1975); J. C. O'Neill, *Paul's Letter to the Romans* (Baltimore: Penguin Books, 1975); Heinrich Schlier, *Der Römerbrief* (HTKNT; Freiburg: Herder, 1977); Ulrich Wilckens, *Der Brief an die Römer* (EKKNT; vol. 1; Zürich: Benziger / Neukirchen-Vluyn: Neukirchener Verlag, 1978); Dieter Zeller, *Der Brief an die Römer* (RNT; Regensburg: Friedrich Pustet, 1985); Paul J. Achtemeier, *Romans* (IBC; Atlanta: John Knox, 1985); James D. G. Dunn, *Romans* (vol. 1; WBC; Dallas: Word Books, 1988); Walter Schmithals, *Der Römerbrief* (Gütersloh: Gütersloher Verlagshaus Gerd Mohn, 1988); Peter Stuhlmacher, *Der Brief an die Römer* (NTD; Göttingen and Zürich: Vandenhoeck & Ruprecht, 1989); John Ziesler, *Paul's Letter to the Romans* (TPINTC; London: SCM Press, 1989); Joseph A. Fitzmyer, *Romans* (AB; New York: Doubleday, 1993); Robert H. Mounce, *Romans* (NAC; Nashville: Broadman & Holman, 1995); Douglas J. Moo, *The Epistle to the Romans* (NICNT; Grand Rapids: Eerdmans, 1996); Brendan Byrne, *Romans* (SP; Collegeville, Minn.: Liturgical Press, 1996); Luke Timothy Johnson, *Reading Romans: A Literary and Theological Commentary* (New York: Crossroad, 1997); and Thomas R. Schreiner, *Romans* (BECNT; Grand Rapids: Baker, 1998); also Countryman's translation in *Dirt, Greed, and Sex* (p. 112); and Robert Jewett, "The Social Context and Implications of Homoerotic References in Romans 1:24-27" (*Homosexuality, Science, and the "Plain Sense" of Scripture*, 223-41); and, in the same work, David E. Fredrickson, "Natural and Unnatural Use in Romans 1:24-27: Paul and the Philosophic Critique of Eros," 197-222.

2. Rom 1:25 is a parenthetical flashback to 1:23, reminding the reader of the previous context. Because it does not directly address the issue of same-sex intercourse, it is not given special attention in the translation notes.

phrase by Sanday and Headlam captures the connection with the preceding line of thought: "Such were the beginnings of idolatry. And as a punishment for it. . . . " Some manuscripts follow *dio* with *kai* ("also") but the overwhelming external attestation speaks against its originality.

in the context of. Gk. *en.* Most translate literally as "in." The sense could be: (1) concomitant circumstances ("entangled as they were in," "in their abandonment to," "with"); the sphere, circumstances, moral condition, or state in which gentiles were found or involved at the time of God's giving over; (2) cause ("because of, on account of"); (3) instrumental means ("through"); or (4) a pleonastic use of *en* as a simple dative, referring to that to which people are given over ("to"). My own preference is for the first option (cf. Sir 5:2).

desires. Gk. *epithymiais.* LSJ: "desire, yearning; (also) longing, passion; (generally) appetite; (especially) sexual desire, lust"; BAGD: "desire, longing, craving." In Greek thought generally the word can have a neutral or positive sense, though from the time of Plato on and particularly with the Stoics the word typically acquires the negative sense of a desire for what is not one's own, forbidden, and outside one's moral purpose. Thus, Plato, *Phaedo* 83B: "the soul that truly belongs to philosophy thus abstains from both pleasures (*hēdonōn*) and desires (*epithymiōn*)"; Maximus of Tyre, *Or.* 24.4a: "the greatest evil for a human is desire (*epithymia*)." In Stoic thought, desire, along with pleasure, fear, and grief, was regarded as one of the four chief passions (F. Büchsel, *TDNT* 3.168-71). Paul usually uses *epithymia* in a negative sense to refer to the desires of the sinful impulse operating in the Spirit-less flesh of human existence (Rom 6:12; 13:14; Gal 5:16-24; cf. Eph 2:3; 4:22). Like other Jews, Paul could summarize the Mosaic law with the opening phrase of the tenth commandment "You shall not desire/covet," from which commandment "sin produced in me every kind of desire" for forbidden things (Rom 7:7-8; 13:9; cf. 4 Macc 2:6; *L.A.E.* 19:3; Philo, *Decal.* 142-43, 173; *Spec. Laws* 4.84-94; Jas 1:14-15; 4:2). Thus sinful *epithymia* was by no means restricted for Paul to unbridled or illicit forms of *sexual* desire, though manifestations of such consistently stand first or second in Pauline vice lists and obviously are foremost in Paul's mind here in Rom 1:24-27. It is important to be clear that the negative valence for *epithymia* is mandated by the context, not by the inherent meaning of the word in Paul. Elsewhere, Paul could refer to *epithymia* in a positive sense (e.g., Paul's "intense desire" to be reunited with the Thessalonian converts [1 Thess 2:17; 3:2] or his "desire to depart and to be with Christ" [Phil 1:23]). Desire becomes a problem only when people are "desirers of evil things," such as idolatry and sexual immorality (1 Cor 10:6; cf. Col 3:5). The context for Rom 1:24 rules out any possibility that the term is to be taken in a morally neutral sense (*contra* Countryman). Dunn sees an allusion to a "classic example of human craving which brought divine wrath upon it (Num 11:31-35) which is twice referred to in the Psalms with the formula that God gave them their desire" (Pss 78:29; 106:14-15; *Romans*, 62).

gave them over. Gk. *paredōken autous.* LSJ and BAGD give as meanings of *paradidōmi* "give or hand over, give up, deliver" (LSJ, BAGD); "surrender" (LSJ); "turn over, abandon" (BAGD). In Christian and Jewish literature of the period, *paradidonai tina eis* usually denotes a transference and subjection to imprisonment, slavery, death, destruction, sword, affliction, or judgment.[3] According to Acts 7:42 God, as a result of the idolatry of the golden calf episode, "turned and gave them over (*paredōken autous*) to worship the host of heaven."

uncleanness. Gk. *akatharsian.* LSJ: 1a. "uncleanness, foulness" (of a wound or sore); b. "dirt, filth"; 2. (in moral sense) "depravity"; 3. "ceremonial impurity"; BAGD: "impurity, dirt; (in a moral sense) immorality, viciousness (esp. of sexual sins)." That by "uncleanness, impurity, filthy conduct" Paul primarily had in mind immoral *sexual* behavior is evident from the direct connection between 1:24 and 1:26-27, the use of the word as a description of sexual immorality (adultery) in 1 Thess 4:6-7, and the close conjunction of *akatharsia* with sexual immorality in vice lists (2 Cor 12:21; Gal 5:19; cf. Col 3:5; Eph 4:19; 5:3). Cultic or ceremonial uncleanness is no longer at issue; the sense is moral. A contemporary parallel is the use of the words "smutty" or "dirty" for sexually immoral material and practices. A secondary allusion in Rom 1:24 to a wider range of "filthy" behavior is likely given the extension of the vice list in Rom 1:29-31 and the use of *akatharsia* in 1 Thess 2:3 with reference to the "impure practices" of deceit, trickery, and flattery as a pretext for greed.

consisting of their bodies being dishonored among themselves. Gk. *tou atimazesthai ta sōmata autōn.* Commentators are divided over the precise sense of the genitive articular infinitive. Options include: (1) final (purpose), "in order that, so that"; (2) consecutive (result), "so that, with the result of/that"; and (3) epexegetical (additional explanation), "that is, in that, consisting of." If the sense is epexegetical, then Paul would be merely expanding on what he means by "uncleanness." If one gives it a final sense, then God's deliberate punitive intent in turning people over to their degrading passions is stressed. If consecutive, then one is able to think of the process in a less personal, more mechanistic way: God handed them over to their sinful desires, which carried with it the inevitable result of self-degrading bodily behavior. Usage of the genitive articular infinitive in Paul elsewhere provides no certain

---

3. For texts, see my "Heart of Wax and a Teaching That Stamps: TYPOS DIDACHES (Rom 6:17*b*) Once More," *JBL* 112 (1993): 669-70.

direction (cf., e.g., the different findings of BAGD s.v. *ho*, II.4γ; BDF §400; Moo, *Romans*, 112 n. 100). A comparison with Rom 1:26 and 1:28 at first glance suggests a final or consecutive sense for 1:24. However, the structure of 1:24 is a little different from 1:26 and 1:28 since the verse states not that "God gave them over to the desires of their hearts" but rather that "God gave them over *in* the desires of their hearts *to* uncleanness." The "giving over" in 1:24 thus appears to be a giving over to sinful conduct in the context of sinful desires. "Uncleanness," like "sexual immorality" (*porneia*) and "licentiousness" (*aselgeia*) in the vice lists, stands primarily for immoral activity, not a desire that in turn aims at or leads to such activity. Heinrich Meyer therefore appears to have been correct when he stated that the genitive is epexegetical, giving a "more precise definition" of "uncleanness," inasmuch as the "being dishonored" "already constitutes the impurity itself, and does not merely attend it as a result" (*Romans*, 64).

For the meaning of the verb *atimazō*, cf. LSJ: "hold in no honor, esteem lightly, bring dishonor upon; (pass.) suffer dishonor/insult, be put to shame"; BAGD: "dishonor, degrade, treat shamefully, insult." The word appears elsewhere in Paul in Rom 2:23 (Jewish transgression of the law as a dishonoring of God). Opinion is split on whether the infinitive *atimazesthai* should be taken as a passive ("being dishonored") or as a middle ("dishonoring") possibly in conjunction with a reflexive or reciprocal sense given to *en autois* ("in/among themselves"). The matter can be fairly easily resolved. Since no other instances of the occurrence of the middle form in ancient Greek literature have been produced (Cranfield), and since the passive makes perfectly good sense, there is little reason for not construing *atimazesthai* as a passive.

among them. Gk. *en autois*. The precise meaning of the preposition *en* is exceedingly difficult. The options are: (1) "among," which in turn could be stretched to a reciprocal sense such as "between themselves" or "with one another"; (2) instrumental "through," a view espoused mainly by German commentators; and (3) "in," as a way of stressing that the dishonoring is something done to, in, or on their bodies. In favor of "in" is the remark in 1:27 regarding "receiving back in themselves (*en heautois*) the recompense" (cf. 1 Cor 6:18-19: *porneia* as a sin "into/against" [*eis*] one's own body"). Nevertheless, the stress of the immediate context of 1:24 appears to be more on the fact that human beings, left unrestrained by God to gratify their own desires, end up by dishonoring themselves. In other words, their own behavior toward one another constitutes the initial "payback" for their "error" of idol worship. The meanings "by" (perhaps agency is better than instrumental "through") and "among" become difficult to disentangle since the dishonoring that occurs "among" them is done "by themselves." That Paul chose to use *en* rather than *hypo* or *dia* tilts the scales in favor of "among."

Romans 1:26

Because of this. Gk. *dia touto* ("because of this, on account of this, therefore, for this reason, that is why"). The function of the phrase is resumptive, picking up the *dio* in 1:24 and introducing a more specific description of the statement made there. We now discover the specific form in which this dishonoring of their bodies took. Rom 1:25, then, is parenthetical. Its purpose is to remind readers that God's "giving over" was not an arbitrary action on the part of a hateful god but rather the right and righteous response of the creator God.

to dishonorable passions. Gk. *eis pathē atimias* (lit., "to passions of dishonor"). The abstract noun *atimia* means "dishonor, disgrace" (LSJ, BAGD); "shame," here "shameful/disgraceful passions" (BAGD) or "degrading passions" (Zerwick/Grosvenor). It is found in the NT only in Pauline literature. In 1 Cor 11:14, Paul describes the "dishonor" or "disgrace" of a man feminized by long hair, the closest parallel to our text (cf. also Rom 9:21; 1 Cor 15:43; 2 Cor 6:8; 11:21). The dishonoring in Rom 1:26, as in 1:24, is a dishonoring not merely of society nor even primarily of God but rather of one's own self as a human being "gendered" by God in creation and discernable in the material constitution of the human body. The genitive is a "Hebraic" or qualitative genitive, taking the place of an adjective. Cranfield's translation ("which brings dishonor"; also Byrne), though, captures the sense of the genitive nicely.

The word *pathos,* "passion," appears elsewhere in the NT only in 1 Thess 4:5 and Col 3:5. In the former, men should select wives primarily with a view to their holy character, not "in the passion of lust" (*en pathei epithymias*), that is, not out of an all-consuming and blind desire for physical beauty. Zeno, the founder of Stoicism, defined *pathos* as "an irrational and unnatural (*para physin*) movement of the soul or an impulse *in excess*" (Diogenes Laertius 7.110). While not an exclusively negative term (note the qualifier "of dishonor"), it tends to convey something more than mere emotion: an intense, and thus potentially overpowering, impulse to act in a manner contrary to right reason and nature. Plato refers to "erotic passion" as a "madness" of sorts that causes one to be "led away" (*Phaedr.* 265B; cf. Jewett). Greco-Roman moral philosophy centered around the control of improper passion.

for even. Gk. *te gar.* Most English translations needlessly leave out the "for." The sense is explanatory rather than causal (*contra* BAGD, s.v. *gar,* 1b). In other words, the fact that women engage in same-sex intercourse is not the reason why "God gave them over to dishonorable passion." Rather, this fact is a prime example of an action arising from such a controlling passion. Barrett's "for example" and Schreiner's "that is" ("nämlich": Wilckens, Stuhlmacher) capture the sense. The meaning of *te* in this context is not clear. It may begin the "both . . . and" sequence which continues at the start of v. 28 with another *te*. Or, it could carry the sense of "indeed" (BAGD, s.v. *gar*, 1b) or "even," as in Rom 7:7; 2 Cor 10:8. In that event, Paul may be expressing greater astonishment at the behavior of women taking on the male sex role.

their females. Gk. *hai . . . thēleiai autōn*. The use of *thēleiai* rather than *gynaikes* ("women"), and later in v. 27 of *arsenes* ("males") rather than *andres* or *anthrōpoi* ("men"), suggests an allusion to Gen 1:27 (*arsen kai thēlu epoiēsen autous*: "male and female he made them"). Most English translations, however, translate here as "women" and "men" respectively, thus obscuring the link to Gen 1:27 for readers. Some translations omit any translation of *autōn* or translate "among them," apparently because of the offensive implication that wives belonged to their husbands in a way that husbands did not belong to their wives. Yet, since such a conception of marriage existed in antiquity, one should beware of sweeping this word under the rug. Paul's use of the phrase "his own vessel" possibly for a man's wife in 1 Thess 4:4 (otherwise, of the male member, cf. 1 Sam 21:4-5) and his use of the adjective *hypandros* (under [the power of] or subject to a man/husband") to describe a "married" woman in Rom 7:2 carry similar meanings. Less likely, though not impossible, is that "their" is also to be inferred for "males" in 1:27 (such an inference is possible in Greek; so NEB, Fitzmyer), indicating that "their" merely continues the third-person references in Rom 1:18-25.

the natural use (of the male as regards sexual intercourse). Gk *tēn physikēn chrēsin*. In Rom 1:26-27 (as often elsewhere in Greek literature), *physikos* is equivalent to *kata physin* ("in accordance with nature"), an antonym of *para physin* in 1:26. In the NT the word occurs only here and in 2 Pet 2:12. The noun *chrēsis* (cf. the verb *chraomai*, "to use, make use of; desire, yearn after, enjoy") fundamentally means "use, usage, usefulness" (LSJ also: "employment, practice"). Yet it is sometimes applied to sexual intercourse (cf. BAGD, s.v. *chrēsis*, 2; see now the numerous examples cited in Fredrickson, "Romans 1:24-27," 199-207); for example, Pseudo-Lucian, *Affairs*, 25 ("I will show that the womanly [use] is better by far than the *use* of a darling boy"). LSJ puts Rom 1:26 under its definition (3): "intimacy, acquaintance," BAGD under "relations, function (esp. of sexual intercourse)." The noun appears in its broad sense, along with *kata physin* in Philo, *Names*, 112 (envy and malice drive the seven faculties of the unreasoning element from "the use that conforms to nature" and to the rational principle in the mind). The phrase "the natural use *of the male"* in Rom 1:27 suggests that the ellipse in 1:26 is to be filled out as "the natural use (of the female)," and in both cases should be understood as "as regards (or: in) sexual intercourse." Less likely, one could supply "the natural use of (their own bodies in sexual intercourse with) a male/female." However, the genitive "the male" is more precisely the object of the use (objective genitive). Fredrickson argues that *chrēsis* in Rom 1:26-27 should not be translated "relation" or "intercourse" because *chrēsis* generally refers not to mutual gratification but to "the activity of the desiring subject, usually male, performed on the desired object, female or male," implying perhaps that Paul thinks of the husband as the primary or exclusive "user" of the wife ("Romans 1:24-27," 199). However, Paul's application here presumes a mutuality in the male-female sexual relationship so far as sexual "use" is concerned: not only is there a natural "use" of the female by the male (1:27) but also there is a corresponding natural "use" of the male by the female (1:26; cf. ibid., 201). Sexuality in Paul's understanding has its "function" or "use" in giving pleasure to a complementary sexual "other"; sex here is first and foremost self-giving rather than self-gratifying (cf. 1 Cor 7:3-5 with the pattern of self-emptying set forth in the "Christ hymn" in Phil 2:5-11).

for that which is contrary to nature. Gk. *eis tēn para physin.* It is sometimes argued that *para* here should be translated neutrally as "beyond, more than." See the discussion on pp. 389-90. Most render as "contrary to nature," "against nature," or "unnatural."

Romans 1:27

having left behind. Gk. *aphentes,* aor. ptc. of *aphiēmi*: "leave" and so "leave behind, give up, abandon, neglect" (BAGD; cf. LSJ). The adverbial nuance of the circ. ptc. is ambiguous: temporal ("after/when they had left behind"), causal ("because they had left behind"), or, more likely, attendant circumstances ("leaving behind").

were inflamed. Gk. *exekauthēsan,* aor. pass. indic. 3d pl. of *ekkaiō*; *kaiō* means "to kindle, light; set on fire, burn; (pass.) be lit, burn, be on fire" (LSJ, BAGD). The *ek-* prefix has the meaning "out, up" or serves to intensify the verb and express completion ("utterly"): "burn out/up; light up, kindle, inflame; (pass.) be kindled, burn up, be inflamed" (LSJ, BAGD). Most translate "burned"; otherwise, "were inflamed" or "were consumed." The association of passion with all-consuming fire is a stock image. In antiquity it could be related physiologically to an excess in the body's "heat," as, for instance, in references to elevated heat levels in the blood of the young (roughly equivalent to our application of the phrase "raging hormones" to adolescents). For a full discussion of heat imagery with reference to erotic desire, see Fredrickson, "Romans 1:24-27," 210-12.

with their yearning. Gk. *en tē̜ orexei autōn.* The noun *orexis* means "(strong or intense) desire, longing, yearning, craving, appetite, appetency" (LSJ, BAGD, *TDNT, TLNT*; most translate here as "desire," "lust," or "passion"). In isolation the word does not necessarily connote a negative desire since the noun, for example, can be used in a definition of philosophy as "the desire for the understanding of things that always are" ([Ps.-] Plato, *Def.* 414B). The related verb *oregō* means in the midd./pass. voice "stretch out oneself, reach out or after, grasp at, yearn for, strive for, aspire to, desire" (so LSJ, BAGD). It is used to denote the supreme goal of human beings as "exercising desire in accordance with nature" (Epictetus, *Diatr.*, 1.21.2). When the *orexis* does not follow reason or nature, it becomes a negative quality. Stobaeus defines *epithymia* (bad desire) as "*orexis* disobedient to reason" (*Anth.* 2.87.21-22; cf. H. Heidland, "*oregomai, orexis*," *TDNT* 5:447-8; *TLNT,* 2.591 n. 2; further Fredrickson, "Romans 1:24-27," 213-14.) The verb is used three times in the NT, twice in a positive sense (Heb 11:16; 1 Tim 3:1), once in a negative sense (the desire for money, 1 Tim 6:10). The only occurrence of the noun, here in Rom 1:27, clearly has a negative sense since the context speaks of desire for things "contrary to nature," and specifically of sexual desire for other males. The translation "lust" is not inaccurate for the context (*contra* Countryman), though the word in isolation is not restricted to sexual desire.

committing. Gk. *katergazomenoi,* circ. ptc. denoting attendant circumstances. The verb means "to effect by labor, achieve; work at, practice" (LSJ), "to achieve, accomplish, commit (Rom 1:27); bring about, produce, create" (BAGD); "do, perpetrate" (ZG). It is possible that the meaning is ironic: "achieving" indecency rather than something of value.

indecency. Gk. *tēn aschēmosynēn.* The noun *aschēmosynē* is related to *schēma* ("form; appearance; bearing, dignity"), with alpha-privative prefix ("un-"). The *-synē* suffix is added to adjectives (in this case, *aschēmōn,-on,* "misshapen, ugly; unseemly, shameful, indecorous, indecent") to convert to an abstract noun, often expressing a quality. Thus: "want of form, disfigurement; 'bad form,' indecorum, obscene or disgraceful conduct (Rom 1:27)" (LSJ); "shameless deed" (BAGD); "indecency" (ZG). Translations vary: "indecent acts," "shamelessness," "what (or: that which) is shameless/shameful," "shameful things," "shame," "obscenity," "unseemly acts." The noun appears elsewhere in the NT only in Rev 16:15 and the adj. only in 1 Cor 12:23, both times with reference to one's private parts (BAGD). The related verb *aschēmoneō* ("to behave unseemly, disgracefully, indecently, dishonorably") appears only in 1 Cor 7:36. The Septuagint uses the noun as a translation of Hebrew ʿerwâ, "nakedness, genital area," derivatively, "indecency, disgrace" (REB: "private parts"), and the vast majority of instances appear in Lev 18:6-19 and 20:11, 17-21, usually in the phrase "you shall not uncover the nakedness of (= have indecent, disgraceful, shameful sexual intercourse with)" one's near-of-kin (i.e., incest) or one's wife during menstruation. The allusion is another indication that Paul is hearkening back to Levitical law. It is possible that the abstract form of aschēmosynē is being used in Rom 1:27 for concrete acts (cf. Philo, Alleg. Interp., 2.66; BDF §110[2]). The translation "committing indecency" is a mediating solution since "indecency" oscillates in meaning between "the quality or state of being indecent" and "something that is indecent." Another option, which would pick up more clearly the Levitical background, would be to translate as "indecent exposure and intercourse."

and in return receiving. Gk. *kai . . . apolambanontes,* another circ. ptc. denoting attendant circumstances (connected to *katergazomenoi*). The verb *apolambanō* means "to take or receive from; receive what is one's due, have one paid; regain, recover" (LSJ), "to receive (Rom 1:27); receive in return, recover, get back" (BAGD). The *apo-* prefix can have different senses: "from," "back again" or "in return," "what is one's own," "in full" (cf. LSJ, s.v. *apo,* D). Sometimes it has no special significance (as in Gal 4:5: "receive" adoption; cf. Col 3:4, the only other usage in Pauline texts). Both "in return, back" and "what is one's due" are pertinent in this context given the *anti-* prefix in the object *antimisthian,* the sense of "due" conveyed by *edei,* and the fact that *apolambanontes* is characterized as the return for *katergazomenoi.* Most translations have simply "receiving"; otherwise, "receiving back" (Dunn, Jewett) or "being paid in turn" (Fitzmyer).

the payback. Gk. *tēn antimisthian.* According to BAGD, *antimisthia* is found only in Christian writers, though the related words *misthos* ("wages, pay; recompense, reward, requital") and *antimisthion* ("reward"), among others, are common in non-Christian texts. LSJ gives as its meaning "requital, recompense"; BAGD as "reward; penalty (Rom 1:27); return; exchange (2 Cor 6:13)"; ZG as "corresponding reward." In the NT it is found only here and in 2 Cor 6:13, where it clearly takes on the added sense of "in return" or "in exchange." The *anti-* prefix brings out "the reciprocal nature of the transaction" (BAGD) and thus the senses "in return, equal to, corresponding" (LSJ, s.v. *anti,* C). Given this and the basic sense of the *misth-*stem as "pay, wages," an appropriate translation would be "payback" (cf. Schmidt; most translate as "penalty"; otherwise, "wages, recompense, reward, punishment").

which was necessitated. Gk. *hēn edei.* Although the construction in Rom 1:27 is awkward, the sense is clear enough: the accusative "which" (antecedent: *tēn antimisthian*) is the thing that was made necessary (specifying the "it") and the genitive *tēs planēs* is an objective genitive belonging with *tēn antimisthian*, denoting the cause or reason why the *tēn antimisthian* was required. Thus, "(the payback) for their straying which (viz., payback) was necessary"; or "(the payback, recompense) which was necessary for (= on account of) their straying," "which was necessitated by their straying," "which their straying necessitated." Most translations treat the *hēn edei* more loosely, as if it were an attributive adjective between *tēn* and *antimisthian* (e.g., the due penalty); thus, "due," "inevitable," "fitting," "appropriate." The last two translations weaken the sense of necessity, requirement, compulsion, or inevitability inherent in *dei*.

by their straying. Gk. *tēs planēs autōn.* The basic meaning of *planē* is "wandering, roaming; going astray" and from this it takes on the sense of "deceit" (LSJ, BAGD), "deception, delusion, error" (BAGD).

In the discussion that follows, I begin with the particular historical context of the letter to the Romans and the literary context, first of Rom 1:18–3:20 and then more precisely of 1:18-32. Next I analyze the meaning of "contrary to nature" within this context. Finally, I treat five questions that have been raised with regard to the meaning of Rom 1:24-27.

Romans 1:18–3:20 Within the Sweep of Paul's Letter and the Situation at Rome

The overarching context of our passage in Romans is Paul's argument that "all are under sin" (3:9, a verdict that Paul claims he has "previously charged" in the letter); that "there is no one righteous, not even one" (3:10; cf. 3:20), that "the whole world is liable to God's judgment" (3:19), and that "all sinned" (3:23). Paul's aim is to demonstrate that the Jews, and not just gentiles ("for there is no distinction"), are culpable before God. Therefore Jews and gentiles alike are dependent on the way that God chooses to manifest his merciful fidelity and salvation (righteousness); that is, in the atoning death of Christ (3:21-26). If even Jews cannot be justified "on the basis of works of the law" but only "apart from the law" (3:20-21), then gentiles too are justified apart from observing the requirements of the Mosaic law. Paul here has in view primarily those requirements that in the first century were regarded as distinctively Jewish such as circumcision, special dietary laws, and special holy days (the sabbath, Jewish festivals). And, further, only the gospel can effect liberation from sin's power because in it the gift of Christ's Spirit is dispensed to those who believe.[4]

Within Romans as a whole, Paul's presentation of the gospel has a socio-ethical edge. In Rome, believers were receiving others into their house churches and then debating with them over different attitudes toward meat and possibly also over the observance of special days (14:1–15:13). Paul was determined to end this divisive pattern. He contended that the "strong" (liberal) Christians in Rome who thought it permissible to eat meat and treat all days alike should not look down

---

4. The problem of Paul's view of the law is a thorny one. An excellent overview and critique of different approaches can be obtained in: Stephen Westerholm, *Israel's Law and the Church's Faith: Paul and His Recent Interpreters* (Grand Rapids: Eerdmans, 1988). Cf. Frank Thielman, *Paul and the Law: A Contextual Approach* (Downers Grove: InterVarsity, 1994); idem, "Law," *DPL*, 529-42; James D. G. Dunn, *The Theology of Paul the Apostle* (Grand Rapids: Eerdmans, 1998), 128-61; C. K. Barrett, *Paul: An Introduction to His Thought* (Louisville: Westminster/John Knox, 1994), 74-87; Douglas J. Moo, " 'Law,' 'Works of the Law,' and Legalism in Paul," *WTJ* 45 (1983): 73-100; C. E. B. Cranfield, " 'The Works of the Law' in the Epistle to the Romans," *JSNT* 43 (1991): 89-101; idem, "St. Paul and the Law," *SJT* 17 (1964), 43-68; idem, *Romans*, 845-62; Heikki Räisänen, *Paul and the Law* (Philadelphia: Fortress, 1983); E. P. Sanders, *Paul, the Law, and the Jewish People* (Philadelphia: Fortress, 1983); idem, *Paul and Palestinian Judaism* (Philadelphia: Fortress, 1977), 431-556; Hans Hübner, *Law in Paul's Thought* (Edinburgh: T. & T. Clark, 1984); Thomas R. Schreiner, *The Law and Its Fulfillment: A Pauline Theology of Law* (Grand Rapids: Baker, 1993); N. T. Wright, *The Climax of the Covenant: Christ and the Law in Pauline Theology* (Minneapolis: Fortress, 1991); also the collection of essays in James D. G. Dunn (ed.), *Paul and the Mosaic Law* (WUNT 89; Tübingen: Mohr [Siebeck], 1996). One of the main points of contention is whether Paul thought the law was still binding on gentile Christians or, for that matter, Jewish Christians. In my view, the argument in both Galatians and Romans decidedly favors the position that Paul believed that the law had been abrogated in Christ. Paul could not speak of continued adherence to the Mosaic law given his jettisoning of circumcision, dietary laws, and calendric observances as requirements. Nevertheless, for Paul, the contingent expression of God's will for the nation of Israel in the dispensation leading up to the coming of Christ obviously overlapped with the enduring and universal will of God for all peoples at all times. The same God who had given the law to Moses had also given Christ to the world; significant continuity was inevitable. Paul believed that the atoning death of Jesus and the concomitant gift of the Spirit made possible fulfillment of the fundamental requirement of the law in the lives of believers (Rom 6:15-23; 7:4-6; 8:3-14; 13:8-10) without actually renewing the Mosaic law.

on, or attempt to coerce, "weak" (conservative) Christians. The "weak" who abstained from eating meat and regarded some days as particularly holy should, in turn, not judge the "strong."[5] Paul hoped that his proclamation of the gospel to the Roman Christians would so fill them "with all joy and peace in the course of their believing" (15:13) that they would be able to overlook differences on minor matters and stop judging one another. Overwhelmed with gratitude for being included as gentiles among the people of God, they would "welcome one another" for the purpose of praising "together with one mouth the God and Father of our Lord Jesus Christ" (15:6-7; cf. 14:1, 3).

---

5. The occasion behind Paul's letter to the Romans is the subject of an enormous amount of literature. It is not possible to explore its complexities here. The main issue concerns whether Rom 14:1–15:13 can be used to reconstruct an actual (and significant) problem at Rome which at least partly explains Paul's purposes in writing or whether Rom 14:1–15:13 is just generalized parenesis. Among those who hold the former position (which I also adopt) are: Mark Reasoner, *The Strong and the Weak: Romans 14:1–15:13 in Context* (SNTSMS; Cambridge: Cambridge University Press, 1999); Robert Jewett, *Christian Tolerance: Paul's Message to the Modern Church* (Philadelphia: Westminster, 1982); idem, "Ecumenical Theology for the Sake of Mission: Romans 1:1-17 + 15:14–16:24," *Pauline Theology: Volume III: Romans* (D. Hay and E. Johnson, eds.; Minneapolis: Fortress, 1995), 89-109; Anthony J. Guerra, *Romans and the Apologetic Tradition: The Purpose, Genre and Audience of Paul's Letter* (SNTSMS 81; Cambridge: Cambridge University Press, 1995); James C. Walters, *Ethnic Issues in Paul's Letter to the Romans* (Valley Forge: TPI, 1994); A. J. M. Wedderburn, *The Reasons for Romans* (Edinburgh: T. & T. Clark, 1988); Francis Watson, *Paul, Judaism and the Gentiles: A Sociological Approach* (SNTSMS 56; Cambridge: Cambridge University Press, 1986); Mark D. Nanos, *The Mystery of Romans: The Jewish Context of Paul's Letter* (Minneapolis: Fortress, 1996); Walther Bindemann, *Theologie im Dialog: Ein traditions-geschichtlicher Kommentar zu Römer 1–11* (Leipzig: Evangelische Verlagsanstalt, 1992); William S. Campbell, *Paul's Gospel in an Intercultural Context: Jew and Gentile in the Letter to the Romans* (SIHC 69; Frankfurt: Lang, 1992); Jeffrey A. Crafton, "Paul's Rhetorical Vision and the Purpose of Romans," *NovT* 32 (1990): 317-39; John M. G. Barclay, " 'Do We Undermine the Law?' A Study of Romans 14.1–15.6," *Paul and the Mosaic Law*, 287-308; Sam K. Williams, "The 'Righteousness of God' in Romans," *JBL* 99 (1980): 241-90; among commentators, cf. Dunn, Moo, Fitzmyer, and Schreiner.

These authors differ on the degree of importance to assign 14:1–15:13 as a reason Paul wrote the letter, relative to other putative reasons: enlist support for Spanish mission; rehearse defense speech in Jerusalem; combat misrepresentations of his gospel by Judaizers at Rome; provide the Roman church with a general presentation of his gospel which functions as a self-recommendation and/or as a general exhortation to the Roman church. They also differ on the direction of Paul's

While one might want to argue that a possible inference to be drawn from this larger social context is that contemporary believers should cease judging homosexual Christians, this would be an erroneous application from the perspective of Pauline thought. When Paul enjoins believers in 14:1–15:13 to stop judging one another, he emphasizes that mutual toleration is the proper approach for matters of indifference such as diet and calendar (accommodation, though not necessarily commendation).[6] He does not take the same approach of accommodation on all matters, however. In matters involving sexual ethics, community relations, singular veneration of Christ, and circumcision, Paul does not countenance accommodation. One need only contrast Paul's flexible approach in 14:1–15:13 with his unbending exhortation immediately preceding in 13:12-14, where Paul calls on the believers at Rome to "lay aside the works of darkness" such as "wild partying and bouts of drunkenness, sleeping around (or: sexual excesses; *koitai*) and unrestrained and depraved sexuality (*aselgeiai* or: acts of licentiousness, debauchery), quarreling and jealousy."

---

argument in Rom 14:1–15:13 (critiquing alike both the strong and weak, or primarily critiquing one side or the other) and the ethnic identity of the "strong" and "weak" (some identify the weak primarily as Jewish Christians, others as primarily or exclusively gentile Christians; Nanos is exceptional in regarding the weak as non-Christian Jews). While the greetings list in Romans 16 indicates the presence of some Jewish Christians at Rome, the implied readers of Paul's letter are clearly gentile Christians (1:5-7, 13-15; 6:19; 11:13; 15:14-16). Some have also disputed that the discussion of diet and calendar in Rom 14:1–15:13 has anything to do with faithfulness to Mosaic law, pointing out that the Torah does not require abstinence from all meat. However, there is evidence that some Jews in antiquity abstained from meat altogether in an effort to avoid any contamination from idols, to distance themselves from the excesses of pagan life, to check the passions of the flesh, and/or to mourn Israel's "captivity." The focus of Romans 1–11 on the Mosaic law speaks in favor of linking the dispute in 14:1–15:13 to Torah observance, as does the address in 7:1 ("I am speaking to those who know [the] law"). Certainly when Paul speaks in 14:6 of some treating a particular day or days as especially holy in relation to the Lord, he can hardly be referring to pagan holy days. He must have in mind the sabbath. For a collection of essays representing diverse positions on the "Romans debate," see Karl P. Donfried (ed.), *The Romans Debate* (rev. ed.; Peabody: Hendrickson, 1991). See also my articles, "Why the 'Weak' at Rome Cannot Be Non-Christian Jews," *CBQ* 62 (2000): 64-82; and "The Meaning of [*hymōn to agathon*] in Romans 14:16" *JBL* 117 (1998): 675-89.

6. Paul does not adopt a relativist stance on matters of diet. For him no food is inherently defiling (14:14, 22).

In short, homosexual practice whether among men or women was *not* a matter of indifference for Paul (in Stoic terms, an *adiaphoron*) and certainly not an issue for which he would have encouraged mutual toleration and acceptance. To the contrary, for Paul, same-sex intercourse comes under the heading of "depraved sexuality" that is to be "laid aside" along with the other vices of 13:13.

The social context of Romans establishes this about Rom 1:18–3:20: the demonstration of universal human sinfulness affirms the indispensability of the gospel for rescuing people both from sin's penalty and also from sin's power. Only the gospel both reconciles sinners to God and transforms sinners into God's holy people (saints) living within "the obedience of faith" (1:5; 15:18; 16:26). We will come back to the extended argument for the necessity of righteous conduct on the part of believers in 6:1–8:17 but, for now, it may be helpful to have in mind the series of earnest exhortations in that section:

> What then shall we say? Should we continue in sin, in order that grace may increase? May it not happen! We who died in relation to sin, how can we live in it? . . . . We were buried with [Christ] . . . , in order that . . . we might walk in newness of life. . . . Our old human was crucified with him, in order that the body of sin might be put out of commission, that we might no longer be serving as sin's slave. . . . Consider yourselves to be dead in relation to sin but alive in relation to God in Christ Jesus. Don't let sin continue to rule in your mortal body for the obeying of its desires, nor continue to present the members of your body to sin as weapons of unrighteousness, but present yourselves to God as if alive from the dead and the members of your body to God as weapons of righteousness. For sin shall not manifest its lordship over you. . . .
>
> What then? Should we sin . . . ? May it not happen! Don't you know, the one to whom you present yourselves as slaves for obedience, you are slaves of the one whom you obey, whether of sin for death or of obedience for righteousness? . . . For just as you presented the members of your body to *uncleanness* as slaves and to lawlessness for the purpose of doing lawless acts, so now present the members of your body to righteousness as slaves for holiness. For when you were slaves of sin, you were free with respect to righteousness. What fruit were you bearing at that time?—for which things you are now ashamed, for *the end result of those things is death*. But now, having been freed from sin and enslaved

to God you are bearing fruit for holiness, and the end result is eternal life. For the wages of sin is death. . . .

You were put to death in relation to the law . . . for the purpose of you becoming another's, the one who was raised from the dead, in order that we might bear fruit for God. . . . We were discharged from the law . . . so that we might serve as a slave in newness of Spirit. . . . The "law" of the Spirit of life in Christ Jesus freed you from the "law" of sin and of death.[7] . . . God, having sent his own Son . . . as a sin-offering condemned sin in the flesh, in order that the righteous requirement of the law might be fulfilled in us who walk not in conformity to the [sinful impulse operating in the members of the] flesh but in conformity to the Spirit. . . . For *if you are living in conformity to the flesh, you are going to die; but if by the Spirit you put to death the deeds of [sin-controlled] flesh, you will live. For as many as are being led by the Spirit, these are the children of God.*

A transformed existence that entails death to self and life for God is both a free gift and a grace-empowered requirement for those adopted into God's family. To return to the old ways of the sin-controlled life after one's deliverance is to deepen one's rebellious suppression of the truth, to immerse oneself again in self-degrading and indecent practices, and finally to face anew the apocalyptic repercussions for such sin.

Thus, the rejection of homosexual conduct in Rom 1:24-27 and of other sins mentioned in 1:28-31 is not just a trap for self-righteous people who judge others, as some commentators claim (see below). It is, also, a prelude to Paul's defense of the moral claims of the gospel on individuals and on the community. Rom 1:18–3:20 depicts what life *used to be like* before believing in Christ and receiving the Spirit but which has *now* been fundamentally transformed for those who are in Christ. It portrays the predicament of all unsaved humanity, a predicament that requires not only forgiveness but also deliverance from sin's power to inflict human self-degradation (6:1–8:17). In response to this experience of forgiveness and absolution the community unites in "bragging"

---

7. By "the law of sin and death" is meant the sinful impulse as an internal regulating force, which prior to faith ruled the bodies of Roman Christians and compelled to sin even those whose minds concurred with the righteous demands of the law.

about what God has done in Christ (chs. 5 and 8:18-39).[8] When gratitude for God's grace fails to motivate believers to right conduct, a
reminder of the apocalyptic consequences of not living in the Spirit is
required. Christ's atoning death as a God-given, amends-making restitution for human sins takes salvific effect for any single individual only
when that individual is joined to Christ through the indwelling Spirit
of Christ, a joining that in turn allows and requires Christ to live
through that individual. In short, in Pauline thought, a transfer of sin
to Christ requires a transfer of self to Christ; justification and ethics are
inseparably joined.

The Argument of Romans 1:18-32: The Suppression of Truth in Creation/Nature

In Rom 1:18-32, Paul employs a typical Hellenistic-Jewish critique
of gentile sin in order to set up an imaginary dialogue partner. In this
instance, the partner is a Jew who rejects gentile inclusion apart from
observance of Torah and who excuses himself from God's judgment on
the basis of knowing the Law and being circumcised. Rom 1:18-32
does not describe the origin of sin itself; Rom 5:12-21 (the sin of Adam)
comes closest to doing that. Rather, 1:18-32 shows how sin runs amok
particularly among idol-worshipers and explains why God is fully justified in judging them ("so that they are without excuse," 1:20; cf. 2:1).[9]

Paul's purpose is to show that God's verdict is just and right. This is

---

8. My choice of words, "bragging," is deliberate. Paul uses *kauchasthai* ("to brag,
   boast") to describe the Christian's proper response to the work of God in Christ
   (5:2-3, 11), in contrast to bragging or boasting in works of the law (2:17, 23; 3:27;
   4:2). Paul's rhetorical strategy appears to be based in part on Jer 9:23-24: one should
   boast not in wisdom, might, or wealth, but rather in knowing that God acts with
   "righteousness in the earth" (cf. Rom 2:29, which alludes to Jer 9:25-26; also, "let
   him who boasts boast in the Lord" in 1 Cor 1:31 and 2 Cor 10:17 is a synthesis of Jer
   9:23-24). By building a reservoir of gratitude among the Roman Christians for the
   revelation of God's righteousness through faith in Christ (3:21-26; ch. 5; 8:18-39;
   11:32-36), Paul hopes to unite them in a chorus of peace, joy, and praise and thereby put an end to mutual judgment in the community over matters of indifference
   (15:5-13; 14:17). Cf. my article, "Why the 'Weak' at Rome Cannot Be Non-Christian
   Jews," 73-74.
9. Naturally, idol worshipers are primarily found among the gentiles, though there may
   be a subtle allusion in v. 23 to the Golden Calf episode mentioned in Ps 106:20.

so precisely because the gentiles do indeed know that what they are doing is wrong. God does not judge them for their ignorance but for acting contrary to the knowledge that they do have. This suppression of knowledge shows itself especially in two ways: idolatry and same-sex intercourse. In the case of idolatry, gentiles should know better than to worship statues and wood carvings of human and animal images. Why? Paul points to the majesty, power, beauty, and order of God's creation as clear evidence of God's awesomeness. In the view of any first-century Jew, the act of creating the cosmos obviously could not be restricted to the work of human hands, an idol. A pagan who honors an idol has to deliberately suppress the truth about God's greatness, a greatness that shatters all icons and manifests itself in the vast created order.

A similar argument is made from a Jewish writing from Alexandria, Egypt, dating to within eighty years or so of the date of Romans: the pseudepigraphical work known as the Wisdom of Solomon:

> All people who were ignorant of God were foolish by nature; and they were unable from the good things that are seen to know the one who exists, nor did they recognize the artisan while paying heed to his works; but they supposed that either fire or wind or swift air, or the circle of the stars . . . were the gods that rule the world. . . . let them know how much better than these is their Lord, for the author of beauty created them. And if people were amazed at their power and working, let them perceive from them how much more powerful is the one who formed them. For from the greatness and beauty of created things comes a corresponding perception of their Creator. Yet . . . perhaps they go astray while seeking God and . . . trust in what they see, because the things that are seen are beautiful. Yet again, not even they are to be excused; for if they had the power to know so much that they could investigate the world, how did they fail to find sooner the Lord of these things?
>
> But miserable, with their hopes set on dead things, are those who give the name "gods" to the works of human hands, gold and silver fashioned with skill, and likenesses of animals, or a useless stone. . . . A skilled woodcutter may saw down a tree. . . . He forms it in the likeness of a human being, or makes it like some worthless animal . . . and sets it in the wall. . . . When he prays . . . , he is not ashamed to address a lifeless thing. . . . But the idol made with hands is accursed, and so is the one who made it. . . . For equally hateful to God are the ungodly and their

ungodliness. . . . For the idea of making idols was the beginning of fornication. . . . For through human vanity they entered the world. . . . it
was not enough for them to err about the knowledge of God. . . . All is
a raging riot of blood and murder, theft and deceit, corruption, faith-
lessness, . . . confusion over what is good,. . . defiling of souls, inter-
change of sex roles,[10] disorder in marriages, adultery, and debauchery.
For the worship of idols. . . is the beginning and cause and end of every
evil. For they. . . prophesy lies, or live unrighteously, or readily commit
perjury; for because they trust in lifeless idols they swear wicked oaths
and expect to suffer no harm. But just penalties will overtake them. . . .
the just penalty for those who sin . . . . (13:1-11, 13-17; 14:8-9, 12, 14,
22, 25-31 NRSV [slightly modified])

Here gentile idolaters "are not to be excused" (a different Greek word
than the one at the end of Rom 1:20, but the same point) because they
should have been able to deduce (1) that "the good things that are
seen" were fashioned by a divine Artisan and (2) that such an Artisan

10. The translation of this phrase, *geneseōs enallagē* (14:26) is by David Winston (*The
Wisdom of Solomon* [AB; Garden City: Doubleday, 1979], 280). A literal translation
would be "change/interchange of origin/birth (or: coming into being, creation, kind,
generation)." The verb related to *enallagē* is used also in *T. Naph.* 3:4 for the sin of
Sodom: "don't become like Sodom which changed (*enēllaxe*) the order of its nature";
the verb "exchanged" in Rom 1:26 merely uses a different prefix for the same stem.
Although the phrase in Wisd 14:26 may have a broader reference to a general "inter-
change (or inversion) of the works of (i.e., prompted by) nature" (*phuseōs ergōn
enallagē*), including sleeping in the day and keeping "vigil by night to indulge . . .
insatiable lust" (Philo, *Cher.* 92; cf. NJB: "sins against nature"), the use of "birth/
origin" suggests an inversion of one's gendered birthright. A sexual sin is confirmed
by the subsequent list: "disorder in marriages, adultery, and debauchery." While a
general reference to distorted sexuality is possible, the parallel language in *T. Naph.*
3:4 and Rom 1:26 indicate that at the very least same-sex intercourse is at the forefront, perhaps along with incest and bestiality (cf. NRSV, REB: "sexual perversion";
NAB: "unnatural lust"; *contra* Bailey, *Homosexuality*, 45-48). Scroggs writes in *The
New Testament and Homosexuality*, 92: "I do not myself see how the Greek can bear
this translation [of "sexual perversion"], but if it is correct, it probably refers to homosexuality." Countryman rejects a specific reference to homosexual acts but admits
that it would be included under the broader sense of "the whole range of nonpro-
creative sexual activities" (*Dirt, Greed, and Sex*, 63). Brooten thinks that the phrase
"could mean same-sex relations" (*Love Between Women*, 296 n. 112). According to
Nissinen, the expression "can refer to any change in what is considered customary—
to homoeroticism, among other things. By itself this expression does not contain a
direct reference to same-sex conduct, but the following components of the list suggest that sexual issues are indeed at stake here" (*Homoeroticism*, 90).

must be greater than the things made, for "from the greatness and beauty of created things comes a corresponding perception of their Creator." Having become "foolish" (related to a verb in Rom 1:21), they engaged in the self-degrading worship of the likenesses of worthless animals. This in turn unleashed a host of vices, including (apparently) same-sex intercourse, because people now perceived themselves as subject only to the discipline of gods of their own making, leaving them free to act on their own impulses and open to self-deception.

As with Rom 1:18-32, though the author seems to attribute all evil in the world to the development of idolatry ("the beginning and cause and end of every evil"), elsewhere in the book he makes clear that corruption was introduced into creation at the fall of Adam (2:23-24; 10:1) and admits that the Jews themselves sin, even though they are not idolaters (15:6); the language is hyperbole. Already, by virtue of succumbing to idol worship and falling prey to their own passions, a punishment of sorts takes place: "miserable (or: wretched), with their hopes set on dead things, are those who give the name 'gods' to the works of human hands. . . . [the idolater] is not ashamed to address a lifeless thing" (13:10, 17). Yet the emphasis is on the active intervention of God to punish, engaged as the author is in a description of the plagues that befell the Egyptians during the time of Moses: "just penalties will overtake them. . . . the just penalty for those who sin."

In a more pronounced fashion than the author of the Wisdom of Solomon, Paul contends that the worship of idols already precipitates divine wrath.[11] By saying that "the wrath of God is being revealed" already in the present time (1:18a), Paul is not denying a future, final expression of God's wrath in the eschaton. Texts in 1:32–2:12 make clear that the manifestation of God's anger in the present time does not exhaust the wrath of God:

- "the decree of God that those who do such things are worthy of death" (1:32a)

---

11. Another major difference between the two texts is that Paul uses the motif of idolatry, understood as a deliberate suppression of the truth, not as a way of distinguishing gentiles from Jews but rather as a basis for setting a trap for Jews. If gentiles cannot escape God's judgment precisely because they know that they are engaging in behavior worthy of death, how much more so is this true of those who know the law but violate its precepts?

- "Do you count on this, O human who judges the ones who do such things [described in 1:18-32] and does the same that you will escape the judgment of God?" (2:3)
- "storing up wrath for yourself on the Day of Wrath" (2:5)
- "wrath . . . [will come] on every soul among humans who continually do evil, the Jew first and the Greek" (2:8-9)
- "all who have sinned without the law will also perish without the law, and all who have sinned in the law will be judged by the law" (2:12)

Indeed, Paul's contention that the wrath of God is even now being revealed against sin is probably intended as clear and convincing proof of the certainty of a future, more cataclysmic judgment on all those who continue to lead sinful lives and do not opt for the revelation of God's righteousness recently manifested in Christ. While the sinning Jew, like the sinning gentile, might construe the absence of fire and brimstone in the present time as evidence of God's approval, the present time ought to be viewed as a time of divine "forbearance" designed to lead the sinner "to repentance" (2:4).[12] In any case, Paul contends

---

12. Käsemann's quotable statement must therefore be qualified: "Paul paradoxically reverses the cause and consequence: Moral perversion is the result of God's wrath, not the reason for it" (*Romans*, 47). Similarly, Hays: "Homosexuality, then, is not a *provocation* of 'the wrath of God'. . . ; rather, it is a *consequence* of God's decision to 'give up' rebellious creatures to follow their own futile thinking and desires. The unrighteous behavior . . . is a list of *symptoms*. . . . Homosexual activity will not *incur* God's punishment: it is its own punishment, an 'antireward' " ("Awaiting the Redemption of Our Bodies," 8-9). Contrary to these overstatements, the "moral perversion" to which God hands over human beings as a manifestation of divine wrath results in a build-up of sinful behavior that culminates in the catastrophic "day of wrath." Moreover, degenerate passions antedate idolatry; idolatry leads to enslavement to such passions, not to their origination. Horst Balz goes too far on the other end: "It is not correct to speak [in 1:24, 26, 28] already of punishment, for the punishment of these people occurs according to Paul at the judgment: they are worthy of death (1:32; cf. 2:8-9; 3:19). Rather, their consciously chosen . . . behavior is a punishable condition, which God lets them get into, in order to hand them over to the punishment of judgment" ("Biblische Aussagen zur Homosexualität," *ZEE* 31 [1987]: 65). While Balz is correct to stress that the definitive judgment is yet to come, the fact that Paul declares that God's wrath is and has been revealed already (1:18) and refers to same-sex intercourse as its own "payback" or "recompense in return" (1:27) establishes that same-sex intercourse is not only a "punishable condition" but also a preliminary punishment.

that already in the present time God's wrath is being manifested against idolaters. And it is manifested in an indirect way, not by God hurling thunderbolts but rather by God stepping back and allowing the sinful passions of the flesh to take control of those who have turned their back on the living and true God. Here God acts in a way familiar to many parents who allow rebellious teens to reap the penalty of their own misconduct by simply not intervening to rescue them from their own destructive behavior. Committing sin, satisfying one's own perverse desires, being subjected to one's own degrading passions—this becomes its own punishment (with a future punishment still to follow).[13]

Three times in Rom 1:18-32, Paul speaks of God "giving them over" to the "uncleanness" of passions that dishonor their own bodies (1:24), to the "dishonorable passions" of same-sex eroticism (1:26), and to an "unfit mind" that seeks to do "what is not proper" (1:28). For rhetorical effect, each "handing over" follows a reference to a conscious human "exchange": an exchange of "the glory of the imperishable God" for idols resembling perishable creatures (1:23), of "the truth of God for the lie" of idol worship (1:25), and of the "natural sexual function" of intercourse with members of the opposite sex for unnatural intercourse with the members of the same sex (1:26).

The literature on Rom 1:18-32 often displays unnecessary confusion about the sequence and interrelationship of these two tripartite actions. The first two exchanges are identical. Rom 1:25 is simply a flashback to 1:23 designed to remind the reader that the punishment to which God hands over the idolater fits the crime perfectly. Rom 1:28*a*

---

13. As Paul Achtemeier puts it: "So here we are, we rebellious peoples, glorying in the freedom we think to be grace, only to be told by Paul it is instead the fearful punishment of sin and a manifestation of God's wrath. The permissiveness we celebrated as a world 'come of age' we now find to be nothing more than the permission to fall deeper into sin. . . . Divine discipline is the measure of grace, as divine permissiveness is the measure of wrath. A society in which discipline is disappearing and in which anything is permitted is, in light of this passage, clearly a society suffering under the wrath of God" (*Romans*, 42). There is a distinct tension here between the definition of wrath as permissiveness and the definition of Christianity as freedom—a tension that Paul works toward resolving in Rom 6:1–8:17 (esp. 6:15-23; cf. Gal 5:13–6:10). Freedom is never absolute. It is always freedom in relation to something else, either from sin for righteousness or from righteousness for sin.

("just as they did not see fit to acknowledge God") implies the same exchange. The exchange of natural intercourse for unnatural intercourse in 1:26 represents the appropriately absurd and self-debasing outcome for people who foolishly exchange God for idols.

The three "giving overs" (1:24, 26, 28) do not represent temporal sequences but rather are speaking of the same fundamental act. Possibly, the first "giving over" in 1:24 states the outcome in generic terms ("to an impurity consisting of their bodies being dishonored in them"). This outcome is, then, vividly exhibited by the specific behavior described in the second "giving over" of 1:26 ("to dishonorable passions" leading to the indecency of same-sex intercourse and "in return receiving in themselves the payback") but which ultimately embraces the wide array of sinful excess catalogued in 1:28-31.[14] More likely, the "giving over" of 1:24 is identical with the "giving over" of 1:26 (and, by implication, other sexual sins). "Uncleanness" in Paul primarily refers to sexual sins (1 Thess 4:7; Gal 5:19; 1 Cor 7:14; 2 Cor 12:21; cf. Col 3:5; Eph 4:19; 5:3). The "dishonoring" of 1:24 is picked up in the "dishonorable passions" of same-sex intercourse in 1:26, and, in Paul's view, "sexual immorality" (*porneia*) was uniquely a sin "against one's own body" (1 Cor 6:18). The "giving over" of 1:28-31 should then be understood as a concomitant action. One can diagram the "plot structure" of the "exchanges" and "giving overs" as follow:

Stage 1: God's invisible transcendence and majesty is visibly manifested in creation (1:19-20).

Stage 2: Humans knowingly and thus foolishly *"exchange"* the true God for idols (1:21-23, recapitulated in 1:25 and 1:28a).

Stage 3: God *"gives over"* humans to their desires/passions and to an "unfit mind" which aim at self-degrading and self-destructive forms of conduct (1:24, 26, 28).

---

14. Without excluding this option altogether, Peter von der Osten-Sacken thinks that 1:24 probably refers specifically to unchaste behavior with prostitutes (*porneia*; "Paulinisches Evangelium und Homosexualität," *BTZ* 3 [1986]: 36). He reasons that *porneia* usually appears in Pauline vice lists and, since it does not appear elsewhere in 1:28-31, it may be alluded to in 1:24. However, it is more likely that same-sex intercourse is in view in 1:24 as the epitome of a broader array of sexual immoralities.

Stage 4: Many humans then dishonored themselves by *"exchanging"* natural intercourse for manifestly self-degrading and unnatural intercourse (1:26-27); all engaged in some form of "improper" and evil conduct (1:28-31).

Stage 5: The self-degrading evil behavior to which God "gives over" humans ends in the ultimate recompense of "death" (1:32).

Quite appropriately, an absurd exchange of God for idols leads to an absurd exchange of heterosexual intercourse for homosexual intercourse. A dishonoring of God leads to a mutual dishonoring of selves. A failure to see fit to acknowledge God leads to an unfit mind and debased conduct.

In terms of rhetoric, the argument in 1:18-32 can be classified as a "forensic" or "judicial" indictment. First, 1:18 provides an opening summary statement that focuses on the *present* manifestation of God's wrath (cf. "is being revealed") against humanity for knowingly suppressing the truth about God (*propositio*). Second, 1:19-23 describes idolatry as an inexcusable denial of the truth about God visible to human eyes in "the things made," an "exchanging" (*ēllaxan*) of God's obvious glory for statues in human or animal forms (*narratio* or statement of facts). Third, 1:24-31 validates God's course of action (cf. *dio*, "therefore," in v. 24 and *dia touto*, "for this reason," in v. 26) in "giving over" (*paredōken*) these idolaters to their sinful impulses (*probatio* or proofs), both (a) their desires for same-sex intercourse as the epitome of self-degradation, an action utterly "contrary to nature" (1:24-27; general statement: v. 24; recapitulation of the root sin of idolatry: v. 25; female homosexual intercourse: v. 26; male homosexual intercourse: v. 27) and (b) various other evil desires elaborated in the form of a vice list, which fill out the picture of depraved conduct that results from shunning the one true God (1:28-31). Finally, 1:32 supplies the conclusion which stresses both the culpability of the participants (doing and even approving, despite knowing) and the ultimate fate of death awaiting those who engage in such depraved conduct ("knowing . . . worthy of death"; *peroratio*).[15]

---

15. For an alternative assessment of the rhetoric, cf. Calvin L. Porter, "Romans 1.18-32: Its Role in the Developing Argument," *NTS* 40 (1994): 216-19. Porter classifies 1:18-32 as an epideictic speech which strengthens "the disposition toward action

Romans 1:26-27: Same-Sex Intercourse as "Contrary to Nature"

Same-sex eroticism functions as a particularly poignant example of human enslavement to passions and of God's just judgment precisely because it parallels in the horizontal-ethical dimension a denial of God's reality like that of idolatry in the vertical-divine dimension. In other words, idolatry is a deliberate suppression of the truth available to pagans in the world around them, but so too is same-sex intercourse. Paul emphasizes this in his adoption of the phrase "contrary to nature." Given the meaning of "contrary to nature" (*para physin*) and comparable expressions used by Jewish writers of the period to describe same-sex intercourse, the meaning of the phrase in Paul is clear. Minimally, Paul is referring to the anatomical and procreative complementarity of male and female.[16] Put in more crude terms, Paul in effect argues that even pagans who have no access to the book of Leviticus should know that same-sex eroticism is "contrary to nature" because the primary sex organs fit male to female, not female to female or male to male. Again, by fittedness I mean not only the glove-like physical fit of the penis and vagina but also clues to complementarity provided by procreative capacity and the capacity for mutual and pleasurable stimulation. These clues make clear that neither the anus, the orifice for excreting waste products, nor the mouth, the orifice for taking in food,

---

by increasing adherence to values it lauds" and defends "traditional and accepted" values. The difference between our two classifications, forensic and epideictic, is not great in this particular case. Paul is presenting for the interlocutor's approval his forensic indictment of the gentile world. This indictment reflects shared values with the interlocutor (hence the epideictic element). At the same time, Paul converts the indictment of gentiles into an indictment of Jews, including the interlocutor. This indictment in turn serves to persuade both the interlocutor and the audience at Rome to a future course of action (a deliberative element). As regards the subdivision of 1:18-32, Porter treats 1:18 as the introduction or *exordium*; 1:19-21 as the *narratio*; 1:22-31 (subdivided into 1:22-24, 25-27, 28-31) as the "division" (*divisio*), "which should set forth 'the things we intend to praise or censure'" (*Rhet. Her.* 3.7.13); and 1:32 as the conclusion. Different from Porter, I place the main break between 1:23 and 1:24 rather than between 1:21 and 1:22. I do so for the following reasons: the *dio* in 1:24 indicates a decisive shift from human behavior to divine response; the first occurrence of the threefold use of *paredōken autous ho theos* appears in 1:24; and 1:28, which nearly all commentators agree starts a new subdivision, likewise begins with the phrase *paredōken autous ho theos*.

16. Others who point to male-female "complementarity" as the key to understanding Paul's use of *para physin* include Hays, "Relations Natural and Unnatural,

are complementary orifices for the male member. For Paul it was a
simple matter of commonsense observation of human anatomy and

184-215; Schmidt, *Straight and Narrow?*, 81-2; and Wright, "Homosexuality: The
Relevance of the Bible," 295. Most commentators speak vaguely of same-sex
intercourse as a violation of the "order of nature" or "natural order" created and
intended by God (cf. *T. Naph.* 3:3-5). Fitzmyer, however, explicitly mentions "the
order seen in the function of sexual organs themselves, which were ordained for an
expression of love between man and woman and for the procreation of children"
(*Romans*, 286). Cranfield takes "nature" as a metonym for "the intention of the
Creator" or "the way God made us" (*Romans*, 125-26) as does Springett
(*Homosexuality*, 129-30). Karl Hoheisel recognizes that Paul viewed same-sex
intercourse as standing outside "the order of God or of creation," but appeals to
Rom 11:24 for modern reappropriations of Rom 1:26-27 to allow for a "changeable
divine order" ("Homosexualität," 338-39). A. M. J. M. Herman van de Spijker
believes that "nature" refers not only to "the bodily sexuality or genitalia" (citing
S. J. Ridderbos) but to "the human nature in its spiritual, soulish, and somatic components" (*Die gleichgeschlechtliche Zuneigung* [Olten: Walter, 1968] 83-84). In the
view of Balz, "it is a matter of an offense against the human body given with creation. . . . : false use of one's sexual potency, a renunciation of offspring, an offense
against the creation-appropriate combination of man and woman and finally probably also the disturbance of the bodily relationships of life willed by God. . . . Paul
appeals, when he speaks of *physis*, to an insight accessible to everyone in the reality of creation given in all that is" ("Biblische Aussagen," 66).

According to Hays, "[T]he understanding of 'nature' in this conventional language does not rest on empirical observation of what actually exists; instead, it
appeals to a conception of what ought to be, of the world as designed by God and
revealed through the stories and laws of Scripture" (*The Moral Vision of the New
Testament*, 387). It seems to me that this statement has something important to say
but is not completely accurate. In Rom 1:24-27 Paul is *not* appealing to the stories
and laws of Scripture—which he could not assume that gentiles had knowledge
of—but he *is* appealing to "empirical observation of what actually exists" inasmuch
as "the world designed by God" still showed the marks of the Creator's hand. This
was true of the grandeur of the created world and was true as well of the anatomical and procreative complementarity of male and female. Hays is correct that
"nature" in the sense used by Paul here does not embrace everything that existed
as a good. Some things that are innate, such as many of "the desires of the human
heart," listed in 1:24-31, have been skewed by the fall and are not safe indicators
of God's intention for human sexuality. However, in the anatomical and procreative
complementarity of male and female, empirical observation of what is and intuitive
understanding of what ought to be merge because the fall did not obliterate this
physical and functional aspect of human sexuality. The Stoics too appealed to
empirical observation of sexual differences between men and women as a way of
determining right behavior.

Brooten identifies two meanings of "nature" in Rom 1:26-27: nature as "the order
of creation" and as "the gendered nature of human beings" (*Love Between Women*,
272-80). By the former she means deriving "a heterosexual norm for humans from

procreative function that even pagans, otherwise oblivious to God's direct revelation in the Bible, had no excuse for not knowing.[17]

That Paul was thinking of "nature" not as "the way things are usually done" (i.e., cultural convention) but rather as "the material shape of the created order" is also apparent from his previous illustration that

---

the presumed exclusive heterosexuality of animals" or "an order of creation as laid down in the Genesis creation narratives" which in turn promoted the "priority of man over woman" (i.e., woman made from and for man as in 1 Cor 11:8-9; pp. 273-75). In response to Brooten, the heterosexual proclivity of animals may have played some role in Paul's thinking but, to judge from the limited attention it gets in Jewish writings of the period, it is unlikely to have played a major role. At most, it probably functioned as a subsidiary, corroborating argument. The order of creation laid down in Genesis 1–3 undoubtedly informed Paul's own thinking but, in the context of the argument in 1:18-32, Paul could not (and did not) presume that gentiles had access to such written revelation. The focus is on visible clues in creation and nature, not on a *written* text (access to the latter is what distinguishes Jew from gentile in Romans 2, though Paul undermines that very distinction by pointing to the internal, unwritten "law" possessed even by gentiles). By nature as "the gendered nature of human beings" Brooten means "the particular nature of man and the particular nature of woman," the specific character traits or dispositions that define masculine and feminine "natures." It is a woman's "nature" to play the passive, subordinate sexual role and the male's "nature" to play the active, dominant sexual role (pp. 275-77, 280). Strangely, and without justification, Brooten completely neglects any discussion of "nature" as anatomical complementarity.

Nissinen similarly regards "unnatural" as a synonym for "(seriously) unconventional." Unlike Brooten, he occasionally gives at least backhanded reference to anatomical complementarity as a factor in denoting same-sex intercourse as "unnatural" (*Homoeroticism*, 105). "Evidently, 'natural intercourse' implies *not only gender difference and the complementarity of sexes* but also gender roles. . . . *Gender role categories . . . are not determined by anatomical sex only* but also by an appropriate self-presentation and conformity to established gender roles" (ibid., 107; my emphases). Yet even between these two sentences he can speak as if anatomical complementarity in heterosexual intercourse played no role in Paul's evaluation of it as natural. "Paul's understanding of the naturalness of men's and women's gender roles is *not* a matter of genital formation and their functional purpose, which today is considered the main criterion for the unnatural" (my emphasis). This strict "either/or" approach is Nissinen's usual way of formulating the issue.

For a refutation of the thesis that Paul regarded same-sex intercourse as "unnatural" primarily because it put some women in dominant sexual roles and some men in subordinate sexual roles, see the discussion in ch. 5.II. Given Paul's argument in 1 Cor 11:2-16 it cannot be denied that confusion of "headship" factored into Paul's thinking but this factor alone hardly constituted Paul's *primary* reason for rejecting same-sex intercourse.

17. On the rejection of natural theology as a sufficient medium for knowing God, cf. Karl Barth, *Natural Theology: Comprising "Nature and Grace" by Professor Dr.*

idolatry entails the suppression of truth. Paul says that God's will as regards the worship of idols is "plainly visible" or "obvious" (*phaneron*) because "from (the time of) the creation of the world his unseen qualities (*ta aorata*) are clearly seen (*kathoratai*), capable of being mentally apprehended by means of the things made (*tois poiēmasin*)." In other words, *visual* perception of the *material* creation that God has made (certainly including observation of heavenly bodies, a stock philosophical appeal) should lead to a mental perception about the nature of God and God's will.

Similarly, the reader should expect that the appeal to nature in 1:26-27 has to do, at least primarily, with the visual perception of male-female bodily complementarity (the fittedness of the sex organs). Passions, which are not material and hence not visible to sight, are

---

Emil Brunner and the Reply "No!" by Dr. Karl Barth (London: Centenary, 1946). It is certainly true that, for Paul, at least since the coming of Christ definitively redemptive knowledge of God was possible only through (1) the communication of the gospel, a gospel which announced the salvific work of Christ on the cross and in his resurrection; (2) an individual's embrace of Christ's lordship (Rom 10:9-15); and (3) God's "sealing" of the believer with the Spirit of Christ. Nevertheless, Rom 1:18-32 makes quite clear that Paul allowed for sufficient knowledge of God accessible through observation of the material creation to enable gentiles to deduce that idolatry was wrong and to justify God's expression of wrath against those who commit it. He also apparently regarded some knowledge of moral absolutes among gentiles as possible through the "natural" faculties of reason and conscience (Rom 2:14-16). However, he did not regard such knowledge as any more fruitful for redemption than the access that Jews had to the direct revelation of Mosaic law. (The image of gentiles who keep the law in 2:26-29 alludes to believers in Christ who have the gift of the Spirit, not to gentiles in general.) Indeed, Paul uses the argument in Rom 2:14-16 not to establish that gentiles know enough to be saved but rather to confirm that the Jews are not exempted from God's judgment simply because they know what Scripture says and occasionally comply with it. "Nature," according to Paul in 1 Cor 11:14-15, should have made clear to the Corinthian believers, even if Scripture did not, certain distinctions between the sexes and the implications of such for worship praxis. Paul's reference in 1 Cor 5:1 to incest as an instance of "sexual immorality" accepted "not even among the gentiles" may also have natural law in the background. For Paul, then, nature provided the unbeliever (and believer) with access to some information about God and God's will that enabled compliance with the truth at some level. It also justified God's condemnation of those who violated certain basic principles concerning idolatry and immorality. Yet the knowledge that nature/creation communicated about God was insufficient for salvation—only the word of the gospel and the gift of the Spirit could convey that. Cf. James Barr, *Biblical Faith and Natural Theology* (Oxford: Clarendon, 1993).

excluded from consideration as indications of God's intentions manifest in nature. Other allusions to Genesis in Rom 1:18-32 (see below) also refer the reader back to God's creation of male and female as complementary sexual beings in Gen 1:27-28. The reference in 1:24 to same-sex intercourse as a "dishonoring of their bodies," combined with the reference to "natural use" in 1:26-27, confirms that Paul viewed same-sex intercourse as an "unnatural" use of the gendered body because of the clear anatomical "discomplementarity" of such intercourse. The fact, too, that ancient philosophical discussions about nature's provision for gender differentiation often appealed to visible, bodily characteristics of men and women (including 1 Cor 11:14) confirms the understanding proposed here for "nature" in Rom 1:26-27 (see ch. 5.II).[18]

---

18. Given these considerations, Helmut Koester's attempt to contrast the "technical" usage of nature in 1 Cor 11:14 with its use in Rom 1:26-27 of "the natural order" is inexplicable. Koester tries to split the forms of argumentation in 1:18-25 and 1:26-27 by pointing to the fact that *physis* "does not occur at all when Paul speaks of the knowledge of God from His works of creation in the visible world" (*"physis"* *TDNT* 9:273). However, Koester himself admits that in sayings in Philo which parallel Rom 1:18-25 *physis* is "repeatedly used," personifying nature as creator and sustainer of the world (ibid., 267, 273 n. 215). Moreover, as in Rom 1:18-27, the author of *T. Naph.* 3:3-4 exhorts the readers to "recognize the Lord who made all things . . . in all the products of his workmanship" and compares the actions of gentiles who "changed their order" by devoting themselves "to stones and sticks" to the actions of the men of Sodom who "exchanged the order of their nature."

Pim Pronk follows Koester's point about the absence of *physis* in Rom 1:18-23 (*Against Nature? Types of Moral Argumentation Regarding Homosexuality* [Grand Rapids: Eerdmans, 1993], 227). Pronk continues: "Paul viewed homosexual behavior as. . . a classic example of *paganism*. . . . And he further illustrates this by referring to the nature known to him and all men in its normal functioning, hence to empirical observation. Paul regards this being-given-up to the . . . non-normal— the unnatural—as a consequence of God's wrath. Not because the non-normal is morally unnatural but because the unnatural is a sign of *unbelief*. The thrust of Paul's argument, therefore, is directed not against 'nature' but against 'unbelief.' Hence Paul calls homosexual behavior 'unnatural' in order to furnish factual information. That homosexuality is unnatural is a reason—for Paul—to view it as a form of unbelief. . . . I, therefore, conclude that, seeing Paul does not equate creation (= normative creation order) and nature, the word 'unnatural' in Romans 1 cannot without qualification be taken as referring to Genesis 1" (ibid.). It is difficult for me to assess this argument because, frankly, I do not understand the logic of it. If Pronk means that Paul condemns same-sex intercourse as unnatural solely because it is characteristic of pagans and therefore must be, by definition, a sign of unbelief,

When gentiles engage in same-sex eroticism they "in return receive in their own persons the payback necessitated by their straying" (1:27).

---

then Pronk has ignored the close parallels to 1:26-27 in Philo and Josephus, the allusions to Genesis throughout 1:18-32, the clear lines of connection with the argument from observable creation in 1:18-23, and the parallel form of argument from nature in 1 Cor 11:14.

Oda Wischmeyer emphasizes that "Creation and nature in Paul, as in the Old Testament and early Judaism, are not independent theologumena. Rather [ktisis] and [physis] in Paul are secondary and tertiary concepts in the context of Pauline talk about God" ("[Physis] und [Ktisis] bei Paulus: Die paulinische Rede von Schöpfung und Natur," ZTK 93 [1996]: 352-75; quote from p. 370). Wischmeyer is correct that creation alone cannot lead one to reconciliation with God in Christ, that the creation is only provisional in view of the "new creation." However, too great a divide between creation and new creation leads one to a point closer to Marcion than to Paul. As noted above, 1:18-32 argues that enough knowledge of God is mediated by creation/nature to justify God holding people accountable for their sins, particularly idolatry and same-sex intercourse. Simply abstaining from idolatry and same-sex intercourse is not enough to be saved; but engaging in these provides adequate grounds for condemnation. A distinction between creation and nature as secondary and tertiary concepts, respectively, also requires qualification. To be sure, Paul in 1 Cor 11:2-16 does put forward a proof pertaining to the creation of Adam and Eve (11:7-12; the verb ktizō appears in 11:9) separately from a proof pertaining to nature (11:13-14). In this sense, creation refers to an event at the beginning of time while nature refers to the ongoing semi-timeless state or result issuing from that event. Depending on the information needed, discerning creation may require some knowledge of divine revelation (viz., God's specific actions in Genesis 1-3, such as woman's derivation from man), whereas discerning nature presupposes only human observation of created things. In the case of Rom 1:18-27, the distinction between creation and nature collapses because there Paul means by "creation" the way things turned out after the initial act of creating. True, ktisis in 1:20 ("from the creation of the world") refers to the primal event, but it does so in a context that emphasizes the aftermath of that event: "the things made" which are now subject to human observation. The use of ktisis in Rom 1:25 (worshiping the creature rather than the Creator), like its use in Rom 8:19-22 (the creation groans in expectation of redemption), refers to created things or things reproduced after the pattern of the initial creation, which are still accessible to sense perception. One could easily substitute nature for creation in Rom 8:19-22 and not materially affect Paul's meaning. The only difference would be that the term creation necessarily requires the notion of a Creator, whereas the term nature does not. Yet in Paul's thinking, as for first-century Jews generally, nature is by definition the Creator's handiwork. Consequently, when Nissinen (citing Wischmeyer) states that "creation and nature are not interchangeable concepts in Paul's theology," he is mistaken, at least insofar as the uses in Romans are concerned (Homoeroticism, 107). What is "contrary to nature" is at one and the same time contrary to divinely created structures.

The "straying" or "error" (*planē*) is that of not acknowledging the true God (i.e., idolatry).[19] The use of *planē* in Wis 12:23-27 provides the closest parallel:

> Therefore, too, the unrighteous who lived in a life of folly you tormented through their own abominations. For they strayed (*eplanēthēsan*) very far on the paths of straying (or: error; *planēs*), taking for gods things which—even by the standard of animals—were regarded as dishonorable (*ta atima*) by their enemies (or: among loathsome things), deceived like foolish infants. Because of this, as to unreasoning children you sent your judgment to mock them. But those [idolaters] who have not heeded the warning of mild rebukes will experience a judgment worthy of God. For they were indignant at those [animal deities] they thought to be gods, because they themselves were suffering, being punished by them. Having seen the One whom they were formerly refusing to know, they recognized the true God. Therefore the outer limit of judgment came on them (i.e., the death of the firstborn and the drowning at the sea).

Here the "unrighteous" Egyptians committed the "straying/error" of idolatry, the worship of despicable animals instead of the one true God, and in return were mockingly punished by the real animals they worshiped in statue form. The more general discussion of the beginning of idolatry in the human race in Wis 13–14 moves from idolatry to self-deception as regards right conduct and thence to various forms of evil

---

19. This is, rightly, the consensus view. Cf. the commentaries by Calvin, Hodge, Godet, Meyer, Lietzmann, Murray, Schlier, Cranfield, Dunn, Wilckens, Byrne, and Schreiner; also, BAGD; Herbert Braun, "planaō," *TDNT* 6:243 ("The later LXX use is very obviously the background here"); *EDNT*; Countryman, Schmidt, Nissinen, Balz, and Jewett. Moo, Fitzmyer, and Schmithals are alone in designating the "error" as homosexual activity. Such an interpretation leaves one fishing for a referent for "payback" beyond the text itself, when the text already supplies an adequate referent: being handed over by God to the dishonoring of their own bodies in shameful, self-degrading conduct. The reminders in 1:25 and 1:28a that those whom God gives over to dishonorable passions and disapproved desires are the very same ones who dishonored and disapproved of God confirms that the "error" that leads to punishment is idolatry. Both Countryman and Schmidt also point out that Paul consistently used *planē* and related words (the verb *planaō* and the adjective *planos,-on*) of wrong belief rather than wrong conduct. A similar critique can be leveled against Fredrickson's claim that the "error" is passion (i.e., excessive sexual desire; "Romans 1:24-27," 215).

conduct. In Rom 1:18-32 the sequence is the straying/error of idolatry (worshiping the creature rather than the Creator), God's role in expressing wrath through the giving over of humankind to their sinful impulses (Paul's distinctive contribution), followed by human commission of self-degrading acts. Consequently, there can be little doubt that what Paul meant by "payback" or "recompense" (*antimisthia*, often translated as "penalty") in 1:27 was the act of being given over by God to "dishonor their bodies" (1:24) and to be overtaken by their "dishonorable passions" (1:26). Such activity worked an "indecency . . . in themselves" that transparently contradicted the divine design visible in male/female anatomy and in sexual and procreative function.[20] "One is

---

20. The majority of scholars correctly regard the perversion of same-sex intercourse as its own penalty. Cf. already Martin Luther, *Lectures on Romans*, 27; and Calvin, *Romans*, 35, 37 ("to bring disgrace upon ourselves. . . .[is] the most suitable punishment for a dishonor done to the divine Majesty. . . . those who were not ashamed to extinguish . . . the glory of God which alone gives us light deserve to become blind at noonday"). Moo defines the penalty as either "the sexual perversion itself" or "eternal punishment" (*Romans*, 116). Given 1:32 (behavior "worthy of death"), there may indeed be a secondary allusion to eschatological destruction. Still, the focus of 1:18, 24-31 is on the *present* experience of divine wrath—a point confirmed by the present tense of *apolambanontes* ("receiving," though a future ptc. would be rare). Murray sees two punishments: "the gnawing unsatisfied lust itself, together with the dreadful physical and moral consequences of debauchery" (*Romans*, 1.48, quoting W. Shedd). Although Schmithals was convinced that the recompense was not homosexuality itself, he expressed uncertainty over what it might be; perhaps childlessness, or "disappointment of the soul," or "the self-offense," or sickness (*Römerbrief*, 81). Brooten also leaves the question open: the penalty is either the "diseased" sexual activity itself, with the receptive male partners made effeminate by a passive sexual role and the active partners becoming sterile, or possibly venereal disease (*Love Between Women*, 258). Bartlett supposes that Paul was alluding to "venereal disease or other kinds of physical infirmity" ("A Biblical Perspective on Homosexuality," 140). Yet in general such conditions do not factor into the criticisms of same-sex intercourse by ancient moralists. Examples in Philo suggest that Paul may have had partly in mind the feminizing of the receptive male partner and masculinizing of the active lesbian partner, and hence the "degeneration" of both body and soul attending the alteration of nature's stamp on gender. The active male homosexual experiences the debilitating effect of unrestrained passion. Yet the context of Rom 1:18-32 puts the emphasis squarely on the "dishonoring" of the bodies (1:24, not the physical effects on them) of both partners in same-sex intercourse—a dishonoring that takes place when the obvious indicators of God's will in creation and nature are ignored. Cf. now Fredrickson who argues that "punishment consists of being handed over to passion—itself dishonorable to have. . . . Punishment was a central metaphor for the

being punished by the very things by which one sins" (Wis 11:16).[21] In the same way, idolatry is its own punishment because it mocks its practitioners, who have blinded themselves to the truth that silently screams at them in the created world and reduces them to "foolish," unwise, pitiable creatures.[22] The wrath of God, which will manifest itself fully on the day of final judgment (2:5), already "is being revealed from heaven against all ungodliness and unrighteousness of humans" (1:18) in that God is even now giving over those who have exchanged the true God for substitute gods to the self-degradation of indecent and shameless forms of conduct.

That this payback "was necessitated" (*edei*) by the error of idolatry could mean that it was the inevitable, almost mechanistic outcome. As BAGD notes, *dei* can refer to "divine destiny or unavoidable fate," as well as to the "compulsion" of duty, law, what is fitting, or a specific goal. In the context of 1:18-32, it is true that there is a certain logic to the sequence of events. First, a false wisdom suppresses the truth about God in creation. This leads, second, to the foolishness of worshiping objects sculpted in the image of created things. Finally, this leads, in turn, to an inevitable distortion of one's moral compass and the satisfaction of desires that are inherently self-degrading.[23] Nevertheless,

---

ill effects on the lover of his own passionate love. . . . taking its toll on the finances, mental equilibrium, and the honor of the lover" ("Romans 1:24-27," 217).

21. The parallel to Wis 11:16 is only a partial one since the context refers to the plagues involving "irrational creatures" that befell the Egyptians, who worshiped such animals. The worship of animals is not being conceived by the author as its own penalty, nor does Paul view the punishment for worshiping animals as an animal-related series of plagues. One could argue that, in Paul's thinking, humans who worship animals become like animals in that rational reflection is subjugated by unreasoning passion. However, such a point would have to be tempered by the observation of Greco-Roman moralists that not even animals engage in same-sex intercourse. Cf. *T. Gad* 5:9-11 where "Gad" states that "God brought on me a disease of the liver. . . . For by whatever human capacity anyone transgresses, by that he is also chastised. Since my anger was merciless in opposition to Joseph, through this anger of mine I suffered mercilessly, and was brought under judgment for eleven months, as long as I had it in for Joseph" (the liver is here viewed as the seat of strong emotions, including anger).

22. Cf. Wis 13:10-14:1, among other early Jewish texts, for similar rhetoric about the self-debasement involved in idol worship, a theme also familiar to Israel's prophets (e.g., Isa 44:9-20).

23. Cf. Dodd, *Romans*, 55; *EDNT*, s.v. *dei* ("the logic of events frequently overshadows divine determination").

the threefold *paredōken autous ho theos* ("God gave them over") in 1:24, 26, 28 emphasizes God's "semi-active" role in the process. God is "semi-active" because, on the one hand, God actively "gives over" humans to their own desires as a deliberate act of divine judgment ("wrath"), but, on the other hand, God manifests this wrath (at least initially) by passively allowing these sinful desires to take their own course rather than by bringing supernatural destruction.

God deliberately decides not to intervene to thwart the control of sinful passions in order that the punishment might fit the crime. In this way, we learn that the dishonoring of God leads to a dishonoring of self. The place of Rom 1:24-27 within the larger context of the revelation of God's righteousness for a world trapped in sin (2:4; 3:21-26; 6:1–8:17; 11:32; cf. Gal 3:22; 1 Cor 5:5) suggests that the hopeful intent of the punishment is reformatory. Humans disgusted by their self-debasing conduct become good candidates for receiving the gracious transforming power of the gospel and Spirit of Christ (cf. Wis 11:23; 12:2, 10, 20).[24] Yet Paul also subscribed to a common theme of early Jewish texts that the unrepentant are allowed by God to continue to heap up the measure of their sins until their total destruction is warranted (Rom 2:5; cf. Wis 12:26; 19:4).[25]

---

24. Cf. Godet (*Romans*, 178) who compares the parable of the prodigal son: "when man has reached a certain degree of corruption, he can only be cured by the very excess of his own corruption."

25. Cf. Dunn, *Romans*, 65, 73 ("'God handed them over'. . . denotes a measured and deliberate act, but also the resigning of direct control over what is thus passed on. . . . God handed them over to the freedom for which they yearned; not their freedom to them, but them to their freedom"); Moo, *Romans*, 111 ("God does not simply let the boat go—he gives it a push downstream"); Murray, *Romans*, 44 ("The giving over . . . cannot be reduced to the notion of non-interference. . . . God's displeasure is expressed in his abandonment of the persons concerned to more intensified and aggravated cultivation of the lusts of their own hearts with the result that they reap for themselves a correspondingly greater toll of retributive vengeance"); Sanday and Headlam, *Romans*, 45 ("the force of [*paredōken*] is not merely *permissive* . . . , through God permitting men to have their way; or *privative*, through His withdrawing His gracious aid; but *judicial*, the appropriate punishment of their defection: it works automatically, one evil leading to another by natural sequence"; citing *m. ʾAbot* 4:2: "every transgression is punished by another"; *b. Šabb.* 104a: "whosoever will be impure to him is it [the door of vice] thrown open"). Similarly, Cranfield, Zeller, Schmidt, Zahn, Hodge, Godet, Meyer, Lagrange; Leon Morris, *The Epistle to the Romans* (Grand Rapids: Eerdmans, 1988): 93; S. L. Johnson,

The power of Paul's argument lies precisely in its simplicity: if one disregards the book of Leviticus and asks oneself what clues existing in nature might aid in discerning the Creator's will for sexual expression, then human anatomy and procreative function comprise the most unambiguous indications of divine intent. One can debate the "naturalness" of homosexual urges. Many human emotions (for example, lust, anger, jealousy, covetousness) obviously run counter to God's intended design for nature and cannot be pronounced good simply because they are felt. Paul attributes such sinful impulses to the fall of Adam (Rom 5:12-21). However, anatomy is not quite as skillful a deceiver and for that reason is a more effective mediator of the truth.

All of this explains why Paul selects female and male homosexual conduct as "exhibit A" of culpable gentile depravity. First and foremost, along with idolatry, same-sex intercourse represents one of the clearest instances of conscious suppression of revelation in nature by gentiles, inasmuch as it involves denying clear anatomical gender differences and functions (leaving them "without excuse").[26] Second, it

---

"'God Gave Them Up': A Study in Divine Retribution," *BSac* 129 (1972): 131-32. Both Luther and Calvin viewed God as actively involved through the manipulating of Satan. "This 'giving up' is not so much a permission as a commission, a command, of God. . . . the Lord orders the devil or the flesh to tempt and overwhelm a man" (Luther, *Lectures on Romans*, 27). God "not only permits men to fall into sin. . . but . . . He also ordains it by His just judgment, so that they are forcibly led into such mad folly not only by their own evil yearnings but by the Devil as well . . . the minister of the wrath of God and His 'executioner'" (Calvin, *Romans*, 35). At first glance bringing Satan into the picture might appear highly dubious. Yet Paul undoubtedly believed in the Devil's role as tempter and punisher whose activities God could utilize for grander divine purposes (esp. 1 Cor 5:5; 2 Cor 12:7; also Rom 16:20; 1 Cor 7:5; 2 Cor 2:11; 11:3, 14; 1 Thess 2:8; cf. Eph 4:27; 6:11; 2 Thess 2:9; 1 Tim 1:20; 3:6-7; 5:15; 2 Tim 2:26). In Rom 9:18; 11:7, 25, Paul spoke of God's active role in "hardening" the hearts of humans (here Israel) to serve the divine plan. It is thus conceivable that Paul understood the "giving over" of Rom 1:24-32 as more active than most commentators indicate. However, Paul makes no reference to Satan in Romans until the very end of the letter (16:20). Generally he was content to speak simply of the sinful passions operating in human members. Even when he alluded to God's use of Satan or God's hardening of hearts, he did so with the understanding that these actions were in accord with the desires of those affected and initiated for the ultimate purpose of maximizing salvation.

26. Martin Stowasser is quite right to point to the fact that idolatry and sexual sin are an expected combination, given that there was a growing tendency in early Judaism to group the first five commandments of the decalogue under the rubric of idolatry and the second five under desire, particularly sexual desire ("Homosexualität

stakes out the common ground between Paul and his imaginary Jewish interlocutor since for Jews in antiquity homosexual conduct was a particularly repulsive example of gentile depravity.

A number of commentators mention the second reason given above as an explanation for why Paul highlighted same-sex intercourse before introducing a vice list, but I am not aware of anyone who explicitly mentions the first reason.[27] Yet the evidence is strong for concluding that the selection was based in large measure on the obvious visible

---

und Bibel: exegetische und hermeneutische Überlegungen zu einem schwierigen Thema," *NTS* 43 [1997]: 517). But this does not explain why same-sex intercourse is singled out from among all sexual sins.

27. Hays comes close but focuses more on scripture (Genesis 1–3) than on empirical observation accessible to gentiles: "Paul singles out homosexual intercourse for special attention because he regards it as providing a particularly graphic image of the way in which human fallenness distorts God's created order. God the Creator made man and woman for each other, to cleave together, to be fruitful and multiply. When human beings engage in homosexual activity, they . . . [reject] the Creator's design" ("Awaiting the Redemption of Our Bodies," 8). Schmithals comments that "the exchange of God and idols corresponds to the exchange of the sexes" (*Römerbrief*, 81). While this is an element picked up in the text (the verb "exchanged" is applied to both idolatry and same-sex intercourse), it does not tell the whole story since all vices involve an "exchange" of right behavior for wrong behavior. The explanation does not pick up the creation/nature parallelism. The same qualification can be given for Luther's assessment (adopted by Achtemeier): "What is more just than that those who turn away from the glory of God should be dishonored, not only in their hearts (and this is idolatry) but also in their bodies?" (*Lectures on Romans*, 31).

Brooten pays more attention than anyone else to the question of why Paul gave "special prominence to unnatural sexual intercourse." She suggests three possibilities. (1) Perhaps Paul, cognizant of the fact that "Rome was a center of debate and discussion about same-sex love" sought to build consensus with the Roman believers and/or to persuade them "not to practice acts of same-sex love and to oppose them actively." This may have been a factor but at best a minor one in view of the number of vices Paul could have chosen for this urban area; it does not establish why Paul singled out this particular vice. (2) Paul is attempting to build consensus by "employing a traditional Jewish anti-idolatry diatribe, which, like any polemic in this period, typically includes charges of sexual misconduct." Again, this does not explain why Paul highlighted the particular sexual vice of same-sex intercourse. As noted above, Wis 14 probably mentions same-sex intercourse but devotes only two words in the midst of a long vice list. The special attention that Paul gave to same-sex intercourse is striking by comparison. (3) Paul combined these two reasons, adapting "traditional Jewish anti-Gentile polemic" to the situation at Rome. This solution is simply an acknowledgment of the weaknesses of the two previous suggestions. Brooten concludes by saying that "we cannot definitively

manifestation in creation of same-sex discomplementarity. First, both the opening and closing lines of Rom 1:18-32 put the emphasis square-ly on human culpability for doing what God has clearly shown to be wrong through the visible evidence in creation.[28] Singling out same-sex intercourse was consistent with this emphasis on an obvious squelch-ing of the truth, a truth which was visibly manifest in male and female human bodies. To some extent this is true of all the vices enumerated in 1:29-31, but it is especially true of same-sex intercourse precisely because of the visible grounding of the truth in human anatomy.

Second, in the case of both idolatry and same-sex intercourse Paul emphasized their self-degrading character. Idol-worshipers are foolish for trading the transcendent glory of God for statues made in the images of animals, the Creator for the creature (1:21-23, 25). Similarly, those who participate in homosexual activity dishonor their own bodies, pursue dishonorable passions, ignore the natural "use" of the opposite

---

establish Paul's strategy in composing Rom 1:24-31 as he did" (*Love Between Women*, 261-62).

Nissinen's solution is not clear to me. "Changing the Creator to a creature leads to the altering of *conventional orders*, which is manifest in disordered sexual behavior. . . . Paul seems to have chosen same-sex sexual relations as an example of an indecent life precisely for the reason that they best rhetorically illustrate the exchanging of God for idols. . . . *The natural order is the divine order*, and to change the Creator to a creature means converting order to disorder" (*Homoeroticism*, 106; my emphasis). With the last sentence, Nissinen appears to be saying that both idolatry and same-sex intercourse are distortions of the created order—unless he is making an arbitrary distinction between "divine order" and "created order." However, sentences before, he referred to same-sex intercourse as an "altering of conventional orders" and later says that Paul is not referring to "an order of creation" in 1:26-27, that "creation and nature are not interchangeable con-cepts in Paul's theology" (pp. 106-107). Yet if we accept Nissinen's contention that creation and nature are not interchangeable in Rom 1:18-32, it is difficult to see why same-sex intercourse, among all sins, provides the best parallel to idolatry. Surely *Paul* did not view same-sex intercourse as a disruption of mere societal convention.

28. Thus: "humans who suppress the truth" (1:18), "God has made it visibly clear to them" (1:19), "readily seen because they are capable of being mentally grasped through the things made . . . so that they are without excuse" (1:20), "although they knew . . . " (1:21); and "although they knew. . . " (1:32). It is precisely this point which makes the connection with the following section: "you are without excuse . . . for . . . you judge. . . . we know . . . you who judges those who do such things. . . . But if you call yourself a Jew . . . and know . . . " (2:1-3, 17-18). Paul argues in ch. 2 that Jews know on the basis of a clearer, more explicit, and more direct reve-lation than the created order: Scripture.

sex, and commit acts that are clearly "contrary to nature" and indecent (1:24, 26-27). The self-degrading and shameful character of both actions, idolatry and same-sex intercourse, is integrally linked to the obviousness of their error.

Third, this similarity between idolatry and same-sex intercourse explains the peculiar construction of 1:24-27. The description in 1:24 of God turning the idolaters over to "an uncleanness that consisted of *dishonor*ing their bodies *in themselves*" clearly refers in the first instance to same-sex intercourse described in 1:26-27 ("God turned them over to *dishonor*able passions . . . receiving *in themselves* the payback"; also the parallel terms of "uncleanness" and "indecency"). Rom 1:24-27 forms an obvious subsection, as does 1:19-23 and 1:28-31. Yet Paul interrupted the connection between 1:24 and 1:26 with the parenthetical reminder of who these people engaging in same-sex intercourse were: "who exchanged the truth about God for a lie and worshiped and served the creature rather than the Creator who is blessed forever" (1:25). The insertion of 1:25 was Paul's way of reminding the reader of parallels between idolatry and same-sex intercourse that made the punishment so appropriate for the crime. In their vertical relationship to God the gentiles ignored the obvious truth about God visible in creation in order to pursue an absurd course of action— a course of action that they alleged was a product of wise rational reflection. God responded to their idolatry with the punishment of allowing them to debase their bodies in their horizontal relationships with one another. With no divine restraint on their passions, they continued to ignore the obvious truth—now about heterosexual complementarity so evident in nature—and pursued the absurd course of action of having sexual intercourse with members of the same gender. The correspondences can be laid out as follows:

Idolatry	*Same-Sex Intercourse*
vertical relationship with God	horizontal relationships with each other
suppressing visible evidence in creation	contrary to visible evidence in nature

in the sphere of the mind	in the sphere of body and passions[29]
human decision	divine handing-over
exchange of God for idols	exchange of opposite-sex for same-sex
not glorifying God	dishonoring themselves
foolish act	self-degrading behavior

The key parallel is the *absurd denial of natural revelation* in one's worship of God and intercourse with other humans.

Fourth, Greco-Roman moral discourse against the blurring of gender distinctions in general and same-sex intercourse in particular often mocked violators by appealing to the transparent character of divine design in nature. Philo, for example, highlighted the absurdity of same-sex intercourse when he described the situation at Sodom in this way: "Although they were men, (they began) mounting males, the doers not standing in awe of the nature held in common with those who had it done to them. In the process of trying to beget children, they were given convincing proof of their error inasmuch as they were sowing procreative sperm without result" (*Abr.* 135).[30]

It has become commonplace among interpreters of Rom 1:26-27 to state that Paul did not regard same-sex intercourse as more egregious than any other immoral act.[31] The treatment in 1:24-27 suggests otherwise, as is apparent from the compounding of such expressions as

---

29. The distinction between mind and passions is a slippery one since the range of sinful actions enumerated in 1:28-31 is described as the result of being handed over to "an unfit mind" (1:28). A disoriented mind, cut free from the moral direction found in the one true God, can provide no guidance for the restraint of sinful passions in the body.

30. Author's translation. Cf. 1 Cor 11:14: "does not *even* nature itself teach you. . . ."

31. Hays's opinion is representative: "Homosexual acts are not . . . specially reprehensible sins; they are no worse than any of the other manifestations of human unrighteousness listed in the passage (vv. 29-31)—no worse in principle than covetousness or gossip or disrespect for parents" ("Awaiting the Redemption of Our Bodies," 8-9).

Lance puts it this way: "Paul's illustrations are not chosen with great care or intentionality. . . . Paul did not set out specifically to address the issue of homosexuality. . . . he makes his point in passing" ("The Bible and Homosexuality," 148). On the contrary, Paul's illustration was chosen with great care and intentionality.

"the uncleanness of their bodies being dishonored" (1:24), "dishonorable passions" (1:26), and "indecency" or "obscene behavior" (1:27). In addition, the emphasis on the transparent self-degradation of the act ("in themselves") and the singling out of same-sex intercourse as a prime example before developing the extended vice list in 1:29-31 point in this direction. The depth of Paul's visceral feelings toward same-sex intercourse finds parallels not only in the level of disgust toward same-sex intercourse exhibited by other Jewish writers of the period but also in the responses to homosexual behavior in Paul's scripture: the narratives of homosexual rape (Ham, the men of Sodom, and the Benjamites at Gibeah) as examples of the zenith of detestable behavior; the intense revulsion against homosexual cult prostitutes manifested in Deuteronomic and Deuteronomistic texts; the special attachment of the label "abomination" to all male homosexual intercourse in the Levitical prohibitions; and possibly the unmentionable character of same-sex intercourse in Ezekiel, who refers to such behavior only by the metonym "abomination."

Paul will shortly (2:1–3:20) employ this visceral response to good advantage, as a means of snaring the law-possessing Jewish interlocutor into the trap of universal sin. Yet he gives no indication, either in 1:18-32 or in 2:1–3:20, that his assessment of same-sex intercourse in 1:26-27 was little more than a piece of rhetorical exaggeration. For *both* Paul and the interlocutor, gentiles generally sinned more frequently and more atrociously (cf. Gal 2:15). The difference between Paul and the interlocutor was not over whether, on average, gentiles or Jews were greater sinners. On that they would clearly agree. Instead, Paul was interested in two other matters. First, can Jews who sin, albeit in less shameful fashion and in fewer instances on average than gentiles, escape divine wrath for the transgressions they do commit (2:1-24; 3:1-20)? Second, can gentiles (i.e., Christian gentiles) who attain a higher level of righteousness than some Jews stand in judgment over transgressing Jews (2:25-29)? On the one hand, Jews may sin less qualitatively and quantitatively; but, on the other hand, since they have access to the direct revelation of Scripture they know more and, consequently, have even less of an excuse for sinning (2:1: "without excuse"; 2:2: "we know . . . "; 2:7: "tribulation and distress for . . . the Jew first"). Regardless of how Jews stack up in relation to gentiles, their level of "achieved" righteousness will be measured not against gentile standards but against the law (2:6-29) and against the God whom they may be tempted to charge with unfairness (3:1-8). The end result is— must be—that every mouth is shut when God rises in theophany to present the lawsuit for judgment (3:4-20).

Did Procreation for Paul Have Heuristic and Prescriptive Value?

For Paul, homosexual acts were sinful, first and foremost, because they demonstrated the rejection of God's intention that sexual inter-course be between sexual "others," an intention revealed by the anatomical complementarity of male and female sex organs. But were there additional reasons as well? That Paul might also have had in mind the heterosexuality that prevailed in the animal kingdom is possible though, if he did, it is unlikely that it played a crucial role in his thinking. As we have seen in extant Jewish texts of the period, such reasoning was employed but not with great frequency. More significant is the question of whether Paul, like Josephus and Philo (and many Greco-Roman moralists), rejected homosexual behavior on the grounds that all sexual activity that did not lead to procreation was wrong.

A sophisticated variant of this view is presented by Margaret Davies.[32] Davies argues that the "web of relations" that undergirded

---

32. Margaret Davies, "New Testament Ethics and Ours: Homosexuality and Sexuality in Romans 1:26-27," *BibInt* 3 (1995): 320-21. Cf. Dozeman, "Creation and Procreation," 178-80. Dozeman views Rom 1:26-27 as a "metaphorical extension" of the Levitical prohibitions, characterizing same-sex eroticism not only as wrong but also as "an act of self-worship and therefore idolatry for Paul" in that sex is "performed as an end in itself rather than for the purpose of procreation." Nissinen focuses on the problem of gender role reversal but in his concluding chapter he does refer to ancient misunderstandings about procreation. "Behind the distinction between active male and passive female roles are undoubtedly also ancient ideas about reproduction. . . . Losing [sperm] was a harmful waste of life." To say today that "life against anatomy is against nature" would "mean that also all heterosexual expressions of sexuality . . . are against nature if they do not aim directly at procreation" (*Homoeroticism*, 130, 133). Appealing to the influence of Plato's *Timaeus* (30A-B, 41A-D, 42A-B, 90E, 91A-C) on Hellenistic Judaism, Roy Bowen Ward believes that Paul's critique of same-sex intercourse in Rom 1:26-27 was based primarily on the belief that the genitals were used *kata physin* when employed for procreation only ("Why Unnatural? The Tradition Behind Romans 1:26-27," *HTR* 90 [1997]: 263-84). He appears to regard a concern for hierarchical disorder as

the anti-homosexual view of the Priestly writer was subverted by Paul's theology and practice. Where the Priestly writer promoted a mandate to procreate, the limitation of women's roles to childbearing, the need for more land and hence the socializing of men to violence, Paul sought the devaluation of the mandate to procreate, a stronger valuation of women's roles in ministry, and the devaluation of war. Consequently, for Davies, Paul's opposition to homosexuality should be treated as an unwarranted "emotional hangover."[33] Quite apart from the very dubious connections she draws between anti-homosexuality on the one hand and procreation and war on the other,[34] it is precisely Paul's adamant stance against homoerotic activity in spite of his relative disinterest in procreation and war that suggests Davies has misunderstood the reason for Paul's opposition.

(merely?) secondary and derivative. "This antipleasure, pro-procreation argument could and did result in an active/passive dichotomy between men and women engaged in penile-vaginal intercourse and the notion that there was a 'natural' difference between the sexes that applied generally to societal relationships" (p. 284). Jürgen Becker contends that Paul "presupposes that his readers know [what the "contrary to nature" consists of], namely that the aim of reproduction is cancelled in the case of homosexuality. If asked, Paul probably would have argued on the basis of Gen 1:27f." However, Becker also attributes other elements to Paul's thinking: the rejection of all sexual activity outside of marriage as inherently "excess" and "sexual immorality"; and the treatment of monogamy under the idea of a "reciprocal giving and taking" which "refers precisely to the specific sexual differences of man and woman" ("Zum Problem der Homosexualität in der Bibel," 53, 58). Stowasser follows Becker, noting that attempts to explain Rom 1:26-27 on the basis of an idolatrous form of cultic prostitution are "not compelling." "The text itself points with its allusions to the order of creation rather to the orientation of sexuality toward propagation . . . and implies perhaps also marriage. . . . The context, which is very strongly stamped by Gen 1, makes this conclusion appear to be probable. . . . Sexuality . . . stands exclusively in the service of propagation" ("Homosexualität und Bibel," 518-19).

33. Davies, "New Testament Ethics and Ours," 320-28. Davies is also impressed by the fact that in terms of chromosomes males and females differ by only one chromosome and thinks the only appropriate response to this discovery is to "see ourselves primarily as people rather than primarily as either men or women" (pp. 323-24, 329-31). Others, who have no wish to deny that both men and women are human beings first and foremost, are equally impressed by the differences that research has discovered between men and women (behavioral as well as anatomical, hormonal as well as chromosomal). In this vein, they emphasize the distinctiveness of each gender along the lines of the now popular phrase "men are from Mars, women are from Venus."

34. If failure to procreate was the major reason why the Holiness Code rejected homosexual behavior, what accounts for their rejection of incest? Why didn't the

The parallel with idolatry in Rom 1:18-32 indicates that, in Paul's view, the fact that sexual intercourse could potentially lead to childbirth only in heterosexual pairing provided clues or insights as to God's design for the sexual complementarity of the male and female organs. Consequently, for Paul procreation had more of a heuristic rather than prescriptive value, which in turn implies that those who argue that sexuality involves more than procreation miss the point. Unlike Philo, Josephus, and most Jews of his day, Paul did not emphasize (at least not in extant writings) the supreme importance of procreation in sexual pairing. His expectation of an imminent coming of Christ led him to promote the benefits of a singlehood that he himself modeled (1 Corinthians 7). Unlike Philo, Paul could hardly have been concerned about the depopulating of urban areas since, in his view, there was precious little time before the return of Christ. Furthermore, even Philo does not make the non-procreative capacity of male same-sex intercourse the sole or main reason for rejecting such behavior. Rather, the desire to have sex with another male and the demasculinization of the passive partner are his primary concerns.

Paul recommended marriage not for the purposes of procreation but for the purpose of avoiding sexual immorality (1 Cor 7:2-5). He regarded sexual intercourse in marriage as a legitimate (indeed, necessary) activity because it provided an appropriate escape valve for sexual desire that might otherwise result in adultery and promiscuity. Sex did not have to lead to procreation; it had real value as a release for sexual desire. Paul's exhortation in 1 Thess 4:4-5 that each gentile male believer "know how to procure for himself his own vessel (= wife) in holiness and honor, not in the passion of (sexual) desire as do the gentiles who do not know God" is not a denial of the role of sexual desire in marriage. Instead, it gives advice on how to select a mate, suggesting that one should look beyond a prospective mate's physical appeal to broader issues of character (cf. Sir 36:26-29; Tob 6:12; 8:7).[35]

Holiness Code also prescribe the death penalty to men who stayed married to barren women or men who masturbated or men who did not get married at all? Is the only problem with bestiality that it did not lead to human conceptions? Cf. pp. 128-41 for motives behind the Levitical prohibition.

35. Cf. Schmidt, *Straight and Narrow?*, 53. Brooten, among others, also recognizes that Paul did not condemn homoerotic behavior on the grounds of being nonpro-

It may be, though, that the argument for procreation factored in Paul's criticism not only as a clue to God's design for sexuality but also secondarily as an indication of the irresponsibility and excess of homo-erotic passion. The purpose of sex in marriage was not limited to pro-creation but *if* one were going to have sex it should be in the context of establishing stable family structures that includes a lifelong commit-ment in marriage and an intent at least to try to fulfill God's command to multiply. Sex for pleasure is permissible (and even necessary to avoid temptation to adultery) but conducted in isolation from stable family structures it becomes unbridled excess. Other potentially prob-lematic corollaries of the Hellenistic "contrary-to-nature" argument will be discussed in ch. 5 (II) and (III); namely, that same-sex inter-course upsets male dominance over women and, in many circles at least, was regarded as a product of over-heated heterosexual lust. What is clear at this point is that the capacity for procreation, in Paul's thought, serves as an additional clue of God's will for human sexuality. He does not limit sex to reproduction alone and so to argue for a broader view of sex does not undermine his argument against same-sex intercourse in any way.

Did Paul Think That Homoerotic Behavior Was "Dirty" But Not Sinful?

A plain reading of Rom 1:26-27 makes clear that Paul regarded same-sex intercourse and unrestrained passion for such practices as sin. However, there are some who argue that Paul treated same-sex intercourse either as not sinful or as sin only in a very diminished and vitually inconsequential sense. L. William Countryman is the most vigorous proponent of the view that Paul did not consider homosexuality

---

creative (*Love Between Women*, 248, 252-53). She makes the additional point that, "Although other ancient sources do condemn male-male sexual relations as non-procreative (e.g., Philo), those on female homoeroticism do not attack women involved in relationships with other women for not bearing children, but rather for lives that are shameful, impure, unnatural, and monstrous" (pp. 252-53). Similarly, William R. Schoedel: "One important component of the attack on same-sex eros (in Plato and later in Philo) is missing in Paul: the emphasis on procreativity" ("Same-Sex Eros: Paul and the Greco-Roman Tradition," *Homosexuality, Science, and the "Plain Sense" of Scripture*, 48).

to be sin.[36] According to Countryman, Paul merely regarded homosexuality as an "unpleasingly dirty aspect of Gentile culture . . . visited upon the Gentiles as recompense for sins, chiefly the sin of idolatry but also those of social disruption." "The argument is simply this: 'We all know Gentiles have sinned. Only look at the dirtiness into which God plunged them as a consequence. But what of the Jew who criticizes them? Are you claiming to be sinless?' "[37]

Countryman's analysis ignores obvious signals in 1:18-32 and the larger context of Romans and other Pauline letters. With regard to the language of 1:18-32, there is a clear parallel between the statements that "God handed them over in the desires of their hearts to the uncleanness of dishonoring their bodies among themselves" (1:24) and "God handed them over to dishonorable (homoerotic) passions" (1:26) on the one hand and "God handed them over to an undiscerning mind, to do what is not proper, having been filled with all unrighteousness, evil, greed, malice . . . , (things) worthy of death" (1:28-32) on the other hand. The implication is clear: same-sex intercourse, like the vices enumerated in 1:29-31, was sinful conduct deserving of death.

Countryman stretches credulity when he contends that, in Paul's mind, God handed gentiles over to homosexual behavior only *after* they "were already filled" with the sinful vices in 1:29-31. Paul clearly viewed these vices as a *concomitant* sinful consequence, along with the same-sex intercourse of 1:26-27, of being handed over by God to sinful passions after they had "exchanged" the true God for false gods (cf. 1:28: "and just as they did not discern the correctness of acknowledging God . . . "). Same-sex intercourse is simply singled out at the start as a particularly egregious example, among many examples, of the gentiles' sinful violation of God's truth available in nature. Countryman's attempt to discern a sequence from sinful vices (1:29-31) to "dirty" (but not "sinful") same-sex intercourse (1:26-27) has no warrant in the text—to say nothing of the fact that the discussion of same-sex intercourse precedes the enumeration of vices. The fact that Paul normally began vice lists with a list of sexual sins,[38] yet lists no specifically sexu-

---

36. *Dirt, Greed, and Sex*, 117, 123 (see pp. 104-23).
37. Ibid., 117, 123.
38. This is true of the two most extensive and "formal" vice lists in the undisputed

al vices in Rom 1:29-31, suggests that Paul intended the treatment of same-sex intercourse in 1:26-27 as an initial listing of sinful vices.[39]

Countryman also unconvincingly attempts to distinguish "what is not proper" (*ta mē kathēkonta*) in 1:28 from the category of "what is sinful" and then connect the former phrase only with homosexual behavior. Yet the phrase "what is not proper" clearly belongs with the sinful vices that follow (". . . to do the things that are not proper, filled with all unrighteousness, wickedness, . . . "). No distinction between "what is not proper" and sin can be made. Countryman also argues that "things worthy of death" in 1:32 does not include homosexual behavior, despite the fact that Lev 20:13 prescribes the penalty of death for male-male intercourse.[40]

To maintain his position that Paul evaluated same-sex intercourse as "dirty" but not "sinful," Countryman also has to insist that the additional descriptions of homosexual behavior in 1:24, 26-27 as "uncleanness," "the dishonoring of their bodies among themselves," "dishonorable passions," "contrary to nature," "burned in their yearning for one another," and "committing indecency" did not connote sin for Paul. However, all of these terms refer to sinful behavior in a range of Hellenistic Jewish literature.[41]

In addition, Countryman's assumption that the gentile audience in Rome would not have construed the homosexual behavior described in 1:26-27 as sin ignores the universal condemnation of lesbianism in the ancient world, not to mention the widespread condemnation of male homoerotic behavior by Greco-Roman moralists. To think that Paul, a

---

Pauline letters outside of Rom 1:29-31. 1 Cor 6:9-10 begins with the "sexually immoral (or: fornicators; *pornoi*), idolaters, adulterers, males who play the sexual role of females, men who take males to bed." Gal 5:19-21 begins with "sexual immorality (or: fornication; *porneia*), uncleanness, licentiousness" (similarly, Eph 5:3-4; Col 3:5-8). Unrestrained sexual activity also figures prominently in the middle of Rom 13:13 (cf. 1 Tim 1:9-10) and at the very end of 2 Cor 12:20-21. The latter is really two lists, the second of which consists only of "uncleanness and sexual immorality (*porneia*) and licentiousness." The prominence given to sexual vices does not necessarily mean that sexual vices are the worst of all sins but it may suggest that sexual vices are the most pernicious in terms of temptation and addiction.

39. Brooten, *Love Between Women*, 260-62.

40. Cf. the observation by von der Osten-Sacken: Rom 1:32 "must be referring principally to Lev 20:13" ("Paulinisches Evangelium und Homosexualität," 35).

41. Cf. the excellent discussion by Schmidt, *Straight or Narrow?*, 68-85.

Jew, regarded homoerotic conduct as merely "dirty" rather than "sinful" behavior flies in the face of historical probability, especially since all other Jewish texts from antiquity express not only disapproval but abject horror at such conduct.

Finally, the context surrounding 1:26-27 makes clear that same-sex intercourse is sin for Paul. First, all the other conduct described in 1:18-32 is evaluated as sinful, so surely same-sex intercourse is as well. Second, the heading for 1:18-32 as a whole refers to God's wrath "upon *every* ungodliness and unrighteousness of human beings who suppress the truth in unrighteousness" (1:18). Third, same-sex intercourse parallels the sin of idolatry since both suppress the truth about God and God's creation. Fourth, the description of gentile behavior in 1:18-32 is presented as partial proof of the "charge" that "all are under sin" (3:9; cf. 3:23: "all have sinned").

More broadly, an examination of Pauline texts outside Rom 1:18-32 also confirms the assessment of same-sex intercourse as sin. In Rom 6:19 Paul alludes to 1:24, 26-27 when he speaks of the former life of the Roman Christians as one in which they had presented their "members as slaves to uncleanness and to lawlessness for the purpose of lawlessness."[42] Here Paul places the phrase "slaves to uncleanness" parallel to being slaves of sin (6:16-17, 20). As in Rom 1:24, 27, 32, this "uncleanness" is associated with "things of which you are now ashamed" and which lead to death (6:21). Rom 6:19 thus intimates that Paul sees the unclean and shameful condition of humanity described in 1:24, 26-27 as sinful behavior, as behavior which must now belong to a *past* stage of the believer's life. And, in Rom 13:12-14, Paul says believers must now "put away" such things as "sleeping around and licentiousness," actions described as "works of darkness."

Paul also uses purity language for sin/holiness contrasts elsewhere in

---

42. von der Osten-Sacken is right to note that "uncleanness" in Rom 6:19 cannot be narrowed solely to homosexual behavior or even to illegitimate sexual behavior generally ("Paulinisches Evangelium und Homosexualität," 37), though it probably has the latter in the foreground. Given the prominence that homosexual intercourse has among the list of vices in Rom 1:24-31 and the likelihood that "uncleanness" in 1:24 has same-sex intercourse first and foremost in view, "uncleanness" in Rom 6:19 certainly includes same-sex intercourse at the head of a list of sinful behaviors.

his letters. At the end of 1 Thess 4:3-8, Paul justifies his commands regarding sexual purity by appealing to the fact that "God has not called us to uncleanness but in holiness." In 1 Corinthians 5, where Paul treats a comparable "abomination" of the Levitical Holiness Code, incest, Paul employs the language of purity ("clean out the old yeast . . . ," 1 Cor 5:7) not to distinguish incest from sin but to aid in the characterization of such behavior as "sexual immorality" (*porneia*, 5:1). Paul even goes so far as to recommend the offender's expulsion from the community in the hopes of saving him and expunging the community of the "leaven of malice and evil" (5:5, 8). The vice list in 1 Cor 6:9-11, *contra* Countryman, indicts homosexual behavior and characterizes it as a form of conduct not to be practiced any more by believers for "you were washed, you were sanctified." Thus, the evidence is quite clear that Paul considered same-sex intercourse to be sin.

Does Romans 2:1–3:20 Condemn Those Who Condemn Homosexual Practice?

The material that follows Rom 1:18-32 is significant in determining Paul's ultimate reason for citing homosexual practice and other sins. Paul's point is not merely to condemn homosexual activity but to begin with a very clear example of unethical conduct and then to continue widening the net until it captures all of humanity. For Paul, even the pinnacle of goodness, the Jew, is subject to judgment. All deserve condemnation and hence all are beholden to the grace of God in Christ. In Rom 11:32, Paul writes: "God confined together all into disobedience in order that he might have mercy on all."

Accordingly, he begins broadening the indictment with the vice list in 1:29-31. The list is aimed mainly at gentiles but many of the vices (for example, arrogance, bragging, strife, envy, greediness) blur the boundary between gentile and Jew. This culminates in the statement at the start of 2:1-2 that the moral person (primarily the Jew) who condemns the people described in 1:18-32 likewise is "without excuse" because he or she commits the same sorts of acts despite "knowing that God's judgment against those who practice such things is true." If gentiles who are ignorant of Scripture are culpable because they know from creation/nature that what they are doing is wrong, how much more guilty are those who have access to the direct revelation of Scripture?

The rest of 2:1–3:20 sets out to demonstrate that not even the moral person, the Jew, is exempted from God's judgment. Jews may have undergone circumcision and possess God's law, but they do not thereby escape condemnation. In a sweeping "sting operation," the Jew who nods his or her head at the judgment of God against gentile sinners described in 1:18-32 is compelled by the end of the argument to acknowledge the just judgment of God against him or her.[43] If gentiles deserve judgment (and they do), then so do Jews. Apart from God's mercy shown in Christ there is no hope for redemption from sin's penalty and power.

Does this larger context mean that Paul thought that those engaged in same-sex intercourse were no worse sinners than the rest of humanity and that therefore homosexual conduct should be a non-issue among believers? This is the view of many advocates for the legitimacy of homosexual conduct, including Victor Paul Furnish, who writes:

> In Rom. 1:24-32 Paul is not enumerating specific "sins" but listing some representative consequences of sin. . . . Far from singling out any particular group or practice for special criticism, the apostle is insisting that when people condemn others they are also condemning themselves (Rom. 2:1). This "bad news" about the human condition is followed in Rom 3:21–8:39 with the "good news". . . that . . . saving grace is bestowed as a sheer gift (e.g., 3:24), with absolutely no conditions (e.g., 5:6, 8). Clearly, he has not written the earlier paragraphs in order to "condemn sinners," to frighten them into repenting, or to specify what one should and should not do.[44]

---

43. From the *Rhetorica ad Herennium* (the oldest Latin technical manual on the art of rhetoric), Porter cites the following passage. "If the hearers have been convinced, if our opponent's speech has gained their credence . . . , we shall make our Subtle Approach to the cause by the following means: the point which our adversaries have regarded as their strongest support we shall promise to discuss first; we shall begin with a statement made by the opponent . . . " (1.6.10; "Romans 1.18-32," 222).

44. V. P. Furnish, "The Bible and Homosexuality," 29; cf. idem, *The Moral Teaching of Paul: Selected Issues* (2d ed.; Nashville: Abingdon, 1985): 78-80; Charles D. Myers, Jr., "What the Bible Really Says About Homosexuality," *Anima* 19 (1992) 54-55; among commentators, Byrne, *Romans*, 70. Nissinen makes a similar point: "What

Is the worst sin the sin of judging others who sin (as Furnish implies), including the sin of judging others who commit same-sex intercourse? Paul does indeed lay a trap for the Jewish interlocutor who appears from 2:1 on, but not so that Paul may end all moral judgment in the Christian life. Paul did not point out the universal sinfulness of humanity in order to trivialize sin for believers. Paul is ensuring that *even the Jew* (not just the gentile) will have to accept God's just judgment and be open to the way that God chooses to set things right in Christ. The point to the interlocutor is that "salvation is apart from the law for all who believe in Christ" (i.e., "Christ alone"), not that "Gentile sin should be left uncriticized." Paul underscores universal sin in order to show how God relativized the differences between Jew and gentile, thereby removing the Mosaic law as an entry requirement

---

matters here is the theology of justification by faith, not homoeroticism as such. Paul's rhetorical strategy in Romans 1–2 seems to be to stimulate his readers' moral indignation . . . —but this is a rhetorical trap. . . . His words about same-sex conduct in Romans 1:26-27 are one example he chose from his tradition to illustrate how badly the world needs grace and, at the same time, to set a trap for anyone who would read his words with feelings of moral superiority or religious bigotry" (*Homoeroticism*, 111-12). George Edwards also views the shift to the Jewish interlocutor in 2:1 as decisive for the interpretation of 1:18-32 in general and 1:26-27 in particular. The "rhetorical context" of Rom 1:26-27 "forbids the use of that passage for the moral condemnation of homosexuality in itself. . . . Paul's preoccupation in Romans throughout is with the inadequacy of legal rectitude. Analogously, the theology of gay/lesbian liberation in no way presumes that confession, absolution, or the means of grace is not applicable to the homosexual. But when access to the means of grace is prefaced by the demand to adopt the culture of heterosexuality, the very meaning of grace itself is reduced to a legal requirement" (*Gay/Lesbian Liberation*, 98-99). For Edwards, "the threefold Levitical tradition (idolatry-adultery-homosexuality) common to 1 Corinthians 6:9f. and Rom 1:18-32 is alien to the spirit of Paul's theology in its discontinuity with the legal rectitude at the bottom of the Holiness Code" so that these texts must be subjected to the same critique that patriarchal texts in Paul's letters receive from "liberated Christians" (ibid.). One wonders if Edwards would take the same approach to the relationship of grace and ethics in Paul's core gospel on such matters as incest, promiscuous premarital intercourse, prostitution, bestiality, adultery, and pedophilia (among sexual sins); or murder, theft, blatant economic exploitation of others, extreme verbal abuse, and racism (among non-sexual sins; cf. the list of vices in Rom 1:29-31). Isn't Paul's description of Christian existence in 1 Cor 6:11 ("and these things some of you were [engaged in], but you washed [these sins] off, . . . were made holy, . . . were made righteous in . . . Christ and in the Spirit") part of the hope of the gospel? Or is this too just a Levitical holdover of "legal rectitude"?

for gentile and Jew alike. As a consequence, it is only the power of the gospel that is able to transfer Jew and gentile from the dominion of sin to the dominion of God.

Rom 1:18-32 in no way gives the impression that Paul questioned the correctness of God's judgment on "humans who in their wickedness suppress the truth" (1:18). Indeed, the point of the discussion is that God is wholly justified in judging. Even without access to Scripture, people knew that what they were doing was wrong. God is in the right to judge people who "though recognizing that those who do such things are worthy of death, . . . do them" (1:32). Paul does not disavow the threat of divine judgment in ch. 2 either. Rather, he places the Jews too under God's sentence. "We know (viz., Paul and the imaginary interlocutor) that the judgment of God on those who do such things (viz., those described in 1:18-32) is in accordance with the truth" (2:2). This statement makes absolutely clear that Paul is not retracting the fundamental point of 1:18-32. Indeed, Paul goes on to argue that not even the Jew will escape God's judgment. The trap that Paul sets in 1:18-32 is for those Jews who think that they can be justified in God's sight through observance of the Mosaic law and apart from faith in Christ.[45]

Commentators often have problems with Paul's logic in ch. 2 because they assume (mistakenly) that Paul is attempting to argue there that all Jews are sinners. Paul will not make that point until ch. 3. Here in ch. 2 Paul has a more limited purpose in mind; namely, to get the interlocutor to concede that God would be justified in subjecting to destruction "some" circumcised, law-possessing Jews who sin in egregious ways. With this point conceded, he can then widen the net in 3:1-8. If God is not unfaithful for condemning "some" Jews, then neither can God be unfaithful for holding all Jews under divine indictment, for "every human being is a liar" relative to God's "truthfulness" (3:3-4*a*, citing Ps 116:11).

Even David acknowledged that God was in the right to sentence him

---

45. As we noted above, 1:18-32 is a "layered" trap. The trap is also set for Paul's audience at Rome. In matters of indifference in Torah observance (diet and calendar), matters over which a Christian's salvation was not at stake, they had no right to judge one another.

for his sin (3:4*b*, citing Ps 51:4). When God is the standard of righteousness rather than sinful gentiles, even "we Jews" are unrighteous (3:5). The interlocutor attempts to evade the indictment by appealing to a special dispensation of grace for Jews who are, to be sure, unrighteous but not "sinners" of the same magnitude as gentiles (3:7). But Paul silences him by noting the irony: in asking God to overlook his sins because "the truthfulness of God abounded in my lie" (3:7), the interlocuter is coming dangerously close to the position that some slanderously charge Paul with advocating: "Let us do evil that good may come" (3:8). The argument in 2:1–3:8 is then concluded with the affirmation that all stand under God's judgment for their sin—*not* that the whole notion of God judging sinners is a bad thing (3:9-20).

From 3:21 on, Paul does show that God has provided a way out of eschatological judgment for those who embrace the new work of God in Christ. Jew and gentile have an equal opportunity to be saved through faith in Christ. Nevertheless, it is clear as the letter proceeds that Paul has not jettisoned the motif of judgment, either for unbelievers or for believers. For Paul, God's judgment is *still* coming on those who do the things described in Rom 1:18-32. Paul believes that those who become redeemed in Christ will, and must, no longer live like the people described in 1:18-32; otherwise, they too will perish.

Rom 6:1–8:17 provides an emphatic response to those who might conclude from Paul's earlier argument regarding the abundance of divine grace in Christ (Rom 5) that one need not change one's sin-controlled, pre-Christian life. "Should we [believers] continue to sin" in order to make God look even better ("that grace might abound," 6:1) or because believers are free from retribution on the day of judgment ("we are not under law but under grace," 6:15)? "May it not be the case." God's intent for believers is made clear by Paul's understanding of baptism as the occasion when believers die to their sin-controlled lives and become open to the destiny of a resurrected life lived for God. It is self-evident that God's intent in graciously saving people was that believers lead righteous lives. That this is so is apparent from Christ's deliverance of believers from past enslavement to sin, Christ's resurrected life for God as an example for the present, and the firm hope that Christ gives believers of being resurrected like him in the future (6:1-14).

The confession "Jesus is Lord" (cf. Rom 10:9) is no magical charm. If one lives as a slave to sin, it is sin and not Christ or God that is Lord of one's life and it is sin that will pay one back with death. In other words, the "free gift" does not remain with those who do not experience liberation from sin's power (6:15-23). Those who lead lives under sin's primary control will die and be excluded from the life of God's kingdom, whether they are believers or not. Only those who are fundamentally led by the Spirit will live (8:5-14). Although salvation does not come by personal merit, unrighteous conduct can disqualify one from salvation.[46] One must recapitulate the Christ event in one's own life by undergoing the transformative experience of dying to one's self and rising to a new life for God, through the indwelling power of Christ's Spirit.

For Paul, God's goal is clear: lives transformed into living and holy sacrifices (12:1-2; 15:16) and united in praise (15:6-13). The power of the gospel is denied if it is not embodied in the moral and social life of the individual within the context of the community of faith (12:9-21; 13:8-14; 14:1–15:13). Paul summarized his own mission as an attempt to secure an "obedience of faith" among the gentiles (1:5; 15:18; 16:26), which implies both faith as an act of obedience and faith manifested in obedience. Homosexuality is not to be excused in the Christian life any more than adultery, fornication, incest, bestiality, or pedophilia would be. 1 Cor 6:9 and 1 Tim 1:10 make clear that homosexual conduct on the part of anyone, including believers, is among the serious sins that can disqualify one from "inheriting the kingdom of God." If God's punishment for idolatry was to step back and allow degrading human passions to control human life (1:18-32), how can God's deliverance be anything less than liberation from the control of such passions? What kind of salvation would leave people trapped in degrading behavior and continually subject to the ongoing wrath of God?

A more subtle variation of the view espoused by Victor Furnish is Robin Scroggs's notion that, although Paul is clearly opposing homosexuality, he is not especially concerned with it. "[S]ince Paul's intention is theological, not ethical, and since the two verses [Rom 1:26-27]

---

46. Cf. Rom 11:22: "God's kindness to you, *if* you continue in that kindness; otherwise, you also will be cut off."

ultimately stem from his Jewish tradition, it cannot fairly be said that Paul is *especially incensed* against homosexuality."[47] However, the fact that Paul singled out homosexual conduct in 1:26-27 does indicate that he found this to be a particularly egregious sin—precisely because it constituted a clear and willful suppression of the knowledge of God's will for humans in the created order.

While it is true that Paul did not explicitly instruct his audience not to commit homosexual acts but instead put the discussion in the service of his argument that gentiles are under sin, it seems clear that Paul regarded homoerotic actions as particularly revolting sin that should be avoided. If Paul had singled out bestiality instead of homosexuality in 1:26-27, few would argue that Paul was being purely descriptive here, not prescriptive, and not "especially incensed" just because the opposition to bestiality also "stems from his Jewish tradition." As we have seen, bestiality is considered a comparable sexual sin to same-sex intercourse not only in Leviticus but also in Philo's writings and other Jewish texts. In 1:18-32 Paul also never explicitly said to his audience "don't commit idolatry." As with homosexuality, he would not have had to say it to the Jewish interlocutor. In fact, he used the theme of gentile idolatry to snare the interlocutor. Surely this does not mean Paul was not "especially incensed" with the gentile sin of idolatry. The vices in 1:29-31 (including murder), despite being mentioned to reinforce a descriptive theological argument, definitely have a strong implicit element of ethical proscription.[48]

Paul was trying to bait the Jewish interlocutor by appealing to a form

---

47. Scroggs, *The New Testament and Homosexuality*, 114, 116 (my emphasis). Scroggs's primary argument against a contemporary application of Rom 1:26-27 (namely, Paul is thinking only of pederasty and other oppressive models of homosexual relations) is discussed in ch. 5.I.

48. I can agree with Hays statement that *"no direct appeal to Romans 1 as a source for rules about sexual conduct is possible"* (*The Moral Vision of the New Testament*, 394; his emphasis), but only to a point. The genre of Rom 1:24-27 is not legal material so one must stop to think whether drawing ethical prohibitions from this text is hermeneutically appropriate. To that extent, "direct" is the operative word. However, the text itself, particularly set as it is within the larger context of Romans with clear textual interconnections with Romans 6, makes clear that Paul regarded same-sex intercourse as a form of sinful behavior incompatible with Christian existence (6:1, 15, 19; cf. 1:24). Hays's argument thus appears to me to be out of balance when he goes on to state: "To use these texts appropriately in ethical

THE BIBLE AND HOMOSEXUAL PRACTICE

of sexual conduct that nearly all Jews in the first century found especially revolting. Yet there is no indication that Paul himself felt any less
strongly about the subject. That Paul was seeking to establish that
all/any sin equally rendered people culpable to God's judgment does
not mean that all sins were equally egregious for Paul. The case of
incest mentioned in 1 Corinthians 5, for example, was for Paul a matter of a different caliber from many of the other issues treated in
1 Corinthians, requiring the most extreme measure of expulsion from
the community.

Paul cautioned against the judging of others when it led one to
exempt oneself from personal scrutiny and the call of the gospel (as
with the Jewish interlocutor in Romans 2). He counseled believers
engaged in the task of turning straying believers back to the right path
to be conscious of their own failings. "Brethren, if in fact a person is
taken unawares by any trespass, you the spiritual ones, restore such a
one in a spirit of gentleness, being on the lookout lest you too be
tempted" (Gal 6:1). Paul also rejected judgment within the community of believers over matters of indifference, such as dietary practices
(Rom 14:1–15:6), and matters that involved personal vengeance, such
as the lawsuit discussed in 1 Cor 6:1-8. Yet he retained a place for
admonition in the church, recognizing the need to adapt one's
approach to different types of believers (1 Thess 5:12-14). With regard
to a case of gross sexual misconduct such as incest, an exasperated Paul
asked the Corinthian church the rhetorical question, "Is it not those
inside (the church) whom you are to judge?" (1 Cor 5:12).

Did Paul Think Only Idol Worshipers Could Engage in Same-Sex Intercourse?

Another misunderstanding of Rom 1:26-27 requires correction.
Contrary to what some critics of Paul's argument suggest, Paul is not

reflection about homosexuality, we should not try to wring rules out of them, nor
should we abstract principles from them. Instead we should attend primarily to the
way the texts function to shape the *symbolic world* within which human sexuality
is understood. . . . Romans 1 . . . must function as a diagnostic tool" (ibid., 396).
Rom 1:18-32 is a "diagnostic tool"; but it does not require much "wringing" to produce legitimately the essential "rule" or "principle" that same-sex intercourse is
forbidden to believers. Indeed, Hays himself draws just such a rule.

saying in Rom 1:18-32 that idolatry, the worship of statues or images, is the *necessary* prerequisite for homosexuality.[49] However, based on this erroneous interpretation, many advocates of homosexual behavior contend that since homosexuals today are generally not idolaters in the strict sense, Paul's understanding of homosexuality and its causes is misguided and irrelevant. The most insistent on this score is Dale Martin.[50] Martin argues that Rom 1:18-32 alludes not to the fall of Adam and Eve but to a Jewish decline-of-civilization myth that traces the evils of gentile society to the origins of idolatry (a myth appearing in *1 Enoch* 6 and *Jubilees* 11). According to Martin, Rom 1:18-32 thus is based on a worldview in which homosexuality is "not a symptom of 'the Fall' but of Gentile polytheism."[51] He writes:

> Modern scholars read the Fall into Romans 1 because it renders the text more serviceable for heterosexist purposes. . . . Most of us do not believe that all of humanity was once upon a time neatly monotheistic, only later, at a particular historical point, to turn to polytheism and idolatry; nor are we likely to believe that homosexuality did not exist until a sudden invention of polytheism. . . . Most of us . . . probably do not believe that the abolition of idolatrous cults and polytheism would spell the end of homosexuality.[52]

Martin is correct that the divine "giving over" of which Rom 1:18-32 speaks does not refer to the fall. Yet he overlooks the fact that elsewhere in Rom 5:11-21, which does relate the story of the origin of sin, Paul makes clear that he understands that sinful passions entered into human flesh with Adam's transgression. Rom 7:5, 7-23 also assumes

---

49. Some scholars reject a rigid connection between idolatry and homosexuality in Paul. Cf., e.g., Klaus Haacker, "Exegetische Gesichtspunkte zum Thema Homosexualität," *Tbei* 25 (1994): 176; Georg Strecker, "Homosexualität in biblischer Sicht," *KD* 28 (1982): 134.
50. D. Martin, "Heterosexism and the Interpretation of Romans 1:18-32," *BibInt* 3 (1995): 332-55. William Countryman has made the same point; so too Klaus Wengst, "Paulus und die Homosexualität," *ZEE* 31 (1987): 74. Cf. Bartlett, "A Biblical Perspective on Homosexuality," 140: "Those who really want to be 'pauline' in their understanding of homosexual practices today would have to argue that people who engage in homosexual acts are being punished by God for their idolatry. One wonders whether people who engage in homosexual practices have been more idolatrous than heterosexual people."
51. Ibid., 355.
52. Ibid., 338-39.

that sinful impulses are the lot of human existence. Although it is clear that Rom 1:18-32 does not refer to the fall, it is equally clear that for Paul the sinful passions to which God hands gentiles over did not originate with the beginning of idolatry, but with Adam. In other words, the full range of sinful passions and the behavior arising from them (including homoerotic behavior) at least potentially preceded the worship of idols for Paul.

In Rom 1:18-32 Paul is seeking to explain why homosexual behavior, along with rampant expression of sinful passions in general, is so prevalent among gentiles, at least in comparison with Jews. He is speaking in terms of collective entities, not individuals, and in terms of widespread effect, not origin. Paul is not excluding the presence of the vices mentioned in 1:26-31 prior to first act of idolatry or in the context of other groups besides the gentiles.[53] Even though Paul characterizes such vices as arising from people who do not "see fit to acknowledge God" (viz., in turning to idols, 1:28a), Paul surely knows that the vices mentioned in 1:29-31 can also be found among Jews who are not idolaters in the strict sense. Indeed, this is the point he wants to make in ch. 2. "You who preach not to steal, do you steal? You who say not to commit adultery, do you commit adultery? You who abhor idols, do you rob temples?" (2:21-22).

The point Paul is making is simple: sin in all its most degrading expressions is going to be more rampant in cultures where people turn from the worship of the true, living God to the worship of gods of their own making. Those who turn their backs on God, particularly in the absurd manner of worshiping lifeless statues, are going to be handed over by the real God to their own *pre-existing* foolish desires. Idolatry and homosexual behavior are in some measure parallel (not just successive) phenomena since both are presented as willful suppressions of the obvious truth about God and God's design in the natural world.

Contrary to Martin's belief, 1 Cor 6:9-11 implies that Christians who had joined the church and left behind their same-sex relationships could turn back to their homosexual desires. Martin contends that in 1 Cor 6:9-11 the vices are described by Paul as part of the past (not

---

53. A similar point is made by Haas, "Exegetical Issues," 397.

present) of believers. He writes that for Paul "the abolition of . . . poly-theism [spells] the end of homosexuality."[54] To arrive at this conclusion, Martin has to ignore the context. When Paul says "Don't you know that the unjust (*adikoi*) shall not inherit the kingdom of God; do not be deceived," he clearly intends his comments as a veiled warning to the Corinthians. They should not deceive themselves into thinking that they can get away with engaging in *porneia* or with "wronging" or "acting unjustly toward" (*adikein*) fellow believers by taking them to pagan court. If a return to vice were not a possibility for Christians, such a warning would not have been necessary.

Moreover, the list of vices in 6:9-10 is simply an expansion of the list of vices in 5:10 and 5:11. The four vices in 5:10 are included in the six vices of 5:11 and all six vices in 5:11 are included in the ten vices of 6:9-10. The vice lists in 5:10-11 appear in the context of Paul's warning to the Corinthians not to associate with or even eat with a person who claims to be a brother but engages in any such vices. The Corinthian church, Paul insists, should expel from the community *Christian pornoi* (sexually immoral persons), which in the context of ch. 5 is applied to a Christian engaged in incest. Three of the four types of sinners added to the vice list in 6:9-10 are simply additional specific categories of sexually immoral persons: adulterers, effeminate men who engage in passive homosexual behavior, and men who take other males to bed. Evidently, then, this vice list, like those in 5:10-11, is inclusive of Christians who engage in such behavior. The church is to separate from such Christians precisely because the latter will not inherit God's kingdom if they do not repent. That includes separating from Christians who engage in homosexual behavior.

Paul did not think that returning to idol worship was a necessary intermediate step before Christians could be tempted back into homosexual behavior, any more than he thought only Christians who worshiped idols could engage in incest, adultery, or theft. Indeed, "idolaters" constitutes a distinct category of sinners in these vice lists; it is not presupposed that the other types of sinners are idolaters. Consequently, it is obvious that Paul did not think that the abolition of polytheism spelled the end of homosexuality.

---

54. "Heterosexism," 339.

Instead, Paul was clearly concerned that believers might return to former patterns of sinful practices, including same-sex intercourse, practices that could lead to loss of salvation. In Rom 6:19, he writes: "just as you (formerly) presented your members as slaves to uncleanness and to lawlessness for the purpose of (living in) lawlessness, so now present your members as slaves to righteousness for the purpose of (living in) holiness." The reference to "uncleanness," identified with "sin" in 6:16-18, 20, 22-23 and shameful practices in 6:21 and leading to "death" according to 6:16, 21, 23, is a clear allusion to the range of sinful behaviors enumerated in 1:24-31, particularly the description of same-sex intercourse in 1:24-27. The entire discussion of 6:1–8:17, including the section of the argument in 6:15-23, is aimed at establishing that gentile believers who return to the pattern of sinful activity that characterized their former pre-Christian existence will not inherit eternal life (8:12-13). There would be no point to this discussion unless there was a realistic possibility in Paul's mind that gentile Christians could once more succumb to and come under the sway of the same sinful impulse operating in the "flesh" in manifold forms.

Regardless of what confession believers may make to being under the lordship of God and Christ, if they continue to live in "obedience" to a pattern of sinful behavior, they are slaves to sin, not to God. And, for Paul, sin will pay the wages of "death" (6:16, 21, 23). The "gift of eternal life" (6:23) is bestowed only on those who have been "given over" to a new "imprint" stamped on their hearts by the teaching of the gospel, only to those who were freed from sin and enslaved to righteousness/God (6:17-18, 22).

In Gal 6:7-9 Paul provides a similar cautionary warning to believers who might be tempted to think that the grace of God in Christ somehow exempted them from moral culpability with apocalyptic repercussions. There we read:

> Do not be deceived; God is not to be mocked,[55] for whatever one sows this one will also reap. For the one who casts seed into one's own flesh

---

55. Or: to be sneered at; to be made a fool of; someone you can thumb your nose at (*muktērizetai*).

will reap a harvest of destruction and decay from the flesh, but the one who casts seed into the Spirit will reap a harvest of eternal life from the Spirit. And let us not grow tired of doing what is right for in due time we will reap, *if* we do not relax our efforts.

Paul understood that believers might return to their old sinful ways while maintaining confessional allegiance to Christ. Indeed, he warned them that God would not tolerate such conduct from them any more than God would tolerate such conduct from unbelievers. In short, all sins constitute a rebellion against God and an "idolatry" in the looser sense of supplanting God's intent for one's own. It is not necessary to worship statues in order to lose one's moral way and be subject to God's judgment.

Did Paul Not Have Creation in Mind When He Spoke of Same-Sex Intercourse?

Others, including Martti Nissinen,[56] agree with Martin that Paul did not have the Genesis accounts in mind when he wrote Rom 1:24-27. How plausible is the view that Paul in Rom 1:24-27 did not regard

---

56. *Homoeroticism*, 107. Nissinen's view is a little more nuanced than Martin's. "Paul does not refer to the creation narratives (Genesis 1–3)," he argues. Nevertheless, "Even if the idea of creation is not absent from our text" (1:18-32), Paul's "theology of creation is not primarily drawn from Genesis 1–3" but from "Hellenistic Jewish ideas of the law of nature, according to which the order and purpose of creation are visible in conventional patterns—like heterosexuality." Yet the unbending and visceral Hellenistic Jewish posture against same-sex intercourse, which contrary to the prevailing culture of its day permitted no exceptions, is itself in part attributable to Genesis 1–2. First-century Jews did not regard the sexual pairing of male and female in Genesis 1–2 as a mere "conventional pattern." Cf. Abraham Smith, "The New Testament and Homosexuality," *QR* 11 (1991): 25, who (like Nissinen) focuses on status hierarchy but (unlike Nissinen) recognizes that the backdrop of Genesis underscores a more inclusive rejection of same-sex intercourse: "The statement that such acts are 'against nature' refers to the created order in Genesis and suggests that these acts show a disruption of the natural subordinate/superordinate relations between male and female ordained by God in creation. . . . Nevertheless, Paul's cultural interpretation of the Genesis traditions would indeed have left him with only one option for sexual relationships—that between a male and a female." Unfortunately, Smith fails to carry through the latter observation in the rest of his essay, limiting Paul's condemnation of same-sex relationships to abusive, pederastic forms.

same-sex intercourse as a rebellion against, and distortion of, the created pattern of sexuality in Genesis 1–2?

It is not at all plausible. Since Paul traces the origin of all sinful passions ultimately back to the fall, it is not surprising that the biblical creation stories serve as a backdrop to the narrative in 1:18-32.[57] Obvious allusions to Genesis 1 include the words "ever since the creation of the world" (1:20) and "the Creator" (1:25). Paul's denotation of the sexes in 1:26-27 as "females" (*thēleiai*) and "males" (*arsenes*) rather than "women" (*gynaikes*) and "men" (*andres* or *anthrōpoi*) follows the style of Gen 1:27 (LXX): "male and female (*arsen kai thēlu*) he made them." The intertextual connection between Rom 1:23 and Gen 1:26 (LXX) is unmistakable:[58]

And they exchanged the glory[59] of the immortal God for the likeness (*homoiōmati*) of the image (*eikonos*) of a mortal human (*anthrōpou*) and of birds (*peteinōn*) and of four-footed animals (*tetrapodōn*) and of reptiles (*herpetōn*). (Rom 1:23)

---

57. Cf. especially Ulrich W. Mauser, "Creation, Sexuality, and Homosexuality in the New Testament," *Homosexuality and Christian Community*, 45-49; also, Hays, *The Moral Vision of the New Testament*, 404 n. 21; Schmidt, *Straight and Narrow?* 81; Grenz, *Welcoming But Not Affirming*, 54; Stowasser, "Homosexualität und Bibel," 518-19.

58. Cf. Niels Hyldahl, "A Reminiscence of the Old Testament at Romans 1.23," *NTS* 2 (1955/56): 285-88; Jacob Jervell, *Imago Dei: Gen 1,26f. im Spätjudentum, in der Gnosis und in den paulinischen Briefen* (FRLANT 76; Göttingen: Vandenhoeck & Ruprecht, 1960), 320; Wilckens, *Römer*, 1.107-108. Knut Holter points also to a link with LXX Deut 4:15-18: "you did not see a likeness on the day in which the Lord spoke to you in Horeb. . . . Do not act unlawfully by making for yourselves a carved likeness, any kind of image (*eikona*), a likeness (*homoiōma*) of male or female (*arsenikou ē thēlykou*), a likeness (*homoiōma*) of any beast (*ktēnous*) of those which are on the earth, a likeness of any winged bird (*orneou pterōtou*) which flies under the heaven, of any reptile (*herpetou*) which creeps on the earth, the likeness of any fish, whatever is in the waters under the earth." The connection to idolatry is mentioned here, not in Gen 1:26-30. "It seems clear to me that Gen 1,26-28 provides a reasonable background for St. Paul's juxtaposition of idolatry and homosexuality in Rom 1, 23-27. Deut 4 is obviously the model for this negative echoing of Gen 1, but both the choice of terminology and the emphasizing of the sexual differentiation point back to Gen 1, rather than to Deut 4" ("A Note on the Old Testament Background of Rom 1, 23-27," *BN* 69 [1993]: 21-23).

59. For a description of man as "the image and glory of God," cf. 1 Cor 11:7.

Let us make a human (*anthrōpon*) according to our image and according to our likeness (*homoiōsin*); and let them rule over the fish of the sea, and the birds (*peteinōn*) of the air, and the cattle (*ktēnōn*), and over all the earth, and over all the reptiles (*herpetōn*) which creep upon the earth. (Gen 1:26)

Also striking is the fact that the limited threefold combination of birds/animals/reptiles in Rom 1:23 appears in Gen 1:30: "wild animals (*thēria*) . . . , birds . . . , reptiles." Other allusions to Genesis 1–3 may appear in the references to "the lie" in Rom 1:25,[60] shame in Rom 1:27 (cf. Gen 3:1, 8), knowledge in Rom 1:19, 21, 28, 32 (cf. the tree of the knowledge of good and evil),[61] and the sentence of death in 1:32 (cf. Gen 2:17; 3:4-5, 20, 23).

What is Paul trying to communicate by these intertextual echoes? For Paul, both idolatry and same-sex intercourse reject God's verdict that what was made and arranged was "very good" (1:31). Instead of recognizing their indebtedness to the one God in whose image and likeness they were made, humans worshiped statues made in their own image and likeness. Instead of exercising dominion over the animal kingdom, they bowed down not only to images of themselves but also to images of animals. Instead of acknowledging that God had made them "male and female" and had called on them to copulate and procreate, they denied the transparent complementarity of their sexuality and engaged in sex with the same sex, indulging themselves in irresponsible sexual passion on which stable and productive family structures could not be built. As with Jesus, so with Paul: the creation story in Genesis does not leave room for a legitimate expression of same-sex intercourse. Even though Rom 1:18-32 speaks of events after the fall, for Paul all human rebellions are in one way or another rebellions against God's will for humankind set in motion at creation.

---

60. "The prophets had referred to idolaters as speaking and trusting in 'lies' about God (Hosea 7:13; Jer 14:25; cf. Isa 59:13), but the singular use of 'the lie' in Romans implies an antecedent act, from which all later lies about God derive, namely the primordial desire of humans to 'be like God,' defining evil and good for themselves (Gen 3:5)" (Jewett, "Homoerotic References, " 227).

61. In Genesis 2–3, eating from the tree of the knowledge of good and evil not only acquaints humans with evil but also gives humans the capacity to discern for themselves what is right and wrong. In Rom 1:18-23, humans exchange the knowledge of God available in creation for a knowledge of their own making.

So in Rom 1:18-27 it is apparent that Paul has the Genesis account of the creation of male and female humans in view. And yet we are asked by Martin, Nissinen, and others to believe that when Paul spoke of same-sex intercourse as an act "contrary to nature," he really was not thinking about human rebellion against the sexual pairing of male and female humans in Gen 1:26-31. It is strange that Paul should so soon forget the creation stories of Genesis, particularly since the creation and fall of Adam and Eve figure in remarks throughout Romans (for example, Rom 3:23; 5:12-21; 7:7-13; 8:19-21).

Their proposal appears even more far-fetched in the light of Paul's use of Genesis 1–3 elsewhere. Only two or three years before writing the letter to the Romans from Corinth, Paul wrote to the church in Corinth about the subject of *porneia* or "sexual immorality."[62] After discussing a case of incest (1 Corinthians 5) and an intra-Christian dispute taken to pagan court (6:1-8), Paul launches into a more general treatment of the relationship of the use of one's own body to the gospel's proclamation of freedom in Christ (6:12-20).[63] In so doing he

---

62. *Porneia*, in the ancient Greek world, meant primarily "prostitution." However, in Hellenistic Judaism and Christianity, the word could have the broader sense of "sexual immorality."

63. Will Deming argues that the issue of lawsuits treated in 6:1-11 relates to the incident of incest described in the previous chapter ("The Unity of 1 Corinthians 5–6," *JBL* 115 [1996]: 289-312). According to Deming, the man may have married his stepmother, had her as a concubine, or paid for her sexual services. Outraged by this, some members of the Christian community at Corinth took the man to court while others supported him. The former lost the case but tension from the dispute continued to hang over the community. Paul's discussion of prostitution in 6:12-20 might then be about not a distinct instance of sexual immorality at Corinth but instead either a hypothetical analogy or an allusion to the incestuous man paying his stepmother for sexual favors. While I find Deming's arguments intriguing, the notion that the lawsuit in 6:1-8 has to do with the incestuous man fails on three counts. First, why would Paul encourage the Corinthian believers to be "wronged" and "defrauded" (6:7-8), that is, to let the matter drop *within* the Christian community and not just in the courts? Paul himself has already urged the community to expel the incestuous man. Second, Paul's claim in 5:1 that the case of incest is a kind of sexual immorality found not even among the gentiles would have been undermined if the courts had taken no action. Third, Paul refers to this lawsuit in question as an example of "the least (most insignificant, trivial) cases" (6:2) and "everyday/ordinary matters" (6:3), unlikely characterizations of incest; 6:1-8, then, should probably be regarded as an excursus. The theme of judging those inside the community in 5:9-13 brought up in Paul's mind an occasion where not only did the

draws on the specific example of sex with a prostitute to make his general point. In 1 Cor 6:16 Paul cites Gen 2:24 ("a man . . . shall be joined to [*proskollēthēsetai pros*] his wife and the two will become one flesh") to establish that intercourse with a female prostitute makes a Christian man "one body" with her, "joins himself to the prostitute" (*ho kollōmenos tē pornē*), which in turn causes "the (bodily) members of Christ" to become "members of a prostitute" and defiles the man's body which is "a temple of the Holy Spirit" (6:15-20).[64] Here it is clear that when Paul critiques sexual behavior of any sort as immoral his standard remains tied to Genesis 1–2. For Paul, the only legitimate sexual union for Christians is that between one man and one woman in permanent,[65] exogamous, and monogamous marriage. All other forms of sexual intercourse, including same-sex intercourse (6:9), are immoral perversions of this bond (6:18-19). Later in the same letter (11:2-16), when Paul expresses concern that distinctive gender differences between men and women are being ignored at Corinth, he once more refers back to the creation stories in Genesis 1–2.[66] It is hardly plausible, then, that Paul did not have in mind Genesis 1–2 when he spoke in Rom 1:24-27 of one of the most flagrant perversions of gender and sexual practice known to first-century Jews.

Corinthians not judge those inside their community but, worse, they brought their dirty laundry before pagan courts of justice. Deming is right, however, in regarding 6:12-20 as a continuation of the discussion of sexual immorality in ch. 5 (with 6:9-11 as a transition) and convincing in his argument that 6:12-20 does not indicate that some Corinthian men were having intercourse with prostitutes.

64. For a link to Romans at this point, cf. Rom 6:13: "Don't continue to present your members to sin as weapons of unrighteousness, but present . . . your members to God as weapons of righteousness."

65. I.e., as long as one's spouse is alive, 1 Cor 7:39.

66. In attempting to justify the use of head coverings for women while praying and prophesying as a sign of male headship, Paul alludes to Gen 1:26-27 when he speaks of "man" (albeit, not woman) as "the image and glory of God" and also to Gen 2:18-23 when he points out that "woman is from man" and "created for the sake of man" (11:7-12). On the question of how much the concern for male-female hierarchy factored into his discussion of same-sex intercourse, along with additional discussion of 1 Cor 11:2-16, see ch. 5.II. Other obvious citations or echoes to Gen 1–3 in Pauline letters other than Romans include: 1 Cor 14:34 (Gen 3:16?); 1 Cor 15:21, 38-39, 45, 47 (Gen 1:11-12, 20, 24; 2:7; 3:17); 2 Cor 4:6 (Gen 1:3); 2 Cor 11:3 (Gen 3:13); cf. Eph 4:24 and Col 3:10 (Gen 1:26-27); Eph 5:31 (Gen 2:24); 1 Tim 2:12-14 (Gen 1:27; 2:7, 22; 3:6, 13, 16); 1 Tim 4:4 (Gen 1:31).

Before closing our discussion, a final point can be drawn from 1 Cor 6:12-20. There, as in Romans, Paul makes a distinction between the moral significance of dietary matters and sexual behavior. On the one hand, what can lawfully be eaten is a matter of indifference so long as one's choices do not cause another to stumble. On the other hand, sexual sins were never matters of indifference. The Corinthians may have adopted the slogan "Food is for the stomach and the stomach is for food" (6:13*a*) and done so to legitimize freedom from a variety of dietary taboos that they regarded as mere societal convention. Paul let this slogan stand but then drew a stricter line on issues of sexuality: "*but* the body is *not* for *porneia* but for the Lord and the Lord for the body" (6:13*b*). Believers, Paul argued, do not have the luxury to utilize their freedom in Christ to do with their bodies as they wish, "for you were bought with a price; so glorify God in your body" (6:20; cf. 7:23). What a believer does with his or her body drags into the muck the indwelling Christ, for "the one who is joined to the Lord is one spirit (with him)" (6:17). The slogan "all things are within my authority and power" (*panta moi exestin*) thus required the qualification that "I will not be placed under the authority and power (*exousiasthēsomai*) of anything" (6:12).[67]

The point that Paul makes in 1 Cor 6:12-20 is similar to the one he

---

67. There are three options as to the origin of these slogans. One or more of these slogans were (1) formulated by the Corinthian "strong"; (2) formulated by Paul during a visit to Corinth or his previous letter and picked up and misinterpreted by the Corinthians; or (3) formulated by Paul in 1 Corinthians, "enlisting a popular tradition to parody the Corinthians" (so Deming, "Unity," 311; i.e., "there is a tradition familiar to both of us in which I see a distinct similarity to you—is your situation not a *classic case* of XYZ?" [ibid., 310]). Whatever interpretation one adopts, it is doubtful that the Corinthians believed they had license to do anything (cf. the sexual asceticism Paul combats in the next chapter). The Stoics believed that "only the wise person was free to 'do what he wanted,' for only he had brought his moral disposition into perfect harmony with the divine will" (ibid., 301). For the one who had knowledge about what was truly right and truly wrong (as opposed to popular convention), what was within one's control and outside it, and conformed his/her desire accordingly, no one could interfere with the exercise of his right. The phrase "all things are permitted me" could also be used to denote that which is legally permitted by the larger society. If the Corinthians applied the slogan "all things are permitted me" at all, they probably restricted it to food, specifically idol meat (the slogan reappears in 10:23 in that context).

would make a few years later when writing to Rome from Corinth. In the letter to the Romans, Paul stressed that believers had come under the dominion of a new Lord. Whereas previously they were "free in terms of righteousness" (i.e., free to avoid living rightly) and headed for destruction, they were now "freed from sin and enslaved to God" with prospects for eternal life (6:16-23). There is no sexual license for believers. Indeed, the Corinthians had left behind sexual license when they became believers. "These things some of you *were*; but you washed these away, but you were made holy, but you were made right, in the name of *the Lord* Jesus Christ and in the Spirit of our God" (1 Cor 6:11). In short, "Flee *porneia!*" (1 Cor 6:18).

Ignoring 1 Cor 6:12-20, David Bartlett appeals to Galatians 5 to justify same-sex intercourse for those with an exclusively homosexual orientation.

> One of Paul's basic premises is the freedom of the Christian from the obligation of observing the Jewish law. . . . Paul's insistence is that God's favor is never earned by anything we do. God's favor is a free gift. . . . [Gal 5:13] suggests that the test of whether the Galatians are living as faithful Christians is not their obedience to a law (even as important a law as circumcision was) but their ability responsibly to turn to one another in love. . . . When Paul writes of the gifts of the Spirit, the marks of the life lived in faith, he writes primarily of relationships. . . . the gifts of God's Spirit are equally available to heterosexual people and to homosexual people. . . . It is my hope that openness to empirical studies, to the testimony of homosexual people, and to the deepest insights of the Bible will move us toward that place where we can honestly paraphrase Paul: "In Christ Jesus, neither heterosexuality, nor homosexuality—in themselves—are of any avail, but faith working through love."[68]

The problem with Bartlett's line of reasoning is that Paul nowhere treated sexual expression as a matter of indifference or a discarded relic of the Torah (like circumcision and dietary and calendar observances) when it deviated either from celibacy or from enduring and faithful heterosexual marital union. As the discussion of immorality in 1 Cor 6:12-20 makes clear, sexual intercourse for Paul involved the whole person in union with another person; it never engaged people

---

68. "A Biblical Perspective on Homosexuality," 144-46.

only peripherally. Indeed, Paul goes so far as to say that, among all sins, there is something "uniquely body-defiling" about immoral sexual intercourse. "Flee *porneia*! Every (other) sin, whatever a man does, is outside of the body; but the one who commits *porneia* (*ho porneuōn*) sins into/against (*eis*)[69] his own body" (6:18). As Bruce N. Fisk has appropriately stated, 1 Cor 6:18

> declares sexual sin to be profoundly (and even uniquely) self-destructive. . . . Sexual sin, as a bodily act, . . . forges a bodily union. . . . Other sins may be physically destructive (e.g. suicide, gluttony), corporately destructive (e.g. gossip, divisiveness), or spiritually defiling (e.g. idolatry) but for Paul, because sexual sin is uniquely body-joining, it is uniquely body-defiling.[70]

No matter how the participants may view sexual intercourse, it is never a casual act like shaking hands. Even sex with a prostitute, which some today would understand as a "non-bonding" impersonal experience, Paul understood to be a merger that brought with it the total denigration of one's own body. Sexual intercourse was too important a matter to be left up to some arbitrary self-justification based on a dubious application of the general principle of love. Fornicators, persons engaged in incest, pederasts, and even those participating in adultery, prostitution, and bestiality could all argue that in their allegedly special circumstances the conduct in question was ultimately "loving."

Few areas are so given to self-deception as the area of sexuality. Where the potential for pleasure is greatest, the potential for clever and self-serving sophistry is also greatest. Consequently, Paul and all other New Testament writers adamantly resisted a "situational ethic" in the area of sexual expression. Instead they claimed that God had laid

---

69. The use of *eis* ("into") in the sense of "against" with the verb *hamartanein* ("sinning") is common enough (cf. LXX Prov 8:36; 20:2; Sir 10:29). The contrast with "outside (*ektos*) the body" suggests, though, a double entendre: immoral sexual intercourse is a sin "into" and so "against" the body.

70. "[PORNEUEIN] as Body Violation: The Unique Nature of Sexual Sin in 1 Corinthians 6.18," *NTS* 42 (1996): 540-58 (quote from pp. 557-58). Fisk points to a parallel in Sir 19:2-4: "The man who unites with prostitutes (*ho kollōmenos pornais*) is shameless. Decay and worms will possess him, and the shameless person will be removed. . . . the sinner commits an offense against his life." Cf. Prov 6:32 (LXX): the adulterer "acquires for himself destruction for his life."

down clear rules that brooked no exceptions. To paraphrase Paul as saying "neither heterosexuality nor homosexuality are of any avail" is as misguided as saying "neither monogamy nor multiple sexual partners are of any avail" or "neither exogamous relationships nor incestuous relationships are of any avail." Moreover, to intimate that the list of vices in Gal 5:19-21 is concerned primarily with "relationships" rather than sexual expression not only poses a false dichotomy but also ignores the fact that the first three vices mentioned are *porneia*, *akatharsia* (impurity, uncleanness—usually a sexual category for Paul), and *aselgeia* (licentiousness, usually referring to a lack of sexual restraint). Forms of sexual expression that deviated from the kind of heterosexual union validated by God at creation can never, by definition, be legitimately construed as "loving."

The discussion of 1 Cor 6:12-20 makes a nice segue into an analysis of the only other text in the undisputed Pauline corpus that speaks directly to the question of homosexuality. This text, 1 Cor 6:9, appears just three verses earlier.

Excursus: The Claim That Romans 1:26 Refers to Heterosexual Intercourse

James E. Miller and others claim that Rom 1:26 refers to *heterosexual* anal or oral intercourse.[71] Miller makes three arguments. First, he notes that Rom 1:26 does not explicitly say that "their females" engaged in sexual intercourse with other females. He then argues that the "likewise" (*homoiōs*) introducing the description of male same-sex intercourse in 1:27 need not suggest that 1:26 is about female same-sex intercourse. In support he cites *T. Naph.* 3:4-5: ". . . [do] not become like Sodom, which changed the order of its nature. And likewise also (*homoiōs de kai*) the Watchers changed the order of their nature. . . ." Both Sodom and the angels known as the Watchers "changed the order of their nature," but the "likewise" does not mean that they did so in precisely the same way. The former engaged in homosexual intercourse, the latter in

---

71. James E. Miller, "The Practices of Romans 1:26: Homosexual or Heterosexual?" *NovT* 37 (1995): 1-11. Also: Fredrickson, "Romans 1:24-27," 201 n. 15; Peter J. Tomson, *Paul and the Jewish Law* (CRINT 3.1; Assen: Van Gorcum; Minneapolis: Fortress, 1990), 94; Stowasser, "Homosexualität und Bibel," 516, 519. Greenberg thinks that a definitive statement cannot be made, one way or the other (*Construction*, 214-15).

heterosexual intercourse with human women. The point of comparison in Rom 1:26-27 is not two forms of homosexual intercourse but two forms of non-coital (anal, oral) sexual intercourse. Second, according to Miller's key argument, classical and Hellenistic Jewish sources rarely mention male and female homosexuality in the same context and, when they do, "male homo-sexuality is the primary topic and is introduced first." "In other words, we have minimal evidence that a single category 'homosexual' existed in Classical culture. Rather male and female homosexuality were treated as separate categories."[72] Third, both anal and oral heterosexual intercourse were sometimes practiced as a form of contraception (e.g., by courtesans "to attract and keep lovers"). Miller cites Ps.-Phoc. 189 as his sole example of Hellenistic-Jewish revulsion for such conduct ("do not outrage [your] wife by shameful ways of intercourse").

Against Miller's position, though, the following arguments can be raised, corresponding to his three points. First, although Rom 1:26 does not explicitly state that females had sexual intercourse with females, the parallel wording in 1:27 strongly infers it:

1:26: their females exchanged the natural use for that which is contrary to nature
1:27: and likewise also the males, leaving the natural use of the female, burned in their desire for one another . . .

The expression "natural use *of the female* (as a sexual partner)" in 1:27 suggests that the implied objective genitive for "natural use" in 1:26 is "natural use (of the male as a sexual partner)," which in turn implies that the converse "that which is contrary to nature" refers to the unnatural use of females as sexual partners. The continuation of 1:27 makes clear that the exchange for men is not that of coital intercourse for non-coital intercourse but rather an exchange of sexual relations with women for sexual relations with men. It is precisely just such a continuation of thought that is lacking in the analogy from *T. Naph.* 3:4-5, which states only that Sodom "changed the order of its nature" and "the Watchers changed the order of their nature." Neither clause specifies what the "order of nature" was changed for, which makes possible a loose comparison. However, Rom 1:27 is quite explicit about what "the natural use of the female" was exchanged for: sex with members of the same sex. For the "likewise" of 1:27 to be appropriate, both the thing exchanged and the

---

72. Miller, ""Romans 1:26," 6-7.

thing exchanged *for* must be comparable. Hence, sex with members of the same sex, not non-coital sex, is the point of comparison between 1:26 and 1:27.

Second, even Miller admits of five instances in which male homosexual intercourse and female homosexual intercourse are discussed in the same context: Aristophanes's speech in Plato's *Symp.* 189D–191E; *Phaedrus* 4.16; Plutarch, *Lyc.* 18; Pseudo-Lucian, *Affairs* 28; and Ps-Phoc. 190-92. Brooten's work has supplied many others. Moreover, Miller has neglected early Christian texts that pair male and female homoeroticism, including those that interpret Rom 1:26 as a reference to lesbian intercourse. Miller's contention that Paul's audience would not have caught the reference to female same-sex intercourse in 1:26 is thus unconvincing.

Third, Miller fails to cite a single ancient source that explicitly refers to anal or oral intercourse as "unnatural" or "contrary to nature." Yet female same-sex intercourse is cited as being just that (Brooten refers to Plato, Seneca the Elder, Martial, Ovid, Ptolemy, Artemidoros, and probably Dorotheos of Sidon). Anal and oral intercourse did not carry much of a stigma in Greco-Roman society. Even most later rabbis did not forbid such intercourse between a husband and a wife (*b. Ned.* 20a-b; *b. Sanh.* 58b; both cited by Brooten). Ps.-Phoc. 189 does not specify what is meant by "shameful ways of intercourse" (probably any deliberate act of non-procreative sex), but even if it does refer to oral or anal sex it is important to note that the author blames men, not women. The fact that Rom 1:26 puts the blame squarely and solely on women indicates that unnatural forms of heterosexual intercourse are not at issue.

A similar critique can be levelled against the view of Klaus Haacker that Rom 1:26 is referring to bestiality.[73] Another can be added: sex between women and beasts would appear to be ruled out by 1:24 ("dishonoring their bodies among themselves") and 1:27 ("burned in their desire for one another"); in other words, the context suggests sex between humans.[74]

Excursus: Why Paul Mentions Female Same-Sex Relations First

Scholars have speculated on Paul's reasons for mentioning female same-sex intercourse before male same-sex intercourse. Otto Michel viewed the order

---

73. "Exegetische Gesichtspunkte," 173-80.
74. For a critique of Miller, Haacker, and others who interpret Rom 1:26 as something other than female homoeroticism, see the apt comments by Brooten, *Love Between Women*, 248-52.

as "an outworking of the story of the Fall," where God addresses first "woman" and then "man" (Gen 3:16-19), symbolizing perhaps a disruption of the order of creation (Gen 1:27: "male and female"; cf. 1 Cor 11:8-9).[75] Brooten regards this as an additional, possible explanation.[76] Some have suggested that Paul left male same-sex intercourse for last "because the more aggressive character of male sexuality, as indicated in v. 27, makes for a better crescendo" (Dunn) and allows Paul to treat it "more fully" (Cranfield).[77] Jewett speaks of "a strikingly egalitarian note in Paul's treating same-sex intercourse among females as an issue in its own right, holding women to the same level of accountability as men."[78] The same conclusion was reached by John Nolland: "Rom 1:26 is a natural place to get to from Lev 18:22 and 20:13, once a gospel perspective had pressed upon one the need to address the situation of women as seriously as the situation of men."[79] Others have argued the reverse; namely, that female same-sex intercourse was mentioned first and given less detailed attention because it was a more shocking phenomenon to Paul (so Hodge, Murray, Brooten, and Nissinen).[80] Already John Chrysostom, *Hom. Rom. 4* wrote: "It is even more shameful that the women should seek this type of intercourse, since they ought to have more modesty than men."

That Paul found female homosexuality more shocking than male homosexuality may be supported by the phrase *"their* females" in 1:26 and would justify the rendering of *te* as *"even* their females." Elsewhere Paul focused only

---

75. *Römer*, 105. He is followed tentatively by Wilckens (*Römer*, 109 n. 200).
76. *Love Between Women*, 240.
77. Dunn, *Romans*, 64; Cranfield, *Romans*, 125, followed by Morris, *Romans*, 92.
78. "Homoerotic References," 233.
79. "Romans 1:26-27 and the Homosexuality Debate," *HBT* 22 (2000): 49.
80. See Hodge, *Romans*, 63 ("Paul first refers to the degradation of females . . . because they are always the last to be affected in the decay of morals, and their corruption is therefore proof that all virtue is lost"); Murray, *Romans*, 1.47 ("[it] is undoubtedly for the purpose of accentuating the grossness of the evil. . . . It is the delicacy which belongs to the woman that makes more apparent the degeneracy of homosexual indulgence in their case"); Brooten, *Love Between Women*, 240 (the "commonly held assumption" that same-sex intercourse is more shameful for women since women ought to be more modest "may help to explain why Paul mentions women first and why he does not spell out the exact form of their sexual contact. Perhaps . . . female homoeroticism is unspeakable for Paul, making him hesitant to describe it precisely"); Nissinen, *Homoeroticism*, 108 (Paul "could hardly accept women exercising their sexual energy in any other way than with their husbands—not to mention the possibility that a woman would assume a man's role as an active partner. It is possible that Paul mentions women's homoerotic relations first in order to make men's comparable acts appear particularly 'unnatural' ").

on male homosexual activity (1 Cor 6:9; cf. 1 Tim 1:10) but this may have been because that was where the debate in antiquity raged most hotly. Female homoeroticism was universally regarded by men in antiquity as wrong and rare by comparison with male homosexual behavior, so it would have required less attention by Paul. Cf. the argument of Charicles, an advocate for the superiority of heterosexual love, against Callicratidas, an advocate for pederasty, in Pseudo-Lucian, *Affairs* 28: "Therefore, . . . Callicratidas, . . . if the intercourses with males are proper for the males, in the future let women love one another also. Come now, O newer time and lawgiver of strange pleasures, since you contrived new paths for male wantonness (*tryphē*; or: softness, daintiness, luxury, indulgence), graciously give the equal right (*isē exousia*; or: equal license, authority) to women and let them have intercourse with one another as men do. Let them fasten below a cunning contrivance (*technasma*; or: artificial contraption, piece of handiwork) consisting of licentious instruments (*aselga organa*), a monstrous riddle without sperm-sowing capacity, and let a woman sleep with a woman like a man. And let the name that has seldom come into our hearing—I am ashamed even to mention—of tribadic (*tribakē*; lit., rubbed, from *tribas*, i.e., lesbian) licentiousness (*aselgeia*) parade as if in ostentatious procession. And let every one of our women's chambers be (*sc.* as?) Philainis (a fourth-century B.C.E. female poet who allegedly wrote an obscene book about sexual positions), behaving obscenely (*aschēmonousa*) with androgynous (*androgynoi*) loves. And how much better it is for a woman to force herself into male wantonness (*tryphē*) than for what is noble among men to be feminized (*thēlunesthai*) into a woman?" (my translation). Even Callicratidas recoiled at this thought and declared women to be suited only for childbearing (38). Charicles's intent was to bring forward lesbianism as an example designed to elicit shame on the part of supporters of male homosexual practice. If one admits that it is inappropriate for women to play the part of men in sexual intercourse, then for the sake of consistency one should also oppose males playing the role of women. Paul's citation of female homosexuality first may have been part of a rhetorical strategy adapted to his cultural context: lead with one's strongest suit.

If Paul thought lesbianism was not only more surprising than male homosexual practice but also morally more reprehensible, then he would have differed from *some* later rabbis who, largely on the basis of the silence of the Torah on lesbianism and the fact that normally no penetration was involved, treated female homoeroticism as a lesser offense akin to masturbation. The Jerusalem Talmud (*Git.* 8:10, 49c.70-71) records a debate over whether two women who "rub" with each other can continue to eat priestly offerings and be eligible to marry a priest. The School of Shammai allegedly disqualified them from doing so, on the grounds that it was equivalent to harlotry (Lev 21:7, 9), while the School of Hillel permitted them to do so on the grounds that it was a mere "obscenity." There are good reasons for supposing, though, that the debate goes back only to the mid-third century (cf. the attribution of the "Shammai" position not to Shammai but to Rav Huna, a Babylonian rabbi of the mid-third century, in the Babylonian Talmud, *Yebamot* 76a). *Sipra*, a rabbinical commentary on Leviticus composed before the third century C.E., appears to put marriage between two women on the same level of sexual offense as marriage between two men and incest, all alleged practices of the Canaanites and Egyptians forbidden to Israelites (*Sipra* on Lev 18:3).[81]

While it is hard to discount an element of chauvinism in Paul's remarks, misogyny would be an inappropriate label. Paul believed that same-sex intercourse was a disgusting form of sexual behavior whether it was done by males or by females. In his mind, he would hardly have been doing women a favor by believing that they were just as prone to such behavior as men. It would have been a relatively benign slight of women if Paul had said in another context, "Even a large number of their women commit murder, rape, and child molestation." Indirectly, he would have been paying women a compliment: women do not normally engage in the kinds of sordid activity typically associated with men. The fact that some women do engage in such activity makes their conduct all the more shocking. Similar viewpoints prevail in our own society even among feminists. Some feminists proclaim women to be, on the whole, less prone to severe aggression and irresponsible sexual behavior. Statistical evidence supports such a conclusion. A population group that had as many women incarcerated as males would occasion shock in our own society. There is also statistical evidence that in the United States male homosexuality is twice as common as lesbianism. In Paul's day, with women's freedom of sexual expression subject to far greater regulation and lesbianism probably much rarer than male homosexual behavior, we should not be surprised that Paul was surprised by the occurrence of lesbian activity among some women.

Women's sexual purity was closely guarded by males in antiquity. Part of this had to do with male concerns for property rights (see, e.g., Exod 20:17: "you shall not covet your neighbor's wife, or . . . slave, or ox, or donkey, or anything else that belongs to your neighbor"). Part of it can be traced to compassionate desire to protect women from predatory males. The fact that special concerns for the sexual purity of women were sometimes tainted by chauvinistic beliefs, even in biblical texts, should not lead to the conclusion that the

81. For further discussion and literature, cf. Brooten, *Love Between Women*, 64-70.

church should no longer lift up sexual purity as an important value to maintain in society. Few in the church today would contend: "Since adultery in antiquity was often conceived as a threat to male honor, we should do away entirely with the notion that adultery is a bad thing." Rather, we draw the appropriate conclusion that female honor should be regarded as just as important as male honor; no double standard should be permitted. Why then should anyone intimate that, because Jewish and Christian resistance to same-sex intercourse may have had a partially chauvinistic element in it (a desire to protect male status), the church today should completely disregard the historic prohibition of homosexual behavior?

II. The Vice Lists in 1 Corinthians 6:9 and 1 Timothy 1:10

Two other texts in Pauline (or deutero-Pauline) literature besides Rom 1:24-27 mention same-sex intercourse explicitly: 1 Cor 6:9 and 1 Tim 1:10. These verses bolster my reading of Rom 1:24-27 as they define homosexual sex as vice or sin that cannot be practiced by those who wish to inherit God's kingdom. Below I offer my own translations of the two passages. Following this, I engage in an extended discussion of the terms at issue, *malakoi* and *arsenokoitai*, in each of the verses in turn. I end this chapter with remarks that conclude part 1 as a whole.

Translation and Introduction

1 Corinthians 6:9-11

[9]Or do you not realize that unrighteous people will not inherit God's kingdom? Stop deceiving yourselves. Neither the sexually immoral (*pornoi*),[82] nor idolaters, nor adulterers, nor *effeminate males who play the sexual role of females (malakoi)*,[83] nor *males who take other males to*

---

82. "Fornicators" (NRSV, NAB, REB, NASB, ASV, KJV), "the sexually immoral" (NIV, NJB), "the immoral" (RSV), "one who is immoral" (CEV), "those who indulge in sexual sin" (NLT).

83. "Males performing the female role in homosexual relations" (Turner, "Biblical Texts," 441), "men who assume the female role in sex" (Furnish, *Moral Teaching of Paul*, 70), "men who assume a passive sexual role with other men" (Brooten, *Love Between Women*, 260), "male prostitutes" (NRSV, NIV, NLT), "boy prostitutes" (2d ed. of NAB [1987]), "effeminate call boys" (Scroggs), "the self-indulgent" (NJB),

bed (arsenokoitai),[84] [10]nor thieves, nor greedy people, not drunkards, not verbally abusive people, nor swindlers will inherit the kingdom of God. [11]And these things some (of you) were. But you washed yourselves off (or: were washed off), and you were made holy, and you were made righteous in the name of the Lord Jesus Christ and in the Spirit of our God.

1 Timothy 1:8-10

[8]Now we know that the law is good, if anyone uses it lawfully, [9]knowing this: that law is not laid down for the righteous, but for the lawless and disobedient, the ungodly and sinners, the unholy and profane, killers of fathers and killers of mothers, murderers, [10]the sexually immoral *(pornoi)*,[85] *males who take other males to bed (arsenokoitai)*,[86] kidnap-

---

"effeminate" (NASB, ASV, KJV, Dale Martin; W. F. Orr and J. A. Walther: "effeminate men"), "perverts" (R. F. Collins), "(one who is) a pervert" (CEV), "homosexual perverts" (NAB, 1st ed. [1970]), "catamites" (JB; i.e., boys kept by pederasts; cf. F. Lang, J. Becker: "Lustknaben"), "sensualist" (A. Robertson and A. Plummer), "masturbators" (Countryman, Boswell); "Weichlinge [soft or effeminate men]" (W. Schrage, H. Conzelmann, E. Fascher). Both the second edition of the RSV (1971) and the REB combine this and the next term in a single translation: "sexual pervert[s]." The result is an overly vague revision of earlier readings (RSV, 1st ed.: "homosexuals"; NEB: "homosexual perversion"; cf. TEV: "homosexual perverts"). Fredrickson translates "those who lack self-control" ("Romans 1:24-27," 197).

84. "Those who have sex with men" (Brooten, *Love Between Women*, 260), "men who have sex with [men who assume the female role in sex]" (Furnish, *Moral Teaching of Paul*, 70), "mit Männern Schlafende [those who sleep with men]" (Schrage), "the arrogant who penetrate boys" (Fredrickson), "sodomites" (NRSV, NJB, 1st ed. of the NAB, Robertson and Plummer), "practicing homosexuals" (2d ed. of NAB), "homosexual offenders" (NIV; cf. NEB, cited above), "homosexuals" (Collins, NLT, NASB; cf. 1st ed. of RSV, cited above), "male homosexuals" (Orr and Walther), "(one who) behaves like a homosexual" (CEV), "abusers of themselves with mankind" (KJV; ASV: ". . . with men"), "Knabenschänder [violaters of boys, boy abusers]" (Conzelmann, Fascher, Lang, J. Becker, Christian Wolff).

85. "Fornicators" (NRSV, REB, ASV), "immoral persons" (RSV, NASB: "men"), "the unchaste" (NAB), "the promiscuous" (NJB), "adulterers" (NIV), "whoremongers" (KJV), "people who are sexually immoral" (NLT), "people who are sexual perverts" (CEV), "the incestuous" (Quinn and Wacker).

86. "Sodomites" (NRSV, RSV), "practicing homosexuals" (NAB), "homosexuals" (NJB, NLT, NASB, Quinn and Wacker, Knight), "(people) who live as homosexuals" (CEV), "perverts" (NIV, REB), "abusers of themselves with men" (ASV), "them that defile themselves with mankind" (KJV), "pederasts" (Dibelius and

pers (who sell free people into slavery) (*andrapodistai*),[87] liars, perjurers, and whatever else is opposed to sound teaching that accords with the gospel. . . .

These verses make clear that certain behaviors, including certain sexual behaviors, cannot be a part of faithful Christian living. In 1 Corinthians Paul associates the washing of baptism with an end to sinful ways of being. The author of 1 Timothy notes that, while the righteous are free from the law, they yet live freely according to its precepts, not returning to the unrighteous behavior of the past.

In 1 Cor 6:9-11, *pornoi* is listed first before "idolaters" and detached somewhat from the list of three sexual vices that follow. On the one hand, this peculiar ordering may be accounted for by the fact that a specific case of *porneia* was the focus of discussion in 1 Corinthians 5. Becker conjectures that "the original series began first with the idolaters, followed by four vices from the sphere of sexuality."[88] Stowasser thinks that *pornoi* was added by Paul to a pre-existing vice list.[89] We recall that in Rom 1:18-32 sexual vices follow immediately upon idolatry.[90] On the other hand, in Gal 5:19-21 "idolatry" is mentioned only after a series of three sexual vices. Moreover, in other lists where sexual vices figure prominently idolatry is not mentioned at all (e.g., Rom 13:13; 1 Cor 5:10; and 2 Cor 12:20-21).

Paul clearly tailored his vice lists to the needs of the specific communities he addressed. The secondary significance of idolatry in some vice lists probably owes more to the type of audience Paul was addressing[91]

Greeven). In the view of Jerome Quinn and William Wacker, "Unless the *pornoi* here . . . are the catamites (and that is lexically possible), the *malakoi* have been edited out of the source (Pauline or pre-Pauline) that is being used. The reason is that the *arsenokoitai* are now understood to be all homosexuals, active or passive, old or young" (*The First and Second Letters to Timothy* [Grand Rapids: Eerdmans, 2000]: 101).

87. "Kidnappers" (RSV, NAB, NJB, REB, NASB, CEV), "menstealers" (ASV, KJV), "slave traders" (NRSV, NIV, NLT, Quinn and Wacker).

88. Becker, "Zum Problem der Homosexualität in der Bibel," 51.

89. Stowasser, "Homosexualität und Bibel," 510-11.

90. Cf. the discussion of Israelite sins during the wilderness wanderings in 1 Cor 10:7-8: ". . . nor become idolaters just as some of them. . . . Nor let us commit *porneia* just as some of them committed *porneia*."

91. That is, gentile Christians who were more prone to lapse into sexual immorality than to fall back into idolatry.

than to any absolute devaluation of idolatry relative to sexual immorality. Idolatry and sexual immorality were closely conjoined in Jewish thought inasmuch as both were sins of infidelity to the covenant relationship established between God and God's people. Indeed, infidelity to one's spouse became a metaphor for infidelity to God. As Rom 1:18-32 and Wisdom of Solomon 12–15 indicate, a wrong-headed view of God would invariably lead to a wrong-headed view of God's will for human behavior—particularly in the area of sexuality where the temptation of erotic pleasure goes hand-in-hand with self-deception. However, this did not mean for Jews that certain forms of sexual behavior were wrong only because they were associated with foreign cults. In fact, Jewish exaggeration of the presence of sexual immorality in Greco-Roman cults was a standard means for discrediting such cults.

Of critical importance in determining the relevance of 1 Cor 6:9 and 1 Tim 1:10 for contemporary discussions of same-sex intercourse is the meaning of the terms *arsenokoitai* and *malakoi*. Some scholars argue that the meaning of these terms cannot be known, or that they refer to something other than participants in same-sex intercourse, or that they designate only distinct types of homosexuals that bear little resemblance to contemporary expressions of homosexuality. If any of these positions were true, it might discredit their use by those opposed to homosexual practice. Clarification of these words in their historical context will occupy us for much of the rest of this chapter.

The Meaning of Malakoi *in 1 Corinthians 6:9*

In the vice list of 1 Cor 6:9-10, I have translated *malakoi*, which literally means "the soft ones," as "effeminate males who play the sexual role of females"; and *arsenokoitai*, which literally means "male-bedders," as "males who take other males to bed." Advocates of homosexuality among Christians offer other readings. Some narrow the meaning and others expand it.

In his translation of *malakoi*, Robin Scroggs offers the narrow meaning "effeminate call-boys."[92] Taking a different tack, Dale Martin con-

---

92. Scroggs, *The New Testament and Homosexuality*, 106-8 ("the youth who consciously imitated feminine styles and ways and who walked the thin line between

tends that in Greek literature *malakoi* carries the broad sense of "the effeminate." He goes on to say that in the ancient world, for men, *malakoi* can denote such diverse things as a penchant for "soft" or decadent living, a fondness for expensive clothes and gourmet foods, excessive attention to the care of one's hair, long hair, wearing perfume or makeup, gluttony, too much heterosexual sex, laziness or aversion to the rigors of a philosopher's life, cowardice, and acceptance of phallic penetration by another male. Martin's point is that, since the term reflects a belief that feminine traits are inferior, it is misogynist and contemporary interpreters should abandon an appeal to "what the Bible says" here.[93] Both Scroggs and Martin seek to render the word *malakoi* unusable for those who regard all homosexual behavior as sin: Scroggs by showing the word is too narrow to embrace non-prostituting passive homosexual males; Martin by demonstrating that the word is too broad to be taken seriously today, embracing as it does not only passive homosexual males but also any heterosexual males who display effeminacy.

In my own reading, the meaning of *malakoi* in 1 Cor 6:9 probably

---

passive homosexual activity for pleasure and that for pay," p. 106); followed by Smith in emphasizing the prostitution angle ("The New Testament and Homosexuality," 20, 23). Greenberg contends that "Boswell's confidence that homosexuality is not intended seems misplaced" and that "Scroggs's idea that *malakos* refers to an effeminate call-boy is simply speculative." However, his own preference, namely that "the term in this context referred to homosexual cult prostitutes," merely adds a religious dimension to Scroggs's view (*Construction*, 212-13).

93. Dale B. Martin, "*Arsenokoitēs* and *Malakos*: Meanings and Consequences," *Biblical Ethics and Homosexuality*, 117-36 (*malakos* is discussed on pp. 124-31, 134-36); similarly, Fredrickson, "Romans 1:24-27," 219-20 (*malakoi* refers broadly to any persons who lack self-control, not excluding the passive, penetrated male but in the context of 1 Cor 6:1-11 specifically directed at the "unjust" who run the law courts); and Boswell, *Homosexuality*, 339-41 (*malakos* "refers to general moral weakness, with no specific connection to homosexuality," possibly masturbation or prostitution). Countryman follows Boswell in adopting the meaning "masturbator," referring not to one who occasionally masturbates but to "the person so devoted to the pursuit of private pleasure as to be devoid of responsibility" (*Dirt, Greed, and Sex*, 119, 202). Scanzoni and Mollenkott translate as "self-indulgent," heterosexuals obsessed with sexual conquest (*Is the Homosexual My Neighbor?*, 68-69). For an extensive treatment of the effeminate person in antiquity, cf. H. Herter, "Effeminatus," *RAC* 4 (1959): 620-50.

lies somewhere in between "only prostituting passive homosexuals" and "effeminate heterosexual and homosexual males." Because the word has a broad range of meaning in Greek literature, what it specifically means for any given writer will vary. However, here, Paul places this vice alongside a list of offenses that lead to exclusion from the kingdom. This suggests he refers to an offense more serious than simply a "limp wrist" (*contra* Martin). For instance, in 1 Cor 11:2-16, Paul argues strongly that women who pray and prophesy should wear a veil. He notes that short hair is natural for men and long hair for women. In his many types of appeals, he at no time suggests, however, that inappropriate headgear or hairstyle will lead to exclusion from the kingdom of God. If then *malakoi* refers to a general critique of effeminacy in men, what kind of effeminacy would generate such a serious penalty for a Jew? In 1 Cor 6:9 *malakoi* are sandwiched in between adulterers (people who commit an act of immoral sexual intercourse) and *arsenokoitai* (people who have something to do with an immoral act of same-sex intercourse). Immoral sexual intercourse, then, would appear to be an identifying mark of the *malakoi*.[94] Furthermore, the epithet "soft" itself suggests males playing the female role in sexual intercourse with other males.

These suppositions are confirmed by reference to the views of another first-century Jew, Philo. Philo twice uses the word *malakia* ("softness, effeminacy," alongside of the term *anandria*, "unmanliness") in his discussion of homosexual behavior in *Spec. Laws* 3.37-42 to refer to the behavior of passive homosexual partners (*hoi paschontes*) who cultivate feminine features. He describes men who braid their hair and who use makeup and excessive perfume in an effort to please their male lovers.[95] He does not limit himself here to "call boys"; the effeminate partner could become the active partner's mistress or even wife. The issue of sex-for-sale or prostitution never

---

94. Cf. Stowasser, "Homosexualität und Bibel," 511: "The bracketed position of [*malakos*] between the sexually-connotated vices [*moichoi*] and [*arsenokoitai*] makes a non-sexual meaning, as e.g. a sissy or effeminate person [*Weichling*], unrestrained [*zügelloser*] person, extremely improbable." Similarly, Springett, *Homosexuality*, 134.

95. Other standard attempts at effeminacy included wearing women's clothes and plucking hair from the face and body.

even comes up in Philo's critique. Admittedly, Philo does refer to the fact that some of these "male-females" (*androgynoi*) can be seen strutting at the head of festal processions celebrating the mysteries of Demeter. Some of these "unholy ministers," Philo says, have mutilated their genitals in a desire to be permanently transformed "into women." We may presume that some of these cultic functionaries brought in temple revenue as prostitutes. Nevertheless, Philo does not restrict his description of the phenomenon of feminized passive partners to such figures. Indeed, his critique focuses not on idolatrous associations or the exchange of money but rather on the deliberate effacement of the masculine stamp by these male-females, first by allowing themselves to be penetrated as women by other men, second by taking the further step of feminizing their appearance. They are those "who, accustoming themselves to be infected with a female disease, drain away both their souls and their bodies, leaving no ember of the male gender to smolder. . . . and with devotion practicing as an art to transform the male nature into female, they do not blush." The law sentences to death this "male-female (*androgynon*) who counterfeits the coin of nature." These are the kinds of effeminate men that for Philo are judged "worthy" to be killed (cf. Rom 1:32: "worthy of death") by "those who obey the law" (*Spec. Laws* 3.38, alluding to Lev 20:13). Similarly, in his description of the men of Sodom in *Abr.* 135-37, Philo uses the word *malakotēs* ("softness, luxury, decadence") to denote the whole feminizing process of receptive male partners in homosexual intercourse. Their feminization began with the act of sexual intercourse, irrespective of subsequent effeminate dress and mannerisms: "men mounted males, the doers not standing in awe of the (male) nature held in common with those who had it done to them. . . . Then, little by little, by accustoming those who had been born men to put up with feminine things, they equipped them with a female disease . . . not only feminizing their bodies with *malakotēs* and daintiness but also bringing their work to completion by making their very souls more degenerate."[96]

The collective evidence from Philo and 1 Cor 6:9-11 puts to rest the qualifications imposed on the term *malakoi* by Martin and Scroggs.

---

96. My translations.

(a) Against Martin, it is evident that "soft men" in 1 Cor 6:9 refers not to any male with effeminate traits but instead to males who function in the role of the passive homosexual partners and who also undertake to erase their distinctively masculine nature.

(b) Against Scroggs, although some of the "effeminate men" may exchange homosexual sex for money, the term is by no means restricted to homosexual prostitution. The "soft" stimulate outrage from Philo primarily for their attempts at removing all signs of masculinity given by nature, not for selling their services (the latter reason Philo does not even mention).

(c) Furthermore, although Philo treats the discussion in *Spec. Laws* 3.37-42 under the rubric of pederasty (*to paiderastein*) and alludes to the active partner (*ho drōn*) as a *paiderastēs*, it would be a mistake to limit his discussion of the passive partners only to adolescent boys. Philo makes clear that these male-female hybrids include adults who employ various means to prolong "their youthful beauty." Philo apparently had in mind the *cinaedus* (Gk. *kinaidos*), a man who, out of a desire to be penetrated by other men, "permanently, even as an adult, assumed the role of the passive partner, with effeminate mannerisms."[97] Philo does not aim his criticism at the age disparity in the relationship.

(d) A connection to idolatrous cults on the part of some of the "soft" does not seem to have been the central concern for Philo, or for Paul in Rom 1:24-27.

(e) Nor is it likely that Paul's primary concern was the non-procreative quality of their actions. In addition to the evidence from Rom 1:24-27, we can point to Philo's treatment. Unlike Paul, Philo adhered to the view that sex should only be for the purposes of procreation. Yet, although Philo briefly mentions that the *active* (insertive) partner "destroys the procreative sperm," his emphasis is on the passive partner's deliberate self-demasculinization. It is this element that explains why Philo regarded the "evil" of pederasty as "greater by far" than the non-procreative acts of heterosexual intercourse treated in *Spec. Laws* 3.32-33 (sex with a menstruating woman) and 3.34-36 (mating with a barren woman).

---

97. Nissinen, *Homoeroticism*, 68, 72, 83.

THE WITNESS OF PAUL AND DEUTERO-PAUL

(f) As for concerns about exploitation, Philo criticizes the older, active partner for serving as "a tutor and instructor in the grievous vices of unmanliness and softness by prolonging the bloom of the young and emasculating the flower of their prime" (*Spec. Laws* 3.39). Even so, at the same time he holds the passive partner accountable for willingly, and sometimes zealously, working at the removal of masculine traits. To argue that Philo or Paul were only concerned with exploitative same-sex relationships is to argue from an oxymoron, because for both Philo and Paul same-sex relationships were inherently exploitative. The moment a man takes another male to bed he distorts and diminishes the other male's sexual identity as created and ordained by God, regardless of whether the relationship is fully consensual and non-commercial.

(g) Finally, it would be a mistake to assume that, for Paul or Philo, only those passive homosexual partners who feminized their appearance would be considered worthy of exclusion from God's kingdom or of death. Clearly, both Paul and Philo took their cue from the Levitical prohibitions which say not a word about hair style, perfume, makeup, or female attire (cf. Deut 22:5 for a prohibition against men wearing women's clothes). For them, the first and most heinous stage of feminization occurred in the act of sexual penetration: being lain with "as though a woman." It is not realistic to argue that Paul and Philo simply did not know another, more acceptable "masculinized model" for the passive partner in homosexual intercourse. The culturally accepted model for the adolescent male "beloved" in ancient Greece did not entail an effeminate appearance for the passive partner. Philo, with his knowledge of Greek myth, history, and philosophy, surely knew this (he knows, for example, the speech of Aristophanes in Plato's *Symposium*), and it is likely that Paul did too. Even in their own day, arguments were being made that homosexual intercourse was an expression of appreciation for the superiority of the masculine ideal. Yet neither the evidence from Philo nor the evidence from Paul lends any support to the view that a passive partner with masculine affect would have been an acceptable alternative to the *cinaedus*. For them, an attempt by the passive partner to feminize his appearance is simply the logical corollary or symptom of a root problem; namely, playing the receptive female role in homosexual intercourse. What bothered both of them first and foremost was any act of sexual intercourse between two people of the same sex, not the dress or hairstyle of either of the participants.

Therefore, in 1 Cor 6:9, *malakoi* should be understood as the passive partners in homosexual intercourse, the most egregious case of which are those who also intentionally engage in a process of feminization to erase further their masculine appearance and manner.[98]

The Meaning of Arsenokoitai in 1 Corinthians 6:9

The second disputed word, *arsenokoitai* (sg. *arsenokoitēs*) literally means "bedders of males, those [men] who take [other] males to bed," "men who sleep or lie with males."[99] It is a neologism, occurring for the

---

98. For those who construe *malakoi* as a reference to the younger passive partner in a pederastic relationship, cf. Schoedel, "Same-Sex Eros," 63-64; Wolgang Schrage, *Der Erste Brief an die Korinther (1 Kor 1,1-6,11)* (EKKNT 7/1; Zürich: Benziger; Neukirchen-Vluyn: Neukirchener, 1991), 431-32; Gordon Fee, *The First Epistle to the Corinthians* (NICNT; Grand Rapids: Eerdmans, 1987), 243-44; Raymond F. Collins, *First Corinthians* (SP; Collegeville, Minn.: Liturgical Press, 1999), 236; Wold, *Out of Order*, 191-92; Springett, *Homosexuality*, 134; Grenz, *Welcoming But Not Affirming*, 57; David E. Malick, "The Condemnation of Homosexuality in 1 Corinthians 6:9," *BSac* 150 (1993): 487-92. Nissinen thinks the meaning of the term is unclear but leans in the direction of identifying the *malakos* with the *cinaedus* (*Homoeroticism*, 117). Peter Zaas states that *malakoi* "can possibly take the sense of 'catamite,' but only because of its association with the less ambiguous term *arsenokoitēs*" ("1 Corinthians 6.9ff.: Was Homosexuality Condoned in the Corinthian Church?" *SBL Seminar Papers, 1979* [ed. P. Achtemeier; Missoula, Mont.: Scholars Press, 1979], 205-12; quote from p. 209). Zaas attempts to tie Paul's proscriptions of homosexuality closely to the sin of idolatry. Hoheisel gives up on determining the exact meaning of the word ("Homosexualität," 339-41).

99. "Sodomites" is best avoided, both because the Greek word does not incorporate the proper name "Sodom" ("Sodomites" would imply a direct allusion to the story of Sodom whereas *arsenokoitēs* makes no such allusion) and because the inhabitants of Sodom were guilty of many other evils besides same-sex intercourse. The translation "practicing homosexuals" (NAB) is passable but does not convey the probable reference to the active partner. "Homosexuals" alone is problematic because the focus of *arsenokoitēs* is on the act of having sex with other males. Experiencing desires for intercourse with people of the same sex is not in itself sin, though like all impulses it can become sin if such thoughts are embraced and nur-

first time in extant literature here in 1 Cor 6:9 and later in 1 Tim 1:10.[100] Does the term refer exclusively to anyone who engages in homosexual intercourse as the active partner? Scroggs once more proposes a narrower reading, namely, that *arsenokoitēs* refers to "the active partner who keeps the *malakos* as a 'mistress' or who hires him on occasion to satisfy his sexual desires."[101] Martin argues for an interpretation which is at once narrow and broad. He contends that the

---

tured (even apart from action—the Spirit is to be Lord over one's thought life as well as behavior). In other respects, "homosexuals" is too narrow a translation since it does not encompass heterosexuals or bisexuals who have intercourse with members of the same sex. Cf. the critique of David F. Wright's translation "homosexuals" (cited below) by William L. Petersen, "Can [*ARSENOKOITAI*] Be Translated By 'Homosexuals,'" *VC* 40 (1986): 187-91. In a response to Petersen, though, Wright notes that the focus of his article on *arsenokoitai* was indeed on "male homosexual activity," that " 'homosexuals' has come in common parlance to refer also to those who engage in homosexual activity, irrespective of their known or unknown orientation," and that Petersen's approach requires a precision that would make any reference to "homosexuality" in antiquity impossible (even in book titles such as Kenneth Dover's *Greek Homosexuality*; "Translating [*ARSENOKOITAI*] (1 Cor. 6:9; 1 Tim. 1:10)," *VC* 41 [1987]: 396-98). Some looseness in the use of "homosexuals" does seem to be required for ease of public discourse on the subject, though for translation of 1 Cor 6:9 and 1 Tim 1:10 greater precision is advisable.

100. The use of the verb *arsenokoitein* in *Sib. Or.* 2.73 may antedate the occurrence of *arsenokoitēs* in Paul but the date of the former is difficult to establish. See the discussion below.

101. *The New Testament and Homosexuality*, 108. Scroggs notes: "Seen in this way, the list shares the disapproval of this form of pederasty in agreement with the entire literature of the Greco-Roman world on the topic!" (ibid.). That very observation is enough to sink Scroggs's interpretation of *malakoi* and *arsenokoitai*, because, as regards the issue of same-sex intercourse, it fails to discriminate between the views of first-century Jews and the prevailing sentiment in the Greco-Roman world generally. The latter can be characterized as disapproval of same-sex intercourse only in certain circumstances (e.g., when adult, free citizens took on the role of the effeminate passive partner, as opposed to adolescents, slaves, or foreigners). However, even Scroggs acknowledges that Jews and Christians in antiquity (including Paul in Rom 1:24-27) opposed all forms of homosexual intercourse known to them. The rise of the Christian state in the time of Constantine and thereafter spelled the demise of every and any official state tolerance of same-sex intercourse. Scroggs's interpretation blurs this irrefutable historical distinction. Furnish is not certain whether the terms *arsenokoitai* and *malakoi* refer to "male prostitutes and their customers or . . . 'homosexual' acts between any two males" ("The Bible and Homosexuality," 24). Stowasser believes that Scroggs's interpretation show "great plausibility, though one cannot speak in terms of a stringent

word has in view men who exploit other males by means of sex—
"perhaps but not necessarily by homosexual sex."[102] So for him the
word does not take in non-exploitative homosexual sex (hence, a narrow

---

proof" ("Homosexualität und Bibel," 515). Fredrickson restricts the term to the
violent and hybristic (arrogant) pederast who not only experiences a loss of self-
control but also demeans the younger male through the disgrace of penetration
("Romans 1:24-27," 221-22).

102. Martin, "*Arsenokoitês* and *Malakos*," 118-23. Cf. Boswell who construes the word
to refer to "active male prostitutes. . . . capable of the active role with either men or
women" (*Homosexuality*, 341-53 [quote on p. 344]). Boswell contends against a
homosexual connotation largely on the basis of an argument from silence: the term
arsenokoitai and cognate words rarely occur in Christian texts. "The Carolingian
theologian Hincmar of Reims was the first medieval moralist to make use of
1 Corinthians 6:9 in writing about homosexuality, and even he seems to have understood the Vulgate's reference as involving prostitution as well. The passage was not
cited again by a major theologian for four centuries. Saint Thomas Aquinas, in the
thirteenth century, was the first really influential theologian to use the passage . . .
as scriptural basis for hostility to homosexual behavior" (ibid., 353). Boswell makes
much of the term's absence in both John Chrysostom (fourth century) and Peter
Cantor (twelfth century), each of whom combed the scriptures for references to
same-sex intercourse but never mentioned *arsenokoitai* in either 1 Cor 6:9 or 1 Tim
1:10 (ibid., 347-49). Cf. Scroggs's comment: "If [*arsenokoitês*] is a coinage of
Hellenistic Jews taken from rabbinic discussions, this would fully explain what
Boswell finds so remarkable, that the word does not appear in Greco-Roman discussions of pederasty, and that in later patristic authors, the word is either avoided
or given other meanings. To a native-speaking Greek, without contact with Jewish
debate, the word would have made little sense" (*The New Testament and
Homosexuality*, 108 n. 13). David F. Wright gives careful examination of the word's
absence in John Chrysostom (actually, in his fifth homily on Titus, the latter does
mention *arsenokoitai* in 1 Cor 6:9 without discussing the meaning of the term) and
the contexts where one would have most expected Chrysostom to refer to
arsenokoitai in 1 Cor 6:9. He convincingly shows that the term's disuse tells us little ("Homosexuals or Prostitutes," 142-44). "Of itself non-use reveals nothing about
a word's meaning; only use clarifies meaning. And Boswell has signally failed to
demonstrate any use of [*arsenokoitês*] etc. in which it patently does not denote male
homosexual activity. The only possibility is the occurrence in John the Faster, where
even Boswell has to resort to a wholly unprecedented meaning" (ibid., 144). Lance,
however, regards Boswell's arguments as sufficiently persuasive to leave the meaning of *arsenokoitai* and by extension *malakoi* in great doubt ("The Bible and
Homosexuality," 146-47). Nissinen thinks that "the homoerotic interpretation
seems better grounded than Boswell's argument" but (citing Countryman) calls
even the former merely an "educated guess" (*Homoeroticism*, 116, 118).
Countryman, using 1 Tim 1:10 as his starting point, argues without much substan-
tiation that the word signified "the male, slave or free, who used his sexual attractiveness to ingratiate himself with a rich and elderly lover in the hope of receiving a
substantial legacy, thus replacing more legitimate heirs" (*Dirt, Greed, and Sex*, 202).

interpretation) but it may include exploitative heterosexual intercourse (hence, a broad interpretation).

A broadening of the word *arsenokoitēs* to include exploitative heterosexual intercourse or even a restriction to exclude non-exploitative homosexual intercourse appears unlikely in view of the unqualified nature of the Levitical prohibitions. As David F. Wright has persuasively argued,[103] *arsenokoitēs* was probably coined by Hellenistic Jews from a conflation of two Greek words appearing in the Septuagint's rendering of Lev 18:22 and 20:13: *meta arsenos ou koimēthēsē koitēn gynaikeian* (18:22); *hos an koimēthē meta arsenos koitēn gynaikos* (20:13). The Greek word for "male" is *arsēn* and the word for "bed" or "lying" is *koitē* (related to the verb *keisthai*, "to lie"), to which has been attached a masculine personal suffix *-(t)ēs* denoting the agent or doer of the action ("a man / one who . . .").[104] Scroggs himself has observed that the rabbis used the phrase *miškab zākûr* ("lying of/with a male"),[105] drawn from the Hebrew text of Lev 18:22 and 20:13, to refer to homosexual intercourse.[106] It is possible that the Hebrew phrase may have been in circulation prior to Paul's letters, in which case *arsenokoitia* ("homosexual intercourse") and its derivatives would be a straightforward Greek translation. Otherwise, the Hebrew phrase represents an independent but parallel development, still corroborating the link between *arsenokoitia* and the Levitical prohibitions. In a discussion of how one knows that *miškab zākûr* is punished by stoning, *b. Sanh.* 54a cites Lev 20:13 and notes that the man who lies with a male (the active partner) "excludes a minor," but the male with whom

---

103. "Homosexuals or Prostitutes?," 125-53.
104. Outside the NT the word sometimes occurs with the spelling *arr-* rather than *ars-*. According to P. D. M. Turner, "the [*t*' or *tau* of *arsenokoitēs*] has no connection with [*koitē*] 'bed' except the coincidental one of a derivation from [*keimai*] 'I lie'" (Turner, "Biblical Texts," 442). The *-tēs* suffix is added to a verb stem, not a noun; but the noun *koitē* in Lev 18:22; 20:13 would have called to mind the verb to which it was related. However, if the *tau* has no direct connection to the noun *koitē*, why do the related verb (*arsenokoiteō*, not *arsenokeimai*) and abstract noun (*arsenokoitia*) retain the *tau*? Turner also contends that since the words *koitē* and *keimai* did not normally denote sexual intercourse such a use of the root in *arsenokoitēs* in 1 Cor 6:9 and in *koitē* in Lev 18:22; 20:13 strengthens "a deliberate, conscious back-reference by the Apostle" to the Levitical proscriptions (pp. 442-44).
105. Cf. *b. Sanh.* 54a; *b. Šabb.* 17b; *b. Sukkah* 29a; *y. Ber.* 9.50.13c.
106. Scroggs, *The New Testament and Homosexuality*, 83, 108.

he lays (the passive partner) may be "an adult or minor." In other words, in the view of the rabbis, *miškab zākûr* was not restricted to pederasty.

That *arsenokoitai* refers to same-sex intercourse is strengthened by its pairing with *malakoi*. If the first vice, *pornoi*, is bracketed off as a Pauline addition to a pre-formed list, a relatively clear sequence develops. As Martin Stowasser has shown,[107] the first four vices (in a list minus *pornoi*) are joined together in chiastic sequence. The first (*eidōlolatrai*, idolaters) and the fourth (*arsenokoitai*) are both five-syllable words ending in -*ai* and accented on the penult. The second (*moichoi*, adulterers) and the third (*malakoi*) are words ending in -*oi* and accented on the ultima. The fifth (*kleptai*, thieves) and sixth vices (*pleonektai*, the greedy or covetous) exhibit assonance and share a similar content.[108] The seventh (*methysoi*, drunkards) and eighth vices (*loidoroi*, the verbally abusive) are both three-syllable words ending in -*oi* and accented on the antepenult. They are sometimes paired in Jewish literature, inasmuch as drunkenness leads to abusive speech.[109] Only the ninth vice (*harpages*, robbers or swindlers) is left dangling without a partner. Idolatry and adultery (or *porneia*) are linked in early Jewish tradition.[110] OT prophets frequently compared Israel's idolatry to an adulterous woman. If adultery is paired with idolatry, then *malakoi* and *arsenokoitai* constitute a pair of sexual sins distinct from adultery. Given such a pairing, our identification of *malakoi* with passive homosexual partners confirms the supposition that the term *arsenokoitai* refers to the active partners in homosexual intercourse.

Furthermore, in every instance where the *arsenokoit-* word group occurs in a context that offers clues as to its meaning (i.e., beyond mere inclusion in a vice list) it denotes homosexual intercourse. Wright provides the most thorough study of the evidence. His work is now disputed by Dale Martin, however. What follows is based on Wright's work but addresses Martin as well. Martin limits his study to what he

---

107. Stowasser, "Homosexualität und Bibel," 512-13.
108. *T. Ash.* 2:5; *T. Dan* 5:7.
109. Prov 20:1, 3; Philo, *Dreams* 2.168; cf. *T. Jud.* 14:8.
110. Wis 14:13, 26-27; 1 Cor 10:7-8; cf. *T. Levi* 17:11; Clement of Alexandria, *Paed.* 3.89.

considers the five earliest attestations after the New Testament. Even these make clear that homosexual conduct is at issue. I address five other texts or groups of texts that Martin leaves out of his discussion.

(1) In *Sib. Or.* 2.73, the term occurs in the context of a vice list: "do not *arsenokoitein* [Collins, *OTP*: practice homosexuality], do not betray information, do not murder." The preceding vices have to do with accepting gifts from unjust sources and stealing "seeds" (hoarding grain?); the vices cited immediately after this verse are those of withholding wages and oppressing the poor. The surrounding context suggests to Martin that *arsenokoitein* refers to "economic exploitation by means of sex," homosexual or heterosexual.

Given *Sib. Or.* 3.185-87 (ca. 165–45 B.C.E.), the author may indeed have had in mind homosexual intercourse with call boys: "Male will have intercourse with male and they will set up boys in houses of ill-fame . . . and it will throw everything into confusion." The error, though, would be to limit the reference to the economic exploitation of prostitution ("betraying information" and "murder," the two immediately following vices, are not strictly "economic exploitation"). Homosexual intercourse with an adolescent boy was regarded as a theft of sorts not so much because sex for money or sex with a teenager was wrong as because the act of penetration robbed the teenage boy of his masculinity by treating him as a female. In this connection, one may compare the ancient view of adultery as theft and the use of the Greek word *gamoklopeein* (literally, "to steal or commit theft against a marriage") in Ps.-Phoc. 3 to mean "commit adultery," alongside the prohibition against "rousing love for another male." Similarly, *Sib. Or.* 5.430 speaks of a future time in which there will be "no marriage-stealing (adulteries, *gamoklopiai*) and unlawful love of boys." As we have seen, Philo's disgust for same-sex intercourse had to do primarily with the passive partner's willingness to discard his masculine nature. Even among some Greco-Roman moralists, condemnation of same-sex intercourse was by no means limited to exploitative forms. Or, perhaps better stated, male-male intercourse was by its very nature exploitative because it made the penetrated partner (willingly or not) play the role of the female.

Moreover, as Wright notes,[111] *Sib. Or.* 2.73 is part of an extract (2.56-

---

111. Wright, "Homosexuals or Prostitutes?" 136-38.

148) from *The Sentences of Pseudo-Phocylides* "replete with Levitical associations" which had been transferred here by a Christian editor sometime after 150 C.E.[112] *Sibylline Oracle* 2.73 is actually absent from the text of Pseudo-Phocylides and was likely added to the extract by the (Christian) editor. Its addition was probably influenced both by line 3 of Pseudo-Phocylides (immediately preceding the block of material incorporated into the Sibyllines), a general prohibition of "male Cypris" ("Cypris" is a name for Aphrodite, "love"), and by the general prohibitions in Leviticus. Both sources of influence indicate that the editor was not restricting the meaning of *arsenokoitein* only to exploitative forms of homosexual practice.

(2) In the second-century *Acts of John*, "John" pronounces a "double measure" of eschatological judgment for the rich and adds: "So also the poisoner, sorcerer, robber, swindler, and *arsenokoitēs*, the thief and all of this band . . . " (36).

(3) Similarly, Theophilus of Antioch (a second-century Christian) in his *To Autolychus* twice uses the term in vice lists (1.2, 14). In the first instance it appears sixth (after adultery, *porneia*, thief, plunderer, defrauder/robber, and before savagery, abusive behavior, wrath, jealousy, etc.). In the second instance it occurs third (after adultery and *porneia* and before greed and idolatry). The issues here, and the conclusion that should be drawn, are the same as for *Sib. Or.* 2.73.

(4) Hippolytus uses the term in his description of the "Naasene" Gnostic myth (*Haer.* 5.26.22-23). In the myth, the evil "Naas (a Greek transliteration of the Hebrew word for serpent) approached Eve and after deceiving her committed adultery with her, which is contrary to the law; and he also approached Adam and possessed him like a boy (an allusion to pederasty), which is also itself contrary to the law. From that time on, adultery and *arsenokoitia* have come into being." The reference is clearly here to homosexual (not heterosexual) behavior which in antiquity usually (though not always) took the form of pederasty. To

---

112. Alternatively, with John J. Collins, the material in 2.56-148 was written by a non-Christian Jew ("the polemic against homosexuality [v. 73] . . . is also typically Jewish") but inserted into the *Sibylline Oracles* by a Christian sometime between 70 and 150 C.E. (*OTP* 1.330-31).

suggest, as Martin does, that the issue here may be rape and not homosexual penetration is like saying that the only type of adultery being condemned here is adultery involving deception or coercion.

(5) A second- to third-century Christian, Bardesanes, is quoted in Eusebius's *Preparation for the Gospel* (6.10.25) as saying: "From the Euphrates River (eastward) . . . a man who is derided as a murderer or thief will not be the least bit angry; but if he is derided as an *arsenokoitēs,* he will defend himself to the point of murder. [Among the Greeks, wise men who have male lovers are not condemned.]" The line in brackets is omitted in important witnesses and may have been added by Eusebius. In a desperate move Martin dismisses a mid-fourth-century interpretation of the meaning of the word as too late and suggests that *arsenokoitēs* and "[men] who have male lovers" might just be similar (and not exactly equal) concepts. Yet even *if* the line is an interpretation coming one century later, there is no credible reason for dismissing it as an inaccurate interpretation. Moreover, "[men] who have male lovers" is clearly intended as a definition of *arsenokoitēs.*

To these texts treated by Martin one can add others cited by Wright, mostly later, that confirm the general meaning of *arsenokoitēs* as "men who have sexual intercourse with males."

(6) In his *Apology* (ca. 125-45 C.E.), Aristides indicts the gods for committing acts of "mutual slaughter and poisoning/witchcraft and adultery and theft and *arsenokoitias*" (13:7). Probably an allusion is being made to a statement in 9:8-9 that if a human imitated the gods he would become "an adulterer or a man who has intercourse with men" (*androbatēn,* lit., "a man-coverer").[113] Chapter 9 narrates the sexual escapades of Zeus who had sex with many women (human and divine) and carried off the handsome shepherd boy Ganymede to be his

---

113. Boswell tries to avoid the obvious connection with homosexual intercourse by asserting that in context Aristides is referring to criminal violations of the laws of nations. "In no city within the Roman Empire in the second century were there laws in effect against homosexual relations per se" (*Homosexuality,* 350). Cf. Nissinen: "Homoerotic relationships between free men. . . were not generally accepted and may have been even prohibited by law" (alluding to *Lex Scantinia* and Valerius Maximus; *Homoeroticism,* 70).

"beloved";[114] hence the two charges of adultery and *arsenokoitias*.[115]

(7) The abstract noun *arsenokoitia* is grouped together with *porneia* (sexual immorality, fornication, prostitution, incest) and *moicheia* (adultery) in Origen, Theodoret of Cyrrhus (ca. 450), a homily dubiously ascribed to Cyril of Alexandria (where *malakia* also appears), Nilus of Ancyra (ca. 410; where *aselgeia*, "licentiousness," also appears), and the *Sacra Parallela* attributed to John of Damascus (where *arsenokoitia* is linked explicitly to Lev 20:13). This grouping of *arsenokoitia*,

---

114. The word "catamite" (a boy kept by a pederast) is derived from the Latin name for Ganymede (*Catamitus*).

115. Mention of the allusion to Zeus and Ganymede is made by William L. Petersen, "On the Study of 'Homosexuality' in Patristic Sources," *Studia Patristica 20* (ed. E. A. Livingstone; Leuven: Peeters, 1989), 284. Petersen also notes with regard to the Hippolytus reference cited above that some 65 lines later (5.26.35) Naas is identified with the eagle (Zeus) that carried off Ganymede, and Adam is identified with Ganymede. The two references lead Petersen to debunk two translations of *arsenokoitai*, "active male prostitutes" (Boswell) and "homosexuals." Petersen is correct in arguing that neither Zeus nor Ganymede were homosexuals in the sense of being exclusively oriented toward members of the same sex, although both engaged in homosexual acts. He eschews even the translation "pederasty," "for connotations of 'pederasty' today are completely at odds with the ritual courting of a youth by an older man, and the youth's eventual surrender and/or abduction by the man. . . . During certain periods in Greek society, this public ritual was sanctioned by all concerned" (pp. 284-85). I do not understand Petersen's point with regard to pederasty. He seems to be saying that "pederasty" is a bad translation because "pederasty" has negative connotations in our society but had a positive valence in antiquity. Yet the usage of the term *arsenokoitai* in these two texts and in Paul is clearly negative, as are Philo's references to pederasty (to say nothing of locating the meaning of a "C.E." term in a "B.C.E." context). Petersen goes on to say:

Perhaps implicit in the word is the idea of *all* male-male sexual acts, but that is *not* self-evident from the context. Indeed, the . . . context . . . would seem to argue against such a conclusion. . . . I am *not* suggesting that early Christianity tolerated or approved of same-sex sexual acts. On the contrary, I think it is clear from the *intensification* of Old Testament ethics . . . , the stress on chastity and virginity, and the pervasive aversion to all sex, even within marriage, that early Christians continued the Levitical prohibition against "men lying with men." But it does *not* follow from this general observation, that *this* particular word, [*arsenokoitai*], must necessarily reference *all* male-male sexual acts. . . . Rejecting the translation 'homosexuals' does not mean that the Christian tradition viewed same-sex sexual acts positively, for it did not. . . .

Paul and Patristic writers were oblivious to [the crucial distinction between act and orientation]. For them, the external act was all that mattered. (pp. 285, 287; his emphases)

Petersen has trapped himself in a logical fallacy. He correctly observes that the

porneia, and *moicheia* parallels the grouping of *porneia, moicheia,* and *paidophthoria* (corruption of boys) in *Barn.* 19:4; *Did.* 2:2; Clement of Alexandria, Origen, and *The Apostolic Constitutions.*[116]

(8) In his *Demonstration of the Gospel* Eusebius (d. ca. 340) at one point states: "Moses issued commands to adulterers and to the unbridled (*akolastois*) not to commit adultery, nor (*mēde*) to *arsenokoitein,* nor to pursue pleasures contrary to nature. . . , but I do not want my disciples to even look at a woman with unbridled desire" (1.6.67). Although Boswell has argued otherwise,[117] *arsenokoitein* is probably a reference to the prohibitions in Leviticus against homosexual conduct.[118] Shortly before in the same work, Eusebius lists the following

---

act of same-sex intercourse, not the exclusive or inclusive predisposition of the participants, "was all that mattered." Yet he incorrectly deduces that the meaning of *arsenokoitai* should be restricted to older men who court male youth in accordance with established conventions. If the act of male-male intercourse was all that mattered, what difference does it make if the participants are old or young, in love or paying clients, aroused only by members of the same sex or by members of both sexes, in accord with societal conventions or not? The focus of the term *arsenokoitai* on homosexual acts rather than orientation only makes the term more inclusive, not less so, because it renders all reasons for entering into homosexual intercourse irrelevant to the condemnation of the act itself.

116. Wright, "Homosexuals or Prostitutes," 135. See Origen, *Comm. Matt.* 14:10; idem, *Fr. 1 Cor.* 27; idem, *Fr. Exod.*, on Exod 12:15; Theodoret, *Hist. eccl.* 4:22.9; (Pseudo-) Cyril of Alexandria, *Homil. Div.* 14; Nilus, *Ep.* 2.282; *Sacra Parall.* 2.11; Clement of Alexandria, *Paed.* 2.10.89; *Ap. Const.* 7.2.10.

117. Boswell argues that the text distinguishes between the *arsenokoitai* and those who "pursue pleasures contrary to nature"; but cf. the following statement from *The Apostolic Constitutions* (fourth century): "the sin of Sodom is contrary to nature (*para physin*), as is also that with brute beasts, but adultery and fornication are contrary to law (*paranomon*)." Boswell goes on to argue: "There can indeed be no question of homosexuality here, since the sentence immediately following makes it obvious that the . . . discussion concerns the proper attitude of Christian men toward *women*" (*Homosexuality*, 351). The last argument makes little sense. Boswell implies that "pleasures contrary to nature" refers to homosexual intercourse. But, given that assumption, how can the following sentence regarding immoral heterosexual intercourse preclude a homosexual connotation to *arsenokoitein?* Eusebius probably had in mind: Moses commanded not to commit adultery, nor to have homosexual intercourse, nor to pursue *any other* pleasures contrary to nature" [lesbianism and/or bestiality?], . . . but I do not want my disciples to even look at a woman with unbridled desire [to say nothing of looking at a man with unbridled desire]." Cf. Wright, "Homosexuals or Prostitutes," 134.

118. Later in the same work, Eusebius speaks of Moses' ban on "sexual intercourse both of women with women and of men with men" (4.10.6).

commands: "do not murder, do not commit adultery, do not steal, do not swear falsely, that males not be mad for males (*ouk arrenas arresin epimainesthai*) . . . " (1.6.33). A parallel appears in his *Preparation for the Gospel* (1.4.6): "nor that males be mad for males and permit pleasures contrary to nature."

(9) In a collection of homilies attributed probably falsely to Macarius of Egypt (ca. 425) the men of Sodom are charged with "wanting to commit *arrenokoitia*" with the angelic visitors (*Homo. Spir. 50* 4.354; *Serm.* 64 49.5.6).

(10) The translations of *arsenokoitai* in the early translations of Scripture confirm a general reference to "men who have sex with males": in Latin, *masculorum concubitores* ("men lying together with males"); in Syriac, "those who lie with men"; and in Coptic, "lying with males."[119]

---

119. Three late occurrences can be mentioned.

(11) In a sixth-century-C.E. work by the Egyptian astrologer Rhetorius, *arsenokoitas* twice appears among a list of vices inculcated by Aphrodite in those born during the constellations of Aries (*Cat. Cod. Astrol. Graec.* 8.4.82, p. 196). For a translation, cf. Malick, "1 Corinthians 6:9," 483 n. 18.

(12) The *Anthologia Graeca* (a collection of epigrams) records an inscription at Thessalonica honoring Basil I of Macedon (a ninth-century Byzantine emperor), addressed to the city of Thessalonica and commemorating Basil's defeat of the Arabs: "You do not tremble at a barbarian, not at males (who are) men who lie with males (*arrenas arrenokoitas*; epigram 9.686). Boswell contends that *arrenas* (acc. case) must be the direct object of *arrenokoitas*; otherwise *arrenas* would be "purely pleonastic—which would be odd in an inscription, where one would ordinarily expect terseness." That being the case, then the *arreno-* prefix of *arrenokoitas* must serve as the subject (male prostitutes who bed others, both male and female) rather than as the object (those [men] who lie with males; *Homosexuality*, 344 n. 22). However, the former meaning makes little sense in the context: why should the Thessalonians tremble at "active male prostitutes"? It is more likely that homosexual assault would be the cause of fear. Moreover, *arrenokoitas* is a noun, not a verb. If "males" were the object of *arrenokoitas*, one would expect an objective genitive (*arrenōn*), not an accusative.

(13) The only truly problematic text is one from a comparatively late date, between the ninth and tenth century C.E., in a work falsely attributed to John the Faster, Patriarch of Constantinople (582-95), entitled *Penitential*: "Likewise one must inquire about *arsenokoitia*, of which there are three varieties. For it is one thing to get it from someone, which is the least serious; another to do it to someone else, which is more serious than having it done to you; another to do it to someone and have it done to you, which is more serious than either of the other two. . . . One must inquire into which of these (practices) the penitent has fallen, and how often, and for how long, and if it happened before marriage or after, if

Given the attested occurrences, Martin's unwillingness to admit that *arsenokoitēs* is limited to homosexual behavior is surprising. That it is so limited is confirmed by its morphology. The suffix on the second element of the compound noun (*-koitēs*) indicates that "bedders of, the ones taking to bed or lying with" is masculine. The first element of the compound (*arsen-*, "male[s]") is the object, not the subject, since "in all, it seems, of the comparable compounds [of *-koitēs*] the first element in fact specifies the object of the 'sleeping' or its scene or sphere."[120] Martin makes much of the point that it is ridiculous to define the meaning of a word by "its (assumed) etymology" rather than

---

before the age of thirty or after. . . . One must also ask about the . . . sin of incest. . . . One type is committed with two sisters. . . . Some even do it with their own mothers, and others with foster sisters or goddaughters. In fact, many men commit the sin of *arsenokoitia* even/also/and (*kai*) with their wives" (*to mentoi tēs arsenokoitias mysos polloi kai meta tōn gunaikōn autōn ektelousin*; translation in Boswell, *Homosexuality*, 364; cf. Hoheisel, "Homosexualität," 340). Boswell and Hoheisel understand *arsenokoitia* here as anal intercourse. That interpretation also poses problems for Boswell's interpretation of *arsenokoitēs* as an "active male prostitute" who has sex with men or women. Boswell explains the discrepancy by saying that the word *arsenokoitai* "became confused and lost its original significance, so that by the sixth century it was used to designate activities as different as child molesting and anal intercourse between husband and wife" (p. 353; as regards a sixth-century date, note that Boswell incorrectly attributes the "Penitentials" to John the Faster). Is it not just as plausible that an original meaning of "a man who lies with a male" had become confused by the ninth or tenth centuries, extrapolating a defining feature of homosexual sex, anal intercourse, and applying the term to men who engage in anal sex, whether with men or women? Another possibility is that *arsenokoitia* here still means "(men) lying with males." The context indicates that incest is at issue. The author may be saying that some men have sex both with their wives and men who are kin of their wives. In a slightly different vein, Wright understands the text to say: "'Incredibly enough, some men even go as far as having incestuous intercourse with their own mothers. . . . Indeed, (would you believe it that) many men even engage in homosexual activity in the company of their own wives' i.e. three to a bed, or while the wives likewise indulge each other homosexually?" ("Homosexuals or Prostitutes?" 140).

120. Ibid., 130. Particularly in view of the actual usage discussed above, I do not understand Nissinen's claim that of the two alternatives, taking the male affix of *arsenokoitēs* as the object of the sexual intercourse or as the subject, "neither is thoroughly documented" (*Homoeroticism*, 116). He argues that "Not everyone who has used the term . . . [has] necessarily taken into consideration the Septuagint or the etymology of the word in general" (ibid.). Even if this were true of other authors (and the evidence adduced above does not lend support for such an assumption), it certainly is not likely to have been true of Paul who made use

by actual usage.[121] While in general this is good advice, it is misleading with regard to this particular word (and, in any case, the actual usage brings us to the same verdict about the word's meaning). "Men who take males to bed" can hardly be understood to refer to exploitative *hetero*sexual intercourse.[122]

Less obvious on the surface is the problem with Scroggs's proposal that *arsenokoitēs* refers to "the active partner who keeps the *malakos* as a 'mistress' or who hires him on occasion to satisfy his sexual desires." Some of the occurrences of the *arsenokoit-* word group cited in the texts above have to do either with prostitution or rape but other occurrences cannot be so limited. The pairing of *malakoi* and *arsenokoitai* suggests that the *malakoi* would be among the consensual male partners of the *arsenokoitai*, though the pairing certainly does not preclude other, less effeminate partners than transvestites and transsexuals with homosexual proclivities.

Nissinen speaks for many (including Scroggs and Martin) when he argues otherwise; namely, that the term *arsenokoitēs* cannot be applied to all forms of same-sex intercourse.

The modern concept of "homosexuality" should by no means be read into Paul's text, nor can we assume that Paul's words in 1 Corinthians 6:9 "condemn all homosexual relations" in all times and places and ways . . .

---

of the Septuagint and shows contacts with the Levitical Holiness Code in his discussion of same-sex intercourse in Rom 1:24-27. Nissinen also admits that "the law" in 1 Tim 1:8-11 refers to OT law (p. 114), which strengthens the link between *arsenokoitēs* and the Levitical prohibitions.

121. Martin, "*Arsenokoitês* and *Malakos*," 119.

122. Martin's contention that "the *scripture* for the church is traditionally the text, not a historically reconstructed authorial intention" makes no sense to me (ibid., 136 n. 38). To the extent that authorial meaning is recoverable, it must be recovered. Otherwise, one might as well forget about exegeting the meaning of a text. A curious problem for Martin is that in his "Heterosexism and the Interpretation of Romans 1:18-32," written just a year earlier, he took the opposite approach. There he contends that because Paul thought both that homosexuality could exist only concurrently with idolatry and that homosexuality was merely an excess of heterosexual desire Paul's words could be discounted. Isn't this an appeal to authorial meaning, however misguided? Even in his article "*Arsenokoitês* and *Malakos*," Martin is not aiming at a flat, timeless reading of scripture but seeking an "historically reconstructed" meaning.

Regardless of the kind of sexuality meant in 1 Corinthians 6:9 and 1 Timothy 1:10, in their current contexts they are examples of the exploitation of persons. . . . What Paul primarily opposes is the wrong that people do to others.[123]

Is it really true that Paul's paramount concern was with the exploitation of others brought about by only some forms of homosexual behavior? Let us take a couple of parallel examples.

When Paul opposed incest in 1 Corinthians 5, based on the Levitical and Deuteronomic law codes, was he only opposed to exploitative forms of incest? Very little in 1 Corinthians 5 suggests concern for exploitation of another, except perhaps insofar as he might classify incest as inherently exploitative. This was a case of gross sexual immorality (*porneia*), pure and simple.

Did Paul only oppose exploitative instances of adultery, fornication, and sex with prostitutes or did he oppose every instance? In 1 Cor 6:12-20, immediately following the vice list where *malakoi* and *arsenokoitai* appear, Paul gives no indication that sex with a prostitute might be acceptable under certain non-exploitative circumstances. Instead, for Paul the whole phenomenon of prostitution, like the whole phenomenon of incest, was *porneia* and as *porneia* it had to be completely shunned in every and any circumstance. And yet Nissinen, Scroggs, Martin, and others would have us believe that it is an open question whether *arsenokoitai* in Paul's mind would have applied to all forms of same-sex intercourse, including the kinds of non-exploitative forms allegedly manifested in our contemporary context. This dubious hope has to be maintained in the face of many additional obstacles.

First, the term *arsenokoitēs* itself indicates an inclusive sense: all men who play the active role in homosexual intercourse. Had Paul intended to single out pederasts he could have used the technical term *paiderastēs*.

---

123. *Homoeroticism*, 118. The argument may have a slightly disingenuous quality. Are Nissinen, Scroggs, and others, who at least acknowledge that the *arsenokoitai* are probably people who have intercourse with the *malakoi*, inferring that they would accept a strong stance on the part of our contemporary religious denominations against sex between men and adult male transvestites/transsexuals? Both transvestites and transsexuals come under the protective umbrella of gay-rights organizations.

Second, the likely derivation of the word from the Levitical prohibitions (LXX) strengthens the case for an inclusive meaning. What kind of same-sex intercourse would have hurdled the obstacle of Lev 18:22 and 20:13 in Paul's mind? Surely none since these prohibitions speak generically of all men who have sexual intercourse with any and every kind of male.

Third, to adopt the position of Nissinen and others, we would have to ignore the viewpoints on same-sex intercourse of two prominent first-century Jews, Josephus and Philo, undoubtedly representative of first-century Jews generally. As we have seen, both reject homosexual intercourse on the grounds that it is not intercourse between a man and a woman. Josephus clearly adopted the most inclusive understanding of the prohibitions in Lev 18:22 and 20:13: "The law recognizes only sexual intercourse that is according to nature, that which is with a woman, and that only for procreation of children. But it abhors the intercourse of males with males" (*Ag. Ap.* 2.199). As noted in our discussion of Philo's perspective on the *malakoi*, what Philo abhorred more than anything else about homosexual intercourse was not its procreative incapacity but rather its inherent distortion of male sexuality; namely, a man substituting a male for a female in sexual intercourse. Clearly, for both Philo and Josephus, the only acceptable, complementary partner for sexual intercourse was someone of the opposite sex. If all the forms of homosexual intercourse known to the human species could have been paraded before Josephus and Philo, surely none would have met with their approval.

Fourth, the meaning which Paul gave to *arsenokoitai* ultimately has to be unpacked in light of Rom 1:24-27. Scholars who want to adopt a very restricted meaning for *arsenokoitai* usually treat 1 Cor 6:9 in isolation from Rom 1:24-27. Is it not logical to assume that what Paul says in Rom 1:24-27 tells us precisely what it is about the *malakoi* and *arsenokoitai* that Paul rejects? When Paul speaks of the sexual intercourse of "males with males" (*arsenes en arsesin*) in Rom 1:27, he obviously has in mind *arsenokoitai*. In Paul's view, the "dishonoring of their bodies" mentioned in 1:24 occurred *whenever* a woman had sexual intercourse with a female instead of a male, and *whenever* a man had sexual intercourse with another male instead of a female. Men and women exchanged the "natural use" of the opposite sex as the appropriate complementary partners in sexual intercourse for an "unnatural use" of the same sex as sexual partners. There were no exceptions for Paul. Genesis 1–2 provided only one acceptable model. Paul, like all other first-century Jews, opposed same-sex intercourse between men because he believed that woman was created by God to be man's one and only sexual partner. And he believed that the anatomical and pro-creative complementarity of male and female visible in nature sup-ported this conclusion. What was wrong, first and foremost, for Paul in the case of same-sex intercourse was the fact that the participants were members of the same sex rather than the opposite sex. It was not a question of whether the sexual relationship was characterized by mutual affirmation or exploitation, parity in age or age disparity, pro-creative capacity or procreative incapacity, innate sexual urges or con-trived sexual urges, or any other extrinsic set of antinomies. In order to determine the semantic spread of the term *arsenokoitai*, it is a mistake to focus exclusively on the one or two most common forms of same-sex intercourse in Paul's day at the expense of ignoring Paul's reason for opposing same-sex intercourse, which had little or nothing to do with factors that could distinguish unacceptable forms of same-sex inter-course from acceptable forms.

Fifth, the context of the passage in 1 Corinthians makes clear why the *malakoi* and *arsenokoitai* belong with other forms of sexual immorality (*pornoi* [those who fornicate, commit incest, or have sex with prostitutes] and adulterers): they participate in a form of sexual behavior other than that sanctioned in the context of a monogamous, lifelong, non-incestuous, opposite-sex marriage bond. In 1 Corinthians 5 Paul draws on the Levitical proscription of incestuous behavior (*porneia*) in Leviticus 18 and 20, which reinforces our supposition that Paul had in mind the proscriptions against male same-sex intercourse in Lev 18:22 and 20:13 when he referred to *arsenokoitai* in 6:9. The overlap of the vice lists in 1 Cor 5:10-11 and 6:9-10 indicates that all unrepentant participants in *porneia*, be it incest, fornication, adultery, or same-sex intercourse, are to be expelled from the community of believers in a final, desperate bid to keep them from being excluded from God's coming kingdom. 1 Cor 6:12-20 forbids all *porneia*, here sex with a prostitute, on the grounds that it joins in a "one-flesh" union two people other than a husband and a wife in holy matrimony. This reinforces our supposition that a responsible hermeneutic today should understand the combination of *malakoi* and *arsenokoitai* in the broadest possible sense, as violaters of the model of marriage put forward in Genesis 1–2, specifically, a union between a man and a woman. In 1 Corinthians 7 Paul takes up the subject of marriage. There he once more expresses concern that there be no *porneia*. It is because of such a concern that he modifies his wish that all Christians be unmarried like himself and advises married couples against abstaining from sex for any lengthy period of time (7:1-9, 36). Picking up Jesus' own command, he forbids remarriage of divorced women, apparently on the grounds that remarriage while one's first spouse is still alive constitutes adultery (7:10-11). At the end of the chapter he again affirms that "a wife is bound to her husband as long as he lives" (7:39). Given this exclusive attention to heterosexual unions, is it reasonable to conclude that Paul had only some forms of same-sex intercourse in view in 6:9?[124]

As if this were not enough, we can add one more element from 1 Corinthians. There is no chance that the very same Paul who was concerned about blurring the distinctions between the sexes even over such relatively minor matters as hair coverings in 1 Cor 11:2-16 could have limited the meaning of *arsenokoitai* in the same letter to only specific types of same-sex intercourse. If in Paul's view inappropriate hairstyles and head coverings were a source of shame because they compromised the sexual differences of men and women, how much more would a man taking another male to bed be a shameful act (Rom 1:27), lying with another male "as though lying with a woman"? Paul did not make head coverings an issue vital for inclusion in God's kingdom, but he did put same-sex intercourse on that level. Suppose the Corinthians had written back:

> Paul, we have a brother in our church who is having sex with another man. But that other man does not put on makeup or heavy perfume, wear women's clothing, braid his hair, or otherwise try to look like a woman. And the other male is an adult. The two men really do love each other and are committed to spend-

---

124. Cf. Coleman, *Gay Christians: A Moral Dilemma* (London: SCM Press; Philadelphia: TPI, 1989), 84-85.

ing the rest of their lives together. Neither are involved in idolatrous cults or prostitution. When you mentioned that *arsenokoitai*
would be excluded from the coming kingdom of God, you were
not including somebody like this man, were you?

Given the context of 1 Cor 5–6 and 11, can anyone seriously propose
that Paul would have said, "That's right, such a man would not be an
arsenokoitēs"?

Sixth, if Paul (like Philo and Josephus) condemned both active and
passive partners, how does exploitation factor in the equation? A condemnation of both partners indicates that the relationship is consensual. Paul is certainly not condemning any passive partners who might be
raped. Granted, even consensual relationships can have an exploitative
dimension. However, if exploitation were Paul's principal concern,
surely he would not have pronounced the same sentence on exploited
passive partners. Nissinen and others who believe only exploitative
forms of same-sex intercourse are condemned have the logic of Paul's
thinking backwards. It is precisely those who *willingly* engage in same-
sex intercourse, who follow their sinful innate impulses for forbidden
sex, who enjoy it, who show no remorse for their conduct and are
under no coercion from others, that Paul and Philo reserve their greatest scorn for. Not the exploitative forms of same-sex intercourse but
the non-exploitative and fully consensual forms are the most heinous
because then the participants are entirely without excuse.[125]

Seventh, the list of vices 1 Cor 6:9-10 contain intertextual echoes to
Deuteronomic law that indicate a contrast between same-sex intercourse in all its forms and heterosexual marriage. Brian Rosner has
shown that the vice list in 1 Cor 5:11 has been constructed largely on

---

125. It is strange that Nissinen, who vigorously argues that biblical writers rejected
same-sex intercourse because it upset conventional male-female hierarchical patterns, should here in 1 Cor 6:9 make exploitation the issue for Paul (by "exploitation" here he means something other than hierarchical roles per se, which Paul
did not regard as inherently exploitative). What do those two concerns have in
common? As for Nissinen's contention that "The modern concept of 'homosexuality' should by no means be read into Paul's text," the "modern concept"—
Nissinen talks as if there is some sort of uniform view—is entirely irrelevant to the
basis for the condemnation. See ch. 5.IV.

the basis of the contexts in which the refrain "Drive out the wicked person from among yourselves" (quoted in 1 Cor 5:13) occurs in Deuteronomy: 17:7 (idolatry); 19:19 (malicious false testimony); 21:21 (the rebellious son who is also a drunkard); 22:21 (sexual promiscuity, here specifically adultery); and 24:7 (theft).[126] What is true of 5:11 is also true of 6:9-10 since 6:9-11 contains all six vices of 5:11, merely adding three additional sexual vices (adulterers, *malakoi*, *arsenokoitai*) to the one already mentioned (*pornoi*) and one additional economic vice (thieves) to the two already mentioned (the greedy and swindlers). What that indicates is that for Paul the four sexual vices in 6:9 are there because they all constitute forms of sexual intercourse which occur outside of the context of marriage between a man and a woman. In that case, the terms *malakoi* and *arsenokoitai* are meant to signify, at least as representative types, all who participate in same-sex intercourse. As we shall see, the appearance of *arsenokoitai* in 1 Tim 1:10 makes a similar point, since there it comes under the rubric of the decalogue commandment against adultery.

It is self-evident, then, that the combination of terms, *malakoi* and *arsenokoitai*, are correctly understood in our contemporary context when they are applied to every conceivable type of same-sex intercourse. A first-century Jew or Christian would regard the prohibitions in Lev 18:22 and 20:13 as absolute and affecting any male-to-male sexual intercourse, even if the primary examples of his/her culture were confined to pederastic models.[127]

First Corinthians 6:9 confirms that Paul's rejection of homosexual conduct is just as applicable for believers as for unbelievers. Paul's

---

126. Brian S. Rosner, *Paul, Scripture, and Ethics: A Study of 1 Corinthians 5–7* (AGJU 22; Leiden: Brill, 1994), 69-70.

127. Both Schrage (p. 432) and Fee (p. 244) understand the word to refer to men who engage in sex with other males, at least in the active role. They do not limit the word to the procuring of boy prostitutes or even to pederastic relationships. Similarly, Schoedel, "Same-Sex Eros," 63-64 (adding that the distinction between *malakoi* as passive homosexual partners and *arsenokoitai* as active homosexual partners "even if intended, may not have meant all that much to Paul"); Greenberg, *Construction*, 213-14; Schmidt, *Straight and Narrow?*, 95-96; Wold, *Out of Order*, 193-95; Grenz, *Welcoming But Not Affirming*, 57-58; Malick, "1 Cor 6:9," 483-87, 490; P. Michael Ukleja, "The Bible and Homosexuality, Part 2: Homosexuality in the New Testament," *BSac* 140 (1983): 351.

warning in 1 Cor 6:9-11 is to the believers at Corinth to remember that those who live their lives under the control of sin will not inherit the kingdom of God. The Corinthians used to live in sin, but now they have been transformed in Christ to lead righteous lives. Unfortunately, they are acting in a manner inconsistent with that transformation. In response, Paul underscores that Christians who decide to plunge back into a life of sin face the same consequences as unbelievers; hence, the injunction to "stop being led astray" or "stop deceiving yourselves" (*mē planasthe*).[128] The fact that vice lists are often traditional and conventional does not diminish the seriousness of the offense of homosexual conduct for Paul (especially in light of Rom 1:26-27). The cleansing, sanctifying, and justifying action of Christ through the Holy Spirit calls people away from homosexual behavior (and all other past sinful behaviors) and into a lifestyle of holiness.

Nissinen contends that to use 1 Cor 6:9-10 and 1 Tim 1:10 "as a basis for threatening people with eternal damnation leads to a kind of scriptural positivism, which may turn out to be a matter of the cruel abuse of religious power."[129] Would Nissinen make the same claim against those who quote Scripture to condemn the oppression of the poor? I suppose the question of whether a "cruel abuse of religious power" occurs when one cites such texts depends on two factors: (1) whether the one citing the texts has a loving or hateful affect; and (2) whether people who engage in same-sex intercourse, persistently and without repentance, do in fact run the risk of being excluded from God's eternal presence. If the eternal destiny of unrepentant, practicing homosexuals is at stake, or even a full relationship with God in the present life, then it would be a "cruel abuse of religious power" to give false assurance that these texts do not condemn homosexual behavior. It can be as much a cruel abuse of religious power not to say what Scripture says, however unpleasant it is to hear, as to say what it says in a cold and callous manner. To think otherwise is to indict Jesus himself, who was

---

128. The same phrase appears in 1 Cor 15:33; Gal 6:7; and Jas 1:16. Coleman notes that the verb here shares the same stem with the noun *planē* ("straying, error") in Rom 1:27 (*Gay Christians*, 82-83). A similar warning to the Corinthians against thinking that they are immune from falling from the faith appears in 1 Cor 10:5-10, 22 with regard to eating idol meat in an idol's temple.

129. *Homoeroticism*, 125.

not shy about using Scripture to warn people of impending judgment. Similarly, within the story line of Genesis 2–3, should we say that the serpent, upon reassuring Eve that she would not die if she ate from the tree forbidden by God, was adopting a more loving and inclusive stance than God?

The Meaning of Arsenokoitais in 1 Timothy 1:10

1 Tim 1:10 reinforces rather than provides an additional or alternative understanding to 1 Cor 6:9. It is, however significant because *if* the Pastorals were not written by Paul (as most scholars think), it confirms that Paul's opposition to homosexual behavior continued on in the early post-Pauline churches.[130] Scroggs attempts to blunt the impact of the text by arguing that *pornois, arsenokoitais*, and *andrapodistais* are to be taken as a topical unit. He gives *pornoi* its more restrictive sense of "male prostitutes" (normal Greek usage) rather than "sexually immoral persons" (the broader sense it usually takes in the New Testament), then construes *arsenokoitai* in the limited sense as men who lie with the aforementioned male prostitutes. The word *andrapodistēs* means "slave dealer, kidnapper" (LSJ, BAGD) but Scroggs thinks that the preceding context of sexual terms implies that *andrapodistai* has a particular type of slave dealer in mind: people who sell boys or girls to be "slaves for brothel houses."[131]

---

130. To be sure, the author of 1 Timothy gives only qualified approval to the law in a context where some "desiring to be teachers of the law" (1:7) are promoting Jewish myths, genealogies, and commandments. For the author, in distinction to the opponents, the function of the law is largely negative: it pronounces judgment on those who act in a manner "contrary to the sound teaching that conforms to the glorious gospel of the blessed God" (1:10-11). Yet it is not to be equated with "the glorious gospel" since the law has no power to save and transform sinners by grace (1:12-17). This does not mean that the author regarded the vice list in 1:9-10 as irrelevant for believers, as if believers could now engage freely in murder, sexual immorality (including same-sex intercourse), stealing, and lying without fear of apocalyptic repercussions (cf. the reference to the "shipwreck" of Hymenaeus and Alexander in 1:19-20). "Godliness is valuable . . . for both the present life and the life to come. . . . For to this end we toil and struggle" (4:8-10; for warnings to believers as regards conduct, cf. 2:15; 4:1; 5:8, 15, 20; 6:9-10, 14, 19, 21).

131. Scroggs, *The New Testament and Homosexuality*, 119-20; followed by Smith, "The New Testament and Homosexuality," 29.

Scroggs's interpretation of *andrapodistai* has recently received support from an article by J. Albert Harrill.[132] Harrill shows that *andrapodistai* (literally, "men-stealers") was a derogatory term applied to slave dealers who were notorious for procuring slaves through illegal means and for sordid gain. Rather than restrict the slave trade to foreigners or war captives, many slave traders illegally abducted free citizens, or the slaves of such, from their own country.[133] They had a reputation for covering up the defects of slaves in order to sell slaves at higher prices (much like used-car salespersons today who conceal defects in automobiles). Slave dealers were also known for practicing pseudomedicine and pseudopharmacology to retard puberty in male slaves and thereby enhance "softness." Such techniques included using red-hot nutshells to soften leg hairs, flour to whiten the skin, barley-gruel to cover up defects in complexion, and certain plant extracts to slow the onset of puberty. They also removed facial and armpit hair. When these methods no longer did the trick, some slave traders were not averse to castrating slaves. In perpetrating such acts, slave dealers obviously hoped to appeal to the homoerotic interests of some of their cliental. Not surprisingly, they acquired for their efforts the label of "pimp." Sometimes they sold effeminate slaves to houses of prostitution.[134]

Given the association between the practices of some slave traders and the homosexual desires of some buyers, the close proximity of the two terms is not surprising. The mention of *arsenokoitai* may well have called to mind the *andrapodistai*. However, there is a difference between recognizing some overlap in the semantic fields of the two terms on the one hand and restricting the semantic fields of each term only to such an overlap on the other hand. The criminal conduct of *andrapodistai* was hardly confined to feminizing male slaves for masters with same-sex erotic designs. More central still to the derogatory epithet of *andrapodistēs* was the illegal kidnapping of freeborn citizens,

---

132. "The Vice of Slave Dealers in Greco-Roman Society: The Use of a Topos in 1 Timothy 1:10," *JBL* 118 (1999): 97-122.
133. Pollux, a second-century C.E. rhetorician, defined an *andrapodistēs* as "one who reduces a freeborn person to slavery or who kidnaps someone else's slave" (*Onom.* 3.78).
134. Ibid., 108-12.

with or without an accompanying feminization for homoerotic clients. In this connection, Philo treats the sins of *andrapodistai* in *Spec. Laws* 4.13-19 without once mentioning homosexual prostitution.[135]

Once again, the derivation of *arsenokoitai* from Lev 18:22; 20:13 (a formulation that is not limited to prostitution), its actual usage in Judeo-Christian literature, and the unqualified Judeo-Christian rejection of all forms of homosexuality make an overly narrow interpretation of the word implausible. In fact, that *arsenokoitai* has in mind the broad prohibitions in Leviticus against all forms of male-to-male intercourse is even clearer in 1 Tim 1:10 than in 1 Cor 6:9 since the vice list is described as coming from "the law" in 1:8-9.

According to Scroggs, whether "the law" refers to the Mosaic law or to civil law cannot "be finally answered."[136] Yet four considerations settle the case decisively in favor of the Mosaic law. First, in 1:7, the author refers to Christians "desiring to be teachers of the law." Promotion of civil law in a religious context makes little sense. In addition, these teachers are people who "occupy themselves with myths and endless genealogies that promote speculations" (1:4).[137] Second, the phrase "now we know that the law is good" (1:8) is likely to be an allusion to Paul's description of the Mosaic law as "good" in Rom 7:12, 16 (*kalos* in both cases). Third, this law legislates not merely against social disorder but against whatever is opposed to "the sound [religious] teaching that conforms to the glorious gospel" (1:10-11). Finally, the order of the last half of the list of vices corresponds to the order of the Decalogue. "Killers of fathers and killers of mothers" corresponds to the fifth commandment to honor one's parents; "murderers" corresponds to the sixth commandment; "the sexually immoral, males who take other males to bed" corresponds to the seventh commandment against adultery; "kidnappers" corresponds to the eighth command-

---

135. He focuses on the heinous character of stealing the freedom of a human being (far worse than stealing lifeless articles) and doing so for the sake of unjust profit. Especially despicable to him are kidnappers who sell fellow Jews to foreigners.

136. Scroggs, *The New Testament and Homosexuality*, 118, 120.

137. Cf. Tit 1:10, 14: "idle talkers and deceivers, especially *those of the circumcision* . . . teaching for sordid gain. . . . rebuke them sharply . . . not paying attention to *Jewish* myths or to *commandments* of those who reject the truth."

ment against stealing; and "liars" and "perjurers" correspond to the ninth commandment against bearing false witness.[138]

That the vice list in 1 Timothy corresponds to the order of the Decalogue also speaks against too close a connection between "males who take other males to bed" and "kidnappers." The latter would appear to introduce a distinct commandment, the eighth command- ment against stealing, rather than belong with the seventh command- ment against adultery. This is consistent with the rabbinic application of the eighth commandment to kidnapping (Str-B 1:810-13). In addi- tion, the summary of the Decalogue in *Ps.-Phoc.* 3–8 connects homo- sexual behavior with adultery ("Neither commit adultery nor stir up passion for males" [3], as in 1 Cor 6:9) and disconnects the two from the command against stealing.[139] Philo regarded the seventh (LXX: sixth) commandment against adultery as a rubric embracing the "spe- cial laws" not only against adultery but also against incest, intercourse during menstruation, *pederasty*, bestiality, prostitution, and other mat- ters pertaining to sexual intercourse (*Spec. Laws* 3.1-82). The crime of kidnappers/men-stealers (*andrapodistai*) he placed under heading of the eighth commandment against stealing (*Spec. Laws* 4.13-19).

Similarly, the *Didache* (a manual of Christian teaching written in Syria at the end of the first century) depended on the Decalogue for its construction of the second commandment of the "way of life," plac- ing the prohibition of pederasty within the heading of the seventh commandment against adultery:

---

138. There is probably also an allusion to the first three commandments in the first three pairs of vices ("the lawless and disobedient, the godless and sinners, the unholy and profane"; cf. Becker, "Zum Problem der Homosexualität in der Bibel," 54). In any case, there is a general consensus that the reference to "the law" in 1:8 and "law" in 1:9 is to the Old Testament law (*inter alios*, Springett, Nissinen, Stowasser; and, for authors of commentaries on the Pastoral Epistles, Quinn and Wacker, G. W. Knight III, L. T. Johnson, M. Dibelius and H. Conzelmann, G. Fee, P. H. Towner, T. C. Oden, L. Oberlinner, J. N. D. Kelly, D. Guthrie, H. Ridderbos, C. Spicq, A. Schlatter, J. Calvin; also, N. J. McEleney, "The Vice Lists of the Pastoral Epistles," *CBQ* 36 [1974]: 206-7). Jürgen Roloff thinks that a more general reference is meant by "law" than the Torah of Israel alone, though for the author of 1 Timothy the Old Testament law constitutes "a significant special case" (*Der erste Brief an Timotheus* [EKKNT 15; Zürich: Benziger Verlag, 1988], 73).

139. The order of the list in Ps-Phoc. 3–8 does not correspond to the order in the

you shall not murder (6); you shall not commit adultery, *you shall not corrupt boys* (*paidophthorēseis*), you shall not commit *porneia* (7); you shall not steal (8); you shall not use magic, you shall not practice sorcery; you shall not murder a child with an abortion, nor kill what is born [infanticide]; you shall not covet your neighbor's goods (10); you shall not violate an oath, you shall not testify falsely (9). . . .[140]

Placing the prohibition of same-sex intercourse under the rubric of the seventh commandment against adultery points to the fact that early Judaism and Christianity rejected same-sex intercourse because it regarded *any* sexual intercourse outside of marriage, a monogamous union between man and woman, as immoral—not just forms of same-sex intercourse that were particularly exploitative such as sex with "call boys."[141] Finally, that *pornoi* in 1 Tim 1:10 should be assigned the narrow meaning of "male prostitutes" is very doubtful. We have seen that *pornoi* in the vice list of 1 Cor 6:9 refers, minimally, to people who commit incest (cf. *pornos/-oi* in 1 Cor 5:9-11), people who have sex with prostitutes (cf. *porneia* in 1 Cor 6:12-20), and people who engage in pre-marital sex (fornication).

The most that can be said for Scroggs's position is that *arsenokoitai* here *might* have in mind *primarily* the most despicable form of homosexual conduct (viz., homosexual sex with boy prostitutes or one's own feminized male slaves). Even if that concession were appropriate (and I doubt that it is), it would still not exclude a wider reference to all men who sleep with other males. Indeed what should be clear is that the references to same-sex intercourse in 1 Cor 6:9 and 1 Tim 1:10 corroborate our understanding of Christian teaching—that all homosexual intercourse is excluded from faithful Christian living.

Decalogue: adultery, murder, stealing, coveting, bearing false witness, honoring God, honoring parents.

140. *Did.* 2:2-3; cf. the *Barn.* 19:4: "you shall not commit *porneia*, you shall not commit adultery, you shall not corrupt boys."

141. Stowasser, "Homosexualität und Bibel," 521.

III. Conclusion

The Pauline and deutero-Pauline texts that directly address the issue of same-sex intercourse unequivocally reject such behavior for believer and unbeliever alike. With regard to Rom 1:24-27, both idolatry and same-sex intercourse are singled out by Paul as particularly clear and revolting examples of the suppression of the truth about God accessible to pagans in creation and nature. People who engage in homosexual intercourse do so in spite of the self-evident clues implanted in nature by God; specifically, male-female anatomical, physiological, psychological, and procreative complementarity. More crudely put, the parts fit and function appropriately male to female and not female to female or male to male. To be sure, Paul and other Jews derived their own opposition to same-sex intercourse, first and foremost, from the creation stories in Genesis 1–2 and the Levitical prohibitions, both of which have intertextual echoes in Rom 1:18-32. Yet, Paul contended, even gentiles without access to the direct revelation of Scripture have enough evidence in the natural realm to discern God's aversion to homosexual behavior.

Participation in same-sex intercourse is partly its own payback for turning away from the one true God, since Paul regards such behavior as itself unclean, a dishonoring of one's own body, and a self-shaming act of obscene indecency. At the same time, it is evidence of God's future judgment, since the participants have no excuse for not knowing that those who do such things are worthy of death.

Contrary to some views that have been put forward in our own time, Paul did not reject same-sex intercourse primarily because of a divine mandate to procreate. Nor did Paul think that same-sex intercourse was merely "dirty," but not sinful, behavior. Nor did he hold same-sex intercourse to be sinful because he could only conceive of idolaters as practicing such behavior. Nor was he arguing that judging those who commit same-sex intercourse is itself sinful.

The overarching context of the letter to the Romans clarifies the place of homosexual behavior in the Christian life. Paul envisaged same-sex intercourse as merely an extreme and obvious case on the horizontal plane of inter-human relationships of what was true of a much wider sweep of sinful behavior. In Romans 2, Paul drew Jews who condemned gross gentile sinners into the net of indictment. Yet Paul's rhetorical strategy in Romans was not to absolve gentiles of gross sin, or to declare that all sins are equal, or to deny God or God's people the right to take action against gross sin. Rather, Paul's rhetorical aim was to demonstrate that Jew and gentile alike had no option but to believe in Jesus Christ or die, to urge believers to unite in common praise in what God's grace had done in Christ, to exhort believers to a transformed life in things that matter, and to caution against judgment over matters of indifference within the Christian community of faith.

Inclusion in the sphere of Christ's lordship and Spirit, made possible by Christ's atoning death, not only brings about forgiveness from past sin but also mandates transformation away from a past life of moral uncleanness, including the uncleanness of same-sex intercourse. Believers who continue to live as if sin is their master will perish along with unbelievers. Unlike issues of diet and calendar, same-sex intercourse still belongs with a range of immoral actions which, if persisted in, invites God's judgment and the community's discipline rather than a "welcome" which ignores such behavior. However, the good news is that God is on the side of believers in sparing no effort to transform them into the image of Jesus. God both empowers believers by means of the Spirit, and motivates them through God's unprecedented accomplishment of redemption in Christ and the hope of a magnificent salvation yet to be revealed. The God who once manifested wrath against those who turned to idols by handing them over to their shameful passions has now handed them over to the life-giving, transformative power of the Spirit of Christ. The former manner of life bore fruit that would lead to death; the new manner of life bears fruit that leads to eternal life.

The occurrence of *malakoi* and *arsenokoitai* in the vice list in 1 Cor 6:9, and of *arsenokoitai* in the vice list in 1 Tim 1:10, confirm our reading of Rom 1:24-27. In 1 Cor 6:9, the term *malakoi* has most in view males who actively seek to transform their maleness into femaleness in order to make themselves more attractive as receptive or passive sexual partners of men; *arsenokoitai* has most in view men who serve as the active sex partners of the *malakoi*. Neither term can be widened in meaning to include heterosexuals or narrowed in meaning to exclude certain non-exploitative forms of homosexual intercourse. The contexts for 1 Cor 6:9 and 1 Tim 1:10, collectively, indicate that the term *arsenokoitai* has intertextual connections to the Levitical prohibitions of homosexual intercourse and to the exclusive endorsement of monogamous, heterosexual marriage in Genesis 1–2, in the Decalogue prohibition of adultery, and in Deuteronomic expulsion texts. Both vice lists clearly establish that, in the authors' view, believers who do not turn away from participating in homosexual intercourse are among those who will be excluded from God's coming kingdom.

We have already found wanting some arguments that have been employed for discounting or sidetracking the relevance of the biblical data for contemporary church discussions of homosexuality. However, there remains the task of treating more thoroughly major objections that have been raised against contemporary application of the Bible's prohibitions of homosexual conduct. It is to this concern that the next chapter is devoted.

Postscript

To the thirteen occurrences or group of occurrences of the *arsenokoit-* stem in antiquity (pp. 317-23) the following can be added:

(14) In the *Chronographia* of Joannes Malalas (ca. 565 C.E.), *arsenokoitountes* (lying with males) (436.5).

(15) In the *Acta Conciliorum Oecumenicorum* for Chalcedon (451 C.E.), *arsenokoitia* (lying with males) (Actio 11.73.5 [= Tom 2, vol. 1, pt. 3, p. 24]).

(16) In two scholia (marginal comments) on the works of Aristophanes, *arsenokoitai/arrenokoitai* (men who lie with males): (a) on a passage in *Nubes (Clouds)* 1080-1104; and (b) on a text in *Plutus (Wealth)* 153.

As with the earlier discussion, these instances employ the *arsenokoit-* stem to refer to sexual desire for males, typically pederastic acts, but not necessarily exclusively so, and without any limitation to commercial sex or expansion to include heterosexual relationships.

5. THE HERMENEUTICAL RELEVANCE OF THE BIBLICAL WITNESS

Given the Bible's clear opposition to homosexual conduct, there remains the question of what these texts mean for the church today. In a case like this, where the Scriptures are clear, the question of hermeneutics centers on whether any contemporary considerations preclude the direct application of the Bible's message to the modern debate. In assessing the Bible's hermeneutical relevance it is helpful to keep in mind some basic principles for guiding application.

1. Is the issue a matter of significant concern in the Bible?

(a) *Is there a consistent perspective in the Bible?*
How often is the issue addressed?
If infrequently addressed, does infrequency imply insignificance or universal agreement?
Is it likely that any biblical writers might have held a different position?
Is there continuity between the Testaments?

(b) *Is it a serious moral issue for biblical writers?*
Does violation lead to exclusion from God's people?
Do any biblical writers regard the issue as a matter of indifference?

Do biblical writers prioritize it as one of the core values of the faith?

2. Does the biblical witness remain valid in a contemporary setting?

    (a) *Is the situation to which the Bible responds comparable to the contemporary situation?*

    (b) *Are the arguments made by biblical writers still convincing?*

    (c) *Do new socio-scientific insights or cultural changes invalidate the biblical witness?*

        Do these new insights directly engage the arguments marshalled by the biblical authors?

        How certain are these new insights?

        Are the writers of Scripture limited or blinded by their cultural horizon?

        Were there other perspectives or options available in the author's own time?

    (d) *Has the church adopted a consistent and strong witness on the issue over the centuries?*

    (e) *Does a new work of the Holy Spirit in the church justify changing the biblical position?*

        Does the biblical position run counter to the "weightier matters" of love/justice?

        Does this alleged "new work" promote God's kingdom?

        Does the change involve a total reversal of the biblical position or only a modification?

This chapter will treat the main objections to applying the biblical texts that reject homosexual practice to the contemporary context. These objections tie in with the principles enumerated above.[1]

---

1. The "diagnostic checklist" that Richard Hays has developed for proper use of scripture in contemporary ethical discourse is similar (*The Moral Vision of the New Testament*, 212-13). I put the "descriptive" and "synthetic" task under one heading (the synthetic task is itself descriptive) and see no reason why the "pragmatic" should not come under the "hermeneutical."

The objection that homosexuality is not a matter of significant concern in the Bible (question 1) has to some extent already been treated, particularly for the authors who explicitly proscribe it, but also for Jesus and early Judaism in general. In section V below we will broaden the discussion to the whole canon.

Question 2—whether the biblical witness remains valid in a contemporary setting— occupies most of the attention of this chapter. The argument that the biblical writers had in mind exploitative, pederastic models of homosexuality is used to suggest that homosexuality then and now are two very different phenomena (2a). I address this in section I.

The contention that the biblical writers mistakenly construed homosexual urges to be a manifestation of inordinate heterosexual desire aims to prove that the rationale for the Bible's rejection of homosexuality is flawed (2b) and at variance with the contemporary understanding of homosexual orientation (2c). I take this up in section III.

Some allege that modern science has demonstrated that homosexuality is a genetically based condition whereas the biblical writers perceived it to be a matter of free choice (2c). I discuss this in section IV.

The view that the Bible's condemnation of homosexual behavior was primarily motivated by a desire to maintain male dominance seeks to expose the Bible's own need for reform based on the core values of love and justice (2e). I explore this in II.

Two arguments frequently employed do not respond so much to the specific questions given above as call into question broader presuppositions. The observation that the church has made an about-face on other biblical positions (e.g., women in ministry) is designed to call into question fundamentalist convictions concerning biblical inerrancy. I address this in section VI. The point that the church is comprised of sinners saved by grace is aimed at demonstrating that the church's judgmental attitudes toward homosexuals are hypocritical when the church singles out this sin for special attention. I address this in section VII.

The issue of church tradition in the last two millennia (2d) is not treated here largely because it is well known that, until the last few

decades, the church has maintained a consistent stance against homosexual behavior as sin.[2]

Because no interpreter of the Bible can pretend to be completely
unbiased, it may be helpful for me to lay out my own premises for a
readership that is likely to cover a broad theological spectrum. My
basic assumption is that the Christian Scriptures are the most significant authority and guide for church decisions. At the same time, the

---

2. Cf. Grenz, *Welcoming But Not Affirming*, 63-80; Soards, *Scripture and
Homosexuality*, 33-46; Wright, "Early Christian Attitudes to Homosexuality," 329-
34; Peter Coleman, *Christian Attitudes to Homosexuality* (London: SPCK, 1980),
124-44; Bailey, *Homosexuality and the Western Christian Tradition*, 82-160;
H. Kimball Jones, *Toward a Christian Understanding of the Homosexual* (New York:
Association Press, 1966), 66-89; on female homoeroticism, Brooten, *Love Between
Women*, 303-57. Boswell's argument in *Christianity, Social Tolerance, and
Homosexuality* that homosexual intercourse was not seriously opposed in the
church's history until the mid-thirteenth century is unconvincing. Boswell tends to
maximize the meager evidence favoring a pro-homosexuality interpretation (construing silence as neutrality or even acceptance and expressions of same-sex friendship as erotic) and minimize the mountain of evidence in opposition to same-sex
intercourse. As Hays notes, "every pertinent Christian text from the pre-
Constantinian period . . . adopts an unremittingly negative judgment on homosexual practice, and this tradition is emphatically carried forward by all major Christian
writers of the fourth and fifth centuries. . . . A critical reading of Boswell's own discussion will confirm the point: he is unable to cite a single early Christian text which
approves homosexual activity" ("Relations Natural and Unnatural," 202). Boswell's
astounding assessment of the New Testament evidence ("The New Testament takes
no demonstrable position on homosexuality," p. 117) is indicative of his treatment of
subsequent church history. The same problems reappear in Boswell's more recent
book, *Same-Sex Unions in Premodern Europe* (New York: Villard, 1994), where
Boswell attempts to show that a quasi-marriage ceremony between men existed in
the Eastern Empire until the early Middle Ages. Schmidt's comments are apropos:
"at every key point Boswell's argument depends on quotations taken out of context,
questionable translations and speculation to fill in very wide gaps between very
small bits of evidence. What he has 'discovered' is a ceremony of ritualized broth-
erhood that borrows a few elements from marriage ceremonies. Although homosexuality may have been present in some such relationships, there is no evidence
that sexual partnership (or even nonsexual marriage) was sanctioned by the ceremony, the church or the culture. Indeed, the ceremony in question typically
includes prayers that the two men avoid 'offense,' 'scandal' and 'temptation'. . . . he
can find no historical data to . . . support the claim that such ceremonies reflected
church or societal acceptance of homosexual marriage" (*Straight and Narrow?*,
135). Cf. Robin Darling Young, "Gay Marriage: Reimagining Church History," *First
Things* 47 (1994): 43-48; and Brent D. Shaw, "A Groom of One's Own: The Medieval
Church and the Question of Gay Marriage," *The New Republic* 211 (1994): 33-41.

Bible consists of writings compiled over a millennium, from diverse locations, and by many different writers. Because of this, the Scriptures contain significant internal tensions at points.

I believe the gospel at its core is a message of liberation. By liberation, I mean something more noble than tolerance or permissiveness. I am convinced that the gospel offers us true freedom, a freedom based in God's will—not in human passions. There is reason to question whether the gospel's liberating message has filtered through in equal measure to every position espoused by every biblical writer.

Further, scientific and historical-critical methodology has advanced considerably over the last two thousand years, though it would be an error to equate science and morality or to assume that "new" is always "improved." For example, there are some pre-scientific cosmogonic and cosmological details that contemporary believers are not bound to embrace.[3] In addition, with regard to questions of historical accuracy, the picture of Jesus found in the Gospels cannot simply be equated with the "historical Jesus." The Gospels are portraits of Jesus pieced together to serve particular theological ends.

On the whole I find Paul's exposition of the gospel to be compelling and an authoritative lens from which to interpret and inform my experience. Nevertheless, even though I generally agree with the ultimate point that Paul wants to make on issues of critical significance for Paul, I sometimes have reservations about the way that Paul gets there. For example, I sometimes find Paul's exegesis of the Old Testament to be less than compelling. Paul is still "my apostle," but he does not (and did not in the first century) have to be inerrant in every matter.

Finally, I believe that criticism of Scripture and of the contemporary worldview is a two-way street. I cannot be a biblical literalist or fundamentalist and still retain intellectual integrity. However, I do not think

---

3. Nissinen argues that "unless we totally oppose homosexuality, we have to diverge from the 'clear word' of the Bible. But this is true also when one professes that the earth is round and revolves around the sun" (*Homoeroticism*, 126). The analogy is hardly credible. Belief in a certain cosmology is never presented in Scripture as essential for salvation. Moral sexual behavior, however, is always considered essential; and homosexual behavior is consistently regarded as incompatible with membership in the redeemed community. In terms of the authoritative claim of Scripture on the church's faith and practice, the two matters are not comparable.

that Scripture and the prevailing cultural sentiment are equal in value. Along with most Christians, I have come to the conviction that the gospel message exists in its purest form in the Bible (particularly in the Gospels and the authentic Paul), for all its warts and problems. For me the Bible is the normative "playing field" for grappling with matters of faith and practice. Experience is also important, but no experience is self-interpreting or self-validating. I know of no better interpretive lens than the gospel as proclaimed in the New Testament. My own view is that the *burden of proof* is on those who would reject a biblical position, particularly a strong and consistently held New Testament position on a moral issue with strong support from the Old Testament and subsequent church tradition. I believe this to be the case with respect to homosexuality.

To overturn such a clear biblical mandate requires strong and unambiguous counter-arguments. Furthermore, one must demonstrate that the new information being brought to bear addresses directly the reasons for the Bible's position. For example, it is not enough to prove that the primary expression of homosexuality in antiquity was an inherently exploitative form (pederasty) or that modern science has demonstrated that homosexuality is primarily a genetic phenomenon (two dubious claims, as we shall see). One must also prove that the Bible condemned homosexuality *primarily* on the grounds of the exploitative mismatch created by pederasty or on the grounds that homosexuality was a willfully chosen rejection of God's design for sexuality. Otherwise, even if one's point were valid it would still have little relevance for ascertaining the deficiencies in the Bible's reasons for condemning homosexual behavior.

In addition, a strong case *for* homosexual conduct needs to be made, one that goes beyond misleading platitudes such as "God loves all people" or "Jesus embraced everyone" or "God made me this way." God loves all people and Jesus did embrace outcasts but both call people to repentance and a transformed life. Many, if not most, innate feelings (including a plethora of sexual desires) stand in direct opposition to God's will for redeemed humanity and are to be brought under the control of the Spirit's power.

In the following presentation, headings in boldface summarize the main arguments against hermeneutical appropriation of the Bible's stance on homosexuality. Each heading is followed by an elaboration of the argument, then by a detailed response.

I. The Bible condemns only exploitative, pederastic forms of homosexuality.

Robin Scroggs, followed by others,[4] argues that since the dominant expression of same-sex love in the Greco-Roman world was pederasty (sex between an adult male and an adolescent boy), Jewish and Christian writers could only have had this in mind, and indeed usually thought of the most exploitative forms of pederasty: sex with "call-boys" or household slave boys.[5] Because contemporary expressions of homosexuality can be mutual, non-exploitative, and caring, no one can predict what the Bible would have said about homosexuality had this been the prevailing model in antiquity. In response, I offer two different criticisms.

(1) The biblical texts themselves nowhere limit their rejection of homosexual conduct to exploitative forms.

(a) The prohibitions in Lev 18:22; 20:13 are unqualified: any man who lies with another male in the manner that men lie with women (i.e., engaging in sexual intercourse) has committed an abomination. There are no exceptions. One finds no specifications regarding age of either participant. Neither is there any mention of the exploitative character of the relationship. If homosexual actions were wrong primarily because they were exploitative, why would Lev 20:13 specify a penalty of death for both participants, the exploited as well as the exploiter?

The prohibitions against homosexual intercourse are as absolute as the injunctions against incest and adultery. It simply does not matter

---

4. Scroggs, *The New Testament and Homosexuality*; *inter alios*, Furnish, *The Moral Teaching of Paul*, 52-82; Waetjen, "Same-Sex Sexual Relations in Antiquity," 107-12; Arland J. Hultgren, "Being Faithful to the Scriptures: Romans 1:26-27 as a Case in Point," *WW* 14 (1994): 315-18.
5. Sex with coerced slave boys could take the form of household boy-slaves being forced to have sex by their masters or boys unwillingly enslaved in brothel houses as prostitutes.

how well homosexual conduct is done; what matters is that it is done at all. Arguing that non-exploitative forms of homosexuality might have been accepted is like contending that the Holiness Code was only opposed to exploitative forms of incest. Although Lev 18:22 and 20:13 do not directly specify why homosexual conduct is an "abomination," the most likely reasons are that homosexual conduct entails a confusion of genders through violation of the anatomical and procreative complementarity of male and female, that it constitutes a rejection of the pattern laid down in the traditional material in Genesis 1-3, and that it serves to destabilize the integrity of the family and the ordered survival of the species.

(b) Romans 1:26-27 is equally absolute in its wording: "their females exchanged the natural use" (i.e., of the male as regards sexual intercourse) and "the males. . . were consumed with passion for one another, males with males." The reference to lesbianism in 1:26 casts a wider net than abusive, male, pederastic relationships, inasmuch as lesbianism in the ancient Mediterranean world was not confined to pederastic models or rigid active versus passive roles.[6] The fact that Paul segues from lesbianism in 1:26 to male homosexual behavior in 1:27 with the words "and likewise also" (*homoiōs te kai*) suggests that he rejects both forms of homosexual behavior for the same reasons; that is, on grounds other than their exploitative or oppressive character.

Moreover, the contrast in 1:27 is clearly not between exploitative homosexual relationships and loving homosexual relationships but between heterosexual and homosexual conduct: "the males, leaving behind the natural use of the female (as regards sexual intercourse). . . . " From Paul's perspective the fundamental problem with male homosexual conduct is not that it is exploitative of young people but

---

6. "Female homosexual practices took many forms, from almost violent nymphomania to bisexuality to homosexual marriage. It is probable that there was no female parallel to pederasty (with the possible, though doubtful, exception of Plutarch's Spartan women). From what we can tell from the available evidence, the most prevalent form of female homosexual practice involved mutually consenting women of roughly equal age" (Mark Smith, "Ancient Bisexuality," 243). "The reference to women itself indicates that Paul's criticism should not be restricted to pederasty, although it is definitely one of the phenomena in the background" (Nissinen, *Homoeroticism*, 110). Cf. Brooten, *Love Between Women*, 359-60.

that it is sexual gratification aimed at other males rather than at females. The blurring of the sexes, doing with the same sex what should be done with the opposite sex alone, is the problem for Paul. Indeed, Paul emphasizes the mutuality of affections: "the males . . . were inflamed in their desire for one another." He is not presuming a situation in which only an allegedly active older partner in the relationship is sexually gratified. But mutuality does not imply moral goodness to Paul.

Additionally, as in Lev 20:13, Paul states that both parties involved are under divine judgment, not just the so-called exploitative active partner: "males engaging in indecency with males, receiving back *in themselves* the recompense which was required of their straying." In Paul's view the divine "recompense" or "wrath" (1:18) was already manifesting itself in the "*mutual* degrading of their bodies" (1:24) that arises when people distort God's intended design for their sexuality by doing what their bodies were not created to do. Just as idolaters degrade their own humanity by choosing to worship an image of another creature rather than the Creator, so too the one engaged in homosexual conduct is degraded by ignoring the obvious design for sexuality in basic human anatomy and physiology.

First Corinthians 6:9 also pronounces judgment both on effeminate males who play the role of females in male homosexual intercourse (*malakoi*) and on active male partners who take the former to bed (*arsenokoitai*). I refer the reader to pp. 310-12, 325-30 for reasons why the combination of these two terms is correctly understood in our contemporary context when applied to every conceivable type of same-sex intercourse.

In short, Paul does not present a picture where one party is being degraded and exploited, but rather portrays both partners as seeking to gratify their urges with one another and together reaping the divine recompense for their mutually degrading conduct. Had Paul wanted to limit his remarks to pederasty he could have used Greek words that refer specifically to such activity. Even if Paul were thinking in the first instance of pederasty while employing the more inclusive language of Leviticus ("men lying with males"), he shows no apparent interest here in the matter of one-sided exploitation. The phrase *contrary to nature* is not a reference to having sex with a youth or exploiting someone.

Like most ancient Jews, Paul viewed the creation story in Genesis 1–3 as endorsing only heterosexual unions. *Contrary to nature* is a reference to erasing the stamp of gender placed on male and female by the Creator.[7] The problem that same-sex intercourse posed for Paul was that it was same-sex, not that it was inherently exploitative. Pederasty was one of the most acceptable forms of same-sex intercourse in antiquity. Undoubtedly Paul would have viewed an adult male who willingly presented his body for penetration by another man (a *cinaedus*) with greater, not lesser, scorn.

(2) It is misleading to argue as if Jewish Christian writers had nothing but negative images from which to base their judgment of homosexuality.

Even on the surface of it, the notion that mutually caring same-sex relationships first originated in modern times sounds absurd. Are we to believe that nobody with homosexual or lesbian urges in all of antiquity was able to provide a healthy example of same-sex love? In fact, moving statements about the compassionate and beautiful character of same-sex love can be found in Greco-Roman literature. Among the examples[8] are the speeches in Plato's *Symposium.* In it is narrated a

---

7. In Plutarch's *Dialogue on Love*, the character Daphnaeus speaks negatively even of consensual intercourse between males: "to consort with males (whether without consent, in which case it involves violence and brigandage; or if with consent, there is still weakness [*malakia*] and effeminacy on the part of those who, contrary to nature, allow themselves in Plato's words 'to be covered and mounted like cattle')— this is a completely ill-favored favor, indecent, an unlovely affront to Aphrodite" (751D-E; W. C. Helmbold, LCL). Homoerotic intercourse is inherently exploitative because it confuses the genders.
8. Cf. the pro-homosexual (albeit misogynistic) arguments by Protogenes and Pisias in Plutarch, *Dial. Love,* 750B–751B, 752B-C: "Since [marriage to a woman] is necessary for producing children, there's no harm in legislators talking it up and singing its praises to the masses. But genuine Love has no connection whatsoever with the women's quarters. . . . Love, in fact, it is that attaches himself to a young and talented soul and through friendship brings it to a state of virtue; but the appetite for women we are speaking of, however well it turns out, has for net gain only an accrual of pleasure in the enjoyment of a ripe physical beauty. . . . [Heterosexual love is] an effeminate and bastard love. . . . mere copulation. . . . What insolence! To think that human beings who acknowledge that they are locked like dogs by their sexual parts to the female should dare to transport the god (Love) from his home in the

series of discourses on Love (*Erōs*) by various celebrants (including Socrates), during the time of light drinking after a banquet that occurred in 416 B.C.E.[9]

Phaedrus, the first speaker, states: "I at least am not able to say immediately what it is that is any greater good for someone who is young than a useful lover (*erastēs*, the older and active homosexual partner) and for a lover a darling boy (*paidika*; or: favorite, the younger or boyish passive homosexual partner)" (178C). He argues that "an army of lovers and darling boys" would be the best possible army since each soldier would be inspired by his partner to great heights of valor so as not to be disgraced in the eyes of that partner (178D–179B). He also tells the story of how Achilles ("still beardless, since he was much younger") was honored by the gods with a place in the Isles of the Blest because of his deep devotion to his lover Patroclus (expressed in avenging Patroclus's death and in seeking to join him in death; 179E–180B).

The next speaker, Pausanias, was a "lover" of the host Agathon. Their relationship had started over twelve years earlier when Agathon was eighteen (cf. Plato, *Prot.* 315D-E). Agathon was no longer a youth. Now about thirty-one years old, Agathon had just won a prize for his plays at a dramatic festival and owned the home at which this symposium took place. Pausanias distinguishes between two types of love (*erōs*): the heavenly and the popular. Popular Aphrodite

> is the (love) which the common (*phauloi*; or: bad, inferior) sort of men fall in love with (*erōsin*). And such men first of all fall in love with women not less than boys, then as regards those with whom they fall in love, (*sc.* they fall in love) with the bodies more than the souls; then whenever possible (*sc.* they fall in love) with the most mindless ones. . . . But the (*sc.* other love is) related to the heavenly (*sc.* Aphrodite) who first of all does not partake of the female but only of the male; [and this is the love of boys;] then, (*sc.* this Aphrodite) is elder, without an allotment of wantonness (*hybris*; or: insolence); for which reason those who are

---

gymnasia and the parks with their wholesome fresh-air life in the sun (i.e., the noble venues for pederasty) and confine him in brothels . . . !" (Helmbold, LCL). Cf. also Achilles Tatius, *Leuc. Clit.* 2.38.

9. The following translations of the *Symposium* are my own.

inspired by this love turn their attention to the male, being fond of (*agapōntes*) what is more vigorous by nature and has more mind. . . . For they fall in love with boys only at the point when they begin to have in their possession a mind; and this moment approximates the time when they begin to get a beard. For, I think, *those who begin from that moment to fall in love with them are prepared to love in the expectation that they will be with them all their life* and will share their lives in common; but not (*sc.* prepared)—after having used deception, taken advantage of their lack of prudence as youth, and laughed at them—to go off and run away to another. (181 B-D)

Pausanias acknowledges that pederasty is justly criticized when the lover has only the body in view and not also the soul. "For at the same time with the bloom of the body ceasing, (the body) which he used to love, 'he has taken flight and gone off' [Homer, *Il.* 2.71], having dishonored many speeches and promises. But the lover of the moral character that is good remains throughout life, as if having been fused into a single entity with that which abides (viz., the soul of the beloved)" (183E). A "darling boy" should not capitulate to sex too quickly, nor do so for money or status. Yet "one way is left in our law if a darling boy is going to grant favors to a lover rightly"; namely, to do so "in the cause of virtue" (184C). The darling boy should act "in the belief that he will be granting favors to a good man and that he himself will be made better because of the affectionate regard (*philia*) of his lover" (185A). The lover, in turn, is obliged to attend to the education of his favorite and to make his growth in wisdom and goodness the top priority (184D).

Pausanias is not uncritical towards all forms of pederasty; he is able to make distinctions between exploitative forms (which should be condemned) and non-exploitative forms (which should be commended). Moreover, he stresses that the bonds created between lover and loved ought to be lifelong, a conception which, while not involving age-matched couples, nevertheless takes the phenomenon beyond pederasty. This was certainly true of Pausanias's relationship with Agathon.[10] The ideal of young male beauty and the misogynist exaltation of the masculine mind can be criticized from a contemporary

10. "[Agathon's] relationship with Pausanias is between consenting adults whose age differential is by now irrelevant, who have chosen to continue mutually loving each

standpoint (as can the prevailing heterosexual model of female subordination in antiquity), but the relationship between lover and loved commended by Pausanias is not exploitative of the younger passive partner.

In the fourth speech (189C–193D), the great comic poet Aristophanes (who was earlier prevented from speaking by a hiccup arising from "a surfeit [*plēsmonēs*] or some other cause," now cured) constructs a myth about human origins in which humans were once binary beings, one type consisting of a man-man, another of a female-female, and a third kind of a male-female. When they attempted to extend their power to the heavens, Zeus sliced each in two and closed up the wounds. Ever since then all humans long for their other half.

All of the women who are a cut-off part (*tmēma*; or: section, piece) of a woman (viz., the female-female) do not exactly turn their attention to men, but rather are inclined toward women, and from this race come into being the female sexual companions of females (*hai hetairistriai*). And all who are a cut-off part of a male (viz., the male-male) pursue male things, and so long as they may be boys and inasmuch as they are little slices of the male(-male), they regard with affection (*philousi*) men and rejoice when they lie down with and are locked together with men (viz., in sexual embrace; *sumpeplegmenoi*). And these are the best of the boys and lads, inasmuch as they are by nature (*physei*) the most manly. But some at this point say that they are shameless, falsely; for they do not act this way impelled by shamelessness but by courage and manliness and manly look, fondly welcoming (*aspazomenoi*) that which is similar to them. Now the proof of this is great: for in fact when they reach perfected adulthood only such persons turn out to be men fit for civic activities. And when they reach manhood, they become lovers of boys and are not inclined by nature (*physei*) toward marriage and the procreation of children, yet are compelled to do so by the law or custom (*nomos*). Yet it suffices for them to live their lives out with one another unmarried. So such a person cannot help but become (*pantōs men . . . gignetai*) both a lover of boys (*paiderastēs*) and someone who has affectionate

other, in spite of the possibility of cultural censure. . . . In a later tradition Plutarch describes the love of the tragic poet Euripides for Agathon, who was then well advanced in years. To term either of these a pederastic relationship is a serious stretch of the evidence and the language" (Smith, "Ancient Bisexuality," 235).

regard for his lover (*philerastēs*), always fondly welcoming that which is of the same kind. So of course when he also happens upon that very person who is his half, whether the lover of boys or any other (*sc.* lover?), then they are wonderfully struck with affectionate regard (*philia*) and a sense of kinship (*oikeiotēs*) and love (*erōs*), almost not wanting to be divided even for a short time. And *these are they who continue with one another throughout life.* . . . *[each] desiring* to join together and to be fused into a single entity with his beloved (*erōmenos*) and to *become one person from two.* . . . our race would become happy in the following way, if we would bring love to fulfillment and each would happen upon his own darling boy, going back to his ancient nature (*physin*). (191E–192C, 192E, 193C)

The speech is preceded by banter between Aristophanes and Eryximachus in which Eryximachus cautions Aristophanes not to spin absurdities but rather to "speak as though intending to give a reasonable argument" (*lege hōs dōsōn logon*), while Aristophanes states that he is "afraid not that I may say something amusing, for that would be gain and native to my (or: our) Muse, but that (*sc.* I may say something) absurd" (189B). After the speech, Aristophanes charges Eryximachus to not treat what he has said as though he said it "after the manner of comedies" (193D).

Regardless of the degree of seriousness or lack thereof of Aristophanes's presentation, however, the speech even as satire reflects or plays off of the positive view of same-sex eroticism expressed by Phaedrus and Pausanias and current among some in antiquity: a view that applauds the naturalness, beauty, and longevity of same-sex love ("who continue together throughout life"), even conjecturing a genetic basis for such love between women on the one hand and between a younger male and an older male on the other. The final lines also suggest that even though homoerotic relationships were often characterized as gratification of the older male by the younger male, with the latter giving sexual favors in return for the former's instruction, the younger partner too could be "wonderfully struck with affectionate regard and a sense of kinship and love."[11]

---

11. Later an inebriated Alcibiades barges in on the symposium and recounts how Socrates had previously withstood his youthful attempts to give himself sexually to

A lengthy defense of the love of boys also appears in the much later work, the Pseudo-Lucianic *Affairs of the Heart* (ca. 300 C.E.).[12] In it Lycinus recounts a debate between two men over whether love of women or love of boys is superior. The case for the latter was made by Callicratidas (30-49), whom Lycinus describes as a man who hated women and who kept plenty of male slave-boys and servants around his household but only "until the first signs of down on their chins appeared" (10). However, the speech of Callicratidas also enshrines some

---

Socrates. "Regarding him to have been in earnest for my bloom of youth (*hōra*), I regarded it (viz., this situation) to be a gift of Hermes (*hermaion*; or: a godsend) and a wonderful piece of good luck for me, supposing that by granting favors to Socrates I would earn the right to hear whatever things he knew; for I would take exceedingly great pride in my bloom of youth. So with these things in mind, . . . I would send the attendant away and alone keep company with him. . . . I would think that he would immediately converse with me as a lover might converse with his darling boy in private, and I would rejoice. But none of these things would ever happen. . . . After that . . . I would exercise in the gymnasium with him in anticipation of making some progress there. . . . And what need I say? For I got no further. And since I accomplished nothing by that method, it seemed to me that I had to impose myself upon the man forcefully. . . . At last I invite him to have supper with me, just like a lover plotting against his darling boy" (217A-C). After convincing Socrates to stay the night, Alcibiades propositioned him. "You seem to me . . . to have become the only lover worthy of me, and you appear to me to be hesitating to mention it to me; I understand (*sc.* things) in this way: I regard it to be entirely senseless not to grant you even this favor. . . . For to me nothing is more important than that I become the best person possible, and I think that in this I have no helper more able than you. So I would feel far more shame before sensible people if I did not grant favors to such a man than I would feel before the senseless many if I did grant such favors" (218C-D). When Socrates rebuffed this offer, pointing to the superior beauty of the mind over the body, Alcibiades tried one last ploy. He wrapped his body around Socrates and slept with him all night. "I rose from sleep having no more slept with Socrates than if I had been lying down to sleep with a father or older brother. After this you can well imagine what thoughts I had: on the one hand regarding myself as dishonored; but on the other hand admiring the nature of this man and his sexual self-control and manliness. . . . Accordingly, then, I neither had the capacity to be angry and deprive myself of social intercourse with this man nor did I know the means by which I might draw him to myself" (219D). Alcibiades is portrayed as someone who, far from being exploited, prided himself in his ability to attract older men through his youthful beauty, pursued Socrates as though he himself was the active "lover," counted the giving of himself sexually to an eminent older man as a high honor, and was almost tempted to feel angry at Socrates' rebuff. Mark Smith cites other texts that point to youths experiencing sexual pleasure from pederastic relationships ("Ancient Bisexuality," 231).

12. The translations of *Affairs* that follow are my own.

nobler values. According to Callicratidas, "only the male love (viz., love of males) is an activity that pleasure and virtue share in common. . . . For marriage has been devised as a remedy to ensure the necessary succession (*sc.* of the human race) but only the male love is a noble injunction of a wisdom-loving (*philosophos*) soul"; the latter is "artistically formed with beauty in view," not out of some necessity (31, 33). He grants that love for women is the older of the two practices but argues that its antiquity only proves its primitiveness, for only with the advance of civilization and culture could love for boys come about: "we should deem the old customs among our pursuits (*epitēdeumata*) as necessary, but the ones which life devised when it had leisure for reasoning should be honored (*timēteon*; or: valued) as better than those" (35).

Likewise, for Callicratidas, an appeal to the heterosexual practices of animals proves only that love of boys requires the exercise of reason (which animals lack), while love of women is mere brute animal passion. "Lions do not so love because they are also not philosophers. . . . But for men practical wisdom coupled with scientific knowledge, from experimenting many times, having chosen what is most noble, deemed the most steadfast (*bebaiotatoi*; or: most secure, durable, sure) of loves to be the male ones (viz., the love between males)" (36). Although "love" (*erōs*) goes by one name, there are really two: the love for women which is "unbridled pleasure (*akolastos hēdonē*)" and love of boys which is "goodwill that is temperate (*hē sōphronousē eunoia*)" (37).

Callicratidas goes on to contrast "the evils associated with women" with "the manly life of a boy" (38-45), ending with a moving tribute to the selfless and self-sacrificing love of the older partner.

> Who would not be a lover of such a young man (*ephēbos*, age eighteen and over)? And who could have eye beams so blind, and have reasoning faculties so maimed? And how could one not love a Hermes in the wrestling schools, and an Apollos with the lyre, and a horseman like Castor, and one who pursues divine virtues by means of a mortal body? But as for me, O divine powers of heaven, may my life be continuously this: to sit right opposite my dear friend and to hear him speaking pleasantly nearby, and to go out with him when he goes out and to have joint involvement (*koinōnia*) in every activity. So any lover might well pray

that the one of whom he is fond should travel through life without stumbling and without swerving unsteadily, reaching old age without sorrow, after having experienced from no Fate malicious abuse. But if indeed, because of the law of human nature, a disease should lightly touch him, I shall be sick with him when he is ill and I shall sail with him when he sets out through stormy sea. And if a violent tyrant should fasten chains around him, I shall put iron fetters that are equal on myself. Everyone who hates him will be my enemy, and I will have affectionate regard for those who are kindly toward him. But if I should behold robbers or hostile men rushing headlong toward him, I would arm myself even beyond my strength. And if he dies, I shall not put up with living. And I will lay final commands on those of whom I am fond next most after him, to heap up a common grave for both of us, and after having mixed up together my bones with his bones, not even to separate our mute ashes from one another. (46)

When the boy reaches maturity, it becomes difficult to distinguish between "lover" and "beloved":

> When the earnest love bred in us from childhood reaches manhood upon the age that now enables reasoning, what for a long time was a recipient of affectionate regard gives back reciprocal expressions of love, and *it is difficult to perceive which of the two is a lover of which,* as though from a mirror, when an image resembling the goodwill of the one who (*sc.* first) had affectionate regard fell onto the beloved. Why then do you reproach it (viz., this love of males) as a strange indulgence (*tryphē*; or: softness, daintiness, luxury, wantonness) of the world we live in (*tou kath' hēmas biou*; or: of our life) when *it was ordained by divine laws* and has come down to us from succession? And having received it gladly, we cherish it with a pure thoughts as though caretakers of its temple. (48)[13]

Mark Smith cites a series of examples of homoeroticism in antiquity that broaden the standard model of love between a man and a boy: those

---

13. Lycinus sides with Callicratidas: "Though marriage is a thing useful for men's lives and blessed whenever it turns out well, I regard the loves (or: erotic desires) for darling boys, so long as they woo the pure rules of friendship, as the activity of philosophy alone. Therefore marriage is a must for all men, but let the boy-loving (*paiderastein*) be permitted only for the wise; for complete virtue grows least among women" (51).

between young adult males, between adult males of unequal age, between adult males of roughly equal age, between adult males who alternate in the roles of "lover" and "beloved," and between bisexuals and members of the same and opposite sex, with many of these relationships characterized as stable and even as lifelong "marriages." "In sum, the extant sources for Greco-Roman homosexual practices demonstrate many exceptions to pederasty and a decline in the prominence of pederasty in the last three centuries immediately preceding Paul."[14] After citing the evidence for female homosexuality in antiquity (often "relationships of mutual consent without reference to active/passive distinctions or age differentiation or exploitation"), Smith concludes that:

> Paul probably did know of at least several different types of homosexual practices among both men and women. He used general language in Rom. 1, because he intended his proscription to apply in a general way to all homosexual behavior, as he understood it. In context, then, homosexual activity, in all its manifestations (as understood by Paul), is evidence of God's judgment on human sinfulness.[15]

---

14. Smith, "Ancient Bisexuality," 236-37. For example, "Xenophon of Ephesus in his second-century C.E. novel, *Ephesiaca*, introduces Hippothoos, a truly versatile man who is consecutively in love with a male of his own age, an older woman, and a younger man." Springett cites Suetonius's reference to the emperor Galba who "showed a preference for mature and sturdy men. It is said that when Icelus, one of his old-time bed-fellows, brought the news of Nero's death, Galba openly showered him with kisses and begged him to get ready and have intercourse with him without delay" (*Galba* 21).

15. Ibid., 246. James E. Miller, in a short critique of Smith's article, argued: "Though I would not argue that Paul felt homosexual relations between adult males were acceptable, I doubt very much that such practices were on his mind when he wrote Romans 1:27 or that any of his first-century audience would have thought of two adult males when they heard this verse" ("Pederasty and Romans 1:27: A Response to Mark Smith," *JAAR* 65 [1997]: 861-66, quote from p. 864). He further contends that "Paul is attacking an accepted Gentile practice. Homosexuality between adult males was not an accepted activity, but pederasty was" (ibid., 863). He faults Smith for allegedly claiming "that first-century sexual attitudes and practices were rather like modern attitudes and practices" (ibid., 864). Smith emphasized in his rejoinder that: (1) although there "were differences in cultural attitudes toward sexuality," "the differences in sexual practices were few, if any"; (2) since pederasty in Paul's day was only part of a broader range of homosexual activity, it is not likely that Paul's reference to males "consumed with passion for one another" referred to

Indeed, one might expect to see in the homosexual community a negative reaction against stereotyping all expressions of homoerotic behavior in antiquity as sordid, since such a stereotype would deprive the homosexual community of ancient precedents for healthy homoerotic relationships. Indeed, this was already the case made in Boswell's book, *Christianity, Social Tolerance, and Homosexuality*, published three years before Scroggs's book.[16] To be sure, one partner usually retained the higher status but, for that matter, the same could

---

"only one of many options available for homosexual expression" (Miller's own admission that he "would not argue that Paul felt homosexual relations between adult males were acceptable" makes essentially the same point); and (3) to assert that Rom 1:27 attacks only "an accepted Gentile practice" becomes problematic in view of the fact that the vices cited in Rom 1:18-32 are not limited to practices "accepted" in Roman sources ("Paul and Ancient Bisexuality: A Rejoinder," *JAAR* 65 [1997]: 867-70). Smith had the better of the exchange. My only criticism of Smith's article is that he contends that "Paul (as well as other biblical authors) does not place any special emphasis on censuring homosexual activity" (p. 247), regarding homosexuality as "a minor issue (as far as human sinfulness can ever be a minor issue)" (p. 250). Although he insists that "Rom. 1 is relevant to the modern discussion" of homosexuality, Smith does not take a stance in his article on whether Paul's perspective was "correct" (pp. 250-51).

16. Thus Boswell: "If the difficulties of historical research about intolerance of gay people could be resolved by simply avoiding anachronistic projections of modern myths and stereotypes, the task would be far simpler than it is. Unfortunately, *an equally distorting and even more seductive danger* for the historian is posed by the tendency to exaggerate the differences between homosexuality in previous societies and modern ones. One example of this tendency is the common idea that gay relationships in the ancient world differed from their modern counterparts in that they always involved persons of different ages: an older man (the lover) and a young boy (the beloved). . . . It is clear that in many cases it was superior beauty which earned one the position of beloved, not inferior age. . . . In any event, one did not have to be young in any accepted sense: Euripides was the lover of Agathon when Euripedes was seventy-two and Agathon forty; Parmenides and Zenon were in love when the former was sixty-five and the latter forty; Alcibiades was already full bearded when Socrates fell in love with him. . . . [I]t does not seem likely that, with a few exceptions, the apparent prevalence of erotic relationships between adults and boys in the past corresponded to reality. It was, rather, an idealized cultural convention. . . . [T]erminology is also misleading on this point. . . . Beautiful men were 'boys' to the Greeks just as beautiful women are 'girls' to modern Europeans and Americans. The actual age of the male involved may have mattered to some Greeks; to others it obviously did not. . . . Most used terms which suggested erotic attraction for young men and for older males interchangeably, clearly implying that age was not a consideration. The term 'pederasty' frequently has no more relation to the age of the objects of desire than 'girl chasing' "

be said for heterosexual relationships in antiquity. There were certainly instances of exploitative homosexual relationships in antiquity and pederasty was the most common form of homoerotic expression. Yet that is a far cry from making the case that homosexuality in Greco-Roman society was inherently exploitative or that it was so prone to exploitation that Jews and Christians could not make the distinction between exploitative and non-exploitative forms. Victimization simply did not factor significantly in the arguments that Jews and Christians made in the ancient world. All forms of homosexual and lesbian conduct were wrong simply because of what it was not: natural sexual intercourse with the opposite sex.[17]

Scroggs claims that the biblical texts are without hermeneutical relevance for the contemporary debate because "the context which called the biblical statements into existence" does not "bear a reasonable similarity" to the contemporary context; homosexuality then and now are two fundamentally different phenomena.[18] On the contrary, there is "reasonable similarity" between the two cultural contexts because the fundamental aspect of homosexuality and lesbianism that accounts for their rejection remains the same: the lack of gender complementarity

---

(*Christianity, Social Tolerance, and Homosexuality*, 27-30 [28 n. 52]; my emphasis). I suspect a similar concern lies behind Brooten's critique of Scroggs: "Robin Scroggs argues that Paul must be referring to pederasty. . . . If, however, the dehumanizing aspects of pederasty motivated Paul to condemn sexual relations between males, then why did he condemn relations between females in the same sentence? . . . Scroggs . . . maintains his thesis concerning pederasty even though the sources on women do not support it. . . . Rom 1:27, like Lev 18:22 and 20:13, condemns all males in male-male relationships regardless of age, making it unlikely that lack of mutuality or concern for the passive boy were Paul's central concerns. . . . The ancient sources, which rarely speak of sexual relations between women and girls, undermine Robin Scroggs's theory that Paul opposed homosexuality as pederasty" (*Love Between Women*, 253 n. 106, 257, 361).

17. Indeed, as Schoedel intimates, in the Greco-Roman world homosexual intercourse between an adult male and a male youth was regarded as a *less* exploitative form of same-sex eros than intercourse between two adult males, precisely because the key problem with homosexual intercourse—behaving toward the male passive partner as if the latter were female—was exacerbated when the intercourse was aimed at adult males who had outgrown the "softness" of immature adolescence ("Same-Sex Eros," 50). When Jews like Philo and Paul rejected pederasty they were rejecting the best, not the worst, in the homosexual practice of their day.

18. Scroggs, *The New Testament and Homosexuality*, 123-29.

in same-sex couples. Two thousand years of history have not changed that basic fact of human existence.

II. The Bible primarily condemns homosexuality because of its threat to male dominance.

Bernadette Brooten has argued in her recent, well-documented book on early Christian responses to female homoeroticism that the primary reason why early Christian leaders condemned female homoeroticism was because it constituted "gender role transgression."[19] In other words, female (and male) homoeroticism threatened to undermine the prevailing cultural pattern of male dominance and female subordination. Sexual intercourse between males and females was conceived in antiquity as a role-play between an active male exercising his dominance over a woman through mounting and phallic penetration, with the woman playing the passive role of being mounted and receiving the man's "seed." Lesbians who played the active role were often conceived in masculine terms, and, thereby, guilty of confusing the gender-stratified social order. Similarly, many ancient moralists criticized the passive male in homosexual relationships for taking on a weak and submissive role appropriate only for women. In sum, the passive, subordinate role of women in sexual intercourse and the active, dominant role of men were in keeping with the respective "natures" or inherent character traits of women and men (for example, a woman's disposition toward domestic life and submission to a man, a man's disposition toward public, military, political, and philosophical roles).[20] According to Brooten, Paul and the early Church Fathers absorbed these cultural values. "Paul's condemnation of homoeroticism, particularly female homoeroticism, reflects and helps to maintain a gender asymmetry based on female subordination. I hope that churches today,

---

19. Brooten, *Love Between Women*. A similar view is given by Stanley K. Stowers, *A Rereading of Romans* (New Haven: Yale University Press, 1994), 94-97; Martin, "Heterosexism," 344-46; Edwards, *Gay/Lesbian Liberation*, 78-80; Wolfgang Stegemann, "Paul and the Sexual Mentality of His World," *BTB* 23 (1993):163-65; among commentators, Byrne, *Romans*, 69 (though "a more theological note may also be present: such behavior is contrary to the design inserted into the natural order by the Creator").

20. *Love Between Women*, 275-80.

being apprised of the history that I have presented, will no longer teach Rom 1:26f as authoritative."[21]

Martti Nissinen takes a similar approach. "In antiquity, *physis* expresses a fundamental cultural rule or a conventional, proper, or inborn character or appearance, or the true being of a person or a thing rather than 'nature' in a genetic-biological sense, as a modern reader would perceive it." Nissinen includes in his contrast to "genetic-biological" not only "conventional" but also "inborn." Since inborn or innate traits encompass genetic traits and biological traits include both innate and genetic traits, the contrast is somewhat muddled. The truth is that the ancients classified some things as natural which we would likewise attribute to nature, and some things as natural which we would regard as conventional or cultural. Each case has to be handled individually to determine whether the terms *natural* and *nature* in any given author are being correctly applied from a contemporary perspective. Nissinen, in any case, views the usage of *physis* in Paul's letters, particularly in 1 Cor 11:14-15, as proof that Paul meant by *natural* "the common order of things," "conventional patterns," and by *unnatural* "something that goes beyond the ordinary realm of experience."[22] "Paul's understanding of the naturalness of men's and women's gender roles is not a matter of genital formation and their functional purpose, which today is considered the main criterion for the unnatural."[23] "It was women's active sexual role that was regarded as truly 'contrary to nature.'. . . The patriarchal role structure was disturbed also by the female role assumed by the passive partner in a homosexual relationship of two men."[24] The biblical authors, including Paul, were locked into an "ideology of hierarchical polarization." Their visceral response to homosexual behavior stems from their outrage at men adopting the passive, penetrated role of socially inferior women and women attempting to take on the active role of socially superior men.[25]

---

21. Ibid., p. 302.
22. *Homoeroticism*, 105, 107.
23. Ibid., 107.
24. Ibid., 108.
25. Ibid., 129, 133. Cf. Abraham Smith, "The New Testament and Homosexuality," 25. Stephen D. Moore takes a similar approach ("Que(e)rying Paul: Preliminary

Ancient sources, including Jewish sources, do indeed indicate that gender stratification was an element in the critique of homoeroticism. However, this was not the only argument employed in antiquity against male and female homoeroticism (procreation and heterosexual inter-

---

Questions," *Auguries* [eds. D. J. A. Clines and S. D. Moore; JSOTSup 269; Sheffield: Sheffield University Press, 1998], 250-74). Drawing on Winkler's *Constraints of Desire* (pp. 37-40), he interprets Paul's remarks in Rom 1:26-27 in the light of the second-century C.E. work *The Interpretation of Dreams* (*Onirocritica*) of Artemidorus. In 1.78-80 Artemidorus discusses dreams of sexual intercourse (for additional discussion of this text, cf. also Brooten, *Love Between Women*, 175-86; Nissinen, *Homoeroticism*, 76-77).

Artemidorus develops three basic categories. "The best set of categories for the analysis of intercourse is, first, intercourse which is according to nature [*kata physin*] and law/convention [*nomos*] and customary usage [*ethos*], then intercourse against law/convention [*para nomon*], and third, intercourse against nature [*para physin*]" (1.78). Generally assuming the dreamer to be a man, Artemidorus classifies under "intercourse which is according to nature and law/convention" intercourse with all types of women (one's wife, mistress, prostitute, a woman who is a stranger, a female servant), intercourse with males (his active male lover or his male slave), and masturbation (by stroking). He classifies under "intercourse against law/convention" various acts of incest (including both opposite-sex and same-sex incest), but also intercourse which involved penetrating one's friend (i.e., intercourse between social equals) and fellatio with others. Under "intercourse against nature" the following: orally stimulating or kissing one's own penis (self-fellatio), sex with a god or goddess, sex with a corpse, and sex with an animal. A woman who dreams either of "possessing" or "being possessed" by another woman is also listed as "intercourse against nature."

Following Winkler, Moore argues that what gets placed under the category of "unnatural" is any act of sexual intercourse that does not involve penetration of social inferiors; that is, any act of sexual intercourse that does not recreate proper human social hierarchy. He concludes his article with an "amplified translation" of Rom 1:26-27:

> Their women exchanged natural relations (of domination versus submission, designed to display social hierarchy, they themselves assuming the inferior position by accepting penile penetration) for unnatural relations (in which no display of domination or submission occurred and consequently no social hierarchy was exhibited, because no penile penetration took place), and the men likewise gave up natural relations with women (the male assuming the dominant position, penetrating the woman and thereby exhibiting and reaffirming his social superiority over her) and were consumed with passion for one another, men committing shameless acts with men (in which one partner would necessarily end up the loser in the zero-sum game of honour versus shame, passively accepting penetration and thus defeat at the hands of the other). (p. 273)

For Moore "it seems to matter very little in the end whether Paul himself

course among animals are two others). Indeed, behind the various arguments was the simple recognition of a "fittedness" of the sex organs, male to female. This fittedness, the ancients observed, included not only the compatible physical dimensions of the penis and vagina but also the complementarity of these organs in terms of sexual pleasure and procreative capacity.

Homoeroticism may have appeared as a threat to the gender-stratified societies of the first-century Mediterranean basin but the degree of revulsion against same-sex eroticism held by many in antiquity was not limited to this when they spoke of the passive male homosexual partner as effeminate and the active lesbian partner as masculine. A male who allowed himself to be penetrated was acting like a female

was fully cognizant of what he was saying or whether he was merely a dummy on the knee of a ventriloquist culture" (p. 272).

In addition to the discussion below, two immediate responses can be given to Moore's reconstruction of the logic of Rom 1:26-27. Artemidorus's classifications of natural and conventional, unconventional, and unnatural are indeed heavily marked by concerns revolving around human social hierarchy and the importance of the symbolism of penile penetration. Hence, sex between women is inherently unnatural (no penis is involved) while sex between two men of unequal status is natural. However, not all the classifications are so neatly placed under a concern for social hierarchy. For a man to have sex with his daughter or son is "against law/convention," even though no disruption of human social hierarchy takes place; indeed human social hierarchy is affirmed (to be sure, incest is not "contrary to nature"). Sex with a god or with an animal does not establish a human social hierarchy but neither does it disrupt human social hierarchy. If a man penetrates a dog, human social hierarchy is not inverted (the same can be said for self-fellatio and sex with a corpse). Might we not suspect that additional issues are involved here, for example, "union between two radically different spheres of existence" (to use Brooten's expression)? And why is masturbation by self-stroking listed as intercourse which is "according to nature or convention/law" but self-fellatio as intercourse "contrary to nature"? Neither act of masturbation establishes human social hierarchy. Attempts to define everything in the list according to whether human social hierarchy is affirmed may be overly reductionistic.

More important is the rather obvious point that Paul was not simply mimicking the cultural milieu inhabited by Artemidorus. If he had been, he would not have regarded all male homosexual intercourse as unnatural. The fact that he does regard all homosexual intercourse as against nature suggests that more was at stake for him than the creation of human social hierarchy. Men are in socially subordinate positions to other men as much in Jewish culture as in Greco-Roman culture. Why not permit a socially superior male to penetrate a socially inferior male if the only issue is one of status differentiation?

quite apart from issues of dominance and submission: the appropriate receptacle was absent from the male sex. The receptive male was trying to receive something that only females were made to receive. A female who attempted to have sex with another female could not penetrate a woman's vagina without a prosthesis substituting for the male organ. This is simply a basic biological difference that was as obvious in antiquity as it is today. Males have a sex organ suited for penetration and no orifice appropriate for sexual receptivity. Females have genital organs suited for receiving male penetration and no penetrating organ of their own. Sexual intercourse is complementary for males and females, not males with males or females with females.

In the contemporary context, one hears repeatedly the objection that not all sexual activity involves penetration by a phallus, even in heterosexual relationships. Why, then, should the absence of such penetration in homoerotic relationships (particularly lesbian) deny their legitimacy? Yet that misses the point. The point is not that sexual intimacy must always and only involve phallic penetration (as if all kissing, caressing, and other forms of sexual contact would have to cease) but rather that the fittedness of the penis and vagina provide clues as to how God desires sexual pairing to be organized by gender. The anatomical clues point to God's intention that human sexuality involves opposite-sex pairing as opposed to same-sex pairing.

When Epictetus (a first-century C.E. Stoic philosopher) criticized a young student of rhetoric for plucking the hairs out of his legs, he did not focus his argument on the obscuring of male dominance. Instead he argues that the student was taking extraordinary pains to erase the masculine stamp given to him by nature:

> Woman is born smooth and dainty by nature, and if she is very hairy she is a prodigy, and is exhibited in Rome. . . . But for a man not to be hairy is the same thing, and if by nature he has no hair he is a prodigy, but if he . . . plucks it out of himself, what shall we make of him? . . . "I will show you," we say to the audience, "a man who wishes to be a woman rather than a man." What a dreadful spectacle! . . . Man, what reason have you to complain against your nature? Because it brought you into the world as a man? . . . Make a clean sweep of the whole matter; eradicate . . . the cause of your hairiness; make yourself a woman all over, so

as not to deceive us, not half-man and half-woman. Whom do you wish to please? Frail womankind? Please them as a man. "Yes, but they like smooth men." Oh, go hang! And if they like sexual perverts, would you have become such a pervert? . . . Leave the man a man. . . . How treat your paltry body, then? As its nature is. . . . What then? Does the body have to be left unclean?—God forbid! but the man that you are and were born to be, keep that man clean, a man to be clean as a man, a woman as a woman. . . . No, but let's pluck out also the lion's mane . . . and the cock's comb, for he too ought to be "cleaned up"! Clean? Yes, but clean as a cock, and the other clean as a lion . . . ! (*Diatr.* 3.1.27-45 [Oldfather, LCL])[26]

---

26. Epictetus extended this argument to beards in *Diatr.* 1.16.9-14: "Has not nature used even [the hairs on a chin] in the most suitable way possible? Has she not by these means distinguished between the male and female? . . . Again, in the case of women, just as nature has mingled in their voice a certain softer note, so likewise she has taken the hair from their chins. . . . Wherefore, we ought to preserve the signs God has given; we ought not to throw them away; we ought not, so far as in us lies, to confuse the sexes which have been distinguished in this fashion" (LCL). Similarly, in Athenaeus's *Deipnosophists* the story is recounted of Diogenes of Sinope, who once accosted an effeminate man with shaven chin for "finding fault with nature" for making him a man rather than a woman, a story that is then used to blast pederastic philosophers for "indulging in passion contrary to nature" (13.565C). Musonius Rufus, Epictetus's teacher, taught that the beard should not be cut; but he also had an explanation for why some cutting of the hair on one's head was not unnatural. "A man should cut the hair from the head for the same reason that we prune a vine, that is merely to remove what is useless. . . . the beard (should not) be cut . . . (for it) has been provided for us by nature as a kind of cover or protection (compare Paul's argument that the hair on a woman's head is given to her by nature for a covering, 1 Cor 11:14-15). Moreover, the beard is nature's symbol of the male just as is the crest of the cock and the mane of the lion. . . . The remark of Zeno was well made that it is quite as natural to cut the hair as it is to let it grow long, in order not to be burdened by too much of it nor hampered for any activity. For *nature plainly keeps a more careful guard against deficiency than against excess*, in both plants and animals, since the removal of excess is much easier and simpler than the addition of what is lacking. In both cases *man's common sense ought to assist nature.* . . . Therefore the hair should be cut only to get rid of too much of it and not for looks . . . " (XXI, Lutz). No one today would accept the argument that to shave is to "confuse the sexes" and so one may justifiably point to a flaw in the argument. Still, the general point holds: those who go to extraordinary lengths to deny what nature has bestowed bodily to distinguish the sexes (and most today would still put men plucking hairs for beautification purposes in that category) are engaging in an "unnatural" activity.

The same principle ultimately lies behind the critique of homeroti-cism: It denies the sexual, bodily gender differences of male and female and attempts a merger that nature never intended, that is, for which complementary sex organs were not provided. It amounts to a complaint against the "gendered body" that God/nature gave.

To be sure (as Brooten points out), Paul's discussion of veils in 1 Cor 11:3-16 maintains a distinction in gender dressing for the sexes on the grounds that God has ordained man to be the "head" of the woman. Paul understands men as the image and glory of God while women are only the glory of man, and that woman was made from and created for man. The problematic v. 10 ("the woman ought to have authority on/over her head") possibly means that the women prophets ought to wear the appropriate head covering as a sign that they are under the authority of men; more likely, though, that they ought to have or take authority over their own head by wearing the appropriate covering.[27] In any case, it would not be surprising, given some of the arguments he employs in 1 Cor 11:1-16, if gender hierarchy were one of Paul's concerns in his discussion of homosexuality in Rom 1:26-27. Nevertheless, there are good reasons for thinking that for Paul in Rom 1:26-27 the blurring of gender stratification, if a factor at all, was secondary to the blurring of gender itself.

---

27. This is the view taken by Schrage, Fee, and Collins; also Richard B. Hays, *First Corinthians* (IBC; Louisville: John Knox, 1997), 187-88. Alternatively, the head covering functions as the sign of, or means by which a woman exercises, her right to prophesy. The remark "because of the angels" at the end of the same verse probably picks up on the rationale of the Corinthian women prophets and turns it against them. The Corinthian women prophets may have claimed that they could not wear a head covering because, having been made like angels by virtue of their participation in Christ, gender boundaries had been transcended (cf. Gal 3:28)—particularly at those moments when they exercised angelic authority in prophesying or speaking the language of angels (1 Cor 13:1). Paul countered: it was precisely "because of the angels" that the women prophets should exercise their newly acquired authority by taking responsibility for their own head, for they "must be covered to keep the heavenly host from a misplaced worship of man whose glory [they] reflect" (Antoinette Clark Wire, *The Corinthian Women Prophets* [Minneapolis: Fortress, 1990], 121). Scholars disagree over whether Paul's remarks in 11:1-16 refer to a covering in addition to the woman's hair or to a distinctive hairstyle (tying the hair up on top of the head rather than having the hair hang loose). The language of "covering down" that Paul recommends for women prophesying and the shameful alternative of having the hair shorn or shaved (11:5-6) suggest the former.

First, not even in 1 Cor 11:3-16 is total male dominance the overriding consideration. Paul is careful to qualify his argument for male headship with the point that neither male nor female exists without the other and that men are born from women (11:11-12). Paul is not trying to take away the right of women to prophesy but only to have them prophesy with sensitivity to gender distinctions. Elsewhere in his letters Paul undermines conventional, subordinate roles for women. In Romans 16, for instance, he mentions numerous female co-workers. In 1 Cor 7:3-4, he insists on the mutuality of conjugal rights. Finally, he pronounces that in the community of the baptized there is "neither male and female" (Gal 3:28). Scholars have long recognized a distinction between the more liberating perspective of the genuine Pauline epistles and the less liberating stance toward women in the deuteropauline letters (especially the Pastorals).

Second, given the previous point and the significantly more severe responses that Paul takes toward homoeroticism in Rom 1:26-27 and 1 Cor 6:9, it seems unlikely that Paul's main concern with homosexual practice is that it threatens male dominance.[28] A more credible interpretation is that for Paul homoeroticism constitutes an extreme expression of human revolt against the divinely ordained natural order and not just a subversion of customary gender roles. In fact, Paul regards homosexual intercourse as such an obvious violation of the natural order that gentiles who do not know Scripture are without excuse when they engage in such behavior. Something even more basic than gender stratification is at stake: nothing less than gender differentiation itself. The case is similar to that of incest, which Paul treats in 1 Corinthians 5 and for which he recommends expulsion from the community. Even the "pagans/gentiles" in general recognize this to be sexual immorality. The issue is not primarily about hierarchy and dominance (or about abusive relationships or procreation, for that matter), though social organization is involved. It has to do with mixing two things that were never intended by God to be mixed—in the words of Lev 18:17, they are the same "flesh" (even if, as here, a man and his stepmother are

28. Cf. Balz, "Biblische Aussagen zur Homosexualität," 67: In 1 Cor 11:2-16 "it is a matter of rules for the life of the congregation, whereas homosexuality is connected with fundamental questions of 'righteous' and 'unrighteous' in general, thus with every behavior which divides humans from God."

involved). More than likely Paul was also opposed to bestiality so the same could be said here: the issue went deeper than the matter of dominance.

Third, if one wants to argue that Paul's primary reason for rejecting homosexual behavior was his concern that male social superiority over females not be undermined, then one has to explain why it is that Paul's position toward homosexual behavior (and the position of all biblical writers, and no doubt of Jesus himself) was *more* uncompromising than that of the prevailing Greco-Roman culture. The Greeks and Romans approved of certain forms of homosexual behavior, particularly in cases where the passive or penetrated partners were social inferiors. In a system where social hierarchy is the primary concern, such concessions are quite understandable. The fact that biblical authors made no such concessions suggests that their concern was broader than status differentiation. Brooten, Nissinen, and others have to argue, in effect, that Paul and Jesus were simply more misogynistic than their Greek and Roman contemporaries. Surely, such an argument has little merit. It is more plausible to argue that the biblical writers had in view another concern: gender differentiation, viewed not as a tool for holding women down as social inferiors but as a structural design divinely imbedded in creation for the health and vitality of the human race.

Fourth, on lexical grounds there is little basis for claiming that Paul's references to "nature" refer to contingent cultural norms. Outside of Rom 1:26 Paul uses *physis* in six texts. In four of these the dative *physei* ("by nature") is used (Gal 2:15; 4:8; Rom 2:14; 2:27). The fifth (Rom 11:21, 24) contains three occurrences of *kata physin* and one occurrence of *para physin*.

(1) Gal 4:7-9: "You (gentiles) are (now) children of God. . . . However, at one time, not knowing God, you were enslaved to things (or: beings) which by nature (*physei*) are not gods; but now, knowing God—or rather, having been known by God—how can you turn back again to the weak and wretched elements (*stoicheia*) which again, once more, you want to serve as slaves? You are observing days and months and set times and years!"[29]

29. Works consulted include: J. Louis Martyn, *Galatians* (AB; New York: Doubleday, 1997); Richard N. Longenecker, *Galatians* (WBC; Dallas: Word Books, 1990);

The specific, contextual sense of *physei* in Gal 4:8 hinges on the meaning of the referent for "things which by nature are not gods": the "elements." The key to the latter's meaning lies in Wis 13:1-9, a text that we have already seen to be the closest parallel to Rom 1:18-23. Gentiles who were foolishly "unable from the good things that are seen to know the one who exists . . . supposed that either fire or wind or swift air, or the circle of the stars, or turbulent water, or the luminaries of the heaven were the gods that rule the world" (13:1-2 NRSV). Ancient Greek sophists centuries earlier had already distinguished between gods that were so "by nature" (*physei*, though "in reality" astral bodies) and gods that were so only "by human convention" (*thesei*; cf. Plato, *Laws* 889E, 904A). *Nature* here for Paul, as a Jew, is that which something truly is by virtue of its creation. The things that the gentiles once foolishly worshiped as "gods" were in reality the good "works" or "created things" that God made (Wis 13:1, 5). "By nature" in Gal 4:8 thus means "in their created essence, their natural essence as established by the Creator," *as opposed to* popular opinion and convention.[30]

(2) Gal 2:14-16: "If you (Cephas), being a Jew, live like a gentile and not like a Jew, how can you compel the gentiles to 'Judaize' (= live like Jews)? We, by nature (*physei*) Jews and not sinners from gentile peoples,. . . even *we* believed in Christ Jesus, in order that we might be justified from the faith in/of Christ and not from works of the law."

Here Paul points out the irony of Peter, a Jew who lives like a gentile, compelling gentiles to live like Jews (2:14). Even though Peter and Paul were "Jews by nature" and not gentiles, they nevertheless proved themselves to be no better off then gentiles, both alike seeking justification through faith in Christ. Here "by nature" means something like "by physical or biological descent," "by ethnic lineage," or (as in most English translations) "by birth."[31] It thus refers to what one physically is through birth inheritance, not one what one feels or desires, much less to conventional ways of doing things.

(3) Rom 2:14-15: "For when gentiles who do not have the law by nature

---

James D. G. Dunn, *The Epistle to the Galatians* (BNTC; Peabody, Mass.: Hendrickson, 1993); Hans Dieter Betz, *Galatians* (Hermeneia; Philadelphia: Fortress, 1979).

30. Cf. "in their essential nature" (Koester; similarly, Betz, NEB); possibly, though perhaps too loosely, "in the true nature of things" (Dunn), "in reality" (Dunn, Longenecker), or "really . . . at all" (NJB; cf. REB).

31. BAGD has "natural endowment or condition (inherited from one's ancestors)." Koester refers to "by original descent, in essence, in their true nature" (*"physis,"* TDNT 9:272).

(*physei*)[32] do the things required by the law, these (gentiles), not having the law, are a law to themselves; who demonstrate the work required by the law (to be) written in their hearts, their conscience bearing them joint witness. . . . "

The meaning of "by nature" in Rom 2:14 appears to be something like "through a natural, inborn capacity" (Moo), "by instinct" or "instinctively" (Sanday and Headlam, MOFFATT, NRSV, NLT), "through their own innate sense" (NJB).[33] The reference, however, is not to any innate desire (excluding, for example, those produced by sin operating in the flesh since birth, the "law of sin" in Rom 7:23) but to a capacity for moral discernment implanted by God in humans at creation, a capacity which some gentiles are still able to follow some of the time (but without any greater prospect of justification than Jews). A good paraphrase would be: "by the natural faculty of reason implanted by the Creator in human bodies."

(4) Rom 2:27: "And the person who by nature (*physei*) is uncircumcised (lit., the uncircumcision by nature) will, by fulfilling the law, judge you who (even) through (the medium of the) letter (of the law) and circumcision (are) a transgressor of the law."

The probable meaning of "by nature" in Rom 2:27 is one that approximates its sense in Gal 2:15: "by birth or 'natural' origin" (Moo), "by virtue of his birth" (Cranfield), "owing to his Gentile birth" (Sanday and Headlam), "as a result of his natural, gentile ethnicity," "because of biological descent" (cf. Barrett: "by race"; not, as Byrne translates, "by upbringing"); that is, gentiles who are uncircumcised because they are biologically descended from people groups other than the Jews (the biological descendants of Abraham). Possible but less likely is the meaning "physically" (NRSV, NAB, NIV, REB, RSV, NASB,

---

32. It is not entirely clear whether "by nature" goes with what precedes (so Stanley Stowers, C. E. B. Cranfield, Paul Achtemeier) or with what follows (so nearly everyone else). If the phrase goes with what precedes, then it must have the pregnant meaning "by birthright" (Stowers) or "by virtue of their birth" (Cranfield); that is, it would refer to "Gentiles who do not have the law by right of physical descent." In that event the meaning would closely approximate the sense suggested for Gal 2:15. However, the standard interpretation (viz., that "by nature" goes with the following "doing") is more likely given: (1) the placement of the word after rather than within the preceding participial clause (as in Gal 4:8; cf. Rom 2:27); (2) the subsequent references to "law written in their hearts" and to "conscience"; and (3) the widespread Greek tradition of "unwritten law" or "law of nature" (cf. Rom 7:23; Cicero, *Leg.* 1.6.18; Philo, *Good Person* 46 and *Abr.* 275-76).

33. Given extra-biblical parallels, the translation preferred by BAGD is unlikely to be correct: "when Gentiles fulfill the law's demands *by following the natural order* (of things)." BAGD adds: "[*physei*] may mean instinctively."

PHILLIPS, MOFFATT, Käsemann), not just in the sense "by physical descent" but perhaps in the sense "bodily." In favor of this reading is the context: the person who is uncircumcised "in body" but who, by virtue of keeping the law, shows himself to be circumcised in heart (2:26, 29) will judge the Jew who is circumcised in body only. However, the context does not demand this interpretation. Had Paul intended this sense one might have expected the phrase *en sarki* ("in the flesh," 2:28) rather than *physei*. Yet, regardless of which of the two senses one chooses, the meaning of "nature" in Rom 2:27 goes beyond mere social convention.[34]

(5) Rom 11:21, 24: "For if God did not spare the natural (*kata physsin*) branches, (do not become high-minded [11:20]) lest somehow[35] he spares not even you. . . . And even those (branches; unbelieving Jews), if they do not persist in unbelief, will be grafted in. . . . For if you were cut off from the wild olive tree (to which you belonged) by nature (*kata physin*) and were grafted, beyond nature (*para physin*), into a cultivated olive tree, how much more can these natural (*kata physin*) (branches, the Jews) be grafted into their own olive tree."

Here nature clearly has to do not with innate desires or social convention but with the organic unity of branches to the tree from which they originally sprouted. What is "beyond" or "contrary to" nature is the circumvention of natural processes of growth with artificial, human intervention. In this particular case, however, such a circumvention of nature is not treated as a negative act because olive trees do grow branches; *while supplementing or aiding nature, one is not trying to fit together two discordant entities.* The same could not be said for sexual intercourse between two males, in the view of Paul, Philo, Josephus, and many Greco-Roman moral philosophers, since no two males possess complementary sex organs. To attempt to join two members of the same sex is to act contrary to nature's bodily and physiological provision for human sexuality.[36]

---

34. Paul was not referring in Rom 2:27 to the uncircumcised state of gentiles as "natural," as if in so doing he hoped to denigrate circumcision as an "unnatural" practice (cf. NEB: "uncircumcised in his natural state"). Neither did he imply that the act of circumcising a Jew was "natural," as though forgetting that cutting is an unnatural act because of "the close identification between circumcision and the Jewish race" (Dunn). Nor did he intend to designate those who had remained gentiles in distinction to gentiles who had become circumcised as proselytes (*contra* Koester, *TDNT* 9:272; Fitzmyer).

35. The reading "lest somehow" (*mē pōs*) is omitted by a number of important manuscripts and is textually suspect.

36. For a discussion of the meaning of *kata physin* and *para physin* here in relation to Rom 1:26-27, see n. 68, pp. 390-91 below.

In all of these instances, "nature" corresponds to the essential material, inherent, biological, or organic constitution of things as created and set in motion by God. Neither in Paul's thinking nor in our own do any of these uses pertain merely to personal preferences or prejudices, custom, a culturally conditioned sense of what is normal, or social convention. "Nature" in these verses goes beyond what one feels and thinks to what simply "is" by divine design. The elements earth, water, fire, air, and the celestial bodies (sun, moon, stars) are what they are by virtue of the way God shaped them (Gal 4:8). Branches grow from trees without any say in the matter (Rom 11:21, 24). In general Jews are biological descendants of Abraham (Gal 2:15) and gentiles are biological descendants of other ancestors (Rom 2:27), irrespective of what they feel.[37] Even Jews must admit that gentiles, although often acting like animals, from time to time exhibit an instinctive, rational capacity for moral discernment that bears some resemblance to the written law (Rom 2:14). To whatever extent their consciences have not been seared, gentiles owe this faculty to God's handiwork in creation. Moreover, in none of these instances does Paul use "nature" to refer to conditions that are innate but due to sin operating in human flesh since the fall of Adam.[38]

One final usage of *physis* occurs in Paul that deserves special attention. Unlike the other occurrences of *physis* in Paul, 1 Cor 11:14-15 appears at first to demonstrate that Paul's use of the concept *nature* does at times conflate with cultural customs.[39] The text reads:

---

37. We recognize, and indeed to some extent Paul himself must have recognized (based on OT genealogical lists, the fictive kin relationships of covenants, and the phenomenon of proselytes), that the question of the biological connectedness of every Jew to Abraham was complex. Paul, however, is speaking in general terms. The exceptions merely establish the rule.

38. This is not to say that Paul could never have used "nature," especially "by nature," in a sense that has little to do with "nature" in the proper sense (e.g., in the sense "fundamentally" or "essentially") or used it with reference to things that are morally bad; probably he did. Cf. Eph 2:3 which may or may not reflect Pauline idiom, but which clearly gives a different sense to "nature" than that found in Rom 1:26: "we were children of wrath by nature," that is, "in our natural condition (as descendants of Adam)" (BAGD; NLT correctly paraphrases as "we were born with an evil nature"). Rather, the point is that the extant evidence provides some guidance as to Paul's usual use of the word.

39. Cf. Boswell: "The only instance in which 'nature' seems to have a moral signifi-

Does not even nature itself teach you that if a man lets the hair on his head grow long (*komą*) it is a disgrace for him, but if a woman lets the hair on her head grow long (*komą*) it is a glorious thing for her? For the hair of the/her head (*hē komē*) has been given to her[40] for a covering. (1 Cor 11:14-15)

Even here, there appears to be an element in Paul's reasoning that we would ascribe to nature in the proper sense—and Paul himself clearly distinguishes this argument from the next one based on church "custom" in 11:16. The interpretive confusion surrounding this text stems from the assumption that Paul thinks that nature proves that women can grow longer hair than men. Yet the explanatory clause ("for") in 11:15 establishes that for Paul long hair on women was an inference that could be drawn from direct observation of nature, that women have hair on their head for a covering, not that nature itself directly granted *long* hair only to women.[41]

Nature in the proper sense (not custom) has indeed given to a woman

---

cance for Paul greater than simply 'human nature' is 1 Cor. 11:14. . . . But it would be fatuous to imagine that 'nature' even in the most idealized sense could have an effect on the length of a man's hair. . . . Clearly Paul here uses 'nature' in the sense of custom, tradition, or ethical heritage, ignoring (or rejecting) the usual dichotomy in Greek between custom and nature" (*Homosexuality*, 110 n. 63). Countryman thinks that Paul used "nature" in 1 Cor 11:14 to mean "something like 'widespread social usage.'" However, he does not think that such a sense is relevant to Paul's understanding of "nature" in Rom 1:26-27 because there an argument from "widespread social usage" would "fall flat" in view of widespread acceptance of homosexual intercourse in the Greek world. Instead, he thinks "nature" in Rom 1:26-27 referred to the fact "that Gentiles experienced only heterosexual desire before God visited uncleanness on them and have therefore changed their 'nature,' that is, lost a certain continuity with their remotest past" (*Dirt, Greed, and Sex*, 114; similarly, Scanzoni and Mollenkott, *Is the Homosexual My Neighbor?*, 63-64).

40. "To her" is textually uncertain.

41. The consensus among interpreters is that the causal clause in v. 15 at the very least infers "long hair" and indeed a few translations (W. Schrage, NAB, NIV, PHILLIPS) reflect this: "for the (i.e., her) *long hair* has been given to her for a covering." BAGD translates "(long) hair." However, despite the meaning of the related verb *komaō* as "to let the hair grow long, to grow long," LSJ gives as the meaning of the noun *komē* "hair of the head," not "long hair." The usage in the LXX (twelve times), Josephus (nineteen times), Philo (three times), and Greek Pseudepigrapha texts (two times) bears out this sense. With the possible sole exception of Josephus's *Ant.* 14 §45, "long hair" is never required as a translation of *komē* in these texts and usually is positively excluded by the context.

the hair on her head. It might then be a reasonable conclusion to say with Paul that nature gives us a clue that head coverings (including veils) are appropriate for women: "for the hair on her head has been given to her for a covering" (11:15b). The logic of Paul's argument goes something like this:

(1) Nature has given women hair on their heads, and this hair serves as a covering.
(2) This should teach us that long hair is appropriate for women, not for men.
(3) This should in turn teach us that a head covering, such as a veil, is appropriate for women and not for men.

As readers, we might say, "Why not attribute the same to men since nature also gives men hair for a covering?"

Perhaps Paul allows his judgment to be blinded by cultural convention but the inconsistency in the argument appears so obvious that one has to wonder whether Paul does not have some other basis from nature itself for drawing his conclusion. In my view the most likely explanation, and one that is consistent with the Stoic rationale of the time, is that Paul is thinking of the tendency for many men (including himself?) to develop baldness.

There are, of course, also some women who go bald, but the notion of baldness as a condition generally associated with men still remains. Just as the phenomenon of the "bearded lady" would not undermine Epictetus's point that chin hairs are one of nature's ways of differentiating men from women, so bald women do not destroy the general truth that baldness is a characteristically male trait. Around 400 C.E., the Neoplatonist philosopher Synesius of Cyrene argued that "hair of the head" (*hē komē*) is more "fitting" for women than men, a fact

doubtlessly determined by both custom (or: convention, law: *nomos*) and nature; by custom, since the hair of the head is good (or: beautiful: *kalos*) neither for all males, nor everywhere, nor at all times for the same men. . . . but for women it is always and for all women and everywhere a good (or: beautiful) thing to give serious attention to the treatment of her hair. Yet nature also agrees with the law. . . . If any shedding of hair occurs, (you will say) that this woman suffers from some kind of disease or illness, and by the least bit of attention it returns to what it is by nature (i.e., a full head of hair). But of men who are also worthy to be called men it is not easy to say who has not first arrived at this condition (of hair loss as a result) of nature. In fact, because of this very thing, it (i.e., baldness) seems also to be the ultimate goal (*telos*) of nature, even though it does not befall all men. And just as the children of farmers, understanding from the impulse of healthy plants how they want by nature to grow straight up, support as many of them as do not have strength from themselves to do this with poles and stakes, so since all those whose nature is best appear to be in a condition (of baldness) approaching my own, we must set straight with a razor those who do not share our condition and be of assistance to nature. (*Baldness* 14)[42]

The significant loss of head hair on a woman immediately occasions speculation that she is afflicted by some illness or disease; it is "unnatural." The reaction to baldness in a man is altogether different, for people recognize that baldness is a natural course of affairs for men. Nature, by depriving many men of some or all of the hair on their head (particularly with advancing age) and making that phenomenon much rarer among women, provides a clue for us all. In other words, men who allow the hair on their head to grow long are debasing their masculine stamp, while women who maintain short hair are debasing their feminine stamp.

The perspective of Musonius Rufus, cited above, is pertinent: "nature plainly keeps a more careful guard against deficiency than against excess." In other words, not the excess of hair on the heads of some men but the deficiency that many men experience in contrast to women is the best clue regarding nature's design. Hence, the fact that women have greater success in retaining head hair than do men is, in

---

42. The following translations were consulted: Augustine Fitzgerald, ed., *The Essays and Hymns of Synesius of Cyrene* (London: Oxford University Press, 1930), 2.243-74; George H. Kendal (ed.), *In Praise of Baldness* (Vancouver: Pharmakon, 1985). The treatise is a semi-lighthearted response to a discourse by Dio Chrysostom (40–115 C.E.) in praise of hair, a discourse that made Synesius feel ashamed of being bald already in his twenties. About ten years after writing this work, Synesius was baptized and elected bishop of the Cyrenean diocese of Ptolemais.

Paul's view, nature's way of teaching us that long hair is appropriate for women and inappropriate for men. Women *must* have a covering for their head; for men it is at best only an option. It is thus consistent with nature's teaching that women wear an additional covering on their heads when worshiping (11:5). The "glory" of men, however, evidently does not consist in having a covering for their heads; otherwise nature would not promote hair loss for men. Therefore, it would be dishonorable for men to go out of their way to supply an additional head covering (11:4).[43]

Even if we grant that this is what Paul is thinking, however, it does not make the overall argument credible. Few Christians today follow Paul in arguing that Christian women should wear hats when attending church. Paul himself seems to have recognized that his point was hardly self-evident. He adds this argument from nature only after making several other pleas, including the cryptic "because of the angels." He also immediately adds another appeal to ecclesiastical "custom"[44] since he suspects the Corinthians will not find his logic convincing (contrast the argument from nature in Rom 1:26-27 which is the *only* argument Paul needs inasmuch as the complementarity of male and female sex organs is obvious and convincing). My only point here is that, for Paul, *physis* means "nature" in the strict sense, although the

43. In light of this interpretation of *nature* in 1 Cor 11:14, I cannot understand Koester's comment: the technical use of *physis* here "is of no theological significance" (*TDNT* 9:273). An alternative explanation of what Paul may have been thinking of is hinted at by Schoedel ("Same-Sex Eros," 60-61 nn. 23, 26): Paul may have thought that female "softness" and "moistness," like good soil, allowed for the growth of long and luxuriant hair on the head, whereas male "hardness" tended to produce short, rough hair (citing Pseudo-Lucian's *Affairs* 26 and Galen's *De usu partium* 11.14).
44. *Custom* in v. 16 probably refers not to the custom of covering women's heads in worship (*contra* H. Conzelmann, *1 Corinthians* [Hermeneia; Philadelphia: Fortress, 1975], 191). Such a construal would cut against the grain of the argument in 11:2-15, which strongly advocates such a covering. Nor does it refer to a custom of being contentious (as in "it is not our custom to be contentious"; *contra* Calvin). Rather, *custom* probably alludes to a custom of women worshiping *without* a covering (correctly, G. Fee, C. K. Barrett, apparently W. Schrage): "but if anyone wants to be a lover of conflict (by advocating that women should be able to worship without a head covering), we do not have such a custom (i.e., of women worshiping with uncovered heads), nor do the churches of God."

inferences Paul draws from nature have to be evaluated on a case-by-case basis.

What is clear from these texts is that Brooten and Nissinen have ignored or downplayed the importance of the anatomical (and procreative) complementarity of male and female for Paul's negative assessment of same-sex intercourse. For Paul, same-sex intercourse was not just a dishonoring of gender dispositions, much less of cultural conventions, but a dishonoring of gendered "bodies" (Rom 1:24) through a blatant and foolhardy disregard of the visible physical (and functional) differences of men and women. Further, same-sex intercourse is comparable to idolatry in its deliberate suppression of the visible evidence in creation for the attributes of the true Creator (Rom 1:18-23).

Boswell's approach to the meaning of *nature* shares some similarities with that of Brooten. According to Boswell:

> The concept of "natural law" was not fully developed until more than a millennium after Paul's death, and it is anachronistic to read it into his words. For Paul, "nature" was not a question of universal law or truth but, rather, a matter of the *character* of some person or group of persons, a character which was largely ethnic and entirely human: Jews are Jews "by nature," just as Gentiles are Gentiles "by nature." "Nature" is not a moral force for Paul: men may be evil or good "by nature," depending on their own disposition. A possessive is always understood with "nature" in Pauline writings: it is not "nature" in the abstract but *someone's* "nature," the Jews' "nature" or the Gentiles' "nature" or even the pagan gods' "nature". . . . "Nature" in Romans 1:26, then, should be understood as the *personal* nature of the pagans in question. . . . Romans 1 did not condemn homosexual behavior as "against nature" in the sense of the violation of "natural law." No clear idea of "natural law" existed in Paul's time or for many centuries thereafter.[45]

Like Brooten, Boswell refers to nature as a personal disposition or trait. Unlike her, he does not think that Paul operated with a concept of "natural law" or gave his argument from nature any *inherent* moral force. For Boswell, "nature" in Rom 1:26-27 has more to do with the natural predisposition of men and women to be attracted to one

---

45. *Christianity, Social Tolerance, and Homosexuality*, 110-11, 114.

another than with predispositions that justify gender stratification in sexual roles. Boswell's argument will be dealt with more fully in section III below, but some of the issues he raises are similar enough to Brooten's to warrant preliminary discussion here.

The dichotomy that Boswell poses between *natural law* on the one hand and someone's *personal character* or *disposition* is helpful, but only to a point. Natural law often pertains not just to those principles from nature that are equally applicable to all creatures and things but also to principles germane only to specific classes (for example, humans, birds, fish, or stars). Moreover, for this description of Paul's use of the word *nature* to be accurate, the words *character* or *disposition* would have to be taken in their broadest sense and by no means limited to personality traits or inclinations, inborn or otherwise. Being a Jew (Gal 2:15) or a gentile (Rom 2:27) and possessing the faculty of reason and of conscience (Rom 2:14) are not, strictly speaking, personality traits. Character is an even less applicable designation for the essence of stars as created things (Gal 4:8) or the organic unity of a tree and its branches (Rom 11:21, 24). These so-called dispositions are qualities bestowed through the medium of nature. The meaning of personal disposition or essential character of a person or thing does not apply at all to those instances where *physis* is something other than a dative of respect (Rom 1:26; 11:21, 24; 1 Cor 11:14).

The distinction that Boswell raises is perhaps better stated as a distinction not between natural law and personal character but between nature as a teacher of moral principles and nature as what simply is (without reference to morality). It is true that, in general, when Paul uses *physis* as a dative of respect ("by nature") he primarily has the latter sense in mind (Gal 2:15; 4:8; Rom 2:14, 27; cf. Eph 2:3), though even that admission would have to be qualified since every one of the instances cited above has a positive didactic quality. Yet it is apparent that nature is serving as a moral teacher for Paul in Rom 1:26-27 (as in the parallel argument against idolatry in 1:18-23).

Furthermore, the claim that "no clear idea of 'natural law' existed in Paul's time or for many centuries thereafter" is false. We have already seen that both Philo and (to a lesser extent) Josephus, drawing on Greco-Roman popular philosophy, could make appeals to the way things are constituted in nature and creation as a basis for moral instruction concerning God's design for human sexuality. Philo, indeed, uses the expression "law[s] of nature," as well as comparable phrases such as "unwritten [law of] nature."[46] Particularly in connection with issues of sexuality and gender distinction it was commonplace in antiquity to draw conclusions about proper behavior based on the *visible, bodily* differences between male and female in nature. We saw this to be the case both in Epictetus's argument against men shaving their body hair for purposes of beautification and in Paul's argument for why women should have a head covering when praying or prophesying.

Given the context for Rom 1:26-27, where Paul has just critiqued idolatry on the grounds of what can be clearly *seen in material* creation, there is every reason to conclude that by "nature" Paul means the clear anatomical and procreative compatibility of male and female sex organs. From this observable complementarity Paul (like other Jews) argued that gentiles should be able to draw the conclusion that God did not intend sexual intercourse to be conducted among members of the same sex. This, and not the desire to maintain male dominance in human society, is what Paul primarily had in mind when he spoke of same-sex intercourse as "contrary to nature."

III. The Bible has no category for "homosexuals" with an exclusively same-sex orientation; same-sex passion was thought to originate in over-sexed heterosexuals.

Dale Martin and Victor Furnish, among others, have argued that since ancient moralists regarded homosexuality as a manifestation of an insatiable heterosexual lust and we do not, their opposition to homosexuality (including Paul's) must be disregarded in our own society.[47] The main text they cite is from Dio Chrysostom, *Disc.* 7:151-152:

---

46. Koester argues that Philo advanced the Stoic discussion of natural law through his equation of the didactic character of nature with the Mosaic law (*TDNT* 9:265-66, 269).

47. Martin, "Heterosexism," 339-49 (for ancient moralists homoerotic desire was a "natural" but "inordinate desire," not a "disoriented desire," p. 342); V. Furnish, *The Moral Teaching of Paul*, 60-65; idem, "The Bible and Homosexuality," 26-27; Bartlett, "A Biblical Perspective on Homosexuality," 138, 140. Stowasser makes it a "decisive" hermeneutical consideration that Paul allegedly treated homosexual

The man whose (sexual) appetite is insatiate in such things (viz., referring to ready access to female prostitutes through brothels). . . will have
contempt for the easy conquest and scorn for a woman's love, as a thing
too readily given . . . and will turn his assault against male quarters . . .
believing that . . . he will find a pleasure difficult and hard to procure.

---

practice as a willing "turning away from their own actual heterosexuality"
("Homosexualität und Bibel," 519). "The analysis of the biblical texts has led to the
insight that homosexual acts were understood as an act of will, i.e., subjected to
free decision, and could therefore be forbidden and declared to be sinful." Once it
is recognized that homosexuality is not "a conscious choice to turn away from God"
one can no longer apply the concepts of "guilt and sin" to it (ibid., 522; similarly,
Wengst, "Paulus und die Homosexualität," 77-78). Stowasser does not explain why
he seems to regard the acting out of innate desires as beyond the realm of human
responsibility. Nor does he help us to understand why other forms of innate sexual desire (proclivity to multiple sexual partners, sexual attraction to children or animals) or non-sexual desire (violent or aggressive personality types, alcoholism)
which have a biological dimension are not validated along with homosexual desire.

According to Nissinen, "Paul refers to heterosexual people who knowingly and
voluntarily make themselves homosexuals" (*Homoeroticism*, 109). Nissinen is not
clear about what import to give this observation. On the one hand, he seems to suggest that the modern view about innate homosexual orientation would have made
no difference to Paul's opposition. He writes:

> Paul's criticism does not focus on homosexuals or heterosexuals but more gen-
> erally on persons who participate in same-sex erotic acts. The distinction
> between sexual orientations is clearly an anachronism that does not help to
> understand Paul's line of argumentation. Paul does not mention *tribades* or
> *kinaidoi*, that is, female and male persons who were habitually involved in
> homoerotic relationships, but if he knew about them (and there is every rea-
> son to believe that he did), it is difficult to think that, because of their appar-
> ent "orientation," he would *not* have included them in Romans 1:26-27 (109).
> . . . For him, there is no individual inversion or inclination that would make
> this conduct less culpable (110). . . . Presumably nothing would have made
> Paul approve homoerotic behavior (112).

On the other hand, Nissinen contends that Paul's assumption that homosexual
behavior was a voluntary act of heterosexuals means that Paul's views on homosexuality cannot be appropriated in our contemporary context. He writes:

> Paul, like his contemporaries, could not possibly take into consideration
> homosexual orientation or identity (111). . . . It would not be fair to claim that
> Paul would condemn all homosexuality everywhere, always, and in every
> form. Paul's arguments are based on certain Hellenistic Jewish moral codes
> that are culture-specific. . . . Paul cannot be held responsible for things he
> does not appear to know about—such as sexual orientation, which is not a vol-
> untary perversion (124). . . . Other biblical authors. . . . cannot be expected to
> give statements about questions for which they were not sufficiently equipped
> or knowledgeable. . . . Therefore it is dangerous to assume that the biblical

Other texts they cite are from: Seneca, *Ep.* 46, "On Master and Slave," 7 (a male slave is exploited sexually by his "master's drunkenness and his lust"); Philo, *Abr.* 135 (the men of Sodom, "unable to bear the satiety [viz., great wealth due to high crop yields], . . . shake off the yoke of the law of nature from their necks, chasing after . . . unlawful forms of copulation. . . . although being men they began mounting males. . . . they were conquered by a more forcible lust"); and John Chrysostom, *Hom. Rom.* 4 ("all such desire stems from a greed which will not remain within its usual bounds").[48]

A related view to that of Martin and Furnish has been expressed by John Boswell:

> [T]he persons Paul condemns are manifestly not homosexual: what he derogates are homosexual acts committed by apparently heterosexual persons. The whole point of Romans 1, in fact, is to stigmatize persons

---

authors would have opposed homosexuality even if they had shared modern ideas about it. We cannot possibly know what they would say today (125).

I cannot see how to harmonize these two groups of statements in Nissinen. If, as Nissinen has to concede, it is highly unlikely that Paul would have changed his view about homosexual behavior for those who had an innate inclination, how can current perspectives on the innateness of homosexual behavior make any difference in evaluating Paul's words? If "nothing would have made Paul approve homoerotic behavior," how can it be unfair "to claim that Paul would condemn all homosexuality everywhere, always, and in every form"?

48. Chrysostom (ca. 390), concerned to spare Paul of the charge that he was being unduly harsh toward people who experienced no sexual passion toward the opposite sex, interpreted "exchanged" and "having abandoned" in Rom 1:26-27 to mean that all women and men who engaged in same-sex intercourse were capable of satiating their sexual desire with members of the opposite sex (cited by Boswell, *Homosexuality,* 109). To the quotes given above can be added, *inter alia,* Musonius Rufus, "On Sexual Indulgence" XII: "Not the least significant part of the life of luxury and self-indulgence lies also in sexual excess; for example those who lead such a life crave a variety of loves not only lawful but unlawful ones as well, not women alone but also men; sometimes they pursue one love and sometimes another, and not being satisfied with those which are available, pursue those which are rare and inaccessible . . . "; and Pseudo-Lucian, *Affairs of the Heart,* 20: "In the beginning . . . life was in obedience to the authority of the laws that nature framed. . . . But little by little, descending from that magnificent height in the pits of pleasure, time was cutting strange and peculiar paths to enjoyment. Then wantonness, daring all, transgressed the laws of nature herself" (cf. pp. 165-66 n. 10).

who have rejected their calling, gotten off the true path they were once on. It would completely undermine the thrust of the argument if the persons in question were not "naturally" inclined to the opposite sex in the same way they were "naturally" inclined to monotheism. . . . Paul believed that the Gentiles knew of the truth of God but rejected it and likewise rejected their true "nature" as regarded their sexual appetites, going beyond what was "natural" for them and what was approved for the Jews. It cannot be inferred from this that Paul considered mere homoerotic attraction or practice morally reprehensible, since [Rom 1:26-27] strongly implies that he was not discussing persons who were by inclination gay and since he carefully observed, in regard to both the women and the men, that they charged or abandoned the "natural use" to engage in homosexual activities.[49]

It would be a caricature of Boswell's position to say that he is arguing that Paul is explicitly distinguishing between *natural* homosexuals who experience only desires for the same sex and *unnatural* homosexuals who are really overstimulated heterosexuals and then to accuse Boswell of a gross anachronism.[50] Boswell's point is that Paul thought *all* people who desired and engaged in same-sex intercourse were "naturally" heterosexual inasmuch as they were capable of satisfying their desires through intercourse with the opposite sex. Therefore, Paul's

---

49. Ibid., 109, 112-13. Cf. Edwards, *Gay/Lesbian Liberation*, 98; Scanzoni and Mollenkott, *Is the Homosexual My Neighbor?*, 63-66; Byrne, *Romans*, 70, 77; Bailey, *Homosexuality and the Western Christian Tradition*, 38, 157, 169, 173 (frequently distinguishing between homosexual "perverts," whom the Bible condemns, and homosexual "inverts," of whom the Bible does not speak).
50. Richard Hays's otherwise devastating critique of Boswell appears to me to be guilty of this. "His proposal falls apart completely *as exegesis of Paul* when we recognize that the whole conception of 'sexual orientation' is an anachronism when applied to this text. The idea that some individuals have an inherent disposition towards same-sex erotic attraction and are therefore constitutionally 'gay' is a modern idea. . . . It is, in short, a textbook case of 'eisegesis,' the fallacy of reading one's own agenda into a text" ("Relations Natural and Unnatural," 200-201). As noted below, it is not quite true to say that the notion of "inherent disposition" to homosexuality is only a modern concept. Hays and Boswell are actually agreed that Paul supposed homosexual behavior to be "the result of insatiable lust seeking novel and more challenging forms of self-gratification" (ibid., 200). They differ only in what to do with this knowledge: Boswell intimating that Paul might have arrived at a different conclusion about the "unnaturalness" of homosexuality if he had known what we know, Hays contending that it is irrelevant to Paul's point.

argument that same-sex intercourse was *para physin* would be "completely undermined" by the notion of "permanent sexual preference." Both Boswell and Martin also contend that *para* (plus accusative) in the phrase *para physin* in Rom 1:26 should be translated "beyond," "more than," or "in excess of" nature (owing to an excess of passion) instead of (Boswell) or, more precisely than (Martin), "contrary to" or "against."[51]

There are five problems with this position. First, whether *all* moralists viewed *all* homoerotic passion as an overflow of heterosexual desire is doubtful. In fact, there is considerable testimony in ancient sources to the belief that same-sex passions, at least in some cases, are congenital. The myth of human origins expounded in Plato's *Symposium* (189C–193D) seems to presuppose such a view (even as satire, it builds on pro-homosexual arguments in the culture for the innateness of homoerotic passion). In the same work Pausanias extolled love for males as springing not from the common, vulgar love associated with heterosexual desires but from "the Heavenly goddess" (181B). Aristotelian thought speculated that some males who desired to be penetrated by other males ("the effeminate") were so disposed "by nature" (i.e., because of a rectum that discreted small quantities of semen), and others "from habit" (i.e., because they were molested in childhood by men). Yet even the effeminate "by nature" are "constituted contrary to nature (*para physin*)," a mistake or "defect" in nature.[52] Philostratus (early third century C.E.) complained that a youth who failed to respond to his advances was "opposing the com-

---

51. Martin, "Heterosexism," 343-49; Boswell, *Homosexuality*, 111-14.
52. Aristotle, *Eth. Nic.* 1148b, lines 28-34; Pseudo-Aristotle, *Probl.* 4:26 (translations and discussion in Dover, *Greek Homosexuality*, 168-70; Boswell, *Homosexuality*, 49-50). See also the Hippocratic treatise *De victu* 1.28-29 which attributes homosexual development to a preponderance of sperm from the opposite-sex parent (with the female parent contributing sperm) or from an opposite-sex element within the sperm (cited by Schoedel, "Same-Sex Eros," 58). The full text of *Eth. Nic.* 1148b, lines 28-34 is as follows: "the (*sc.* intercourse or disposition) of sexual pleasures for males . . . occurs for some by nature (*physei*), but for others from habituation, as in the case of those who were abused from the time they were boys. So for all those for whom nature is the cause, no one would describe these persons as lacking in self-control, any more than they would women because they do not take the active sexual role but the passive (or: do not take in marriage but are married; or: do not mount sexually but are mounted)." The author of *Probl.* 4:26 has no dif-

mands of nature" (*Ep.* 64). Achilles Tatius (end of the third century C.E.) declared that a boy's kisses were "of nature" (*Leuc. Clit.* 2.38). Callicratidas in Pseudo-Lucian's *Affairs of the Heart* made the case that pederasty was "an ordinance enacted by divine laws" (48).[53] Brooten notes that some ancient medical writers concluded that homoerotic orientation originated in an inherited disease of the mind or (for women) in the anatomical deformity of an overly large clitoris, while astrologers attributed it to the configuration of the stars at birth.[54]

Such views are inconsistent with the notion that all homosexual activity occurs as a result of overstimulation or boredom from too much sex with women. Even the texts cited above from Dio Chrysostom, Seneca, and Philo do not state that all homosexual behavior can be attributed to this single cause. Bisexual individuals, perhaps, could be so described (heterosexuals exploring homoeroticism) but not all forms of homoerotic expression in antiquity were bisexual.[55] At the very least, it is likely that Paul (like Philo who made explicit reference to the creation myth propounded by Aristophanes in Plato's *Symposium*) was familiar with one or more of these theories. Moreover, he could not have been unaware of the existence of men whose sexual desire was oriented exclusively toward other males (the *kinaidoi*, for example).

---

iculty in speaking about what is "by nature" (innate) as "contrary to nature" (in disharmony with nature's usual distinguishing marks of male and female): *"Those who are effeminate by nature. . . are constituted contrary to nature (para physin)* for, though male, they are so disposed that this part of them (the rectum) is necessarily defective." Similarly, when Paul speaks of same-sex intercourse as "contrary to nature" he is not necessarily denying an innate component to homoerotic sexuality but rather emphasizing that same-sex intercourse is contrary to God's intended design for human sexuality manifested in the anatomical complementarity of male and female.

53. Scroggs, *The New Testament and Homosexuality*, 48-49; Boswell, *Homosexuality*, 49.
54. Brooten, *Love Between Women*, 140-41, 172, 242-43, 360-61; also, Boswell, *Homosexuality*, 52.
55. Bisexuality, too, could be regarded as natural: "The noble lover of beauty engages in love wherever he sees excellence and splendid natural endowment without regard for any difference in physiological detail. . . . The hunter has no special preference for male dogs. . . . So too will not the lover of human beauty be fairly and equably disposed toward both sexes, instead of supposing that males and females are as different in the matter of love as they are in their clothes" (Plutarch, *Dial. Love* 767 [Helmbold, LCL]).

Second, claiming that ancient moralists opposed homosexual expression *precisely for the reason that* homoerotic passion was excessive heterosexual lust is, so to speak, putting the cart before the horse. Philo, for example, thought that gluttonous eating by people could stimulate passions "even for brute beasts" (*Spec. Laws* 3.43) but who would seriously argue that Philo opposed bestiality primarily for the reason that it amounted to excess passion? The description of excess passion was a way of demeaning a desire that on other grounds had already been evaluated as abominable; otherwise, how would the author know to characterize the passion as excess? In other words, the characterization of homosexual desire as excessive lust is incidental or supplementary to a prior revulsion toward such conduct.[56]

Third, Martin's contention that in antiquity "homosexual desire is not itself 'contrary to nature'" is false.[57] To make such a claim Martin has to draw too great a divide between homoerotic desire and homoerotic action. He contends that the "'unnaturalness' of the desire has nothing to do with one man's erotic interest in another, but with the 'unnaturalness' of a man desiring to demean himself by enthusiastically assuming the despised, lower position appropriate for women."[58] Yet Philo could describe heterosexual desire as "passions [which] pay tribute to the laws of nature," as opposed to the passions "of men for males" (*Contempl. Life* 59). Moreover, Martin's claim that Paul would just as easily have applied the expression "dishonorable passions" to sexual passion for one's wife (because all passions for Paul were inherently dishonorable) is untenable.[59] It is likely that the expression

---

56. Cf. the comment by Maximus of Tyre in *Or.* 18 (late second century C.E.): "Periander, tyrant of Ambracia, had a young man . . . as his boyfriend, but since their relationship was immorally constituted, it was a matter of lust not love" (*The Philosophical Orations* [trans. M. B. Trapp; Oxford: Clarendon, 1997]). Maximus was distinguishing between virtuous and vicious love among both same-sex and opposite-sex unions, but the principle is the same.

57. Martin, "Heterosexism," 346. Martin himself acknowledges that some Greco-Roman texts speak of "unnatural desires" (p. 344). Philo speaks of "abominable lusts" and a "polluted and accursed passion" (*Spec. Laws* 2.50), and "a pleasure contrary to nature" (ibid., 3.39). Josephus uses the expression "pleasures which were disgusting and contrary to nature" (*Ag. Ap.* 2.275).

58. "Heterosexism," 344-45.

59. Ibid., 347-48.

"dishonoring of their bodies among themselves" in 1:24 does not, and could never for Paul, refer to married heterosexual unions. First Corinthians 7:2-5, 9 presupposes the satisfaction of sexual passion in marriage so that such passion will not "burn" to the point of exceeding divinely ordained boundaries and lead to adultery. One function of sex within a marriage is to prevent passions from boiling over into "dishonorable" passions, not to preclude passion altogether.[60]

Similarly and more recently, David E. Fredrickson has made a special point of arguing that the word "use" (*chrēsis*) in Rom 1:26-27 is indeterminate with respect to gender: "neither the gender of the subject nor that of the object is material to the concept of use."[61] He then combines this observation with another; namely, the association some Greco-Roman moralists made between "natural use" and the avoidance of excess passion or even of passion altogether.[62] From these two points he concludes that the issue for Paul in Rom 1:26-27 is not so much the choice of a *same-sex* sexual partner as the unrestrained pursuit of desire and the loss of sexual self-control.[63] "Sexual activity between males is not portrayed as the violation of a male-female norm given with creation but as an example of passion into which God has handed over persons who have dishonored him. The immediate problem is passion, not the gender of the persons having sex."[64] There are numerous problems with Fredrickson's reasoning. His first point, that in different contexts "use" can be applied to both heterosexual and homosexual relationships, is largely irrelevant to how it is applied in the specific context of Rom 1:26-27. Here, clearly, the sex of the partner *does* make all the difference in defining the "use" of another in sexual intercourse as unnatural: sex with a member of the opposite sex, defined here as natural, is *exchanged* for sex with a member of the same sex, defined here as unnatural. The gender of the persons having sex, not sexual desire per se, is the immediate problem. Following from this, and answering to Fredrickson's second point, same-sex intercourse (like all other forms of sexual immorality) can be defined as

---

60. Ibid.
61. Fredrickson, "Romans 1:24-27," 200-201.
62. Ibid., 204-7.
63. Ibid., 202, 205-7.
64. Ibid., 222.

excess passion only *after* and *on the basis of* some prior understanding of why same-sex passion is unacceptable. Greek and Roman moralists who did not see anything inherently wrong with one or more forms of same-sex intercourse would not have agreed with the blanket assessment of Paul and all other Second Temple Jewish authors that same-sex intercourse was inherently unnatural or excess passion. Excess passion, therefore, is technically not an independent, self-standing argument for why a given behavior is assessed as wrong. As to Fredrickson's conclusion, the intertextual echoes to Gen 1–2 in Rom 1:18-32 and in other discussions of sexual issues in Paul (see pp. 289-93) make an appeal by Paul to the male-female norm in creation obvious. Fredrickson does not explain why Paul singles out same-sex intercourse for special treatment in Rom 1:18-32. The special revulsion felt for same-sex intercourse by all the Jewish authors surveyed in ch. 2, a revulsion that exceeded the revulsion felt for instances of heterosexual immorality, points manifestly to a special problem with same-sex intercourse: its same-sexness, that is, its violation of male-female complementarity embedded in creation and its functional signification of a member of the same sex as if a member of the opposite sex.

Fourth, whether Paul held all homoerotic desire to stem from over-sexed heterosexuals can hardly be established with certainty from Rom 1:27 ("males . . . were inflamed in their yearning for one another"). The language makes clear that the element of "overheating" is present in Paul's thinking, but that does not tell us much about his view of the development of homoeroticism. Paul (like most in antiquity) probably viewed any infraction of God-ordained boundaries of any sort (including sexual) to be an overheating of desire simply because transgression of God's will invariably entailed a victory of the passions of the flesh over the rational mind or Spirit (cf. 7:13-25). If one craved anything that God had forbidden or nature had shown to be unacceptable, and acted on that craving, then logically one was mastered by one's passion, thereby proving that the intensity of passion had been too great to be resisted.

Whether for Paul the source of homoerotic disinterest with the opposite sex was primarily gluttonous eating or luxury that fueled passions to fever pitch, boredom after too much sex with women, some special innate condition, or an unmet need in childhood is difficult to say and, in any case, would surely have been incidental to Paul's opposition. The reference to females who "exchanged" sexual intercourse with men for intercourse with other females and to men who "left (behind)" or "abandoned" sex with women for sex with other men (Rom 1:27) does not necessarily mean that Paul thought every single individual who engaged in same-sex intercourse also experienced heterosexual desire at one time. Paul is speaking in corporate terms of the sweep of history, not the experience of each and every individual practitioner of same-sex intercourse.[65] The text also clearly implies that the "degrading passions" to which God "hands over" are pre-existing; and the "leaving (behind)" intimates awareness of some men who were (or had become) exclusively oriented to other males. Regardless, since it is likely that Paul did not oppose homoeroticism *because* it constituted excessive heterosexual passion but at most interpreted homoeroticism as excessive passion in view of his *prior* opposition to such behavior, the whole objection that we no longer perceive of homoeroticism as due to excessive passion is largely irrelevant to the hermeneutical debate.[66]

Fifth, the translations "beyond nature" and "contrary to nature" for *para physin* cannot be played off against each other and, moreover, "nature" here has little to do with innate desires. The meaning "beyond" (the more common and general meaning of *para* with the accusative) and "contrary to, against, in opposition to" (a specific sense of this general meaning) are not necessarily mutually exclusive. Same-

---

65. Schmidt, *Straight and Narrow?*, 78; Hays, "Relations Natural and Unnatural," 189-90, 200.

66. Cf. Brooten, who regards the "oversexed heterosexual" argument as detrimental to contemporary lesbians and bisexuals: "Thus, both arguments fall short (that Paul condemns only heterosexuals committing homosexual acts and not homosexuals per se, and that the distinction between sexual orientation and sexual acts would have made no sense to him). Paul could have believed that *tribades* [lit., "woman who rub (other women)," i.e., lesbians], the ancient *kinaidoi* [catamites], and other sexually unorthodox persons were born that way and yet still condemn them as unnatural and shameful, this all the more so since he is speaking of groups of people rather than of individuals. Further, even if Paul condemned only homosexual acts committed by heterosexual persons, many lesbians in the church, who feel that they have *chosen* to love women, as well as all bisexuals, would fall under that condemnation and are thereby not helped by this interpretation. In sum, the category of the innate homosexual who is thereby free of shame and whose sexuality counts

sex intercourse is "beyond" or "in excess of" nature in the sense that it transgresses the boundaries for sexuality both established by God and transparent in nature even to gentiles. Only a woman possesses the complementary opening for insertion by the male member, a point confirmed by the procreative capacity of male "seed" when it enters through the vagina into the female womb. That is what nature refers to when *para physin* is used in connection with discussions of same-sex intercourse. That is the means by which one should be able to discern in the creation that same-sex passion is excess (i.e., transgressing) passion. Thus the principal point is that same-sex intercourse is "in transgression or violation of" natural boundaries/"law(s),"[67] perceptible in the way males and females are made, not that the passion for same-sex intercourse is "too much sex" (Martin) or urges experienced only by "constitutional" heterosexuals.[68] In the same way, idolatry is implicitly "contrary to nature," not because people are "constitutional monotheists," but because simple observation of the cosmos should make clear that, as great as the vast and glorious cosmos is, greater still must be the Artisan who fashioned it, greater certainly than a carved block of wood or stone shaped in the image of one of God's creations (1:19-23).

---

as natural does not fit the Roman world and does not address the self-understanding of many contemporary lesbian, bisexual, and gay Christians. I believe that Paul used the word 'exchanged' to indicate that people knew the natural sexual order of the universe and left it behind. . . . I see Paul as condemning all forms of homoeroticism as the unnatural acts of people who had turned away from God" (*Love Between Women*, 244).

67. Cf. the use of "law(s) of nature" in Philo's discussion of same-sex intercourse (*Abr.* 135; *Contempl. Life* 59), as well as such characterizations of same-sex intercourse as "unlawful," "debasing the currency of nature and violating it," "not standing in awe of the (male) nature" of the passive partner, forcing "those who had been born men to submit to play the part of women," and "restamping the masculine cast into a feminine form." LSJ uses the meaning "in transgression or violation of" rather than "contrary to, against" (s.v. *para*, III.4, citing numerous examples with this sense, including *para physin*).

68. Martin, "Heterosexism," 343. In Rom 11:24 Paul does not have in view an overflow or too much of something (not too much "tree" or branches, certainly not too much passion) when he utilizes horticultural imagery to describe the gentiles' inclusion into the community of God's people as a grafting, "beyond nature" (*para physin*), of branches that "in accordance with nature" (or "by nature," "naturally," *kata physin*) belonged to a wild olive tree, into a cultivated olive tree whose "natural" (*kata physin*) branches had been broken off. Nor is Paul with *kata physin* referring

Not the innateness of one's passions, which in Paul's understanding were perverted by the fall, shows us how to behave, but rather the material creation around human beings and the bodily design of humans themselves, guiding us into the truth about the nature of God and the nature of human sexuality respectively. Otherwise, many (if not all) of the vices in 1:29-31 would be *kata physin,* "in accordance with nature, natural."[69] To suppose that Paul was condemning only the participation in homosexual acts by those who are "naturally" attracted to the opposite sex "is equivalent to saying that scriptural condemnations of adultery refer only to such relationships among those who are 'naturally' monogamous."[70]

---

to something that we in our own time would consider to be matters of mere convention, but rather to material and organic processes. Here *para physin* has to do with an artificial, non-natural process (grafting), fooling nature but at the same time helping nature by doing for nature what nature cannot do for itself: replacing one tree's unfruitful original branches with potentially fruitful branches from a different tree. To be sure, *para physin* in Rom 11:24 does not denote an action that runs counter to God's will ("contrary to nature"), though Hays is right to point out that "the metaphor plays secondarily upon the negative connotations of *para physin*: God's action in incorporating Gentiles. . . is a stunning manifestation of the offensive paradox of grace" ("Relations Natural and Unnatural," 199). However, for Boswell to deduce from the usage in Rom 11:24 that *para physin* in Rom 1:26-27 means nothing more than "extraordinary, peculiar" is to ignore completely the widespread and unremittingly negative use of *para physin* for same-sex intercouse in the Hellenistic world (*Homosexuality,* 112, 114). "It is precisely the context [in Rom 1:26] which insures that sexual acts 'contrary to nature' are given a negative moral evaluation" (Hays, "Relations," 199).

As for the other uses of *para* with an accusative object in Paul, two passages clearly demonstrate the meaning "contrary to, against, in opposition to" in connection with teaching that does not merely add "more" to Paul's gospel but contradicts it (Rom 16:17; Gal 1:8-9). In three other passages the sense is "beyond, more than" (Rom 14:5; 1 Cor 3:11; 2 Cor 8:3), and Rom 4:18 may belong here as well (usually translated "who believed *against* hope" but perhaps better "who believed *beyond what hope could conceive*"). The uses in Rom 1:25 ("served the creature *instead of* or *rather than* the Creator") and Rom 12:3 ("not to have exaggerated thoughts *compared with* what one ought to think") are mediate uses between the senses "more than" and "contrary to"). Two other uses (1 Cor 12:15-16: "because of"; 2 Cor 11:24: "less") are in altogether different categories of meaning (cf. BAGD). The variety of usages in Paul confirm that context means everything for defining the meaning in Rom 1:26.

69. Cf. Balz, "Biblische Aussagen zur Homosexualität," 65: "Constitutional homosexuality would be for Paul nothing else than the clearest expression of non-Jews being given over [to unnatural desires]."

70. Boughton, "Biblical Texts and Homosexuality," 152-53.

Nature is material creation, visible to the naked eye, to the extent that it is not distorted or corrupted by the fall. Obviously, from Paul's perspective, the design and complementarity of male and female sex organs was not part of the fall because the command to procreate (Gen 1:27) had been given before the fall. Furthermore, the emphasis in Rom 1:26-27 is on exchanging (*metallassein*) the natural sexual use (*chrēsis*) of persons of the opposite sex for an unnatural use of persons of the same sex, not on the overflow of passions. In the first instance it is the actions of same-sex intercourse, the use and not the passions, that are *para physin*. The passions are *para physin* only to the extent that they yearn to "do" something beyond—and contrary to—what the natural (anatomical and procreative) male-female complementarity dictates as appropriate.

Hence, even innate or genetic homoerotic passions would have been contrary to nature for Paul (as is the "natural" desire by some men to be penetrated, according to Pseudo-Aristotle, *Problemata* 4:26, cited above)—that is, if for argument's sake one granted that the contemporary supposition of a genetic and exclusive attraction to members of the opposite sex were true. However, as the following discussion will argue, the scientific evidence indicates that genetic influence is at best only a relatively small (though not irrelevant) and indirect contributing factor.

A Note on Schoedel's Study of Ancient Causation Theories

William R. Schoedel's recent erudite article on the influence that ancient causation theories regarding homosexual practice may have had on early Jewish and Christian thinking provides excellent background information for the contemporary reader but ultimately fails to carry through the logic of the very texts that Schoedel adduces.[71] Many of Schoedel's views are compatible with my own:

(1) His own analysis of Plato's argument in *Laws* leads him to conclude that Plato's critique of same-sex eros goes beyond his criticism of non-procreative heterosexual eros as excess passion, charging same-sex eros with something far worse: turning the male passive partner into a female, contrary to nature. "Plato provides abundant resources for those who . . . [emphasize] the perversity of same-sex eros as such."[72]

71. "Same-Sex Eros: Paul and the Greco-Roman Tradition," 43-72.
72. Ibid., 45.

(2) Based on the speech of Aristophanes in Plato's *Symposium* and other texts, he finds "problematic the common view that sexual orientation was not recognized in the ancient world."[73] Those who claim that something akin to the modern category of an exclusive, innate homosexual proclivity did not exist in antiquity are wrong.

(3) He recognizes the importance of anatomical complementarity (without using the precise phrase) as a prime reason for the rejection of same-sex intercourse by ancient moralists: ancient writers "who appeal to nature against same-sex eros find it convenient to concentrate on the more or less obvious uses of the orifices of the body to suggest the proper channel for the more diffused sexual impulses of the body."[74]

(4) He rightly sees that Philo's rejection of same-sex intercourse was based on grounds that distinguished it from his rejection of excessive (i.e., non-procreative) heterosexual sex. For Philo, "when the two sexes madly pursue each other for pleasure, their behavior is morally wrong yet within the bounds of 'the laws of nature' ([*Contempl. Life*] 59). That of course cannot be said for the love between two males," where Philo's primary concern was "the feminization of the youth."[75] By inference, the question of how homosexual impulses arise would appear to play only a secondary role in Philo's assessment of homosexual behavior since Philo stresses effects rather than cause.

(5) He entertains briefly the "suggestion that Paul is speaking [in Rom 1:26-27] only of same-sex acts performed by those who are by nature heterosexual" as finding "some support" in Philo, *Abr.* 135. Then he dismisses the suggestion: "But such a phenomenon does not excuse some other form of same-sex eros in the mind of a person like Philo. Moreover, we would expect Paul to make that form of the argument more explicit if he intended it. . . . Paul's wholesale attack on Greco-Roman culture makes better sense if, like Josephus and Philo, he lumps all forms of same-sex eros together as a mark of Gentile decadence."[76]

---

73. Ibid., 46-47.
74. Ibid., 46.
75. Ibid., 50.
76. Ibid., 67-68.

One could be excused for surmising on the basis of such statements that Schoedel would see little value to the argument that Paul rejected homosexual behavior primarily on the grounds that it constituted an excess of sex by naturally inclined heterosexuals. However, the dominant line of Schoedel's reasoning appears to draw the opposite conclusion. Repeatedly he attributes early Jewish and Christian opposition to same-sex intercourse to a characterization of same-sex intercourse as "excessive search for pleasure" and an irrational and unmotivated fear of impurity.[77] He refers to material from Soranus's *De morbis chronicis* (4.9.131-37) in which Soranus diagnoses same-sex desire as a disease of the mind or spirit (akin to Philo's reference to "the disease of effeminacy in their souls," *Contempl. Life* 60), rather than as a disease of the body, and thus as a condition subject to human control.[78] He concludes from all this that in the time of Philo and Paul theories of homosexual causation were undergoing a "shift in emphasis from physical abnormality to psychological disorder" and that this shift in turn made it easier to take a severe stance against all forms of same-sex intercourse.[79]

At this point Schoedel is once more his own best critic. He himself notes that in the same treatise Soranus expresses an openness to the views of "many leaders of the medical school" that ascribe adult homosexual prostitution to an "inherited disease" (yet, Soranus adds, still against nature's best instruction), a biologically rooted condition that societal values could play a part in reinforcing or making "milder" (4.9. 134-37).[80] Moreover, as Schoedel notes, a strict distinction between diseases of the mind and biological inheritance runs counter to the views expressed in Plato's *Timaeus* (86B–87B) where diseases of the mind, though distinguished from diseases of the body, may be traced either "to bad upbringing or a defective *inherited* constitution of the body."[81] Schoedel acknowledges that "a similar conception of a psychological disorder socially engendered or reinforced *and genetically transmitted* may be presupposed" for Philo.[82] This view of things sounds

---

77. Ibid., 51-52, 70-71.
78. Ibid., 54-55.
79. Ibid., 55-57.
80. Ibid., 57-58.
81. Ibid., 56 (quoting Schoedel's summary; my emphasis).
82. Ibid. (my emphasis).

remarkably like the current scientific consensus on homosexual orientation (*contra* Schoedel who seems to assume throughout that modern science has concluded that homosexuality is a fixed genetic state).

Hence, Schoedel's study, far from having the intended effect of proving that the edifice of Paul's stance toward homosexuality rests on an outmoded theory of causation, actually dictates the opposite conclusion: current theories of homosexual causation are, at least in terms of broad strokes, compatible with ancient theories that may have underlain Paul's views. Indeed, Paul's own views on homosexuality did not depend on any one particular theory of causation but rather on the male-female complementarity embedded in creation and accessible to all through either Scripture or nature.

IV. Homosexuality has a genetic component that the writers of the Bible did not realize.

In "III" we examined whether Paul believed that homosexual intercourse was always an act undertaken by over-sexed heterosexuals. Here we need to explore whether or to what extent it may be taken as a scientific given that homosexuality is an unchangeable and static sexual orientation that is relatively immune from environmental factors. The popular view being promoted by homosexual-activist groups and their supporters is that people are either "born gay" or not. All the supporters of proposition "III" above argue that if the writers of Scripture had only known that homosexuality is not a chosen behavior but a genetically determined orientation, they may very well have looked at homosexuality in a different light.

We will explore the current scientific data in the following order: the questions of whether there are distinct homosexual brains and distinct homosexual genes; evidence from identical twin studies; the question of intrauterine hormonal influences on homosexual development; the impact that parents, siblings, and peers have on childhood sexual development generally and childhood gender nonconformity in particular; the contribution of cross-cultural studies for understanding environmental influence on homosexual behavior; the impact of urban life and education on homosexuality in contemporary American society; evidence for movement along the heterosexual-homosexual Kinsey ratings; and the efficacy of attempts by mental health professionals and lay counselors to "change" homosexuals.[83] Finally, we will conclude with a discussion of how this data relates to Paul's understanding of homosexuality.

A Homosexual Brain?[84]

Some scientists have tried to find differences in homosexual and heterosexual brains to confirm the hypothesis that homosexual orientation is at least partly determined by intrauterine hormonal influences on fetal brain development. Are the brains of male homosexuals closer to female brains than male heterosexual brains? Three studies in the early 1990s suggested a difference.

---

83. For the discussion that follows I am particularly indebted to the following works: Neil and Briar Whitehead, *My Genes Made Me Do It! A Scientific Look at Sexual Orientation* (Lafayette, La.: Huntington House, 1999; Neil Whitehead is a research scientist with a Ph.D. in biochemistry); Stanton Jones and Mark Yarhouse, *Homosexuality: The Use of Scientific Research* (Downer's Grove: InterVarsity, 2000) [my thanks to InterVarsity Press for permitting me to see a penultimate version of the book in manuscript form]; Jones and Yarhouse, "The Use, Misuse, and Abuse of Science in the Ecclesiastical Homosexuality Debates," *Homosexuality, Science, and the "Plain Sense" of Scripture*, 73-120; and Jeffrey Satinover, *Homosexuality and the Politics of Truth* (Grand Rapids: Baker, 1996). Also helpful were: Schmidt, *Straight and Narrow?*, 131-59; Grenz, *Welcoming But Not Affirming*, 13-33; Paul Cameron, *The Gay Nineties: What the Empirical Evidence Reveals About Homosexuality* (Franklin, Tenn.: Adroit, 1993); Sherwood O. Cole, "The Biological Basis of Homosexuality: A Christian Assessment," *JPT* 23/2 (1995): 89-100. For material in scientific journals, cf. esp. William Byne, "Science and Belief: Psychobiological Research on Sexual Orientation," *JHomosex* 28 (1995): 303-44; idem, "The Biological Evidence Challenged," *Scientific American* 270 (May 1994): 26-31; idem and Bruce Parsons, "Human Sexual Orientation: The Biologic Theories Reappraised," *Archives of General Psychiatry* 50 (1993): 228-39; Paul Billings and Jonathan Beckwith, "Born Gay?" *Technology Review* (July 1993): 60-61; J. Maddox, "Wilful Public Misunderstanding of Genetics," *Nature* 364 (1993): 281; M. Barinaga, "Is Homosexuality Biological?" *Science* 253 (1991): 956-57; T. R. McGuire, "Is Homosexuality Genetic? A Critical Review and Some Suggestions," *JHomosex* 30 (1995): 115-45; R. C. Friedman and J. Downey, "Neurobiology and Sexual Orientation," *Journal of Neuropsychiatry and Clinical Neurosciences* 5 (Spring 1993): 134-48; L. Gooren, "Biomedical Theories of Sexual Orientation: A Critical Examination," *Homosexuality / Heterosexuality* (ed. D. McWhirter et al.; New York: Oxford University Press, 1990), 71-87; A. Banks and N. K. Gartrell, "Hormones and Sexual Orientation: A Questionable Link," *JHomosex* 30 (1995): 247-68.

84. In addition to the Whiteheads and Jones/Yarhouse, cf. Paul and Kirk Cameron, "Homosexual Brains?" *Family Research Institute Special Report* (1996).

The one which has received by far the most media attention is the 1991 study done by Simon LeVay, a homosexual neurobiologist who in 1992 left the Salk Institute to found the Institute of Gay and Lesbian Education. LeVay studied an area of the hypothalamus[85] known as INAH3[86] in 19 homosexual males,[87] 16 heterosexual males, and 6 females. He concluded that INAH3 was two times larger in the heterosexual males (.12) than in the females (.056) and homosexual males (.051).[88] The media immediately trumpeted LeVay's results as proving that homosexuality is caused by immutable brain differences that distinguish homosexuals from heterosexuals.

Such a conclusion is irresponsible, for two reasons. First, there were six problems with LeVay's study. (1) It was a single-author study. Measurements were not made by more than one investigator. (2) His sample size was so small that it is impossible to conclude that the group constituted a representative sample of the larger population. Animal research will not be able to confirm LeVay's results because there is no homolog to a hypothalamic nucleus governing sexual orientation in animals. (3) LeVay may have misjudged the sexual orientation of some of the individuals. The fact that over a third of the allegedly heterosexual males died of AIDS raises suspicions that they were not heterosexual after all. LeVay made his determination on the basis of medical charts. If the medical chart for a given individual did not specifically state a homosexual orientation, LeVay simply assumed that the individual was heterosexual.[89] If all six of the AIDS "heterosexuals" had in fact engaged in homosexual activity, then the distinction between the two groups would not be significant. (4) LeVay's study also did not confirm that *all* homosexuals had a smaller INAH3. Three of the nineteen homosexuals had a larger INAH3 than the average heterosexual male

85. A region of the brain connected with sexual behavior.
86. Interstitial Nucleus of the Anterior Hypothalamus, four different sections of which have been examined to date.
87. The number includes one bisexual.
88. Simon LeVay, "A Difference in the Hypothalamic Structure Between Heterosexual and Homosexual Men," *Science* 253 (1991): 1034-37.
89. Only two of the fourteen heterosexuals had denied before their deaths that they had ever engaged in homosexual behavior. There was no information about the sexual orientation of the rest of the "heterosexuals."

INAH3. Three of the "heterosexual" males had an INAH3 smaller than that of the average homosexual male. Minimally, this means that the size of the INAH3 is not a direct or sole determinant of homosexual orientation. (5) A more careful (blind) study by William Byne did not find a difference between male homosexual and male heterosexual INAH3s.[90] (6) Furthermore, there is no proof that INAH3 has any bearing on sexual behavior, to say nothing of sexual orientation. It is simply a hunch on LeVay's part.

Second, there is no proof that the size differential (if one exists) is largely attributable to prenatal development of the brain. Even if LeVay's small sample were representative of the larger population and his findings could be replicated, and even if he correctly identified the sexual orientation of each individual, a different size of the INAH3 for heterosexual and homosexual males (on average but not in all cases) could be due to any of a number of other post-natal factors typical of each of these population groups: for example, early childhood trauma, patterns of sexual behavior in adolescent or adult life (such as the sex of one's partner, degree of promiscuity, or contact with fecal matter), involvement in sports, intravenous drug use, stress, diet, or general emotional health. Both the AIDS virus and some AIDS drugs are associated with lower testosterone levels which, in turn, may have affected the size of INAH3 at the time of death. Within limits, plastic structures in the brain can be altered through nutrition, disease, exercise, traumatic experiences, learning, pleasure stimuli, interpersonal dynamics, repetitious behavior, and adolescent and adult hormonal changes. Experiments on monkeys have shown that exercise of three fingers can increase the area of the brain associated with that function and decrease other regions proportionately. A similar phenomenon has been documented among violinists.[91] An NIH study discovered that people who had become blind and taken up Braille increased the size

---

90. Whitehead, *Gene*, 129.
91. Whitehead, *Genes*, 127. "[T]he average carbon atom stays about seven years in brain tissues. This means that the complete material of the brain is changed during a lifetime by substitutions of different atoms and brain cells—even in 'permanent' nerve tissue. Nothing is hardwired. Anyone determined to change any behavior should be able to make a substantial difference in thinking and habit patterns within a decade. Biological determinism is a myth" (ibid., 131).

of the area of the brain controlling the reading finger. Baby monkeys repeatedly subjected to traumatic separation from their mothers experience significant changes in brain function.[92] One recent article argues from research on rats that sexual behavior can effect changes in both the brain and nervous system.[93] Commenting on LeVay's research, the editor of *Nature* stated: "Plastic structures in the hypothalamus [might] allow . . . the consequences of early sexual arousal to be made permanent."[94] LeVay himself admitted in his study that "the results do not allow one to decide if the size of the INAH3 in an individual is the cause or consequence of that individual's orientation."

A Homosexual Gene?

In 1993, scientist Dean Hamer found what the media immediately hailed as the discovery of the "gay gene."[95] What did Hamer and his colleagues really claim to find? They recruited forty pairs of homosexual brothers who also had a high incidence of homosexual relatives on the maternal side of the family (20% of the maternal uncles and male cousins). Since women have two X and no Y chromosomes and men have one X and one Y chromosome, any genetic factor for homosexuality in this group would have to show up on the X chromosome passed on by the mother. In the case of thirty-three of these pairs (83%), the scientists claimed to have discovered a particular genetic sequence in the region of the X chromosome known as Xq28. Just by random chance, one would expect 50% of the brothers to share the same variation since the mother has two X chromosomes. Hamer's team concluded that "one form of male homosexuality is preferentially transmitted through the maternal side and is genetically linked to chromosomal region Xq28."

Almost immediately the alleged finding was greeted with considerable criticism from the scientific community, a fact which the media conveniently failed to report. Hamer was criticized for failing to check

---

92. Satinover, *Homosexuality*, 79-80.
93. S. Marc Breedlove, "Sex on the Brain," *Nature* 389 (Oct. 23, 1997): 801.
94. J. Maddox, "Is Homosexuality Hardwired?" *Nature* 353 (Sept. 1991): 13.
95. Dean Hamer, et al., "A Linkage Between DNA Markers on the X Chromosome and Male Sexual Orientation," *Science* 261 (1993): 321-27.

his results against a heterosexual control group and inflating the statistical significance of his findings. One of his young researchers accused him of neglecting to report findings that would have undermined the significance of his results. That researcher was fired.

Hamer and colleagues then conducted a second study that was published in 1995.[96] This time the results were less dramatic: Twenty-two out of thirty-two brothers (67%) shared the same genetic sequence in Xq28, albeit a 34% increase over the random 50% figure. Unlike the previous study, this study checked for the same genetic sequence among the test group's heterosexual brothers, who were found to be less likely to carry the variation in Xq28. Homosexuals who had bisexual brothers showed no linkage (i.e., only a 50% match occurred). Lesbian sisters from other families were also checked, but none carried the chromosomal marker in Xq28.

For the sake of argument, let us suppose the 67% figure is correct. What has Hamer proved? Hamer himself has acknowledged that "We have not found the gene—which we don't think exists—for sexual orientation." "There will never be a test that will say for certain whether a child will be gay. We know that for certain."[97] Hamer's team did not locate a chromosomal marker for lesbians or bisexuals. Moreover, Hamer's alleged discovery applies only to a relatively small segment of the exclusively homosexual population: those who have both a homosexual brother and homosexual maternal relatives. Even within that relatively narrow band of the homosexual population, a significant percentage of the test group of homosexuals did not carry the Xq28 variation, while many of the heterosexual brothers of the test group did bear the marker in the X chromosome. As a commentator for the *New Scientist* noted, Hamer's marker was neither a necessary nor a sufficient cause of homosexual orientation for this very limited segment of the homosexual population. Finally, there is no proof that the marker provides any direct bearing on sexual orientation. It is possible that the marker codes for some other trait that may increase the chances of becoming homosexual; for example, traits that may contribute to a child's gender nonconformity or a penchant for the exotic and novel.

---

96. S. Hu, et al., D. Hamer, "Linkage Between Sexual Orientation and Chromosome Xq28 in Male But Not in Females," *Nature Genetics* 11 (1995): 248-56.
97. For the source of the quotes, cf. Whitehead, *Gene*, 135, 146-47.

Yet the discussion above presumes that Hamer's 67% figure is correct. Even that result may be false. In the last decade or so, claims of genetic linkage for manic depression, schizophrenia, and alcoholism have been made by researchers. Subsequent research, however, has not been able to replicate these findings. Hamer's claims may suffer the same fate. In a 1999 issue of *Science*, a group of Canadian researchers failed to replicate Hamer's findings. Although they used a larger sample size (fifty-two pairs of homosexual brothers), no significant connection between Xq28 and homosexual orientation was detected.[98]

A theory of genetically determined behavior does not coincide with scientific assessments of the role of genes. As Neil and Briar Whitehead put it:

> Science has not yet discovered any genetically dictated behavior in humans. So far, genetically dictated behaviors of the one-gene-one-trait variety have been found only in very simple organisms. . . . But if many genes are involved in a behavior, then changes in that behavior will tend to take place very slowly and steadily (say, changes of a few percent each generation over many generations, perhaps thirty). That being so, homosexuality could not appear and disappear suddenly in family trees the way it does.[99]

In short, genetic influence on homosexuality is, if existent at all, relatively weak in comparison with family, societal, and other environmental influences. The 1992 United States National Research Council Report on violence and genes provides an example of a healthier, depoliticized conclusion about the relationship of genes to behavior. According to the report, violence can be attributed to

98. G. Rice et al., "Male Homosexuality: Absence of Linkage to Microsatellite Markers at Xq28," *Science* 284 (April 23, 1999): 665-67.

99. Whitehead, *Genes*, 209; more detailed discussion on pp. 13-31. Mutations, they note, could appear suddenly in a family tree, but for a behavioral change that would require the implausible scenario of many genes mutating at the same time and would likely not affect more than .025% of the population (ibid., 24-25). The Whiteheads acknowledge that "many conditions . . . have been traced to specific gene locations or chromosome faults: muscular dystrophy, familial colon cancer, Huntington's disease," etc., but these are not behaviors (ibid., 21).

interactions among individuals' psychosocial development, neurological and hormonal differences, and social processes. . . . *These studies suggest at most a weak role for genetic processes* in influencing potentials for violent behavior. . . . If genetic predispositions to violence are discovered they are likely to involve many genes and substantial environmental interaction rather than any simple genetic marker.[100]

A standard textbook on psychiatry reaches a similar conclusion:

> Studies demonstrating a genetic factor in criminality have also acknowledged cultural/environmental influences shaping the behavior. . . . what is inherited may not be a mechanism specific to a behavior but rather something related to qualities of that person that render him or her more vulnerable to social influences. . . . That genes have a role in behavior can be demonstrated; that behaviors are influenced by other forces is also certain, particularly learning through models, instructions, and rewards from the sociocultural environment.[101]

If only the popular understanding of the relationship of genes to homosexuality would be so sober-minded. Few people would want to argue that violent behavior is so genetically predetermined that humans

---

100. Quoted by Whitehead, *Genes*, 215-16. Jones and Yarhouse (*Homosexuality*, 82) refer to a recent study published by none other than Dean Hamer (and others) on "A Genetic Association for Cigarette Smoking Behavior" (*Health Psychology* 18 [1998]: 7-13). Although people without a particular gene were more likely to smoke and not quit, the identified gene "is not a strict determinant of the ability to quit smoking, but rather an influence on an individual's general need and responsiveness to external stimuli, of which cigarette smoking is but one example" (interview of Hamer, *APA News Release*, Jan. 14, 1999). In other words, the genetic influence is indirect, hinges on particular interactions with the environment, and at most constitutes one among multiple influences. This would also be an apt description of any genetic influence on homosexual behavior—should one be discovered some day.

101. Paul R. McHugh and Phillip R. Slavney, *The Perspectives of Psychiatry* (2d ed.; Baltimore: Johns Hopkins, 1998), 185-86. With regard to homosexual behavior, McHugh and Slavney conclude that "genetic factors play some role in the production of homosexual behavior, but . . . sexual behavior is molded by many influences, including 'acquired tastes' (or learning) closely related to the culture in which the individual develops . . . . It is possible . . . to picture a future in which homosexual behavior will be so much in the cultural experience of every individual that the genetic contribution will become undetectable" (ibid., 184-85).

who engage in it should be absolved of responsibility. Yet this and more is precisely the conclusion that the homosexual lobby wants the general public to draw about homosexual behavior.

Evidence from Identical Twin Studies

Identical twins are monozygotic; that is, they are produced from "one egg" and one sperm. In terms of genetic makeup, identical twins are truly 100% identical. Non-identical or fraternal twins, however, are dizygotic; that is, they are formed from "two eggs" and two sperm. Fraternal twins share no greater genetic resemblance to one another than do non-twin siblings (on average, a 50% overlap). Because identical twins are a perfect genetic match, a genetic basis for homosexuality would have to show up in higher "concordance rates" for identical twins in which at least one twin is homosexual. If homosexuality were determined completely by the genes, we would expect the concordance rate in such cases to be 100%. In other words, the identical twin of a homosexual would always be homosexual, much as eye color and sex in identical twins match 100% of the time.

In the early 1990s four major studies were published on the concordance rates for homosexuality in identical twins.[102] In their 1991 study of 110 identical and non-identical male twins containing at least one homosexual member each, Bailey and Pillard reported a concordance rate of 52% for identical twin pairs (i.e., in 52% of the identical twin pairs studied the co-twin was also homosexual) but less than half that (22%) for non-identical twins. In their 1993 study of 71 identical and 37 non-identical female twins with at least one lesbian or bisexual member each, the same researchers reported a concordance rate of

---

102. J. Michael Bailey and Richard C. Pillard, "A Genetic Study of Male Sexual Orientation," *Archives of General Psychiatry* 48 (1991): 1089-96; idem, et al., "Heritable Factors Influence Sexual Orientation in Women," *Archives of General Psychiatry* 50 (1993): 217-23; Michael King and Elizabeth McDonald, "Homosexuals Who Are Twins: A Study of 46 Probands," *British Journal of Psychiatry* 160 (1992): 407-9; F. L. Whitam, M. Diamond, and J. Martin, "Homosexual Orientation in Twins—A Report of 61 Pairs and 3 Triplet Sets," *Archives of Sexual Behavior* 22 (1993): 187-206. Cf. also N. Buhrich, J. M. Bailey, and N. G. Martin, "Sexual Orientation, Sexual Identity, and Sex-Dimorphic Behaviors in Male Twins," *Behavior Genetics* 21 (1991): 75-96.

48% and 16% for identical and non-identical twins respectively. A 1993 study published by F. Whitam and others found a concordance rate of 65% for 34 identical twin pairs and 30% for 23 non-identical twin pairs.[103] These three studies received great fanfare in the media and led many to the false conclusion that homosexual behavior arose from a genetic contribution of 50% or greater. Less widely reported was a smaller, 1992 British study by King and McDonald. They announced concordance rates only half those of Bailey and Pillard: 25% for male and female identical twins (only 10% if bisexual co-twins were not counted), 12% for non-identical twins.[104]

A major criticism of these studies was that the samples were not randomly obtained. Volunteers were recruited through advertisements in gay publications, making it likely that the test groups would have an artificially high number of homosexual twins whose co-twins were also homosexual. This sample bias has been corrected in a more recent study by Bailey himself, with dramatically lower concordance rates. Utilizing the Australian Twin Register, Bailey sent out surveys to 9,112 of Australia's roughly 25,000 twins and tabulated the responses from 4,901 completed questionnaires. Of 27 pairs of male identical twins in which at least one twin of each pair was non-heterosexual, only 3 pairs consisted of two non-heterosexuals (11%). Of 22 pairs of female identical twins in which at least one twin of each pair was non-heterosexual, only 3 pairs were concordant for non-heterosexuality (13.6%). For same-sex male non-identical twins, none of the 16 pairs were concordant (0%); for same-sex female non-identical twins only 1 out of 18 pairs was concordant (5.6%); for opposite-sex non-identical twins, 2 pairs out of 28 (7%) were concordant. Bailey himself now admits that "concordances from prior studies were inflated due to concordance dependent ascertainment bias."[105]

---

103. Four of the identical twin pairs were female.

104. Of 46 twin pairs in the study, 38 were male pairs and 8 were female pairs.

105. J. Michael Bailey, Michael P. Dunne, and Nicholas G. Martin, "Genetic and Environmental Influences on Sexual Orientation and Its Correlates in an Australian Twin Sample," *Journal of Personality and Social Psychology* 78 (2000): 524-36 (quote from p. 533). "In contrast to most prior twin studies of sexual orientation, . . . ours did not provide statistically significant support for the importance of genetic factors for that trait." Commenting on Hamer's study, the authors

Can we then say with some confidence that the genetic contribution to homosexual behavior is probably somewhere between 10 and 15%? No, even that figure would have to be reduced considerably. Some portion could be due to a common prenatal intrauterine environment rather than to genes. More important, common nurture or environment is likely to be a significant factor accounting for concordance rates. All of the twin studies cited above involve twins raised in the same households. So when one subtracts influences arising from being raised in the same family environment and the same larger cultural environment, who knows what smaller figure one might be left with: 8%? 5%? 1%?

Environmental influences are evident in the 1991 study of male twins by Bailey and Pillard. There Bailey reported that the concordance rate for non-identical twins was 22%, for non-twin brothers 9.2%, and for non-twin adoptive brothers 11%. Since non-identical twins have no greater genetic similarity than non-twin brothers, the fact that the former have a concordance rate for homosexuality that is over twice as high as the latter can only be explained from factors other than genes. Equally striking is that non-twin, biologically related brothers had a slightly *lower* concordance rate than non-twin, biologically unrelated adoptive brothers. Only being raised in a similar environment

---

note that "our male [identical-twin] concordance figure suggests . . . that any major gene for strictly defined homosexuality has either low penetrance or low frequency"—that is, any influence on sexual orientation from an X-linked gene is likely to be minimal at best (quotes from p. 534). The authors do note, however, that "our results provided some support" for the "assumption that trait-relevant environment is no more similar for [identical twins] than for [non-identical twins]" (p. 533). Bailey reports higher concordance rates than the ones I give above because in cases where both twins are homosexual he counts each twin separately as a match. This gives him the following inflated concordance rates: 20% for male identical twins, 24% for female identical twins, 0% for male non-identical twins, and 10.5% for female non-identical twins. To this layman, such a method of reporting gives a false impression: given a sample size of one pair of identical twins, if both identical twins were homosexual the concordance rate would be 200% (an oxymoron). Whichever concordance-rate figures one uses, the general public should be aware that Bailey's inflated concordance rates do not represent the percentage of twin *pairs* concordant for homosexuality. Also important to be aware of is that Bailey counts as "non-heterosexual" anyone who numbers a "2" (heterosexual with substantial homosexual feelings) or above in Kinsey's 0-6-point graduated scale of sexual orientation. See Jones and Yarhouse, *Homosexuality*, 75-78.

can explain such parity in concordance rates for the two groups, and explain why adoptive brothers of homosexuals would be four times more likely than the general population to be homosexual.[106]

Twins, and especially identical twins, have additional non-genetic influences on them that could artificially elevate concordance rates. King and McDonald reported in their twin study that same-sex twins, particularly in identical twin sets, had an abnormally high incidence of sexual relations (hence, homosexual relations) with each other. They usually have the same peer group. Parents, siblings, and peers often treat twins as mirror images of the same person. Research on twins has amply documented high behavioral imitation rates. On average, twins also experience significantly higher rates of child abuse and same-sex peer ridicule. In their early years the average twin has to play catchup in physical development and in the acquisition of social skills. Twins may be twice as likely to remain unmarried. Any of these factors may contribute to the development of a homosexual orientation. Indeed, there is evidence that identical twins may be four times more likely to become homosexuals than the general population.[107] Thus a significant factor in the higher concordance rates for identical twins than for non-identical twins may be the distinctive socialization of identical twins.

The best way to rule out the environmental factor in identical twin studies is to assess concordance rates among identical twins raised in different households. Unfortunately, the difficulty in locating such twins where at least one is homosexual has made it virtually impossible to study this phenomenon. However, a 1986 study of very small sample size examined four sets of female identical twins raised in different households, where at least one twin in each set self-identified as lesbian. In *none* of the four pairs of twins was the co-twin also lesbian.[108]

---

106. The figures for the 1993 study of female twin homosexuality by Bailey and Pillard are concordance rates of 16% for non-identical twins, 14% for non-twin sisters, and 6% for adoptive sisters. Even here the incidence of lesbianism among adoptive sisters of lesbians is still three times higher than the national average. Cf. Jones and Yarhouse, *Homosexuality*, 78-79.
107. For references to twin research in the scientific literature, cf. Whitehead, *Genes*, 152, 155-56.
108. E. Eckert, et al., "Homosexuality in Monzygotic Twins Reared Apart," *British Journal of Psychiatry* 148 (1986): 421-25. The researchers also located two sets of male identical twins reared separately. In one instance the co-twin was also homo-

Intrauterine Hormonal Influences?

Intrauterine hormonal influences should be distinguished from genetic influences, even if the two are innate and possibly interdependent. We know that a testosterone surge in the embryo produces male genitals and other typically male characteristics; without that surge, the embryo develops female characteristics. Genetically coded female embryos exposed to male hormones develop large clitorises, and as adults excessive hairiness, and deep voices (the condition is called adrenogenital syndrome). Could it be, then, that male embryos that receive inadequate doses of testosterone, and female embryos that receive too much develop a homosexual orientation? Lab research has shown that rats injected in the womb with abnormally high doses of hormones have an increased incidence of homosexual mating behaviors (though the same effect does not occur with primates). An East German researcher in the late 1940s concluded that stress experienced by German mothers during World War II led to a delayed testosterone surge, which in turn brought about a very high incidence of bisexuality and homosexuality. However, more recent studies on humans in high-stress conditions have not been able to confirm these results.[109] A 1995 study indicates that females born to mothers who took an estrogen drug during pregnancy were more likely to identify themselves as bisexual. However, the increase in exclusive lesbian orientation was tiny and many of the females exhibited no homosexual proclivity.[110] Other studies, including one in 1992, showed no difference in sexual orientation when pregnant mothers were given artificial female sex hormones.[111] Even if extraordinarily high prenatal estrogen levels created by human drugs exert a moderate effect on bisexuality, that would still not prove that homosexual behavior under normal circumstances is traceable to intrauterine hormonal influences. Moreover, there is general agreement that significant hormonal differences between adult

---

sexual, in the other instance the co-twin was heterosexual. Cited in Jones and Yarhouse, *Homosexuality*, 74.

109. Cf. the discussion in Whitehead, *Genes*, 118.

110. H. F. L. Meyer-Bahlburg, et al., "Prenatal Estrogens and the Development of Homosexual Orientation," *Developmental Psychology* 31 (1995): 12-21.

111. Cf. Whitehead, *Genes*, 114.

homosexual and heterosexual men do not exist. Adult male homosexuals given male hormones developed a higher sex drive but did not become heterosexual. To say that homosexual behavior is caused by abnormal hormone levels during pregnancy is to go beyond the current data, though some indirect influence may be possible.

Childhood Gender Nonconformity and the Socialization of Children

The life stories of many (though not all) homosexuals include early childhood memories of feeling out of place with respect to members of the same sex. There is a consensus in scientific literature that children who exhibit a high degree of gender nonconformity have an increased likelihood of developing a homosexual identity as an adult.[112] Such gender nonconformity might include interest in toys, games, activities, or clothing associated with the opposite sex; primary association with members of the opposite sex; and feelings of not "fitting in" with or being accepted by peers of one's own sex. The "sissy" boy and "tomboy" girl are classic types of gender nonconformity. There is no consensus, though, over the causes of early gender nonconformity. It is consistent with the hypothesis of some type of genetic or intrauterine causation, which at best is likely to exert only an indirect influence (e.g., in bestowing physical or personality traits that are culturally identified as compromising traditional gender identity). But it is also plausible that gender nonconformity is a precipitating cause for some forms of developing homosexuality rather than an effect of a latent homosexual orientation.

According to one psychoanalytic theory,[113] children learn to behave

---

112. Even gay-gene researcher Dean Hamer acknowledges as much. "Most sissies will grow up to be homosexuals, and most gay men were sissies as children. Despite the provocative and politically incorrect nature of that statement, it fits the evidence. In fact, it may be the most consistent, well-documented, and significant finding in the entire field of sexual-orientation research and perhaps in all of human psychology" (*The Science of Desire* [New York: Simon and Schuster, 1994] 166). Similarly, Simon LeVay, *Queer Science* (Cambridge: MIT Press, 1996) 6, 98.

113. Cf. the discussion in Whitehead, *Genes*, 49-75; Jones and Yarhouse, *Homosexuality*, 54-60, 65-66; Satinover, *Homosexuality*, 104-8, 184, 221-28; Schmidt, *Straight and Narrow?*, 144-48, 214-16; Grenz, *Welcoming*, 15-21. Also: Joseph Nicolosi, *Healing Homosexuality: Case Stories of Reparative Therapy* (New York: Jason Aronson, 1993); idem, *Reparative Therapy of Male Homosexuality* (New York: Jason Aronson, 1991); Elizabeth Moberly, *Psychogenesis: The Early Development of Gender Identity* (London: Routledge &

in ways appropriate to their gender through their interaction with their same-sex parent and, later, with same-sex peers. When a proper relationship with the same-sex parent or with same-sex peers is disrupted, the formation of a secure sexual identity in the child is likewise disrupted. Gender nonconformity in the child and attendant feelings of being different from others of the same sex can be created or significantly exacerbated by such experiences.

At an early period in the child's life, if the child perceives the same-sex parent to be distant, rejecting, or unappealing (whether correctly or not), the child may find it hard to identify fully with the image of sexuality conveyed by the same-sex parent. For boys identification with the same-sex parent is particularly susceptible to complications because, unlike girls, boys must make the difficult crossover from a prior primary identification with mother. If gender identification with the same-sex parent cannot be completed, the child may defensively detach from the same-sex parent. However, such detachment subsequently only heightens the child's anxiety regarding acceptance from members of the same sex. Not all homosexuals experience poor relationships with their same-sex parent and not all children who experience such impaired parental relationships become homosexual. Nevertheless, some studies have indicated that poor emotional bond-

---

Kegan Paul, 1983): eadem, *Homosexuality: A New Christian Ethic* (Cambridge: Clark, 1983); eadem, "Homosexuality: Restating the Conservative Case," *Salmagundi* 58/59 (1982/83): 281-99; Irving Bieber et al., *Homosexuality: A Psychoanalytic Study of Male Homosexuals* (New York: Basic Books, 1962); Gerard van den Aardweg, *On the Origins and Treatment of Homosexuality: A Psychoanalytic Reinterpretation* (Westport, Conn.: Praeger, 1986); idem, *The Battle for Normality: A Guide for (Self-)Therapy for Homosexuality* (San Francisco: Ignatius, 1997); idem, *Homosexuality and Hope: A Psychologist Talks About Treatment and Change* (Ann Arbor, Mich.: Servant Books, 1986); Elaine V. Segal, *Female Homosexuality: Choice Without Volition* (Hillsdale, N.J.: The Analytic Press, 1988); Charles Socarides, *Homosexuality: Psychoanalytic Therapy* (New York: Jason Aronson, 1989); idem, *Homosexuality: A Freedom Too Far* (Phoenix: Adam Margrave, 1995); idem, "Advances in Psychoanalytic Theory and Therapy of Male Homosexuality," *The Sexual Deviations* (Oxford: Oxford University Press, 1996), 252-78; Lawrence J. Hatterer, *Changing Homosexuality in the Male: Treatment for Men Troubled by Homosexuality* (New York: McGraw-Hill, 1970); Ruth Tiffany Barnhouse, *Homosexuality: A Symbolic Confusion* (New York: Seabury, 1977); Edmund Bergler, *Homosexuality: Disease or Way of Life* (New York: Collier Books, 1962).

ing with the same-sex parent characterizes a significantly higher percentage of homosexuals than heterosexuals.

Some psychiatrists also give a secondary role to the opposite-sex parent in predisposing a child to homosexual behavior as an adult. For example, a close-binding or demanding mother may impair her son's attachment to his father or same-sex peers by criticism of the father or of males in general. Or she may smother the son's attempts to assert himself and break out of her primary influence. For girls, the loss of a father through death or divorce, or mistrust of males exacerbated by an alcoholic, angry, or abusive father, may have a bearing on later lesbian development. Again, we are dealing here primarily with a child's perceptions, perceptions which may not conform to reality or to a parent's intent.

While interaction with parents is an important factor in many, possibly most, cases of homosexual development, it is not a factor in every single case and even where it is a factor it may or may not be the most important factor. Often just as, or more, important is the relationship between a child and same-sex peers or siblings. A child may possess physical traits that make the child feel awkward, inadequate, or out of place in the presence of same-sex peers. Indirect genetic or intrauterine influences and/or unusual features to the early socialization of a child may dispose the child toward interests which stand outside the norm for one's gender. Same-sex peers may isolate the child for ridicule as much because of the way the child responds to teasing as because of any gender nonconformity. Both the child and same-sex peers can exaggerate initially small differences in an effort to resolve uncomfortable tensions and reduce the potential for conflict in overlapping interests. Because childhood and adolescent relationships with same-sex peers play a critical role in shaping sexual identity, persecution or isolation from same-sex peers may pervert the child's normal need to be wanted and desired by members of the same sex into an eroticization of same-sex love. For example, a boy who is bad at sports because of slight build or poor eye-to-hand coordination may develop a weak masculine identity due to trauma inflicted by male peers. When such a boy transitions from the phase of male "chum" bonding to the phase of erotic attraction, the healthy and normal needs for same-sex affirmation may become confused with impulses for erotic gratification. The high incidence of "other-destructive" behavior in homosexual circles (unsafe sex, sadomasochism, "fisting," high rates of non-disclosure of HIV/AIDS status to partners) may be attributable in part to buried anger arising out of the pain of rejection and taunting from boyhood same-sex peers. In the case of females, an aversion to the opposite sex may arise out of failed or abusive romantic relationships. Alternatively, the sheer loneliness that comes from waiting for males to take a sexual interest in them may push some females by default into exploring homosexual behavior.

Daryl Bem, a professor of psychology at Cornell University, has made a case for an "exotic becomes erotic" theory of homosexual development; namely, "the proposition that individuals become erotically or romantically attracted to those who were dissimilar or unfamiliar to them in childhood." Contrary to the heterosexual norm, those whose behavior is characterized by gender nonconformity regard members of the same sex as more "exotic."[114]

Bem's theory may be of value as a complementary explanation, rejecting as it does the theory that gender non-conformity arises out of a prior homosexual identity. Its weakness, as psychologist Joseph Nicolosi points out, is that it "gives no consideration to the boy's authentic needs for acceptance, affection and approval from members of the same sex." Nicolosi cites a memory of a 35-year-old homosexual client that well illustrates the point:

> "I recall the exact moment I knew I was gay. I was twelve years old and we were taking a shortcut to class. We were walking across the gym and through the locker room, and an older guy was coming out of the shower. He was wet and naked and I thought, Wow!"

> I asked the client to again tell me exactly what his experience was. He became very pensive. Then he answered,

> "The feeling was, 'Wow, I wish I was him.' "[115]

---

114. Daryl J. Bem, "Exotic Becomes Erotic: A Developmental Theory of Sexual Orientation," *Psychological Review* 103 (1996): 320-35. Bem, a homosexual who "came out" after thirty years of marriage and two children, hopes his theory will promote a "non-gender-polarizing culture" (ibid., 332).
115. Joseph Nicolosi, "A Critique of Bem's E.B.E. Theory," n.p. [updated Aug. 5, 1999]. Online: http://www.narth.com/docs/critique.html.

If this dynamic is reflective of homosexual experience it points to an important difference between heterosexual and homosexual attraction—the difference between wanting to *have* a member of the opposite sex as a complementary other and wishing to *be* someone else of the same sex as a replacement of one's sexual self. When children regard members of their own sex as more "exotic" than members of the opposite sex, then something is clearly wrong, as the very expressions "same sex" and "opposite sex" imply. Such children may be reacting to an insecure gender identity by becoming sexually attracted to what they would like to see in themselves. This is not a healthy reaching-out to a sexual "other," but rather an unhealthy, narcissistic attraction to one's own sex and a symptom of an unmet need for sexual self-acceptance.

Homosexual relationships, especially for males, may also serve for many as a refuge from the anxiety associated with societal expectations around heterosexual courtship and intimacy. Consistent with this explanation is the fact that promiscuous, casual sex and "open," short-term relationships are hallmarks of male homosexual activity. It also fits with the much higher rates of substance abuse reported among homosexuals, inasmuch as the adoption of one self-soothing response to internal distress is usually accompanied by other methods of self-soothing.[116]

There is also evidence that self-identified homosexuals and bisexuals are three to nine times more likely to have experienced sex as a child (usually with an adolescent or adult male) than their heterosexual counterparts.[117] The higher correlation suggests that sexual abuse

---

116. Satinover, *Homosexuality*, 189-95.
117. Cf. Jones and Yarhouse, *Homosexuality,* 57-58. According to the 1992 National Health and Social Life Survey, among those who had been sexually touched as a child by an adult, 7.4% of the men and 3.1% of the women identified themselves as homosexual or bisexual. Yet self-identified homosexuals/bisexuals accounted for only 2.8% of the men and 1.4% of the women in the survey (Edward O. Laumann et al., *The Social Organization of Sexuality: Sexual Practices in the United States* [Chicago: University of Chicago, 1994], 297, 344). A nationwide survey by Family Research Institute found that homosexuals and bisexuals were nine times more likely to have been sexually molested as a child (Paul Cameron et al., "Child Molestation and Homosexuality," *Psychological Reports* 58 [1986]: 327-37). A review of the literature on molestation of boys in the *Journal of the American Medical Association* noted that adolescents who were sexually molested by men

may be at least *a* causative factor in predisposing *some* people to adult homosexual behavior. An early association of sexual arousal with an adult or adolescent of the same sex (particularly in the case of boys), or an association of heterosexual sex with trauma (particularly in the case of girls), may incline the child in the direction of homosexual relationships.

It is probably not possible to pinpoint any one socializing factor that leads a person to develop a homosexual orientation. Nevertheless, environmental factors and reactive psychological development (where choice in some limited sense may be included) appear to be key ingredients. This point is perhaps most strikingly demonstrated by the following observation. Roughly 90% of children born with ambiguous genitalia choose as adolescents or adults to retain the gender identification bestowed on them in their upbringing, even if their gendered upbringing is subsequently discovered to be at odds with the child's genetically determined sex. In such cases, gender socialization clearly has a greater impact than genes.[118]

Cross-cultural Studies: Extreme Variations in the Cultural Manifestations of Homosexuality

From previous discussion in this book, it is evident that a comparison of ancient Greek culture and ancient Israelite culture provide two very different examples of how cultural reactions to homosexual behavior can affect its social expression or whether it is expressed at all. In the case of the former, pederasty pervaded male society to a point where it achieved conventional status, at least among the upper classes.

---

were up to seven times more likely to identify themselves later as homosexual (W. C. Holmes et al., "Sexual Abuse of Boys," *JAMA* 280 [1998]: 1855-62).

118. Whitehead, *Genes*, 85-95. The Whiteheads also refer to an interesting experiment on animals, in which researchers at the Babraham Institute in Cambridge "allowed ten ewes to raise goats from birth and ten nanny goats to raise lambs from birth. . . . Once mature they ignored their own species and tried to mate 90% of the time with the foster mother species. . . . even after years of mixing with their own species, the males did not revert (but females did). If the sexuality of these lower animals was so influenced by learning, human sexuality will be more so" (ibid., 59; referring to: K. M. Kendrick et al., "Mothers Determine Sexual Preferences," *Nature* 395 [1998]: 229-30).

In the case of the latter, all forms of homosexual behavior were virtually non-existent.

David Greenberg has written the most comprehensive account of the social construction of homosexuality from earliest times to present day. He categorizes the historical and social manifestation of homosexuality according to four ideal types: (1) transgenerational (the partners are from different generations); (2) transgendered (one of the partners takes on the gender identity of the opposite sex); (3) class-structured (partners belong to different social classes, for example, the dominant partner as a free adult citizen, the subordinate partner as a slave or prostitute); and (4) egalitarian (the partners are social equals).

As an example of transgenerational homosexuality, he focuses on New Guinea. In 10% to 20% of New Guinea cultures, an institutionalized form of pederasty exists, though the specifics vary from tribe to tribe. For example, in the case of the Etoro tribe, a boy around the age of ten enters into a homosexual relationship with his brother-in-law, which continues until he develops a full beard (roughly fifteen years). He then serves as the older partner for his wife's younger brother. When he reaches the age of forty, he discontinues homosexual relationships altogether, except at collective initiation ceremonies or if he takes a second wife. In the case of the Sambia tribe, homosexual relationships begin when the boy is seven. He regularly fellates an adolescent boy until he reaches puberty; then he is regularly fellated by a pre-pubescent boy until he marries, at which time he gives up all homosexual relations. All males must participate in these activities at the appropriate stages of their life. The mode of homosexual intercourse is different for different tribes: oral in some (e.g., Etoro, Sambia), anal in others, and smearing semen over the younger partner in one or two cases. The rationale for these practices is that semen from an adult male implants virility in the boy. In other tribes of New Guinea homosexual behavior was practiced by only a tiny minority of men, and in still others it was non-existent or virtually so.

One of Greenberg's examples of transgenderal homosexual relations occurs in connection with some North American Indian tribes. Indian men known to French explorers and settlers as "berdaches" dressed up in female clothes and adopted a feminine manner. They were conceptualized as a third sex of "not-men" with whom other men could have sex. Female berdaches who adopted male social roles and had sex with other women were also known to exist.

As an example of egalitarian homosexual behavior he mentions, among others, the Akan women of the Gold Coast (Ghana) who until marriage (and sometimes even after marriage) almost universally participated in lesbian affairs. "Whenever possible, the women purchased extralarge beds to accommodate group sex sessions involving perhaps half-a-dozen women."[119]

Greenberg also cites "quite a few societies in which all forms of homosexuality are reported to be extremely rare," and in some cases apparently non-existent. Sometimes this occurs in societies that explicitly proscribe homosexual behavior but at other times in societies lacking such prohibitions.[120]

Even though Greenberg is thoroughly supportive of gay rights, he regards as indefensible the position of "essentialists" who view homosexuality as an immutable, genetic condition.

> The years some homosexuals spend trying without success to conform to conventional expectations regarding gender and sexual orientation tell against the most extreme claims of sexual plasticity. However, in the absence of any evidence linking the peculiar sexual practices of Melanesia with genetic difference, it is reasonable to suppose that if a bunch of Melanesian infants were to be transported in infancy to the United States and adopted, few would seek out the pederastic relationships into which they are inducted in New Guinea, or take younger homosexual partners when they reached maturity. Similarly, American children raised in New Guinea would accommodate themselves to the Melanesian practices. *Where social definitions of appropriate and inappropriate behavior are clear and consistent, with positive sanctions for conformity and negative ones for nonconformity, virtually everyone will conform irrespective of genetic inheritance* and, to a considerable extent, irrespective of personal psychodynamics.[121]

All of this suggests that cultural norms, not some form of genetic

---

119. *The Construction of Homosexuality*, 66.
120. Ibid., 74-77.
121. Ibid., 487 (my emphasis).

determinism, play the dominant role in manipulating how and whether homosexuality will come to expression. Cultures that become increasingly accepting of one or more forms of homosexuality can expect to see over a period of time marked increases in the incidence of homosexual behavior in the population.

The Impact of Urban Life and Education

In the United States today, the odds of a given child becoming homosexual increase dramatically depending on the social environment. We will focus on two cultural markers, though others could be noted (e.g., religion or income): urban/rural differences and the level of education. Data from the 1992 National Health and Social Life Survey (NHSLS) conducted by Edward Laumann, Robert T. Michael, Stuart Michaels (all of the University of Chicago) and John Gagnon (State University of New York), combined with data from the 1988 General Social Survey, confirm the conventional wisdom about homosexuality being primarily an urban phenomenon:[122] 9.2% of men in the central cities of the twelve largest urban areas identified themselves as homosexual compared with a mere 1.3% in rural areas and 2.8% generally; hence, a 708% increase from rural to urban, 329% increase from general to urban. Lesbianism and female bisexuality is much less of an urban phenomenon, though significant increases still appear: 2.6% compared to 1.4% generally (a 186% increase) and less than 1% rural. The authors write that a relatively uniform distribution of homosexuality in different social groups "would fit with certain analogies to genetically or biologically based traits such as left-handedness or intelligence. *However, that is exactly what we do not find.* Homosexuality . . . is clearly distributed differentially within categories of . . . social and demographic variables."[123] Migration may account for some of this, but cannot explain all, especially since the differences also show up for those aged fourteen and sixteen. Thus, *"an environment that provides*

---

122. Cf. the chart in Laumann et al., *Social Organization*, 305-6. The NHSLS study is the most extensive survey to date of sexual practices of Americans. The addition of the GSS adds 5,585 more adults to the NHSLS sample size, bringing it to a total of 8,744 adults.
123. Ibid., 307 (my emphasis).

increased opportunities for and fewer negative sanctions against same-gender sexuality may both allow and even elicit expression of same-gender interest and sexual behavior.[124]

As regards education,[125] among those whose level of education does not extend beyond high school only 1.8% of men and .4% of women identified themselves as homosexual/bisexual. Among college graduates the rates are 3.3% of men and 3.6% of women, a 183% and a 900% increase respectively. Women who are college graduates are thus nine times more likely to identify themselves as lesbian or bisexual than women who only graduated from high school. One might argue that education opens up women to their "true" sexuality, or that women's studies programs on many college campuses indoctrinate women with ideologies supportive of lesbianism. Laumann and others attribute the dramatic rise in rates of female homosexuality either to "greater social and sexual liberalism . . . and . . . greater sexual experimentation" that coincides with higher education or to "a higher level of personal resources (human capital)" that can allow women to please themselves rather than men.[126] The fact that the incidence of homosexual self-identification in men is affected far more by urban location than educational attainment, whereas for women it is just the opposite, suggests that the two sexes respond differently to different types of cultural stimuli. Male homosexuality appears to be governed more by pure libido, whereas female homosexuality is more cognitive and relational.

However one explains the increases, it seems clear that consistent exposure to a smorgasbord of variant sexual behaviors and the intense questioning of a heterosexual norm in educational settings can result in sevenfold to ninefold increases in the numbers of people identifying themselves as homosexual or bisexual. Given the fact that there still are major cultural reservations about homosexual behavior in the United States,[127] there is every reason to believe that the further erosion of such reservations could lead to significantly higher increases of homosexuality in the population. Possibly with time the current 2-3% rates

---

124. Ibid., 308 (my emphasis).
125. Ibid., 305.
126. Ibid., 310.
127. Polls consistently show that a significant majority of all Americans still regard homosexual intercourse as inherently wrong.

of self-identifying homosexuals and bisexuals could "max out" in the population at 15-25%. This suggests that it is possible for aggressive homophile instruction in the schools to recruit some additional children into a homosexual lifestyle who otherwise would have gone through life as self-identifying heterosexuals.

The Elasticity of Sexual Behavior

Advocates of homosexual behavior usually dismiss the notion that increased public support for homosexuality will lead to increased numbers of homosexuals. They do so on the assumptions that homosexuality is an immutable condition; that people who identify themselves as homosexual are locked into a lifelong condition; and, consequently, that clear lines separate homosexuals from bisexuals and bisexuals from heterosexuals.

The evidence to date, however, points to considerable fluidity in a spectrum from heterosexual to homosexual. People who at one time or another experience homosexual impulses do so at different levels of intensity, at different times of life, and for periods of different duration. Many exclusive homosexuals come to a "realization" about their "true" sexual identity relatively late in life. Many who identify themselves as exclusively homosexual early in life subsequently become predominantly or exclusively heterosexual later in life. None of this corresponds to a doctrine of biological determinism.

According to the 1992 NHSLS study,[128] of the 1.4% of females who identified themselves as lesbians or bisexuals, a third (.5%) identified themselves as bisexuals. Of the remaining .9%, only one third of these, a miniscule .3%, said that they were *exclusively* attracted to females at the time of the survey (let alone ever). Of the 2.8% of males who identified themselves as homosexuals or bisexuals, .8% were bisexual and the remaining 2% stated that they were attracted exclusively to other males. Of those who reported any same-sex behavior since turning eighteen *or* any same-sex desire at the time of the survey, *or* identified themselves as homosexual or bisexual at the time of the survey,[129] roughly

---

128. *Social Organization*, 298-300, 311.
129. That is, 8.6% and 10.1% of the total number of women and men surveyed, respectively.

8 out of every 10 (74% of men, 85% of women) did not meet all three criteria. Greater than 9 out of every 10 Americans (90.7% of all men and 94.9% of women) who have had any same-gender sex since puberty have also had opposite-gender sex. Presumably, many, if not most, of these experienced some amount of sexual arousal with a member of the opposite sex.

A nationwide random survey of 4,340 adults in five U.S. cities, conducted in 1983 by the Family Research Institute, reported that more than three quarters of all homosexuals (73% of men and 88% of women) had been sexually aroused at one time or another by the opposite sex, while one in ten heterosexuals (12% of men, 7.8% of women) had been homosexually aroused. Sixty-six percent of all homosexual men and 82% of homosexual women said that they had been in love with someone of the opposite sex. Sixty-seven percent of homosexual women and 54% of homosexual men reported current sexual attraction to the opposite sex. Over half of all people who had ever been homosexually aroused (59% of women and 51% of men) were currently heterosexual.[130]

The earlier (1970) study by Bell and Weinberg had arrived at similar figures.[131] More than three-quarters of all homosexuals (74% of men and 80% of women) had at one time or another been sexually aroused by the opposite sex; 33% of heterosexual men and 6% of heterosexual women had been aroused by people of the same sex. Even among those who identified themselves as exclusively homosexual (category 6) in terms of feelings, two-thirds stated that they had experienced heterosexual arousal at least once in their lives. Sixty-three percent of all homosexual men and 58% of all homosexual women reached orgasm at least once in their lives with an opposite-sex partner.

---

130. Paul Cameron et al., "Sexual Orientation and Sexually Transmitted Disease," *Nebraska Medical Journal* 70 (1985): 292-99; Paul Cameron, Kirk Cameron, and K. Proctor, "The Effect of Homosexuality upon Public Health and Social Order," *Psychological Reports* 64 (1989): 1167-79; results cited in Cameron, *The Gay Nineties*, 71-74.

131. Alan P. Bell and Martin S. Weinberg, *Homosexualities: A Study of Diversity Among Men and Women* (New York: Simon and Schuster, 1978), 53-61, 286-94. In the following discussion, it is useful to keep in mind Kinsey's 7-point graduated scale: (0) exclusively heterosexual, (1) predominantly heterosexual, (2) mostly heterosexual, (3) equally heterosexual and homosexual, (4) mostly homosexual, (5) predominantly homosexual, and (6) exclusively homosexual.

Half of all "exclusive" homosexuals had at one time or another experienced orgasm while having heterosexual sex. Nine out of ten homosexuals (97% of women, 84% of men) and one out of every five heterosexuals (15% of women, 29% of men) shifted along the Kinsey categories of sexual orientation at least once during their lives. A second shift was reported by 60% of homosexual males, 81% of homosexual females, 10% of heterosexual males, and 2% of heterosexual females. A third of homosexual males (32%) and half of homosexual females (52%) had a third shift. According to Bell, Weinberg, and Hammerstein (1981), 2% of the heterosexual population said that they had once been exclusively homosexual (compare to an estimated 4% homosexual population).[132]

Given such fluidity across the Kinsey spectrum, it seems far-fetched to think that exclusive homosexuals have a gene that does not permit them to become heterosexually aroused under any cultural parameters or individual life experiences, while another group of homosexuals has a gene that permits them to be predominantly homosexual, and a third group of homosexuals has a gene that permits them to be mostly homosexual, and so on.

Can Homosexuals Change?[133]

Given the lifetime fluctuation of large numbers of homosexuals across the Kinsey spectrum and the experience of heterosexual arousal (and often orgasm) even among the overwhelming majority of self-identified exclusive homosexuals, the initial and obvious answer to the question "Can homosexuals change?" is yes. Of course, change can take different forms: a reduction or elimination of homosexual behavior, a reduction in the intensity and frequency of homosexual impulses, the experience of heterosexual arousal and marriage, or reorientation from exclusive or predominant homosexuality to exclusive or predominant heterosexuality.

---

132. A. P. Bell, M. S. Weinberg, S. K. Hammersmith, *Sexual Preference: Its Development in Men and Women* (Bloomington: Indiana University Press, 1981).
133. Particularly helpful for the following discussion are Jones and Yarhouse, *Homosexuality*, ch. 5; Satinover, *Homosexuality*, chs. 11–13; and Whitehead, *Genes*, ch. 12.

For over half a century, psychoanalysts and other therapists have been reporting beneficial results for homosexuals who have sought such change. Jones and Yarhouse provide tables which list the results of treating homosexual patients from 14 individual therapists (1950s–1990s) and from group treatments (1950s–1970s). Tallying up the numbers, "positive outcomes" (defined as considerable to complete change) were reported for 623 of 2161 patients (28.8%). "Most psychotherapists will allow that in the treatment of *any* condition, a 30% success rate may be anticipated."[134] Alcoholics Anonymous has a success rate of somewhere between 25-30%.

In 1997 NARTH (National Association for Research and Therapy of Homosexuality) surveyed 882 clients who, it was thought, had experienced some amount of change in sexual orientation. The pre- and post-therapy self-ratings of the clients is given below:

Kinsey Rating	BEFORE	AFTER
0 - exclusively heterosexual	0%	15%
1 - almost entirely heterosexual	0%	18%
2 - more heterosexual than homosexual	0%	20%
3 - equally heterosexual and homosexual	9%	11%
4 - more homosexual than heterosexual	22%	23%
5 - almost entirely homosexual	31%	8%
6 - exclusively homosexual	36%	5%

In the group of clients who identified themselves pre-treatment as exclusively homosexual, post-therapy 18% rated themselves as exclusively heterosexual, 17% as almost entirely heterosexual, 12% as more heterosexual than homosexual. Those surveyed also reported significant decreases of homosexual thoughts. Although critics of change sometimes charge that reorientation therapies do harm to clients, the survey indicated substantial improvements in clients' self-esteem and emotional stability.[135]

Unfortunately, most of the significant research was done prior to the

---

134. Satinover, *Homosexuality*, 186.
135. "The Results of the 1997 NARTH Survey on Change," self-published and distributed by NARTH (www.narth.com).

"big chill" brought on by militant gay-rights activism in the American Psychiatric Association and the American Psychological Association beginning in the early 1970s.[136] Despite such obstacles to fair inquiry, the results achieved to date indicate sober hope with respect to change of homosexuals, even the change of those who identify themselves as exclusively homosexual. Certainly the notion of genetic immutability cannot stand up to scrutiny. Indeed, significant shifts in sexual orientation often occur apart from *any* therapeutic treatment, on both ends of the Kinsey spectrum.[137] Not surprisingly, therapists have found that homosexuals are most likely to achieve significant movement in the direction of heterosexuality when clients have had some history of heterosexual arousal, did not engage in homosexual activity early in life, and begin treatment highly motivated to change. Long-term success depends on the existence of a strong support network for their move out of the gay community, including the development of close but non-erotic same-sex relationships. Forgiveness of the same-sex parent, overcoming the anxiety associated with living up to heterosexual stereotypes, overcoming fear of heterosexual courtship customs, assertiveness training, and healing of sexual abuse may constitute important elements in the restoration process for many homosexuals.

In addition to the secular treatment of homosexuality, there are also numerous faith-based ministries which seek to assist homosexuals in the process of change. Among the most prominent are Exodus

---

136. Cf. Satinover's description of the sordid politics behind the American Psychiatric Association's decision to normalize homosexuality in 1973 (*Homosexuality*, 32-35). The "big chill" is most dramatically illustrated in the sharp decline in articles in medical and psychological journals, as listed in the Medline database: from 1,021 for the years 1966 to 1974; to 42 for the years 1975 to 1979; to a paltry two for the years 1992 to 1994 (ibid., 169).

137. This is particularly true of lesbians, where it is not at all uncommon in midlife for exclusively lesbian females to become bisexual or exclusively heterosexual females to become bisexual. Cf. M. Nichols, "Bisexuality in Women: Myths, Realities and Implications for Therapy," *Women and Therapy* 7 (1988): 235-52; J. K. Dixon, "Sexuality and Relationship Changes in Married Females Following the Commencement of Bisexual Activity," *JHomosex* 11 (1985): 115-33 (both cited by Whitehead). In 1993 a case was reported in which a man who was being treated for social phobia with the drug phenelzine incidentally switched orientations from exclusive homosexuality to primary heterosexuality (Satinover, *Homosexuality*, 189-90).

International (actually an umbrella organization for about a hundred faith-based ministries)[138] and Homosexuals Anonymous (which has about fifty chapters throughout North America and is modeled after Alcoholics Anonymous). Denominational ministries include Courage (Roman Catholic; headquartered in New York City), OneByOne (Presbyterian [PCUSA]; Rochester, New York), and Regeneration (Episcopal; Baltimore).[139] Thousands have experienced significant help from such groups in managing, and significantly decreasing or eliminating, homosexual impulses.

Much of the results that have been obtained to date have been criticized as having insufficient scientific controls to measure change.[140] At the same time, studies in other areas have employed similar measures and standards without receiving the same kind of scathing criticism and scrutiny.

---

138. Included here is Desert Stream (headquartered in Los Angeles), founded by Andrew Comiskey, an ex-homosexual. Among independent ministries two in particular merit special mention: Redeemed Life Ministries, which is based in Wheaton, Illinois, and founded by Mario Bergner (another ex-homosexual); and Pastoral Care Ministries, also operating out of Wheaton, Illinois, and founded by Leanne Payne.

139. For further information, see Satinover, *Homosexuality*, 196-209, 268-69; Jones and Yarhouse, *Homosexuality*, 133-38. Among the books providing pastoral help to homosexuals seeking to change, see Mario Bergner, *Setting Love in Order: Hope and Healing for the Homosexual* (Grand Rapids: Baker, 1995); Andrew Comiskey, *Pursuing Sexual Wholeness: How Jesus Heals the Homosexual* (Lake Mary, Fla.: Creation House, 1988); William Consiglio, *Homosexual No More: Practical Strategies for Christians Overcoming Homosexuality* (Wheaton: Victor Books, 1991); Joe Dallas, *A Strong Delusion: Confronting the "Gay Christian" Movement* (Eugene, Ore.: Harvest House, 1996); Bob Davies and Lori Rentzel, *Coming Out of Homosexuality: New Freedom for Men and Women* (Downers Grove, Ill.: InterVarsity, 1993); Father John E. Harvey, *The Homosexual Person: New Thinking in Pastoral Care* (San Francisco: Ignatius, 1987); idem, ed., *The Truth About Homosexuality: The Cry of the Faithful* (San Francisco: Ignatius, 1996); Jeanette Howard, *Out of Egypt: Leaving Lesbianism Behind* (Nashville: Thomas Nelson, 1994); Ed Hurst, *Overcoming Homosexuality* (Elgin, Ill.: David C. Cook, 1987); Leanne Payne, *Healing Homosexuality* (Grand Rapids: Baker Books, 1996); Michael R. Saia, *Counseling the Homosexual* (Minneapolis: Bethany House, 1988); Frank Worthen, *Helping People Step Out of Homosexuality* (Manila: OMF Literature, 1991).

140. For a strident and biased critique, see Douglas C. Haldeman, "The Practice and Ethics of Sexual Orientation Conversion Therapy," *Journal of Consulting and Clinical Psychology* 62 (April 1999): 221-227; idem, "Sexual Orientation

THE BIBLE AND HOMOSEXUAL PRACTICE

Critics have attempted to explain away reports of change in sexual orientation in one of two ways. (1) So-called homosexuals who have changed to heterosexuals were really not true homosexuals to begin with, but at most only bisexuals. (2) True homosexuals who think they have changed are kidding themselves, for they have only momentarily suppressed homosexual urges through "internalized homophobia." Homosexuals re-classified as heterosexuals may have discontinued homosexual behavior but they continue to feel homosexual impulses and will some day relapse.

There are three main problems with these arguments: First, they exhibit circular reasoning and blatant dogmatism; second, they apply standards for cure that are stricter than those required for other conditions; and, third, they develop an impractical, unworkable standard. Let us take each point in order.

With regard to the first problem, there is no need for such critics to examine the evidence for change because they have ruled change out of bounds on a *priori* grounds. Their reasoning is dogmatic, based primarily on ideological conviction rather than evidence. The greatest fear of the homosexual lobby is that some "true" homosexuals somewhere, somehow, might change in sexual orientation. Intellectually, such a change cannot be permitted because that would discredit the fundamental premise of many activists; namely, that homosexual orientation is immutable. If you press them for how they know homosexuality is an immutable condition they will say that it is obvious that homosexuals are "born that way," implying some sort of genetic or hormonal determinism. In effect, such critics must completely reject environmental influences, even though the consensus in the scientific community—even among homosexual researchers such as Hamer and LeVay—is that environmental and psychological factors still play a significant role in the development of homosexuality. They must ignore the identical twin studies which have conclusively demonstrated that genetic influence is at best small and, in any case, certainly not

Conversion Therapy for Gay Men and Lesbians: A Scientific Examination," *Homosexuality: Research Implications for Public Policy* (ed. J. C. Gonsiorek and J. D. Weinrich; Newbury Park, Calif.: Sage Publications, 1991), 149-60. For a critique of Haldeman, see Jones and Yarhouse, *Homosexuality*, 140-48.

immutable. They must ignore cross-cultural comparisons which show incredible malleability in rates and forms of homosexuality, not to mention intra-cultural comparisons such as the effect of urban settings, education, income, and religion on the incidence of homosexuality. They must discount the capacity of rearing to override the genetic gender of people born with ambiguous genitalia. Indeed, they must reject out of hand all the psychological and psychoanalytic data we have about the enormous effect that parental upbringing and peer socialization has on sexual development of children generally (not just homosexual development). They must toss countless studies on behavior modification. They must overlook the fact that sexual orientation shows remarkable elasticity, including the fact that even the overwhelming majority of people who classify themselves as exclusively homosexual (not bisexual) have, at one time or another, experienced heterosexual arousal. They must pretend that, even though a category 5 (predominant) homosexual can make shifts along the Kinsey spectrum in the direction of heterosexuality, a category 6 (exclusive) homosexual never can. They must further pretend that a person who is exclusively homosexual in orientation from the ages of fourteen to eighteen can never, no matter what experiences she or he encounters in the next sixty years of life, develop heterosexual passions. They must not only deny that homosexuals can become heterosexuals but also—if they want to be consistent—deny that any heterosexual can ever become homosexual. Here they must even ignore the testimony of countless "midlife" gays and lesbians who claim to have experienced some level of heterosexual arousal and orgasm for the first part of their post-pubertal life.[141] And, of course, they have to explain away all the testimonies from ex-homosexuals, many of whom claim to have changed from exclusive homosexual attraction to exclusive heterosexual attraction. Sooner or later, those who make dogmatic claims about

---

141. One study of women becoming lesbian in midlife found that they broke into two groups: those who thought they had always been lesbian and those who believed that they had made a conscious choice to become lesbian (C. Charbonneau and P. S. Landers, "Redefining Sexuality: Women Becoming Lesbian in Midlife," *Lesbians at Midlife* [eds. B. Sang et al.; San Francisco: Spinsters Book Co., 1991], 35-43).

the inherent immutability of "true" homosexuality have to acknowledge that "the emperor has no clothes."

The second problem with such a claim is that it applies a stricter definition of change to sexual orientation than would be applied to various other conditions which have a partial genetic, hormonal, or biological component. It is surely unrealistic to demand that a person who comes out of a homosexual lifestyle and into a heterosexual one never again, under even the most stressful circumstances, experience homosexual urges if she or he is to claim a sexual-orientation change. An acceptable standard of "cure" in other conditions is not the removal of every last vestige of temptation but rather the ability to successfully manage such temptations. Many happily married ex-homosexuals testify that, although homosexual impulses may arise in moments of high stress, they are more a slight nuisance than an intractable problem. Is it fair to say that such persons have not changed their sexual orientation or to call conversion therapy in such cases a failure? At the very least, to refer to them as homosexuals or even bisexuals is misleading, particularly if the homosexual urges are neither intense nor acted upon.

That changes in sexual orientation usually do not come about easily should occasion no surprise. Many pleasurable forms of behavior, particularly sexual behavior, tend toward compulsion and addiction. They cannot be turned on and off like a light switch. A close friend of mine, who has worked for over a decade counseling sex offenders in prisons, has shared with me the pessimism that prison mental health staff have about effecting permanent change. Despite the best effort of clinicians, the recidivism rate for rapists and child molesters is extremely high. The reason why is clear: there is a biological or physiological component to their peculiar experience of sexual arousal. Yet few would claim that change is impossible for such offenders. If society believed that, there would be no point to providing prison counseling services. If once incarcerated sex offenders learn to manage and control their aberrant sexual impulses, it is appropriate to say that satisfactory change has occurred. Why not be able to say the same about once homosexually oriented people who are able to effectively manage such impulses? One can also make comparisons with non-criminal forms of immoral or inappropriate sexual behavior (e.g., sadomasochism, bestiality, addiction to pornography, and intense dissatisfaction with single-partner monogamous relationships) or with non-sexual compulsions, addictions, and disorders which have a genetic or biological aspect (e.g., alcoholism, smoking addictions, eating disorders, depression, pathological gambling, aggression, and criminal behavior). We have no difficulty acknowledging significant change in a "recovering alcoholic" who generally stays away from the bottle but from time-to-time struggles with an internal, physiologically connected desire to drink. Nor do we accuse Alcoholics Anonymous of being a failure because they have only a 25-30% success rate, where "success" is not defined as the complete abolition of temptation.

It is more than a little ironic that the very same gay activists who criticize the success rate of sexual reorientation programs have themselves made it far more difficult for homosexuals to change. The Whiteheads correctly point out that

> when governments begin granting political protections, and homosexuality begins getting official ecclesiastical endorsement, support from medical and caring professions, "scientific" backing, and media affirmation, change is not something a self-identified gay person needs to give much thought to—especially if there are rewarding patterns of sexual gratification to give up.[142]

Imagine a society that endorsed pedophilia—how much more difficult would it be to induce pedophiles to change their behavior? In the current political climate, not only do ex-homosexuals not receive societal congratulations, they also are villified by homosexual-activist groups. Change of any behavior requires strong personal motivation to change. When society and even the church states that change is both impossible and wrong (homophobic), very few will be inclined to change.

A third problem with the contention that changing "true" homosexuals is impossible is that the position is completely impractical. Even if there were such a category as a "true" homosexual, someone who not only exhibits exclusive homosexual behavior and feelings at any given

---

142. *Genes*, 197.

period of time but also can never change under any circumstances, how would society be able to distinguish a true homosexual from a bisexual or heterosexual who is acting just like a true homosexual? The answer is clear: society could not make the distinction, at least not apart from active attempts at changing homosexuals into heterosexuals. As Warren Throckmorton, past president of the American Mental Health Counselors Association, puts it:

> If there is no research [on the longitudinal stability of sexual orientation over the adult life span], how can professional associations be certain that sexual orientation cannot change? . . . Even if one accepts the presumption that sexual orientation cannot be changed, how does one know when a client's sexual orientation is settled? Without a more certain way to objectively determine sexual orientation, perhaps we should place considerable weight on the self-assessment of clients. Clients who want to change cannot reliably be told that they cannot change, since we cannot say with certainty that they have settled on a fixed trait.[143]

So long as people who identify themselves as homosexuals continue to exhibit shifts and even apparent changes in sexual orientation, the functional value of critics' arguments against homosexual change is nil.

We have argued strongly up till now that homosexuals *can* change; or, more precisely, that at least *some* homosexuals, including some who claim to have been exclusively homosexual in orientation, are capable of change. Of course, *empirically* not all homosexuals will change, if by *change* we mean make a major adjustment in sexual orientation. Christian faith entails a strong belief in the power of the Spirit of God to change the lives of those who submit themselves to the lordship of Jesus Christ. Based on testimony of many ex-homosexuals, even secular treatment can sometimes achieve radical changes in sexual orientation; how much more possible, then, is it for homosexuals who turn to Christ to develop heterosexual desires? We have a "cloud of witnesses," thousands of ex-homosexuals in Christian communities across

---

143. Warren Throckmorton, "Attempts to Modify Sexual Orientation: A Review of Outcome Literature and Ethical Issues," *Journal of Mental Health Counseling* 20 (Oct. 1998): 283-304 (quote from p. 286).

the nation and countless thousands more throughout the world who testify to the power of God's Spirit to transform their lives and give them sexual fulfilment in heterosexual marriages. At the same time, we have Christians who appear on the surface at least to have made sincere efforts to change, and yet have been unable to move from a homosexual to a heterosexual orientation. Patterns of sexual arousal embedded in the brain are not easily removed. When the apostle Paul referred to warfare between the flesh and Spirit in the Christian life, he spoke optimistically of the Christian's ability to "walk" or behave in accordance with the wishes of the indwelling Spirit. Yet even that victory presupposes an ongoing struggle with sinful desires. Christians are not guaranteed that they will be freed from such desires altogether, but rather that their identity is not defined by such desires. It is fair to say that Christians who no longer participate in the homosexual behavior of their pre-Christian life are ex-homosexuals. "These things some of you were" (1 Cor 6:11). No longer obeying homosexual impulses but now obeying the will of God for their lives, they have been transformed into the adopted children of God. In the same way, heterosexuals who continue to experience temptations to lust after members of the opposite sex other than their spouse, yet resist such temptations and refuse to act on them, are ex-fornicators and ex-adulterers. Christians are not promised an end to sexual temptation in its various forms. They are given the anchored hope that those who endure to the end will be saved.

The best hope for change in the sexual orientation of homosexuals comes not in attempts to treat homosexuals after years and years of homosexual behavior but rather in limiting the options that young people have in terms of sexual experimentation. Some people will experiment under any cultural conditions. Nevertheless, cross-cultural studies prove beyond a shadow of a doubt that strong cultural disapproval of homosexual behavior can significantly curtail the incidence of such behavior. So perhaps a better question to ask than "Can homosexuals change?" is "Can the numbers of self-identifying homosexuals in the population be affected by cultural attitudes toward homosexual behavior?" The answer to that question, I would contend, is "Yes, significantly so."

Relation of the Scientific Data to Paul's Views

It is evident, then, that the genetic or intrauterine component of homosexual orientation is indirect and not dominant. Indeed, the latest scientific research on homosexuality simply reinforces what Scripture and common sense already told us: human behavior results from a complex mixture of biologically related desires (genetic, intrauterine, post-natal brain development), familial and environmental influences, human psychology, and repeated choices. Whatever predisposition to homosexuality may exist is a far cry from predestination or determinism and easy to harmonize with Paul's understanding of homosexuality. It is often stated by scholars supportive of the homosexual lifestyle that Paul believed that homosexual behavior was something freely chosen, based on the threefold use of "they exchanged" (*metēllaxan*) in Rom 1:23, 25, 26. The use of the word *exchange* may indeed suggest that Paul assumed an element of choice was involved, though for the phenomenon globally conceived and not necessarily for each individual. Certainly, the larger context in which these verses are found indicates a willing suppression of the truth about God and God's design for the created order (1:18). And indeed who would debate the point that homosexual *behavior* is void of all choice? Even a predisposition does not compel behavior.

Romans 1–8 indicates as well that Paul considered the sinful passions that buffet humanity to be innate and controlling. Corresponding to the threefold "they exchanged" is the threefold "God gave them over" (*paredōken autous ho theos*) in 1:24, 26, 28. Rather than exert a restraining influence, God steps aside and allows human beings to be controlled by preexisting desires.[144] Paul paints a picture of humanity subjugated and ruled by its own passions; a humanity not in control but controlled. The irony that results from turning away from God is not more human independence but less. Based on a reading of Rom 5:12-21 and 7:7-23, it is clear that Paul conceived of sin as "innate" (a category available in antiquity which is close enough for our purposes to the concept of genetic). Paul viewed sin as a power operating in the "flesh" and in human "members," experienced since birth as a result of being

---

144. Haacker, "Exegetische Gesichtspunkte," 177.

descendants of Adam. The transmission of Adam's sin to all his descendants was in Paul's view not simply a legal sleight of hand, a judicial verdict that all are sinners because Adam sinned. Rather, Adam transmitted sin, conceived as an impulse, a power, or congenital defect or disease, through the reproduction of human flesh. For Paul, all sin was in a certain sense innate in that human beings do not *ask* to feel sexual desire, or anger, or fear, or selfishness—they just *do*, despite whether they want to experience such impulses or not. If Paul could be transported into our time and told that homosexual impulses were at least partly present at birth, he would probably say, "I could have told you that" or at least "I can work that into my system of thought."

The experience of homosexual urges is part of a larger phenomenon of various sinful impulses that all humans experience, though in different proportions for different kinds of sin. According to Rom 8:1-7, the power of sin, that internal "law" or regulating force which thwarts that other internal "law" of the mind (i.e., the mind's recognition of and desire to do the right enshrined in the external law of Moses), can now be mastered by a third internal "law," the Spirit, which indwells those who believe in Christ. Sinful impulses remain, even among those who have been saved, but for believers it is now possible to live Spirit-led lives, at least in the main.

Advocates of homosexual behavior regard it as cruel to forbid persons who have homosexual impulses from ever acting on their sexual urges. However, there are other cases where people are required to repress their sinful sexual urges. Pedophiles who are only stimulated by sexual encounters with children are required by the church (not to mention civil law) to abstain from carrying out those urges even if it means remaining celibate for the rest of their lives. Heterosexuals who grow tired of being restricted to one sexual partner and/or lose all sexual interest in their spouse do not—from the church's perspective—have the option of committing adultery (nor is this sufficient grounds for divorce from a biblical perspective). Millions of single heterosexuals hold no certain prospect that they will one day be married; yet, from a biblical perspective, premarital sex is not an option. In fact, the 1992 NHSLS study by Laumann and others found that there are twice as many people in the population who have had no sex partners since the age of eighteen (2.9%) than people who classify themselves as (non-bisexual) homosexuals (1.5%). Moreover, as we have noted above, telling male and female homosexuals that they cannot act on same-sex urges is not the same as consigning them to a life without hope.

The bottom line is that no biblical writer regarded individual "self-realization," "self-fulfillment," or "self-gratification" as a good that allows one to disregard clear norms for sexual behavior. Carrying out the will of God and concern for the other (the two great commandments according to Jesus), not the freedom to gratify one's sexual urges, stand at the center of Jewish and Christian self-identity. As Richard Hays puts it, the Bible promotes a "demythologizing of sex": "The Bible undercuts our cultural obsession with sexual fulfillment. Scripture (along with many subsequent generations of faithful Christians) bears witness that lives of freedom, joy, and service are possible without sexual relations."[145] In the current cultural climate, where freedom of sexual expression is often touted as a God-given right, such a claim may sound shocking and offensive, but it constitutes a healthy critique of a new form of idolatry. Scripture presents only two choices for obtaining sexual intercourse: become involved in a lifelong monogamous heterosexual relationship or remain celibate.

V. There are only a few biblical texts that speak directly to homosexuality.

The number of texts that speak directly to the issue of homosexuality is relatively small, though not as small as some have alleged: Gen 9:20-27; 19:4-11; Judg 19:22-25; Lev 18:22; 20:13; Ezek 16:50 (possibly too 18:12 and 33:26); Rom 1:26-27; 1 Cor 6:9; 1 Tim 1:10; and probably also Jude 7 and 2 Pet 2:7. As we argued in ch. 1, texts referring to homosexual cult prostitution should be added to these (Deut 23:17-18; 1 Kgs 14:24; 15:12; 22:46; 2 Kgs 23:7; Job 36:14; and Rev 21:8; 22:15). Some conclude from the limited number of biblical references that homosexual practice is a marginal issue in the Bible. The

---

145. *The Moral Vision of the New Testament*, 390: "The Bible's sober anthropology rejects the apparently commonsense assumption that only freely chosen acts are morally culpable. Quite the reverse: the very nature of sin is that it is *not* freely chosen. That is what it means to live 'in the flesh' in a fallen creation."

church, they say, should use its precious time and resources to address issues other than this. Of course, many of those who argue that homosexuality is a minor issue in the Bible devote considerable time and resources to normalizing homosexual practice in the church. Yet apart from this inconsistency, are their claims for the Bible accurate?

There are at least three problems with this way of thinking. First, such an argument confuses frequency with degree of importance. There are other forbidden forms of sexual conduct that receive little negative documentation in the Bible (bestiality, prostitution) but are not for that reason insignificant sins. The Bible is essentially a series of *ad hoc* documents. That is to say, the authors of the Bible often only treated issues which were problems in the communities of faith being addressed. That homosexuality appears so infrequently as an issue in the Bible is an accident of history, not a sign of its lack of importance. The writers of Scripture generally did not encounter among their readers public displays of homosexual conduct. They also considered the egregious sinfulness of same-sex intercourse as axiomatic and thus requiring little if any instruction. If homosexuality had arisen among members of the communities being addressed, there doubtless would have been more explicit discussion of the matter.[146]

Paul's treatment of incest is illustrative. Only once in all his letters does he address the issue: 1 Corinthians 5. Incest does not even appear explicitly in any of the vice lists. It only appears in 1 Cor 5 because one of the Corinthian believers was sleeping with his stepmother. Had this never happened in Corinth, there would not be a single text forbidding incest in the entire New Testament. Does that mean that the New Testament writers probably waffled on the issue of incest? Obviously not. Paul's exhortation to the community to expel the incestuous man from their midst was as strong a denunciation as could be given.

That leads to the second point. The idea of determining the importance of an issue by counting up the number of texts that speak directly to it is a rather constricted and ahistorical way of viewing Scripture.[147]

---

146. Balz, "Biblische Aussagen zur Homosexualität," 64. Biblical writers used catch-all terms for sexual immorality and licentiousness which readers would have understood to include same-sex intercourse.

147. Even Hays succumbs to the temptation of confusing frequency of mention with importance: "In terms of emphasis, [homosexual behavior] is a minor concern—

Behind every text stands an author(s) who wrote it and a commu-
nity(-ies) of faith to whom the text was addressed. To say that homosexuality was a marginal issue for Paul because he addressed it only two
or three times in his letters is to think of his letters as systematic, self-
contained works wholly disconnected from his life as a historical person.
The fact that Paul cited the issue twice, once as a prime example for
establishing the extreme depths of depravity to which gentiles without
Christ have sunk and once among a series of vices that exclude even
believers from inheriting the kingdom of God,[148] is more than enough
evidence to establish that Paul regarded homosexual conduct as an
extremely serious offense in which Christians should not be engaged.
That means that one of the most important authors of New Testament
texts (if not *the* most important) was unequivocally opposed. Moreover,
the authors of the deuteropauline corpus, the Catholic Epistles,[149] and
the book of Revelation were even more conservative than Paul in
upholding traditional ethical values.[150] If Paul was opposed to homo-

---

in contrast, for example, to economic injustice. The paucity of texts addressing the
issue is a significant fact for New Testament ethics. What the Bible does say
should be heeded carefully, but any ethic that intends to be biblical will seek to
get the accents in the right place, not overemphasizing peripheral issues. Would
that the passion presently being expended in the church over the question of
homosexuality were devoted instead to urging the wealthy to share with the
poor!" (*The Moral Vision of the New Testament*, 381). I would say a hearty
"Amen" to the last sentence if the "instead" were changed to "in addition,"
emphasizing that the passion for generous distribution of material resources
should attain to the same level of passion for sexual purity (to be sure, heterosexual and not just homosexual), not that the latter should be diminished in significance. Frequency of New Testament mention is not in itself a decisive factor in
determining significance, as the incest example in 1 Corinthians 5 clearly shows.
I see no reason from a biblical perspective to rank various forms of sexual
immorality lower on the scale of sin than economic injustice. Both are egregious,
though individual culpability for economic injustice is more difficult to establish
in all but the most severe cases. The debate on same-sex intercourse receives
greater stress in the contemporary context than it does in most writings of the
Bible because it has now become affirmed by a large minority of Christians,
whereas in the first century there was no serious debate about its legitimacy.
148. Twice in vice lists if one accepts the Pastoral Epistles as Pauline (1 Tim 1:10).
149. The deuteropauline texts are Ephesians, Colossians, 2 Thessalonians, and the
Pastoral Epistles (1 Timothy, 2 Timothy, Titus). The so-called Catholic Epistles
are James, 1–2 Peter, 1–2–3 John, and Jude.
150. See, for example, the negative references to homosexuality in 1 Tim 1:10; Rev
21:8; 22:15; Jude 7; 2 Pet 2:7; the conservative household codes, which presup-

sexual conduct, the likelihood of these writers adopting a more liberal stance toward homosexuality is not even "slim to none"—it is just "none."

Although the author of Luke–Acts does not speak directly about same-sex intercourse, his opposition can be easily surmised. According to the "Apostolic Decree" cited in Acts 15:20, 29; 21:25, gentiles did not have to be circumcised but they still had to abstain from *porneia*. That *porneia* would have included same-sex intercourse is evident from the fact that the prohibitions of the "Apostolic Decree" derive from the laws of Leviticus 17–18, among the few laws in the Hebrew Bible expressly enjoined even on resident aliens (Lev 17:8-10, 12-13, 15; 18:26).[151] This approach was consistent with the development of

---

pose only one acceptable sexual relationship; and Revelation's uncompromising stance against eating idol meat.

151. According to the Apostolic Decree, gentiles were to abstain from: (1) "things sacrificed to idols" (*eidōlothyta*), encompassing both sacrificing to a god other than Yahweh and eating food offered to idols (alluding to Lev 17:1-9 which mandates that all sacrifices be brought "to the entrance of the tent of meeting" so that "they may no longer offer their sacrifices for goat-demons, to whom they prostitute themselves"); (2) "blood" (*haima*; alluding to Lev 17:10-12 where the eating of blood is prohibited), possibly containing a secondary allusion to not shedding blood (i.e., "bloodshed," murder) since the command to Noah and his descendants in Gen 9:4-6 couples the prohibition against eating animals from which the blood had not been drained with a prohibition against shedding human blood; (3) "what is strangled (or choked to death; *pnikton*), that is, eating animals that were killed without having the blood drained from them (alluding to Lev 17:13-14 which refers to pouring out the blood of animals that have not died from a shedding of blood); and (4) "sexual immorality" (*porneia*; alluding to Lev 18:6-23, which forbids incest, adultery, intercourse between males, and bestiality). The fact that the sequence of the commands of the Apostolic Decree corresponds to the sequence in Leviticus 17–18 further confirms the former's derivation from the latter. Obviously the Decree was not exhaustive but was designed to treat disputed matters.

The historicity of the Apostolic Decree has been subject to much debate, largely because Paul's own account of the Jerusalem Conference emphatically states that the only stipulation placed on gentile believers was the collection for the poor Christians in Jerusalem (Gal 2:10) and because Paul advocated a more liberal stance toward the eating of idol meat when discussing the issue in 1 Corinthians 8–10 (for Paul it was permissible to eat idol meat so long as one did not eat it in a pagan temple or eat it in the presence of fellow believers or pagans who might be "stumbled"). There is also no extant evidence from the Pauline corpus that Paul would have objected to the eating of meat that had not been properly drained of blood. Some have speculated that the author of Luke–Acts was

so-called "Noahide laws" in early Judaism, commandments regarded as binding on all the descendants of Noah and constituting minimum standards for "righteous Gentiles." Noahide laws always included a prohibition of sexual immorality, which for Jews in antiquity would have included same-sex intercourse.[152] There is also every reason to believe that the use of *porneia* in Mark 7:21 (par. Matt 15:19) should be taken in this broadest possible sense to include homosexual behavior.

---

describing an event that occurred after Paul's meeting with the "pillars" of the Jerusalem church, whether still during the lifetime of Paul (but perhaps without Paul signing off on it) or in the author's own day. Regardless, it certainly represents the view of the author of Luke-Acts and, at least with respect to the proscription of *porneia* (including same-sex intercourse), undoubtedly represented the sentiments of Christian leadership everywhere in the first hundred years of Christian history. It is possible that the prohibition against eating meat improperly drained of blood was implemented purely for the sake of avoiding offense in dealings with Jews and some Jewish Christians, especially given that no other NT text mentions a problem with eating blood. The same may also be true of the injunction against eating idol meat (though Rev 2:14, 20 and the "weak" gentiles at Corinth also objected to this). However, no early Christian leader (certainly not the apostles of the early church or their disciples) viewed worship of idols and sexual immorality as a mere "convention" that one should respect so as to avoid offending the scruples of others. Codex Bezae (D) dropped the prohibition against "what is strangled" and added the Golden Rule in order to conform the Apostolic Decree more closely to moral law (prohibitions against idolatry, "bloodshed," and sexual immorality). For discussion of text-critical problems, see B. Metzger, *A Textual Commentary on the Greek New Testament* (2d ed.; Stuttgart: German Bible Society, 1994), 379-83.

152. By the early third century C.E., rabbis generally identified at least seven "Noahide" commandments, having to do with judicial injustice, idolatry, blasphemy of the divine name, "sexual immorality" (literally, "the uncovering of nakedness," a reference to forms of sexual intercourse forbidden by the Torah in Leviticus 18), "the shedding of blood" (murder), robbery, and eating the flesh of living creatures (i.e., meat that had not been drained of blood; cf. *t. ꜥAbod. Zar.* 8:4; *b. Sanh.* 56a-b). According to *b. Sanh.* 58a, sexual intercourse between males was included in the prohibition against sexual immorality (cf. Maimonides, *Kings* 9:5). Whether this precise series existed in the first century C.E. is a matter of debate but certainly many of the elements (including idolatry and sexual immorality) were part of the minimal expectation on moral behavior for gentiles, as the Apostolic Decree suggests. In *Jub.* 7:20-21 (ca. 150 B.C.E.) Noah is said to have commanded his descendants to "do justice and cover the shame of their flesh (= avoid incest) and bless the one who created them and honor father and mother, and each love his neighbor and preserve themselves from *porneia* and pollution

In addition, the author of the Gospel of Matthew, given his stress on doing the Law, fulfilling the commands, and having a righteousness higher than the Pharisees also makes him a likely candidate for agreeing with Paul on this issue. Nothing in the Gospel of John, the most sectarian of all the Gospels, suggests a more "enlightened" position (cf. 4:17-18). Finally, as I have attempted to show in the case of Jesus, Jesus' silence on the issue points overwhelmingly in the direction not of neutrality, let alone support for homosexual relationships, but instead of definite disapproval.

In short, the odds of any major positive figure connected with earliest Christianity having either no opinion or a positive opinion about homosexual conduct in any form is extremely remote. To assert otherwise is to lose all touch with the historical personalities behind the texts and to foster an arbitrary, gnostic exegesis. The burden of proof is decidedly on anyone who would want to argue that Jesus or any New Testament writer would have been open to same-sex intercourse. Textual silence cannot be equated with neutrality or openness, let alone support, without grossly distorting history.

Third, although there are a limited number of texts that speak directly to the issue, these texts are part of a much larger biblical worldview that consistently portrays only one model for sexual relations, that between a man and a woman in lifelong partnership.[153] This is true of Genesis 1 (where male and female are created to procreate) and Genesis 2–3 (where the only "cleaving" that is said to result in "one

---

and from all injustice." *Sibylline Oracle* 4:24-34 (ca. 80 C.E.) pronounces happy "those of humankind on earth" who worship the true God and reject idolatry, "commit no wicked murder, nor deal in dishonest gain. Neither have they disgraceful desire for another's spouse (= adultery) or for *hateful and repulsive abuse of a male* (= homosexual intercourse)." The *Didache* (Syria, early second century) mentions prohibitions against murder, adultery, idolatry, theft, and blasphemy (3:1-6; the same five appear in *b. Yoma* 67b; *Sipra* on Lev. 18:4). Cf. David Novak, *The Image of the Non-Jew in Judaism: An Historical and Constructive Study of the Noahide Laws* (New York: Mellen, 1983), 3-51, 199-222; Mark D. Nanos, *The Mystery of Romans*, 50-55; Alan F. Segal, *Paul the Convert* (New Haven: Yale University Press, 1990), 195-200; Emil Schürer, *The History of the Jewish People in the Age of Jesus Christ* (vol. 3.1; rev. and ed. F. Millar, et al.; Edinburgh: T & T Clark, 1986), 171-72; Str-B 2.722; 3.37-8; Moore, *Judaism*, 1.274-75; 3.86; *JE* 7.648-50; *EncJud* 12:1189-91.

153. See the helpful treatment by Dearman, "Marriage in the Old Testament," 53-67.

flesh" is the sexual bond between male and female, 2:24, and this before the fall). Taken together with the stories of Ham's crime in Gen 9:20-27 and of Sodom and Gomorrah in Genesis 19, and the Levitical prohibitions in 18:22; 20:13, the Yahwist's (J's), Priestly Writer's (P's), and Holiness Code's (H's) strongly negative stance in the Tetrateuch toward homosexual intercourse is evident. The Deuteronomic prohibitions against cross-dressing (22:5) and against homosexual cult prostitutes ("dogs," 23:17-18) leaves little doubt regarding the position of the editors of the Deuteronomic law on homosexual intercourse. The same can be said for the Deuteronomistic Historian's considerable antipathy toward homosexual cult prostitutes.

On a descriptive level, throughout the Bible there is not a single hero of the faith that engages in homosexual conduct: no patriarch, no matriarch, no prophet, no priest, no king (certainly not David), no apostle, no disciple. The Song of Solomon is devoted to singing the praises of committed heterosexual love. On a prescriptive level, every regulation that affirms the sexual bond affirms it between a man and a woman—without exception. In addition, every proverb or wisdom saying refers to heterosexual—not homosexual—relationships as fitting for the lives of the faithful. There is an abundance of Old Testament laws and proverbs regulating and establishing proper boundaries for sexual intercourse between male and female (e.g., regarding virginity, mate selection, engagement, marital fidelity). By way of contrast, there are no laws distinguishing proper homosexual conduct from improper homosexual conduct, because in every law code homosexual conduct is presumed to be forbidden *in toto*. This includes the Ten Commandments. The fifth commandment stipulates "honor your father and your mother." The seventh commandment says "you shall not commit adultery."[154] The tenth commandment requires that "you shall not covet . . . your neighbor's wife." These only make sense where heterosexual couplings alone are sanctioned. Likewise, every discussion in the New Testament about marriage or sexual unions always and only seeks to regulate heterosexual unions because there is no concep-

---

154. Adultery for same-sex unions would be a *non sequitur* because a union that has no standing from the start cannot be violated.

tion of a proper homosexual union.[155] There was no need to talk about fidelity and loving concern in same-sex unions because it was universally understood that homosexual unions were abominable. The relationship between Yahweh and Israel and between Christ and the church is imaged as a marriage between a husband and a wife.[156] It would have been absolutely unthinkable for any prophet or New Testament author to conceive of this relationship in homosexual terms.

In short, the universal silence in the Bible regarding an acceptable same-sex union, when combined with the explicit prohibitions, speaks volumes for a consensus disapproval of homosexual conduct. To say that there are only a few texts in the Bible that do not condone homosexual conduct is a monumental understatement of the facts. The reverse is a more accurate statement: there is not a single shred of evidence anywhere in the Bible that would even remotely suggest that same-sex unions are any more acceptable than extramarital or premarital intercourse, incest, or bestiality.

Gerald Sheppard, an Old Testament scholar and former student of Brevard Childs, plays off authorial intent and "canonical context," arguing that the particular position of a text within the larger context of other texts "as often as not, invites a reading against an author's original intent." "It is not the voice of the 'genuine' Paul any more than that of the 'historical Jesus' which is normative for the church." He refers also to "a larger theological claim" of the word of God (presumably, "the demands of the Gospel in terms of love and justice") upon all the words of Scripture and the relevance of both "advances in human knowledge" and the witness of people's lives.[157] There are elements in all of these statements that I find acceptable. Nevertheless, Sheppard draws too great a divide between authorial intent and authority.

The various "voices" of Scripture cannot be heard and compared with one another apart from discerning original authorial meaning, to

---

155. E.g., Mark 6:18 par.; 10:2-12, 17-22 par.; 13:18-27 par.; Luke 16:18 par.; Rom 7:1-6; 1 Cor 7; 9:5; 11:1-16; 1 Thess 4:3-8; Col 3:18-19; Eph 5:22-33; 1 Tim 3:2, 12; 5:14; 1 Pet 3:1-7.
156. E.g., Isa 5:1-7; 54:5-7; 61:10; 62:4-5; Jer 2:2, 20–3:3; 31:32; Ezekiel 16, 23; Hosea 1–3; Mark 2:19-20 par.; Matt 22:1-14; 25:1-13; John 3:29; Eph 5:30-32; Rev 19:7-9.
157. "The Use of Scripture," 18, 27, 29, 30, 32.

the extent that such meaning is recoverable (and in many cases, contrary to the claims of post-modernist interpretation, such meaning is recoverable). Otherwise, one is consigned to a sophisticated form of allegory, reading into the text whatever one wants it to say with no controls coming from the text itself. If the recovery of original authorial meaning is not always secure, discerning how the shape of the canonical context impacts a particular text is even less predictable.

Sheppard can appeal to no text anywhere in the canon of Scripture that unambiguously counters the texts explicitly rejecting same-sex intercourse. Indeed, as pointed out above, all the inferential or indirect evidence suggests complete concordance with these explicit texts. The best Sheppard can do is appeal to the later presentation of Paul in 1 Tim 4:1-5 (do not heed those who "forbid marriage. . . . For everything created by God is good") as a corrective to Paul's allegedly limited frame of reference for sexual ethics.[158] Yet the author of 1 Timothy clearly viewed same-sex intercourse as sin (1 Tim 1:10) and thus not a part of God's good creation. Innate impulses cannot be simply equated with creation.

For someone who downplays the original intent of biblical authors, it is surprising to see Sheppard referring frequently to the allegedly antiquated motives of the framers of Levitical law and of Paul[159] as a basis for dismissing the authority of anti-homosexuality texts. Should one not rather say, if one is primarily concerned with the final form of the text and not with the original reasoning of the authors, that since the canonical text lays little explicit stress on the reasons for rejecting same-sex intercourse the reader should take the cue that same-sex intercourse is always wrong, no matter what rationale is given for engaging in it?

Ultimately, although Sheppard on the surface appeals to canonical context, it seems to me that in reality he abandons scriptural guidance altogether. Instead he assumes on the basis of anecdotal evidence (i.e., his own limited observations of same-sex relationships, not the statisti-

---

158. Sheppard claims, wrongly in my view, that Paul recommended marriage "only if it prevent[ed] one from being consumed by lust." Ibid., 27.
159. E.g., sperm as the self-sufficient seed of life or same-sex orientation as a voluntary choice.

cal data regarding the extraordinary promiscuity and health risks typically associated with such relationships) that same-sex intercourse has the capacity to "build up . . . the hope of each person's humanity" and therefore must be right.[160] In this particular instance the basis for his decision making (notwithstanding his protests to the contrary) is not Scripture, or even scriptural principles, but some watered-down, generic application of love that bears little resemblance to the applications one finds among any biblical writers (not to mention the "historical Jesus," whom Sheppard finds irrelevant).

In addition, Sheppard does not explain what he means by "building up a person's humanity" beyond contending that "same-sex love [is] capable of establishing a covenant of trust and love between human beings."[161] This appears to me to be a rather constricted test of morality. A marriage between more than two people (say, three men and two women) could develop into a "covenant of trust and love," as could a marriage between a boy and a woman, or between two siblings, and so on. Presumably, Sheppard would not condone these but he fails to explain what distinguishes these relationships from one involving only two members of the same sex. Two or more people sharing the same distorted view of sexuality could easily form relationships of mutual trust and pleasure, but that does not justify the union.

VI. We do not follow all the injunctions in the Bible now, so why should those against homosexual conduct be binding?

There are indeed a host of injunctions in the Bible that the church today does not heed; so why be such a stickler for this one? There are Old Testament prohibitions (not all ritual or civil) that Christians no longer follow. Few would require women to wear veils during worship as Paul does in 1 Cor 11:1-16. A host of texts in the Old and New Testaments that would seem to be an impediment to women's ordination have been swept aside or thought to be less a word of God than texts affirming women's equality and involvement in ministry. The church now takes a "kinder and gentler" approach to divorce, despite

---

160. Ibid., 30.
161. Ibid.

Jesus' strict prohibition of it. Slavery, which is tolerated in many biblical texts, would be vehemently opposed today. David Bartlett and Gerald Sheppard make a particular point of the analogy from slavery.[162]

The problem with this line of reasoning is that, in cases where the church deviates in its moral practices from portions of the Bible, one can usually find a trajectory within the Bible itself that justifies a critique or moderation of such texts. For example, on the question of *divorce*, there are New Testament authors that moderate Jesus' stance. Jesus' words were so radical that both Matthew and Paul found ways to qualify them. Matthew allowed for the exception of "sexual immorality" (Matt 5:32; 19:9; agreeing with the school of Shammai), while Paul permitted divorce for believers married to unbelievers who wanted to leave (1 Cor 7:12-16). Of course, one could also point to the availability of the option in the Old Testament (Deut 24:1-4). These kinds of qualifications at least provide a basis for further exploration of the issue. Some divorce is permissible for some biblical texts so that one cannot say that the Bible has achieved a unanimous position on the subject. Alternatively, one could argue that the church has become too lenient on the issue in recent years and needs to do what Jesus did: stand against rather than with the culture.[163] There are other factors that make divorce a very different issue than that of homosexual intercourse. First, few in the church today would argue that divorce is to be "celebrated" as a positive good. The most that can be said for divorce is that in certain cases it may be the lesser of two evils. Second, unlike the kind of same-sex intercourse attracting the church's attention, divorce is not normally a recurring or repetitive action. For the situation to be comparable to a self-affirming, practicing homosexual a person would have to be engaged in self-avowed serial divorce actions. Third, some people are divorced against their will or initiate divorce for justifiable cause against a philandering or violent spouse. Such people should be distinguished from those who divorce a spouse in order to

---

162. Bartlett, "A Biblical Perspective on Homosexuality," 142; Sheppard, "The Use of Scripture," 19, 30-31.
163. For application of the divorce sayings to our contemporary context, see Hays, *Moral Vision of the New Testament*, 366-76.

have love affairs with others or to achieve "self-fulfillment." Distinctions between victims and victimizers within a homosexual relationship cannot be used to justify homosexual intercourse. The same can be said for *Sabbath observance*, since Paul in Romans 14 states that no one day is more sacred than another. As for *women's roles* in the church and in the home, the contemporary church does take, on the whole, a more enlightened perspective than can generally be found in the Bible. However, there are so many positive examples of women in leadership positions in the Old Testament (e.g., Miriam, Deborah, Huldah, Esther), of women involved in the ministry of Jesus, and of women serving as co-workers with Paul in the proclamation of the gospel (Romans 16 among other texts), that the Bible contains within its own canonical context the seeds for liberating women from oppressive male structures (cf. Gal 3:28: "there is no male and female; for all of you are one in Christ Jesus"). On this point the Bible is often its own critic and inspiration for change.[164]

Slavery is not a good parallel for the homosexuality debate because the New Testament nowhere affirms slavery as an institution; the best that can be said is that it tolerates slavery and regulates it even in Christian households.

Excursus: The Biblical View of Slavery[165]

Antecedents for a critical view of slavery appear in the Old Testament. Although people from other nations could be enslaved by Jews for life, early

---

164. For a recent treatment along these lines, explaining why "we find a significantly different situation with regard to homosexuality from that with regard to the ordination of women," cf. R. T. France, "From Romans to the Real World: Biblical Principles and Cultural Change in Relation to Homosexuality and the Ministry of Women," *Romans and the People of God* (FS Gordon Fee; eds. S. K. Soderlund and N. T. Wright; Grand Rapids: Eerdmans, 1999), 234-53.

165. The literature on slavery in the Bible and in the ancient world is enormous and no attempt will be made here to provide a comprehensive citation of even the most significant treatments. For a general treatment, cf. M. A. Dandamayev, "Slavery (ANE)" and "Slavery (OLD TESTAMENT)," and Scott S. Bartchy, "Slavery (Greco-Roman)," *ABD* 6:58-73; for Philemon, Norman R. Petersen, *Rediscovering Paul: Philemon and the Sociology of Paul's Narrative World* (Philadelphia: Fortress, 1985); idem, "Philemon," *HBC* (San Francisco: Harper & Row, 1988), 1245-48; Bartchy, "Philemon, Epistle to," *ABD* 5:305-10; for 1 Cor

law dictated that Hebrew slaves had to be released after six years of service (unless the slave declared his desire to remain a slave out of love for his master) and supplied with food and flock (Exod 21:1-11; Deut 15:12-18).[166] Deuteronomic law even forbade the return of runaway slaves (23:15-16). Levitical law required that all Hebrews held as slaves be released every Jubilee (fiftieth) year; yet it also stipulated that Hebrews should not be made to serve as slaves (i.e., be treated with harshness) but rather as "hired laborers" and that the kin of someone who sold himself to a resident alien should have the right to buy him back at any time (Lev 25:39-55). Both the Deuteronomic and Levitical law codes justified their aversion to enslaving fellow Hebrews on theological grounds: Yahweh had redeemed the Hebrews from enslavement in Egypt (Deut 15:15; Lev 25:42, 55; cf. Exod 22:21; 23:9). On the whole, slave law in Israel was more enlightened than in the rest of the ancient Near East. Moreover, Israel did not have a slave economy.[167]

Consistent with his Jewish heritage, Paul showed discomfort with the notion of Christians keeping Christian slaves. The letter to Philemon, and 1 Cor 7:21 should be read as Paul's attempts to support freedom from slavery as at least a penultimate good. For Paul, the ultimate good was freedom from captivity to sinful passions for a life of service to God. In the letter to Philemon, Paul writes to an affluent Christian, probably converted by Paul, who had opened up his home in Colossae as a meeting place for believers and in many other ways "refreshed" their hearts. Paul addresses a situation in which Onesimus (a slave of Philemon) had come into contact with Paul while Paul was in prison, possibly in the hopes of having Paul intercede on his behalf for some wrong he had committed against Philemon (v. 18). Paul converted Onesimus to the Christian faith (v. 10) and, now, in a letter of intercession car-

---

7:21, G. Fee, *The First Epistle to the Corinthians*, 315-20; Bartchy, *MALLON CHRESAI: First Century Slavery and the Interpretation of 1 Cor 7:21* (SBLDS 11; Missoula, Mont.: Scholars Press, 1973; but Bartchy's translation of *chrēsai* as "live according to [God's calling]" is implausible); Dale B. Martin, *Slavery as Salvation: The Metaphor of Slavery in Pauline Christianity* (New Haven, Conn.: Yale University Press, 1990).

166. The ancient "Book of the Covenant" or "Covenant Code" (Exod 20:22–23:33) distinguished between male and female slaves. The latter were not required to be released in the seventh year, since they were sold by fathers into slavery as concubines (Exod 21:7-11). Later, Deuteronomic law eradicated any distinction between male and female slaves (15:12, 17).

167. The law of the Sabbatical year was often not enforced in Israel's history (cf. Zedekiah's actions during the siege of Jerusalem by Babylon in Jer 34:8-17; cf. also Neh 5:1-13; 2 Kgs 4:1). Our concern here, however, is with the statements of Scripture, not human disobedience.

ried by Onesimus requests that Philemon do three things: explicitly, (1) to welcome Onesimus back as if he were Paul himself (v. 17, meaning, minimally, not to punish Onesimus); and, implicitly, (2) to manumit Onesimus (". . . have him back, no longer as a slave but more than a slave, a beloved brother, . . . both in the flesh and in the Lord," i.e., in the sphere of human society and not just the church; vv. 15-16) and (3) to send Onesimus back to Paul so that Onesimus "might be of service to me on your behalf during my imprisonment for the gospel" (vv. 13-14).[168]

Paul did not directly command Philemon to free Onesimus, living as he did in an empire where slavery was a normal part of human existence and sometimes the only alternative to starvation.[169] Paul's authority to command Philemon to make the significant personal and financial sacrifice of releasing Onesimus was also limited (vv. 17-20). Paul, further, indicates that he desired that Philemon voluntarily "do the right thing" as a spur to the growth of his own faith and as an example to his house church (vv. 6, 8-9, 13-14, 22). Finally, Paul was confident of Philemon's good character and of his capacity to do the right thing without command (vv. 4-7, 21).

Yet, in this masterful display of rhetorical skill, Paul does everything possible short of an outright command to free Onesimus. He points to his own acts of self-sacrifice such as his imprisonment for the gospel (vv. 1, 9, 10, 13, 23) and his return of Onesimus to Philemon (vv. 13-14). He also notes his abandonment of authoritarian ways toward Philemon (vv. 8-9, 19) as a model for Philemon to emulate in his dealings with Onesimus (vv. 1, 12-13). He turns Philemon's private matter into an event with public ramifications for his house church by addressing the letter not only to Philemon but also to "the church in your house" and alluding to a future visit (vv. 2, 22). He appeals to

---

168. For points (2) and (3), cf. also v. 21: "I know that you will do *even more* than what I am (explicitly) asking."

169. Like the pre–Civil War American South, ancient Greece and Rome had slave economies. As much as one-third of the population of the major cities consisted of slaves. However, slavery in the Roman Empire had significant differences from antebellum American slavery. Regarding the former, first, slavery was not based on race (Rome was an equal-opportunity oppressor). Second, for most slaves (particularly urban or domestic slaves) slavery was not a permanent condition. Third, for some people, slavery was a means of climbing the social ladder or obtaining special jobs or rights (depending on the status of one's owner). Even if slavery did not bring any elevation in status, many undoubtedly considered it preferable to starvation. Fourth, slaves could own property. Still, despite these "benefits," slaves were treated as pieces of property (a "speaking tool"), were often sexually abused by masters, and were required to be tortured to verify any testimony given in court.

Philemon's goodwill and character (vv. 4-9). He highlights the fact that Onesimus is an entirely new person in Christ (note the repeated relative clauses in vv. 10-13). He points to Onesimus's previous departure as an act of divine providence that would ultimately benefit Philemon.[170] He makes clear that whatever Philemon now did to his "client" Onesimus he would also be doing to his spiritual "partner"—indeed, patron—Paul, since Onesimus had become Paul's "heart" (*splanchna*, "guts"; vv. 7, 12, 17, 19-20). Finally, he even offers to compensate Philemon for any loss he might have incurred from Onesimus's "wrong," despite the fact that Philemon himself owed Paul his very life (vv. 18-19).

That Paul was seeking the manumission of Onesimus is also evident from the general treatment of slavery in 1 Cor 7:21-23. In formulating policy regarding marriage and singleness in 1 Corinthians 7 Paul was guided by the basic principle that believers should remain in whatever condition they were in when called in Christ. However, each policy statement is followed by exception clauses which permitted a different course of action under certain circumstances (normally introduced by "but," "but if," or "but if indeed," 7:2, 7b, 9, 11, 15, 28, 36, 39). In 7:17-24, Paul draws on analogies from circumcision (7:18-19) and slavery (7:21-23) to reinforce his general principle. With regard to the latter, he began with the general policy: "you were a slave when called; don't let it trouble you" (7:21a). Significantly, Paul does not say, as he does in all other general positions, that it is *better or necessary* to remain in this condition. Like the Stoics, Paul regarded true freedom as ultimately an inner condition that transcended the harsh realities of first-century life and enabled one to remain at peace when conditions could not be changed. Moreover, *freedom* and *slavery* were relative terms. "For the slave who was called in the Lord is the Lord's freedman; likewise, the one called as a free person is a slave of Christ" (7:22; cf. Rom 6:16-23). Here, as well, Paul supplies an exception clause to the general rule: "but even if (or: but if indeed) you can become free, make use of (it, i.e., your freedom) more (or: rather)" (*all' ei kai dynasai eleutheros genesthai, mallon chrēsai*). In other words, if believers can become free, they should take advantage of that freedom to redouble their efforts to be slaves of Christ.[171] Like unmarried persons who

---

170. Paul contends that Philemon is not losing a slave but gaining a Christian brother for fellowship, for the work of the gospel, and for assistance to Philemon's spiritual patron Paul (vv. 15-16).

171. Perhaps the biggest mistake made by the NRSV translation committee in the entire NT is the flipflop done on 1 Cor 7:21. In the RSV, the main reading was "avail yourself of the opportunity" (i.e., to become free) and the marginal reading

can give more undivided devotion to the Lord, freed slaves should not do whatever they want, but dedicate themselves to God's service. Both Christian slaves and Christian free(d) persons have an obligation to serve Christ. Just as the Deuteronomic and Levitical law codes referred to the paradigmatic event of deliverance in Israelite history (the Exodus) as a warrant for socio-political freedom for God's people, so too Paul could appeal to the Christ event: "you were bought with a price: stop becoming slaves of human beings" (7:23). While in 7:23 Paul is primarily, though not exclusively, referring to spiritual transcendence of any bondage that humans might impose, his encouragement of slaves to accept civil freedom is real.

---

was "make use of your present condition instead" (i.e., stay a slave). The NRSV reversed the order, making the marginal reading the new main reading (replacing "instead" with "now more than ever"; cf. NJB: "you should prefer to make full use of your condition as a slave"). The main NRSV reading presumes that Paul instructed the Corinthians not to become free even if they had an opportunity to do so. This is surely a nonsensical interpretation, which not even the Stoics recommended. (Cf. the old Stoic adage to eat from the plate if it passes before you but not pant after it if it does not). Moreover, it requires that 1 Cor 7:17-24 be the only major section in 1 Corinthians 7 lacking an exception clause, and this despite containing the "but if" that introduces most of the other exception clauses (all' ei in 1 Cor 7:21, elsewhere ei de). Furthermore, one usually supplies the word missing in an ellipse with the closest antecedent, in the same sentence if possible. The closest referent is "becoming free" at the beginning of the sentence, not "slavery" (which appears in the preceding sentence). Finally, the statement "do not let it trouble you" is not of the same character as the expected "let him remain a slave"; the apparent reason is that Paul was not adamant about a slave remaining in bondage if that slave could obtain freedom. I have read of no convincing counterargument for advancing the interpretation adopted by the NRSV (1 Tim 6:2 does not provide a persuasive parallel and the usual sense of ei kai as "even if" can support either interpretation). Apparently, the committee was swayed by the similar readings adopted by Conzelmann ("remain the more readily as you are"), Barrett ("put up rather with your present status"), and Orr and Walther ("rather make use of [slavery]") in their respective commentaries on 1 Corinthians; possibly also by the misplaced idea that a translation that made Paul look less appealing to contemporary interpreters was more likely to be the correct reading. Significant arguments against that interpretation had already been advanced by Bartchy, Peter Trummer ("Die chance der Freiheit. Zur Interpretation des [mallon chrēsai] in 1 Kor 7, 21," Bib 56 [1975]: 344-68), and Peter Stuhlmacher (Der Brief an Philemon [EKKNT; Zürich: Benziger, 1975], 45); cf. NIV: "do it"; NEB: "take it." Since the 1980s, the dominant interpretation has been that Paul was recommending that believers take their freedom if they can get it: G. Fee ("by all means make use of it"); W. Schrage ("use it [= the freedom] all the more so"); J. Albert Harrill, "Paul and Slavery: The Problem of 1 Corinthians 7:21," Biblical Research 39 (1994): 5-28 ("use [freedom] instead [of remaining a slave]");

From both the letter to Philemon and 1 Cor 7:21 it can be seen that Paul preferred that Christian masters free Christian slaves for three reasons. First, for Paul, the status of slave was incompatible with the status of *brother*. Second, the status of slave was in tension with the liberating, redemptive event of Christ's death. Third, freedom gave believers greater latitude for unhindered devotion to Christ. This is not to say that Paul's perspective corresponds to the Enlightenment critique of slavery as an institution fundamentally in conflict with natural human rights. Paul nowhere advocates freedom for unbelievers, though, in his defense, neither he nor anyone else in the Mediterranean basin of the first century C.E. had any power to effect such. Nonetheless, Paul's stance is a long way off from *affirming* the institution of slavery. To be sure, in the deuteropauline corpus and General Epistles, there developed (as in most other matters) greater accommodation to prevailing cultural values, including the encouragement of Christian slaves to remain slaves of Christian masters (Col 3:22-25; Eph 6:5-9; 1 Tim 6:1-2; Tit 2:9-10; 1 Pet 2:13-20). However, even this was not an endorsement of slavery, much less a proscription to Christian slave masters not to release slaves. Thus there is very little that commends the use of changing Christian views on slavery as an analogous basis for disregarding what Scripture has to say about homosexuality.

While mentioning the slavery analogy, Walter Wink concentrates on the Bible's changing views on "sexual mores." He acknowledges that Christians are right to continue rejecting incest, rape, adultery, and bestiality. But, he argues, Christians disagree with the Bible's stance on sixteen other sexual mores, both those that the Bible "condemned or discouraged" (intercourse during menstruation, celibacy, exogamy, naming sexual organs, nudity, masturbation, birth control; also the belief that semen and menstrual blood render unclean) and those that the Bible permitted but we do not (prostitution, polygamy, levirate marriage, sex with slaves, concubinage, treating women as property, early marriage for girls; also divorce which Jesus rejected but his scrip-

---

Gregory W. Dawes, "'But If You Can Gain Your Freedom' (1 Corinthians 7:17-24)," *CBQ* 52 (1990): 681-97 ("by all means make use [of this opportunity to gain your freedom]"); Norbert Baumert, *Ehelosigkeit und Ehe im Herrn* (Würzburg: Echter, 1984) ("make use of it rather for yourself [i.e., . . . 'concern yourself' rather with this 'being-able-to-become-free'"); similarly, Will Deming, "A Diatribe Pattern in 1 Cor. 7:21-22," *NovT* 37 (1995): 130-37. Stuhlmacher and Schrage are exceptional, however, in recognizing that Paul was not just saying "take the opportunity to become free"; he was exhorting believers to "use that freedom all the more to serve Christ."

ture permitted). Given this state of affairs, he concludes, Christians are free to reevaluate the Bible's stance against homosexuality.[172] Wink's analysis has all the theological sophistication of a math test or football game: sixteen sexual policies in the Bible we no longer heed versus just four that we do. One may half wonder why Wink does not take his logic full circle and disregard the other four "mores," particularly incest and bestiality.[173]

Quite apart from the fact that Wink misreads some of the biblical data and/or the contemporary stance of the church on many of the sixteen sexual mores (e.g., the Bible nowhere approves of prostitution, nowhere requires celibacy), what Wink fails to do is to weigh truly comparable sexual issues from a biblical perspective. What makes the biblical mandate concerning homosexuality so hard for Christians to ignore or downplay are seven considerations.

First, it is *proscribed* behavior, which as a minimalist approach to ethics is less demanding than a positive prescription and therefore more doable (or, better, "non-doable") and fundamental—a sin of commission rather than omission. For example, a command not to harm another is a minimalist expectation in relation to the Golden Rule and thus its violation constitutes a more severe infraction.

Second, it is proscribed *behavior*, not proscribed thoughts, theories, or worldviews. As such, the ethic is again more "bottom-line," more doable, and more basic for human social interaction.

Third, it is behavior proscribed *by both Testaments*. The change of salvation-historical dispensations sometimes results in shifting assessments of what is expected of God's people, especially as regards ritual requirements or civil law for a state theocracy; hence, the preeminence of the New Testament. Yet the Old Testament, because of its sheer size and unique experiences of God, can also balance out or fill in gaps in the New Testament. When the two Testaments are in complete agree-

---

172. Walter Wink, "Homosexuality and the Bible," in *Homosexuality and Christian Faith: Questions of Conscience for the Churches* (ed. W. Wink; Minneapolis: Fortress, 1999), 33-49.

173. Cf. Countryman who argues "the gospel allows no rule against" bestiality, polygamy, pornography, and for "those who have no other access to sexual gratification," sex with prostitutes (*Dirt, Greed, and Sex*, 243-44, 264). Countryman conspicuously leaves unbroached incest between consenting adults.

ment that a given action is morally wrong, the biblical witness is hard to circumvent.

Fourth, it is behavior proscribed *pervasively within each Testament.* There are no dissenting voices anywhere in either Testament. All the inferential evidence that we have for authors who do not speak explicitly to the issue confirms the supposition of pervasive opposition. The best that Wink and others can do is attempt to appeal to the "big picture" of the Bible, by which they mean some general statements about love and tolerance—none of which any of the biblical writers, or Jesus, found to be in conflict with opposition to homosexual conduct. The "big picture" consists not of this misunderstood application of love but rather of the heterosexual model for sexual intercourse provided in Gen 1–2, consistently affirmed throughout the history of Israel and the church.

Fifth, it is *severely* proscribed behavior. The revulsion expressed for homosexual intercourse, across both Testaments, is as strong as it could possibly be, given the different parameters for each Testament: grounds for the death penalty in the Old Testament and grounds for exclusion from the kingdom of God in the New Testament. In Rom 1:24-27, it epitomizes the height of gentile depravity and folly in the ethical sphere.

Sixth, the proscribed behavior is proscribed *absolutely*; that is, the proscription encompasses every and any form of homosexual behavior. The proscription is not limited, for example, only to select types of exploitative homosexuality.

Seventh, it is proscribed behavior *that makes sense.* The complementarity of male and female is a clear indication in the natural order of God's will for sexuality—much clearer than the urges homosexuals experience. Contrary to Wink's view, such urges or "orientation" can never be *natural* in the sense Paul uses the term since they (a) manifestly contradict God's creation design of male and female; (b) arise at best from only a partial and indirect genetic influence; and (c) have no more validity than orientations toward bestiality, incest, multiple partners, sadomasochism, or any of the sinful orientations cited in the vice lists of Rom 1:29-31.

When these seven tests are applied to the lists of sexual mores col-lated by Wink, the first four mores he mentions—those which believers still adhere to—provide much closer analogues than the allegedly sixteen others that differ from contemporary Christian standards.

Human passions are notoriously unreliable indicators of God's will. "I feel this, therefore I should be allowed to do it" would not pass muster on any viable reading of biblical ethics. "I would be living a lie to deny who I am." A believer's identity does not consist of the satisfaction of sexual urges. The issue is not "who I am"—self-avowed homosexuals sometimes justify their behavior by claiming that this is who they are, they cannot deny *their* "true selves"—but "who does God intend me to be." The life lived in a lie is the life that refuses to conform to the truth of God: "who exchanged the truth of God for a lie. . . . exchanged the natural use for that which is contrary to nature" (Rom 1:25-26). God, not ourselves, is the standard of truth. Any other position is idolatry. "But it will be painful for me to have to deny these urges constantly." The New Testament does not assure believers that the process of being transformed into the image of Christ or of having Christ formed in us is always painless.[174] God is the great plastic surgeon, only here the transformation is not cosmetic but aimed at conforming believers into the image of Christ. Often one has no recourse but to "take up one's cross and deny oneself" (Mark 8:34), to die to oneself and self-interest in the hope that Christ may rule in a life lived for God (Rom 6:1-14; Gal 2:19-20). The good news is that even in our sufferings we have the opportunity to confirm to ourselves our election by obedient endurance, helped by the Spirit who translates our inner groans into the things we truly need, awaiting all the more eagerly the transformation of our earthly bodies into glory, and consoled by the certainty that nothing outside of ourselves can separate us from the love of God who loved us when we were enemies (Rom 5:1-11; 8:18-39). "You are consigning me to loneliness for the rest of my life?" No, the intimate fellowship of other believers (the communion of the saints) remains; only same-sex intercourse is forbidden. With the help of fellowship, counseling, prayer, and the Holy Spirit, God may even restore the homosexual to a fulfilling sexual life in lifelong union with

---

174. Rom 8:29; 2 Cor 3:18; 4:11; Phil 3:10; Gal 4:19.

a member of the opposite sex. If that does not happen, the church must inwardly groan together with all the sexually broken and offer support.

The Dearth of Lifelong, Monogamous Homosexual Relationships

Many will still argue that homosexuality *must* be something good because it is able to foster mutually loving relationships. There are two problems with this view.

First, the fact that homosexual unions are sometimes formed in an atmosphere of mutual love says nothing one way or the other about the legitimacy of homosexual intercourse. It merely confirms that caring bonds can and should be established between members of the same sex. There is an appropriate category for such bonds: friendship. Sexual intercourse is not a vital component for establishing a healthy bond between members of the same sex—at least not from a biblical perspective. To maintain that a sexual bond must be sanctified by God if it develops in the context of a mutually caring relationship is a strange form of logic. No one thinks that because pedophiles can express care and love for children that their sexual relations with children are legitimate (even if the children express approval). Few would argue that a consensual incestuous relationship between adult siblings or a consensual sexual relationship between more than two adults must be sanctified by God, no matter how nice such people may otherwise be. Pedophiles and even wife-beaters can be nice people in other areas of their life. A friend of mine who counseled sex offenders in prisons for many years often remarked how indistinguishable these people would be from nice neighbors if the prison garb were removed. My point here is *not* to compare homosexuality in all its features with pedophilia or spousal abuse but rather simply to assert the comparison at one level: positive moral conduct in many areas of one's life does not establish the legitimacy of all of one's conduct. Homosexuals do not turn into werewolves simply because they commit same-sex intercourse. Nor should we commend them for engaging in such conduct when they do so within a larger context of being decent people. Quite simply, there is no way to demonstrate that homosexual intercourse, in and of itself, is a good thing.

Second, all the data for homosexual conduct indicates that it has a very poor track record so far as enduring monogamous relationships are concerned. A non-random study of nearly 1,000 homosexuals in the San Francisco Bay Area was conducted by Bell and Weinberg in 1970.[175] It reported that 84% of white homosexual males (= WHMs) and 77% of black homosexual males (= BHMs) had 50 or more homosexual partners in their lifetime. Within this group of 50+ partners, 28% of WHMs and 19% of BHMs had over 1,000. Only 3% of WHMs and 6% of BHMs had fewer than 10 homosexual partners during their lifetime. The statistics for lesbians were significantly less shocking, though still high. About a quarter of homosexual females had fewer than 5 homosexual partners in their lifetime; an additional 30% had 5 to 9 partners. Only 7% of white homosexual females (= WHFs) and 12% of black homosexual females (= BHFs) had 50 or more partners. As for the number of homosexual partners in the *year* previous to the study, 66% of homosexual males and 6% of homosexual females had more than 10. Only 10% to 11% of homosexual males had fewer than 3 partners in a year, compared to 71% of WHFs and 59% of BHFs. Since the information was gathered exclusively in an urban area of the pre-AIDS period, the statistics undoubtedly reflect higher numbers than one would expect of a cross-section of society today. Nevertheless, the enormous disparity between male and female homosexual activity is significant, since both sexes lived under similar cultural conditions. Furthermore, since the survey was undertaken in San Francisco, it is hard to attribute the high rates of sexual promiscuity primarily to society's homophobia.

The 1992 National Health and Social Life Survey (NHSLS; Laumann et al.) focused on the sexual habits of all Americans, surveying 1,749 women and 1,410 men. The number of homosexuals/bisexuals included in the survey was small (39 males, 24 females) so the statistics have to be used with some caution. Even so, the figures suggest that homosexual/bisexual men have two to six times more sex partners than heterosexual men, while women who have same-gender partners have three to four times more sex partners than women who have no same-gender partners. Lesbians/bisexuals may have a slighter higher

---

175. *Homosexualities*, 81-102, 312-25.

number of sex partners than heterosexual men but still significantly fewer partners than homosexual men.[176]

One of the largest studies to date of the sexual habits of homosexual men (nearly 5,000) was the Multicenter AIDS Cohort Study (published in 1987). It found that "a significant majority of these men . . . (69% to 83%) reported having fifty or more lifetime sexual partners."[177] By contrast, the NHSLS study cited above reported that at least 83.4% of mostly heterosexual *males* have had fewer than twenty-

---

176. *The Social Organization of Sexuality*, 313-16. According to the study, the mean number of sex partners in the last year for men who self-identify as homosexual or bisexual (= H/BM) is higher, but not extraordinarily higher, than heterosexual men (= HetM): 3.1 (H/BM) to 1.8 (HetM). Given the very small sample size of homosexual men for this study and the much higher rates for homosexual men suggested in the studies cited below, the NHSLS figure of 3.1 is probably too low (the authors report a "confidence level" that the real figure for H/BMs is no higher than 4.2 partners). Even so, the difference between a relationship having no extra-relational outlets in a given year and one having one or two additional sex partners is enormous. The same study noted that three quarters of all adult males (a composite of the 97.2% heterosexual and the 2.8% homosexual or bisexual) had just one partner or less in the preceding year. I do not know any husband who, upon telling his wife that he only had one or two extramarital outlets that year, would be congratulated on his fidelity to the relationship. When the time interval is stretched to the number of sex partners in the last five years the increase is even more significant: means of 18 for H/BMs to 4.9 for HetMs (an increase of 367%). The authors acknowledge that the real figures could be as high as 26.7 for H/BMs and 5.6 for HetMs (a 477% increase). As for the number of partners since age eighteen, H/BMs have a mean of 42.8 sex partners and HetMs 16.5 (an increase of 260%). Here again the figures could be as high as 73.1 sex partners for H/BMs and 19.4 for HetMs (a 377% increase).

Unfortunately, because the sample size for current self-identified female lesbians or bisexuals was under thirty, NHSLS did not report their findings for this group. However, for women who at one time or another since the age of eighteen had at least one same-gender sex partner (and who currently may or may not self-identify as a lesbian), the mean number of sex partners since age eighteen was 19.7, compared to 4.9 for women who have never had any same-sex partners since the age of eighteen (a fourfold increase). These figures can be compared with the same category for men, those who had any same-gender partners since age eighteen (44.3 sex partners) and those who did not (15.7 sex partners). In effect, females who had any same-gender partners since age eighteen had slightly more sex partners than men who have never had same-gender partners, but still less than half the number of sex partners had by men with any same-gender partners since age eighteen.

177. R. A. Kaslow et al., "The Multicenter AIDS Cohort Study: Rationale, Organization, and Selected Characteristics of the Participants," *American Journal*

one sex partners since the age of eighteen, nearly half had four or fewer, and nearly one-quarter had one or none.[178]

A 1997 study of 2,583 homosexually active men in Australia found that, of those over forty-nine years old, one-quarter (26.6%) had more than 10 male partners in the past *six months* alone, half (44.9%) had between 2 and 10, and a quarter had just one (28.5%). In the course of their lifetime *to date*, only 2.7% of the older men (and just 2.9% of those under 50 years of age) reported having had just one male partner. The percentages for the other response categories are astounding: 2-10 male sex partners, 10.2%; 11-20, 14.1%; 21-50, 12.9%; 51-100, 11.8%; 101-500, 21.6%; 501-1,000, 11%; 1,000 or more, 15.7%. Thus, nearly 9 out of every 10 of those over 49 years old had lifetime more than 10 male sex partners, and of these the majority had over 100.[179]

In 1994, the largest gay magazine in America, *The Advocate*, published the results of questionnaires returned by 2,500 of its adult male homosexual readers. In the course of the relatively short average lifespan of the respondents (thirty-eight years old), only 2% had had sex with just one man. Fifty-seven percent had more than 30 male sex partners, and 35% had more than 100. In the past year alone, about two-thirds (63%) had more than one male sex partner and the large majority of these (over 60%) had five or more; only 28% had just one partner. About half (48%) said they had engaged in three-way sex in the last five years, 24% group sex (four or more).[180] The 1995 *Advocate* survey of 2,500 of its lesbian readers indicated far fewer sexual partners

---

of Epidemiology 126 (August 1987): 310-18 (cited by Satinover). A Boston study of 481 homosexual men published in 1992 reported that 77% had more than ten partners in the previous five years. For this and other studies, cf. Schmidt, *Straight and Narrow?*, 106-7, 199.

178. *Social Organization*, 179: 0 partners (3.4%), 1 partner (19.5%), 2-4 partners (20.9%), 5-10 partners (23.3%), 11-20 partners (16.3%), 21 or more partners (16.6%). Note that among those males surveyed, roughly 2.8% identified themselves as homosexual or bisexual; removing them from the sample would mean a slightly higher rate of heterosexual males having 20 or *fewer* sex partners.

179. Paul Van de Ven, et al., "A Comparative Demographic and Sexual Profile of Older Homosexually Active Men," *Journal of Sex Research* 34 (1997): 349-60 [and personal correspondence]. The study was done for the National Centre in HIV Social Research at Macquarie University.

180. Janet Lever, Ph.D., "The 1994 *Advocate* Survey of Sexuality and Relationships: The Men: Sexual Relations," *The Advocate* (Aug. 23, 1994): 16-24.

for lesbians on average: 2% had never had sex with a woman; 1 in 7 had only one female sex partner; 23% had eleven or more female sex partners (compare the 8% figure for American women generally who had more than eleven male sex partners, NHSLS); but only 1% had more than one hundred lifetime same-sex partners (compare to homosexual men in the *Advocate* survey where 1% reported having more than one hundred sex partners *in a single year*). On average they had ten sex partners during their lifetimes as of the time of the survey.[181]

Even within the context of a relationship, homosexual males rarely exhibit serial monogamy, let alone lifelong monogamy. A Dutch study of the sexual habits of one hundred fifty-six male homosexual couples published in 1994 reported that, on average, each partner had seven other sex partners in just the one year preceding the survey.[182] Nearly two-thirds (62%) of these "close-coupled" gays were non-monogamous in that same one-year period. The number of outside partners in the first year of the relationship averaged 2.5; *by the sixth year of the relationship the number increased to eleven.* Another study in the late 1980s discovered that 79% of close-coupled gays had sex with one or more persons other than their primary partner, compared to 19% of close-coupled lesbians, 10% of married heterosexuals, and 23% of unmarried cohabiting heterosexuals.[183] Other surveys indicate that the percentage of male homosexuals living in monogamous relationships for just the preceding year is very low: somewhere between 10% and 25%.[184] The rates for the American adult population as a whole are the

---

181. Janet Lever, "The 1995 *Advocate* Survey of Sexuality and Relationships: The Women: Lesbian Sex Survey," *The Advocate* (Aug. 22, 1995): 25, 29. Lever does not list the number of female sex partners in just the prior year for all respondents; but she notes: "Long periods of celibacy are common among lesbians" (ibid., 26).

182. A. A. Deenen, L. Gijs, and A. X. van Naerssen, "Intimacy and Sexuality in Gay Male Couples," *Archives of Sexual Behavior* 23 (1994): 421-31.

183. P. Blumstein and P. Schwartz, "Intimate Relationships and the Creation of Sexuality," *Homosexuality/Heterosexuality* (eds. D. P. McWhirter et al.; New York: Oxford University Press, 1990), 317.

184. Cf. the series of studies cited by Paul Cameron, "Same Sex Marriage: Til Death Do Us Part?" (Colorado Springs: Family Research Institute, 1997). Briefly, the percentage of gays in monogamous relationships for the preceding year alone was: in London, 23% (though here only for the preceding *month*; 1987); in Toronto, 12% (1990); in Australia, 25.5% (with 35% in non-monogamous rela-

mirror opposites: 80% of all men and 90% of all women had only one sexual partner or none in the preceding year;[185] 75% of all men and 85% of all women have *never* had an extramarital affair.[186]

In 1984 a homosexual couple, one a psychiatrist and the other a psychologist, published a book that focused on the sexual habits of the most "stable" gay couples. Of one hundred fifty-six couples, only seven had remained monogamous, and not one of the seven relationships had yet reached the six-year mark. The consensus among the couples interviewed was that the heterosexual model of monogamy did not work for gay relationships.[187] Another book published in 1984, reporting on the sexual habits of several hundred male couples in Chicago, found only slightly better results: a mere 9% of male homosexual couples who lived together more than five years did so in an "exclusive" partnership.[188]

In short, the rule of monogamy for heterosexual relationships is the exception for male homosexual relationships. Indeed, male homosexuals

---

tionships and 29% participating only in casual sex; 1991); in San Francisco, 14% (1993). Two combined Dutch studies (1992) indicated that 78% of homosexual males had more than five partners in the past year alone (P. J. Veugelers et al., "Estimation of the Magnitude of the HIV Epidemic Among Homosexual Men," *European Journal of Epidemiology* 9 [July 1993]: 438; cited by Schmidt). The Bell and Weinberg study (1978) reported that only 10% of homosexual males and 28% of homosexual females could be classified as "close-coupled," a classification that required a "low" number of sexual partners (under four per year?), minimal "cruising," and minimal sexual problems. Another large survey from the 1970s, interviewing 4,329 homosexual men, found that over a third had *never* been in a relationship lasting longer than a year, over half for more than two years, and only 7% for more than ten years (K. Jay and A. Young, *The Gay Report* [New York: Summit, 1979], 339-40).

185. The NHSLS study found that 76.7% of all male respondents had either just one (66.8%) or no sex partners (9.9%) in the preceding year, 18.3% had 2-4 partners; 5.1% had five or more, 88.3% of all women had only one partner (74.7%) or none (13.6%); 10% had 2-4 partners; and only 1.7% had five or more (*Social Organization*, 177). Another major survey, published at roughly the same time, reported that 83% of all men and 90% of all women had either one sex partner in the previous year or none (C. Leigh, et al., "The Sexual Behavior of U.S. Adults," *American Journal of Public Health* 83 [October 1993]: 1404; cited by Schmidt).
186. *Social Organization*, 216.
187. David P. McWhirter and Andrew M. Mattison, *The Male Couple: How Relationships Develop* (Englewood Cliffs, N.J.: Prentice-Hall, 1984).
188. J. Harry, *Gay Couples* (New York: Praeger Books, 1984), 115 (cited by Schmidt).

themselves often argue that the stifling model of heterosexual monogamy should not be foisted on homosexuals.[189] The vast majority of male homosexual relationships do not last beyond a few years.[190] Although their record of success at serial monogamy is significantly worse than heterosexual females, homosexual females do significantly better than homosexual males. However, limited data suggests that lesbian relationships on average are actually of *shorter* duration than male homosexual relationships.[191]

---

189. In the April 1994 issue of *Genre* magazine (a publication geared toward homosexuals), Doug Sadownick examined the phenomenon of gay partnerships and concluded that "to adapt heterosexual relations [to homosexual ones] is more than just foolhardy; it's an act of oppression." Andrew Sullivan, a homosexual and editor of the *New Republic*, has written: "there is more likely to be greater understanding of the need for extramarital outlets between two men than between a man and a woman; and again, the lack of children gives gay couples greater freedom. . . . marriage should be made available to everyone. . . . But within this model, there is plenty of scope for cultural difference. There is something baleful about the attempt of some gay conservatives to educate homosexuals and lesbians into an uncritical acceptance of a stifling model of heterosexual normality" (*Virtually Normal: An Argument About Homosexuality* [New York: Vintage Books, Random House, 1996], 200-204).

190. The Project SIGMA study of nearly one thousand homosexual men in England and Wales found that the median length of cohabitation with a regular male sex partner was twenty-one months. The number of homosexual couples is also extremely small relative to the number of homosexuals. Many estimates put the number of homosexuals/bisexuals in the population as 2–3%. Yet the 1990 U.S. Census indicated that there were only 88,200 homosexual couples and 69,200 lesbian couples—less than one-fifth of 1% of the total number of couples (Cameron, *The Gay 90s*, 31). Denmark has legalized a form of homosexual marriage since 1989. Yet, six years later, only 5% of Danish homosexuals had married (Cameron, "Same Sex Marriage," 3).

191. One study found that only 8% of homosexual men and 7% of homosexual women ever had relationships that lasted four years or more (M. T. Saghir and E. Robins, *Male and Female Homosexuality: A Comprehensive Investigation* [Baltimore: Williams Wilkins, 1973]; cited by Schmidt). A large non-random survey of almost 8,000 heterosexual and homosexual couples indicated that the average length of relationships was 3.5 years for male homosexual couples and 2.2 years for lesbian couples (P. Blumstein and P. Schwartz, *American Couples* [New York: Morrow, 1983]; cited by Cameron). The recent *Advocate* surveys confirm the shorter terms for lesbian relationships. Twenty-six percent of the male respondents *who were in a relationship at the time of the survey* claimed that they had been with their partner for at least ten years (albeit often in an "open" relationship; a nearly equal number, 23%, said that the relationship had been going on for less than a year (Lever, "Men," 24). By comparison only 14% of the female respondents had been

One could argue that the inability of male homosexuals in particular to form enduring monogamous unions is due to society's ongoing disapproval of homosexual relationships and to the denial of a right to civil marriage. Undoubtedly, some portion of the imbalance can be attributed to such things. Yet the ratios are *so* disproportionate that two other significant factors must be involved. One is the obvious fact that homosexual unions do not produce children (though adoption is increasingly becoming an option) and children (especially one's own biological children) *can* be a stabilizing factor in a relationship. However, this factor, like society's disapproval, does not explain why lesbians have far fewer sexual partners on average than homosexual men (though still higher than their heterosexual female counterparts). The most important factor probably has to do with the nature of male sexuality. As a general rule, men who are left to their own devices have great difficulty forming enduring monogamous relationships. Men need to be "civilized" and "domesticated" into such unions by women. *In general*, because men are for the most part sexually stimulated by sight (rather than by a caring relationship, as with women), men are more easily aroused, more often aroused, and hence more likely to succumb to that arousal.[192] For the same reason, men are more likely to cheat on their wives than the reverse. In short, to put two males together in an erotic relationship is not exactly a recipe for long-term fidelity. Exceptions to the rule will always exist but the

---

with their partner at least ten years and of these 14% only 2% in a relationship longer than twenty years; 22% said their current relationship had gone on for less than a year. A full 30% had seriously considered ending their relationship within the prior twelve months (Lever, "Lesbian Sex Survey," 27).

192. Of course it would be foolish to suggest that women are not at all sexually stimulated by sight or that men are not at all sexually stimulated by a demonstration of concern. Nevertheless, there are basic differences in the way men and women are stimulated sexually. What married man does not know this? Wives get sexually stimulated when they see their husbands taking the initiative to wash and wax the kitchen floor (more precisely, it is the conveyance of caring and compassion that translates into greater receptivity to sexual intimacy). Husbands get stimulated when they see their wives wearing something sexy. Wives need the big buildup all throughout the day; husbands can get visually stimulated on a moment's notice. The far greater popularity of pornography among males than among females is also clear testimony to the different ways in which men and women are sexually aroused.

consistent pattern confirms the divine wisdom of prohibiting homosexual intercourse.[193]

The Analogy Between the Early Church's Inclusion of Gentiles and Contemporary Affirmation of Homosexuality

One other analogy from the Bible has sometimes been used to discount the Bible's rejection of same-sex intercourse: the inclusion of gentiles into the church. Its primary proponent is Jeffrey Siker, though

---

193. Cf. Donald Symons, *The Evolution of Human Sexuality* (New York: Oxford University Press, 1979), 292-300. Symons emphasizes "the male's tendencies to be sexually aroused by visual stimuli, the specifically genital focus of male sexual arousal and relief, and the autonomous, fantasizing, initiatory, appetitive, driving aspects of male sexuality. . . . The function of these male characteristics is to generate reproductive opportunities in a milieu in which such opportunities were always competitive" (292). According to Symons, women evolved differently because it was not in their reproductive or nurturing interests to be sexually promiscuous. Differences in the sexual behavior of men and women are most evident in male and female homosexual relationships. The former are much more given to pornography, one-night stands with strangers, multiple partners, and the lure of youth and physical beauty; the latter are more successful at serial monogamy and put greater stress on the social status of partners. An illustration of the differences is the absence of the phenomenon of lesbian baths. Male homosexuals, Symons argues, do not exhibit different tendencies in sexual behavior than their heterosexual counterparts; they simply lack the restraints imposed by female partnership. Symons acknowledges that different social conditions may have some effect on transforming evolutionary patterns, but within limits. He notes that cross-cultural studies confirm significant differences between homosexual and heterosexual relationships. These transcultural differ-ences can be explained by the fact that "heterosexual relations are structured to a substantial degree by the nature and interests of the human female" (300). In commenting on Symons's work, Steven J. Pope is a little more hopeful about change in male homosexual patterns of behavior. "If modification of male sexual patterns has in fact been effected by conditions attending the formation of pair-bonds with females, perhaps the same is possible, if more difficult, in moral commitments of male same-sex partners" ("Scientific and Natural Law Analyses of Homosexuality: A Methodological Study," *JRE* 25 [1997]: 89-126; quote from p. 120). Pope overlooks Symons's point: males can be resocialized when their partners are females. But males will remain males; when a male's partner is a male both will share these proclivities.

My faculty colleague Charles Partee pointed me to the following citation in David M. Buss's *The Evolution of Desire: Strategies of Human Mating* (New York: Basic Books, 1994): "Imagine that an attractive person of the opposite sex walks up to you on a college campus and says: 'Hi, I've been noticing you around town

others such as Luke Timothy Johnson have argued similarly.[194] Siker contends that, like homosexuals today, gentiles were treated by many among the first generation of Jewish Christians with revulsion as "by definition sinful and unclean in the eyes of God," who could not be granted membership in the people of God "as Gentiles" but only as converts to Judaism.

According to Acts 10–11, Peter and the church at Jerusalem were led to embrace gentile inclusion without circumcision only after observing the work of the Holy Spirit in their lives. In the same way, Siker claims, the testimony given by the holy lives of some homosexual Christians should force the contemporary church to rethink its opposition to same-sex intercourse.

The analogy breaks down at four points. First, being a gentile is not like being a homosexual. We have already noted that homosexuality arises from a complex array of factors, including nurture, environment, and choice. If genetics alone accounted for homosexual orientation, then one would never find an instance where identical twins had different sexual orientations. As it is, in most cases where one identical twin has a homosexual orientation the other does not—and this in cases where identical twins are even raised in the same household and thus come under similar influences from nurture and environment. Gentile ethnicity is a different ball of wax: it has to do with ancestry, not desire. At birth, *all* the offspring of gentile parents are gentile, even if later in life there are fictive, legal (covenantal) mechanisms for grafting such a person into the descendants of Abraham (see Rom 11:17-24).

---

lately, and I find you very attractive. Would you go to bed with me?' How would you respond? If you are like 100% of the women in one study, you would give an emphatic no. You would be offended, insulted, or plain puzzled by the request out of the blue. But if you are a man, the odds are 75% that you would say yes. You would most likely feel flattered by the request" (p. 73).

194. Jeffrey S. Siker, "Homosexual Christians, the Bible, and Gentile Inclusion: Confessions of a Repenting Heterosexist," *Homosexuality in the Church*, 187-90; idem, "Gentile Wheat and Homosexual Christians: New Testament Directions for the Heterosexual Church," *Biblical Ethics and Homosexuality*, 145-46; Luke Timothy Johnson, *Scripture and Discernment: Decision Making in the Church* (Nashville: Abingdon, 1996), 144-48 (see already the 1983 edition, pp. 96-97); idem, "Debate & Discernment, Scripture & the Spirit," *Commonweal* (Jan. 28, 1994): 12-13.

Second, in the case of same-sex intercourse, the Bible is primarily condemning an activity or form of behavior, not a state of being. Like any desire for what God has forbidden, the desire for same-sex intercourse can also be a sin but only if consciously nurtured and "fed." The mere inclination or the experience of temptation is not sin. The issue is whether one is mastered by the desire. Being gentile, on the other hand, is not in itself a behavior or desire. Though first-century Jews spoke of typically gentile behavior and often made sweeping generalizations (as in Rom 1:18-32), they were also capable of making distinctions among individual gentiles. For example, some gentiles were embraced under the category of "God-fearer" or "righteous gentile" and welcomed into synagogues. Paul himself is an example of a Jew who could make negative generalizations about gentiles (1 Thess 4:5; Gal 2:15) and yet vigorously defend the inclusion of many of them in the kingdom of God. The problem with gentiles, in Paul's view, was not that they were gentiles—gentile Christians could and did live holy lives before God—but that they typically did not know the God of Abraham, Isaac, and Jacob.

The link between passion for intercourse with a member of the same sex and the commission of such an act is direct. The link between gentile ancestry and being controlled by sinful passions is at most indirect, the controlling desire arising directly out of the absence of a relationship of God, which in turn is only a typical (not inherent) form of "gentile behavior." Because there is no "inherently gentile" form of behavior, a gentile potentially could lead as moral a life as any Jew (minus, of course, the specifically "Jewish" commandments). Yet gratifying a desire for same-sex intercourse is always inherently immoral because the biblical prohibitions are against same-sex intercourse *per se*. The existence of "righteous gentiles" might have been a rare or unusual phenomenon in the eyes of the first generation of Jewish Christians, but the concept of a righteous participant in same-sex intercourse would not only have been rare or unusual, it would have been a complete oxymoron to all first-century Jews.

There were various levels of Jewish acceptance of and association with gentiles, and various levels of gentile adherence to Jewish faith and attachment to Jewish institutions, but it was not a sin *per se* for gentiles to remain uncircumcised. The debate about requiring circumcision for gentiles in first-century Judaism was first and foremost a debate about the degree of participation in the community life of the Jewish people, not primarily or everywhere a debate about sin and salvation. The failure to fulfill a positive ritual command, even the command to circumcise, cannot be equated with the commission of an egregious sexual offense unambiguously proscribed by the Law.

Third, unlike the Bible's stance on same-sex intercourse, the Hebrew Bible or Greek Septuagint is not unequivocally and univocally opposed to gentiles. Christians could find legitimization for the inclusion of gentiles in Scripture itself, whereas no such legitimization could be given for same-sex intercourse. Richard Hays puts it aptly when he writes:

> Experience must be treated as a hermeneutical lens for reading the New Testament rather than as an independent, counterbalancing authority. This is the point at which the analogy to the early church's acceptance of Gentiles fails decisively. The church did not simply observe the experience of Cornelius and his household and decide that Scripture must be wrong after all. On the contrary, the experience of uncircumcised Gentiles responding in faith to the gospel message led the church back to a new reading of Scripture. This new reading discovered in the texts a clear message of God's intent, from the covenant with Abraham forward to bless all nations and to bring Gentiles (*qua* Gentiles) to worship Israel's God. . . . Only because the new experience of Gentile converts proved *hermeneutically illuminating* of Scripture was the church, over time, able to accept the decision to embrace Gentiles within the fellowship of God's people. This is precisely the step that has not—or at least not yet—been taken by the advocates of homosexuality in the church. . . . it is difficult to imagine how such an argument could be made.[195]

In short, the experience of the Spirit's presence in the lives of gentiles opened the eyes of Jewish Christians to see precedents in Scripture that they had previously overlooked. They did not have to override pointed proscriptions such as would have been the case had they attempted to affirm same-sex intercourse.

---

195. Hays, *The Moral Vision of the New Testament*, 399.

Certainly there are significant elements of ancient Israelite tradition that spoke pejoratively of gentiles and advocated only very limited association between Jews and gentiles (this is particularly true in the period of Restoration under Ezra and Nehemiah). However, more often than not the reason for aversion to gentiles was not gentile ethnicity or uncircumcised status but gentile worship of foreign gods, the typically immoral conduct of gentiles, and/or the oppression of Israel by various nations. Alongside such aversion one finds ample evidence of a positive outlook toward at least some gentiles.[196]

In addition to the promise to Abraham that "in you all the families of the earth shall be blessed,"[197] Ruth (a Moabite) stands out as a model proselyte. Jesus is said by Luke to have referred to the widow at Zarephath in Sidon (1 Kings 17) and Naaman the Syrian (2 Kings 5) as two righteous gentiles that put Israel to shame (Luke 4:26-27). Second Isaiah could refer to Cyrus the Persian as God's "Shepherd" and "Anointed" (Isa 44:28; 45:1) and interpret Israel's new role in the post-exilic period as a "light to the nations" (Isa 42:6; 49:6; 51:4; cf. 60:3). The book of Jonah too is a monument to strands in post-exilic Judaism that rejected xenophobia and thought in terms of God's concern for the welfare of all creatures of God's creation (4:10-11). The Ninevites showed evidence of their genuine repentance not by being circumcised but by fasting and turning "from their evil ways" (3:5-10). Many of the prophets predicted a future time of salvation for at least some nations, with Jerusalem as the focal point for disseminating the revelation of Yahweh to the nations.[198] No explicit mention is made in any of these texts of circumcision as an entry requirement. Even the Levitical Holiness Code, so insistent on Israel maintaining holiness in distinction to the abominable practices of the nations, required love of the resident alien "as yourself" (Lev 19:33-34). Thus there were plenty of texts in the Scriptures of Jewish Christians that would lend support to a gentile mission.[199]

---

196. See Donald Gowan, *Eschatology in the Old Testament* (Philadelphia: Fortress, 1986), 42-58.

197. Gen 12:3; 18:18; 22:18; 26:4; 28:14; illustrated already in the blessings of Ishmael and Esau.

198. Cf., e.g., Isa 2:2-4 (par. Mic 4:1-4); 19:18-25; 25:6-7; 45:22-23; 49:6; 56:7; 66:19; Zech 8:22-23; 14:16-19.

199. Even the "Judaizers" that dogged Paul's law-free mission were not opposed to active gentile mission (indeed, they themselves undertook such a mission). The

Fourth, in complete contrast to the issue of same-sex intercourse, the attitude toward gentiles taken by all the authors of texts that subsequently made it into the New Testament canon was one of affirmation of gentile entry into the people of God without requiring circumcision. The premier exponent of a gospel to gentiles, the apostle Paul, for all his emphasis on the freedom of the believer took a radically different approach when it came to matters involving violations of sexual standards. These he regarded as transparently sinful even for gentiles. The Torah, that contingent expression of God's will for a particular people and at a particular time of salvation history, had been abrogated for Paul by the death and resurrection of Christ, which meant for him an end to the distinctively "Jewish" requirements expressed therein. Yet for Paul—as also for Luke's "Apostolic Decree" (Acts 15:20, 29; 21:25) and the "Noahide laws" in early Judaism—there was nothing contingent or especially "Jewish" about certain fundamental sexual norms like the prohibitions against same-sex intercourse, incest, adultery, fornication, and (presumably) bestiality. Thus the canonical case for affirming same-sex intercourse is a long way off from the canonical case for the inclusion of gentiles.

I readily grant that there may exist today, as there did in antiquity, a statistically small percentage of homosexuals who are not sexually promiscuous *and* are able to form long-term monogamous sexual unions *and* do not engage in medically dangerous sexual practices (particularly anal intercourse or sadomasochistic acts) *and* appear to be involved in mutually affirming relationships. The same, of course, could be said for a small percentage of those who participate in incestuous relationships, or who participate in polygamous relationships, or who engage in sexual intercourse with "mature" minors, and so forth. For some strange reason, in the case of these other forms of aberrant sexual behavior, those who affirm same-sex intercourse have no trouble identifying the problems with legitimizing a generally destructive form of sexual behavior for the sake of a tiny minority that seems to "do it right." Furthermore, "doing it right" does not mean "it" is good but

---

disagreement existed only over whether gentile believers should observe the Mosaic law *in toto*, particularly those elements that in the ancient world defined a Jew as a Jew (i.e., circumcision, dietary laws, sabbath and festival observances).

rather that "it" is done in the best way that "it" can conceivably be done. Yet clearly not every sexual act that is engaged in with noble intent is good or right in the truest sense. Some couples who engage in sadomasochistic sex insist that it helps their relationship to thrive. Should this too be condoned as a good? The clearest clue that God gives for appropriate expressions of sexuality, the anatomical and pro-creative complementarity of male and female, suggests that something greater is at stake than even sexual fidelity and physical health.

Excursus: Circumcision and Salvation in Judaism

The Hebrew Bible does not undertake a systematic discussion of require-ments for gentile conversion to Judaism, because being a Jew was primarily a matter of ethnic birthright rather than religious choice. Reflection on gentile inclusion accelerated only in the post-exilic period and even then without complete consensus. Circumcision is presented in Gen 17 (P) as "a sign of the covenant" between God and Abraham's descendants (including foreign slaves in their care). Jacob's sons insisted that only a circumcised man could marry their sister Dinah (Gen 34:13-24). According to Exod 12:48-49 (P), "if an alien who resides with you wants to celebrate the passover to Yahweh, all his males shall be circumcised; then he may draw near to celebrate it; he shall be regarded as a native of the land. But no uncircumcised person shall eat of it; there shall be one law for the native and for the alien who resides among you" (i.e., the law does not make an exception for the resident alien; cf. Num 9:14). The resident alien was held culpable for violating Israelite law and allowed participation in the cult only when in compliance with the rules prescribed for Israelites, but at the same time accorded protection by the law from arbitrary mistreatment.[200] Yet there appears to have been little expectation of, or even zeal for, full integration of resident aliens into Israelite tribal society. The "conversion" of Naaman the Syrian, who was not a resident alien, followed immersion in the Jordan River for the healing of his leprosy, a self-initiated acknowledgment that "there is no God in all the earth except in Israel," and a commitment to sacrificing only to Yahweh (2 Kgs 5:14-19); circumcision was not an issue. A more proactive approach to converts was taken by Second Isaiah, who assured "the foreigners who join themselves to Yahweh [through circumcision or merely a declaration to sacrifice to Yahweh alone?] . . . , all

---

200. Exod 12:18-19; 20:10-11; 22:21; 23:9; Deut 5:14; 16:11, 14; 29:11; 31:12; Leviticus 17-18; 24:22; Num 15:14-16, 29-30.

who keep the sabbath . . . and hold fast to my covenant" that their offerings and prayers would be welcome in the rebuilt Temple (Isa 56:6-8; cf. Isa 14:1). In the late Second Temple period, circumcision was the usual requirement for male entry into Judaism, particularly in Israel. The book of Judith (ca. 160 B.C.E.) refers to a gentile's (Achior's) admission "to the community of Israel" after "he believed in God completely" and was circumcised (14:10). Josephus viewed circumcision as an entry requirement, as did the Jewish-Christian Judaizers who attempted to thwart the Pauline mission. Talmudic sources state that a proselyte in the Second Temple period not only had to be circumcised but also had to undergo baptism and make an offering to the Sanctuary (*Sipre* on Num. 15:14; *b. Yebam.* 46a; *b. Ker.* 9a; cf. *m. Ker.* 2:1; *m. Pesaḥ* 8:8; *m. ʿEd.* 5:2). However, uncircumcised gentiles were certainly not excluded by all Jews everywhere from all participation in Jewish religious life, nor were all consigned by all Jews everywhere to destruction. Obviously gentile women converts could not be circumcised. This simple reality alone would have undermined attempts to make circumcision a *sine qua non* of Jewish identity, particularly since most gentile converts to Judaism were women.[201] In *Joseph and Aseneth* (first century C.E.?) Aseneth's conversion to Judaism was marked not by any standard ritual, not even by baptism, but by repenting of sin and throwing away her idols.

John J. Collins concludes, after sampling the requirements placed on gentiles by some Diaspora literature (*Sib. Or.* 3 and 5, the *Letter of Aristeas*, and Pseudo-Phocylides), that: "What these Jews asked of Gentiles was primarily that they worship the one true God. This was usually thought to entail a rejection of idolatry. *They also insisted on an ethical code with special emphasis on avoiding adultery and homosexuality*. The lack of reference to circumcision is impressive. . . . [These works] show little interest in proselytizing . . . . Salvation is seldom restricted to membership of the Jewish people."[202] Although Philo did not think Jews in Alexandria should interpret the command to circumcision in a purely allegorical fashion, he shows an awareness of some Jews who questioned whether literal circumcision was an essential mark of Jewish identity (*Migr.* 89-94). Philo himself could say: "in reality the proselyte is one who circumcises not his uncircumcision but his desires and sensual pleasures and other passions of the soul. For in Egypt the Hebrew

---

201. Schürer, *The History of the Jewish People*, vol. 3, 162-63.

202. John J. Collins, "A Symbol of Otherness: Circumcision and Salvation in the First Century," *To See Ourselves as Others See Us* (eds. J. Neusner and E. Frerichs; Chico: Scholars Press, 1985), 164-69 (my emphasis). Also: idem, *Between Athens and Jerusalem: Jewish Identity in the Hellenistic Diaspora* (New York: Crossroad, 1986), 137-74, esp. 142-43.

nation was not circumcised" (*QE* 2.2). In the conversion of the royal house of Adiabene (ca. 40 C.E.) a Jewish merchant assured the king that "he could worship God even without circumcision"—though it is not clear whether this assurance was a special exemption owing to the particular circumstances of the king (a subsequent visit by a Galilean Jew convinced the king to be circumcised; Josephus, *Ant.* 20.35-49).

Scot McKnight argues that even though circumcision "by and large . . . was seen as a requirement . . . in light of the debates over the matter, it is probable that circumcision as a requirement had not yet become established custom or tradition prior to the first century A.D."[203] Regardless of whether "God-fearer" was everywhere a technical term for semi-proselytes or not, Jewish, Christian, and pagan literature attests to attendance at synagogues by uncircumcised gentiles, intermarriage, charitable contributions by uncircumcised gentiles to the Jewish people, and the widespread adoption of Jewish practices by gentiles (e.g., Sabbath observance, food laws such as abstinence from pork, fasts, abandonment of idols, worship of and prayer to the God of Israel, certain fundamental ["Noahide"] moral laws).[204] Josephus reported that in Antioch (Syria) large numbers of Greeks were attracted to synagogue services and that Jews "had made these, in a certain way, part of their own community" (*J.W.* 7.45). "The wall between Judaism and paganism may have been high, but it was a wall made from steps and there were Gentiles at each level."[205]

203. *A Light Among the Gentiles: Jewish Missionary Activity in the Second Temple Period* (Minneapolis: Fortress, 1991), 81-82.
204. Cf. Josephus, *Ag. Ap.* 2.123, 282; *J.W.* 2.463; *Ant.* 14.110; Luke 7:1-10; Acts 10; 13:16, 26, 43-50; 14:1; 16:14; 17:4, 12, 17; 18:4, 7; Rom 2:19-20; the category of "fearers of Heaven" and "righteous gentiles" in the Talmud; the inscription from Aphrodisias, ca. 210 C.E., which records a group of donors distinct from Jews and proselytes known as "God-fearers"; the inscription on a theater seat in Sardis, "Place for the Jews and God-fearers" (or: ". . . 'Jews' [i.e., gentile adherents to Judaism] who are also [more precisely called?] God-fearers"); the inscription from Panticapeum, which refers to a manumission "under the guardianship of the synagogue of the Jews and God-fearers"; Juvenal, *Sat.* 14.96-106; and Tertullian, *Nat.* 1.13.
205. McKnight, *A Light Among the Gentiles*, 100. See: ibid., 78-101, 108-15; Collins, "Otherness," 163-86; Schürer, *History*, 3.1:160-74; Louis H. Feldman, *Jew and Gentile in the Ancient World* (Princeton: Princeton University Press, 1993), 342-82; idem, "The Omnipresence of the God-Fearers," *BAR* 12:5 (Sept/Oct 1986): 58-63; Paul R. Trebilco, *Jewish Communities in Asia Minor* (SNTSMS 69; Cambridge: Cambridge University, 1991), 145-66; Bernd Wander, *Gottesfürchtige und Sympathisanten: Studien zum heidnischen Umfeld von Diasporasynagogen* (WUNT 104; Tübingen: Mohr [Siebeck], 1998). For the rejection of the notion of a formally recognized status of gentile "God-fearers"

The fact that large segments of first-generation Jewish Christians (including the "pillars" of the Jerusalem church and the major Christian center at Antioch) could so quickly embrace uncircumcised gentiles as fellow believers in Christ is itself testimony to a blurring of boundaries between Jews and gentiles already in pre-Christian Judaism. As E. P. Sanders notes, "There was wide variety in views about what would happen to the Gentiles."[206] To be sure, some Jews thought that gentiles who did not convert fully to Judaism as proselytes would be consigned to destruction. Acts 11:18 states that when the Jerusalem church heard Peter's report of the gift of the Spirit on Cornelius they concluded that "Then God has given even to the gentiles the repentance that leads to life"—suggesting a change of heart from an earlier conviction that uncircumcised gentiles would not inherit eternal life. Yet even Jews who discounted the salvation of uncircumcised gentiles knew that the matter was still a highly debatable one within Judaism. The circumstances were entirely different in the case of homosexual intercourse, where the issue was sexuality and not Jewish ritual, where the Bible was quite explicit about its character as egregious sin, where "nature" itself made clear its abhorrent quality, and where Jews everywhere agreed on this.

VII. Since we are all sinners anyway, why single out the sin of same-sex intercourse?

This is a very tempting, final fall-back argument: let the person without sin cast the first stone. Maybe homosexuality is a sin after all. Yet since we are all sinners, with equally broken lives, and equally in need of God's grace, heterosexuals have no right to come down so hard on the sin of homosexuality.

The problem with this argument is that, followed to its logical conclusion, it would result in a church that never takes a stand against sin and evil, a church that neither exhibits its own redemption to the world nor calls the world to responsible conduct. All people are sinners; but not a single writer of a biblical text, not a single protagonist of the gospel, ever concludes from this that the church should cease to take

---

before the second century C.E., see Martin Goodman, *Mission and Conversion: Proselytizing in the Religious History of the Roman Empire* (Oxford: Clarendon, 1994), 47, 87-88, 117-19. Goodman, however, at least acknowledges the pre-second-century existence of gentiles who "filled a role equivalent to that filled in later centuries by 'Godfearers.' "

206. *Judaism: Practice and Belief, 63 BCE–66 CE* (London: SCM, 1992), 295.

a stand against sin in all its forms. No biblical text treats grace and holiness as incompatible goals of the church. Few people in the church today who argue for toleration or affirmation of homosexual conduct would want to argue that the church should tolerate or affirm adultery, pedophilia, incest, polygamy, sexual harassment, spousal abuse, discrimination against women, racism, economic oppression, or a host of other societal ills. In such cases, few would say, "Hey, we're all sinners; who am I to judge you?"

The church must always approach the rebuking of sin among its members with humility and sensitivity, repenting of its own faults, and providing offending members with support for change. We all sin but not all sin is equally offensive to God and not all sin is to be treated in the same way. Pocketing a single company pen is not equivalent to committing adultery; the two acts call for radically different responses on the part of the church. Jesus and Paul took firm stances against hypocritical judging and judging in trivial matters but never exhorted the community of God to give up altogether its role of admonishing members. "Be on your guard! If your brother sins, rebuke him, and *if he repents* forgive him; and if he sins against you seven times a day and turns to you seven times and says, 'I repent,' forgive him" (Luke 17:3-4; cf. the instructions for church discipline in Matt 18:15-20; also Gal 6:1; 1 Thess 5:12-14).

Two situations in Paul's churches are illuminating. One is the circumstance in which one of the believers at Corinth was sleeping with his stepmother (1 Corinthians 5), a sexual sin of comparable seriousness to homosexual conduct.[207] Just as today many promote an "enlightened" attitude toward homosexual behavior, so too then many in the church at Corinth expressed support for the incestuous man's conduct. Paul had to criticize them for taking no action against this sin. According to Paul they should have "mourned" for their brother rather than become inflated with pride (5:2). Paul's advice to the community was to expel the member from the church (5:2*b*, 5). The reason is interesting: not only so that the church might not be overtaken by a lax attitude toward sin ("a little leaven leavens the whole lump") but also

---

207. Like the homosexual offender, "the man who lies with his father's wife" is to be given the death sentence according to the Holiness Code (Lev 20:11).

so that the offending believer might somehow be "saved" from judgment "on the day of the Lord" (5:5-6). The same concern for the offending party is manifested in 2 Cor 2:5-11: *After* the offender had experienced discipline from the church, Paul exhorted the Corinthian community to quickly "forgive and comfort him" and "to reaffirm your love for him" in order that Satan might not be able to take advantage of the situation.

The Negative Effects of Societal Endorsement of Homosexuality

There are at least five negative effects that affirming homosexuality can have on the church and society. First, ecclesiastical and societal affirmation will lead to an increase in the incidence of homosexuality and bisexuality, which in turn will lead to a larger number of people afflicted with serious health problems and shortened life expectancy. In section IV above we noted that cultural support for homosexual behavior can significantly increase the incidence of homosexual behavior and the numbers of self-identifying homosexuals. The impact of disease on the homosexual population is well documented. In *Homosexuality and the Politics of Truth,* psychiatrist Jeffrey Satinover has argued that one way to determine the moral desirability of homosexuality is to examine the medical facts. What, he asks, should society think if a relative, friend, or colleague had a condition that is routinely, even if not always, associated with the following problems:

- A significantly decreased likelihood of establishing or preserving a successful marriage
- A five- to ten-year decrease in life expectancy
- Chronic, potentially fatal, liver disease—hepatitis
- Inevitably fatal esophageal cancer
- Pneumonia
- Internal bleeding
- Serious mental disabilities, many of which are irreversible
- A much higher than usual incidence of suicide
- A very low likelihood that its adverse effects can be eliminated unless the condition itself is eliminated
- An only 30% likelihood of being eliminated through lengthy, often

costly, and very time-consuming treatment in an otherwise unselected population of sufferers (although a very high success rate among highly motivated, carefully selected sufferers)

Satinover adds:

> We can add four qualifications to this unnamed condition. First, even though its origins are influenced by genetics, the condition is, strictly speaking, rooted in behavior. Second, individuals who have this condition continue the behavior in spite of the destructive consequences of doing so. Third, . . . many [with this condition] deny they have any problem at all and violently resist all attempts to "help" them. And fourth, these people who resist help tend to socialize with one another, sometimes exclusively, and form a kind of "subculture." (p. 50)

Obviously, Satinover states, society should consider the condition worth treating and worth persuading other members of society to avoid the behavior that brings on these terrible medical risks. Then Satinover lets his reader in on a secret. The condition he was alluding to was not homosexuality but alcoholism. The medical downside of homosexuality is worse:

- A significantly decreased likelihood of establishing or preserving a successful marriage
- A *twenty-five to thirty*-year decrease in life expectancy[208]
- Chronic, potentially fatal, liver disease—infectious hepatitis, which increases the risk of liver cancer

---

208. Cf. Paul Cameron, Kirk Cameron, and William L. Playfair, "Does Homosexual Activity Shorten Life?" *Psychological Reports* 83 (1998): 847-66. Another study estimated "life expectancy at age 20 for [Canadian] gay and bisexual men [to be] 8 to 20 years less than for all men" (Robert S. Hogg, et al., "Modelling the Impact of HIV Disease on Mortality in Gay and Bisexual Men," *International Journal of Epidemiology* 26 [1997]: 657-61). The twenty-year figure assumes homosexual and bisexual men account for 3% of the total male population aged over twenty; the eight-year figure assumes they account for 9% of the population. (By contrast, smoking is estimated to reduce lifespan by two years.) With advances in AIDS treatment, we might expect that figure to come down a little.

- Inevitably fatal immune disease, including associated cancers
- Frequently fatal rectal cancer
- Multiple bowel and other infectious diseases
- A much higher than usual incidence of suicide
- A very low likelihood that its adverse effects can be eliminated unless the condition itself is
- An at least 50% likelihood of being eliminated through lengthy, often costly, and very time-consuming treatment[209]

The additional qualifications given for alcoholism also hold true for homosexuality: a behavior with a partial and indirect genetic component; participation in the behavior despite its destructive effects; participants' rigorous denial that there is a problem; and the formation of a subculture. "Yet despite the parallels between the two conditions, what is striking today are the sharply different responses to them."[210]

The Centers for Disease Control and Prevention (CDC) has kept tabs on the number of AIDS cases by exposure category from 1981 on.[211] Through the end of 1999, among AIDS cases where an exposure category has been identified for adults and adolescents, 52% (341,597) have occurred in men who have sex with men; another 7% (46,582) occurs in men who have sex with men and inject drugs. An additional 28% (184,429) can be traced to injecting drug use and 11% (74,477) to heterosexual contact. What this means is that roughly 2% of the population has accounted for about 60% of all adult/adolescent AIDS cases and 84% of those due to sexual activity. Although the percentage of AIDS cases arising from heterosexual contact has risen in the last decade, in 1999 alone homosexual intercourse still accounted for 50% (17,270) of all new adult/adolescent AIDS cases (34,954) where an exposure category is known and 71% of those due to sexual activity (24,409). A considerable part of the problem is anal intercourse, which is never safe and

---

209. The data that Jones and Yarhouse (*Homosexuality*, 123) have accumulated regarding the success rate of sexual orientation conversion therapy suggests that the 50% figure may be high. The 30% figure given for treatment of alcoholism is about right for homosexuality as well.
210. *Homosexuality and the Politics of Truth*, 49-51.
211. Cf. cdc.gov/nchstp/hiv_aids. A 1997 Australian study indicated that among homosexually active men from ages twenty-five to fifty roughly 11% of those who had been tested were HIV positive (Van de Ven, "Older Homosexually Active Men,"

yet remains the preferred sexual activity among homosexual men. Multiple sexual partners, cruising, and sex with strangers—all hallmarks of typical male homosexual behavior—also factor into the picture.

As the list above indicates, the problem is not just AIDS. On average those who engage in homosexual behavior contract sexually transmitted diseases at a rate two to three times higher than those who do not.[212] Oral-anal contact (where feces can be ingested),[213] penile-anal con-

---

357). A self-selected survey of American homosexual men put the figure at 13% (Lever, "The 1994 Advocate Survey," 21). Both studies also indicated that the majority of men who were homosexually active in the preceding year did not use condoms, either sometimes or always. The Young Men's Survey studied the prevalence of HIV infection among 3,492 fifteen- to twenty-two-year-old males who have sex with males, in seven American cities from 1994 through 1998. It found that the HIV infection rate was high, averaging 7.2%, and rising to 9.7% already by the tender age of twenty-two. Making matters worse, only 18% of the HIV-positive men knew before the survey that they had the disease. Overall, 41% had unprotected anal sex during the previous six months. John Hylton et al., "HIV Prevalence and Associated Risks in Young Men Who Have Sex with Men," *JAMA* 284:2 (2000):198-204.

212. Two studies reached similar results: a study in the early 1980s conducted by the Family Research Institute (Paul Cameron et al., "Sexual Orientation and Sexually Transmitted Disease," *Nebraska Medical Journal* 70 [1985]: 292-99) and a British national sexuality survey conducted in the early 1990s (A. M. Johnson et al., *Sexual Attitudes and Lifestyles* [London: Blackwell, 1994]). Schmidt lists in order of prevalence among homosexuals the following nonviral infections: amebiasis (inflammation of the rectum and colon), giardiasis, gonorrhea, shigellosis, chlamydia, syphilis, and ectoparasites; of viral infections: condylomata (anal warts, linked to anal cancer), herpes, and hepatitis B and A (*Straight and Narrow?*, 116-22; HIV/AIDS is discussed on pp. 122-26).

213. The 1994 *Advocate* survey makes especially clear the attraction that homosexual males have toward the anus. The most popular way to have an orgasm involves anal intercourse (so 45% of respondents: 26% via masturbation while being penetrated; 19% via insertive anal intercourse). The next most popular way to have an orgasm is by receiving oral sex (17%). In the past year alone, 58% performed insertive anal intercourse and 56% engaged in receptive anal intercourse; 41% performed anilingus (tongue on or in the anus), 47% received it. Only 15% expressed an aversion to fingering another male's anus (Lever, "The 1994 Advocate Survey," 21, 23). By contrast, lesbians' "least favorable activities included giving or receiving anal stimulation: More than half will neither perform nor receive anilingus, and almost as many express dislike of anal penetration" (Lever, "Lesbian Sex Survey," 26). Similarly, the 1997 Australian survey found that over 60% of homosexually active men had had anal intercourse during the six months prior to interview; about half had engaged in "rimming" (oral-anal contact); and about 10% had engaged in "fisting" (Van de Ven, "Older Homosexually Active Men," 355-56).

tact,[214] and oral-penile contact[215] account for a number of infections.[216] Homosexuals experience significantly higher rates of alcohol and drug abuse, major depression, and thoughts of suicide and suicide attempts (often over partnership breakups).[217] There is debate over how much of the fault for these indications of distress rests with homosexual behavior itself (e.g., high relationship turnover) and how much is attributable to social hostility against homosexuality. The fact, though, that significantly higher rates of substance abuse has been documented for homosexuals in San Francisco (as compared to heterosexuals in San Francisco) suggests that pinning the lion's share of the blame on societal homophobia is unfair.[218] The high incidence of sadomasochistic sex, sex with strangers, the deliberate infection of partners with STDs, and domestic violence among homosexuals is consistent with the profile of high-risk, aggressive, and dehumanizing behavior.[219]

Higher rates of substance abuse may be related to the same obsessive, compulsive, or addictive needs for self-soothing that made same-sex intercourse an appealing form of sexual expression in the first place. Higher rates of depression and suicide attempts are probably exacerbated by the inherent deficiencies of same-sex unions, and not just by societal opposition to such unions. These deficiencies include:

---

214. For the serious medical risks associated with anal intercourse, cf. Schmidt, *Straight and Narrow?*, 117-18; Satinover, *Homosexuality*, 22-23, 66-68.

215. "Semen contains many of the germs carried in the blood" and "the penis often has tiny lesions (and often those of homosexuals will have been in unsanitary places such as a rectum)" (Cameron, *The Gay Nineties*, 40). According to the 1997 Australian survey cited above, about half had engaged in oral-genital contact that involved ejaculating into the mouth of the partner; over 90% had engaged in oral-genital sex without ejaculation. According to the 1994 *Advocate* survey, 71% said they were fond of receptive oral intercourse, 72% of insertive oral intercourse. In the past year, 58% had another man ejaculate into their mouths, while 44% (including 26% of HIV-positive men) ejaculated into another male's mouth.

216. Cameron, *The Gay Nineties*, 39-44; Schmidt.

217. Jones and Yarhouse, *Homosexuality*, 102-106; Schmidt, *Straight and Narrow?*, 110-14.

218. Cf. Schmidt, *Straight and Narrow?*, 110-11, citing a 1989 study.

219. Cameron, *The Gay Nineties*, 47-50; idem, "Same-Sex Marriage." The *Advocate* survey of homosexual males found that 20% engaged in bondage and discipline, 10% in sadomasochism; 45% made use of a cock ring, 19% nipple clamps; among lesbians: 25% engaged in bondage and discipline, 14% in fisting, 7% in sadomasochism; 6% made use of nipple clamps.

- an endemic dearth of long-term, monogamous relationships (further rejection by members of the same sex)
- an inability to procreate with one's same-sex partner
- an obsessive centering on self that may occur when sexual intercourse can be obtained without having to learn how to relate to a sexual "other" and when erotic attraction is directed toward the very physique and traits that one shares in common with another
- the dismal association of same-sex intercourse with debilitating, sometimes terminal, sexually-transmitted diseases
- shame and guilt over one's abnormal and unnatural sexual practice (a realization that stems from visible evidence of same-sex dis-complementarity or the inability to relate properly to the opposite sex, not from "internalized homophobia")

No one can pretend to know all the causes for the current health crisis and pinpoint the exact percentage of "blame" on each cause. Nevertheless, the bottom-line statistics speak for themselves.

Two recent studies in the *Archives of General Psychiatry* (56 [1999]) also support the conclusion that there is something pathological about homosexual orientation itself. One study by Richard Herrell, et. al., examined 3,400 male twin pairs (so 6,800 subjects) in which both had served in the United States military between 1965 and 1975.[220] About 2% (120) of these reported participation in same-sex intercourse; all but sixteen of these had a co-twin who reported only female sex partners. The authors found that those men who had at least one male sex partner in their lives were six times more likely to report attempted suicide than those who had no male sex partners generally and three times more likely than their heterosexual co-twin. After reviewing scientific literature over the last forty years, showing a fairly consistent six- to sevenfold increase in claims of attempted suicide among homosexuals, the authors concluded:

> There does not appear to be a reduction in the [suicide rate for homosexuals] that one might expect given social change in recent years. . . .

---

220. "Sexual Orientation and Suicidality: A Co-Twin Control Study in Adult Men," 867-74. Quote below from p. 873.

In conclusion, reports of lifetime measures of suicidality are strongly associated with a same-gender sexual orientation. These effects cannot be explained by abuse of alcohol and other drugs, non-suicidal depressive symptoms, or the numerous unmeasured genetic and non-genetic familial factors.

The second study by D. M. Fergusson, et al., followed 1,007 children from birth to the age of twenty-one in Christchurch, New Zealand, deriving information from self-report, parental report, and observations by the authors.[221] Unlike some previous studies that implicated societal homophobia as the problem for disturbances among homosexual youth, this study was not based on one-time anonymous self-reports and did not implicate societal homophobia as the prime culprit. Comparing the self-identified heterosexuals with the twenty-eight young adults identified as "gay, lesbian, or bisexual,"[222] the authors found that the homosexual/bisexual young people were significantly more likely to experience psychiatric disorder: major depression and conduct disorder (four times more likely), nicotine dependence (five times), generalized anxiety disorder (three times), other substance abuse/dependence (two times), and multiple disorders (six times). They also had higher rates of suicide ideation (three times) and suicide attempts (six times). At the same time, the authors found that

> there was some evidence to suggest small tendencies for the GLB [gay, lesbian, and bisexual] group to have experienced more troubled childhoods, with this group having greater exposure to parental change including separation and/or divorce and remarriage and higher exposures to parents with a history of criminal offense.

Neither of these two upbringing factors can be traced to societal homophobia.

Commentary in the same issue by J. Michael Bailey (of identical-

---

221. "Is Sexual Orientation Related to Mental Health Problems and Suicidality in Young People?" 876-80. Quote below from p. 879.
222. Twenty (2%) of these identified themselves as homosexual or bisexual. Another eight (.8%) "self-identified as heterosexual but . . . had had sexual relationships with a same-sex partner since the age of 16 years" (p. 877).

twin-study fame and himself an advocate of gay rights) followed the two studies, in which Bailey concluded: "These studies contain arguably the best published data on the association between homosexuality and psychopathology." He noted that, although antihomosexual attitudes probably play a part in increased suicidality of homosexuals ("but this remains to be demonstrated," he admits), other factors were likely to be involved: "developmental error" (there is "a possibility . . . that homosexuality represents a deviation from normal development . . . that may lead to mental illness"); the tendency of effeminate homosexuals to experience female-like types of "neuroticism"; and "lifestyle differences" associated with sexual orientation (especially "receptive anal sex and promiscuity" and the attendant fear of sexually transmitted diseases).[223]

The argument might be made that, as dire as the health risks associated with homosexuality are, they are risks faced only by those who freely engage in homosexual behavior. If homosexuals are willing to take such risks, why should heterosexuals care? Four responses come to mind. First, it is hardly a compassionate response on the part of society to ignore, let alone laud, participation in same-sex intercourse by those with a homosexual orientation. At a time when society is becoming increasingly vocal against smoking, drinking to get drunk, drug use, and unsafe sex, society's openness to homosexual intercourse, with its score of attendant problems, is strangely inconsistent. I am not advocating the enforcement of sodomy laws against consenting, same-sex adults who have intercourse in the privacy of their own homes. Yet, minimally, the state might promote, through education and counseling, programs of abstinence from same-sex intercourse. Second, the enormous health costs generated by same-sex activity are borne by the whole society, not by the homosexual community alone. These costs are nothing short of staggering. Third, the argument for ignoring the health risks of same-sex intercourse mistakenly assumes a rigid dividing wall preventing any sexual contact between homosexuals and heterosexuals. The reality, of course, is much different. The categories we

---

223. "Homosexuality and Mental Illness," pp. 883-84. Bailey also cites the stress on "physical attractiveness and thinness" in the gay culture, which may explain why male homosexuals are "vastly overrepresented among male patients with eating disorders."

have created to define people by discreet acts are broad strokes which often do not do justice to the complexity of human life and community. The overwhelming number of homosexuals and a minority of heterosexuals undergo one or more shifts along the 0 to 6 graduated Kinsey scale of sexual preference during the course of their lives. Bisexuals compose roughly a third of the homosexual-bisexual population. What this means practically is that some who engage in same-sex intercourse also engage in opposite-sex intercourse, exposing their partners to certain risks. In addition, microbes are transmitted in other ways, such as the sharing of needles by intravenous drug users from the homosexual population to the heterosexual one, and vice versa. Fourth, and perhaps most important, societal approval of same-sex intercourse will probably increase both the number of homosexuals and the incidence of same-sex intercourse in the population. Along with this increase will be the unintentional but inevitable exposure of more members of the population to the numerous, serious health risks associated with homosexual activity than would otherwise be the case.

A second negative effect of societal endorsement of homosexuality has to do with the problem of pedophilia and its role in "recruiting" homosexuals into the fold. There can be little doubt that affirmation of a same-sex lifestyle will increase the incidence of pedophilic activity, or at least adult-adolescent same-sex activity, regardless of society's attempt to distinguish the two. The greater the latitude given to sexual expression, the more likelihood there will be of people crossing the line into illicit conduct. Indeed, a substantial body of literature emanating from the homosexual community entertains the morality of adult-adolescent sex. The homosexual community as a whole has not vigorously and swiftly rejected this development. Indeed, homosexual groups in other countries have been at the forefront of efforts to lower the age for sexual consent.

Although the majority of homosexuals are not pedophiles and do not publicly promote pedophilia, the incidence of same-sex pedophilic behavior is disproportionately high. The 1992 NHSLS study (Laumann, et al.) found that 21% of all instances of adult-child (preteen) sexual touching was same-sex. A 1983 Family Research Institute study arrived at a similar 22% figure.[224] Other studies have reached figures as high as 35-40%.[225] Cameron summarized the data as follows: "About a third of the reports of molestation by the populace have involved homosexuality. Likewise, between a fifth and a third of those who have been caught and/or convicted practiced homosexuality. Finally, a fifth to a third of surveyed gays admitted to child molestation. All-in-all, a rather consistent story."[226] On average, homosexual pedophiles also molest seven to eight times more children than heterosexual pedophiles.[227] We have already noted that same-sex molestation of children increases the chances that the child will later identify his orientation as homosexual. The problem of molestation pertains not only to adult male homosexual molesters but also to adolescent male homosexual boys who are increasingly being encouraged by sex-ed programs and gay-activist groups to engage in same-sex sexual experimentation with their peers.

A third negative effect arising from affirmation of homosexuality, perhaps far more dangerous than that of pedophilia, is greater permissiveness as regards sexual promiscuity. Homosexual expression is harmful to sexual mores and the maintenance of stable families in heterosexual society. It is not just that homosexual unions fail to contribute to the development of stable family units through the inability to procreate, the inability to provide complementary modeling of the sexes to adoptive or neighboring children, or their apparent incapacity

---

224. Paul Cameron et al., "Child Molestation and Homosexuality," *Psychological Reports* 58 (1986): 327-37.
225. Cf. Cameron, *The Gay Nineties*, 61.
226. Ibid., 63.
227. K. Freund and R. I. Watson, "The Proportions of Heterosexual and Homosexual Pedophiles Among Sex Offenders Against Children: An Exploratory Study," *Journal of Sex and Marital Therapy* 18 (Spring 1992): 34-43; cited by Schmidt. A study by C. Jenny et al. ("Are Children at Risk for Sexual Abuse by Homosexuals?," *Pediatrics* 94 [1994]: 41-44) is often cited as "proving" that 98% of men who molest boys self-identify as heterosexuals. In fact, the authors only checked hospital charts and never interviewed the molesters, victims, or those who prepared the charts. The only study in a refereed journal that based its findings on self-reports by molesters concluded that 86% of the molesters identified themselves as homosexual or bisexual (W. D. Erickson et al., "Behavior Patterns of Child Molesters," *Arch. Sexual Behavior* 17 [1988]: 77-86; cited in *FRR* 14:1 [Jan./Feb. 1999]).

for longevity. It is, rather, that typical homosexual behavior undermines society's standards for sexual fidelity across the board, inasmuch as acceptance of homosexuality by heterosexual society seems to require an acceptance of patterns of irresponsible and unstable sexual behavior prevailing among homosexuals. An ethic that embraces only monogamous, lifelong unions between members of the same sex will, it seems, encompass such a tiny fraction of the homosexual population that heterosexual acceptance of homosexual unions in theory will have to appear to homosexuals as rejection of such unions in reality. Homosexuals will (rightfully) insist that heterosexuals are imposing an unfair heterosexual norm on the reality of homosexual orientation and that true acceptance of homosexuals must be acceptance of who homosexuals really are and what they really do, not some abstract ideal that hardly any homosexual unions appear capable of sustaining. Having already made a commitment to affirm the legitimacy of homosexual intercourse and facing guilt over heterosexual failures in the area of stable relationships, church and state will likely capitulate to a standard of sexual fidelity for heterosexual and homosexual alike that will wreak havoc on the institutions of marriage and family. The scenario sounds alarming, but it is quite realistic in view of the statistics on promiscuity in the homosexual community and the propaganda on sexual liberation put forward by leading figures in the homosexual movement. Perhaps the best that one can realistically hope for is that, when the smoke clears and society has made its peace with the homosexual norm, a person who has cohabited with "only" four or five people and had a half dozen "one-night stands" over the course of a lifetime will be regarded by society as someone with a relatively stable sexual life.

Doubtlessly, appeals can be made, as counter examples, to particular cases of same-sex couples who have maintained long-term monogamous relationships and live as stable and productive citizens of society. Yet the occasional anecdotal evidence does not stack up against the cumulative statistics culled from numerous scientific studies, let alone deal with the question of God's revealed design for sexuality in Scripture and the anatomical puzzle of same-sex coupling. Approving same-sex unions because a tiny percentage of the total number appear on the surface to be positive arrangements is like dropping society's moral strictures against incest, pederasty, and polygamy because in isolated instances such arrangements seem to be working out. One may wish for a utopian society where homosexuals will "behave" like the average heterosexual (in accordance with some fictionalized dramatic representations of gays and lesbians in film, television, and the print media), but wishing will not make it so. Nor is it fair to harshly criticize homosexuals for failing to achieve seemingly unrealistic standards. Males will be sexually stimulated as males, regardless of whether they are heterosexual or homosexual. By this I mean that, relative to females, males have a stronger visual (figural) component to sexual attraction, intimacy needs that require less interpersonal communication, and thus a greater willingness to sacrifice long-term, monogamous relationships for short-term sexual gratification. To put two men together in a sexual bond and then to expect a lifelong union of monogamous fidelity to develop is, to my mind, a recipe for failure. One can also politely request that male homosexual unions abstain from anal intercourse, but such restrictions on specific behaviors are unlikely to win converts. Nor is the problem of short-term relationships limited to male same-sex unions. The average length of homosexual relationships appears to be slightly less for women than for men.

A fourth harmful effect to church and society is the total annihilation of societal gender norms. Indeed, this is one of the explicit goals of homosexual activist organizations, and a predictable one given (1) the override of God-given gender differences in acts such as a man penetrating another male's anus and (2) the high incidence of effeminate males and "butch" females among homosexuals. In its most bizarre forms we will be asked as a culture to accept as perfectly normal and well-adjusted a man wearing lipstick, panty hose, and a pink dress. Already homosexual-lobby groups are pushing for laws that will impose hefty fines on any who would "discriminate" against transvestites and transsexuals in the *public* sector, with "discriminate" left ambiguous enough to include such things as denying a school teacher the "right" to come to work in drag or denying an in-process transsexual man the "right" to use female bathrooms.[228] One may grant that

---

228. As this book was going to press the California State Assembly had passed by a single vote a bill that would extend special employment protections to transsexuals and transvestites. Lobbying on behalf of these "transgendered" people and spon-

different cultures have developed varying ways of encouraging some clear differences between the sexes, sometimes with oppressive results for women. Nevertheless, to assert that there are no natural sexual differences between males and females is a distortion of reality in its own right; and misogyny and cultural appreciation for legitimate gender differences can be distinguished. Attempts to obliterate all gender norms can only increase sexual confusion among the young—in fact, it will encourage it—and lead to the further erosion of Christian ethical standards and the institution of marriage.

A fifth harmful effect that we can mention only briefly here is the public marginalization of all those who in good conscience regard homosexual intercourse as sin. This is already a reality in many career paths—certainly in the arts, the media, many institutions of higher learning, and increasingly in major corporations, in public primary and secondary schools, and in federal, state, and local governments. People who "come out of the closet" about their negative evaluation of same-sex intercourse risk not being hired, or, if hired, being demoted, fired, or stalled in their careers. Within the last few years some American colleges and universities have withdrawn recognition of Christian student groups that deny self-affirming practicing homosexuals the "right" to hold office. Ostensibly, these Christian groups have violated the institution's anti-discrimination policy on sexual orientation, although no one made the connection at the time such policies were put in place. The de-recognition usually means the loss of thousands of dollars in school funding, of the use of school facilities for meeting, and of the use of the school's name—not to mention being branded with a terrible social stigma. And why not, since homosexual interest groups equate "homophobia" with racism. In the name of anti-discrimination those who uphold moral values are discriminated against while those who violate such values receive affirmative action. This is only the

---

soring workshops debunking "transphobia" has become part of the portfolio of mainstream homosexual organizations in recent years. Based on an ordinance passed by the city council of Boulder, Colorado, which granted broad civil rights protections to transsexuals, a pre-operative transsexual working in a bagel shop recently appealed to the Office of Human Rights for the "right" to come to work in a pink skirt and lipstick. Similar ordinances are already on the books in Cambridge (Massachusetts), Pittsburgh, Seattle, and San Francisco.

beginning. Children in the public school system will be indoctrinated through government mandated and funded programs to regard every conscience-directed opposition to homosexual behavior as homophobia. Christian schools and universities that "discriminate" on the basis of "sexual orientation" will suffer in many ways (loss of accreditation for some or all of their programs, loss of government funding or research grants, exclusion from interscholastic sports). This will happen regardless of religious exemption clauses which, in any case, are now under attack from homosexual activists who, apparently, all along have employed such exemption clauses as part of a "bait and switch" strategy. Parents who raise their children to revere God's creation design for human sexuality will one day do so in the knowledge that their children will be treated as the equivalent of racists—all in the name of societal tolerance.

Finally, it is not only the church and society that suffer when homosexuality is approved. Ultimately it is the individual homosexual who suffers in his or her relationship to God when the church shirks its duty to call a sin a sin. Far from being an unloving act, a sensitive refusal to condone homosexual conduct is the responsible and loving thing to do. The church deceives the homosexual by affirming a lifestyle that God deems to be sin. It is a nice, easy way out. No one is offended, the arguments go away, the tension dissipates—all at the "minimal" cost of forestalling the redemptive work of Christ. God did not offer up Jesus Christ for the purpose of rubber stamping and affirming all human desires. Christ died in order that human beings might be reconciled to God and begin the process of sanctification that will ultimately lead to glorification. To simply assert that God loves us and forgives us as we are, without holding out the necessity and hope of a life conformed to the will of God, is to deny

> God's power to do for us what we cannot do for ourselves. . . . To fly in the face of scripture in a pale call for acceptance and inclusion is a failure to do the costly work of reconciliation that liberates us from the bondage of our sinful selves. . . . Acceptance is not forgiveness. Affirmation is not transformation. And inclusion is not reconciliation.[229]

---

229. The quote is from an unpublished essay by Marion Soards. Used by permission.

The church must not shirk its duty to effect the costly work of reconciliation that liberates persons from bondage to a sinful self. It is not a kindness for a parent to allow a child to play with a scorpion or touch a hot radiator; nor is it a kindness for the church to give its blessing to forms of sexual expression that, as Paul notes, degrades the body created by God. The church should reject the notion that the only alternatives are to affirm homosexual behavior or to hate and harass the homosexuals. Rather, the church must affirm a third option: to love the homosexual by humbly providing the needed support, comfort, and guidance to encourage the homosexual not to surrender to homosexual passions.

Summary

With two millennia and more dividing the biblical texts that speak about homosexual behavior from our own time, it is inappropriate to simply assert the Bible's authority at face value. At the same time, the strong biblical testimony against homosexual practice sets the burden-of-proof bar very high for Christians who wish to discount the Bible's witness. We have investigated the main arguments employed to discount the normative force of the Bible's perspective for our own day and found each of the arguments wanting. The Bible does not limit its rejection of same-sex intercourse to particular, exploitative forms. It does not condemn same-sex intercourse (at least not primarily) because of the threat that such intercourse poses to male dominance over females. The Bible's stance is not weakened by an alleged failure to understand the genetic or innate orientation of homosexuals, partly because scientific data indicates that the genetic influence pales in comparison to environmental influences, partly because the Bible recognizes an innate character to sin. Despite the limited number of texts in the Bible that speak directly to the question of same-sex intercourse, there is very little likelihood that any writer of Scripture, or Jesus, would have supported homosexual behavior of any sort. Comparisons drawn with such issues as women's roles as church leaders, slavery, and divorce are poor analogues for contemporary disagreement with the Bible's stance on same-sex intercourse. Finally, on grounds of health and sexual morality, same-sex intercourse cannot be regarded as a "light" or relatively harmless sin. The clear implication, then, is that the unambiguous rejection of same-sex intercourse that we find in Scripture remains in force for the church.

Conclusion

I. Recapping the Arguments

Drawing from the material in the preceding chapters, we see emerging at least four reasons why those who engage in same-sex intercourse act contrary to God's intentions for human sexual relations.

(1) Same-sex intercourse is strongly and unequivocally rejected by the revelation of Scripture. Arguments put forward by advocates of homosexuality to undermine the contemporary relevance of Scripture are weak. Scripture does not reject same-sex intercourse because of some alleged ignorance of non-exploitative forms of homosexual behavior or genetic causation factors. It does not reject homosexual intercourse because of some misperception that only idolaters in the strict sense could engage in such behavior or because of some superstition about defilement and purity. It does not reject homosexual practice, at least not primarily, out of some need to assert the rule of men over women. Rather, Scripture rejects homosexual behavior because it is a violation of the gendered existence of male and female ordained by God at creation. Homosexual intercourse puts males in the category of females and females in the category of males, insofar as they relate to others as sexual beings. That distorts the sexuality intended by God for the health and vitality of the human race. God

487

intended the very act of sexual intercourse to be an act of pluralism, embracing a sexual "other" rather than a sexual "same." The biblical proscription of same-sex intercourse, like those against incest, adultery, and bestiality, is absolute (encompassing all cases), pervasive (by both Testaments and within each Testament), and severe (mandating exclusion from God's kingdom).

(2) Same-sex intercourse represents a suppression of the visible evidence in nature regarding male-female anatomical and procreative complementarity. Complementarity extends also to a range of personality traits and predispositions that contribute to making heterosexual unions enormously more successful in terms of fidelity, endurance, and health than same-sex ones. Acceptance of biblical revelation is thus not a prerequisite for rejecting the legitimacy of same-sex intercourse. However, for those who do attribute special inspired status to Scripture, at any level, there is even less warrant to affirm same-sex intercourse.

(3) Societal endorsement of homosexual behavior will only accelerate the many negative social effects arising from such behavior by, first, undermining efforts to deter those already engaged in same-sex intercourse from continuing that behavior and, second, substantially increasing the number of people who both participate in same-sex intercourse and view themselves as homosexual, bisexual, or transgender. We have delineated five such negative effects:

- an increase in serious health problems (disease including but not limited to HIV/AIDS, hepatitis, and rectal cancer; substance abuse; mental illness, including depression and suicide attempts) and hence a significant decrease in life expectancy
- an increase in the incidence of same-sex pedophilic and adult-adolescent sexual activity
- a significant erosion in ecclesiastical and societal expectations of long-term monogamous relationships and thus a further cheapening of the institutions of marriage and family
- the annihilation of all societal gender norms, which in turn will normalize the most bizarre elements of the homosexual movement (transsexualism, transvestism) and increase sexual-identity confusion among the young

- the public, political, educational, professional, and legal marginalization of any (both organizations and individuals) who make known their opposition to homosexual behavior, as the societal equivalent of racists

(4) The practicing homosexual's own relationship with the Creator will be put in jeopardy. If we are to believe Scripture, the failure of the church to help the homosexual make the transition out of homosexual practice and into sexual wholeness will make the church an accomplice to the very form of behavior that God finds detestable. The church will become an enabler of the practicing homosexual's loss of spiritual transformation and, possibly, salvation.

In sum, it is not hard to see the wisdom of God in sanctioning only heterosexual unions.

II. Church and Civil Policy Matters

These conclusions about the morality of same-sex intercourse have implications for both church and civil policy.

With regard to church policy, practicing, self-affirming homosexuals should be treated as any other persons engaged in persistent, unrepentant acts of immoral sexual behavior. They should be loved and ministered to; the church of God must struggle along with them and share in the groanings of the Spirit. They should also be called to a higher standard of behavior. Minimally, this means that those who will not abstain from same-sex intercourse are ineligible to hold church office.

In addition, if same-sex intercourse is sin, churches must make hard decisions regarding membership and discipline. If a church body (whether a denomination or local congregation) has no problems with enrolling or retaining as a member someone engaged in persistent *and unrepentant* acts of incest, polygamy, adultery, prostitution, or fornication, then practicing, self-affirming homosexuals should be fully accepted as well. However, if a church body would deny membership to such persons or put those who are already members under church discipline, then the same should be applied to practicing and unrepentant homosexuals. The key here is not whether the person is homosexually inclined but whether he or she is having same-sex intercourse and doing so in a "self-affirming" manner. The church can and ought to be generous in extending numerous opportunities for the homosexual who "backslides" into homosexual intercourse to be restored to the community of faith. I take seriously the words about the church forgiving "seven times a day" those who say "I repent" (Luke 17:3-4; cf. Matt 18:21-22: "seventy-seven times" or "seventy times seven"). The church should retain a certain "holy gullibility" about the genuineness of repentance in order to err on the side of grace. However, what the church has to be concerned about is allowing *members* to be free to engage in grossly immoral behavior (and homosexual behavior is so defined in the Bible), indefinitely refusing to repent, and substituting their own moral standards of behavior for those of Scripture without any expectation of sanctions implemented by the church. If persons indefinitely refuse to repent of such acts—declaring them to be wrong, expressing sorrow and regret, and renewing a commitment to refrain from such acts—some type of ecclesiastical discipline is surely called for. Otherwise the church ceases to stand under the lordship of Christ in any meaningful sense. Otherwise, too, it is impossible to make sense of Paul's approach to the comparable issue of a man engaged in incest in 1 Corinthians 5.

As regards the blessing of same-sex erotic unions by clergy, the appropriate position of the church could hardly be clearer. A union of two or more people who enter that union in whole or in part for the purpose of engaging in sexual intercourse, where the aforementioned intercourse is of a kind that can only be sinful in any and every circumstance—such a union cannot be blessed without sanctioning the form of sexual intercourse in question. Some pro-homosexuality clergy defend the blessing of homosexual unions on the grounds that all sorts of things are blessed, from boats and houses to friendships; that blessings are inherently good things; and that a blessing does not mean approval of all facets of the persons or things blessed. Such an argument is ludicrous at best, duplicitous at worst. Quite apart from the obvious fact that there are few people banging down church doors to receive blessings for non-erotic friendships, none of these examples mentioned above involves sin as a constitutive part of what is being blessed. Who would accept the contention that blessing a sexual relationship between a man and his horse, a man and a ten-year-old girl, an adulterous man and his mistress, a man and his three wives, or a brother and a sister would be an innocuous event? Clearly, blessing such unions would send an unmistakable signal that the sexual intercourse that bonds the parties together is acceptable.

At the same time, there should be no impediment to church office for someone with a homosexual orientation or preference who remains celibate, does not endorse homosexual behavior, and gives every evidence of wanting to remain committed to the Bible's and church's teaching on homosexuality. In order to join as a member, or continue in good standing, the lesser standards of abstaining from homosexual intercourse or, in cases of occasional lapses, a willingness to repent should be adequate. In addition, even to those who cannot meet these minimal standards for membership, the church could show hospitality in other ways (for example, welcoming them as visitors to church meetings and reaching out to them in their homes). Through these means, as well, the church will have opportunities to communicate the gospel message.

On matters of public policy, Christians should work toward a society that neither prosecutes nor promotes homosexual behavior. In effect, this means, positively, Christians should support the decriminalization of homosexual behavior and full prosecution of crimes against homosexuals. At the same time, the church should oppose any attempts to make "sexual orientation" a *specially* protected class, or to grant to same-sex relationships status and benefits comparable to those married couples receive. The issues are too complex to address adequately here and will have to await elaboration in a future publication.[1]

III. A Final Word

The final word on the subject of homosexuality is and should always be: love God and love the homosexual "neighbor." The homosexual and lesbian are not the church's enemy but people in need of the church's support for restoring to wholeness their broken sexuality

---

1. For a helpful collection of essays on the subject, see Christopher Wolfe, ed., *Homosexuality and the American Public Life* (Dallas: Spence, 1999).

through compassion, prayer, humility, and groaning together for the redemption of our bodies. The old saying "Hate the sin but love the sinner" holds true, despite the shortcomings that it shares with all slogans. As David Wright notes, "It may sound simplistic, but it . . . goes right to the heart of the gospel."[2] The core proclamation of the gospel declares that God made amends for human sin while humans were still ungodly and hostile sinners, that God experienced the pain and agony of offering Christ up to death in order to rescue the maximum number of people from sin and transform them into Christ's image. To denounce same-sex intercourse and then stop short of actively and sacrificially reaching out in love and concern to homosexuals is to have as truncated a gospel as those who mistake God's love for "accepting people as they are" and who avoid talk of the gospel's transformative power. It is to forget the costly and self-sacrificial work of God in our own lives, past and ongoing.

The policy stances that the church must take toward same-sex intercourse do not diminish the believer's call to love the individual homosexual. Indeed, a keener understanding of the theological, social, and physical consequences of same-sex intercourse can *potentially* perform the salutary task of helping our "love abound still more and more in knowledge and all insight so that [we] may figure out the things that make a difference, in order that [we] may be pure and blameless heading into the day of Christ, having been filled with the fruit of righteousness that comes through Jesus Christ, to the glory and praise of God" (Phil 1:9-11). An ill-informed love can be just as destructive as hatred. Knowledge of truth is therefore essential to any appropriate exercise of love. It is not enough to want to love. One must know how to express one's love to particular people in particular situations. At the same time, it is not enough to know what is right. Knowledge can "puff up" or "inflate" the ego. It can become a weapon for exalting oneself over others in a smug attitude of moral superiority. It can turn into a tool for "depersonalizing" others. Love must be wedded with knowledge, faith must express itself in love.

In Christian faith this love comes about primarily by continual meditation on the good news of what God did for our own selves in Christ

---

2. *The Christian Faith and Homosexuality*, 25.

Jesus. God reached out to us in our sin. God paid the ultimate price to release us from self-centeredness for a relationship with our Creator. We have won something better, something more exciting and joyous, than the state lottery—not by luck, but by God's gracious design. No truly good thing will God spare us since on our behalf God did not spare even God's own Son. Even through the difficult times God can transform us into the image of Christ. We can be free from fear, from anger, from hate, from greed, from self-pity because the relationship with God in Christ transcends all else. We need not feel that we are "missing out on something" when we pursue only the abundant pleasures permitted by God for our own health. We are free to love, motivated to do so and instructed by the example of God's own love for us. We can redirect our love of self to a love of others, knowing that God has and will provide all we need. Thereby, we fulfill the command to "love our neighbors as ourselves." Out of our overflow of joy and peace and gratitude we are "constrained" to pursue others in love, whether we like what they do or not.

This book has been aimed at showing that affirming same-sex intercourse is *not* an act of love, however well meaning the intent. That road leads to death: physically, morally, and spiritually. Promoting the homosexual "rights" agenda is an awful and harmful waste of the church's energies and resources. What does constitute an act of love is befriending the homosexual while withholding approval of homosexual behavior, working in the true interests of the homosexual despite one's personal repugnance for same-sex intercourse, pursuing in love the homosexual while bearing the abuse that will inevitably come with opposing homosexual practice. It is the harder road to travel. It is too hard for many people to live within that holy tension. Yet it is the road that leads to life and true reconciliation; it is the calling of the church in the world. The real difficulty for the church lies not in assessing whether the Bible's stance toward same-sex intercourse is unremittingly negative, nor even (as is increasingly being suggested) in assessing whether the hermeneutical appropriation of the Bible's stance for our contemporary context sustains that witness. No, the real difficulty for the church lies in the pastoral dimension: the "nuts-and-bolts," day-to-day compassionate response to people whose sexual actions are recognized to be sinful and harmful to themselves, to the church, and to society at large.

INDEX

INDEX

Ancient Sources

Old Testament

New Testament

Ancient Near Eastern Literature

Other Rabbinic Works

Apostolic Fathers

New Testament Apocrypha and Pseudepigrapha

Classical and Ancient Christian Writings

INDEX

INDEX